Facts
about Germany

Facts
about Germany

Societäts-Verlag

Picture Sources

t = top, b = bottom, r = right, l = left

ACON: 331 b l; Adam Opel AG: 127, 229; AEG: 227, 411; AID/Henke: 263 b r; AKG, Berlin: 77 t l, b r, 447, 449; Architekturphoto/Dieter Leistner: 68, 243, 454; Architekturphoto/Ralph Richter: 222, Architekturphoto/Friedrich Busam: 431 t r, 458; Karl-Günter Balzer: 383; Charles Barker: 401 t l, b r; BASF AG: 60, 267; Bayerische Verwaltung der Staatlichen Schlösser, Gärten und Seen: 472; Bilderberg: 310, bb/Peter Ginter: 266, 367, bb/Wolfgang Keub: 284, bb/Michael Engler: 329, bb/Thomas Ernsting: 428, bb/Rainer Drexel: 468; bpk, Berlin: 77 t r, 81, 82, 88, 91; Bremer Lagerhaus-Gesellschaft: 215 b r; Bundesbildstelle Bonn: back cover t l, b r, 17, 76, 83, 96, 98, 103-119, 121 t, 131 t l, b l, 133, 142-143, 146, 156 t, 165, 169 t l, b r, 185 t r, b l, 187-203, 215 b l, 230, 232, 234, 253, 298, 335, 364, 387, 462, 467; Bundesministerium für Arbeit und Soziales: 237, 331 t r, 339, 347, 351; Bundesministerium für Verteidigung: 260; Bundesministerium für wirtschaftliche Zusammenarbeit: 207, 211; CMA: 309; DAAD: 212; Deutsche Aerospace Airbus: 44, 215 t l; Deutsche Börse AG: 215 t r; Deutsche Bundesbahn: front cover b r, 314; Deutsche Messe AG: 292; Deutscher Bundestag, Bonn: 147; Deutscher Volkshochschulverband: 420; DFJW: 359 t l; DLR: 401 b l, 425, 429; dpa: 77 b l, 121 b, 155, 157, 483; FAG Foto M. Skaryd: 319; Forschungszentrum Karlsruhe: 175; Gundel Kilian: 403, 431 b l, 473; KNA-Bild: 384 ; Bildagentur Helga Lade: 7 t l, t r, 21 t l, b l, 29, 30/31, 32, 34/35, 45, 47, 48, 50, 51, 57, 62, 65, 66/67, 73, 131 b r, 151, 183, 185 t l, 209, 263 b l, 271, 274, 283, 299, 303, 314/315, 318, 328, 331 t l, b r, 343, 359 t r, b r, 399, 405, 408, 412, 417, 431 t l, 444, 461, 469, 472; Wolfgang Lechthaler: 7 b l, 21 t r, 131 t r; Mainbild: 169 t r, 242, 334, 378 t; Rainer Martini/LOOK: back cover t r, 375; Bildagentur Mauritius: 7 b r, 125, 169 b l; Max-Planck-Gesellschaft: 225, 226, 424, 431 b r; Bernd C. Möller/FOCUS: 293; Horst Müller: 374, 376; NATO Photos: 185 b r; Isolde Ohlbaum: 437, 439; Bildarchiv OKAPIA: 21, 40, 42, 49, 231, 250, 251, 278, 281, 286, 305, 326/327, 357, 361, 378 b, 455; Rheinisches Bildarchiv Köln/Museum Ludwig Köln: 450/451; s.e.t. photo productions: 470; Wolfgang Saucke: 438; Schlossfestspiele Heidelberg: 481; Georg Schreiber: 474; Bildagentur Schuster/Jogschies: back cover b l; Siemens AG: 179, 213, 258, 272, 297, 426; Ronald Siemoneit: 477, 479; Gerhard Steidl: 435; STIEF PICTURES, Frankfurt: front cover t l, 39, 53, 54, 56, 70, 71, 263 t l, t r, 275, 287, 311, 355, 362, 381, 392; Stiftung Warentest: 247; Süddeutscher Verlag: 95; Telekom: 322, 323; Thüringer Landesfremdenverkehrsverband: 75; TRANSDIA, Mosler: 153; ULLSTEIN: front cover t r, 26, 36; VISUM/Dirk Reinartz: 436; VISUM/Thomas Pflaum: 63; ZDF: 359 b l, 397

Maps: Westermann Schulbuchverlag GmbH, Braunschweig

Editors: Dr. Arno Kappler, Adriane Grevel M. A.
Translator: Gerard Finan
Cover and Layout: Peter Lenz
Correct as at Oktober 15, 1993

Typesetting and conversion work:
Societätsdruck, Frankfurt/Main
Graphics: Icon, Bonn
Reproductions: Gehringer, Kaiserslautern
Printed by Westermann, Braunschweig
Printed in Germany 1993
Printed on chlorien-free bleached paper
ISBN 3-7973-0553-2

Contents

Contents

Country and people

· The country · The people

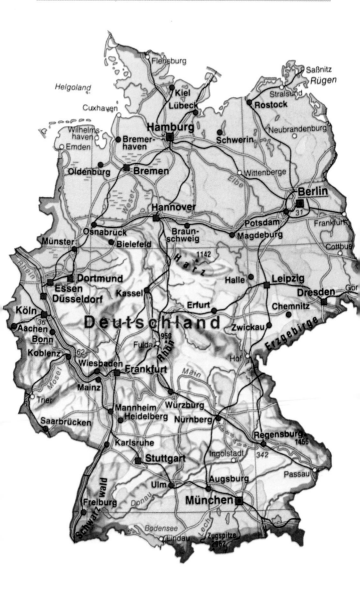

The country

The Federal Republic of Germany is situated in the heart of Europe. It has nine neighbours: Denmark in the north, the Netherlands, Belgium, Luxembourg and France in the west, Switzerland and Austria in the south, and the Czech Republic as well as Poland in the east. This central location has been more pronounced since 3 October 1990 when Germany was reunited. The Federal Republic is more than ever a link between east and west, but also between Scandinavia and the Mediterranean. As an integral part of the European Community and NATO, Germany is a bridge to the countries of Central and Eastern Europe.

The Federal Republic of Germany covers an area of 357,000 sq km. The longest distance from north to south as the crow flies is 876 km, from west to east 640 km. Its extremities are List on the island of Sylt in the north, Deschka, Saxony, in the east, Oberstdorf, Bavaria, in the south, and Selfkant, North-Rhine/Westphalia, in the west. The total length of the country's borders is 3,767 km. Germany has a population of 80 million, the largest in Europe after Russia's, followed by Italy (population 58 million), the United Kingdom (57 million) and France (56 million). In size, however, Germany is smaller than France (552,000 sq km) and Spain (505,000 sq km).

■ ▪ **Geographical features.** Germany has various charming landscapes. Low and high mountain ranges intermingle with upland plains, terrace country, hilly regions and lakelands, as well as wide, open lowlands. From north to south Germany is divided into five regions with different topographical features: the North German Plain, the Central Upland Range, the terrace panorama of the southwest, the alpine foothills in the south, and the Bavarian Alps.

In the north are dry, sandy lowlands with many lakes as well as heaths and moors. There is also the fertile land south of the Central Upland Range. These lowland penetrations include the Lower Rhenish Bight, the Westphalian Bight and the Saxon-Thuringian Bight. The marshes along the North Sea coast extend as far as the geest. Characteristic features of the Baltic Sea coastline are, in

Schleswig-Holstein, the fjords, in Mecklenburg-Western Pomerania the lakes and the counterbalancing coastline. The main islands are, in the North Sea, the East Frisian Islands such as Borkum or Norderney, the North Frisian Islands of Amrum, Föhr, Sylt and the Halligen as well as Helgoland in the Helgoland Bight. Situated in the Baltic Sea are the islands of Rügen, Hiddensee and Fehmarn. Some parts of the Baltic coast have flat, sandy shores, others steep cliffs. Between the North and Baltic Seas lies the low-hill country called "Holsteinische Schweiz" (Holstein Switzerland).

The Central Upland Range divides north Germany from the south. The central Rhine valley and the Hessian depressions serve as the natural north-south traffic arteries. The Central Uplands include the Rhenish Slate Mountains (Hunsrück, Eifel, Taunus, Westerwald, Bergisches Land and Sauerland), the Hessian Mountains, the

---

Mountains, rivers, islands

Zugspitze (northern Alps)	2962 m
Watzmann (northern Alps)	2713 m
Feldberg (Black Forest)	1493 m
Großer Arber (Bavarian Forest)	1456 m
Fichtelberg (Erzgebirge)	1214 m
Brocken (Harz)	1142 m
Rivers within Germany	
Rhine	865 km
Elbe	700 km
Main	524 km
Weser	440 km
Spree	382 km
Shipping canals	
Mittellandkanal	321 km
Dortmund-Ems-Kanal	269 km
North-Sea-Baltic-Kanal	99 km
Lakes and Dams	
Lake Constance (Total area)	538 sq km
Lake Constance (German part)	305 sq km
Müritz	115 sq km
Schwammenauel	205 cubic metres
Eder Dam (Lake Eder)	202 cubic metres
Islands	
Rügen	926 sq km
Usedom (German part)	354 sq km
Fehmarn	185 sq km
Sylt	99 sq km

Weser and Leine Mountains in western and central Germany. Right in the centre of Germany are the Harz Mountains. In the eastern region are the Rhön Mountains, the Bavarian Forest, the Upper Palatinate Forest, the Fichtelgebirge, the Frankenwald, the Thuringian Forest and the mountains of the Erzgebirge.

The terrace landscape of the Central Uplands in the south-west embrace the upper Rhine valley with the adjacent mountain ranges of the Black Forest, the Odenwald and Spessart, the Palatinate Forest with the Haardt and the Swabian-Franconian terrace country with the Alb.

In a narrow valley between Bingen and Bonn the river Rhine, the main north-south axis, slices through the Rhenish Slate Mountains, whose not very fertile highland areas (Hunsrück, Taunus, Eifel, Westerwald) are considerably less densely populated than the sheltered wine-growing areas on both sides of the Rhine which are very popular with tourists. The alpine foothills embrace the Swabian-Bavarian highlands and lakes, the broad, gravel plains, the hilly landscape of Lower Bavaria, and the Danube valley. Characteristic features of this region are the moors, dome-shaped hill ranges and lakes (Chiemsee, Starnberger See) as well as small villages.

The German part of the Alps between Lake Constance and Berchtesgaden is limited to the Allgäu, the Bavarian Alps and the Berchtesgaden Alps. In this alpine world lie picturesque lakes, such as the Königssee near Berchtesgaden, and popular tourist resorts such as Garmisch-Partenkirchen or Mittenwald.

■ ■ ■ **Climate.** Germany is situated in the temperate zone between the Atlantic Ocean and the eastern part of the European con tinent. Sharp changes in temperature are rare. There is precipitation all the year round. In winter the average temperature is between 1.5° C in the lowland areas and minus 6° C in the mountains. In the warmest month of the year, July, temperatures are between 18° C in low-lying regions and 20° C in the sheltered valleys of the south. Exceptions are the Upper Rhine Trough with its extremely mild climate, Upper Bavaria with its warm alpine wind (Föhn) from the south, and the Harz Mountains, a climatic zone of its own with cold winds, cool summers and heavy snow in winter.

The people

Germany has a population of over 80 million (including 6.5 million foreigners) and is one of the most densely populated countries in Europe (222 people per sq km). Only Belgium and the Netherlands have a higher population density.

The population is distributed very unevenly. Greater Berlin, which has been growing rapidly since Germany's unification and now has 3.4 million inhabitants, will probably have eight million by the end of the millennium. More than four million people (about 5,500 per sq km) live in the Rhein-Ruhr industrial agglomeration where towns and cities are so close together that there are no distinct boundaries between them.

Other concentrations are to be found in the Rhein-Main area around Frankfurt, Wiesbaden and Mainz, and the Rhein-Neckar region focusing on Mannheim and Ludwigshafen, the industrial area around Stuttgart, as well as the catchment areas of Bremen, Dresden, Hamburg, Cologne, Leipzig, Munich and Nuremberg/Fürth. These contrast with the thinly populated moorlands of the North German Plain, parts of the Eifel Mountains, the Bavarian Forest, the Upper Palatinate, the March of Brandenburg, and large parts of Mecklenburg-Western Pomerania.

The western part of Germany is much more densely populated than the five new states in the east, where only about a fifth of the population (16 million) live on roughly 30% of the national territory. Of the 20 cities with more than 300,000 inhabitants, four are in the eastern part of Germany.

Nearly a third of the population live in the 85 cities (of more than 100,000 inhabitants). They number about 26 million. But the great majority live in small towns and villages: over 7 million in municipalities with a population of less than 2,000, 46 million in towns with between 2,000 and 100,000 inhabitants.

The population in both the old and new federal states began to decline in the 70s because the birthrate was falling. In the west, however, there has been a slightly upward trend since 1990. With eleven births a year to

Age structure of the population of Germany on 1 Jan. 1992

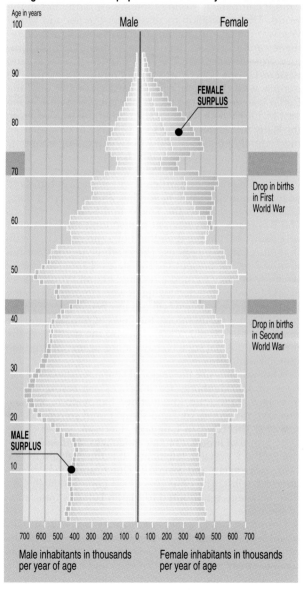

Age in years

Male   Female

FEMALE SURPLUS

Drop in births in First World War

Drop in births in Second World War

MALE SURPLUS

700 600 500 400 300 200 100 0 100 200 300 400 500 600 700

Male inhabitants in thousands per year of age

Female inhabitants in thousands per year of age

every 1,000 inhabitants (in West Germany prior to unification) Germany has one of the lowest birth rates in the world. The population increase after the Second World War was mainly due to immigration. Some 13 million refugees and expellees entered the present German territory from the former German eastern provinces and eastern Europe. There was a continuous strong flow of people who fled from east to west Germany until the Berlin wall was erected by the communist regime in the east in 1961 which hermetically sealed the border. From the early 60s large numbers of foreign workers came to the Federal Republic of old whose expanding economy needed additional labour which was not available at home.

■ ■ ■ **Regional disparities.** Over the past thousand years or so the German nation has grown out of a number of tribes, such as the Franks and Saxons, Swabians and Bavarians. They have of course long since lost their original character, but their traditions and dialects live on in their respective regions. Those ethnic regions are not identical to the present federal states (Länder), most of which were only formed after the Second World War in agreement with the occupying powers. In most cases the boundaries were drawn without much consideration for old traditions. Furthermore, the flows of refugees and the massive post-war migrations, but also the mobility of the modern industrial society, have more or less blurred the ethnic boundaries.

What remains are the regional characteristics. The natives of Mecklenburg, for instance, are reserved, the Swabians thrifty, the Rheinländer happy-go-lucky, and the Saxons hardworking and shrewd, and so on.

■ ■ ■ **The German language.** German is one of the large group of Indo-Germanic languages, and within that one of the Germanic languages. It is thus related to Danish, Norwegian and Swedish, Dutch and Flemish, but also to English. The emergence of a common High German language is attributed to Martin Luther's translation of the Bible.

Germany has a wealth of dialects but it is usually possible to determine a person's native region. If, on the other hand, a Frisian or a Mecklenburger and a Bavarian were to speak in pure dialect they would have great difficulty understanding one another. Moreover, whilst the country was divided the two German states developed a different political vocabulary. New words were also coined which were not necessarily understood in the other part of the country. But basic vocabulary and grammar remained the same in east and west. The common language was one of the links which held the divided nation together.

German is also spoken as the native language in Austria, Liechtenstein, large parts of Switzerland, South Tirol (northern Italy) and in small parts of Belgium, France (Alsace) and Luxembourg along the German border. And the German minorities in Poland, Romania and the republics of the former Soviet Union have partly retained the German language.

German is the native language of more than 100 million people. About one in every ten books published throughout the world has been written in German. As regards translations into foreign languages, German is third after English and French, while more works have

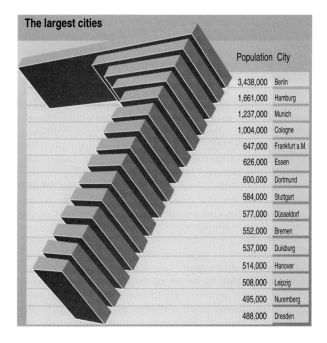

The largest cities	
Population	City
3,438,000	Berlin
1,661,000	Hamburg
1,237,000	Munich
1,004,000	Cologne
647,000	Frankfurt a.M.
626,000	Essen
600,000	Dortmund
584,000	Stuttgart
577,000	Düsseldorf
552,000	Bremen
537,000	Duisburg
514,000	Hanover
508,000	Leipzig
495,000	Nuremberg
488,000	Dresden

been translated into German than into any other language.

■ ■ ■ **Foreign nationalities.** For years Chancellor Helmut Kohl has been saying that Germany is friendly towards foreigners. And quite rightly so, as the statistics prove. Of Germany's more than 80 million inhabitants 6.5 million are from abroad. They were all glad to come and stay in Germany. For decades there were no racial problems. The category of "guest workers", initially consisting of Italians, was extended to include Greeks and Spaniards, and then Portuguese, Yugoslavs and Turks. Occasional tensions within the community were far outweighed by the friendships made with neighbours and colleagues at work.

Integration within the European Community and the western world, the dissolution of the eastern bloc, and the immigration of people from Asian and African countries naturally meant a considerable increase in the number of foreigners of different colour in Germany.

The Turks, who number 1,855,000, have long been the largest foreign community, followed by people from the states which belonged to the former Yugoslavia, whose number, including war refugees, can only be roughly assessed at one million because of the many war refugees. Next are the Italians (558,000), the Greeks (346,000), Poles (286,000), Austrians (185,000), Romanians (167,000) and Spaniards (134,000). Iranian, Portuguese, British, Americans and Dutch each number between 100,000 and 115,000, and the Bulgarians, Hungarians, Czechs, Slovaks and Frendch each between 60,000 and 90,000. When speaking of foreigners we today think of people of non-European origin, the 86,000 Vietnamese, 80,000 Moroccans, 53,000 Lebanese, 44,000 Sri Lankans, 42,000 Afghans and 36,000 Indians. The 61,000 people from the former Soviet Union are more conspicuous in the eastern part of the country than in the west.

Nearly 60% of all foreigners have been living in Germany for ten years or more. Over two thirds of foreign children were born here. The Federal Republic has not only proved itself to be an open society by bringing in workers, their families, asylum-seekers and war refugees. It has always been a champion of free movement of labour within the European Community. Germany's

Demonstration condemning attacks on foreigners

willingness to open her doors to foreigners who have
been persecuted on political grounds compares favour-
ably with that of other countries. The new article 16a of
the Basic Law, like the previous article 16, still guarantees
protection from political persecution in the form of an
individual basic right. In 1992, for instance, Germany
alone took in nearly 80% of all people seeking asylum in
the whole of the European Community. In 1989 the number seeking asylum in Germany was 121,318, in 1991 the
figure rose to 256,112, and then to 438,191 in 1992. At the
same time the proportion of those who could be recognized as genuine victims of persecution fell to less than
5%. In 1993, up to the end of August, some 260,000
asylum-seekers entered Germany. Their number fell si-
ginificantly when the new legislation became effective
on 1 July 1993.

Under new legislation (which was carried by a two-
thirds majority in parliament) the right of asylum has
been focused on its true purpose (which is the normal
state of affairs in other countries) of affording protection
to those who actually have been persecuted on political
grounds and really do need protection. As a result,
foreigners who enter Germany from a safe third country

may no longer invoke this basic right. Germany also reserves the right, notwithstanding the Geneva convention on refugees, to draw up a list of countries where, according to official sources of information, no one is subject to persecution so that there is, as a rule, no ground for asylum. Nonetheless, every person whose application for asylum has been rejected may appeal, if necessary right through to the Federal Constitutional Court.

■ ■ ■ **The country's debt to foreigners.** Germany owes a great deal to her foreign workers and businessmen. They have contributed largely to the country's economic growth and every year add some DM 100 billion to the country's gross national product. 40% of the workforce of some of Germany's world-famous companies, such as Siemens AG, are foreigners. Cooperation between German and foreign workmates is good and fosters mutual respect. Hence there are far fewer conflict situations at work than in neighbourhoods where sizeable ethnic communities have formed.

Attacks by Germans on foreigners prior to 1991 were recorded like all other crime statistics, including those by foreigners on Germans. It was only after the GDR became part of the Federal Republic that attacks on foreigners began to occur which focused not on the individual victim but on his identity as a "foreigner", irrespective of the person's actual nationality.

Various factors contributed to the increased violence. The growing number of foreigners who wrongly claimed to have been persecuted on political grounds in order to circumvent the immigration laws aroused much concern and anger among the population. Then there was the ostensibly nationalistic reflex action of many people in the former GDR to a Marxist-Leninist doctrine which had been imposed by the old regime and no longer had to be obeyed. And another obvious cause was the impression gained by some young people, in eastern Germany but also in the west, that they themselves were underprivileged in life and should take it out on foreigners (see also the chapter on youth).

■ ■ ■ **Crime against foreigners.** In the autumn of 1991 foreigners and Germans alike were alarmed by the violence and firebomb attacks in Hoyerswerda, Saarlouis and other towns where it was all too easy for the perpetrators to commit their appalling crimes. To the dismay of the overwhelming majority of the population, their bad example was widely copied. Whereas in 1990, in the Federal Republic prior to unification, less than 200 attacks by right-wing extremists, not primarily against individuals, were registered, the number in 1991 was 1,483, and thereafter as many as 2,285. In this volatile atmosphere the membership of extremist parties of the right increased, which was first reflected in the Bremen and Schleswig-Holstein state elections where they were able to clear the 5% hurdle and enter parliament.

The tragic climax of the attacks on asylum-seekers, following the new wave of violence in Rostock, were the murders committed in Mölln in November 1992 and Solingen in May 1993. In those firebomb attacks eight Turkish women and children died. In both cases the offenders were young people. And in fact the majority who commit such crimes out of blind hatred are youngsters between the age of 12 and 20 acting alone.

Germany leaves no doubt that she condemns xenophobia, that she will resolutely prosecute and severely punish violent attacks, and that she will protect foreign residents and offer all those who stay permanently every chance to become integrated. The government have on many occasions declared their support for foreigners. The public have demonstrated their concern for the foreign members of the community in rallies and candlelight vigils (the one in Munich being the largest demonstration since the Second World War). The unions and the business community have organized many different activities to stress the solidarity of the workforce irrespective of nationality. Their action has counteracted a growing lack of confidence in German companies, products and services, especially in America.

■ ■ ■ **Promoting integration.** The Federal and state governments will not be deterred by xenophobic activities from pursuing their long-term aims. They have in several instances made the laws less restrictive, thus making it easier for foreigners, and especially young people, who have lived in Germany for many years to become naturalized citizens. The government consider this to be the more consistent approach in comparison with the much-debated half-measures of allowing foreigners to vote in local government elections (a proposal which, by the way, was rejected by the Federal

Constitutional Court in 1990) or a merging of the two fundamental principles of nationality, ius soli (place of birth) and ius sanguinis (lineage). And the law is very tolerant towards foreigners who wish merely to work in Germany but not to participate in the social and cultural life of the country by allowing them to practice their native customs and way of life.

The federal states

· Baden-Württemberg · The Free State of Bavaria · Berlin
· Brandenburg · The Free Hanseatic City of Bremen
· The Free and Hanseatic City of Hamburg · Hesse
· Mecklenburg-Western Pomerania · Lower Saxony
· North-Rhine/Westphalia · Rhineland-Palatinate · Saarland
· The Free State of Saxony · Saxony-Anhalt
· Schleswig-Holstein · Thuringia

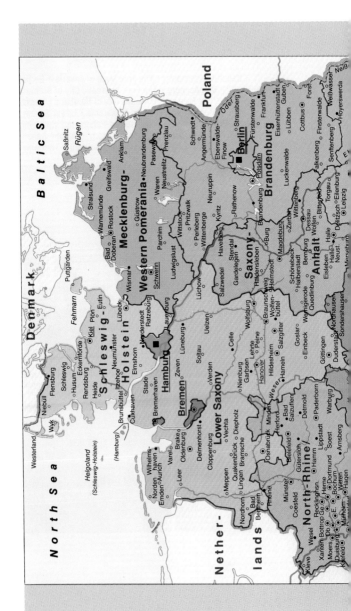

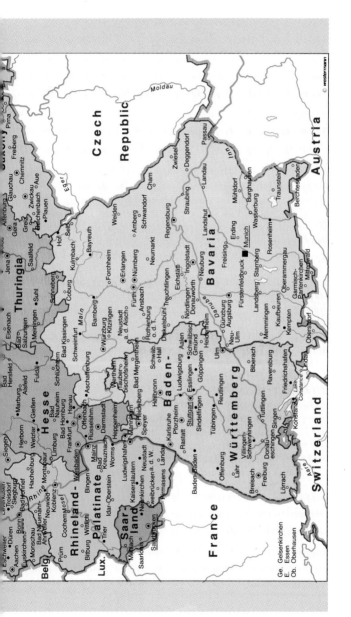

The federal states

The Federal Republic of Germany consists of 16 states known as "Länder": Baden-Württemberg (Stuttgart), Bavaria (Munich), Berlin, Brandenburg (Potsdam), Bremen, Hamburg, Hesse (Wiesbaden), Mecklenburg-Western Pomerania (Schwerin), Lower Saxony (Hanover), North-Rhine/Westphalia (Düsseldorf), Rhineland-Palatinate (Mainz), Saarland (Saarbrücken), Saxony (Dresden), Saxony-Anhalt (Magdeburg), Schleswig-Holstein (Kiel) and Thuringia (Erfurt).

Germany has always been divided into states but the map has changed its shape over the centuries. The most important changes in the modern age resulted from the Napoleonic wars at the beginning of the 19th century, the Austro-Prussian war of 1866, and the First and Second World Wars. After the latter Germany was occupied and divided and the country's largest state, Prussia, dissolved. Most of the federal states as we know them today were established after 1945, but they have largely retained their ethnic traditions and characteristics and some of the old boundaries. Until Germany was reunited in 1989 the Federal Republic consisted of eleven states which had been created in the former western occupation zones and had adopted democratic constitutions between 1946 and 1957.

In the Soviet-occupied zone, which later became the German Democratic Republic, five states were formed, partly along the traditional lines, but as early as 1952 this structure was smashed by the East German regime and replaced by a centralized administration. Soon after the successful peaceful and democratic revolution in Germany in October 1989 the people began to demand the restoration of those former states. Following the first free election in the former GDR on 18 March 1990, the parliament created five federal states.

Then, on 3 October 1990, the German Democratic Republic, and hence the states of Brandenburg, Mecklenburg-Western Pomerania, Saxony, Saxony-Anhalt and Thuringia, acceded to the Federal Republic of Germany. At the same time East Berlin was merged with West Berlin.

State election 1992	
CDU	39.6 %
SPD	29.4 %
Republicans	10.9 %
Greens	9.5 %
FDP/DVP	5.9 %

Population	10.0 mill.
Area	35,751 sq km
Capital	Stuttgart

Baden-Württemberg

■ ■ ■ **Natural beauty, abundance of culture.** Baden-Württemberg has some of the country's most charming countryside. It embraces not only the Black Forest, a very popular recreational area in the Central Uplands, or Lake Constance, known locally as the "Swabian Sea", but also the green valleys of the Rhine and the Danube, the Neckar and the Tauber, the rugged Schwäbische Alb and the gentle Markgräflerland, all major holiday resorts. The different soil conditions are ideal for fruit, wine, asparagus and tobacco.

Not only blessed by nature, it is also an ideal crossroads for transport and communications which heightens its attractiveness to tourists and industry. The inventiveness and business sense of the people are proverbial, and their intellectual and artistic achievements fill many a chapter of German cultural and literary history, as testified by such names as the writers Friedrich Schiller (1759-1805) and Friedrich Hölderlin (1770-1843), or the philosophers Georg Wilhelm Friedrich Hegel (1770-1831) and Martin Heidegger (1889-1976). The central Neckar region with the state capital Stuttgart (population 584,000) is Baden-Württemberg's industrial and cultural centre. Mannheim's Kunsthalle and Reiß-Museum are outstanding landmarks. The minsters of Ulm and Freiburg are monuments to southern Germany's architectural pre-eminence. Heidelberg's castele and the old city centre attract visitors from all over the world. And the Black Forest's traditional cuckoo-clocks are not confined to the Clock Museum in Furtwangen but taken to all corners of the globe by tourists.

■ ■ ■ **Cars and microchips.** Baden-Württemberg is a highly industrialized region and thus, in economic

Stuttgart's Neues Schloss and Jubiläumssäule

terms, one of Germany's most powerful states. Precision engineering, which is concentrated in the Black Forest of cuckoo clock fame, and the automotive industry have the longest tradition.

Traditional crafts and modern industry are the backbone of the economy. In and around Stuttgart are to be found the headquarters of such world famous firms as Daimler Benz, Bosch, IBM, SEL and the sports car manufacturer Porsche. Here, as everywhere else in Baden-Württemberg, there is a highly organized network of small and medium-sized firms who supply state-of-the-art parts and equipment to the big companies.

Adjacent to the central Neckar industrial region are Karlsruhe (273,000) with its oil refineries, Mannheim (308,000) and Heidelberg (136,000), which make buses and printing machinery respectively, but also Freiburg (189,000) and Ulm (106,000) with their extensive service industries. When Germany was reunited Baden-Württemberg began to establish close ties, not only in the economic sphere, with the new state of Saxony, which is similar in structure.

The tower of Freiburg's Minster

■ ■ ■ **Science and research.** Among Baden-Württemberg's numerous academic and scientific institutions is the Nuclear Research Centre at Karlsruhe, the German Cancer Research Centre in Heidelberg, as well as several Max Planck Institutes and nine universities. Heidelberg University, founded in 1386, is the oldest in Germany, whereas Karlsruhe is home to Germany's oldest technical college. That city is also the seat of Germany's supreme courts, the Federal Court of Justice and the Federal Constitutional Court.

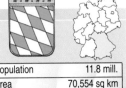

State election 1990	
CSU	54.9 %
SPD	26 %
Greens	6.4 %
FDP	5.2 %

Population	11.8 mill.
Area	70,554 sq km
Capital	Munich

The Free State of Bavaria

■ ■ ■ **A white-and-blue tradition with a future.** Bavaria is by far the largest of Germany's states and has the longest political tradition, there having been a Bavarian tribal dukedom as early as the 6th century. Bavaria owes much of its reputation as a tourist's paradise to its cultural heritage and captivating landscapes. Germany's most popular holiday destination, this state offers the Alps, with the country's highest mountain the Zugspitze (2,963 m), the picturesque lakes in the hilly alpine foreland, the Bavarian Forest with the first German national park, the valleys of the Danube and Main and their tributaries a region of beautiful scenery and towns through which passes the "Romantic Route". In former times Munich was the rural capital of Germany's largest farming area. After the Second World War it enjoyed calling itself "Germany's secret capital" and became the focal point of a rapidly growing industrial region (automobiles and aircraft, electrical engineering and electronics industry, insurance and publishing). And with its university and other institutions of higher education, the Max Planck Institute and its nuclear reactor, Bavaria's capital (population 1.2 million) is also a major academic and research centre. 1992 Munich opened a new international airport named after the late Franz-Josef Strauß, Bavaria's long-serving minister-president.

■ ■ ■ **Industry and agriculture.** Nuremberg (495,000) lies at the intersection of Europe's future motorway network stretching from Naples to Stockholm and from Lisbon via Prague to Warsaw. Together with Fürth and Erlangen, Nuremberg forms an industrial agglomeration focussing on engineering and the electrical and toy industries (Siemens, Quelle, Grundig). Nuremberg's annual International Toy Fair is the most important of its kind.

Augsburg (255,000) is home to the engineering and textile industries. Regensburg (121,000) has a young electrical and an even younger automobile industry (BMW). Ingolstadt, too, is a car-manufacturing centre (Audi). East Bavaria's glassworks (Zwiesel) and porcelain factories (Rosenthal, Hutschenreuther) carry on the region's famous crafts. Large parts of Bavaria, especially the Alps and the alpine foothills, are still mainly farming areas. The region's Franconian wines are highly rated by connoisseurs. There are also hundreds of breweries producing Bavaria's famous beer, which flows in abundance at, for instance, Munich's Oktoberfest.

Stone bridge, Salzstadl and St.Peter's Cathedral, Regensburg

■ ■ ■ **Culture from all ages.** Regensburg has retained most of its medieval townscape. Nuremberg, the city of Albrecht Dürer (1471-1528), has some of the finest examples of late medieval treasures in its churches and museums, whereas Augsburg has the purest Renaissance heritage. The churches in the Banz and Ettal monasteries, Vierzehnheiligen, and Steingaden's "Wieskirche", which appears in UNESCO's list of world cultural assets, as well as Würzburg, former residence of the prince-bishops, are outstanding examples of baroque and rococo architecture.

In Munich we find not only Germany's largest university but also the Deutsches Museum, the world's biggest exhibition of science and technology. The city also boasts numerous historic buildings, famous art galleries

The Olympic area, Munich

Construction Machine Fair (BAUMA), Munich

and theatres. The Herrenchiemsee, Linderhof and Neuschwanstein castles, built by the "fairytale king" Ludwig II in the 19th century, are tourist magnets. So too are the towns of Rothenburg ob der Tauber, Nördlingen and Dinkelsbühl with their traditional semi-timbered houses. Music lovers, too, are well catered for in Bavaria, for instance at the annual Wagner Festival in Bayreuth. Richard Wagner lived there from 1872 to 1883.

State election 1990	
CDU	40.4 %
SPD	30.4 %
PDS	9.3 %
FDP	7.1 %
Alternative List*	5.0 %
Aliance 90 / Greens**	4.4 %

Population	3.4 mill.
Area	889 sq km
Capital	Berlin

Berlin

■ ■ ■ **A city with a turbulent past.** For decades Berlin was the symbol of Germany's division and a flashpoint in the Cold War between the victorious western powers and the Soviet Union. In 1948 only the unforgettable airlift enabled the West Berliners to survive an 11-month Soviet blockade of the city. Aircraft of the American Air Force, supported by the British and French allies, kept the people of West Berlin supplied with vital necessities.

In the 50s the three western sectors and East Berlin grew more and more apart. The city's partition seemed to be cemented for ever when the East Germans began to build that infamous wall on 13 August 1961. With his famous call "Ich bin ein Berliner" in front of Schöneberg town-hall in 1963, US President John F. Kennedy endorsed his support for the city and its people. Among Berlin's governing mayors are such famous names as Ernst Reuter, Willy Brandt and Richard von Weizsäcker. And in 1987 President Ronald Reagan, in a speech near the Brandenburg Gate, appealed to the Soviet Union to "tear down this wall". The wall was indeed opened - on 9 November 1989 - in the wake of the peaceful revolution in East Germany. That was the city's chance to make a new start.

■ ■ ■ **Germany's capital and a European cultural centre.** Prior to its spiritual and cultural decline under the nazi dictatorship, and prior to the destruction caused by the Second World War, Berlin was not only the hub of German industry but, in the "golden twenties", also one of Europe's cultural capitals.

---

* The Alternative List stood in West Berlin only.
** The Alliance 90/The Greens stood in East Berlin only.

Platz der Akademie (formerly: Gendarmenmarkt) with

the Schauspielhaus, French Cathedral and Huguenot Museum

With Germany's division now a thing of the past, cultural roots, severed for decades, can grow together again and complement each other. Berlin boasts three opera houses (Deutsche Oper, Deutsche Staatsoper, Komische Oper), several major orchestras and dozens of theatres, and it continues to be one of the world's greatest museum cities. The leading newspapers are "Berliner Morgenpost", "Berliner Zeitung" and "Tagesspiegel". The university in the eastern part of the city is named after the von Humboldt brothers, Wilhelm (1767-1835), the scholar and politician, and Alexander (1769-1859), a famous naturalist and traveller. In the western part are the Free University and the Technical University, both founded in 1948. Berlin also has many famous research establishments, such as the Hahn Meitner Institute of Nuclear Physics, the Heinrich Hertz Institute of Communications Technology, and the Prussian Cultural Heritage Foundation.

The future seat of the Federal Government continues to grow and it is estimated that the metropolitan area's present population of 3,5 million will almost double by the year 2000. Great efforts are being made to modernize the city's transport systems (roads, city and underground railways, ferries, airports) without destroying its many parks, woods and lakes.

View over the Victory Column and Tiergarten
towards the eastern part of Berlin

The Brandenburg Gate, symbol of German unity

Berlin is still Germany's largest industrial centre, focusing mainly on engineering, food and beverages, pharmaceuticals, textiles and especially electrical goods. Two world famous companies were established there in the 19th century: Siemens and AEG. With Berlin as their base they have successfully coped with the transition to the information age.

The reunited city faces tremendous challenges. The people in both parts of Berlin, having lived for decades under different political systems, are now growing accustomed to one another again and the economic disparity is being overcome. Hundreds of thousands of flats, especially in the eastern districts, are being brought up to standard. Unification has sparked an economic boom but the measures needed to link the two parts together, to develop and modernize the future seat of government and to accommodate the rapidly growing population demand creativity, investment and enterprise. German and foreign investors have meanwhile acquired large plots of land at Potsdamer Platz, which had remained derelict since the Second World War. Planning for the new government quarter in the Spreebogen is well advanced. 835 architects from 44 countries took part in a competition for the area's overall design and layout. The nearby cathedral, having been renovated over the past 20 years, is now resplendent in its former glory.

State election 1990	
SPD	38.2 %
CDU	29.4 %
PDS	13.4 %
Alliance 90 / Greens	9.3 %
FDP	6.6 %

Population	2.5 mill.
Area	29,053 sq km
Capital	Potsdam

Brandenburg

■ ■ ■ **The legacy of Frederick II.** The state of Brandenburg encircles the German capital. Just outside Berlin
lies the state capital of Potsdam (140,000), venue of the
Potsdam Conference where, in the summer of 1945, the
leaders of the United States, the United Kingdom and the
Soviet Union took decisions which greatly affected the
future of conquered Germany. Potsdam had been deliberately chosen for the conference because of its close
association with Prussian-German history, King Frederick
II (1712-1786) having made it his residence. Frederick's
architectural masterpieces in Potsdam, especially those
in the beautiful park of Sanssouci, outlived Prussia's
existence as a state. It was there that the enlightened
monarch held philosophical discussions with his friends,
who included Voltaire (1694-1778). And there he also received other famous guests such as Johann Sebastian
Bach (1685-1750).

■ ■ ■ **Dutchmen and Huguenots.** For a long time
thinly populated Brandenburg remained economically
underdeveloped. In order to rectify this situation its rulers opened the borders to large numbers of foreigners in
the 17th and 18th centuries.

Dutch immigrants as well as Protestants who had been
expelled from France and Bohemia brought their knowledge and skills and played a major part in the region's
advancement. We are still reminded of this by such
names as the "Dutch Quarter" and the "French Church"
in Potsdam.

The countryside around Berlin has been impressively
described by Theodor Fontane (1819-1898), a descend-
ant of French Huguenots, in his famous "Walks in the
March of Brandenburg".

The courtyard of the Cecilienhof, Potsdam

■ ■ ■ **Rye and steel.** Brandenburg is the largest of the
new German states. Agriculture and forestry are important branches of the economy. Thirty-five per cent of the
total area is forest (mainly fir). This region grows rye and
wheat, oilseed, potatoes and sugarbeet and, in a belt
around Berlin and in the Oderbruch near Frankfurt on
the Oder, fruit and vegetables. The industrial centres are
around Eisenhüttenstadt (steel) and Cottbus, where the
lignite mines provide the raw materials for the chemical
industry and energy. 23.6 per cent of the workforce are
employed in engineering and the automotive industry.
Mercedes Benz has a truck assembly works in Ludwigs-
felde to the south of Berlin. The company proposes to
invest one billion marks there. Frankfurt on the Oder is
known for its electrical engineering and appliance construction industries. Increasing numbers of tourists are
attracted to Brandenburg's rugged but none the less
charming landscape of forests and lakes.

The old (1508-1811) and new (since 1991) university
town of Frankfurt on the Oder acquires a new significance as a distribution port for eastern Europe now that
visas are no longer required for travel between Germany
and Poland. Since 1991 a German-Polish intergovernmental commission for regional and transborder cooper-

Boat trips in the Spreewald are popular with tourists

ation has been promoting good-neighbourly contacts in
the Euro-regions of "Viadrina" and "Spree-Neisse-Bobr".

Brandenburg sees good prospects of sharing in Berlin's economic boom. There are plans for merging
Brandenburg and Berlin into one federal state with Potsdam as the capital. This is the task of an inter-state commission.

State election 1991	
SPD	38.8 %
CDU	30.7 %
Greens	11.4 %
FDP	9.5 %
DVU	6.1 %

Population	684,000
Area	404 sq km
Capital	Bremen

The Free Hanseatic City of Bremen

■ ■ ■ **The two-city state.** Two cities, one state: Bremen and Bremerhaven are 65 km apart but nonetheless belong together. They constitute the smallest German state in terms of both area and population. Yet this Free Hanseatic City of Bremen is, next to Bavaria, the oldest body politic in Germany, and after San Marino the second oldest city-republic in the world.

Bremen is also many centuries older than Bremerhaven. Founded as a bishopric in 787, it quickly flourished, thanks to the privileges bestowed upon it as a market town. In the 11th century it was described as the "Rome of the North". In 1358 Bremen became a member of the Hanseatic League, which dominated trade in the North and Baltic Seas until well into the 16th century.

■ ■ ■ **Risk and win.** "Outside and in, risk and win", is the motto which tells of this city's growth and affluence. In 1827, when it seemed that the river Weser would be silted up, mayor Smidt founded a new port at the mouth of the Weser and named it Bremerhaven, which, together with adjacent townships, grew into a city.

Bremerhaven handles mostly (60%) container traffic and since 1983 has had the largest container terminal in the world. Bremen almost has a monopoly of imports of tea and coffee, tobacco and cotton.

Bremen has made itself less dependent on maritime trade and shipbuilding by developing a highly productive aerospace industry. It has also resumed car production and is making its mark in the electronics sector and in the food and beverages industry. Bremerhaven is the focal point of German polar research. Also afloat there are the old barges and men-o'-war of the German Maritime Museum.

Maritime Museum and Columbus Quay, Bremerhaven

■ ■ ■ **Bremen's "parlour".** On the market place stands the Gothic cathedral of St. Peter and the magnificent Renaissance town-hall with its very hospitable wine cellar. In front of it is Roland's column (1404), symbol of the city's freedom and a local landmark, like the nearby "town musicians", a statue of the animals in a Grimms fairy-tale. From the market square the visitor enters the Böttcherstrasse, a narrow street of shops and museums built on the initiative of the merchant Ludwig Roselius (1924-31). It is a brick monument to Bremen's civic spirit. Every year, on the second Friday in February, Bremen's maritime community hold their traditional "Schaffermahlzeit" in the Rathaus. Distinguished public figures are invited.

State election 1993	
SPD	40.4 %
CDU	25.1 %
GAL	13.5 %
STATT	5.6 %

Population	1.7 mill.
Area	755 sq km
Capital	Hamburg

The Free and Hanseatic City of Hamburg

■ ■ ■ **Germany's gateway to the world.** Hamburg is Germany's principal seaport and largest overseas trade and transshipment centre as exemplified by the fact that some 130 Japanese and more than 20 Chinese trading companies are represented there. The port's industrial area encompasses shipyards, refineries and processing plant for raw materials from abroad. In addition to these port-related activities, the aerospace, electronics, precision engineering, optical and chemical industries play an increasingly important role in this city-state.

Hamburg began to flourish as a commercial town in 1189, when it was granted customs and commercial rights. One of the first members of the Hanseatic League, it soon became the main transshipment port between the North Sea and the Baltic Sea. In 1460, and then finally in 1510, Hamburg was raised to the status of an imperial city - an autonomous status it has retained to this day. However, the devastating fire of 1842 and the Second World War spared but few of this commercial centre's medieval buildings.

■ ■ ■ **A green industrial city.** Hamburg is Germany's second largest industrial centre with a population of 2.8 million. Nonetheless the spacious parks (e.g. "Planten un Blomen") and gardens, woodlands, moors and heaths, have retained its character as one of Germany's "greenest cities". As a result of Germany's unification, the port of Hamburg, with its ramified links with the waterway network, has regained its old hinterland. This enhances the city-state's prospects of becoming the hub of trade, services and communications between east and west as in former times. Hamburg is also the banking and service centre for northern Germany. The fact that it is

the world's principal consular city after New York underscores its international status. The Congress Centre,
venue for many international exhibitions, is one of the
most modern conference centres in Europe.

Hamburg's role as a media city is uncontested. It is
home to Germany's largest periodicals, the German
Press Agency (dpa), and various television and radio networks and studios.

■ ■ ■ **Civic pride and passion for art.** Hamburg has always been an attractive cultural city as well. It was here
that Germany's first permanent opera house was established in 1678, where Georg Friedrich Händel (1685-
1759) staged his first opera ("Almira"). One of the city's
famous sons was the composer Johannes Brahms (1833-
1897). In 1767 the Deutsches Nationaltheater was
founded. It was linked with the name of Lessing and
achieved fame chiefly on account of its performances of
Shakespeare. At that time Friedrich Gottlieb Klopstock
(1724-1803) and Matthias Claudius (1740-1815) were
Hamburg's "literary institutions".

In the present century Rolf Liebermann, director of
Hamburg's opera house, and Gustaf Gründgens the
actor, gave to opera and the theatre respectively a strong
international flavour with their avant-garde productions.

Assembling of the Airbus 321 in Hamburg

Cargo being transshipped in containers

Unforgotten is the Hamburg-born actor Hans Albers, especially for his film role as Baron "Münchhausen". Today the city is also host to musical productions, such as Andrew Lloyd Webber's "Phantom of the Opera", for which a new theatre ("Neue Flora") was specially built. Public generosity stemming from civic pride, and a far-sighted buying policy, have given Hamburg's Kunsthalle, Museum für Kunst und Gewerbe and Völkerkundemuseum, to name only three, outstanding collections.

State election 1991	
SPD	40.8 %
CDU	40.2 %
Greens	8.8 %
FDP	7.4 %

Population	5.9 mill.
Area	21,114 sq km
Capital	Wiesbaden

Hesse

■ ■ ■ **The Rhein-Main crossroads.** The central location of Hesse in the Federal Republic of Germany prior to the country's unification was a boon to its biggest city Frankfurt (647,000), Germany's main financial centre, and to its industrial fairs. This city is a huge autobahn intersection and railway junction, and it has the vast (17 sq km) Rhein-Main Airport which is the largest freight and second largest passenger airport in Europe. Frankfurt on the river Main accommodates most of the country's large banks and many branches of foreign banks in Germany. It is also the headquarters of the Bundesbank, which guards the deutschmark's stability.

■ ■ ■ **Industry and beaux arts.** The Rhein-Main region is, with Berlin, Germany's second largest industrial centre after the Rhein-Ruhr district. It is home to such firms as Hoechst, Opel and Degussa. Other major industries (machinery, locomotives and wagons, automobiles) have established themselves in the northern part of the state around Kassel. This city has an excellent reputation among art lovers owing to its excellent collections of Dutch paintings and its "documenta", the largest exhibitions of contemporary art in the world. Southern Hesse is home to the leather industry (Offenbach). This region's centre is Darmstadt with its famous Technical University. From 1899 the Mathildenhöhe (art nouveau museum in the Ernst Ludwig Haus) developed into the city's artists' colony.

Frankfurt, too, birthplace of Johann Wolfgang von Goethe (1749-1832), is a city of art, theatre and publishing. The River Main's "museum embankment" is constantly growing. Also new in the city centre are the "Schirn" art gallery (1986) and the Museum of Modern

Art (1991). The International Book Fair, at which the Peace Prize of the German Book Trade Association is awarded annually, is the largest of its kind in the world.

Amidst charming landscapes are the university towns of Marburg and Giessen, as well as Wetzlar, famous for its optical instruments. The Bergstrasse and the Rheingau are among Germany's best fruit and wine-growing areas. In eastern Hesse is the bishopric of Fulda, a baroque town of considerable historical importance. The state capital Wiesbaden (257,000) is not only an administrative centre but an elegant spa with a much-frequented casino.

■ ■ ■ **Republican tradition.** Hesse has existed in its present form only since 1945. In previous centuries it

The Mathildenhöhe and Wedding Tower, Darmstadt

A landscape in the Taunus, looking towards Walsdorf

had nearly always been split up into small principalities. It became a focal point in the 16th century, when land-grave Philipp the Magnanimous became one of the political leaders of the Reformation. Frankfurt was for a long time a free imperial city and the place where German emperors were crowned. The city's Saint Paul's Church has become a national monument. It was there in 1848/1849 that the National Assembly convened, the first democratic German Parliament. It failed, however, because of the power wielded by Germany's ruling princes.

State election 1990	
CDU	38.3 %
SPD	27 %
PDS	15.7 %
Alliance 90 / Greens	6.4 %
FDP	5.5 %

Population	1.89 mill.
Area	23,598 sq km
Capital	Schwerin

Mecklenburg-Western Pomerania

■ ■ ■ **Land of a thousand lakes.** No other German state is as rural, no other has such a varied coastline, and no other is as thinly populated as Mecklenburg-Western Pomerania. Its greatest treasure is its untouched nature and "thousand lakes".

Its striking brick architecture bears the unmistakable characteristics of the Hanseatic trade centres Stralsund and Wismar, and of the old university towns of Greifswald (founded in 1456) and Rostock. Rostock, an old Hanseatic town, is today the region's largest city (250,000). However, it is Schwerin (130,000) which became the state capital after Germany's unification.

Schwerin's Stadtschloss is now the seat of the state parliament

■ ■ ■ **Nature and art.** Mecklenburg-Western Pomerania is a gently undulating region with hundreds of lakes, a patchwork of fields, woods and livestock enclosures. Mecklenburg's largest lake is the Müritz (117 sq km), which has an extensive nature reserve along its eastern shore. Throughout the region there are some 260 protected areas. There are countless testimonies to its rich cultural history and many of them, such as Schwerin's castle with its 300 towers, are being renovated.

A big attraction are the chalk cliffs of Rügen, Germany's largest island (926 sq km). Caspar David Friedrich (1774-1840), the painter from Greifswald, captured the seascapes with romantic exuberance. The writer Fritz Reuter (1810-1874) vividly described the area and its people in his low German idiom. The sculptor and writer Ernst Barlach (1870-1938) spent his productive period in Güstrow. And Uwe Johnson (1934-1984) erected with his

The container section of the port of Rostock

The chalk cliffs of Rügen, a wonder of nature

novels a literary monument to his native region and its people.

■ ■ ■ **Tourism, the industry of tomorrow.** The most important branches of the economy are farming and animal husbandry. The coastal and inland fishing industries are permanent sources of employment and are therefore being rapidly modernized and adapted to changing consumer demand. The coastal area is the location of eastern Germany's shipbuilding industry with its various suppliers. But the most promising industry is tourism. In 1992 Mecklenburg-Western Pomerania had about ten million visitors. Rambling and biking are extremely popular. The region is striving to develop its tourist infrastructure, but planners want to make sure that this constantly growing industry does not become a burden on the environment.

State election 1990	
SPD	44.2 %
CDU	42 %
FDP	6 %
Greens	5.5 %

Population	7.5 mill.
Area	47,364 sq km
Capital	Hanover

Lower Saxony

■ ■ ■ **A variegated landscape.** This second largest state in Germany (47,349 sq km) can be subdivided into three main regions: the Harz, the Weserbergland (Weser Highlands) and the North German Lowlands around Lüneburg Heath. A world to themselves are the moors of the Emsland, the marshland behind the North Sea dikes, and the East Frisian islands in the shallow coastal waters.

The major north-south and west-east autobahn and railway arteries intersect in Lower Saxony, and here too the Elbe Canal links up the Rhine, Elbe and Oder, the principal waterways of western and eastern Europe.

■ ■ ■ **Mining tradition and Volkswagen.** Nearly two thirds of this region is given over to farming. There is a wide-ranging food industry which produces such famous delicacies as bacon from the Oldenburg area or honey from Lüneburg Heath. It also has a long mining tradition especially in the Harz. Even in medieval times the imperial town of Goslar owed its wealth to silver mining. In 1775 a school for miners and foundry workers was established in Clausthal which developed into a world-famous mining college. Lüneburg gained prominence because of local salt deposits, and the potash industry is a major branch of Lower Saxony's economy. Salzgitter is the centre of Europe's third largest iron-ore deposit. Significant quantities of local oil and gas are also extracted, providing about 5% of the country's requirements. Brunswick is home to the Federal Institute of Physics and Metrology, the national authority for the testing, standardization and licensing of materials. It also determines the exact Central European Time (CET) per radio signal. Emden has Germany's third largest port on the North

Sea. Famous companies produce container vessels and automobiles there.

But one town in Lower Saxony epitomises car manufacturing in Germany: Wolfsburg, home of the famous Volkswagen. Volkswagen is the biggest company in the region and its foundation the largest non-governmental scientific institution in Germany.

■ ■ ■ **Hanover and the industrial fair, Göttingen and its university.** Half a million of this state's 7.3 million inhabitants live in the capital, Hanover. It is the venue for the world-famous industrial fair and the "CEBIT" exhibition of communications technology. Every year they show the present generation the world of tomorrow. Hanover is now looking forward to hosting the World Exhibition in 2000.

The university town of Göttingen has played an outstanding role in the country's political and scientific history. In 1837 a group of professors, the "Göttingen Seven", protested against the sovereign's decision to annul the constitution. For this they were dismissed, but

Lüneburg Heath, an attractive recreational area

The Hanover Industrial Fair is the largest in the World

most of these liberal spirits met again in 1848 as deputies to the National Assembly in Frankfurt. Another famous name associated with Göttingen is that of the mathematician and astronomer Carl Friedrich Gauss (1771-1859).

In the 20th century Göttingen has been a source of major developments in the field of nuclear physics. Of all those who taught or studied in Göttingen one need only mention the Nobel Prize winners Max Born (1882-1970) and Werner Heisenberg (1901-1976).

State election 1990	
SPD	50 %
CDU	36.7 %
FDP	5.8 %
Greens	5 %

Population	17.,7 mill
Area	34,071 sq km
Capital	Düsseldorf

North-Rhine/Westphalia

■ ■ ■ **A powerhouse in the heart of Europe.** The present state of North-Rhine/Westphalia was formed in 1946, when the British, who occupied the region after the war, merged the greater part of the former Prussian Rhine province and the province of Westphalia with the state of Lippe-Detmold. North-Rhine/Westphalia covers an area of 34,000 sq km and is thus as large as Belgium and Luxembourg together. Not only is it the most densely populated state in the Federal Republic (17 million), it is also Europe's largest conglomeration. About half of this region's population live in cities with more than 500,000 inhabitants. The Ruhr district is an a huge web of towns and cities with a total population of about 7.5 million, and it is Germany's, indeed Europe's, largest industrial region. With its 31 giant power stations the Ruhr is Germany's main source of energy.

■ ■ ■ **Tradition and innovation.** In a massive effort on the part of industry, the regional and the federal government over many years, North-Rhine/Westphalia has succeeded in restructuring its economy, which is traditionally based on coal and steel, to meet world market demand. Hundreds of thousands of new jobs have been created through the settlement of innovative industries, with the result that today it is the future-oriented branches alongside such internationally famous companies as Klöckner-Humboldt-Deutz, the world's largest engine manufacturer, that dominate the scene. Proof of the region's economic vitality is the fact that, apart from heavy industry, there are 450,000 small and medium-sized firms, many of them with state-of-the-art technology, for instance those making cloth in Krefeld or cutlery in Solingen. A traditional yet expanding branch of the service sector is that of insurance, while Dortmund is the location of Germany's largest breweries. The northern parts concentrate on farming and animal husbandry, while the Münsterland is famous for horse breeding and riding. The most visible sign of North-Rhine/Westphalia's dynamic economy is the dense network of autobahns, railways and waterways. It incorporates Europe's traffic arteries and links together the region's principal cities of Cologne, Essen, Dortmund, Düsseldorf, Duisburg, Bochum, Wuppertal, Bielefeld, Leverkusen and Aachen. Duisburg has the largest inland port in the world.

■ ■ ■ **Leisure, culture, and higher education.** This coal mining region is undergoing a transformation. For-

Bonn's baroque city hall

The gothic cathedral is Cologne's landmark

mer landscapes of smoking chimney stacks and con-
veyor belts are being turned into green areas and the
open-cast mining areas on the Rhine recultivated. The
Sauerland and the Bergisches Land are popular recreational areas, particularly for people in the Rhine and
Ruhr district. North-Rhine/Westphalia has 44 spas. Cologne, now the region's largest city (over a million) and a
major centre since Roman times, is famous for its romanesque churches and Gothic cathedral, but also for its museums (Wallraf Richartz Museum/Museum Ludwig,
Roman-Germanic Museum, and many more). Düsseldorf (577,000), the state capital, is one of the country's
main financial centres. It has made its name as a cultural
city through its outstanding collections of paintings, its
Deutsche Oper am Rhein (Düsseldorf/Duisburg), and its
famous Schauspielhaus. Münster in Westphalia, with a
most attractive city centre, has a major university. South
of Cologne lies Bonn, until 1949 a medium-sized university town, but from that year until the country's unification capital of the Federal Republic of Germany. Although the seat of the Federal Government, too, is to be
switched to Berlin, Bonn will continue to play an important role as an administrative and scientific centre.

State election 1991	
SPD	44.8 %
CDU	38.7 %
FDP	6.9 %
Greens	6.5 %

Population	3.8 mill.
Area	19,846 sq km
Capital	Mainz

Rhineland-Palatinate

■ ■ ■ **More than sagas and vineyards.** Rhineland-Palatinate was formed in 1946 from parts of Bavarian, Hessian and Prussian territory which previously had never belonged together. In the meantime they have become closely knit and Rhineland-Palatinate has acquired its own identity. Initially one of the poorer regions, it is today the state with the largest export quota and headquarters of Europe's biggest chemical corporation, BASF in Ludwigshafen, and the country's most extensive TV and radio network, Channel II, based in Mainz. Every year seven million visitors to Rhineland-Palatinate seek recreation or curative treatment in such spas as Bad Neuenahr, Bad Ems or Bad Bertrich. Many of the region's mineral-waters gush from springs in the volcanic rocks of the Central Uplands. The vineyards on the Rhine, the Ahr and the Mosel yield two thirds of the country's wine. Extensive forests are a major source of employment.

■ ■ ■ **Yesterday and today.** The Rhineland was settled by Celts, Romans, Burgundians and Franks. In Speyer, Worms and Mainz, all on the Rhine, are to be found the great imperial cathedrals of the Middle Ages. The elector of Mainz was arch chancellor of the "Holy Roman Empire of the German Nation". Worms has Germany's oldest synagogue (construction of which began in 1034 in the romanesque style). It was in Worms too, at the imperial diet of 1521, that the reformer Martin Luther refused to recant his theses. Three hundred years later, in Koblenz, the liberal paper "Rheinischer Merkur" opposed Napoleonic rule and censorship of the press, and Hambach Castle was the scene of the first democratic-republican assembly in Germany (1832). The world-famous Print Museum in Mainz displays the treasures of

Johannes Gutenberg (1400-1468), the inventor of book-printing using movable characters. His epoch-making achievement was the breakthrough for Luther's Reformation. Trier is the birthplace of another kind of revolutionary, Karl Marx (1818- 1883), the philosopher and critic of the national economy.

■ ■ ■ **The Rhine, the region's main artery.** The 290 km section of the river Rhine passing through or bordering Rhineland-Palatinate is the region's main economic artery. On it lie the three main cities: Ludwigshafen

Merl on the River Mosel with the former church tower

The BASF in Ludwigshafen is the largest industrial complex in Europe

(158,000), the chemical centre, Mainz (175,000), the state capital, and Koblenz (107,000), the service centre at the confluence of the Rhine and the Mosel. With a population of just under 100,000 are Kaiserslautern, where Emperor Frederick I (Barbarossa) built a palace, and Trier, the 2,000-year-old city on the Mosel. One of Germany's most beautiful landscapes is the stretch of the Rhine valley between Bingen and Bonn. With its many castles it is steeped in legend and its praises have been sung by countless poets, painters and musicians. The Rhine's tributaries, too, the Mosel, Nahe, Lahn and Ahr, have a charm of their own. At the foot of the Palatinate Forest runs the "German Wine Route". The unusnal light above this lovely hilly area was captured by the painter Max Slevogt (1868-1932). Many of his pictures are to be found in Ludwigshöhe Palace near Edenkoben. Some are also to be found, together with works by Hans Purrmann (1880-1966) who was "ostracized" by the nazi regime, in the Federal Chancellery in Bonn.

State election 1990	
SPD	54.4 %
CDU	33.4 %
FDP	5.6 %

Population	1.1 mill.
Area	2,570 sq km
Capital	Saarbrücken

Saarland

■ ■ ■ **Good-neighbourly relations.** The political evolution of this by far the smallest of Germany's states (apart from the city-states) mirrors the vicissitudes of German history in the 20th century.

This coal and steel region was detached from the German Empire in 1920 and placed under the administration of the League of Nations. In 1935 the population voted with a large majority in favour of its return to Germany. The same happened after the Second World War. The Saar was again severed from Germany, and again it was returned after a referendum, this time as a state of the Federal Republic of Germany. France's agreement to this referendum is a landmark in the process of Franco-German reconciliation. The reintegration of the Saarland on 1 January 1957 was effected in accordance with article 23 of the Basic Law (constitution) - an unprecedented step which was to serve as a model for German unification in 1990.

■ ■ ■ **City, state and river.** This state takes its name from the River Saar, a tributary of the Mosel. The Saar Canal between Dillingen and Konz on the Mosel makes it a major waterway for large vessels. The Saar meanders charmingly through the forested Hunsrück range of the Central Uplands. Its lower reaches are a wine-growing area. The state capital, Saarbrücken (192,000), is a fair and congress centre. It is a symbiosis of the French and German way of life. The Saarländer have a partiality for culinary delights and wine. A native of the city, the director Max Ophüls (1902-1957), made film history with such charming comedies as "Liebelei". Saarland's higher education institutions, the university, the polytechnics, the art college and the music academy, are concentrated in the city and many students come from neighbouring France.

The name of the state's second largest city, Saarlouis, reminds us that here, about 300 years ago, the French King Louis XIV built a fortress to defend his conquests in western Germany. This city is today a location for industry (automobiles, steel, food and electronics).

■ ■ ■ **One of Europe's core regions.** Like science and scholarship, industry, too, has long since crossed national boundaries. The Saarland in Germany, Lorraine in France, and Luxembourg are developing ever closer ties, so that the abbreviation "Saar-Lor-Lux" now stands for one of Europe's core regions. Traditional branches of industry of supraregional importance are glass and ceramics. The distinctive features of goods produced by

The Ludwigskirche, Saarbrücken

Colliers about to descend into the coalmine

large companies such as Villeroy & Boch are high quality as well as richness of form and colour. True, the Saarland has been somewhat affected by the coal and steel crisis, but a restructuring programme and innovations have already prepared the ground for the establishment of modern industries. Today most Saarländer are employed in the capital goods and services sector. The region also hopes to derive fresh impetus from the European internal market that came into effect in January 1993, especially in the mechanical engineering, metal-processing and chemical industries.

State election 1990	
CDU	53.8 %
SPD	19.1 %
PDS	10.2 %
Alliance 90 / Greens	5.6 %
FDP	5.3 %

Population	4.7 mill.
Area	18,338 sq km
Capital	Dresden

The Free State of Saxony

■ ■ ▪ **"Little Paris" and "Florence on the Elbe".** Saxony is the most densely populated and most industrialized of the new German states. More than one fifth of the region's 4.9 million inhabitants live in Leipzig (508,000) and Dresden (488,000). Leipzig, famous for its international industrial fair and referred to by Goethe as "little Paris", was one of the main centres of peaceful resistance to the Communist regime in East Germany. The "Monday demonstrations" in the city culminated on 9 October 1989 in the chant: "We are the people!" And Dresden, that "pearl of baroque architecture" which was reduced almost to ashes in the inferno of the 1945 bombings, has been made capital of the restored "Free State of Saxony".

The Meissen porcelain factory has been producing its famous merchandise continuously since 1710. The year before, Johann Friedrich Böttger (1682-1719) had produced his formula for this "white gold". Also world-famous are the wood carvings and pillow lace from the Erzgebirge.

Chemnitz, with its Technical University and research institutes, focuses on mechanical engineering and, of late, micro-electronics. Zwickau is a car manufacturing centre, though instead of the legendary Trabant ("Trabi") Volkswagen's "Polo" is now produced there. Leipzig, once Germany's most important commercial centre and hub of the publishing world, continues to stage its international trade fair, which makes it a gateway to Eastern Europe.

Dresden, popularly known as "Florence on the Elbe", hopes to be able to live up to its reputation as one of Germany's cultural centres. It is still a leading city in the

world of music, with the Opera House, built in the Italian
Renaissance style by Gottfried Semper in 1870-78, restored to its former glory, the Staatskapelle, and the famous choir, the Kreuzchor. It is an El Dorado of the visual
arts with its extensive collections of precious stones,
pearls and works of art in the Grünes Gewölbe and its
paintings by European masters in the Gemäldegalerie
Alte Meister.

The Elbe Sandstone Mountains in the "Switzerland of
Saxony" is a popular holiday region, but not only on ac-
count of the ideal climbing conditions it has to offer.
Great efforts are being made to expand the tourist trade.
An "Erzgebirge Silver Route" is being developed which
will lead visitors to 150 places of interest.

■ ■ ■ **Creative energy and enterprising spirit.** Saxony
features in many chapters of German cultural history.
The works of Johann Sebastian Bach (born in Eisenach in

A painter demonstrating her skill in the Meissen porcelaine factory

Kronentor, Salon und Wallpavillon in Dresden's Zwinger

The Neues Gewandhaus, Leipzig

1685) are traditionally performed by the St. Thomas's Choir in Leipzig where he was cantor from 1723 until his death in 1750. Gottfried Wilhelm Leibniz (1646-1716), philosopher, mathematician and diplomat, discovered the binary number system and - independently of Newton - infinitesimal calculus. Gotthold Ephraim Lessing (1729-1781) extolled in his drama "Nathan the Wise" the virtues of humanity and tolerance. Other sons of Saxony are the composers Robert Schumann (1810-1856) and Richard Wagner (1813-1883).

Even when eastern Germany had a centrally planned economy the Saxons retained their artistic and business sense. Now their characteristic enterprise is beginning to reassert itself. Of the new federal states, this one is considered to have the best economic prospects.

State election 1990	
CDU	39 %
SPD	26 %
FDP	13.5 %
PDS	12 %
Alliance 90 / Greens	5.3 %

Population	2.82 mill.
Area	20,443 sq km
Capital	Magdeburg

Saxony-Anhalt

■ ■ ■ **Classical central Germany.** Saxony-Anhalt is the classical embodiment of central Germany on the rivers Elbe and Saale, covering the area between the Harz mountains, with the Brocken (3,500 ft), the Blocksberg of Goethe's Faust, and the Fläming, a ridge of hills in the east between the Auwiesen in the north and the vineyards along the Saale and Unstrut. Halberstadt's cathedral, originally built in the romanesque style, and the monument to the "Merseburg spells" which is over a thousand years old, bear witness to a historical continuity from the days of Charlemagne.

In many towns the past has lived on. This region is only thinly populated, particularly in the northern parts, Altmark and Magdeburger Börde, whose loess soil is ideal for farming (wheat, sugarbeet and vegetables). There is an extensive food industry (sugar factories). Nearly one in five of the state's three million inhabitants lives in Halle (310,000), Magdeburg (278,000), and Dessau (101,000). Halle, Bitterfeld, Leuna, Wolfen, and Merseburg, hitherto centres of the chemical and lignite mining industries, are in a phase of radical change as a result of the misguided policies of the former German Democratic Republic. Extensive investment to reverse environmental pollution and create a new infrastructure will have to be maintained for many years - as in all of the new German states. The nucleus of the region's traditional chemical industry is to be preserved, however. The opening of the first Max Planck Institute in eastern Germany, in Halle in 1992, was another step to boost the region's economy.

■ ■ ■ **Testimony to a great past.** The decision in 1990 to make Magdeburg, which has a Technical University and a School of Medicine and is a centre of heavy engineering, capital of Saxony-Anhalt settled the traditional rivalry with Halle, at least in this respect. Both cities have a distinctive medieval past. The cathedral of Magdeburg, seat of emperors and bishops, is one of the largest in Germany. The old salt town of Halle, birthplace of the composer Georg Friedrich Händel (1685-1759), is dominated by the cathedral, the Marktkirche and the Red Tower. The German-American painter Lyonel Feininger (1871-1956) captured the city's landmarks with his fascinating modernistic style. His works and those of his contemporaries can be seen in Moritzburg's Staatliche Galerie. But one of the major centres of 20th century art was Dessau, thanks mainly to its Bauhaus school of architecture.

Industry with a future: a chemical plant in Wittenberg

Merseburg's skyline with the cathedral and palace

Tangermünde, with its brick architecture, is regarded as the "Rothenburg of the North". Wernigerode, a jewel of semi-timbered buildings, is commonly known as the "colourful town in the Harz region". The medieval figures depicting the founders of Naumburg's cathedral are early examples of realistic representation. Eisleben is where Martin Luther (1483-1546) was born and died. He was buried in Wittenberg's Schlosskirche, to the door of which he is said to have nailed his 95 theses in 1517. Eisleben was also the home of the famous Cranach family of painters. At the royal court in Köthen Johann Sebastian Bach composed his six Brandenburg concertos. In 1663, the physicist Otto von Guericke, who was mayor of Magdeburg, demonstrated the effects of air pressure using his "Magdeburg hemispheres".

State election 1992	
SPD	46.2 %
CDU	33.8 %
DVU	6.3 %
FDP	5.6 %
SSW	1.9 %

Population	2.6 mill.
Area	15,731 sq km
Capital	Kiel

Schleswig-Holstein

■ ■ ■ **Forever undivided.** Schleswig-Holstein is the only German state bordered by two seas, the North Sea and the Baltic. An ancient deed says that the region's two parts, Schleswig and Holstein, should remain "forever undivided". Consequently, they have long been linked as Schleswig-Holstein - unlike those regions which were "hyphenated" by the occupying powers after 1945.

Schleswig-Holstein is thinly populated (2.6 million inhabitants). The state capital Kiel (246,000) and the Hanseatic City of Lübeck (215,000) owe their importance to their position on the Baltic. Lübeck-Travemünde is one of Germany's principal ferry ports.

■ ■ ■ **Farming and commerce.** In former times Schleswig-Holstein was an exclusively agricultural area (mainly livestock farming) and this branch of the economy is still predominant in the fertile marshlands along the western coast. The coastal fishing industry on the North Sea and the Baltic is also proud of its tradition.

In the Middle Ages and in early modern times Flensburg had one of the largest sail fleets in the North and dominated the route to the West Indies. Lübeck, on the other hand, owed its prosperity to the grain trade, whereas Kiel grew with the navy.

The region's seafaring tradition led to the development of a major shipbuilding industry. As a result of the crisis in this sector in the late 60s, some companies successfully switched to the construction of special vessels. Another solution was to develop a wide range of small and medium-sized industries.

■ ■ ■ **Tourism - a growth industry.** The North Sea island of Helgoland, where Hoffmann von Fallersleben composed his German anthem in 1841, as well as the

Lübeck's "artists' corner" with the churches of St. Mary and St. Peter

North Frisian Islands, including the fashionable Sylt and Föhr, a popular family resort, have their regular visitors just like the resorts on the Baltic Sea, the modern Damp being no different from the dreamy town of Hohwacht in this respect. Inland, the area known as "Holstein's Switzerland" with its lakes is another tourist attraction. Other towns worth visiting are Mölln and the cathedral town of Schleswig, famous for its late Gothic Bordesholm altar created by Hans Brüggemann between 1514 and 1521, a masterpiece of woodcarving.

■ ■ ■ **World cultural heritage and world literature.** Lübeck, whose 500-year-old gate, the Holstentor, bears the inscription in Latin "harmony at home, peace outside", has been entered in UNESCO's cultural list as a German contribution to world culture.

Thomas Mann (1885-1955), a writer of world fame, was born in Lübeck. He was awarded the 1929 Nobel Prize for literature. In May 1993 the house of the grandparents of Thomas and Heinrich Mann (1871-1950) was opened as "Buddenbrook House", a memorial and place of scholarly research.

Kiel Week denotes the famous regatta which every year in June attracts yachtsmen from all over the world.

State election 1990	
CDU	45.4 %
SPD	22.8 %
PDS	9.7 %
FDP	9.3 %
Alliance 90 / Greens	6.5 %

Population	2.57 mill.
Area	16,251 sq km
Capital	Erfurt

Thuringia

■ ■ ■ **Germany's green heartland.** On account of its position and extensive forest areas Thuringia is also referred to as "Germany's green heartland". The state capital is Erfurt (209,000), which was founded in the eighth century and is proud to be called a "garden city". The old part of the city has an unusually large number of Patrician houses, churches and monasteries which make it a kind of architectural museum. Johann Sebastian Bach was born in Eisenach in 1685, one of a ramified family of musicians. He died in Leipzig in 1750. Martin Luther hid in the nearby Wartburg in 1521/22. There he translated the New Testament into German - a major step in the development of modern written German. And at the same place in 1817 students called for a united Germany.

■ ■ ■ **Territorial fragmentation, culture and barbarity.** Thuringia was particularly affected by Germany's much lamented territorial fragmentation. But culturally this proved to be a good thing since the rulers of even small territories were keen patrons of the arts - albeit mostly at the expense of their subjects who had to pay heavy taxes. By far the most prominent among them was Duke Karl August of Saxony-Weimar (1757-1828). He brought to his court the romantic poet and translator of Shakespeare Christoph Martin Wieland (1733- 1813), the poet and philologist Johann Gottfried Herder (1744-1803), and above all Johann Wolfgang von Goethe (1749-1832). Thus at that time, around 1800, Weimar was a capital of culture, and not only of German culture. In this city Goethe produced some of his most famous works, including the final version of Faust. Weimar was also home to Friedrich Schiller from 1787 to 1789 and from 1799 to 1805. There he wrote, among other works, his

William Tell. Franz Liszt (1811-1886) composed and gave concerts there in the second half of the 19th century. Here the Bauhaus was founded in 1919, a school of architecture which sought to overcome the divisions between art, handicraft and technology. In 1925 the Bauhaus moved to Dessau, and a few years later to Berlin, where, in 1933, it fell victim to the barbarity which followed Hitler's seizure of power. The year 1933 also marked the demise of the first German republic, the "Weimar Republic", whose constitution had been drafted in Weimar in 1919.

■ ■ ■ **Industry and crafts.** In medieval times several Thuringian towns, especially Erfurt, became rich through trade with a blue-dyeing plant, the woad. Other branches of the economy grew up later, including machine tools and precision and optical instruments, which made the city of Jena and the name of Carl Zeiss, the mechanic, world famous. Automobiles have been manufactured in Eisenach for some considerable time (in GDR

Schloss Reinhardsbrunn near Friedrichsroda

Glassblowers in the Jena Glassworks

times a famous make was the "Wartburg"). Since German unification the firms of Opel and Bosch have been operating there. Some of the farmland is of the highest quality. Barley, wheat, potatoes, sugarbeet and fruit are grown.

· German history up to 1945
· From 1945 to the present

German history up to 1945

Up to the last century it was a widely held belief that German history began in the year A. D. 9. That was when Arminius, a prince of a Germanic tribe called the Cherusci, vanquished three Roman legions in the Teutoburg Forest (south-east of modern-day Bielefeld). Arminius, about whom not much else is known, was regarded as the first German national hero and a huge memorial to him was built near Detmold in the years 1838-75.

Nowadays a less simplistic view is taken. The fusing of a German nation was a process which took hundreds of years. The word "deutsch" (German) probably began to be used in the 8th century and initially defined only the language spoken in the eastern part of the Franconian realm. This empire, which reached the zenith of its power under Charlemagne, incorporated peoples speaking Germanic and Romance dialects. After Charlemagne's death (814) it soon fell apart. In the course of various inheritance divisions, a west and an east realm developed, whose political boundary approximately coincided with the boundary between German and French speakers. Only gradually did a feeling of cohesion develop among the inhabitants of the eastern realm. Then the term "deutsch" was transferred from the language to its speakers and ultimately to the region they lived in, "Deutschland."

The German western frontier was fixed relatively early and remained fairly stable. But the eastern frontier moved to and fro for hundreds of years. Around 900 it ran approximately along the Elbe and Saale rivers. In subsequent centuries German settlement, partly peaceful and partly by force, extended far to the east. This expansion stopped only in the middle of the 14th century. The ethnic boundary then made between Germans und Slavs remained until World War II.

■ ■ ■ **High Middle Ages.** The transition from the East Franconian to the German "Reich" is usually dated from 911, when, after the Carolingian dynasty had died out, the Franconian duke Conrad I was elected king. He is regarded as the first German king. (The official title was "Frankish King," later "Roman King," from the 11th century the name of the realm was "Roman Empire," from the 13th century "Holy Roman Empire," in the 15th century the words "of the German Nation" were added.) It was an electoral monarchy, that is to say, the high nobility chose the king. In addition, "dynastic right" also applied and so the new king had to be a blood relation of his predecessor. This principle was broken several times. There were also a number of double elections. The medieval empire had no capital city; the king ruled roving about from place to place. There were no imperial taxes; the king drew his sustenance mainly from "imperial estates" he administered in trust. His authority was not always recognized by the powerful tribal dukes unless he was militarily powerful and a skilful forger of alliances. Conrad's successor, Henry I (919-936), was the first to succeed in this, and to an even greater extent his son, Otto (936-973). Otto made himself the real ruler of the realm. His great power found obvious expression when he was crowned Emperor in 962 in Rome.

From then on the German king could claim the title "Emperor". The emperorship was conceived as universal and gave its incumbent control over the entire east. However, this notion never became full political reality. In order to be crowned emperor by the Pope the king had to make his way to Rome. With that began the Italian policy of the German kings. For 300 years they were able to retain control of upper and central Italy but because of this were diverted from important tasks in Germany. And so Otto's successors inevitably suffered big setbacks. However, under the succeeding Salian dynasty a new upswing occurred. With Henry III (1039-1056) the German kingship and emperorship reached the zenith of its power, maintaining above all a supremacy over the Papacy. Henry IV (1056-1106) was not able to hold this position. In a quarrel with Pope Gregory VII over whether bishops and other influential church officials should be appointed by the Pope or the temporal ruler he was superficially successful. But Gregory retaliated by excommunicating Henry, who thereupon surrendered his authority over the church by doing penance to the Pope at Canossa (1077), an irretrievable loss of power by the emperorship. (To this day Germans use the phrase "A walk to Canossa" for someone having to eat humble pie). From then on Emperor and Pope were equal-ranking powers.

In 1138 the century of rule by the Staufer or Hohenstaufen dynasty began. Frederick I Barbarossa (1115-1190), in wars with the Pope, the upper Italian cities and his main German rival, the Saxon Duke Henry the Lion, led the empire into a new golden age. But under him began a territorial fragmentation which ultimately weakened the central power. This decline continued under Barbarossa's successors, Henry VI (1190-1197) and Frederick II (1212-1250) despite the great power vested in the emperorship. The religious and temporal princes became semi-sovereign territorial rulers. The end of Hohenstaufen rule (1268) also meant the end of the the Emperor's universal rule in the east as well. Internal disintegrative forces prevented Germany from becoming a national state, a process just beginning then in other west European countries. Here lies one of the reasons why the Germans became a "belated nation."

■ ■ ■ **Late Middle Ages to modern times.** Rudolf I (1273-1291) was the first Habsburg to take the throne. Now the material foundation of the emperorship was no longer the lost imperial estates but the "house estates" of the dynasties and house power politics became every emperor's main preoccupation. The "Golden Bull" (imperial constitution) issued by Charles IV in 1356 regulated the election of the German king by seven electors privileged with special rights. These sovereign electors and the towns, because of their economic power, gradually gained influence while that of the small counts, lords and knights declined. The towns' power further increased when they linked up in leagues. The most important of these, the Hanseatic League, became the leading Baltic power in the 14th century. To this day the city-states of Hamburg and Bremen proudly call themselves "Hanseatic cities."

From 1438 the crown - although the empire nominally was an electoral monarchy - practically became the property of the Habsburg dynasty which had become the strongest territorial power. In the 15th century demands for imperial reformed increased. Maximilian I (1483 to 1519), the first to accept the imperial title without a papal coronation, tried to implement such a reform but without much success. The institutions newly

Emperor Charles IV and the seven electors (armorial, ca. 1370)

created or reshaped by him - Reichstag (Imperial Diet), Reichskreise (Imperial Counties), Reichskammergericht (Imperial Court) - lasted until the end of the Reich (1806), but were not able to halt its continuing fragmentation. Consequently, a dualism of "Emperor and Reich" developed: the head of the Reich was offset by various institutions - electoral princes, princes and municipalities. The power ot the emperors was curtailed and increasingly eroded by "capitulations," which they negotiated at their election with the electoral princes. The princes, especially the powerful among them, greatly expanded their rights at the expense of imperial power. But the Reich continued to hold together, the glory of the imperial idea had remained alive and the small and medium territories were protected in the Reich system from attack by powerful neighbours.

The towns became centres of economic power, profiting above all from growing trade. In the burgeoning textile and mining industries, forms of economic activity grew which went beyond the guilds system of the craftsmen and, like long-distance trading, were beginning to take on early capitalistic traits. At the same time an intellectual change was taking place, marked by the Renaissance and Humanism. The newly risen critical spirit turned above all on church abuses.

■ ■ ■ **Age of religious schism.** The smouldering dissatisfaction with the church broke out, mainly through

Peasants in revolt (woodcut by Hans Burgkmair, 1525)

the actions of Martin Luther from 1517, in the Reformation, which quickly spread. Its consequences went far beyond the religious sphere. Social unrest abounded. In 1522/23 the Reich knights rose up and in 1525 the Peasants' Revolt broke out, the first larger revolutionary movement in German history to strive for both political and social change. Both uprisings failed or were bloodily quelled. The territorial princes profited most from the Reformation. After the changing fortunes of war they were given the right to dictate their subjects' religion by the 1555 Peace of Augsburg. This accorded the Protestants equal rights with those of the Catholics. The religious division of Germany was thus sealed.

On the imperial throne at the time of the Reformation was Charles V (1519-56), heir to the biggest realm since the time of Charlemagne but also the last Holy Roman Emperor to aspire to the medieval ideal of universal empire. His international political interests were too demanding for him to be able to assert himself within Germany. After his abdication the empire was split up. The German territorial states and the west European national-states together now formed the new European system of states.

At the time of the Peace of Augsburg, four fifths of Germany were Protestant but the struggle between the faiths had not ended. In the following decades the Catholic church was able to recapture many areas (Counter-Re-

formation). The differences between the faiths sharp-
ened, religious parties - the Protestant Union (1608) and
the Catholic League (1609) - were formed. A local conflict in Bohemia then triggered off the Thirty Years War
which widened into a European conflict over religious
and political differences. Between 1618 and 1648 much
of Germany was devastated and depopulated. The 1648
Peace of Westphalia brought the cession of territories to
France and Sweden and confirmed the withdrawal of
Switzerland and the Netherlands from the Reich.

Frederic II, The Great (1712-1786)

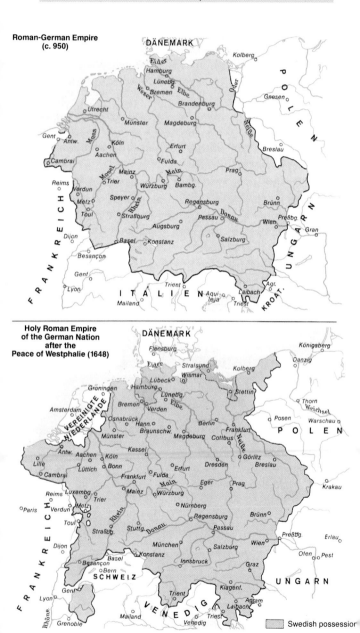

Roman-German Empire (c. 950)

DÄNEMARK
Eider
Kolberg
Hamburg
Lünebg.
Weser
Bremen
Elbe
Brandenburg
Oder
P O L E N
Gnesen
Utrecht
Münster
Magdeburg
Neisse
Gent
Antw.
Maas
Köln
Erfurt
Breslau
Cambrai
Aachen
Fulda
Reims
Mosel
Mainz
Main
Prag
Verdun
Trier
Würzburg
Bambg.
Brünn
Metz
Speyer o
Rhein
Regensburg
Donau
Wien
Preßbg.
Toul
Straßburg
Passau
Gran
F R A N K R E I C H
Augsburg
U N G A R N
Dijon
Basel
Konstanz
Salzburg
Besançon
Genf
Trient
Aqui-
Laibach
Agt.
Lyon
I T A L I E N
leja
Triest
KROAT.
Mailand

Holy Roman Empire of the German Nation after the Peace of Westphalie (1648)

DÄNEMARK
Flensburg
Königsberg
Eider
Stralsund
Wismar
Kolberg
Danzig
Lübeck
Groningen
Hamburg
Lünebg.
Stettin
Amsterdam
Bremen
Elbe
Verden
Thorn
Weichsel
VEREINIGTE
Osnabrück
Hann.
Berlin
Posen
Warschau
NIEDERLANDE
Braunschw.
Magdeburg
P O L E N
Antw.
Münster
Kassel
Cottbus
Neisse
Lille
Aachen
Köln
Frankfurt
Görlitz
Lüttich
Bonn
Dresden
Breslau
Cambrai
Erfurt
Eger
Reims
Frankfurt
Fulda
Prag
Krakau
Luxembg.
Mainz
Main
Paris
Verdun
Trier
Würzburg
Metz
Nürnberg
Brünn
Toul
Rhein
Regensburg
Erlau
F R A N K R E I C H
Straßbg.
Stuttg.
Donau
Passau
Preßbg.
Dijon
München
Salzburg
Wien
Ofen
Pest
Basel
Bern
Besançon
Innsbruck
Graz
U N G A R N
SCHWEIZ
Konstanz
Genf
Trient
Klagenf.
Agram
Rhône
V E N E D I G
Laibach
Lyon
Triest
Grenoble
Mailand
Venedig

Swedish possession

German Empire 1871–1918

DÄNEMARK
Ribe · Kopenhagen
Flensburg
Eider
Groningen · Hamburg · Lübeck · Rostock · Kolberg · Memel · Königsberg · Danzig
Amsterd. · Oldenbg. · Bremen · Lüneburg · Stettin · Thorn · Bialystok
Utrecht · Hannover · Elbe · Küstrin · Posen · Weichsel · Warschau
NIEDERLANDE · Münster · Braunschwg. · Berlin · Frankfurt · Kalisch
Brüssel · Düsseld. · Kassel · Magdeburg · Leipzig · Görlitz · Breslau
BELGIEN · Köln · Erfurt · Dresden · Kattowitz
Lütt. · Aachen · Frankfurt · Eger · Prag · Krakau
Rhein · Mainz · Main · Würzburg · Nürnberg
FRANKREICH · Lux. · Luxembg. · Saarbrücken · Regensbg. · ÖSTERREICH-
Verdun · 1871 · Straßburg · Stuttgart · Donau · Brünn
Toul · München · Passau
Basel · Konstanz · Salzburg · Wien · UNGARN
Besançon · Bern · Innsbruck · Graz
SCHWEIZ · Klagenfurt
RUSSLAND

Boundary of German Confederation (1815–1866)

Germany within the borders of 1937

DÄNEMARK
Ribe · Kopenhagen
Flensburg
Kiel
Groningen · Hamburg · Lübeck · Rostock · Kolberg · Memel · LITAUEN
Amsterdam · Weser · Bremen · Lüneburg · Schwerin · Neu-brandenburg · Stettin · Danzig · Königsberg · DANZIG
Utrecht · Hannover · Elbe · Berlin · Küstrin · Weichsel · Thorn
NIEDERLANDE · Münster · Braunschweig · Potsd. · Frankfurt · Posen · Warschau
Brüssel · Düsseldorf · Halle · Magdeburg · Cottbus · Oder · POLEN
BELGIEN · Aach. · Köln · Bonn · Kassel · Leipzig · Dresden · Görlitz · Breslau
Lüttich · Erfurt · Karlsbad · Prag · Kattowitz · Krakau
Wiesbaden · Frankfurt · Eger · TSCHECHOSLOWAKEI
FRANKREICH · Lux. · Mosel · Mainz · Main · Würzburg
Luxembg. · Saarbrücken · Nürnberg · Brünn
Verdun · Toul · Straßburg · Stuttgart · Regensburg · Donau · Wien
München · Passau
Basel · Konstanz · Salzbg.
Besançon · Bern · Innsbruck · ÖSTERREICH
SCHWEIZ

1 : 15 000 000   0 100 200 300 400 500

The Reich institutions were accorded all major sovereign rights in religious and temporal matters and the right to enter alliances with foreign partners.

■ ■ ■ **Age of absolutism.** The almost sovereign principalities took over the absolutist form of government modelled on the French. Absolutism gave the ruler limitless power while at the same time allowing tight administrations to be built up, an organized fiscal policy to be introduced and new armies to be mobilized. Many princes aspired to making their residences cultural focal points. Some of them, representatives of "enlightened absolutism", encouraged learning and philosophy, albeit within the confines of their power interests. The policy of state control of all economic life also allowed the absolutistically ruled states to gain in economic strength. Thus lands such as Bavaria, Brandenburg (the later Prussia), Saxony and Hanover were able to develop into power centres in their own right. Austria, which repelled the attacking Turks and acquired Hungary as well as parts of the formerly Turkish Balkan countries, rose to a large power. A rival to it developed in the 18th century in the form of Prussia which, under Frederick the Great (1740-86), grew into a first-rank military power. Both states sought to assert their authority in Europe.

■ ■ ■ **Age of the French Revolution.** The nudge which brought the crumbling Reich crashing down came from the west. Revolution broke out in France in 1789. Under pressure from the middle classes, the feudal social order which had existed since the early Middle Ages was swept away; a divison of powers and human rights were to assure the liberty and equality of all. The attempt by Prussia and Austria to intervene by force in events in neighbouring country failed ignominiously and triggered a counter-thrust by the revolutionary armies. Under the stormy advances of the forces of Napoleon who had assumed the revolutionary heritage in France the Reich finally collapsed. France took the left bank of the Rhine. To compensate the former owners of these areas for their losses, an enormous territorial reshuffling took place at the expense of the smaller and particularly the religious principalities. By the "Reichsdeputationshauptschluss" of 1803 some four million subjects had changed rulers. The medium-sized states were the beneficiaries. In 1806 most of them grouped together under French protection in the "Rheinbund" (Rhenish League). In the same year Emperor Franz II laid down the crown and the Holy Roman Empire of the German Nation ceased to exist.

The French revolution did not spread into Germany. Although there, too, various individuals had over the years tried time and again to do away with the barriers between the aristocracy and the common people and although leading thinkers welcomed the overthrow in the west as the start of a new era, one major reason why the spark could not catch easily was that, in contrast to the centrally oriented France, the federalistic structure of the Reich hampered the spread of new ideas. Another big reason was that France, the motherland of the revolution, opposed the Germans as an enemy and an occupying power. Indeed, the struggle against Napoleon forged a new national movement which culminated in wars of liberation. But Germany did not remain unaffected by the forces of social change. First in the "Rheinbund" states and then in Prussia (in the latter connected with names like Stein, Hardenberg, Scharnhorst, W. von Humboldt) reforms were begun aimed at breaking down feudal barriers and creating a society of free, responsible citizens. The objectives were abolition of serfdom, freedom of trade, municipal self-administration, equality before the law, general conscription. But many reform moves were pulled up short. Participation by the populace in legislation was refused almost everywhere. Only hesitantly did some princes grant their states constitutions, especially in southern Germany.

■ ■ ■ **The "German Confederation."** After the victory over Napoleon the Congress of Vienna (September 1814 to June 1815) redrew the map of Europe. The hopes of many Germans for a free, unitary nation-state were not fulfilled. The "Deutscher Bund" (German Confederation) which replaced the old Reich was a loose association of the individual sovereign states. Its sole organ was the "Bundestag" (Federal Diet) in Frankfurt, not an elected but a delegated diet. It was able to act only if the two great powers, Prussia and Austria, agreed. It saw its main task in the ensuing decades in suppressing all aspirations and efforts aimed at unity and freedom. Press and publishing were subject to rigid censorship, the universities were under close supervision and political activity was virtually impossible.

Meanwhile a modern economic development which worked against these reactionary tendencies had begun. In 1834 the "German Customs Union" (Deutscher Zollverein) was founded, creating a unitary inland market. In 1835 the first German railway line went into operation. Industrialization began. With the factories there grew the new class of factory workers. At first they found better incomes, but the rapid growth of the population soon led to a labour surplus. And since there were no social welfare provisions, the mass of factory workers lived in great misery. Tensions exploded violently, for example in the 1844 uprising of the Silesian weavers, which was harshly put down by the Prussian military. Very hesitantly at first, a workers' movement began to form.

■ ■ ■ **The 1848 revolution.** In contrast to the revolution of 1789, the French revolution of February 1848 found immediate response in Germany. In March there were uprisings in all states, and these forced many concessions from the stunned princes. In May the National Assembly (Nationalversammlung) convened in Frankfurt's Paulskirche (St. Paul's Church). It elected Austrian Archduke Johann Imperial Administrator (Reichsverweser) and set up a Reich Ministry which, however, had no powers or authority. The tune was called in the National Assembly by the Liberal centre, which strove for a

The Frankfurt National Assembly of 1848-49

constitutional monarchy with limited suffrage. The splintering of the National Assembly from Conservatives to Radical Democrats which already indicated the spectrum of parties to come made it difficult to draw up a constitution.

But not even the Liberal centre could overcome the differences between the protagonists of "greater Germany" and "smaller Germany" concepts, that is, a German Reich with or without Austria. After hard bargaining a democratic constitution was drawn up which attempted to combine old and new ideas and required a government responsible to parliament. But when Austria insisted on bringing into the future Reich its entire realm, encompassing more than a dozen different peoples, the "smaller Germany" concept won the day and the National Assembly proffered Friedrich Wilhelm IV (Frederick William) of Prussia the hereditary German imperial crown.

The king turned it down, not wanting to owe imperial majesty to a revolution. In May 1849 popular uprisings in Saxony, the Palatinate and Baden which aimed at enforcing the constitution "from below" failed. That was the seal on the failure of the whole revolution. Most of the achievements were rescinded, the constitutions of the individual states revised along reactionary lines. In 1850 the German Confederation was newly founded.

■ ■ ■ **The rise of Prussia.** The 1850s were years of great economic upswing. Germany became an industrial country. Although its production output still lagged far behind England's it was growing faster. Pacemakers were heavy industry and mechanical engineering. Prussia also became the predominant economic power of Germany. Industrial power strengthened the political self-confidence of the liberal middle class. The German Progress Party (Deutsche Fortschrittspartei), set up in 1861, became the strongest party in the Prussian diet and denied the government the funds when it wanted to make reactionary changes to the structure of the army. The newly appointed Prime Minister (Ministerpräsident), Otto von Bismarck (1862), took up the challenge and for some years governed without parliamentary approval of the budget which was required by the constitution. The Progress Party dared offer no further resistance than parliamentary opposition, however.

Bismarck was able to offset his precarious position on the domestic front by foreign policy successes. In the German-Danish war (1864) Prussia and Austria forced the Danes to cede the duchies of Schleswig-Holstein (now forming the Federal Republic's northernmost state) which they initially administered jointly. But Bismarck had from the outset pursued the annexation of the two duchies and steered for open conflict with Austria. In the Austro-Prussian War (1866) Austria was defeated and had to leave the German stage. The German Confederation was dissolved and replaced by the North German Confederation (Norddeutscher Bund) of states north of the River Main, with Bismarck as Federal Chancellor (prime minister).

■ ■ ■ **The Bismarck Reich.** From then on Bismarck worked towards "smaller German" unity. He broke France's resistance in the war of 1870/71, triggered off by a diplomatic conflict over the succession to the Spanish throne. Defeated France had to cede Alsace-Lorraine and pay huge reparations. In the patriotic enthusiasm of the war, the southern German principalities joined up with the northern confederation to form the German Empire (Deutsches Reich). At Versailles near Paris, on the vanquished enemy's territory, King Wilhelm (William) I of Prussia was proclaimed German Emperor on January 18, 1871.

German unity had not come about by popular decision "from below" but by a treaty between princes, "from above". Prussia's predominance was stifling. To many the new Reich seemed like a "Greater Prussia." The Reichstag (Imperial Diet) was elected by universal and equal suffrage. Although it had no say in the formation of the cabinet, it could influence government by its participation in lawmaking and its budgetary power. Although the Reich Chancellor (chief minister) was accountable only to the Kaiser (emperor) and not to parliament, he did have to try to get majorities for his policies in the Reichstag.

Suffrage in the Länder (states) still varied. In eleven it was still class suffrage, dependent on tax paid; in four there was still the old division into estates. The south German states, with their longer parliamentary tradition, reformed their electoral laws after the turn of the century and Baden, Württemberg and Bavaria made theirs the

William beeing proclaimed German Emperor
(painting by A. Werner)

same as the Reich laws. Although Germany's emergence as a modern industrial country strengthened the influence of the economically successful middle class, the people who still called the tune in society were the aristocrats, above all in the army officer corps where they predominated.

Bismarck ruled as Reich Chancellor 19 years. Through a consistent peace and alliance policy he tried to give the Reich a secure position in the new European balance of power. In contrast to this far-sighted foreign policy was his home policy. He had no feeling for the democratic tendencies of his time. To him, political opposition was "hostility to the Reich". Bitterly, but ultimately vainly, he fought the left wing of the liberal middle class, political Catholicism, and especially the organized labour movement which for 12 years (1878-1890) was practically banned by an Anti-Socialists Act (Sozialistengesetz). Hence the vastly growing working class, despite progressive social legislation, were alienated from the state. Bismarck ultimately became a victim of his own system when he was dismissed in 1890 by the young Emperor Wilhelm II.

Wilhelm wanted to rule himself but he lacked the knowledge and staying power. More by speeches than by actions he created the impression of a peace-threatening dictator. Under him there took place a transition to "Weltpolitik" (world policy), with Germany trying to shorten the lead of the great imperialist powers and thereby becoming more isolated. In his home policies Wilhelm soon took a reactionary course after his attempt to win the working class over to a "social emperorship" failed to bring the quick success he had hoped for. His chancellors had to rely on changing coalitions of Conservatives and National Liberals. Social Democrats, although one of the strongest parties, obtaining millions of votes, continued to be excluded from any participation in government.

■ ■ ■ **World War I.** The assassination of the heir to the Austrian throne on June 28, 1914, triggered off the outbreak of World War I. The question as to who was to blame for this war remains in dispute. Certainly, Germany and Austria on the one side, France, Russia and Britain on the other, did not consciously seek it but they were prepared to risk it. From the start, all had definite war aims for which military action was at least not unwelcome. The Germans failed in their aim quickly to vanquish France. The fighting in the west after the defeat of Germany in the Battle of the Marne soon froze into trench warfare, ultimately peaking in senseless material attrition with enormous losses on both sides. With the outbreak of war, the Kaiser receded into the background. As it progressed, the weak Reich Chancellors hat to submit more and more to the will of the army supreme command, whose nominal chief was Field Marshal Paul von Hindenburg but whose real head was General Erich Ludendorff. The entry into the war of the United States in 1917 brought the decision which had long been developing and which could no longer be changed by the revolution in Russia and the peace in the east. Although the country had bled dry, Ludendorff, completely misjudging the situation, continued until September 1918 to insist on "peace through victory" but then surprisingly demanded an immediate armistice. Military defeat also meant political collapse. Unresisting, the Kaiser and the

princes yielded their thrones in November 1918. Not a
hand stirred to defend a monarchy which had lost all
credibility. Germany became a republic.

■ ■ ■ **The Weimar Republic.** Power fell to the Social
Democrats. Their majority had long since abandoned
the revolutionary notions of earlier years and saw their
mission in securing an orderly transition from the old to
the new form of state. Private ownership of industry and
agriculture remained untouched. The mostly anti-repub-
lican civil servants and judges were taken over without
exception. The imperial officer corps retained command
of the armed forces. Attempts by radical leftists to drive
the revolution in a socialist direction were quelled by the
army. In the National Assembly elected in January 1919,
which convened at Weimar and drew up a new Reich
constitution, three unconditionally republican parties —
Social Democrats, German Democratic Party and the
Catholic Centre — had the majority. But through the
1920s the parliamentary parties and popular forces
which were more or less hostile to a democratic state
went from strength to strength. The Weimar Republic
was a "republic without republicans," rabidly fought by
its opponents and only half-heartedly defended by its
supporters. Especially the postwar economic misery and
the oppressive terms of the peace of Versailles Germany
had to sign in 1919 made the people deeply sceptical of
the republic. Growing domestic instability was the result.

In 1923 the confusion of the postwar era reached its
peak (inflation, Ruhr occupation by France, Hitler coup,
communist overthrow attempts). This was followed by
economic recovery and with it some political pacifica-
tion. The foreign policy of Gustav Stresemann regained
political equality for defeated Germany through the Lo-
carno Pact (1925) and accession to the League of Nations (1926). The arts and sciences experienced a brief,
intensive flowering in the "golden 20s." After the death
of the first Reich President, the Social Democrat Friedrich Ebert, former Field Marshal Paul von Hindenburg
was elected head of state in 1925 as the candidate of the
right. Although abiding strictly by the constitution, he
never developed a personal commitment to the republican state.

The ultimate collapse of the Weimar Republic began
with the world economic crisis in 1929. Left and right-

wing radicalism exploited unemployment and the general recession. No more majorities capable of government could be found in the Reichstag, the cabinet being dependent on the support of the constitutionally very strong Reich President. From 1930, the up to then insignificant National Socialist movement of Adolf Hitler which fused extreme anti-democratic tendencies and a raging anti-Semitism with pseudo-revolutionary propaganda grew from strength to strength and by 1932 had become the most powerful party. On January 30, 1933, Hitler became Reich Chancellor. Apart from members of his own party his cabinet included politicians of the right and non-partisan specialist ministers, so that it was hoped that sole rule by the National Socialists could be prevented.

■ ■ ■ **The Hitler dictatorship.** Hitler soon rid himself of his allies. An Enabling Act, approved by all the middle-class parties, gave him practically limitless power. He banned all parties but his own. The trade unions were smashed, basic rights virtually removed and press freedom abolished. The regime exercised ruthless terror and violence against anyone who stood in its way. Thousands disappeared without trial in hastily constructed concentration camps. Parliamentary institutions at all levels were abolished or made powerless. The "Führer" (Leader) principle spread everywhere. When Hindenburg died in 1934, Hitler assumed the roles of president and chancellor. By this he gained control as commander-in-chief of the armed forces, which up to then had still had a certain inner life of their own.

In the few years of the turbulent Weimar Republic the majority of Germans had not acquired any deep-rooted affinity to democracy. More than anything else, years of political turmoil, violence between the various camps - including bloody street battles - and the mass unemployment engendered by the world economic crisis had shattered confidence in government. Hitler, on the other hand, succeeded with job-creation and armament production programmes in reinvigorating the economy and quickly reducing unemployment. He was helped by fact that the world depression come to an end. His position was also bolstered by foreign policy successes. In 1935 the Saar region, until then administered by the League of Nations, returned to Germany and in the same year the

Reich regained its defence sovereignty. In 1936 German troops moved into the up to then demilitarized Rhineland. In 1938 Austria was joined to the Reich and the Western powers allowed Hitler to annex the Sudetenland. Immediately after taking power, the regime began to carry out its anti-Semitic programme. Step by step the Jews were stripped of all human and civic rights. Those who could tried to escape the persecution by fleeing abroad. The persecution of political opponents and the suppression of free speech also drove thousands out of the country. Many of the best German writers, artists and scientists fled the country - an irredeemable loss to German culture.

■ ■ ■ **World War II and its consequences.** Hitler was not to be satisfied. From the outset he prepared for a war he was willing to wage to subjugate Europe. With his attack on Poland on September 1, 1939, he unleashed World War II, which lasted five and a half years, devastated much of Europe and killed 55 million people.

The German armies defeated Poland, Denmark, Norway, Holland, Belgium, France, Yugoslavia and Greece. In the Soviet Union they advanced to a position just short

The ramp of the Auschwitz concentration camp, Poland

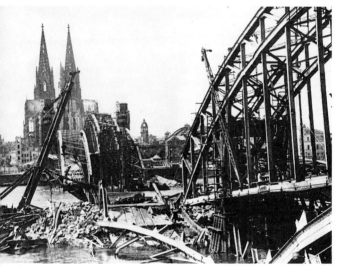

1945: View over Cologne's Hohenzollernbrücke to the cathedral

of Moscow and in North Africa they threatened the Suez Canal. Harsh occupation regimes were set up in the conquered countries. They were fought by resistance movements. In 1942 the regime began the "Final Solution of the Jewish Question": all the Jews the regime could lay its hands on were taken to concentration camps in occupied Poland and murdered. The total number of victims is estimated at six million.

The terror of the regime and the military setbacks strengthened resistance against Hitler in all classes of society. A coup attempt on July 20, 1944, carried out mainly by officers, failed. Hitler survived a bomb planted in his headquarters and took terrible revenge. Outstanding among the many victims were Col. Gen. Ludwig Beck, Col. Graf Stauffenberg, and Carl Goerdeler, former chief mayor of Leipzig.

The war continued, Hitler prosecuting it under enormous losses, until the entire Reich area was occupied by enemies. Then, on April 30, 1945, he killed himself. Eight days later the successor he had willed by testament, Grand Admiral Dönitz, performed the unconditional surrender and was arrested shortly afterwards by the victors.

From 1945 to the present

■ ■ ■ **Reorientation after 1945.** Following the unconditional surrender of the German forces on 8/9 May 1945, the last government of the German Reich, headed by Admiral Karl Dönitz, remained in power for another 23 days. Its members were then arrested and, together with other nazi leaders, tried by the Nuremberg Tribunal for crimes against peace and humanity.

On 5 June the victorious, powers the United States, the United Kingdom, the Soviet Union and France assumed supreme authority in the territory of the Reich. Their basic objective, according to the London Protocol (12 September 1944) and follow-up agreements, was to exercise total control over Germany. They divided the country into three occupation zones, and Berlin, the capital, into three sectors. There was an Allied Control Council composed of the three commanders-in-chief. Once and for all Germany was to be prevented from again aspiring to world domination as she had done in 1914 and 1939. The allies wanted to curb her appetite for conquest, to destroy Prussia as a stronghold of militarism, to punish the Germans for genocide and war crimes, and to reeducate them in the democratic spirit.

At the conference of Yalta (Crimea) held in February 1945, France was coopted as the fourth controlling power and allocated its own occupation zone. In Yalta the only allied intention which remained valid was that of terminating Germany's existence as an independent state but keeping the country intact. Stalin especially was keen to preserve Germany's economic unity. He demanded such huge reparations for the Soviet Union's terrible sacrifices as a result of Germany's invasion that they could not possibly have been made by one occupation zone alone. Moscow wanted 20 billion dollars and control over 80 per cent of all of Germany's factories.

In contrast to the original plans, the British and Americans, too, wanted to preserve a viable rump Germany, not out of greed for reparations but because, as from about the autumn of 1944, US President Roosevelt was aiming to establish a stable Central Europe as part of a system of global balances. Germany's economic stability was indispensable to this plan. He had therefore quickly discarded the notorious Morgenthau Plan (September 1944), which would have reduced Germany to an agricultural country.

Soon the only common aim remaining to the victorious powers was that of disarming and demilitarizing Germany. The original idea of partitioning the country quickly became no more than "lip-service to a dying idea" (Charles Bohlen) when the western powers watched with dismay as Stalin, immediately upon liberating, that is to say conquering, Poland and south-eastern Europe, launched a massive operation to sovietize those regions.

On 12 May 1945 Churchill cabled President Truman that an "iron curtain" had come down in front of the Soviet troops and that no one knew what was going on behind it. But the western powers carefully weighed up the possible consequences of letting Stalin have a say in reparations on the Rhine and the Ruhr. The result was that at the Potsdam Conference (17 July to 2 August 1945), the original aim of which was to create a new European order, agreements were reached which consolidated rather than eased the tensions. The four powers agreed on the matter of denazification, demilitarization, economic decentralization and the reeducation of the Germans along democratic lines. The western powers also

The Potsdam Conference of 1945: Attlee, Truman and Stalin

Germany after World War II

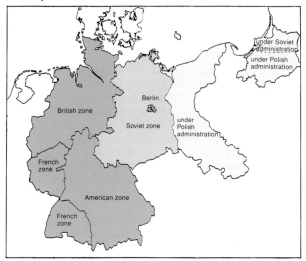

—— German within the borders of 1937

▨ Western zones and Western sectors of Berlin
(Federal Republic of Germany from 1949)

▢ Soviet zone and Eastern sector of Berlin
(German Democratic Republic from 1949)

▢ German eastern territories under Polish or Soviet administration

agreed to the expulsion of Germans from Poland, Hungary and Czechoslovakia. The west had insisted that the transfer be carried out in a "humane" fashion, but in the following years some 6.75 million Germans were brutally deported. They were made to suffer for Germany's war crimes, but also for the shift in Poland's western boundary as a result of the Soviet Union's occupation of Königsberg and eastern Poland. Practically the only point on which East and West agreed was that the four occupation zones should be preserved as economic and political units. At first, each power was to draw its reparations from its own zone. As was to be seen later, however, this set a precedent in that not only the reparations arrangement but also the attachment of the four zones to different political and economic systems made Germany the country where the Cold War manifested itself most of all. This came about in stages.

Meanwhile the task of establishing German political parties and administrative authorities had begun in the occupation zones. This happened very quickly in the Soviet zone under rigid control, with the result that even before the end of 1945 parties and several central administrative bodies had been formed.

In the three western zones the development of a political system was a bottom-to-top process, that is to say, political parties were permitted only at local level at first, then at state level after the Länder had been created. Only later were they allowed to form associations at zonal level. Zonal administrative structures were materializing very slowly, and as the destroyed country's material want could only be overcome by means of generous planning across state and zonal borders, and as quadripartite administration was not functioning, the United States and the United Kingdom decided in 1947 to merge their zones economically into what was known as the bizone.

The conflicting systems of government in East and West and the different approach to reparations in the occupation zones were an obstacle to the introduction of uniform financial, taxation, raw materials and production policy throughout Germany, and led to considerable regional disparities. France was not interested in a common economic administration (bizone/trizone) at first. Stalin wanted to have a say in the management of the Ruhr but at the same time sealed his own zone off to the others.

He would not have any western interference with the appointment of pro-communist officials in the Soviet-occupied zone. The western powers were powerless to prevent such arbitrary measures as the compulsory merger of the KPD (East German Communist Party) and the SPD (Social Democratic Party) to form the SED (Socialist Unity Party) in April 1946.

In view of this development the British and Americans, too, began safeguarding their own interests in their respective zones. The military commanders, most of whom were from the conservative mould, detested socialism. Consequently, the old social structure and system of property ownership were retained in the western zones. Moreover, the state of the economy made it necessary for the authorities, rather than continue the denazification process, to engage efficient, hard-working German specialists to help rebuild the western zones so that they could be protected from Soviet encroach-ments. Thus attitudes on both sides hardened into a cold war. Each accused the other side of being responsible for Germany's division, but these mutual charges hardly concealed the fact that both blocs had gone over to de-fending their bastions.

■ ■ ■ **An enemy becomes a partner.** With his famous speech in Stuttgart on 6 September 1949, US Secretary of State Byrnes had indicated the changed approach. Stalin's occupation of Poland and the redrawing of that country's borders were described as merely temporary measures. As Byrnes saw it, the military role of the west-ern allies in West Germany changed from one of occupa-tion and control to that of protecting powers. And he said that a "soft" reparations policy was intended to deter the Germans from any nationalist thoughts of revenge and encourage their cooperation.

Finally, on the initiative of the United Kingdom and the United States, a trizone was established as a unified western economic area, after initial French resistance. The threat of another Soviet advance westwards follow-ing the coup d'état in Prague on 25 February 1948 in-duced the French to fall into line. Byrnes' views were re-flected first in the Brussels Pact of 17 March 1948 and ul-timately in the North Atlantic Treaty of 4 April 1949.

For such an organization to work West Germany had to have a coherent political and economic system. Thus at the Six-Power Conference in London (23 February to 3 March and 20 April to 1 June 1948), which was attended for the first time by the Benelux countries, France, Britain and the United States agreed that the western occupa-tion zones should have a common political structure.

At the 82nd meeting of the Control Council on 20 March 1948, the Soviet representative, Marshall Soko-lovski, asked for information on the London Conference. When his western colleagues answered evasively Soko-lovski walked out, never to return.

While the western powers were still finalizing their rec-ommendations for a constituent assembly to be con-vened by West Germany's minister presidents (regional premiers), Stalin used the introduction of the deutsch-mark in the West (currency reform of 20 June 1948) as a pretext for imposing a blockade on West Berlin with the aim of annexing it to the Soviet-occupied zone. During the night of 23 June 1948 all land routes between the western zones and West Berlin were closed. Supplies of energy and food from the eastern sector of Berlin and the Soviet zone stopped.

On 3 August 1948 Stalin demanded that Berlin be recognized as the capital of the GDR (German Democratic Republic), which on 7 October 1949 was given a government of its own. But US President Harry Truman refused to budge, having declared on 20 July that the western allies could not forgo West Berlin nor the creation of a west German state ("no Munich of 1948"). Until 12 May 1949 West Berlin was kept supplied by an allied airlift. This visible solidarity with Berlin as a western outpost, together with America's demonstration of strength, evoked a spirit of cooperation in West Germany, with the result that former enemies became partners.

■ ■ ■ **The founding of the Federal Republic of Germany.** West Germany had already begun receiving American foreign aid in 1946 (under the GARIOA Programme), but it was George C. Marshall's programme to combat "hunger, poverty, despair and chaos" (the Marshall Plan) that provided the crucial boost for the country's economic recovery (1.4 billion dollars between 1948 and 1952). While in the Soviet-occupied zone the process of transferring industry to public ownership continued, the "social market economy" system (Alfred Müller-Armack 1947) continued to gain ground in the west after the currency reform. The new economic order was intended to prevent, on the one hand, the "stagnation of capitalism" (Walter Eucken) and, on the other, a centrally planned economy which would be a hindrance to creativity and initiative.

This concept was supplemented by the rule-of-law and the welfare-state principle embodied in the Basic Law and by the country's federal structure. The constitution was deliberately termed the "Basic Law" in order to emphasize its provisional character. The idea was that a definitive constitution should only be adopted after Germany's reunification.

The Basic Law naturally included many of the intentions of the western occupying powers, who, with the Frankfurt Documents presented on 1 July 1948, authorized West Germany's minister presidents (i.e. the heads of government of the Länder) to draw up a con-

In 1948-49 an airlift lasting 462 days maintained supplies to Berlin

stitution. But that document also reflects much of Germany's experience with the Weimar Republic and the "legal" installation of the nazi dictatorship. The constitutional convention held at Herrenchiemsee (10-23 August 1948) and the Parliamentary Council which met in Bonn on 1 September 1948 (65 delegates of the state parliaments) incorporated in the Basic Law (adopted on 8 May 1949) provisions requiring future governments, parties and other political groupings to protect the democratic system. Ever since, all attempts to do away with the liberal, democratic system, or to replace it with a right-wing or leftwing dictatorship, have been treated as criminal offences and the organizations concerned can be banned. The Federal Constitutional Court, the guardian of the constitution, is the authority which decides whether a party is legal or not.

Whereas the authors of the Weimar constitution, naively believing in the uprightness of parliament, had, through article 76, made it possible for enemies of the constitution to destroy what in those days was the most liberal constitution in the world, article 79 of the Basic Law prohibits any change in its article 1 (which ties the use of all public authority to protection of human rights), and any attempt to do away with the country's democratic, social and federal system (article 20 (4)).

These requirements were an immediate reaction to what had happened under the nazi dictatorship, at whose hands most of the "politicians of the Federal Republic's first hour" had suffered, those men and women who were now rebuilding Germany on the democratic traditions of 1848 and 1919 and in the spirit of the "revolt of the conscience" of 20 July 1944. All of them personified in the eyes of the world the "other Germany" and won the respect of the occupying powers. They included the first Federal President Theodor Heuss (FDP), the first Federal Chancellor Konrad Adenauer (CDU), and Economics Minister Ludwig Erhard (CDU), the "locomotive" of the "economic miracle", but also the outstanding leaders of the SPD opposition such as Kurt Schumacher and Erich Ollenhauer, as well as the cosmopolitan Carlo Schmid. It was they who gave the new party system in West Germany its unmistakable character. Gradually, Germany's involvement and political influence increased (Occupation Statute, Petersberg Agreements, membership of GATT, accession to the European Coal and Steel Community). In July 1951 the United Kingdom, France and the United States declared that Germany was no longer a war enemy. The Soviet Union did the same on 25 January 1955.

■ ■ ■ **Security through integration with the west and European reconciliation.** To Chancellor Konrad Ade-

The Paris Treaties 1954: Mendès-France, Adenauer, Eden, Dulles

1957: The singing of the Treatys of Rome

nauer, who until 1963 had largely held the reigns of foreign and domestic policy himself ("Chancellor democracy"), Germany's reunification in peace and freedom was the foremost political objective. To achieve this it was necessary for West Germany to be integrated into the Atlantic Alliance. Accordingly, the restoration of the Federal Republic's sovereignty on 5 May 1955 coincided with its accession to NATO. This alliance was to be the main protective shield, the proposed European Defence Community having proved abortive due to French resistance.

At the same time the European Communities (Treaty of Rome, 1957) were developed into an anti-communist bastion. Adenauer's distrust of Moscow was so deep-rooted that in 1952 he, together with the other western powers, rejected Stalin's offer of reuniting Germany as a neutral country as far as the Oder-Neisse line. To the Chancellor the protection of American troops in Germany was indispensable. His suspicion seemed only too justified when, on 17 June 1953, the people's uprising in East Germany in protest against their life of bondage and against the unbearable productivity norms imposed by the regime, was savagely put down by Soviet tanks. This showed once again that without Moscow little progress could be made on the German question. Thus for sober

US President Kennedy in West Berlin on 26 June 1963

political reasons it was expedient to establish diplomatic relations with the Soviet Union as the largest power in Europe. This was accomplished during Adenauer's visit to Moscow in September 1955, on which occasion he also secured the release of the last 10,000 German prisoners-of-war and about 20,000 civilians.

The crushing of the popular revolt in Hungary by Soviet troops in November 1956, as well as the "Sputnik shock" (4 October 1957), signalled a considerable growth of Soviet power, which manifested itself in the establishment of a socialist system in East Germany, but above all in the Berlin ultimatum issued by Stalin's successor, Nikita Khrushchev, who demanded that the western allies leave West Berlin within six months.

Their adamant refusal caused Khrushchev to try a softer approach on Berlin. His visit to the United States in 1959 did indeed considerably improve the atmosphere ("spirit of Camp David"), and the American President, Dwight D. Eisenhower, to the great concern of the Bonn government, felt that the Russian transgressions of international agreements regarding Berlin were not so serious as to warrant a military conflict outside Germany.

Bonn's disquiet with regard to Berlin's security increased when John F. Kennedy became President of the United States. This represented a change of generation in the American leadership which considerably reduced

Adenauer's influence on US policy towards Europe. True, Kennedy guaranteed with his three "essentials" (25 July 1961) free access to Berlin, the presence of the western powers in the city, and its overall security, but when the Berlin wall was built on 13 August 1961 the allied reaction went little beyond diplomatic protests and symbolic threats. Once again Moscow was able to safeguard its protectorate. Barricades, death strips and repression prevented the people from "voting with their feet" against the East German regime. In July alone, the month before the wall was erected, over 30,000 people had fled from East Germany. The wall had staked out the claims of the superpowers. Although the German question had not been resolved it at least seemed regulated. Even after the Cuba crisis in 1962 the two superpowers continued to seek a better understanding - they had to on account of the nuclear stalemate.

Bonn therefore had no option but to look in other directions, and the temporary estrangement with Washington was in fact outwardly compensated for by the "summer of French friendship". With the Elysée Treaty which they signed in January 1963 Chancellor Adenauer and President de Gaulle laid special emphasis on Franco-German friendship. In order to stress the new quality of this relationship de Gaulle, during his triumphant state

Chancellor Adenauer greeting President de Gaulle in Bonn
on 5 July 1963

visit to Bonn a few months previously, had spoken of the "great German nation". In his view the Second World War had to be seen more in terms of tragedy than of guilt.

As the Federal Republic became increasingly integrated into the western community the atmosphere also began to improve in the relationship with eastern Europe. In December 1963 NATO, at a ministerial meeting in Athens, had signalled this change with its new strategy of flexible response in place of that of massive retaliation.

In an attempt to soften the rigid East-West relationship, the Federal Republic tried to improve contacts at least with the Soviet Union's satellite countries. Without officially abandoning the Hallstein Doctrine, that is to say Bonn's policy of severing relations with any country which recognized the GDR, Adenauer's successors, Ludwig Erhard and Kurt Georg Kiesinger, based their policy on the harsh realities prevailing in central Europe. They were prompted to do so not least by the new approach adopted by the SPD opposition, which promoted Egon Bahr's formula of "change through rapprochement" (15 July 1963).

The establishment of German trade missions in Bucharest and Budapest was a promising start. In the west increasing efforts were being made to merge the European Coal and Steel Community, the European Atomic Energy Community (EURATOM) and the European Economic Community, into one European Community (8 April 1965). The establishment of diplomatic relations with Israel despite pan-Arab protests was a major step in the Federal Republic's policy of rapprochement. At the beginning of 1967 Bonn established diplomatic relations with Romania, and in June the Federal Republic and Czechoslovakia opened trade missions in their respective capitals.

The Harmel Report of December 1967 at least prepared the way for further steps towards detente by laying down the western alliance's twofold aim of maintaining its military strength whilst at the same time being ready to talk to the eastern bloc. In that year Bonn and Belgrade resumed diplomatic relations, they having been broken off by the Federal Republic on account of Yugoslavia's recognition of the GDR. And from Poland came proposals for a non-aggression pact.

Adenauer with Isreal's Prime Minister Ben Gurion (1960)

In addition to the policy of reconciliation with Germany's European neighbours and her integration into the western community, Adenauer too had attached special importance to restitution for the Jews. Six million Jews had been systematically exterminated by the nazis. It was not least the close personal relationship between the Federal Republic's first Chancellor and Israel's Prime Minister Ben Gurion which fostered the process of reconciliation between Jews and Germans. One outstanding event at that time was their meeting in New York's Waldorf Astoria Hotel on 14 March 1960. Addressing parliament in 1961, Adenauer stressed that the Federal Republic could only prove that the Germans had broken completely with their nazi past by making material restitution as well.

As early as 1952 the first agreement had been signed in Luxembourg. It provided for assistance for the integration of Jewish refugees in Israel. Of the total sum of about 90 billion marks provided for restitution purposes, roughly one third went to Israel and Jewish organizations, and especially to the Jewish Claims Conference, a hardship fund which helped Jews all over the world who had been persecuted by the nazis. However, diplomatic relations between the two countries were not established until 1965.

■ ■ ■ **German-German dialogue in spite of the GDR's self-detachment.** In spite of the GDR's continuing efforts to cut itself off completely from the west (e.g. by requiring passports and visas for persons in transit between the Federal Republic and West Berlin) and in spite of the Warsaw Pact's crushing of attempted reforms in Czechoslovakia, the "Brezhnev Doctrine" of the indivisibility of the socialist bloc did not have any serious repercussions on the process of detente. In April 1969 Bonn said it was ready to enter into agreements with the GDR below the level of international recognition.

Obviously, German-German agreements of this kind could hardly be achieved without some kind of prior understanding with Moscow. When the Soviet Union proposed a non-aggression pact, the "new eastern policy" adopted by the Social-Liberal coalition that had assumed power in Bonn on 21 October 1969 quickly began to take on substance. A few months previously (5 March 1969) Gustav Heinemann, who even in Adenauer's day had been a strong advocate of East-West rapprochement, had been elected Federal President. Willy Brandt, who had played an active part in the resistance against the Hitler dictatorship, was now head of a federal government which directed its energies to the construction of a peaceful order throughout Europe. The international constellation was favourable. Moscow and Washington were negotiating on the limitation of strategic arms (SALT), and NATO proposed negotiations on mutual balanced force reductions (MBFR). On 28 November 1969 the Federal Republic became a party to the treaty banning the proliferation of nuclear weapons (NPT). Following the turbulence experienced by its predecessor, the grand coalition government (Viet Nam conflict, emergency legislation, Auschwitz trials, Extra-Parliamentary Opposition, and student revolts), the new cabinet, by embarking on its "Ostpolitik", placed itself under considerable pressure to produce results.

While talks on a non-aggression agreement were being conducted in Moscow and Warsaw, Bonn and East Berlin, too, explored the possibilities of improving relations. On 19 March 1970 the heads of government of both German states, Willy Brandt and Willi Stoph, met for the first time in Erfurt. This was followed by another meeting on 21 May in Kassel. On 12 August 1970 a treaty on the renunciation of force and recognition of the status quo was signed in Moscow. Both sides proclaimed that they had no territorial claims against anyone. In a "letter on German unity" presented to the Soviet Government in Moscow, the Federal Republic stated that the treaty did not contradict its aim of working towards a state of peace in Europe "in which the German people will regain their unity in free self-determination".

On 7 December of that year the Treaty of Warsaw was signed which reaffirmed the inviolability of the existing border (the Oder-Neisse line). Warsaw and Bonn, too, gave an assurance that they had no territorial claims against one another and declared their intention of improving mutual cooperation. In an "information" document on humanitarian measures, Warsaw agreed to the transfer of ethnic Germans from Poland and the reunion of separated families by the Red Cross.

In order to pave the way for the ratification of those treaties, France, the United Kingdom, the United States and the Soviet Union signed an agreement on Berlin which stated that Berlin was not a constituent part of the Federal Republic but that Bonn was entitled to represent West Berlin. In addition, the "ties" between West Berlin and the Federal Republic were to be improved and relations between East Berlin/GDR and West Berlin developed (signing of the Transit Agreement on 17 December). Germany's efforts to foster peace and detente received worldwide recognition which culminated in the award of the Nobel Peace Prize to Willy Brandt (1971).

However, the CDU/CSU, who were in opposition for the first time, considered the results of the negotiations too meagre. Yet their constructive vote of no confidence against Brandt came to grief (247 for, 249 against) and the Bundestag (parliament) ratified the treaties with the Soviet Union and Poland on 17 May. Most CDU/CSU members of parliament abstained. The Bundestag, in an "interpretative resolution", declared that the treaties did not conflict with the aim of restoring German unity by peaceful means.

The series of treaties with Eastern Europe was rounded off by a Treaty on the Basis of Relations between the two Germanies which had been preceded by talks and negotiations since June 1972. After Willy Brandt's reelection as Chancellor on 14 December, the way was clear for the signing of the treaty on 21 December. Both sides undertook not to threaten or use force against one another and to respect each other's independence. The inviolability of the border between the two states was also endorsed. Furthermore, the two sides expressed their willingness to resolve humanitarian problems in a practical manner. It was agreed that, owing to the special nature of their relationship, they would establish "representations" in their respective capitals instead of the usual embassies.

At the signing ceremony the Federal Government again handed over a letter emphasizing its intention to pursue German unity. The government of the state of Bavaria asked the Federal Constitutional Court to confirm that the treaty did not run contrary to this objective. It also noted that the German Empire continued to exist in international law and was partially identical with the Federal Republic. The Court ruled that the GDR could not be regarded as a foreign country, only as domestic territory.

In 1973 the Treaty of Prague between Czechoslovakia and the Federal Republic was signed. It declared the Munich Agreement of 1938 to be null and void "in accordance with this Treaty". The two sides also agreed that their borders were inviolable and that they would not use force against one another.

Whilst negotiations were going on in Vienna on mutual balanced force reductions, the Soviet Union and the United States completed an agreement designed to prevent a nuclear war, and 35 countries attended a Conference on Security and Cooperation in Europe (CSCE) in Helsinki, little change came about in the relationship between the GDR and the Federal Republic. On the one hand, East Berlin benefited both materially and financially from the follow-up agreements to the Basic Treaty, but on the other the East German regime meticulously kept its ideological distance. The East German constitution was amended and the term "socialist state of the German nation" was replaced by "socialist state of workers and peasants". Also omitted was the passage "... fulfilling its responsibility to show the entire German nation the way into a future of peace and socialism".

Nonetheless, Helmut Schmidt, too, strived to continue the policy of developing a balanced relationship. On 16 May 1974 he had succeeded Willy Brandt, who had resigned from the chancellorship when one of his aides, Günther Guillaume, was unmasked as an East German spy. The "swing" arrangement, a facility which allowed the GDR to overdraw by as much as DM 850 million on its credit from the Federal Republic, was extended until 1981.

The GDR continued to profit handsomely from the various transit agreements which were financed by the West, without budging on the political issues. The Final Act of Helsinki (1975), which called for greater freedom of movement in transboundary traffic and more respect for human and civil rights, proved to be a disappointment, not only to the East Germans but to the people of other East European countries as well. There was no end to the chicanery at East Germany's borders. People were arbitrarily turned back, as were visitors to the Leipzig Fair. Western journalists who criticized the GDR were forced to leave the country.

The East German regime suffered a further loss of prestige around the world when it deprived Wolf Biermann, a well-known singer-songwriter, of his citizenship. In spite of all this, the Federal Republic decided for the sake of the people in East Germany to continue its efforts to improve relations. Thus in 1978 an agreement was reached to build an autobahn from Berlin to Hamburg and to repair the transit waterways to West Berlin, the greater proportion of the cost being borne by the Federal Republic. The Federal Government also continued to buy the release of political prisoners from the GDR. In the end Bonn had paid over DM 3.5 billion for the release of 33,755 people, and to have 250,000 families reunited.

■ ■ ■ Missiles versus detente. Whereas the process of European integration continued steadily in the West, the transition from the 70s, the decade of detente, to the 80s was marked by fresh conflicts in Eastern Europe. The Soviet invasion of Afghanistan and the imposition of martial law in Poland, as well as the emplacement of new intermediate-range nuclear weapons (SS 20) in East Germany and Czechoslovakia, worsened the climate of East-West relations.

NATO reacted to this serious upset of the balance of security by deciding that it, too, would introduce new missiles as from 1983. But at the same time it proposed arms control negotiations to the Soviet Union. This was the "two-track" decision. In protest at the invasion of Afghanistan, the United States, the United Kingdom, Canada, Norway and the Federal Republic refused to take part in the Moscow Summer Olympics (1980).

The Americans tried a new initiative, the "zero" solution, by which the Soviets would remove their intermediate-range missiles whilst NATO would promise not to deploy its Pershing II and the new Cruise missiles.

Chancellor Schmidt insisted on the missile modernization alternative so as not to leave any gaps in the Western security shield, but at the same time tried to keep the damage to the German-German relationship within limits. Although East German leader Erich Honekker proposed to introduce a separate East German citizenship, and although the East German regime drastically increased the daily amount of currency which visitors from the West had to exchange on entering the GDR, Schmidt visited East Germany, but without getting any substantial concessions from Honecker. The regime's hardening ideological stance was not least a reaction to the growing protest movements in neighbouring Poland, where the people were demanding economic reform, freedom and disarmament.

But the missile question was not only problematical in the East. In Bonn the FDP decided to change its tack on economic policy and began to drift out of the coalition. Grassroots SPD followers, largely because of pressure from the peace movement and some union factions, withdrew their support for Schmidt for adhering to the NATO two-track decision. As a result, Helmut Kohl replaced him as Chancellor at the head of a CDU/CSU/FDP coalition. He continued Bonn's security policy and close cooperation with Paris and Washington with a view to uniting Europe within a stable and secure framework. In the face of massive protest from the peace movement, sections of the SPD and the Greens (who had polled 5.6% of the votes in the 1983 election for the Bundestag and thus were represented in parliament for the first time), the German parliament approved in November 1983 the deployment of intermediate-range missiles because of "the Warsaw Pact's conventional superiority" (Chancellor Kohl).

Whereas the growing peace movement had been one

of the causes of a change in government in West Germany, protest groups in East Germany, which through the initiative of the Church ("swords into ploughshares") had become more and more vociferous since the beginning of 1982, led ultimately to the disintegration of the entire socialist system.

■ ■ ■ **From the GDR's decline to German unity.** The German Democratic Republic, which had been founded on 7 October 1949, was a product of the Soviet Union. Nonetheless, many Germans, their experience with the nazi dictatorship still fresh in their memories, were at first willing to help develop this anti-fascist model. But the command economy, secret police, the all-powerful SED (the East German communist party), as well as strict censorship, increasingly alienated the people and the regime. In spite of this, very cheap housing, health care and social services gave this self-contained system a certain amount of flexibility which enabled the people to eke out an existence in many different ways. East Germany's great success in international sport was a sort of compensation, just as the "workers" gained satisfaction from the fact that they soon had the highest rate of industrial production and the highest standard of living in the Eastern bloc, despite having to make huge reparations to the Soviet Union. The people's reaction to state control and tutelage was to withdraw into their private sphere.

In spite of all the propaganda about annual production targets having been more than achieved, and behind the facade of anti-imperialist hatred spread in the schools, factories and the armed forces, it became increasingly clear that East Germany's original intention of overtaking the Federal Republic economically would remain a dream. Depleted resources, industry's vicious destruction of the environment, coupled with dwindling productivity as a result of central planning, forced the East German regime to go easy on its promises. It had to raise increasingly large loans in the West. Improvisation became the order of the day with regard to consumer goods. The quality of life and infrastructure (housing, transport, environmental protection) thus deteriorated. All the assurances of socialism's ultimate victory turned out to be nothing more than a caricature. The image of the capitalist class enemy in the West which had been propagated by the regime was completely shattered by the early 80s at the latest. There was a Big-Brother spy network which kept watch on everybody, and the system's indoctrination and strained appeals for solidarity made the claim about the leadership role of "the working class and their Marxist-Leninist party" (article 1 of East Germany's constitution) sound like hollow rhetoric, especially to the young generation. The people began to demand a bigger say in running their own lives, more individual freedom and more and better consumer goods. These wishes were often coupled with the hope that the socialist system, ossified by bureaucratic constraints and anti-Western ideology, would prove capable of reforming itself.

As the atmosphere of diplomatic relations deteriorated as a result of the quarrel over the deployment of medium-range missiles, the proposed Strategic Defence Initiative, a space-based defensive umbrella proposed by the Americans, and East Germany's continued aggravation of the West (for instance, by building a second wall at the Brandenburg Gate and impeding traffic in the air corridor to Berlin), the East Germans themselves put pressure on their own leadership. Some had entered the Federal Republic's "representation" in East Berlin and refused to leave until they had been given a definite assurance that they could move to the West.

In order to make life easier for the Germans in the east, the Federal Government arranged various large bank credits for the GDR. Moscow's fear that this would soften the socialist system was allayed by Erich Honecker, who wrote in "Neues Deutschland", the regime's mouthpiece, in 1984: "Merging socialism and capitalism is just as impossible as merging fire and water." But this self-assurance on the surface could hardly conceal the fact that the reform movements in Eastern Europe had thrown the whole socialist bloc onto the defensive. Honecker's rejection of the accusation made at the CSCE conference in Ottawa (1985) that the people in Eastern bloc countries were denied free speech and freedom of movement was a propagandistic lie.

From the beginning of 1985 more and more people sought admission to the Federal Republic's permanent representation in East Berlin and the German Embassy in Prague. Soon the new General Secretary of the Soviet Communist Party, Mikhail Gorbachev, who had succeeded Konstantin Chernenko (who had died in March), became the main standard bearer for the East German people, who were longing to gain their freedom, but also for international cooperation on security matters.

■ ■ ■ **Meetings and conferences.** In 1986, Gorbachev declared that his main political objective was to eliminate nuclear weapons by the end of the century. His meetings with US President Ronald Reagan in Geneva and Reykjavik, the Conference on Confidence and Security-Building Measures and Disarmament in Europe held in Stockholm, as well as the preparations for negotiations on the reduction of conventional forces in Europe, showed that the East was ready for dialogue. This new approach was conducive to agreements between the two German states on cultural, educational and scientific cooperation. A skeleton agreement providing for cooperation in the field of environmental protection was also signed. That same year Saarlouis and Eisenhüttenstadt made a twinning arrangement, the first of its kind between cities in East and West Germany.

But the East German regime did not want to be infected by Gorbachev's perestroika and glasnost. They didn't want the process of democratic reform in the Soviet Union to spread to the GDR. Kurt Hager, a member of the politburo and the SED's principal ideologue, stubbornly argued that there was "no need to redecorate one's home just because the neighbour is doing so".

The extent to which the East German leaders ignored the expectations of their own people was shown by the protest demonstrations in East Berlin on 13 August, the anniversary of the wall. Chancellor Helmut Kohl spoke against the continuation of Germany's division when, during Honecker's working visit to Bonn (1987), he said: "We respect the present borders but we want to overcome the country's division by peaceful means through a process of mutual understanding. We have a joint responsibility for preserving the vital foundations of our nation."

A step towards safeguarding those vital foundations was the INF Treaty signed by Reagan and Gorbachev. Under that accord, all US and Soviet missiles with a range of 500 to 5,000 km deployed in Europe had to be withdrawn and destroyed. The Federal Republic for its part pledged to destroy its 72 Pershing IA missiles.

The general climate of détente led to increasing demands for greater freedom and reform in East Germany. During demonstrations in East Berlin in early 1988, 120 supporters of the peace movement known as "Church from the Grassroots" were arrested. Prayers were said for them in the Gethsemane Church. Over 2,000 people attended the service, and a fortnight later their number had swollen to 4,000. In Dresden the police broke up a demonstration for human rights, free speech and freedom of the press. In May Honecker used the occasion of a visit by the Soviet Defence Minister Yasov to warn about the danger of imperialism and to call for a stronger Warsaw Pact.

Although Chancellor Kohl, in his state of the nation address to parliament in December 1988, welcomed the lifting of some travel restrictions, he had to denounce the suppression of the reform movement in the GDR. To Erich Honecker, however, the new civil rights movements were merely examples of "extremist intemperance". In response to appeals to remove the wall, he replied on 19 January 1989: "The wall protecting us from fascism will stay there until such time as the conditions which led to its erection are changed. It will still be in existence in 50, 100 years' time."

The stubborn rigidity of the East German leaders at a time when Gorbachev saw a "common European home" taking shape and Helmut Kohl was speaking optimistically about "the disintegration of ossified structures in Europe", aroused even more discontent among the population. At times the Federal Republic's permanent representation in East Berlin had to be closed because of the surge of people wanting to move west. In September 1989 Hungary opened its border, thus permitting thousands of people from the GDR to pass through to Austria and from there into West Germany. This breach of Warsaw Pact discipline encouraged ever more people in the GDR to take to the streets in protest, including growing numbers outside the church. And when the regime, in October 1989, celebrated the 40th anniversary of the founding of the GDR with great pomp and ceremony, mass demonstrations were held, primarily in Leipzig ("We are the people").

Honecker finally realized that his only chance of preserving the essence of the SED regime was for him to re-

The wall is open: free access to West Berlin

sign. He was succeeded as SED secretary general and GDR head of state by Egon Krenz, but the latter's promise of "change" was drowned by the protests of the people, who did not trust him. Under the pressure of events the council of ministers and the SED politburo resigned en bloc. The peaceful revolution seemed to paralyze the authorities. As a result, a mistaken announcement by Günter Schabowski, party secretary in the district of Berlin, that travel restrictions were to be eased prompted thousands of people to cross the border on the evening of 9 November 1989. The authorities could only watch numbly. The wall was open. Soon it was to be broken down and tiny pieces were offered as souvenirs.

News of the breach in the wall reached Chancellor Kohl whilst he was on a visit to Warsaw. He suspended his engagements for a day and hurried to Berlin where he addressed a crowd of 20,000 from the balcony of Schöneberg town-hall. He asked them to remain calm in that joyous hour, and thanked Mr Gorbachev and Germany's friends in the West for their support. He said the spirit of freedom had gripped the whole of Europe. Upon his return to Warsaw he signed a declaration in which Germany and Poland promised to intensify their cooperation in the cause of peace, security and stability in Europe.

The revolution in East Germany opened up the opportunity for the country's reunification after a wait of decades. But caution was required. Paris and London did
not have German unity on the agenda. Mr Gorbachev,
during talks with US President Ronald Reagan off the
coast of Malta (December 1989), warned against any attempt to force the German issue. And in the GDR itself
the new government under Hans Modrow, though demanding rapid reform, also wanted the GDR to keep its
statehood. Helmut Kohl therefore proposed a ten-point
programme for achieving national unity. It envisaged a
"contractual arrangement" based on a confederal system
leading to fundamental political and economic change
in the GDR. The Chancellor proposed that the direct
negotiations with the GDR should take place within a
pan-European setting under the aegis of the European
Community and the CSCE. He avoided specifying a
time-frame for the negotiations so as not to spark any
further comment abroad about Germany seeking super-
power status. The road to unity still seemed long to both
sides, especially when Mr Gorbachev, addressing the
Communist Party Central Committee, said as late as 9
December 1989 that Moscow would not leave East Germany "in the lurch", that it was Moscow's strategic ally in
the Warsaw Pact and that one still had to start from the
assumption of two German states, though there was no
reason why they should not develop a relationship of
peaceful cooperation.

Chancellor Kohl said the people in East Germany
themselves should be the ones to decide on the speed
and the substance of unification. But the government
saw events rapidly slipping from their control. The
people in East Germany distrusted their new government. They became increasingly attracted to the West
and the process of destabilization increased rapidly. But
still Mr Gorbachev held back, particularly as Poland and
Hungary were escaping Moscow's grasp, Ceausescu's
overthrow in Romania was in the offing, and therefore
East Germany's departure from the Warsaw Pact would
upset the balance of power. From western quarters, too,
came exhortations to the Germans to "take account of
the legitimate concerns of neighbouring countries" (US
Secretary of State Baker speaking in Berlin) as they pursued national unity.

Green light for German unification: Chancellor Kohl and Foreign Minister Genscher talking to Mr Gorbachev in the Caucasus

And finally, the unification process could only be continued after Bonn had given an assurance that there would be no shifting of the present borders, that, in the event of unification, NATO's "structures" would not be extended to the territory of the former GDR, and that Germany would reduce its armed forces to offset its strategic advantage. President Bush was in favour of Ger-

Interior Minister Schäuble (West) an State Secretary Krause (East) after signing the German Unification Treaty (1990)

man unification provided the Federal Republic remained a member of NATO.

■ ■ ■ **The "Unification Treaty".** In order that the GDR could be represented in the negotiations with a democratic mandate, free elections were held there on 18 March 1990, the first in 40 years. Lothar de Maizière became the head of a grand coalition made up of the CDU, DSU, DA, SPD and FDP. With him the Bonn government agreed on a time-table for economic, monetary and social union with effect from 1 July 1990, it having become palpably clear that the GDR had no economic basis on which to continue alone, and that the majority of the people in the GDR wanted accession to the Federal Republic.

In August the Volkskammer (East German parliament) voted in favour of accession as soon as possible, and on 31 August GDR State Secretary Günter Krause and Wolfgang Schäuble, Federal Minister of the Interior, were able to sign the "Unification Treaty". Thus on 3 October 1990 the German Democratic Republic officially acceded to the Federal Republic in accordance with article 23 of the Basic Law.

The East German states of Brandenburg, Mecklenburg-Western Pomerania, Saxony, Saxony-Anhalt and Thuringia became states (Länder) of the Federal Republic of Germany. Berlin was made the capital and the Basic Law, after appropriate amendments, applied to the former GDR as well.

The road to unity had been opened by Mikhail Gorbachev, who had given his approval after talks with Chancellor Kohl in Moscow and the Caucasian town of Stavropol in July 1990. He did so on condition that the Federal Republic would forgo NBC weapons and reduce its forces to 370,000, and that NATO's military organization would not be extended to GDR territory so long as Soviet forces remained stationed there. The two leaders also agreed that the Soviet troops would be withdrawn from East Germany by the end of 1994, and that the Federal Republic would provide financial support for their repatriation. Mr Gorbachev's agreement also meant that the so-called Two-plus-Four Treaty could also be signed. Within that framework the Soviet Union, the United States, France and the United Kingdom, as well as the representatives of the two German states, confirmed the unification of Germany consisting of the territories of the former GDR, the Federal Republic and Berlin. Germany's external borders were recognized as definitive. Bonn and Warsaw concluded a separate treaty to take account of Poland's special security needs in the light of history. The two sides agreed to respect each other's territorial integrity and sovereignty.

The ratification of the Unification Treaty and the Two-plus-Four Treaty marked the termination of the rights and responsibilities of the four victorious powers "with respect to Berlin and Germany as a whole". Germany thus regained complete sovereignty over her internal and external affairs which she had lost 45 years previously with the fall of the nazi dictatorship.

■ ▦ ▦ **Germany grows together.** Following the restoration of national unity and the tremendous geopolitical changes that have taken place in connection with the disintegration of the communist systems of eastern Europe, Germany and her partners face completely new challenges. The reconstruction process in the new German states must be vigorously continued so that the country's internal unity can be completed. Europe must develop into a political union. And a global architecture of peace and security must be created.

National, European and global responsibilities are inseparably linked together. Eastern Germany's recovery and consolidation cannot take place unless it is closely bound up with the process of European integration. Europe, on the other hand, cannot acquire its new structure unless it is open to the reformist countries of central and eastern Europe. The countries of the shattered eastern European community must be brought into a close relationship with the common European and Atlantic organizations not only economically but politically as well. The completion of German unity using the nation-state approach of the past is just as inconceivable as creating a „Fortress Europe" to shut out the nations of Asia or the Third World.

The larger Germany is seeking to do justice to her correspondingly larger cooperation in close union with her European and atlantic partners. Her aim, in the words of President Richard von Weizsäcker, is „to serve world peace as part of a united Europe". And Chancellor Helmut Kohl has emphasized that the country will continue to fulfil that role within the ambit of the western alliance. „The Alliance", he said, „which has safeguarded our peace and freedom for decades, can rely on our support." The government is also prepared to increase Germany's involvement in UN peace-keeping measures.

■ ■ ■ **Global assistance.** Germany's assistance for the nations of central and eastern Europe and of the former Soviet Union is in itself an indication of her willingness to involve herself both bilaterally and in the multilateral framework. Since 1989 she has provided DM 37.5 billion for the reform process in central and eastern Europe. The amount made available for Russia and the other successor states of the Soviet Union in the same period is DM 87.55 billion - more than the assistance provided by all western countries together. In addition, Germany contributes, for instance, 28% towards the European Community's aid effort for Yugoslavia, and she has taken in nearly half of all the refugees from the war zones in that country.

Compared with the other west European countries, the proportion of asylum-seekers who came to Germany last year was more than 70%. In 1992 some eight billion marks had to be spent on accommodation and care alone. In spite of drastic cuts in public spending, Germany will maintain her present level of development assistance for developing countries. She is the third largest contributor to the United Nations, a fact which underscores the Government's determination to continue her policy of helping to promote stability and safeguard peace in the bilateral and multilateral framework.

Germany's contribution to stability in central and eastern Europe, and in the newly independent states, is not confined to financial assistance. Great efforts are also being made to further the process of democratization and free-market reform. The financial input has been augmented by the provision of large numbers of experts and the offer of training courses. And in providing assistance for developing countries, too, the government is aiming not only to improve the economic but also the social and political conditions of the local popultions. Protection for human rights is one of the government's chief criteria when it comes to disbursing development assistance.

Training with the latest equipment

■ ■ ■ **On the road to European Union.** In assessing the importance of the Maastricht Treaty for Germany's future role in Europe, Chancellor Kohl said that „Maastricht is the proof that united Germany is actively fulfilling her responsibility in and for Europe and clearly abides by what we have always said, namely, that German unity and European Union are two sides of one and the same coin." Despite the severe damage to the European Monetary System, Germany adheres to the goal of Monetary Union. The common internal market of the twelve EC countries was launched on 1 January 1993. This market embraces 345 million Europeans who form the strongest economic area in the world in terms of purchasing power. With the sole exception of Switzerland, the members of the European Free Trade Association, EFTA, who are Austria, Sweden, Norway, Finland, Iceland and Liechtenstein, have formed the European Economic Area together with the European Community.

The European Monetary Union entered its first phase in mid-1990. Transfers of capital among EC countries have been liberalized, and the coordination of economic policies and cooperation among central banks have been intensified.

The second phase begins on 1 January 1994. From then on preparations will be made for the establishment of the European Monetary Institute (EMI) and of a European Central Bank. The decision on the third phase, which will be the final and irrevocable phase, will not be made until the end of 1996 at the earliest. Complete Economic and Monetary Union presupposes a greater degree of monetary stability and budgetary discipline.

The German Government attaches particular importance to the fact that at the summit meeting in Maastricht in 1991 the heads of state and government not only negotiated the treaty on Economic and Monetary Union but also a treaty on European Union as the superstructure of a further integrating European Community. This is being achieved by means of the new common foreign and security policy as well as cooperation in the fields of justice and home affairs. In the opinion of Chancellor Kohl, this deepening of the Community must go hand in hand with its enlargement to include not only the EFTA countries but, in the longer term, the nations of central, eastern and south-eastern Europe.

■ ■ ■ **Germany's economic unification.** The process of German unification is taking place within the framework of European integration and parallel to a global political and economic restructuring as a consequence of the collapse of the communist system in eastern Europe.

The conversion of the former east German command economy into a well-functioning market economy system is a unique challenge. It requires not only a massive transfer of resources from west to east (in 1993 the gross amount transfer to eastern Germany comes to about 183 billion marks, following 140 billion in 1991 and 152 billion in 1992) but a complete change of management. New markets have to be tapped, supplier systems reorganized, and personnel retrained or enabled to improve their qualifications.

Many factories in the former GDR were in such a derelict condition ecologically as well as technically that their continued operation would have been irresponsible. Nor could the transformation of industry be carried out without painful adjustments to the labour market. Without large-scale redundancies it was impossible to get the economy onto the road of productivity. Competitiveness

Car-building in eastern Germany

is, after all, essential for a company's long-term economic survival.

The government has introduced heavily funded job-creation programmes. Despite this effort, however, it has not been possible in 1993 to improve on the 15% unemployment quota, which is twice as high as that in the western states.

The privatization of state-owned companies that were worth saving was handled by the Treuhandanstalt (Trust Agency) at great cost. Up to the end of August 1993, 12,800 enterprises had been privatized and nearly 3,000 wound up, leaving 1,500 still on the Agency's books. The new owners of the privatized firms have undertaken to retain or to create 1.54 million jobs. On top of this they have bindingly undertaken to invest more than 180 billion marks, which promises a boost for economic growth and renewal in the years ahead. The Trust Agency intends to complete its work by 1994 at the latest.

According to the forecasts of research institutes, eastern Germany's real gross domestic product will increase by 5-6% in 1993. In the opinion of the Bundesbank the worst is over and economic growth there can become increasingly self-sustaining. There has already been a distinct upswing in some branches, for instance building, trades and some services and industries, but many others still face enormous problems, mainly due to the low level of productivity. This year it reached about 36% of the west German level.

As from 1995 the new states will be incorporated in the country's normal financial equalization system. Until then their financial needs will be covered by the „German Unity Fund", which is one of the main ingredients of the „Solidarity Pact" agreed between the federal and state governments in the spring. Under this arrangement nearly 57 billion marks will be available to fund the new states and the local authorities. The new legislation enacted for this purpose also sets aside substantial amounts for housing, transport, postal services and research. All this assistance is designed to put the German economy on a sound footing.

■ ■ ■ **Safeguarding the country's economic future.** Germany's economic development since 1990 has not only been affected by eastern Germany's economic problems. The consequences of a severe global recession have also been increasingly felt, especially since 1992, a trend which began earlier in other industrial countries. After an estimated 1.5% shortfall in the gross domestic product in the western part of the country in 1993, it is expected that this deficit will be made good again in 1994.

The government has ushered in a phase of consolidation with a strict savings policy. It is hoped that new borrowing can be reduced considerably in the next few years. According to IMF statistics, Germany's borrowing is still below the average for western countries, in spite of having to meet the historic challenge resulting from German unification.

However, the savings, consolidation and growth programme is only one of many measures by which the government intends to maintain Germany's attractiveness as a place for industrial investment. Removing the ossified structures and aberrations of past decades is one of the nation's greatest economic and social challenges.

By means of its Investment Promotion Act the government intends, as from 1994, to considerably reduce company taxes and thus spur investment and job creation. New legislation is to be introduced to make working hours more flexible and ensure that machinery can be kept running for longer periods. A new genetic engineering act is intended to prevent some of Germany's top researchers and technology from emigrating. Protecting Germany's economic future is not only a responsibility of government but a challenge to the innovative flair of companies and the flexibility of both sides of industry.

■ ■ ■ **Promoting social integration.** The overwhelming majority of Germans were strongly in favour of national unification, but only gradually did they become aware of the degree of alienation that had developed over a period of more than 40 years when east and west Germans were practically isolated from one another by the communist regime in the east. Understandably, many east and west Germans have different opinions on the contribution which the people in the old states are making to help those in the new. Many east Germans who hoped that the standard of living between eastern and western Germany would quickly be brought into balance are disappointed. They feel they are being neglected by the people in western Germany no less than by the government.

Whilst in Leipzig to lay the foundation stone for the new complex of the city's international fair, Chancellor Kohl said that the Government „knows that the necessary restructuring of the economy is a dramatic process which requires the people in the new states to make incisive adjustments to their private and working lives. It is understandable that such drastic changes evoke fear and concern. But the number who say they are satisfied with the progress of development in eastern Germany is steadily growing.“

In 1993 the pension insurance scheme alone transferred 15 billion marks to the new states in order to boost pensions there once again. Since unification pensions in the eastern part of the country have risen from 30 to the present 73% of those in the west.

A very tricky aspect of coming to terms with 40 years of communist rule in eastern Germany concerns the handling of „government crime“ by the courts, and particularly who is to be held responsible, and to what extent, for the shootings and deaths along the wall and barbed-wire fences that divided the country. Soldiers who actually fired and killed people attempting to flee over the wall have been found guilty but given mild sentences because they were, after all, only obeying orders.

But how should one assess the guilt of the politial leaders who gave the orders? Is it at all possible to assess them in terms of the law?

In 1993 the former East German defence minister, Heinz Kessler, and his deputy Fritz Strelitz, were found guilty by the Berlin regional court of instigating man-slaughter and given prison sentences of seven and a half and five and a half years respectively. Hans Albrecht, for-mer district chief executive, was sentenced to four and a half years for being an accessory to manslaughter. The court also took a previous conviction into account. The trial of Willi Stoph, the former east German prime minis-ter, on charges of having ordered the shootings was ter-minated on account of the accused's poor health. The former head of state and leader of the communist party, Erich Honecker, was released from jail for the same rea-son. In mid-1993 investigations were begun into the past activities of 1,700 members of the East German leader-ship, party functionaries and members of the govern-ment and judicial apparatus.

Another extremely sensitive issue is the scrutiny of the vast quantities of files (filling shelves with a total length of 180 km) maintained by the East German State Security Service („Stasi") by a government authority known by the name of its director, Joachim Gauck (the „Gauck agency"). People in the east want to know what kind of information the Stasi had on them and many of them have discovered that they were spied on by persons they had trusted.

No other development has disturbed the Germans more since 1991 than the outbreak of extremist right-wing violence against asylum-seekers, foreigners and Jewish institutions. In 1992 alone 17 people fell victim to such criminal activity, mainly committed by young people. The wave of violence reached another climax in 1993 with a firebomb attack on a house in Solingen in which five Turkish women and children were burned to death. The authorities and various other organizations are making tremendous efforts to stamp out right-wing extremism. Demonstrations in which nearly three million people have taken part testify to the fact that Germany is still a country friendly towards foreigners and that the German people utterly reject violence.

Political system, constitution, law

- · The Basic Law · The constitutional bodies
- · Federalism and self-government
- · Parties and elections · The legal system

Der Parlamentarische Rat hat das vorstehende
Grundgesetz für die Bundesrepublik Deutschland
in öffentlicher Sitzung am 8. Mai des Jahres Eintausendneunhundertneunundvierzig mit drei-
undfünfzig gegen zwölf Stimmen beschlossen.
Zu Urkunde dessen haben sämtliche Mitglieder
des Parlamentarischen Rates die vorliegende
Urschrift des Grundgesetzes eigenhändig
unterzeichnet.

BONN AM RHEIN, den 23. Mai des Jahres
Eintausendneunhundertneunundvierzig

PRÄSIDENT DES PARLAMENTARISCHEN RATES

Adolph Schönfelder

1. VIZEPRÄSIDENT DES PARLAMENTARISCHEN RATES

Hermann Schäfer

The Basic Law

The Basic Law for the Federal Republic of Germany was adopted in 1949. Its authors intended it as a "temporary" framework for a new democratic system, not as a definitive constitution. The Basic Law called upon the people "to achieve in free self-determination the unity and freedom of Germany". As time passed by the Basic Law proved to be a solid foundation for democracy. Its requirement of national reunification was fulfilled in 1990. The preamble and concluding article of the Basic Law have been amended in accordance with the Unification Treaty, which formed the basis for the accession of the German Democratic Republic (GDR) to the Federal Republic. They now state that, by virtue of the GDR's accession, the German people have achieved their unity. On 3 October 1990 the Basic Law became valid for the whole nation.

The Basic Law's content was greatly influenced by the personal experience of its authors under the Nazi dictatorship. In many parts it clearly indicates that they were trying to avoid the mistakes that had been partly responsible for the demise of the Weimar democracy. Those who drafted the constitution in 1948 were the ministers president (with roughly the functions of a premier or governor) of the states that had been formed in the western occupation zones, and the Parliamentary Council elected by the state parliaments. This Council, chaired by Konrad Adenauer, formally adopted the Basic Law, which was promulgated on 23 May 1949. On the occasion of the Federal Republic's 40th anniversary in 1989 the Basic Law was acknowledged to be the best and most liberal constitution Germany had ever had. As manifest in the life of the community, its principles have largely been put into practice, its requirements by and large fulfilled. More than any previous German constitution, the Basic Law is understood and accepted by the people. It created a state and society which so far has been spared any serious constitutional crises.

■ ■ ▪ **The basic rights.** Pride of place in the constitution is given to a charter of basic rights, the first of which obliges the state to respect and protect the dignity of man. This guarantee is supplemented by the right of self-fulfilment. It affords comprehensive protection from unlawful interference by the state. Both Germans and non-Germans can invoke these constitutional rights. The classical freedoms embodied in the Basic Law include freedom of religion, free speech (including freedom of the press) and the guarantee of property. There are also freedom of art and scholarship, the right to form coalitions, the right to privacy of mail and telecommunications, protection from forced labour, privacy of the home, and the right of conscientious objection. The civil

Signing of the Basic Law on 23 May 1949

rights, which apply only to German nationals, relate for the most part to their involvement in the political process and their free choice of occupation or profession. Basically, they include the right of assembly, the right to form associations and societies, freedom of movement within (including the right to enter) the country, the ban on extradition, and the franchise.

These freedoms are accompanied by rights which guarantee equality. The Basic Law expresses the general principle that all people are equal before the law by providing that no one may be subject to discrimination or privileged on account of his origin, race, language, convictions, religion or political views. It expressly states that men and women must be treated as equals, and it guarantees equal access to public office for all Germans.

The basic rights in the social sphere concern the individual's position with regard to marriage, family, church, school, but also the state, especially in its capacity as a body politic based on social justice. These rights entitle the citizen to certain means of support by the state, for instance in the form of social services, some of which can be claimed direct.

One basic right, which by its very nature can only apply to foreigners, is the right of political asylum. The Basic Law is the first German constitutional instrument to provide refuge in Germany for foreigners persecuted on political grounds. The influx of hundreds of thousands of asylum-seekers over the years, the great majority of whom were not subject to political persecution in their native countries and whose motives are mainly economic, was getting out of control and threatened to undermine the basic right of asylum for genuine cases of persecution.

The German Bundestag has adopted an amendment to the country's asylum law with the necessary two-thirds majority. This was the result of a long and often passionate debate between those in favour of an unrestricted right of asylum - which had been the situation in Germany since 1949 and had no precedent anywhere in the world - and those who felt the time had come to bring the law into line with present-day requirements and the laws of all the other members of the European Community.

Federal Coat of Arms

Federal flag

Thus under a new asylum law which entered into force as article 16a of the Basic Law, asylum procedures have been changed without violating the principle that "anybody persecuted on political grounds has the right of asylum". The essence of the new article is that foreigners from EC countries or "safe third countries" (those where the Geneva Convention on Refugees and the European Human Rights Convention are in force) may not invoke the right of asylum; nor do they have the right to remain in the country temporarily. The procedure for dealing with applications has been shortened; applicants can no longer abuse the system by submitting multiple claims for social welfare; as a general rule asylum-seekers will in future receive payments in kind.

The scope of some basic rights may be restricted by or on the basis of other laws, but these may never encroach upon the essence of those rights. The basic rights are directly applicable law. This was a crucial innovation compared with previous constitutions, whose basic rights were largely non-binding declarations of intent. Nowadays, parliament is just as strictly bound by the basic rights as the government, the courts, the authorities, the police and the armed forces. Thus every citizen has the right to complain to the Federal Constitutional Court about any decisions or actions by the state which he or she feels violate their basic rights. By acceding to the European Convention for the Protection of Human Rights and Fundamental Freedoms in 1952, the Federal Repub-

lic of Germany subjected itself to international control
(with effect from 1953). Under article 25 the citizens of
signatory states have the right to complain to the European Commission of Human Rights and the European
Court of Justice, even if this means taking their own government to task. In 1973 the Federal Republic also ratified the international covenants on human rights of the
United Nations.

■ ■ ■ **Fundamental characteristics of the state.** The
body politic is based on five principles, viz Germany is a
republic and a democracy; she is a federal state based
on the rule of law and social justice; her republican system is constitutionally manifest in the name "Federal Republic of Germany", and in the fact that the head of state
is the elected Federal President. A democracy is based
on the sovereignty of the people. The constitution says
that all public authority emanates from the people. Thus
it opted for indirect, representative democracy, in other
words public authority must be recognized and approved by the people but they have no direct say in the
exercise of that authority, except in elections.

This responsibility is entrusted to the organs specially
established by the constitution for this purpose: the
legislature, the executive, and the judiciary. The people
mainly exercise their constitutional authority by periodi-
cally electing a new parliament. In contrast to some
countries, provision for other forms of direct democracy,
such as referendums, has been made only with regard to
modifications of state boundaries.

The authors of the Basic Law opted for an "adversarial" type of democracy, they having seen the Weimar
Republic undermined by radical parties which were hostile to the constitution. In this context "adversarial"
means that the free play of political forces must stop
where any party or faction attempts to do away with
democracy with democratic means. This explains why
the Basic Law makes it possible for the Federal Constitutional Court to ban political parties who seek to damage
or destroy the country's democratic system.

The constitutional decision in favour of a federal state
implies that not only the country as a whole but its 16
constituent parts, the Länder, have some of the features
of a state. Each has its own powers, though they are restricted to certain spheres, which it exercises through its

Ei - nig - keit und Recht und Frei - heit
Da - nach laßt uns al - le stre - ben

für das deut - sche Va - ter - land!
brü - der - lich mit Herz und Hand!

Ei - nig - keit und Recht und Frei - heit

sind des Glük - kes Un - ter - pfand.

Blüh im Glan - ze die - ses Glük - kes,

blü - he, deut - sches Va - ter - land!

*The national anthem of the Federal Republic of Germany
is the third verse of the "Lied der Deutschen".
The lyrics of the anthem were written by August Heinrich Hoffmann
von Fallersleben (1798-1874) and the melody
was composed by Joseph Haydn (1732-1809).*

own legislature, executive and judiciary. Public responsibility has been apportioned in such a way that law-making, in contrast to the provisions of the constitution, is actually in the hands of the central state, the Federation, whereas the constituent states have the task of implementation.

This division of responsibilities is an essential element of the system provided for in the Basic Law, a principle that is the very foundation of the rule of law. The exercise of public authority has been entrusted to parliament, government and the judiciary, each independent of the others.

The significance of this separation of powers is that the power of the state is qualified by mutual checks and balances. It thus protects the individual's freedom. Another major feature of the rule of law principle is that the executive is strictly bound by the constitution and the laws of the land. Furthermore, encroachments upon an individual's rights or privacy are only permissible on the basis of a law. Any action by the state may be examined by independent judges as to its consistency with the law if the person or persons affected take the matter to court.

The social state is a modern extension of the traditional rule of law concept. Under this system the state is required to protect the weaker members of society and to seek social justice. Numerous laws and court rulings have ensured the application of this principle, which manifests itself in the provision of old-age, invalidity, health and unemployment insurance, social assistance for needy people, rent allowances, child benefit, laws on industrial safety and working hours, etc.

The Basic Law does not, however, state specifically how the country's economy should be run. Where economic policy is concerned it remains for the most part neutral. On the other hand, parliament's freedom to legislate in this sphere is limited by the exigencies of the rule of law principle, and by the fundamental rights of property and inheritance and the free choice of occupation or profession.

■ ■   **Amendments to the Basic Law.** The Basic Law may only be amended with a majority of two thirds of the members of the Bundestag (Federal Parliament) and two thirds of the votes cast in the Bundesrat (Federal

Council). Since one single party or coalition rarely has such a majority in both the Bundestag and the Bundesrat, amendments to the Basic Law require a very broad consensus. This can only be achieved with the support of members of the opposition.

Some provisions of the Basic Law may not be changed at all, not even with a two-thirds majority. Those are the parts relating to the federal system, the separation of powers, democracy, rule of law, and the social state. Likewise untouchable are the commitment to protect the dignity of man and the basic rights and freedoms.

The constitutional bodies

■ ■ ■ **"All public authority emanates from the people"** - this underlying principle of democracy is codified in the constitution. The people exercise that authority directly in elections, indirectly through bodies instituted by the constitution: the legislature, the executive and the judiciary. The constitutional bodies with primarily legislative functions are the Bundestag and the Bundesrat. Executive responsibilities lie principally with the Federal Government, headed by the Federal Chancellor, and the Federal President. Judicial functions pertaining to the constitution are performed by the Federal Constitutional Court.

■ ■ ■ **The Federal President.** The head of state of the Federal Republic of Germany is the Federal President. He is elected by the Federal Convention, a constitutional body which convenes only for this purpose. It consists of the members of the Bundestag and an equal number of members elected by the state parliaments. Sometimes eminent persons who are not members of a state parliament are nominated for the Federal Convention. The Federal President is elected for a term of five years with the majority of votes in the Federal Convention. He may only be reelected once.

The Federal President represents the Federal Republic in its international relations and concludes agreements with foreign states in its name. He also accredits and receives ambassadors, although foreign policy as such is the responsibility of the Federal Government. He appoints and dismisses federal judges, federal civil servants, officers and non-commissioned officers of the armed forces. The President can pardon convicted criminals. He checks whether laws have come about by the proper constitutional procedure and publishes them in the Federal Law Gazette.

He proposes to the Bundestag a candidate for the office of Federal Chancellor (taking account of the majority situation in parliament) and, in response to proposals from the Chancellor, appoints and dismisses cabinet ministers.

If the Chancellor seeks but fails to gain a vote of confidence the Federal President may, on the Chancellor's proposal, dissolve the Bundestag. Premature elections were brought about in this way in 1972 and 1983.

The Federal President personifies the country's political unity in a special way. He is the link between all elements in society regardless of party distinctions. Although his tasks are mainly of a representational nature he can exercise considerable personal authority through his neutral, mediating function. By commenting on the fundamental aspects of current issues he can rise above general party-political controversy and set standards for the public's political and moral guidance.

■ ■ ■ **The Bundestag.** The German Bundestag is the parliamentary assembly representing the people of the Federal Republic of Germany. It is elected by the people every four years. It may only be dissolved prematurely under exceptional circumstances, the final decision lying with the Federal President. The Bundestag's main functions are to pass laws, to elect the Federal Chancellor, and to keep check on the government.

The Bundestag is the scene of parliamentary battles, especially over crucial foreign and domestic policy issues. It is in the parliamentary committees, whose meetings are not usually open to the public, that the extensive preparatory work for legislation is done. Here it is a question of harmonizing political intentions with the detailed knowledge provided by the experts. It is likewise in the committees that parliament scrutinizes and controls government activity. Otherwise it would not be possible to cope with the multitude of technical questions. The Bundestag's committees correspond to the Federal Government's departments and range from the foreign relations via the social affairs to the budget committee, the latter being particularly important in that it represents parliament's control of the budget. The petitions committee is open to requests and complaints from any member of the public.

From 1949 until the end of the last legislative term in 1990 about 6,700 bills were introduced in parliament and 4,400 of them passed. Most of them are initiated by the Federal Government, the others coming from the floor of the house or the Bundesrat. They receive three readings in the Bundestag and are usually referred to the

The Federal Presidents

Theodor Heuss
(FDP)
1949-1959

Heinrich Lübke
(CDU)
1959-1969

Gustav Heinemann
(SPD)
1969-1974

The Federal Chancellors

Konrad Adenauer
(CDU)
1949-1963

Ludwig Erhard
(CDU)
1963-1966

Kurt Georg Kiesinger
(CDU)
1966-1969

appropriate committee once. The final vote is taken after the third reading. A bill (unless it entails an amendment to the constitution) is passed if it receives a majority of the votes cast. Those which affect the functions of the federal states require the approval of the Bundesrat, however.

Walter Scheel
(FDP)
1974-1979

Karl Carstens
(CDU)
1979-1984

Richard v. Weizsäcker
(CDU)
since 1984

Willy Brandt
(SPD)
1969-1974

Helmut Schmidt
(SPD)
1974-1982

Helmut Kohl
(CDU)
since 1982

Members of the Bundestag are returned in general elections, which are direct, free, equal, and secret. They represent the people as a whole, are not bound by instructions and must obey their conscience only. In line with their party allegiances they form parliamentary groups. Freedom of conscience and the requirements of party solidarity sometimes collide, but even if in such a situation a member feels obliged to leave his party he keeps his seat in the Bundestag. This is the clearest indication that members of the Bundestag are independent.

The relative strengths of the party groups determine the composition of the committees. The President (Speaker) of the Bundestag is elected from the ranks of the strongest parliamentary group, in keeping with German constitutional tradition. Members are paid "compensation" reflecting their status as MPs. Anyone who has been a member of parliament for at least eight years receives a pension upon reaching retirement age.

■ ■ ■ **The Bundesrat.** The Bundesrat represents the sixteen federal states and participates in the drafting and implementation of federal legislation. In contrast to the senatorial system of federal states like America or Switzerland, the Bundesrat does not consist of elected representatives of the people but of members of the state governments or their representatives. Depending on the size of their population, the states have three, four, five or six votes which may only be cast as a block.

More than half of all bills require the formal approval of the Bundesrat, which means that they cannot pass into law against its will. This applies especially to bills that concern vital interests of the states, for instance their financial affairs or their administrative powers. No proposed amendments to the constitution can be adopted without the Bundesrat's consent (two thirds majority). In all other cases the Bundesrat only has a right of objection, but this can be overruled by the Bundestag. If the two houses of parliament cannot reach agreement a mediation committee composed of members of both chambers must be convened which, in most cases, is able to work out a compromise.

In the Bundesrat national interests often override party interests. In such cases the voting may not reflect party strengths in the council. This points to an active federalism. The Federal Government cannot always rely on a state government where the same party is in power to follow its lead in every respect, for each state has its own special interests and sometimes takes sides with other states who pursue the same aim, irrespective of the party it is governed by. This produces fluctuating majorities, and compromises have to be made where the parties

Germany's federal structure

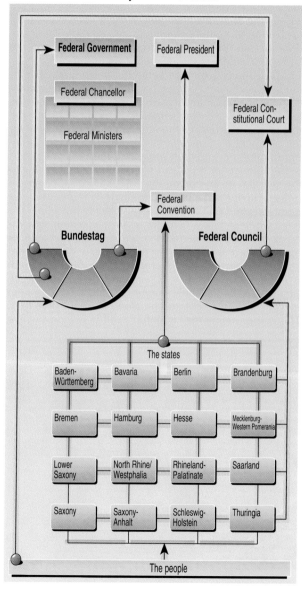

forming the Federal Government do not have a majority in the Bundesrat. The Bundesrat elects its president from among the ministers president of the federal states for a twelve-month term according to a fixed rota. The President of the Bundesrat exercises the powers of the Federal President in the event of his indisposition.

■ ■ ■   **The Federal Government.** The Federal Government, the cabinet, consists of the Federal Chancellor, who is chairman and head of government, and the federal ministers. The Chancellor alone chooses the ministers and proposes them to the Federal President for appointment or dismissal. He also determines the number of ministers and their responsibilities.

The Chancellor is in a strong position mainly owing to the fact that he lays down the guidelines of government policy. The federal ministers run their departments independently and on their own responsibility but within the framework of those guidelines. In a coalition government the Chancellor must of course take account of agreements reached with the other party in the coalition.

This explains why the German system of government is often referred to as a "Chancellor democracy". The Chancellor is the only member of the government elected by parliament and he alone is responsible to it. This responsibility may manifest itself in a "constructive

Meeting of the Federal Cabinet

The Bundestag building on the Rhine, Bonn

vote of no confidence", which was introduced by the authors of the Basic Law in deliberate contrast to the Weimar constitution. Its purpose is to ensure that opposition groups who are agreed only in their rejection of the government but not as regards an alternative programme are not able to overthrow the government. A Bundestag vote of no confidence in the Chancellor must at the same time be a majority vote in favour of a successor. Of the two attempts to bring down a Chancellor with the help of a constructive vote of no confidence, only one has succeeded. That was in October 1982, when a no-confidence motion removed Helmut Schmidt from office and put Helmut Kohl in his place. The Basic Law makes no provision for motions of no confidence in individual federal ministers.

■ ■ ■ **The Federal Constitutional Court.** The Federal Constitutional Court in Karlsruhe is the guardian of the Basic Law. It rules, for instance, on disputes between the Federal Government and the federal states or between individual federal institutions. Only this court has the power to declare that a party constitutes a threat to freedom and democracy and is therefore unconstitutional, in which case it orders that party's dissolution. It scrutinizes federal and state laws as to their conformity with the Basic Law. If it rules that a law is unconstitutional it may no longer be applied. The court acts in such cases only if called upon by certain authorities, such as the Federal Government, state governments, at least two thirds of the members of parliament, lower courts, etc.

In addition, every citizen has the right to file a complaint with the Federal Constitutional Court if he feels his basic rights have been violated by the state. Before doing so, however, he must as a rule have exhausted all other legal remedies.

So far the Federal Constitutional Court has passed judgment in more than 80,000 cases. Some 76,000 of them dealt with constitutional complaints, although only just under 2,000 have been successful. Often matters of great domestic or international significance are dealt with, for instance whether the involvement of German forces in missions of the United Nations is compatible with the Basic Law. Federal Governments of all political hues have had to submit to decisions of the judges in Karlsruhe. The Court has repeatedly stressed, however, that it does not see its task as requiring institutions of the state to follow a specific political course. The Federal Constitutional Court consists of two senates (panels), each with eight judges, half of whom are elected by the Bundestag, the other half by the Bundesrat. The judges serve for twelve years and may not be reelected.

Federalism and self-government

The name "Federal Republic of Germany" itself denotes the country's federal structure. The Federal Republic consists of sixteen states. After 1945 the eleven states of the original Federal Republic were reestablished or newly founded. Following the peaceful revolution in the GDR, the states of former times were restored there too. Since 3 October 1990, when the nation was reunited, they have been part of the Federal Republic. The "Länder" are not mere provinces but states endowed with their own powers. Each has a constitution which must be consistent with the republican, democratic and social principles embodied in the Basic Law. Subject to these conditions they can shape their constitution as they see fit.

Federalism is one of the constitutional principles that may not be tampered with. But this is not to say that the constituent states may not be altered. Provision for boundary adjustments has been made in the Basic Law. The joint constitutional commission of the federal and state governments has proposed simpler procedures.

The federal system has a long tradition in Germany and was interrupted only by the Nazi unitary state of 1933-45. Germany is one of the classical federal states. It is much easier for a country with a federal structure than a centralized state to take account of regional characteristics and problems.

■ ■ ■ **Benefits of a federal system.** German federalism, much as in the United States and Switzerland, binds the country's external unity with its internal diversity. Preserving that regional diversity is the traditional task of the federal system. This function today acquires new substance in the form of regional responsibilities such as landscape management, nature conservation, the protection of monuments and historical sites, the preservation of architectural traditions, and the promotion of regional culture.

But the main purpose of federalism is to safeguard the nation's freedom. The distribution of responsibilities as between the Federal Government and the states is an essential element of the power-sharing arrangement, the checks and balances, as provided for in the Basic Law. This also embraces the participation of the states in the legislative process at federal level through the Bundesrat.

The federal structure also enhances the democratic principle. It enables the citizen to engage in the political process, i.e. in elections and referendums, in his own region. This gives democracy greater vitality. There are other benefits as well. The federal system leaves room for experiments on a smaller scale and for competition among the states. For instance, a single state may try out innovative methods in, say, education which may later serve as a model for nationwide reform. Furthermore, a federal structure can best cope with different regional majorities. Opposition parties at national level may hold a majority in some of the states and thus form the government there.

■ ■   **The powers of the federal states.** The Basic Law determined the powers of the Federation in terms of whether laws should be the same for all states or whether the regions should be allowed to make their own laws. This is illustrated by the fact that the Federation's law-making powers fall into three different categories: exclusive, concurrent or framework legislation. Areas of legislation which fall within the exclusive purview of the Federation are foreign affairs, defence, monetary matters, railways, air transport, and some elements of taxation.

In the case of concurrent legislation, the states may only pass laws on matters not covered by federal law. The Federation may only legislate in such cases where it is necessary to have a uniform law for the whole country. The areas which fall into this category are commercial law, nuclear energy, labour and land law, housing, shipping, road transport, refuse disposal, air pollution, and noise abatement. Since it has proved necessary to have standard laws for these matters, the states have more or less ceased to have any jurisdiction in those areas. Where the Federation has the power to adopt framework laws, the states have a certain amount of legislative latitude. This applies, for instance, in the fields of education, nature conservation, landscape management, regional planning and water management.

There are also a number of other supraregional tasks which, though not mentioned in the Basic Law, are today

The new state parliament, Düsseldorf

jointly planned, regulated and financed by the Federation and the states. They were incorporated in the Basic Law in 1969 as "joint responsibilities". They cover university building, improvement of regional industrial and agricultural structures, as well as coastal preservation.

Direct federal administration is more or less limited to the Foreign Service, the federal railways, posts and telecommunications, labour placement, customs, federal border protection, and the Federal Armed Forces. Most administrative responsibilities are carried out by the states independently.

The Federation's jurisdiction is confined to the Federal Constitutional Court and the supreme courts, which ensure the uniform interpretation of the law. All other courts fall within the ambit of state jurisdiction.

As mentioned above, the states can fill in any gaps left by federal legislation or in areas not specified in the Basic Law. Thus they are responsible for education and culture almost in their entirety as a manifestation of their "cultural sovereignty". They are also responsible for local government law and the police.

The real strength of the states lies in their participation in the legislative process at federal level through the Bundesrat. All internal administration lies in their hands and their bureaucracy implements most federal laws and regulations. Thus state administration is threefold: it handles matters that fall exclusively within its jurisdiction (e.g. schools, police, town and country planning); it implements federal law on its own responsibility (planning for building projects, trade and industry, environmental protection); and it applies federal law on behalf of the Federation (e.g. national highways, promotion of vocational training). Thus in the course of its development the Federal Republic has become a country in which most laws are enacted centrally while the bulk of legislation is administered by the federal states.

■ ■   **Local government.** Local government, as an expression of civic freedom, has a long tradition in Germany. It can be traced back to the privileges of the free towns in the Middle Ages, when civic rights freed people from the bonds of feudal serfdom. (As they said in those days, "town air makes people free".) In modern times local government has primarily been linked, however, to the great reforms of the Prussian Minister Freiherr vom Stein, in particular the Local Government Code of 1808. This tradition of civic liberty is manifest in the self-government of towns and counties expressly guaranteed by the Basic Law. The constitution grants them the right to regulate local affairs within the framework of the law. All municipalities and counties must have a democratic structure. Municipal law falls within the sphere of competence of the federal states. For historical reasons the municipal constitutions vary greatly from state to state, but in practice the administrative system is by and large the same everywhere.

Self-government embraces in particular local transport and road construction, electricity, water and gas supply, sewerage and town planning, as well as the building and maintenance of schools, theatres and museums, hospitals, sports facilities and public baths. Other local responsibilities are adult education and youth welfare. The expediency and cost-benefit aspects of programmes in these fields are the responsibility of the local council. Many such measures are beyond the means of smaller communities and can therefore be taken over by the next higher level of local government, the county (Kreis). The county, too, is part of the system of local government through its own democratically elected bodies. The larger cities do not form part of a county.

Local government and independence are bound to suffer if the municipalities are unable to finance their programmes. Their financial situation is frequently a subject of public debate. Local authorities raise their own

Council meeting in Hanover's New City Hall

taxes and levies, which include land tax and trade tax. They are also entitled to raise local taxes on certain luxury goods. This revenue does not suffice to cover their financial needs, however. They therefore receive from the federal and state governments a share of the nation's income tax. They also receive allocations under the financial equalization arrangement which applies in every state.

Local self-government gives all citizens an opportunity to play their part and have a controlling influence. They can discuss such matters as new building projects with elected councillors at town meetings and inspect budget estimates. The municipalities are the smallest cells in the political system. They must always be able to thrive and develop as the basic source of freedom and democracy.

Parties and elections

In a modern democracy competing political parties are of fundamental importance. They are elected for a specific term during which they either assume the powers of government or keep check on the activities of the current administration. They therefore play a major role in the shaping of public policy. These functions are taken into account in the Basic Law, which devotes a separate article (article 21) to the parties, which defines their task as "helping to form the political will of the people". The parties must be democratically structured and are required to disclose their sources of income and their assets.

■ ■ **Parties in the Bundestag.** Since the first general election to be held in the whole of Germany (1990) there have been six parties in the Bundestag: the Christian Democratic Union of Germany (CDU), the Social Democratic Party of Germany (SPD), the Free Democratic Party (FDP), the Christian Social Union (CSU), the Party of Democratic Socialism (PDS) and the group known as Alliance 90/The Greens. The CDU has no party association in Bavaria, while the CSU puts up candidates for election in Bavaria only. In the Bundestag, however, CDU and CSU have a joint parliamentary group. The SPD, CDU, CSU and FDP were formed in the western states between 1945 and 1947. The SPD was a recreation of the former mainly labour-oriented party of the same name which had been outlawed by the Hitler regime in 1933. The other parties were completely new. The Christian parties, CDU and CSU, in contrast to the Catholic Centre Party of Weimar days, drew their support from both of Germany's two major Christian creeds, Roman Catholicism and Protestantism. The FDP adopted programmes in the tradition of German liberalism.

In the four decades since their establishment these four parties have undergone significant changes. At federal level they have all formed coalitions with one another once or been in opposition. Today they all see themselves as "popular" parties representing all sections of the community. They have distinct right and left wing factions which reflect the various elements of a people's party.

From 1983 to 1990 the Greens party, too, had its own group in the Bundestag. It had been established at national level in 1979 and was gradually voted into some of the state parliaments as well. Its roots lie in a radical ecologist movement which embraces factions opposed to nuclear energy as well as pacifist protest groups. In the 1990 general election, however, the Greens failed to clear the five per cent hurdle, but they are nonetheless represented in the Bundestag, sharing a list with Alliance 90, a product of the civil rights movement which in 1989-90 brought about the peaceful revolution in the former GDR. On 14 May 1993 these two parties merged into one under the name "Alliance 90/The Greens".

The PDS is the successor to the former Socialist Unity Party of Germany (SED), the communist party which ruled in the GDR. It was not able to establish itself as a major political force in united Germany

Helmut Kohl, CDU Chairman for the past 20 years

like the Alliance 90/The Greens group, it is only represented in the Bundestag by virtue of an exception allowing the five per cent clause to be applied separately in the new federal states and the existing ones in the west for the benefit of the parties in the eastern part of the country.

■ ■ ■ **The five per cent clause.** Of the 36 parties which sought election to the first Bundestag in 1949, only four remained in the parliament elected in 1990. This is the result of a "five per cent debarring clause" which was introduced in 1953 and made stricter still in 1957. It stipulates that only parties gaining at least five

Rudolf Scharping, Chairman of the SPD

per cent of the votes or at least three constituency seats can be represented in parliament. This arrangement was explicitly accepted by the Federal Constitutional Court since its purpose was to prevent tiny splinter parties from entering parliament (as had happened in the days of the Weimar Republic) and thus enable the larger parties to obtain majorities that would enable them to govern.

The five per cent hurdle is waived in the case of na-

Klaus Kinkel, Chairman of the FDP

Theodor Waigel, Chairman of the CSU

tional minorities. Thus the South-Schleswig Voters' Association, which represents the Danish minority, has a member in the state parliament of Schleswig-Holstein even though he obtained fewer than five per cent of the votes. Local government elections sometimes produce results that differ greatly from those of federal and state elections. Here the "townhall parties", independent voters' associations, often play an important role.

■ ■ ■ **The electoral system.** Elections for all parliaments in Germany are general, direct, free, equal and se-

Ludger Volmer, Spokesman of Alliance 90/The Greens

Shares of votes at federal elections

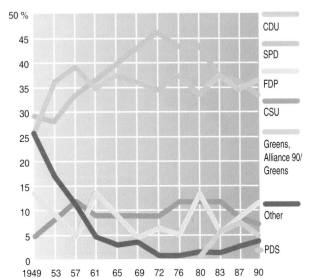

cret. Every German aged 18 or over may vote. There are no primary elections. Candidates are nominated by their parties. Elections for the German Bundestag are based on a system of "personalized" proportional representation. Electors have two votes, the first of which is given to

1990 General Election

Party	Second votes	Percent	M. P. s
CDU	17,055,116	36.7	268
SPD	15,545,366	33.5	239
FDP	5,123,233	11.0	79
CSU	3,302,980	7.1	51
Greens	1,788,200	3.8	-
PDS	1,129,578	2.4	17
Alliance 90/The Greens	559,207	1.2	8
Other	1,952,062	4.3	-
Total	46,455,772	100	662

Turnout was 77,8%.
Size of parlimamentary groups including overhang mandates, as at 1990.

Distribution of seats in the Bundestag *

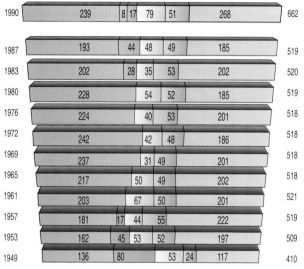

*at beginning of each legislative period; until 1987 including members from Berlin (West)

CDU   SPD   Alliance 90 / Greens
CSU   FDP   PDS   Other

a candidate in their constituency. The successful candidate is elected on a first-past-the-post basis. The second vote is given to a list of candidates put up by the parties.

The votes from the constituencies and those for the state lists are offset in such a way that the composition of the Bundestag almost identically reflects the distribution of votes among the parties. If a party has won more direct seats in the constituencies than its proportion of the votes would justify (they being known as "overhang" seats), it is allowed to keep them. Whenever this happens the Bundestag has more than the 656 members prescribed by law, hence the present 662. The object of having the electorate vote for state lists is to ensure that the strengths of all parties in parliament reflect their shares of the votes obtained. On the other hand, the constituency vote, the first vote, gives people the chance to choose a particular candidate.

Normally, the people take a keen interest in elections. The turnout for the Bundestag election of 1990 was 77.8 per cent. It tends to fluctuate at state and local elections, but it is nearly always around 70 per cent.

■ ■ ■ **Membership and finances.** The memberships of the parties represented in the Bundestag were as follows (February 1993): SPD 905,000, CDU 714,000, CSU 181,700, FDP 100,000, PDS 165,000, Alliance 90/The Greens 39,800. All parties require their members to pay subscriptions which, however, cover only part of their expenses. The donations received, too, are insufficient. Moreover, there is a danger of big donors influencing the parties for their own ends. The Parties Act therefore stipulated that donations of more than DM 40,000 must be made public. The Federal Constitutional Court, however, considered this amount too high and reduced it to DM 20,000. In addition to their own funds the parties receive public grants towards their election campaign costs. All parties who poll at least 0.5 per cent of the votes receive five marks per head on the basis of second votes in the electoral area. The Federal Constitutional Court has banned any public financial support for the parties over and above campaign costs.

The legal system

The law of the Federal Republic of Germany is predominantly written law, most of it federal and comprising more than 4,000 acts and statutory instruments. The states, too, pass laws, mainly on such matters as the police, local government, schools and universities as well as the press, radio and television.

During the forty-odd years when the country was divided the legal systems of the Federal Republic and the GDR became totally different. The crucial decision was taken in 1990 to merge the two legal systems as soon as possible after the GDR's accession to the Federal Republic. This was also of fundamental importance for the process of economic recovery in the new federal states. Extensive adjustments were made in nearly all fields of law in order to take account of the special situation in the GDR and the existing system.

■ ■ ■ **A state based on the rule of law.** German law goes back partly to Roman law and partly to numerous legal sources in the German regions. In the 19th century a uniform system of private law was created for the first time. It applied to the entire German empire. The Civil Code and Commercial Code to this day preserve the liberal spirit of those times. Their underlying principle is freedom of contract.

The guarantees afforded by a democratic state are manifest above all in substantive and procedural law. Criminal law starts from the constitutional premise that no act is punishable unless declared so by law before it was committed (nulla poena sine lege). Thus judges may not make up for gaps in penal law by applying legal provisions which cover similar cases, nor may they apply laws retroactively. Another principle embedded in the constitution is that no one may be punished more than once for the same offence under general criminal law. Personal liberty may not be restricted except on the basis of a formal law. Only a judge may determine whether a person's imprisonment is justified and only he can decide for how long. Whenever a person is detained without a judicial warrant the matter must be brought before a judge for decision without delay.

Although the police may hold someone in temporary custody they may not detain him any longer than the end of the day following the arrest. Everyone has a right to a court hearing - that, too, is guaranteed by the constitution and is a fundamental democratic principle. The administration of justice is entrusted to judges who are independent and answerable to the law only. They may not be dismissed from office nor transferred against their will. Special tribunals are banned.

Nearly all of these fundamental principles had already been established by the judiciary laws of the 19th century. They include the Judicature Act, which governs the structure, organization and jurisdiction of the courts, the Code of Civil Procedure and the Code of Criminal Procedure.

The Civil Code, which entered into force in 1900, and the Codes of Civil and Criminal Procedure were wrested by liberal and democratic forces from the imperial government towards the end of the last century after a long drawn out struggle in parliament. Some German codified laws have found their way into foreign legal systems. The Civil Code, for instance, was the model for its Japanese and Greek counterparts.

■ ■ ■   **The citizen and public administration.** After an evolutionary period of more than 100 years, the Basic Law set the seal on a comprehensive system of legal protection against the actions of public authorities. It enabled the citizen to challenge any measure that affected him on the ground that it violated his rights. This applies to any administrative act, be it a tax assessment notice or a decision whether or not to promote a school pupil to the next grade, be it the withdrawal of a driving licence or the refusal of a building permit.

Administrative courts were unknown in the GDR. Now administration in the new federal states, too, is subject to overall control by the courts.

The legal protection afforded by the specialized courts is complemented by a right of complaint to the Federal Constitutional Court. This "constitutional complaint" is open to every citizen and is an extra form of legal redress against any violations of basic rights by a public authority. The complainant must show that one of his basic rights has been infringed by a public act, for instance a court decision or an administrative measure but also a

The Courts of the Federal Republic of Germany

Federal Constitutional Court — 2 senates

Constitutional courts of the federal states

Joint Senate of the Supreme Courts

Ordinary jurisdiction

Civil jurisdiction	Penal jurisdiction	Administrative jurisdiction	Fiscal jurisdiction	Labour jurisdiction	Social jurisdiction

Federal Court of Justice
- Main civil senate | Main penal senate
- Civil senates | Penal senates

Higher Regional Court
- Civil senates | Family affairs senates | Penal senates — Appellate court | Court of first instance for serious crimes against the state

Regional Court
- Civil divisions | Commercial divisions | Minor penal divisions | Main penal divisions (first instance) | Main penal divisions (second instance) | Juvenile divisions (first instance) | Juvenile divisions (second instance)

Local Court
- Single judge | Family court | Magistrate's court | Judge for penal cases | Magistrate's court | Judge for juvenile cases | Magistrate's court for juvenile cases

Administrative jurisdiction
- Federal Administrative Court — Main senate, Senates
- Higher Administrative Court — Senates
- Administrative Court — Divisions

Fiscal jurisdiction
- Federal Finance Court — Main senate, Senates
- Finance Court — Senates

Labour jurisdiction
- Federal Labour Court — Main senate, Senates
- Regional Labour Court — Senates
- Labour Court — Divisions

Social jurisdiction
- Federal Social Court — Main senate, Senates
- Regional Social Court — Senates
- Social Court — Divisions

law. Normally, such complaints may only be lodged after all other legal remedies have been exhausted.

■ ■   **Social justice.** The Basic Law prescribes the development of the welfare system, hence much greater consideration is now given to the people's social needs than in former times. In the years since the creation of the Federal Republic a whole range of special labour and welfare legislation has been enacted to provide the citizen with various financial benefits in the event of sickness, accident, invalidity, and unemployment, and after retirement.

Labour law is a good example of how these welfare-state principles have been put into effect. Originally, these matters were only briefly dealt with under the heading of "service contracts" in the Civil Code. Today, labour legislation embraces an abundance of laws and collective agreements, but is also largely based on case law. It includes in particular the Collective Wage Agreements Act, the Protection against Dismissal Act, the Works Constitution Act, as well as the various laws on co-determination and the Labour Court Act.

■ ■   **Court structure and the legal profession.** The Federal Republic's courts are largely specialized and provide full legal protection. They fall into five categories:

- The "ordinary courts" are responsible for criminal matters, civil cases (e.g. disputes arising from contracts of sale or lease agreements, family affairs and claims for damages) and voluntary jurisdiction, which includes conveyancing, probate and wardship matters. There are four levels: local court (Amtsgericht), regional court (Landgericht), higher regional court (Oberlandesgericht) and Federal Court of Justice (Bundesgerichtshof). In criminal cases, depending on their nature, each of the first three courts can have jurisdiction, whereas in civil proceedings it will be either the local court or the regional court. One or two other courts may be appealed to on points of fact or law.

- The labour courts (three levels, local, state and federal) handle disputes arising from employment contracts and between management and labour, as well as matters covered by the Works Constitution Act. The labour courts have to decide, for instance, whether an employee has been fairly or unfairly dismissed.

- The administrative courts (local, higher - i.e. state - and federal) handle all proceedings under administrative law that do not fall within the jurisdiction of the social and fiscal courts or, in exceptional cases, the ordinary courts (e.g. cases of public liability), or involve disputes which fall under constitutional law.

- The social courts (local, state, federal) rule on all disputes concerned with social security.

- The fiscal courts (state and federal) deal with taxation and related matters.

- In the five new federal states the old court structure was retained for a transitional period. Although those regions still have county and district courts which deal with all matters which, in the western regions, are the responsibility of five different types of courts, the court structure is being adapted. Ordinary and specialized courts have been established in nearly all of the new states.

- Separate from the five branches of jurisdiction is the Federal Constitutional Court, which is not only the country's supreme court but an organ of the constitution.

There is a complex system of appeals which affords numerous possibilities for judicial review. There are two stages in the appeal procedure. In the first (Berufung), the case can be reviewed both as regards the facts and

Pronouncing judgment in the Federal Court of Justice, Karlsruhe

points of law, i.e. its merits. Thus at this level new evidence can still be introduced. In the second stage (Revision), however, the court will only consider whether the law has been properly applied and the essential procedural formalities observed.

In the Federal Republic of Germany there are approximately 20,000 professional judges, more than three quarters of whom are assigned to the ordinary courts. Most judges are appointed for life and in exercising their profession are bound only by the spirit and letter of the law.

At local court level most proceedings of non-contentious litigation are handled by judicial officers, who are not judges but intermediate-level civil servants. In several types of court lay judges sit with the professional judges. Their experience and specialist knowledge in certain fields, such as labour and welfare matters, enable them to help the courts make realistic decisions. They are also a manifestation of the citizen's direct responsibility for the administration of justice.

The public prosecutors, of whom there are over 4,000, are for the most part concerned with criminal proceedings. It is their responsibility to establish the facts where a person is suspected of a crime. They have to decide whether to discontinue the proceedings or to indict the person concerned. In court proceedings they are the prosecuting counsel. Unlike judges, public prosecutors are civil servants and therefore under orders from their superiors - though within very narrow limits.

More than 60,000 lawyers form a free profession and serve as independent counsel in all fields of law. Through representing their clients in court they play a large part in the administration of justice. They must adhere to their professional code and any violations are dealt with by disciplinary tribunals. All professional judges, public prosecutors and attorneys at law must have the qualifications of a judge, in other words they must have successfully completed the course at a university law school and the compulsory course of practical training which follows, each of which ends with a state examination.

■ ■ ■ **Data protection.** The advance of electronic data processing in the modern industrial society has created new problems for the judicial system. These days computers are used to maintain bank accounts, to book seats on aircraft, to issue tax notices or to collate crime data at police headquarters. EDP has become indispensable in nearly all fields of administration and makes it possible to store and retrieve huge quantities of data.

Modern technology has greatly eased the workload of many companies and public authorities and is increasingly finding its way into even small offices and private homes.

There are hazards as well, however. Stored data can be put to improper use and fall into the hands of unauthorized persons. Anyone with sufficient quantities of data may have access to information on a person's private life, which must remain inviolable.

In 1977 federal and state legislation was introduced to safeguard the community against such dangers. The law specifies those cases where the authorities and, for instance, private companies may store personal data. In all other cases it is forbidden. Staff involved in data processing are bound to secrecy. People are legally entitled to know what data concerning them is held by any agency. They can demand the correction of wrong data and have any that are either disputed or have been improperly obtained erased.

On the recommendation of the Federal Government, the Federal President appoints a Federal Commissioner for Data Protection who is independent of any other authority.

He is a kind of ombudsman to whom any person who feels that his personal data have not been adequately protected may complain. He submits an annual report to the Bundestag. Each of the federal states, too, has a data protection ombudsman. And enterprises who process data must likewise have someone in charge of data protection. The authorities oversee their observance of the law with regard to data protection.

The constitutional significance of data protection emerged in a 1983 ruling of the Federal Constitutional Court. It said that under article 2 of the Basic Law the citizen has the right to determine himself whether his personal data may be disclosed and how it may be used. In 1990 the Federal Data Protection Act was updated in the light of that ruling and the advancement of data processing. It strengthened the rights of persons affected and gave the Federal Commissioner for Data Protection wider powers.

Germany has some of the most up-to-date and comprehensive legislation which has helped increase public awareness of the need for data protection. Parliament will continue to respond to rapid technological change in this field.

State and citizens

· Public finance
· Public service · Internal security

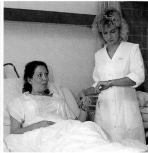

Public finance

In view of the negative experience of the 70s, when the government became overinvolved in the country's management, the present government aims to have a "leaner" state, in other words to cut back on public spending. By dint of budget savings, a consistent privatization policy and deregulation, it was possible in the 80s to reduce the public share of GNP from 50% in 1982 to 45% in 1989.

The purpose of privatization is to enable the state to concentrate on its central role. The proceeds from privatization are not considered a major contribution to the solution of budgetary problems, however. When, for instance, the Salzgitter corporation was sold in 1990 the money was used to establish the German Environment Foundation, one of the largest endowments in Europe, with initial capital of DM 2.5 billion.

But the country's reunification suddenly confronted the government with a host of new responsibilities. The volume and the importance of public finance have increased again accordingly. In 1992 the federal and state governments as well as the local authorities together spent DM 1,051 billion. This was the first time in the country's history that public spending had exceeded the trillion mark. If we add the cost of national insurance, the total came to DM 1,367 billion or 49.3% of GNP. Thus the public share of the national income is back to where it was in the early 80s. Every second mark earned in Germany at present comes from the public authorities. The government plans to reduce this high proportion.

■ ■ ■ **Distribution of responsibilities.** The Federal Republic of Germany has three levels of government, federal, state and local. Their responsibilities in their respective areas are governed by the Basic Law. Generally speaking, they have to meet the necessary expenditure themselves. Hence public revenue does not flow into a joint account but is distributed among the federal, state and local governments.

The lowest level of public administration is that of the municipality, which is concerned with all matters that directly concern the local community and individual citizens. It is thus responsible for water, gas and electricity supply, refuse disposal, the maintenance of local roads, welfare and health services. Together with the state authorities it is also responsible for schools and cultural establishments.

The states have jurisdiction for all aspects of government, unless the Basic Law specifically provides otherwise or leaves open the possibility of a different arrangement. Its main responsibilities fall into the category of cultural affairs and primarily concern schools and education. But the administration of justice, the police and public health services also fall within the states' purview.

Most of the responsibility, and thus the largest financial burden, is borne by the Federal Government. According to the Basic Law, its sphere of competence embraces all matters that directly secure the existence of the state as a whole, viz social security, defence, foreign affairs, national security, the construction of autobahns and national highways, telecommunications, science and research. It is also responsible for energy and the promotion of industry, agriculture, housing and urban development, public health, the environment and overseas development.

There are other various tasks which the federal and state governments plan, implement and finance jointly. They include university building, improvement of regional economic structures, agricultural structure and coastal preservation, as well as cooperation on educational planning and the promotion of science. A fourth level of administration is also assuming increasing importance: the European Community.

■ ■ ■ **Financial planning.** A 1967 Law for the Promotion of Economic Stability and Growth requires the federal and state governments to draw up their budgets in the light of the principal economic policy objectives. These are price stability, a high level of employment, balanced foreign trade and steady economic growth (the "magic square"). The Federal Government and the states must draw up financial plans for their areas of responsibility in which incomes and expenditure are projected for a period of five years. The purpose of this pluri-annual financial planning is to ensure that public revenue and expenditure are commensurate with national economic resources and requirements.

The municipalities, too, must draw up medium-term financial plans. The great importance of the public budgets requires close coordination through all levels of administration. The main body in this process of voluntary cooperation is the Financial Planning Council set up in 1968 and representing the Federal Government, the states and municipalities and the Bundesbank. There is also an Economic Policy Council with a coordinating and advisory function.

■ ■ ■ **Distribution of revenues.** In order to meet their responsibilities the federal, state and local governments must have the necessary funds. Wide-ranging as public responsibilities are, the sources of revenue are equally varied. The main source is taxation. Total tax revenue in 1992 was DM 729.1 billion. The Federal Government's share was 48.1%, that of the states 34.2% and that of the local authorities 12.6%.

Tax revenue has to be distributed according to the size of the responsibilities of the three levels of government. Income, corporation and value-added tax are the „share taxes", that is to say, they are distributed between the federal and state governments according to specific formulas (the value-added tax being renegotiated from time to time). Part of the income tax goes to the local authorities. In exchange they have to surrender to the federal and state governments part of the trade tax they raise, which used to be a purely local government tax. Another part of this VAT goes to the European Community.

Tax revenues 1992
(in millions of DM estimated)

Federal Government	356,849
States	247,363
Municipolities	93,417
EC funds	34,202
Total	731,831

Important taxes:

Wage tax	247,322
Assessed income tax	41,531
Turnover tax, import turnover tax	197,711
Oil tax	55,166
Tobacco tax	19,253

Other taxes apply to only one level of government. The Federal Government obtains revenue from monopolies (e.g. on spirits) and various consumer and transaction taxes (e.g. mineral oil, tobacco and capital transfer taxes).

The states receive the motor vehicle, property, inheritance and beer taxes as well as a number of smaller taxes.

The municipalities obtain revenue from trade tax, less the proportion taken by the federal and state governments, real estate and local excise duties.

There are more than two dozen different taxes. Nearly half of all revenue comes from income tax and corporation tax. Income tax is the one which affects the average person most of all. Employers deduct it from wages and

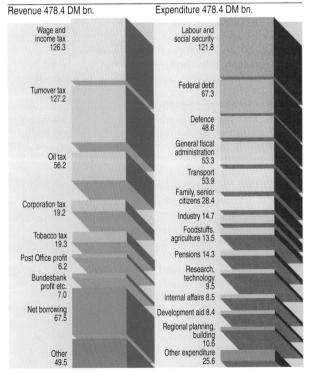

Federal Budget 1994 (draft)

Revenue 478.4 DM bn.	Expenditure 478.4 DM bn.
Wage and income tax 126.3	Labour and social security 121.8
Turnover tax 127.2	Federal debt 67.3
Oil tax 56.2	Defence 48.6
	General fiscal administration 53.3
	Transport 53.9
Corporation tax 19.2	Family, senior citizens 28.4
	Industry 14.7
Tobacco tax 19.3	Foodstuffs, agriculture 13.5
Post Office profit 6.2	Pensions 14.3
Bundesbank profit etc. 7.0	Research, technology 9.5
	Internal affairs 8.5
Net borrowing 67.5	Development aid 8.4
	Regional planning, building 10.6
Other 49.5	Other expenditure 25.6

salaries and remit it to the tax office (the „pay-as-you-earn" principle). The rate of taxation rises with the individual's income. After deduction of certain non-taxable amounts it comprises (until the end of 1993) at least 19% and at most 53%. The new Investment Promotion Act („Standortsicherungsgesetz") will reduce the top rate to 47% as from 1994.

The second largest source of revenue is turn-over tax (value-added tax and turnover tax on imports). It accounts for a quarter of all tax revenue. Mineral oil and municipal trade tax each provide between six and seven per cent.

■ ■ ■ **Financial equalization.** The tax-raising capacity of the states varies considerably because their situation and economic structures are also very different. Thus some states, such as Baden-Württemberg, Hamburg and Hesse, have substantial financial resources while others like Lower Saxony, Saarland, Schleswig-Holstein and Bremen do not. These differences in tax-raising potential are largely balanced out through a sys-

The Nuclear Research Centre. Karlsruhe

tem of „horizontal financial equalization". On the one hand the turnover tax accruing to the states is shared proportionately, on the other the wealthier states make equalization payments to the poorer regions.

A „vertical financial equalization" takes place between states and local authorities. The tax and other revenues of the municipalities are inadequate for their tasks. They therefore depend on subsidies from the states. Some of them are tied to specific purposes but others are freely disposable. The aim of equalization is to reduce the disparity between local authorities with high and those with low tax revenues.

■ ■ ■   **Public debt.** Apart from levying taxes to finance public expenditure the government can also borrow money. In the 70s and especially since reunification the federal and state finance ministers have been drawing increasingly on the capital markets. In 1992 the country's total budget debt came to a record DM 1.21 billion or almost DM 15,000 per head of the population. To this sum must be added the debts of the Federal Railways (1993: DM 48 billion), the Post Office (DM 102 billion) and the Treuhand (about DM 300 billion).

■ ■   **Financial problems in connection with German unity.** When the wall dividing Germany was opened in November 1989 the overall public debt stood at DM 929 billion. Five years later, at the end of 1994, this sum will have almost doubled. This in itself indicates the size of the financial problems relating to Germany's reunification.

Funds which up to 1990 were available to the 11 western states for such things as social security, infrastructure, education and research, individual branches of the economy and the labour market, now have to be spread among 16 states. Public expenditure has naturally increased all round as a result of reunification but the necessary revenue base is only gradually taking shape.

Investment in German unity is therefore correspondingly high. In 1992 public spending on social insurance for the new states exceeded DM 110 billion after deduction of their structural and administrative revenue. The amount in 1993 was almost DM 140 billion, nearly 5% of western Germany's gross domestic product. There are in addition united Germany's considerable international liabilities.

The Unification Treaty provided that the new federal states should from the very beginning be incorporated as far as possible in the financial system established by the Basic Law. Thus since 1991 the new states have been subject to basically the same regulations with regard to budgetary management and tax distribution as the western states. A „German Unity Fund" was set up to provide financial support for the new states and their municipalities. It is fed jointly by the Federal Government and the western states, most of the money being raised in the capital market. This fund will be a substitute until the end of 1994 for a nationwide financial equalization arrangement among the federal states. As from 1995, the financial relations between the Federal Government and all sixteen states are to be completely readjusted. In addition to untied assistance via the German Unity Fund, the states and local authorities in the former GDR receive tied aid from the central government.

In mid-1991 the Federal Government launched a further joint programme known as „Recovery East". In both 1991 and 1992 it provided DM 12 billion for local authority investment, job creation or promotion of regional industry. In order to finance structural reform in the new federal states it was necessary to considerably increase public borrowing, especially that of the Federal Government. A consolidation process over the next few years is intended to reduce the government's public sector borrowing requirement substantially.

Public service

For the average citizen the state as such is an abstract concept. It materializes, however, in the from of public servants who provide the vast range of services for which the federal and state governments and local authorities are responsible. In the western states of the Federal Republic, i.e. those which existed prior to unification, public servants number more than 4.6 million, not counting the armed services. In 1992 eastern Germany's public servants numbered about 1.7 million, a discrepancy that will be gradually reduced.

Public servants have widely differing occupations, for instance departmental officials and dustmen, swimming baths supervisors and professors, judges and nurses, policemen, teachers and engine drivers.

Over the years the public service has assumed many new functions. Today they range beyond the classical police and regulatory responsibilities and cover education and the administration of different public institutions, as well as environmental protection. The number of civil servants is increasing accordingly: In 1950, 9% of all gainfully employed persons were public servants, now the proportion is about 17%. Some 40% of all public servants are civil servants, the remainder workers and salaried employees.

■ ■ ■ **Professional civil servants.** The professional civil service has been part of the German system that has evolved since the 18th century. The Basic Law has guaranteed this proven institution and allows only civil servants to exercise „sovereign powers". The purpose of having a professional civil service is to ensure that public responsibilities are carried out reliably without outside and in particular political influence. On account of the growing significance of public duties, for instance in the fields of infrastructure, education and social affairs, these requirements also apply to a large extent to the service- providing departments. Civil servants also carry out the traditional responsibilities, of course, when they for instance order the demolition of a dangerously dilapidated house, impose fines or go in armed pursuit of criminals. But the range of responsi-

Traffic guidance system on the autobahn

bilities in the modern industrial and social state is far greater.

The civil servant has a special obligation of loyalty to his employer and the constitution. This is prescribed by law. Although civil servants, like all citizens, have the right to participate in political activities, they are required to exercise moderation and restraint. They may also form professional groups but are not allowed to strike.

But as well as special duties they also have special rights. As a rule they are appointed for life. For the period of their active employment and in retirement they and their families receive welfare benefits from the state. If they become incapacitated, or upon reaching retirement age, they receive a civil service pension. Salary scales are related to four service grades: ordinary, intermediate, higher intermediate and higher. Access depends on educational achievement and professional qualifications. Generally, members of the higher grades have a university degree. Judges and members of the armed services are not, in the legal sense, civil servants, but they are subject to similar regulations. Their special status derives from the independence enjoyed by judges and the requirements of military discipline.

■ ■ ■ **Wage earners and salaried employees.** In the 19th century there were very few wage earners in the public service, but their number has increased in the meantime corresponding to the importance of services for the local community. Wage earners and salaried staff in the public sector correspond in many respects to employees in the private sector. They pay social insurance contributions and are not appointed for life. Only after fifteen years' service and having reached the age of at least 40 does their status become permanent. Upon appointment they sign an employment contract which is largely determined by collective wage agreements. They have a right to strike, otherwise their responsibilities and conditions of work have been brought more and more into line with the rights and duties of civil servants. For instance, they are required to maintain official secrecy; they must be incorruptible and loyal to the constitution.

Internal security

The maintenance of public security and order is one of the most important tasks of government. In the Federal Republic of Germany it is carried out by the federal states and the central government. The police are for the most part under the jurisdiction of the states. Only in certain fields does the Basic Law assign responsibility to the Federal Government.

▓ ▓ ▓ **The police in the federal states.** There are the general police forces, the criminal police, river police, and the alert forces.

The general police forces are mainly concerned with the prevention and prosecution of petty crime. They also include traffic police, the law officers with whom the ordinary citizen may, if at all, come into contact.

The criminal police are chiefly concerned with serious offences including organized and industrial crime, sexual offences, robbery, blackmail, serious theft, homicide, drug trafficking and the manufacture and passing of counterfeit money). They have special units, in some cases jointly with the general forces, to combat terrorism and hostage-taking, and for observation and detection.

The river police, as the name implies, control all waterway traffic and monitor in particular the transport of dangerous goods.

The alert forces are responsible for the training of new recruits and provide support for the general and criminal forces during state visits, demonstrations, major sporting events, international fairs and natural disasters. They are trained and deployed as units. They number about 26,000 at present in the western states. New forces are gradually being built up in the new states (since 1991 their strength has been about 6,000).

▓ ▓ ▓ **The Federal Border Guard, a national police force.** The Federal Border Guard is a federal police force responsible to the Federal Ministry of the Interior and numbering about 34,000 (including trainees), plus some 6,250 civilian staff. Its main task is to control the country's borders, which includes checks to prevent the illegal entry of foreigners, organized crime, smuggling and drug trafficking.

The Federal Border Guard also protects key public buildings, such as the office of the Federal President and the Federal Chancellor, the ministries and the Federal Constitutional Court in Karlsruhe. It supports the Federal Criminal Police Office in protecting VIPs and in carrying out responsibilities on the high seas including environmental protection measures.

Since 1 April 1992 the Federal Border Guard has also been responsible for railway and civilian air traffic security. It helps the state authorities cope with particularly dangerous situations, for instance where large forces have to be on duty during state visits or public demonstrations.

The guard is also called in during natural disasters and major accidents. Beyond its statutory functions it carries out international responsibilities, chiefly as part of the police component of UN peace-keeping missions.

■ ■ ■ **The Federal Criminal Police Office.** The Federal Criminal Police Office (BKA), which is based in Wiesbaden with a head department near Bonn, is the focal point of cooperation between the federal and state law enforcement agencies. Concerned with international crime, it collects and evaluates information and other data. The Federal Criminal Police Office is the main body for criminological research and serves as the national centre for INTERPOL, the international criminal police organization.

The BKA handles serious crimes itself, e.g. international drug trafficking, gun-running and terrorist activities. In large-scale operations it supports the police of the federal states. The BKA's security unit in Bonn protects the Federal President, the Chancellor, ministers, etc.

Its staff of about 4,000 come under the authority of the Federal Ministry of the Interior.

■ ■ ■ **Constitution-protection agencies.** Safeguarding the democratic system is defined in the Basic Law as „protection of the constitution". In order to be able to provide effective protection the federal and state authorities collect information on extremist activities and on other developments which constitute a threat to national security and evaluate it for the central and state governments, ministries and courts.

Traffic monitoring centre, Munich

Another important area is counter-espionage. The federal authority charged with these tasks is the Federal Office for the Protection of the Constitution in Cologne. It is accountable to the Federal Ministry of the Interior and cooperates with the corresponding state agencies. This agency has no executive police powers, i.e. it may not arrest or interrogate anyone. A law enacted in 1990 defines the legal basis for its activities more precisely and thus ensures greater protection for rights of privacy.

The federal and state agencies for the protection of the constitution are under the supervision of the competent ministers, parliaments and data protection commissioners. Further control is exercised by the courts.

Germany in the world

Foreign policy
· External security
· Cooperation with developing countries

Foreign policy

In 1990 the German people were reunited in free self-determination. They achieved this goal by peaceful means and with the support of their friends and partners in east and west. The signing of the Treaty on the Final Settlement with respect to Germany (the Two-plus-Four Treaty) in Moscow on 12 September 1990 marked the ending of the post-war era. That accord confirmed that Germany, after the restoration of its unity on 3 October 1990, had regained its sovereignty and was no longer burdened by status and security problems in relation to other countries. Its ten articles regulate the external aspects of unification. Thus, 45 years after the Second World War, the division of Germany, but also the division of Europe, was overcome. United Germany has a greater responsibility to bear. German policy remains above all a policy for peace.

Its objective is to promote the economic and political integration of nation states and to strengthen the international and supranational organizations and institutions so that they will become the foundations of global cooperation and bastions against the dangers of neo-nationalism.

As before, German foreign policy will be based on the country's lasting membership of the community of free democracies, the European Community and the Atlantic Alliance. This translates into four major objectives: the continuing progress of European integration, the further development of NATO, the stabilization of the reform processes in Central and Eastern Europe together with the necessary support, and partnership with the nations of the Third World.

The Federal Republic of Germany will continue to contribute to peaceful progress in the world. It accepts the responsibility deriving from the united country's global importance.

As one of the largest industrial and trading nations it is also dependent upon a stable and well-functioning world economic system. Its main aim is to establish a fair balance of interests between north and south, between the industrial and the developing countries, on the basis

Helmut Kohl being hosted by President William Clinton

of a fruitful dialogue. It pursues that aim chiefly within the United Nations and its sub-organizations.

Currently, the Federal Republic of Germany maintains diplomatic relations with nearly all countries. It has more than 230 embassies and consular posts as well as ten missions at international organizations and two offices protecting its interests in other countries.

■ ■ ■ **European Union.** Ever since it was founded the Federal Republic of Germany has been one of the main advocates of European unification. Together with Belgium, France, Italy, Luxembourg and the Netherlands it formed in 1952 the European Coal and Steel Community, and in 1957 the European Economic Community and the European Atomic Energy Community (EURATOM). In 1967 these three institutions were merged to form the European Community (EC).

The EC developed into a supranational organization with its own institutions, some of whose decisions become directly applicable law in member states. These institutions include especially

- the European Parliament, which since 1979 has been elected direct by the people and has acquired increasing powers
- the Council of Ministers, which plays a large part in Community law-making and decides Community policy

- the European Commission, the Community's executive body, which is independent of national governments, ensures that Community regulations are applied, and draws up proposals for the further development of Community policy
- and the European Court of Justice, which ensures that Community laws and treaties are properly interpreted and applied. The Court's decisions have played a large part in further developing Community law.

The EC has acquired considerable influence not only as an economic community but as a political force and as a champion of democratic values. By 1986 the six founder members of the Community had been joined by the United Kingdom, Denmark, Ireland, Greece, Portugal and Spain. More European countries want to join. The Community has been negotiating with Austria, Sweden, Norway and Finland since 1993 and the aim is for them to become members in 1995. The European Commission has also submitted opinions to the Council on applications for membership from Cyprus and Malta. Turkey's application is still pending.

The Community has meanwhile concluded "Europe agreements" with most of the post-communist democracies of Central and Eastern Europe. They go beyond the association agreements with other countries, such as most of the Mediterranean states. Their purpose is to bring the reformist states of that region economically and politically closer to the Community and pave the way for their accession. As a result of German unification the European Community now has a total population of about 340 million.

From the very outset the aim was to develop the European Community into a political union. The Treaty on European Union of 7 February 1993 is a major step towards this objective.

The Treaty defines the economic and monetary goals of European Union and the Community's further political development. It has meanwhile been ratified by eleven of the twelve member states. As soon as the complaints against the Treaty have been rejected by the Federal Constitutional Court in the autumn of 1993 the German instrument of ratification can likewise be deposited and the Treaty can then enter into force. An intergovernmental conference scheduled for 1996 will re-

Helmut Kohl and French President François Mitterrand

view the Treaty's progress and chart the Community's route into the next century.

One of the Union's basic elements will be the common foreign and security policy which has emerged from European political cooperation (EPC) which, after a modest start 20 years ago, has become a major instrument of European foreign policy and a second pillar of the unification process.

The common foreign and security policy will have the basic features of EPC. There will be new elements, including the principle of majority decision-making and the addition of a security and defence policy dimension to the integration process.

This represents a true breakthrough since the Single European Act of 1987. It will significantly strengthen the European identity in terms of foreign and security policy. It will at the same time broaden the basis of the Alliance and of transatlantic partnership. Furthermore, it will enable the Community and its member states to render a crucial contribution to the stabilization of the security system.

France and Germany have taken a practical step in this direction by proposing, in consultation with NATO and their transatlantic partners, the establishment of a Eurocorps. Other member countries have meanwhile joined in and for the first time in history there will be a 40,000 strong European formation which will be able to engage in NATO operations and missions of Western European Union, which was defined in Maastricht as the European pillar of the Atlantic Alliance.

The Treaty on European Union marked the beginning of the decisive phase leading to the completion of European integration. The course has been charted for the introduction of a common currency before the end of this decade. This will make the Community the world's most important economic area. The political signposts are:
- the merging of the Community treaties into a "Treaty on Political Union"
- the common foreign and security policy
- wider powers for the European Parliament
- the inclusion of domestic affairs and justice in the treaty
- and the start towards social union.

Since the completion of the European internal market on 31 December 1992 nearly all customs and trade barriers between EC member states have disappeared. There is now a huge market much the same size as that of North America allowing free movement of persons, goods, services and capital. In harmony with the Schengen Agreement, under which most of the EC countries have agreed to discontinue border controls from the end of 1993, the internal market will provide a boost for Europe's economies, including Germany's export-led industries.

The European Community has impressively demonstrated its attractiveness as a model community of free nations. But Europe is much larger than the present Community. Numerous important European countries have already applied for or are considering membership. The Community is open to any democratic European country - that is the letter and spirit of the Treaty of Rome.

Several other Austria, Norway, Finland, Iceland and Liechtenstein have signed the European Economic Area Agreement together with the EC and are thus linked up with the internal market.

In the course of its development the European Community has helped enhance Europe's freedom and democracy. As the member with the most powerful economy, Germany makes substantial financial contributions to the Community's expansion. It will continue to make every effort to further the Community's integration.

In accordance with the principle of subsidiarity, the members of the European Union will be in charge of matters they are capable of handling themselves. European Union and national identity are not contradictory. It will not be possible to achieve or preserve the one without the other. That is how the Germans see their unity and European Union - as two sides of the one coin.

The need for progressive integration and the preservation of national identities will increase when the post-communist democracies of central and eastern Europe eventually join the Community. Here, too, seemingly contradictory elements have to be reduced to a common denominator: the enlargement and deepening of the Community. Germany has always advocated the early admission of the reformist states who have discarded communism to help give them political stability and also on account of the economic opportunities their accession will entail for both east and west. But it is also clear that this enlargement will have to go hand in hand with a reform of the Community's institutions and decision-making mechanisms, that is to say, a deepening of the integration process. A larger Community must acquire new rules and procedures if it is to be able to function and develop properly.

The European Community pursues an outward-looking trade policy. It advocates a market-oriented world economic order and is opposed to protectionism. It develops its economic relations with third countries within a close network of trade cooperation and association agreements.

A typical example is the Lomé Convention, which is the basis for cooperation in partnership with 69 African, Caribbean and Pacific developing countries, known as the ACP states.

Meanwhile the Council of Europe, too, is serving as an important bridge to Europe's new democracies. Founded in 1949 with its seat in Strasbourg, it is the oldest European institution and has in the past few years admitted a number of post-communist reformist democracies in central and eastern Europe and given observer status to others. The condition for membership was their irrevocable decision to defend human rights, democracy and the rule of law.

The Council of Europe has thus become a mirror of the democratic renaissance in central and eastern Europe. It has given the new members a stamp of quality, as it were, for their reforms. Germany's attempts to enhance the significance of this institution have been underscored by the scheduling of the first summit meeting of heads of state and government of all member states of the Council of Europe for October 1993 in Vienna.

■ ■ ■ **The Conference on Security and Cooperation in Europe (CSCE).** The CSCE's members include 35 European countries, the former Soviet Union as well as the United States and Canada. It is thus the only forum for pan-European cooperation. The Charter of Paris (1990) marked its entry into a new phase following the end of the east-west confrontation. The participating states are not only committed to human rights, democracy and the rule of law, to economic freedom and social justice as well as European unification but, unlike previously, have a common perception of these principles.

Under the Paris Charter the CSCE has begun assuming operative responsibilities and is creating the necessary structures for this purpose. This applies in particular to early-warning arrangements, conflict-prevention and crisis-management including peace-keeping measures, and the peaceful settlement of conflicts. Within the framework adopted at the 1992 CSCE summit in Helsinki, conflict-prevention and advisory missions have been active in the states adjacent to Serbia/Montenegro, i.e. Kosovo, Sanjak, Voivodina, Georgia, Estonia and the Republic of Moldava. Apart from giving financial support, Germany has from the beginning provided personnel for such missions.

The CSCE's potential for settling disputes by peaceful means has not been sufficiently used. At the end of 1992, therefore, the CSCE Council, meeting in Stockholm, adopted a number of procedural improvements, in particular the agreement on settlement and arbitration procedures within the CSCE, which was the result of a Franco-German initiative which 29 participating states signed immediately and which will become effective after ratification by twelve states, as well as the settlement-by-order procedure.

The German Government welcomes the wide-ranging obligations created by the CSCE in the field of human rights. Although not legally binding they are of a very mandatory nature politically owing to the fact that they have been adopted by all participating states by consensus.

To ensure continuous monitoring of CSCE standards regular implementation meetings are held at which the human rights situation in member countries is critically examined and discussed. CSCE expert missions within the "Moscow mechanism" created in 1991 have, through their investigations and reports, helped to solve problems in several participating states.

The High Commissioner for National Minorities, an office created with strong German support at the 1992 Helsinki summit, identifies potential ethnic tensions at the earliest possible time and helps contain and reduce them through direct consultations with the affected parties.

The CSCE will continue to serve as a forum for dialogue, negotiation and cooperation in order to give fresh stimulus to the process of arms control, disarmament and confidence and security-building. The Helsinki summit established the CSCE Forum for Security Cooperation for this purpose. Germany attaches special importance to the negotiations on a code of conduct in the politico-military sphere. The code is scheduled to be completed by the next summit meeting at the end of 1994 and thus provide a coherent set of rules for the use of military power.

The measures introduced so far have not yet completed the development of the CSCE. One of Germany's aims is to give the CSCE and its institutions more scope for action so that it can better meet its responsibilities as a regional arrangement within the meaning of chapter VIII of the UN Charter.

■ ■ ▨ **Cooperation with eastern neighbours.** For Germany's cooperation with her eastern neighbours it was important to conclude treaties as the framework for a proper relationship. Such accords have meanwhile been signed with Poland, the Czech Republic, the Slovak Republic, Hungary and the successor states of the former Soviet Union. Germany's relationship with the latter is of crucial importance to the whole of Europe, it being essential to create the material foundations for European unity and to establish the fundamental values of democracy and rule of law.

In order to develop a free market economy the nations of eastern, central and south-eastern Europe and those in the new states on the territory of the former Soviet Union need the support of the west as a whole. Germany has strongly backed the reforms in these countries from the very beginning, as shown in particular by the financial assistance of DM 87 billion she has provided for the CIS countries and the approximate amount of DM 37 billion for central and eastern Europe between 1989 and August 1993.

She has thus contributed over 50% of the total aid from the industrial countries. The help provided will ultimately benefit the whole of Europe. Germany remains a strong advocate of European pluralism. The desire for self-determination in eastern Europe will grow the more it coincides with the development of pan-European structures and pan-European solidarity.

■ ■ ■ **The Atlantic Alliance.** The North Atlantic Treaty Organization (NATO) has always been the indispensable foundation of the security of its members in Europe and North America. The Federal Republic of Germany joined NATO in 1955.

The defence preparedness and capability of all NATO member states has, over the decades, safeguarded the free democracies, starting from the dual strategy of defence and dialogue in relation to the Warsaw Pact countries, as expressed in the Harmel Report of 1967. It was not least the Atlantic Alliance which paved the way for the transformation in Europe and Germany.

Meanwhile the political transformation in Europe has removed the confrontation between East and West. The security situation, despite some remaining risks, has improved considerably.

Nevertheless, NATO still has a central role to play in maintaining Europe's stability and security.

NATO's new strategy adopted in Rome in November 1991 represents the alliance's response to the changed security situation. It entails a sizeable reduction in force strengths and new force structures. With the massive communist threat a thing of the past, special importance attaches to the role of mobile and multinational crisis reaction forces in defending the NATO area with fewer forces.

In 1992/93 NATO resolved to support UN and CSCE peace-keeping operations in suitable cases on request. This gives substance to the idea of mutually complementary security organizations. The alliance's military capabilities are also conducive to the instruments of collective security.

Germany played a leading role in bringing about NATO's readjustment, especially in cooperation with the United States.

It was a German-US initiative in late 1991 that led to the establishment of the North Atlantic Cooperation Council, which embraces all members of the defunct Warsaw Pact and the successor states of the Soviet Union. The Council, now institutionalized and meeting regularly, demonstrates the western alliance's readiness for a comprehensive security partnership in Europe. Not only has it proved to be a useful instrument of security dialogue and broad-ranging cooperation among enemies from the days of East-West confrontation who are now friends. It has also contributed to stability in central and eastern Europe.

Foreign Minister Klaus Kinkel
with his Russian colleague Andrei Kosyrev

Disarmament and arms control are indispensable tools of German foreign and security policy. Their purpose is to limit weapon capabilities and establish binding rules for the use of military force.

Cooperative arms control focuses on the implementation of recent accords - to which German too is a party - such as the "Treaty on Conventional Forces in Europe", under which more than 50,000 heavy weapons will be eliminated, the 1992 follow-up agreement on force limitations (CFE Ia), the 1992 "Vienna Document" on confidence and security building measures among the CSCE states, the 1992 "Open Skies Treaty", which renders the airspace of contracting states (i.e. from Vancouver to Vladivostok) accessible for aircraft surveillance, the institution in 1992 of the CSCE Forum for Security Cooperation, which is designed to create a new security relationship among the CSCE states on the basis of cooperation and mutual confidence, as well as the 1993 global ban on chemical weapons, with Germany as one of the main instigators.

A completely new departure in the field of arms control is the provision, also by Germany, of assistance for the destruction of nuclear and chemical weapons. Another task is to prevent the proliferation of weapons of mass destruction and to consolidate the international non-proliferation system. Germany believes that the Non-Proliferation Treaty should be extended indefinitely when the matter is decided in 1995.

Another major event is the session of the Geneva Conference on Disarmament beginning in January 1994, which will be concerned with a comprehensive nuclear test ban.

■ ■ ■ **Relations with the western states.** Germany's and Europe's close ties with the democracies of North America remain unchanged. Transatlantic partnership is based on vital mutual interests and values. Europe, the United States and Canada have manifold historical, human, cultural and political ties. Thus America's and Canada's involvement in Europe continues to be of vital importance to the continent's, and hence Germany's, peace and security. NATO remains an indispensable security bond between Europe and North America.

Biannual summit meetings and various bilateral consultations provide renewed stimulus for the special relationship between Germany and France established by Chancellor Konrad Adenauer and President Charles de Gaulle through the treaty signed in the Elysée Palace, Paris, in 1963. In recent years attention has focused on the question of European Union, progress towards which has been considerably helped by the joint initiatives of Chancellor Kohl and President Mitterrand.

Following German unification, France has also become economically and culturally involved in the development of the new federal states. The stability of Franco-German friendship is guaranteed by the contacts between the citizens of both countries (there being more than 1,400 town and 2,000 school twinnings, as well as cooperation between the regions) and by the close economic relations between the two countries, who are each other's principal trading partner.

Germany's cooperation with other western countries has also been continuously intensified. Semi-annual summit meetings are held with the United Kingdom, and a close network of agreements, consultations and mutual visits makes for a similarly close relationship with Germany's other western partners.

Relations with Israel, too, are intensive and good at all levels and in most spheres. Since the establishment of diplomatic relations in 1965 they have in many respects developed into a genuine friendship.

■ ■ ■ **Germany and the developing countries.** Relations with the developing countries are an important element of German foreign policy. Reducing the prosperity gap between the industrial and developing countries is the biggest task of the 90s. Cooperation based on partnership, not least assistance intended to help the recipients achieve self-sustaining development, serves the common aim of meeting global challenges such as poverty, rapid population growth, disease and drugs, and ensuring mankind's survival. German policy focuses on combating poverty, protecting the environment and natural resources, as well as education and training.

In 40 years of fruitful cooperation prior to unification Germany earned the reputation of a reliable and helpful partner of the nations of the South where four fifths of the world's population live.

The developing nations expect united Germany to assume a larger role on the world stage. At the same time, however, they are afraid she might neglect "the South" in favour of "the East" on account of the economic burden of the unification process and the aid provided for the reformist countries of eastern and central Europe.

Since 1990, therefore, the year of unification, the German Government has often reaffirmed its commitments to the developing countries and its intention to further develop and strengthen the existing bonds of friendship.

The industrial countries must meet their responsibility to create global economic conditions which give the developing countries, too, a fair chance. They must in particular open their markets. In elaborating national policies they must give more attention to their impact on developing countries and increase their assistance in terms of both quality and quantity for the poor countries in particular.

Relations between the European Community and the developing countries are already featuring prominently in Germany's foreign and security policy. Development aid funds in the last three years have not been reduced, rather increased, in spite of the country's additional burdens. When Germany was reunited 106 development projects sponsored by the former GDR were still in progress. 72 of them have been continued, the others were considered unsuitable and abandoned.

Germany, as in the recent past, will participate in international efforts to contain and remove sources of crisis. The aid she has provided since 1991 for the Kurds in Iraq, Somalia and the victims of the civil war in former Yugoslavia is considerably more than in previous years (from DM 90 million in 1989 to DM 162 million in 1992).

For the period 1992-94 Germany has earmarked DM 27 million to help finance the democratization process in the developing and reformist countries and intends to subsequently increase this amount. These countries acquire greater significance as the common foreign and security policy develops.

In the European Community Germany has always urged that the Europeans open their markets wider to the countries of Asia and Latin America, for free trade is, in the final analysis, even more important than development assistance.

■ ■ ■ **Membership of the United Nations.** The day of German unity is also a landmark in Germany's relation-

World Economic Summit, Tokyo 1993

ship with the United Nations, for since 3 October 1990 the interests of all Germans are represented by a single mission to the world organization. And the termination of four-power reservations means that Germany no longer has a unique status in the United Nations. Today it has the same rights and responsibilities as any other member state.

A major aim of German foreign policy is to strengthen the role of the United Nations as the principal institution of the community of nations. Only this will enable the world organization to respond adequately to such global challenges as conflict prevention, population explosion and environmental protection. This applies especially to the Secretary-General, who should be placed in a stronger position to mediate in preventing conflicts. By dint of her own history Germany is particularly committed to freedom, democracy and human rights. All over the world, therefore, her policy is based on respect for human rights and human dignity.

Germany has shown by word and deed that she is prepared to fulfil the global responsibility deriving from the country's unification. In the context of UN peace-keeping and humanitarian missions, which have increased constantly since the end of the East-West confrontation, she has, for instance, sent troops to Cambodia and Somalia. She has also indicated her readiness to assume a larger role in a reform of the Security Council.

■ ■ ■ **Cultural relations.** Cultural policy is one of the main elements of German foreign policy. It consists of
- giving other countries a comprehensive and self-critical picture of the Federal Republic of Germany and her cultural achievements, a picture which reflects the country's pluralist democracy and embraces the whole nation's spiritual and intellectual values
- promoting the German language all over the world
- and fostering cultural exchange with other countries in a spirit of partnership.

The aim of this policy is to remove prejudices and strengthen mutual respect. In this way it helps to promote political and economic cooperation. In the development of cultural relations the Federal Foreign Office cooperates with the state governments, the churches, unions, sports associations, political foundations and many other organizations.

Germany has concluded cultural agreements with 65 countries but also has intensive cultural exchanges with most other countries. Translating cultural policy into practice is largely the responsibility of organizations acting on behalf of the Federal Government. They include
- the Goethe Institute, which has 158 branches abroad and 16 in Germany and whose main tasks are to cultivate the German language abroad and promote international cultural cooperation
- the German Academic Exchange Service (DAAD), which organizes exchanges of academic staff and students
- Inter Nationes, which hosts foreign guests of the government and provides a wide range of information on the Federal Republic of Germany through films, tapes and printed material
- and the Institute for Foreign Relations, which organizes German exhibitions abroad and foreign exhibitions in Germany.

External security

The principal aim of the Federal Republic's security policy is to maintain peace and safeguard the country's freedom and independence. "Maintaining peace with fewer weapons" was the Federal Republic's motto in helping to end the East-West confrontation. Germany is playing a constructive part in shaping Europe's new security relationships. The members of the European Community aim to establish a common foreign and security policy in which Western European Union plays a major role. The close political and military cooperation in the North Atlantic Treaty Organization (NATO) is complemented by cooperation on security matters with the central and eastern European countries in the North Atlantic Cooperation Council.

Through its involvement in disarmament and arms control Germany is helping to build new security structures. Prior to unification Germany undertook by treaty to reduce the size of its armed forces significantly by 1994. With 370,000 servicemen the Bundeswehr of united Germany will be smaller than the armed forces of the Federal Republic prior to unification. Up to 1990 the Bundeswehr had a personnel strength of 490,000, while the GDR's National People's Army (NVA) had 170,000. The Federal Republic of Germany is a member of NATO and still provides the largest contingent of conventional forces for the Alliance in Europe. In the 1990 Treaty on Conventional Forces in Europe the Federal Republic also agreed to sizeable disarmament measures.

As in the past, the Bundeswehr remains a purely defensive army. It has no weapons of mass destruction and does not want any. However, security precautions are still necessary because only a country prepared to defend itself can exercise sovereign powers and thus be in a position to conduct negotiations and play its part in an alliance.

■ ■ ■ **The Bundeswehr.** The Bundeswehr consists of modern armed services based on conscription for men. The basic period of military service is at present twelve months. There are also career servicemen and others on engagements of up to 15 years. For women there are

The Federal President visiting British troops in Germany

careers available in the medical and music corps. The civilian staff of the armed forces number about 186,000.

The Bundeswehr consists of the army, the navy and the air force. In all services considerable disarmament measures are envisaged. Hundreds of tanks and aircraft are to be scrapped and ships decommissioned. The defence budget is dwindling. In the mid-90s new plans will come into effect for the armed forces. Combat forces and the territorial army will be merged. Only a few mobile units of 10,000 to 15,000 men with a large proportion of career servicemen will have a full complement in peacetime.

On 3 October 1990, the day of German unity, the armed forces of the former GDR, the National People's Army (NVA), were disbanded. Some NVA servicemen, after first being given temporary contracts, have been permanently incorporated in the Bundeswehr. In 1992 the first conscripts from eastern Germany were called up for service.

In 1991 the Soviet Union began withdrawing its approximately 340,000 troops as well as 210,000 dependents and civilian personnel from the territory of the former GDR. This process is being partly financed by the Federal Republic and is due to be completed in 1994. The United States and the other NATO countries with troops stationed in Germany are also reducing their military presence.

■ ■ ■ **The Bundeswehr's mission.** The Bundeswehr
- protects the Federal Republic of Germany and its
people from political blackmail and external danger
- promotes Europe's military stability and integration
- defends Germany and her allies
- serves the cause of world peace and international security in accordance with the UN Charter
- and provides support in the event of disasters and other
emergencies, including humanitarian aid programmes.
The Federal Republic of Germany has been a member of
NATO since 1973. The international community now
rightly expects reunited Germany to play a full part in
UN missions and activities. According to the Charter this
can also include military operations.

Germany is prepared to grow into this international responsibility. She is already participating in UN humanitarian missions in Cambodia and former Yugoslavia, the
world organization's verification team in Iraq, the monitoring of the embargo on rump Yugoslavia, and the enforcement of the no-fly rule by NATO AWACS aircraft
over Bosnia-Herzegovina. A Bundeswehr contingent has
been sent to Somalia to support the UN peace-keeping
operations.

The Bundeswehr's involvement in UN peace-keeping
operations has become an important aspect of German
foreign and security policy.

■ ■ ■ **The Bundeswehr and the community.** In peacetime supreme command of the armed forces lies with

Manpower of German armed forces

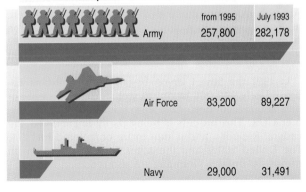

	from 1995	July 1993
Army	257,800	282,178
Air Force	83,200	89,227
Navy	29,000	31,491

the Federal Minister of Defence, in the event of war with the Federal Chancellor. Parliamentary control of the Bundeswehr is exercised by the Bundestag committees, especially the Defence Committee.

An important role is also played by the Parliamentary Commissioner for the Armed Forces, who is elected by parliament for a five-year term. His task is to protect the constitutional rights of servicemen. Every member of the armed services has the right to complain to him directly without going through his superiors. The Commissioner may demand information and access to files from military units and to visit any Bundeswehr facility unannounced. He submits an annual report to the Bundestag on the complaints he has received.

General conscription indicates a country's intention to defend itself and at the same time serves to integrate the armed forces into the community as a whole. Apart from having the civic duty to serve in the armed forces, the individual has a basic right to refuse on grounds of conscience. Under article 4 of the Basic Law, no one may be assigned to armed combat against his conscience. Anyone recognized as a conscientious objector is no longer under obligation to serve in the armed forces. Instead, he must complete 15 months of alternative civilian service.

Cooperation with developing countries

The Federal Republic of Germany is one of the biggest donors of development assistance. At the beginning of 1992 it had economic cooperation partnership agreements with 183 countries.

As early as 1961 a Federal Ministry for Economic Cooperation (in 1993 the words "and Development" were added to the title) was created -the first time any country had appointed a cabinet minister with sole responsibility for development assistance. This showed the determination of the German parliament, government and people to help other nations in need in the light of the country's experience after the war when her own economy had to be rebuilt.

Even after unification and the fundamental changes in central and eastern Europe, Germany has broadened her relations with the developing countries in awareness of her increased global responsibility. All leading members of the government and the opposition want united Germany to honour her commitments to the developing countries and to increase her development assistance further still.

Assistance is also provided for the countries of eastern Europe and the successor states of the Soviet Union, through the Federal Ministry for Economic Cooperation and Development for those who come under the international category of developing countries, through the Federal Ministry of Economics and other departments for the others.

In a period of more than 30 years the German Government, together with non-governmental organizations and private institutions, has gathered valuable experience and created a broad range of instruments for the promotion of overseas development. Through close cooperation with recipient countries it has been possible to adapt assistance measures to the differing economic and social conditions in Africa, Asia and Latin America.

Despite all efforts to reduce the prosperity gap between industrial and developing countries and despite their partial success, the task of removing hunger and poverty has still not been accomplished in many parts of the world. Consequently, combating mass poverty and removing its structural causes is still the foremost objective of German development policy. The world of tomorrow will only be able to live in peace if it proves possible to solve these problems and at the same time ensure respect for human rights.

It is now generally recognized that the people in North and South, in East and West, in poor and rich countries, are interdependent. This is clearly illustrated by the alarming extent of environmental destruction and its interactions between industrial and developing countries. The German Government, apart from pursuing a progressive environmental policy at home, also supports Third World countries in their implementation of environment-friendly development programmes. It does so partly by linking debt relief with environmental protection measures.

Being a leading export nation, the Federal Republic of Germany has an interest in healthy economic progress in the developing countries. It considers itself to have a special responsibility to help liberalize international trade. The more efficient the economy of the developing countries, the more attractive they becomes as partners for trade and investment.

There is also another motive for development cooperation. Improved living conditions in the Third World open up better economic and social prospects for mil-

Modern plant-protection methodes in the Philippines

lions of people who otherwise would leave their native countries in quest of a new life in the industrial countries.

■ ▨ ▨ **Aims of development policy.** It is the recipients themselves who must decide what they want from development cooperation since effective aid can only be a way of helping them help themselves.

But such assistance will only be effective if the countries concerned create conditions which enable the people to participate through the democratic process in the task of building the country's economic and social system and to employ their skills in a meaningful and worthwhile manner.

Experience has shown that such conditions are most likely to be found in countries that have a law-based system with market elements which offer incentives to the people. The governments of developing countries themselves are alone responsible for creating a framework of this kind that is conducive to development.

In the autumn of 1991 the German Government laid down new political criteria for official development aid, viz:

- respect for human rights
- participation of the people in the political process
- the guarantee of security under the law
- a market-oriented economy
- and development-oriented domestic policies (which includes cuts in excessive arms expenditure).

Of course, not all developing countries are able to meet these conditions entirely, but the German Government will even then continue to look for ways and means of helping the people direct, of alleviating their poverty, and of preserving the natural foundations of life. This is achieved through programmes which are implemented directly with the people's self-help organizations.

Development cooperation takes the form of direct bilateral assistance from government to government, multilateral assistance via international organizations, principally the United Nations and its specialized agencies, and through the European Community. It also takes the form of private sector cooperation and the promotional activities of non-governmental organizations, who have long experience with cooperative measures in the Third World.

Advising Peruvian farmers

In 1991 the German Government spent nearly DM 11.5 billion on development cooperation. That is equivalent to 0.41% of the Gross National Product and above the average for all industrial countries.

From 1959 to 1991 Germany's net financial assistance, i.e. after deducting repayments, came to DM 367 billion. DM 302 billion took the form of direct (bilateral) assistance, DM 74 billion having been made available through multilateral agencies. These sums include contributions by Germany's states (1991: DM 137 million) and the NGOs (1991: DM 1.26 million).

■ ■ ■ **Financial and technical cooperation, personnel.** Financial cooperation, or capital aid, is the main instrument in terms of volume. Capital aid mainly consists of concessional loans to finance social infrastructure and environmental protection projects, as well as non-repayable grants.

The money provided is used to finance individual projects (e.g. road construction) or comprehensive programmes, in the field of health, for instance, or to provide credit for small-scale farmers. Capital aid is also granted to developing countries who have little foreign exchange with which to import the machinery, spares and raw materials they need to maintain or improve production, as well as scientific, technical and medical equipment.

Since 1987 the German Government has also been providing what is known as "structural aid" - currency for the speedy import of commodities and services required for structural adjustment programmes. This structural aid is not tied to German supplies and services. The Federal Government attaches considerable importance to mitigating the social repercussions of structural adjustment measures.

■ ▦ ▨ **Financial cooperation.** The terms on which capital aid is granted depend on the economic situation of the recipient. Since 1978 the poorest countries have only been receiving non-repayable grants (financial contributions). The other developing countries receive loans with ten-year grace periods, long maturities, and minimal interest rates.

Assistance within the framework of technical cooperation is generally provided free of charge. Projects or programmes are implemented jointly with existing institutions or by those newly established by the recipient countries. Specialists, advisers and instructors are seconded to developing countries and paid by the German Government; equipment and material for the promoted institutions are either dispatched or financed; and training is provided for local specialists and managerial personnel who assume the responsibilities of the German experts as soon as possible. The training mostly takes place in Germany.

By the end of 1992 182,000 participants had benefited from such programmes, including 15,000 who began their training in 1992. The object of this cooperation is to give people from the Third World suitable opportunities to develop their knowledge and skills on their own responsibility. Thus they are helped to start up in business or employed on development cooperation projects.

In 1992, 3,500 local experts worked alongside 1,407 German experts on technical cooperation projects financed by Germany. Of the 1,850 or so working on financial cooperation projects, approximately 900 were experts from developing countries.

Where personnel training is concerned, distinctions are made. The experts seconded by the German Government are employed as advisers on various technical cooperation projects and programmes. They are under contract to a German organization. Integrated experts, on the other hand, are under contract to an institution in the developing country concerned, from which they receive the usual local salary. Germany tops up salaries and provides social security and temporary assistance.

German development volunteers have a special status within the framework of non-governmental assistance projects. They differ from other specialists in that they "work in closest possible contact" with the population in return for a small allowance.

■■■ **Areas of development cooperation.** Decisions as to which sectors of the economy require priority treatment are made on the basis of proposals and data submitted by the developing country concerned.

Cooperation projects have three main aims: to overcome poverty, to protect the environment and natural resources, and to promote basic education and training. Projects range from industry, crafts and mining, transfer of technology, and the development of administrative infrastructures, to combating drug crime.

In all sectors women are included as key figures in the development process. Even in the planning stage their interests must be taken into consideration. This applies especially to areas where women bear the main burden, as in agriculture, water and fuel supply, and where they

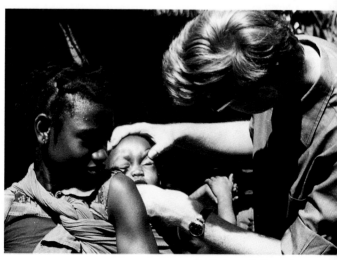

Medical care in Tanzania

are particularly affected by poor conditions, for instance health and housing, food production and training.

The main areas of concentration are food security and rural development. The aim is to help the developing countries maintain food supplies through their own efforts. This is why efforts are being made to increase agricultural production by promoting small farmers, by providing farming equipment, developing efficient marketing systems and promoting agricultural research. These are major contributions towards improving the general supply situation in rapidly growing, densely populated urban areas.

Food aid, which attracts great public attention, is not development assistance. It is only intended as a means of removing supply bottlenecks in the wake of natural disasters, harvest failures or flows of refugees resulting from armed conflict.

The German Government tries to buy an increasing proportion of its food aid supplies, i.e. grain, in regions or localities of developing countries that have a surplus of such commodities. In this way it is able to supply the kind of food which the people affected normally eat. At the same time food production is promoted in surplus countries.

Trainees learning how to use electronic measuring equipment

Training courses for telecommunications engineers

Measures to preserve and restore the natural sources of life constitute an important part of development assistance.

Consequently, every project is examined as to its compatibility with the environment. The German Government also supports national environmental protection programmes, which include land-use planning, afforestation, forest management and measures to prevent soil erosion. Priority is given to measures for the preservation of tropical rainforests and the prevention of desertification.

Other sectoral priorities are energy supply and education, especially educational infrastructure.

Increasing support is being provided for the reform of general and vocational education, and better educational opportunities for rural populations, especially girls and women.

Germany has helped considerably to raise international standards of vocational training. With regard to population control, the German Government promotes family planning programmes in agreement with the governments concerned.

Development aid projects sponsored by the former German Democratic Republic have been continued since unification provided they were still appropriate. As a result, the Federal Ministry for Economic Cooperation and Development has taken over 64 new projects in twelve countries which are supported by grants totalling approximately DM 120 million.

The economy

Economy system and policy

The Federal Republic of Germany is one of the major industrial countries. In terms of overall economic performance she is the third largest, and with regard to world trade she holds second place. She is one of the seven leading western industrial countries (the Group of Seven) who, since 1975, have every year held a summit meeting at which they coordinate their economic and financial policies.

In 1992 the gross national product, that is to say the value of all goods produced and services in the course of a year, came to a record DM 2,775 billion in the western part of the country, a per capita amount of DM 42,000. After price adjustments, GNP has doubled in the past 25 years, and in 40 years increased even fivefold. Expressed in 1985 prices, that is a growth from DM 415.5 billion in 1950 to DM 2,246.3 billion in 1992.

Germany owes her rise from the devastation of the Second World War to her present position among the world's leading industrial nations not to her natural resources or financial reserves but to her skilled manpower. The crucial factors which account for a country's economic efficiency are the training and industry of the labour force, managerial skills, and the broad scope which the social market economy affords to hard-working people.

After the Second World War people often spoke of the German "economic miracle". Ludwig Erhard, the Federal Republic's first Minister of Economics, disliked this term. He said it was no miracle, "merely the result of honest endeavour on the part of a whole nation who were given the opportunity and freedom to make the best of human initiative, freedom and energy".

■ ■ ■ **The social market economy.** Since the war the Federal Republic has developed a socially responsible market economy. This system rejects both the laissez-faire doctrine of the Manchester school and government intervention.

The Basic Law, which guarantees private enterprise and private property, stipulates that these basic rights be exercised for the public good. Under the motto "as little government as possible, as much government as necessary" the state plays a mainly regulatory role in the market economy. It creates the general conditions for market processes, but it is the millions of households and companies who decide freely what they want to produce and consume.

The question as to which and how many goods are produced and who gets how much of what is decided above all in the marketplace. The government forgoes any direct intervention in price and wage fixing.

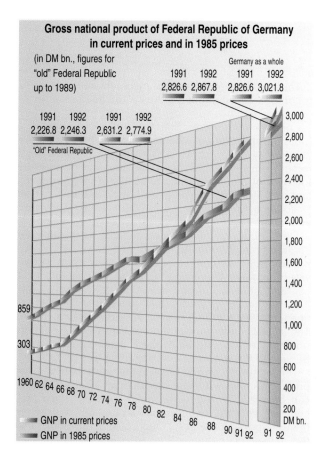

Gross national product of Federal Republic of Germany in current prices and in 1985 prices

(in DM bn., figures for "old" Federal Republic up to 1989)

Germany as a whole

	1991	1992	1991	1992
	2,826.6	2,867.8	2,826.6	3,021.8

1991	1992	1991	1992
2,226.8	2,246.3	2,631.2	2,774.9

"Old" Federal Republic

859

303

1960 62 64 66 68 70 72 74 76 78 80 82 84 86 88 90 91 92   91 92

3,000
2,800
2,600
2,400
2,200
2,000
1,800
1,600
1,400
1,200
1,000
800
600
400
200 DM bn.

GNP in current prices
GNP in 1985 prices

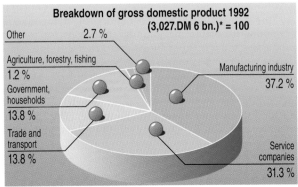

Breakdown of gross domestic product 1992
(3,027.DM 6 bn.)* = 100

Other 2.7 %

Agriculture, forestry, fishing
1.2 %

Government, households
13.8 %

Trade and transport
13.8 %

Manufacturing industry
37.2 %

Service companies
31.3 %

*) In respective prices – provisional figures

The prerequisite for a well-functioning market system is competition. Without it there can be no market economy.

Competition ensures that the individual pursuit of profit translates into a maximum supply of goods for the community as a whole. It encourages initiative and forces companies to improve their market position by lowering prices, improving the quality of their products, and offering better payment and delivery terms as well as additional services. It is also conducive to innovation and rationalization.

Open competition is undoubtedly hard for all concerned. Entrepreneurs time and time again try to neutralize competition, whether through agreements with rivals or mergers. Preventing this is the purpose of a 1957 Law against Restraints on Competition (Cartel Act). It forbids concerted practices and agreements which influence market conditions by restricting competition. The law has undergone numerous improvements and its observance is monitored by the Federal Cartel Office in Berlin and the state anti-trust departments.

The legitimate driving force of the market economy is profit. This is why its rules do not apply where no profit can be made or overriding public interests have precedence. For this reason a number of sectors of the German economy have never been completely subject to the market economy system, for example agriculture, parts of the transportation system and the basic commodities industries.

Many of the former state enterprises in the new federal states, too, have not yet been incorporated in the market system. This is the task of the Treuhandanstalt (Trust Agency). Once this has been achieved the government will revert to its proper role in the eastern part of the country as well.

Mainly for social reasons, agriculture cannot be completely exposed to free market competition. The government aims to gradually privatize such enterprises as the Deutsche Bundesbahn, the Reichsbahn of the former GDR, and the German Federal Post Office in order to increase competition, ease the financial burden on the national budget, and provide more efficient services for the public.

The shortage of housing resulting from the war initially led to the market being state-controlled. In the meantime many of the restrictions have been lifted. The state does, however, ensure that competition does not result in socially intolerable conditions, chiefly by means of laws protecting tenants, the payment of rent supplements to low-income households, the promotion of building projects and the modernization of housing.

In several sectors where, in principle, there is free competition, lawmakers have made entry into the market subject to conditions. Thus craftsmen and retailers, for instance, must prove they have the necessary profes-

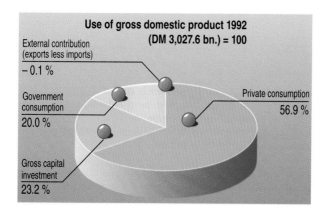

**Use of gross domestic product 1992
(DM 3,027.6 bn.) = 100**

External contribution
(exports less imports)
– 0.1 %

Government
consumption
20.0 %

Gross capital
investment
23.2 %

Private consumption
56.9 %

sional qualifications before they can set up in business. For other occupations the state requires special training and a minimum age, for example in the fields of health, legal practice, accountancy and tax consultancy. It none the less regularly considers whether such government controls are still necessary and are not misused to protect some sectors of the economy from competition.

■ ■ ■ **Industrial relations.** In the labour market, too, the free play of forces applies. There is collective bargaining, that is to say, agreements on pay, working hours, holidays and general working conditions are freely negotiated between labour and management.

Their central organizations, the trade unions and the employers' associations - often called "social partners" in Germany - thus play an important role. Although their main task is to represent their members' interests with both determination and a sense of proportion, they also bear considerable responsibility for the economy as a whole. Their bargaining can greatly affect the functioning of the economic system.

Labour and employers in the Federal Republic have always been aware of this responsibility. The system's stability is due largely to them. This reflects the advantages of the kind of trade unionism that has developed in western Germany since the war.

The unions in Germany are "unitary unions" in a double sense: each represents all the workers in an entire branch of industry (i.e. not only the members of a certain trade), and they are neutral; they have no party or religious ties.

■ ■ ■ **The social component of the economic system.** One major reason why it has been easier to maintain social harmony in Germany than in other countries is that there is a dense social security network. Social protection is considerable, especially for the working community. Whether an employee is old or sick, injured by accident or jobless, affected by the bankruptcy of his employer or undergoing retraining for a more promising occupation - most of the financial hardships are cushioned by the welfare system.

It is based on solidarity. Those in employment pay contributions to the various branches of the social insurance system. It extends far beyond the child benefit, rent supplements, social assistance for the needy and com-

Gross domestic product of major industrial nations 1992

in US$ bn. / in US$ per inhabitant

in US$ bn.	Country	in US$ per inhabitant
5,881	U.S.A	23,319
3,675	Japan	29,661
1,775	Federal Republic of Germany	22,355
1,325	France	23,410
1,224	Italy	21,250
1,041	U.K.	18,104
573	Spain	20,892
562	Canada	14,361

pensation for war victims. Expenditure on social security in 1992 accounted for about a third of GNP, largely owing to the inclusion of the new states, where benefits were twice as high as in the west.

■ ■ ■ **Macroeconomic development.** A market economy, too, can experience undesirable developments. The state must try to counter them through appropriate budgetary, taxation, welfare and competition policies. Since 1967 the Federal Republic has had an economic management instrument in the shape of the Stability Act. Its aims are stable prices, a high level of employment and a balance of foreign trade under conditions of steady, adequate growth. Of late unfortunately, they have not always been achievable. The Bundesbank, which is responsible for money supply, as well as the trade unions and employers' associations, also bear some of the responsibility for the state of the economy. The following bodies are involved in the coordination of economic and fiscal policy:

- The Economic Policy Council, consisting of the federal ministers of economics and finance, one member from each state government and representatives of the local authorities. The Bundesbank may also take part in the consultations, which take place at least twice a year.

- The similarly composed Financial Planning Council, which has the task of coordinating financial planning at all levels of government. The federal and state governments have to draw up pluri-ennial plans so that public revenue and expenditure can be geared to the demands and capacities of the national economy.

- The Panel of Economists, which was set up in 1963. It consists of five independent economic experts (popularly known as the "five wise men") and evaluates overall economic trends every autumn as a basis for government decision-making and pubic judgment.

The Business Promotion Centre, Duisburg

Every January the Federal Government presents to the Bundestag and the Bundesrat an annual economic report, which contains a response to the annual assessment of the panel of experts as well as an outline of economic and financial policy objectives for the current and subsequent years.

■ ■ ■ **The national and the global economy.** Reducing unemployment is a central task of government policy. The key to job creation lies in heavier investment. To secure an adequate return on investment the Federal Government is trying to strengthen the market's own forces, especially through incentives for individual enterprise. State influence on the economy is being reduced, regulations that obstruct market activity are being eliminated. This makes for freer competition and easier adaptation to new developments. Considerable impetus was provided by a major tax reform programme, the final stage of which began in 1990.

Germany is an advocate of free world trade and rejects all forms of protectionism. Because she exports a third of her GNP she depends on open markets. The economy therefore needs a growing European internal market. But outside the European Community as well, Germany must maintain traditional markets and develop new ones. This constant pursuit of open markets and free world trade corresponds with the country's internal market economy.

Germany: an attractive region for investment

Regeneration in the west

■ ■ **In the midst of global disruptions.** The peaceful German revolution and the radical transformations in central, eastern and south-eastern Europe in 1989 have not only dramatically changed the political map of Europe but at the same time plunged the western world, the whole structure of the OECD, into deep recession. The governments of these regions are plagued with falling production and sales as well as growing unemployment.

The Federal Republic of Germany is no exception, recession having arrived there later. Its position is unique in only one respect: It is the only country in the world having to cope with the problems of East and West simultaneously, or as one well-known German author wrote: "We must simultaneously reform the old Federal Republic's market economy and transform the defunct centrally planned economy of the old GDR; we are having to adapt one system and overcome another."

Germany is still a country of high wages, extensive social benefits and corresponding affluence. In order to maintain this level it is essential to adapt to new developments in the field of science and technology and in world markets

An expensive industrial location can hold its own only so long as it is a good location - an exigency reflecting the fierce competition stemming from increasing world economic integration. At the beginning of 1993 the European Community became one huge internal market.

Everywhere the barriers for goods and services are becoming more permeable, communication and transport costs are being reduced, and production technology is increasingly mobile. Hence in other parts of the world a similarly high level of productivity can be achieved with the same technology as in Germany. As a result, wage differentials and load ratios for manufacturers have a greater impact than ever before. And since investment follows the best yield, Germany must make itself more attractive as a place of business.

■ ■ ■ **Traditional factors.** Prior to unification the Federal Republic of Germany had a large current account surplus and a moderate national debt. It had a number of advantages over its international rivals: a high level of productivity, an extensively skilled and motivated workforce, high technical standards, creative scientists, a well-functioning infrastructure, social harmony, a stable currency and a reliable political environment. But of course these assets alone are no longer sufficient. In such matters as labour costs, operating times, company taxes, environmental protection regulations and social security contributions, German firms are at a disadvantage.

Costs additional to wages, for instance, are higher in Germany than anywhere else in the world. In manufacturing industry German companies must pay DM 19.46 on top of the already high hourly wage.

These extra costs are for social insurance, continued wage payments to workers absent through illness, holiday pay and allowances, capital formation contributions and other in-company benefits. For comparison: addi-

Nuclear fusion experiment at the Max Planck Institute, Garching

tional costs in Sweden per hour are only DM 16.66, in France DM 13.18, and in Japan and the United States as little as DM 7.18 and DM 6.93 respectively.

Labour in Germany is dearer than perhaps anywhere else in the world, the Germans work less than their counterparts in other industrial countries. The average annual working time in German industry is about 1499 hours. In the United States it is 1847 hours, in Japan as much as 2139. Industrial plant in Germany is in operation for only 53 hours a week on average, in the United Kingdom 76 hours.

■ ■ ■ **Adaptation and necessary consequences.** On account of these drawbacks - though they do bring considerable social benefit - Germany must ensure that her industries remain competitive, especially those based on the key technologies of the future. Large sections of the traditional branches, such as textiles, have already been switched to cheaper locations. German car makers and chemical firms, too, are increasingly inclined to invest in lower-cost countries.

■ ■ ■ **The Investment Promotion Act.** The answer to this challenge can be neither protectionism nor an industrial policy, for trade restrictions and subsidies do more harm than good. The government supports free international trade and opposes any form of protectionism. Since Germany exports about one third of her gross na-

The multicolor of "Giotto", the European comet probe

Centre of technology near Regensburg

tional product she relies heavily on open markets. It is
vital to the German business community to develop the
internal European market whilst at the same time preserving old markets and developing new ones outside the
Community.

The German Government therefore aims to improve
the general conditions for private enterprise. A first step
has already been taken with the Investment Promotion
Act ("Standortsicherungsgesetz"), which is designed to
attract more business to Germany.

As from 1994, heavy taxes on companies will be reduced. The rate for withheld profits will be cut from 50
to 45%, the maximum income tax rate for trading income from 53 to 47%. The lower rate for companies not
covered by the indirect relief procedure is to be reduced
to 42%, and the corporation tax rate for distributed
profit to 30%. Groups operating internationally benefit
from the fact that earnings abroad are no longer subject
to taxation if they are distributed within the group. Previously, holding companies resident in Germany were at
a disadvantage in this respect. Smaller companies have,
in addition, a write-off saving facility.

The act shows that it has again become necessary for
the market's own batteries to be recharged. Public influence on industry is being cut back, as are anti-market

regulatory mechanisms, and state-owned enterprises are being privatized. This makes for more vigorous competition and eases the task of adapting to new developments. The readjustment of economic and fiscal policy has succeeded once before, during the mild recession of the early 80s. Then, three million new jobs were created within the space of a few years and industry regained its competitive edge.

But these new deregulation measures also concern both sides of industry. More flexible arrangements with regard to working and operating hours, labour costs and social benefits are necessary.

Transformation and reconstruction in the east

■ ■ ■ **Economic recovery in the east and a "solidarity pact", a task for all Germans.** Eastern Germany's economic recovery will remain a major challenge for many years. This task is unique in the country's legal and economic history. An entire national economy has to be remoulded to conform to the principles of the social market economy.

Under socialism, the centrally planned economy made it practically impossible for the people in the former GDR to show enterprise and act on their own responsibility. The small and medium-sized industries, formerly the driving force of the economy, had been almost totally eliminated. Creativity and initiative had to a great extent been paralyzed.

Compared with western levels, productivity was low (in 1970 it was 46% of western Germany's). The regime ruthlessly exploited the environment, causing pollution on a massive scale, and yet the economic gain was but modest. Housing, road networks and communications were not up to present-day requirements. Consequently, the task of modernizing these systems had to be given priority when the country was reunited.

Developing the private sector and promoting investment are cornerstones of an efficient market economy. The building of a well-functioning infrastructure and rapid improvements in public administration are major undertakings in the process of reorganizing the economy of the new German states. This is the only way to establish a solid foundation for competitive industries.

Allembling cars in a new plant at Eisenach

Today, three years after the country's unification, this restructuring process is in full swing. It is at first a painful experience for many people since the transformation comes at a time when the world economy is fraught with problems and the old markets of eastern Europe, which were crucial to the former GDR, are no longer available owing to the revolutionary changes that have taken place there.

In order to cope with this difficult situation, which apart from other problems has caused serious unemployment, extensive measures have been introduced at all levels. Up to March 1993 government and industry in the Federal Republic had invested some DM 225 billion in the new states. In 1992 this investment had peaked at 47% of eastern Germany's gross domestic product. This has rightly been described as an investment boom. Private investment alone in 1992 amounted to DM 60 billion. Over half a million new enterprises have been established.

■ ■ ■ **Strategies for improving eastern Germany's industrial base.** West German companies intend to double by 1995 the 25 billion marks a year they spend on purchases in the new federal states, as part of the country's "solidarity pact".

Annual public funds of at least 100 billion marks have been flowing to eastern Germany since 1990, either from the Federal Government or via joint federal and state facilities such as the "German Unity Fund".

The two-year joint programme "Recovery East" (1991-92) was another Federal Government measure to promote investment. The DM 24 billion set aside for this purpose was primarily used to provide companies with start-up capital or interim financial assistance. By means of a special programme entitled "Regional Industrial Promotion" investments totalling approximately DM 14.5 billion were made in 1991 and 1992, thus preserving or creating 112,000 jobs.

Housing modernization schemes have been financed under the Recovery East programme and from loans provided by the Kreditanstalt für Wiederaufbau (Development Loan Corporation). By 1993 more than one quarter of eastern Germany's total housing stock had been renovated. In 1993 the government has provided another DM 1.18 billion to finance a joint programme for improving agricultural structure and coastal preservation.

In order to attract more industry to eastern Germany the government has so far approved more than 1,250 research projects as qualifying for financial support. More than DM 100 million has been made available to mainly small and medium-sized companies to help them acquire the necessary know-how and become more competitive.

Economic recovery depended on efficient regional and local government and a well-functioning legal system. These foundations, too, had to be established. The

A truck plant in Ludwigsfelde/Brandenburg

Road construction in the new states is making steady progress

Federal Government provided the funds to send 2,300 judges, public prosecutors and court officers to create a judicial system in the mould of that existing in the western part of the country, so that now the legal system is the same in all parts of the country. In addition, experienced administrators from the west are helping to adapt public administration in the east, a process which has now more or less been completed.

■ ■ ■ **The Trust Agency (Treuhandanstalt).** A key role in the restructuring process is played by the Treuhandanstalt, a public privatization agency. Its task is to privatize, reorganize or if necessary wind up former state assets in the GDR, to make companies competitive, and to make land and other property available for industrial or commercial purposes. When established in 1990 it assumed responsibility for some 8,500 combines with 45,000 factories and production plant, in fact practically all of the former GDR's industrial assets. Under the communist regime 90% of all companies belonged to the state.

Up to mid-1993 the agency was able to privatize more than 12,000 companies or parts of companies from among the 12,800 or so on its hands (large combines have been split up into several companies).

The agency's responsibilities also include returning assets (e.g. kindergartens, sports grounds etc.) to local authorities and businesses to their former owners. The primary aim of both the agency and the Federal Government is to make it possible to preserve and revitalize core industries even under the extremely difficult conditions of structural transformation.

Up to the end of May 1993 the new owners of the privatized firms had promised the agency that they would preserve or create together 1.4 million permanent jobs, especially in the industrial sector. They have also guaranteed to invest over 175 billion marks which promises to boost growth and restructuring in the years ahead.

The Trust Agency intends to wind up its operative work at the end of 1993, much earlier than expected. That will mark the end of the biggest privatization programme in history.

Again up to the end of May 1993, the agency had sold more than 2,300 complete or partial companies to east Germans, principally in the form of management buyouts. Saxony leads the way with more than 630 such transactions. This has been a major step in creating a self-sufficient small business community in eastern Germany.

The Treuhand has launched a fresh initiative to continue this development. In a much simplified procedure

A purification plant under construction in Bitterfeld

small firms are to be sold off on very favourable terms, preferably to people in eastern Germany. The same is true of medium-sized firms in eastern Germany who want to buy land to expand or start up a new business.

Up to May 1993 the Agency had spent some DM 38 billion for the redevelopment of companies under its responsibility. One must add to this the 65 billion marks provided so far to adjust old debts of the former GDR and to meet equalization claims in respect of opening deutschmark balance sheets, as well as sureties for company loans totalling DM 20 billion.

The Agency's total payments in the period 1990 to 1993 are expected to be in the region of DM 155 billion.

Redevelopment funds will in future be focused more heavily on product and market-related investment in order to introduce modern production methods and make companies competitive. The Treuhandanstalt, in its present form, intends to wind up its activities by 31 December 1994. Its functions will then be transferred to other agencies and the accumulated debts converted into a fund which the Federal Government will amortize over a period of about 30 years.

■ ■ ■ **Good prospects for the future.** In spite of persistent problems such as rising prices, high unit wage costs and interest rates, the new German states, with a new, efficient infrastructure, will have good development prospects because of their proximity to the burgeoning markets in eastern Europe. This will become one of Europe's most up to date industrial regions. But if eastern Germany is to be lastingly attractive to national and international investors, all political and business leaders, as well as the people in the new federal states, will have to make a great effort requiring continuous support from western Germany.

The Federal Statistical Office forecast that eastern Germany's gross domestic product would increase by 6% in 1992. After a slow start and in spite of the many obstacles to be cleared on the way to recovery, this growth signifies that a process of vigorous adjustment is now under way. The start-up support from the west is having an effect.

The signs of change and progress are unmistakable. Considerable infrastructural improvements have been made and the development of telecommunication sys-

Restoration work on Merseburg Cathedral

tems and the enlargement of road and rail networks are making considerable headway. The heavy demand in the building sector continued in 1992 as well. Industrial plant is being adapted to western standards, agriculture is being modernized, and more and more successful strategies for marketing local products are emerging, with support from a variety of west German companies.

Since the beginning of the Economic and Monetary Union on 1 July 1990, incomes (and hence purchasing power) of private households have increased significantly. A wide choice of training opportunities opens up new prospects to young people. Government programmes, such as trade training and retraining courses, are helping to prepare people for new jobs.

Much importance attaches to the "Recovery East" restructuring process, but not only for the sake of the new German states. The enormous changes in Europe are particularly obvious in this part of the continent along the interface of the old bloc systems. The challenges resulting from these developments confront the changing, opening Europe as a whole and thus can only be mastered if all Europeans pull together.

The labour market

The German labour market has time and again had to cope with critical situations. In the early post-war years the Federal Republic was preoccupied with finding jobs for millions of expellees from Germany's former eastern territories and for resettlers from East Germany. But they in particular made a large contribution to the country's economic upswing.

From the mid-50s to the early 70s hardly anyone was out of work, but as a result of the subsequent crises unemployment became a major and increasing problem. Not until the eighties did the situation substantially improve, but there remained a basic stock of jobless people.

When the country regained its unity in 1990 there suddenly arose the problem of a divided labour market. While the ranks of the jobless decreased in the western states on account of the favourable economic situation, their numbers swelled at first in the new states. This was primarily due to the transition from socialist central planning to a social market economy.

■ ■ ■ **Employment.** The labour force in the old federal states increased from 20.4 million in 1950 to over 29 million at the end of 1992. In the new federal states the number of employed in 1992 was about 6.7 million. Up to 1989 the employment rate increased in both parts of Germany in spite of the fact that periods of training had lengthened and the life-work span shortened. This means that ever more people (especially women) have found employment.

From about 1960 onwards the increase in the workforce was due mainly to ever larger numbers of foreign workers streaming into the Federal Republic. In 1965 the number of foreign workers had risen above a million, and in 1973 it was more than 2.6 million, the highest level.

Since then, recruitment of foreign workers, with the exception of those from European Community member countries, has been halted. In September 1992 the number of registered foreign workers was about 2.1 million. The biggest contingent are the Turks, followed by workers from former Yugoslavia, Italy, Greece, Austria and Spain.

Vocational counselling in a labour exchange

Full employment in the old federal states reached its peak in 1970 when only 150,000 were out of work. At the same time there were almost 800,000 job vacancies. During the subsequent recession the labour force diminished and the number of unemployed increased. It rose above one million in 1975 and two million at the beginning of the 80s.

Government policy in the western part of the country since 1982 has improved the conditions for economic growth and considerably reduced the obstacles to employment. As a result some 1.5 million new jobs were created between 1984 and 1990, and a further 1.5 million between 1989 and 1991.

In the former GDR there was always full employment - at least that was the official version as presented by the communist regime. In actual fact, however, there was much concealed unemployment, estimated at between one and a half and three million. The problem's full dimensions only became apparent when Germany was united and the ruined East German economy collapsed. Various government initiatives at first prevented any sharp increases in unemployment there, but old, unproductive jobs have been written off faster than new ones have been created.

For a transitional period, therefore, the Federal Institute for Employment is has employed considerable government funds to finance job creation, retraining and further training programmes in order to reduce unemployment (currently over two million), to give workers better prospects and to accelerate the modernization process. With economic activity picking up the employment situation, too, will improve considerably.

Some groups are especially hard hit by unemployment, i. e. those with inadequate vocational qualifications, women and older people, as well as those who have been out of work for long periods of time. Government and industry are making great efforts to help them. Because of the increasing use of modern technology greater importance attaches to vocational skills. But it is also important that those affected by unemployment should receive adequate social security.

■ ■ ■ **Unemployment insurance.** Germany's statutory unemployment insurance scheme was introduced in 1927. It is now governed by the Labour Promotion Act of 1969. The authority administering the scheme is the Federal Institute for Employment in Nuremberg.

Insurance is obligatory for all employees (except professional civil servants). Contributions are paid half by the employee and half by the employer. Any unemployed person whose previous employment was subject to insurance contributions and who is ready to accept "reasonable" employment offered by the labour exchange is entitled to draw unemployment benefit, which may be as much as 68% of the last net pay. As a rule it is paid for a maximum period of one year, in the case of older unemployed people at most for 32 months. Anyone then still unemployed can apply for unemployment support of up to 58% of the net wage or salary, other sources of income, including those of family members, being taken into account.

The employment agency also pays benefits to those on short time or unable to work during the cold winter months (e.g. construction workers).

■ ■ ■ **Labour promotion.** The Institute for Employment is also responsible for job placement and vocational guidance as well as the promotion of vocational training, which is particularly important. The Institute gives juveniles and adults subsidies and loans for vocational training if they cannot raise the funds themselves.

It also promotes vocational advancement by granting loans and covering all or part of the cost of training.

Labour market and vocational research is another of the agency's functions. The research findings are submitted to the Federal Minister for Labour and Social Affairs as an aid to decision-making.

Bundesanstalt für Arbeit
(Federal Institute for Employment)
P.O. Box 90327, Nuremberg

Incomes and prices

■ ■ **Incomes.** In recent decades incomes have increased constantly in Germany. In the western part of the country disposable income of private households rose from DM 188 billion in 1962 just under DM 1,710 billion in 1992. The family budget has grown in real terms, too, that is to say, allowing for inflation. Income derives from many different sources, but the main one by far is employment, i.e. wages and salaries including social security contributions.

In addition there are dividends from shares, income from property and other assets as well as public support in the form of child and unemployment benefit, pensions and other remittances.

Disposable income is what is left over after deduction of taxes and social insurance contributions, and also regular remittances (e.g. by foreign workers to their natives countries). Just under half of the disposable income is accounted for by net wages and salaries, almost a third by profit-drawing and net income from assets, and about a fifth by social security contributions.

■ ■ **Standard of living.** The five decades since the Second World War have seen the growth of unprecedented prosperity in Germany. The social market economy has raised the country from destruction to one of the most powerful economies in the world with widespread affluence. Nearly half of the employed members of the community own their own houses or apartments. And eastern Germany, too, in only a few years since the country's unification, is already approaching the level of prosperity of the west.

In 1964 the average disposable monthly income of a four-person household was DM 904. Of this, DM 823 was spent on private consumption - nearly two thirds of this on food, clothing and housing. In 1992 the same type of household in western Germany disposed of more than DM 4,500 a month, of which only about half went on the three items mentioned. But spending on other items has increased substantially, e.g. leisure, transport, education and telephones. The Germans in the western states spent DM 1,500 billion on private consumption in 1992.

Assets and disposable income are distributed unevenly, however. At the top of the incomes pyramid are the self-employed, followed by farmers, public employees, civil servants and wage-earners. Whereas the social structure in the new federal states is still being shaped, a process has taken place within the old states which has led to the approximation of most social groups. Beneath a top layer of about two per cent of the population there has emerged a very broad middle class. However, the relatively high standard of living can only be maintained because both man and wife have a job. The great majority of the working population live entirely or predominantly from the fruits of their labour, while only a small minority can live on their assets.

■ ■ ■ **Assets.** Assets, however, have increased at an even faster rate than disposable incomes. They have doubled in fact. At the end of 1992 private assets in the old federal states stood at approximately DM 3,200 billion. They include cash, savings, bonds, life insurance and other forms of property.

The per-capita average in western Germany is about DM 50,000. This does not include landed property. In the relatively short period to the millennium land and premises worth about DM 350 billion will pass to the

Working time required to pay for certain household goods *
To purchase the specified goods an industrial worker had to work the stated number of hours and minutes:

	1950 hrs. min.	1960 hrs. min.	1980 hrs. min.	1990 hrs. min.	1992 hrs. min.
1 l milk	14	8	5	3	3
1kg rye bread	17	15	10	9	9
1kg pork	2 50	2 08	45	33	31
1kg butter	3 39	2 08	38	23	20
Men's shoes	21 15	13 01	7 33	6 44	6 14
Soup plate, china	41	21	18	21	23

* "Old" Federal Republic

next generation of heirs.
Thus the post- war gener-
ation who rebuilt the
country will bequeath
more than any other
generation in Germany.

Since the 50s the gov-
ernment has promoted pri-
vate capital formation by
means of various bonuses,
tax and other allowances.
Tax incentives are given to
people saving with build-
ing societies or through insurance policies, or contri-
buting to house-building
schemes. There is a yearly
limit, of course, and the
housebuilding bonus is
also tied to incomes.

In addition to the
general incentives for all

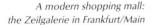

Sales day!

*A modern shopping mall:
the Zeilgalerie in Frankfurt/Main*

Cost of living index in various countries
(1985 = 100)

Country	1990	1991	1992
Federal Republic of Germany (old)	107.0	110.7	115.1
Belgium	111.0	114.6	117.4
Denmark	121.2	124.1	126.7
France	116.5	120.2	123.0
Great Britain	133.3	141.1	146.4
Ireland	117.6	121.4	125.1
Italy	131.8	140.2	147.6
Netherlands	104.3	108.4	112.5
Austria	111.4	115.0	119.7
Switzerland	113.2	119.7	124.7
Spain	136.8	144.9	153.3
Canada	124.5	131.5	133.4
USA	121.5	126.6	130.4
Japan	107.0	112.3	112.4
Australia	146.4	151.1	152.6

special bonuses have been available to employees since the 60s. Since 1991 they have also been applicable in the new federal states. Under the Capital Formation Act the bonus is paid on limited amounts and has to be transferred direct by the employer to the employee's building society account, a capital formation account with a bank (including investment certificates and shares), or the employer's capital formation scheme.

Savings of up to DM 936 a year qualify for this bonus. It can only be claimed by people whose earnings do not exceed a particular limit. In the western part of Germany capital formation savings arrangements are made for most employees, primarily within the scope of collective wage agreements, in addition to their normal wage. Employees can also obtain bonuses for parts of their wages which they save.

In 1992 about 13 million employees in western Germany received bonuses totalling well over a billion marks for capital formation savings. They also receive tax concessions on limited amounts which they invest with their employer.

■ ■ ■ **Prices.** The standard of living depends not only on income but also on prices. Consumer prices are therefore a major domestic issue. Opinion polls have consistently shown that for many people the chief consideration is stable prices. This is mainly because Germans know from personal experience what devaluation of money means. They have suffered two enormous inflations this century, each resulting in

A cash machine

collapse of the currency and huge losses of assets.

Although the Federal Republic has not been able to evade worldwide inflation entirely it has managed to keep prices under control better than many other countries.

The cost of living rose at times by more than 6% annually, especially in the 1970s, then fell considerably, so that in December 1986 it was lower than in December of the previous year for the first time in almost 30 years. In the whole of 1986 the cost of living was 0.1% lower than in the previous year. In later years, too, the Federal Republic managed quite well by comparison, its inflation rates not rising above 3%. The strongly fluctuating prices of the 70s and 80s reflected the sharp movements in the price of oil. Since mid-1990, however, heavy demand in connection with the country's unification as well as steep increases in wages and taxes to finance the recovery of the East German economy have accelerated prices with the result that the inflation rate in 1992 was about four per cent. The government, and especially the Bundesbank, give high priority to monetary stability. Price growth is expected to slow down in 1994.

Consumer Protection

The range of goods and services is growing. Every year more than 1,000 new products come onto the market in Germany alone. Since the launching of the single market on 1 January 1993, the range has become even greater and even more confusing.

Products made in Germany compete with goods imported from all over the world. But such a wide variety is a problem for consumers, too, since it is hardly possible to judge quality and value for money. In addition, there are dangers to health and dishonest sales methods.

As a result, consumer protection now plays an important role in the life of the community. Its purpose is to make the market more transparent and help people make rational decisions on the basis of objective information. But they also need advice on their rights with regard to contracts, insurance, loans, investment, travel, etc.

Thus in 1964 the Federal Government set up a foundation in Berlin known as "Stiftung Warentest" which tests goods of all kinds from the ballpoint pen to the personal computer as to quality, value for money and compatibility with the environment. Services, too, are tested. This organization now screens about 1,700 articles in 100 comparative testings a year. To date it has screened more than 30,000 products and services. Warentest only calls upon independent experts and institutes and has earned a good reputation from consumers and manufacturers alike, the latter being glad to advertize the fact that their products have been approved by "Stiftung Warentest".

The foundation's main publications are "Test", which appears monthly and has a circulation of about a million, and "FINANZ-Test". Furthermore, the test results are regularly publicized in some 160 newspapers and periodicals, and on radio and television.

The public can also seek advice from a number of other organizations, including more than 250 regional centres which provide information on the quality and prices of goods and services and receive financial support from the government.

Razors being put to the test

Before parliament introduces new consumer protection legislation it consults the associations. The Consumers' Association (AgV) has 38 member organizations ranging from the German Tenants Federation via the German Housewives Union to the Otto Blume Institute of Social Research.

Consumer protection has been considerably improved by legislation. The General Conditions of Sale Act protects customers from the pitfalls contained in small print; the Consumer Credit Act enables the borrower to cancel the loan and requires information to be provided by the Länder; the Foodstuffs Act protects customers from damaging substances in food; the Travel Contract Act forces operators to fulfil their promises; the Product Liability Act makes manufacturers liable for flawed products. There are also many other laws to protect consumers. They concern such matters as the labelling of foodstuffs and detergents, pharmaceutical products and price tags on goods in shop windows.

This legislation is being increasingly switched to the European Community, however. The Community issues directives that must be converted into national law in member states. The European Commission has a "Consumer Advice Council" composed of 39 members. The most important consumer organization at European level is the "Bureau Européen des Unions des Consommateurs (BEUC)" which represents 24 national consumer organizations.

Arbeitsgemeinschaft der Verbraucherverbände
(Union of Consumer Associations),
Heilsbachstr. 20, 53123 Bonn
Stiftung Warentest,
Lützowplatz 11-13, 10785 Berlin

Housing and urban development

■ ■   **Housing.** Living accommodation in Germany can be anything from a single room, a self-contained flat, a single family house or a mansion. There are about 34.2 million dwellings, over 27 million of them in the old (western) states. Roughly 40% of these are occupied by the owners themselves, the rest being rented.

Flats in apartment buildings are traditionally rented, hence most of those inhabited by their owners are in houses for one or two families. Owner-occupied housing has increased steadily since the late 70s.

Twenty per cent of dwellings in the western states have been subsidized by the government. This "social" accommodation is intended for large families, the disabled, old people and those with low incomes.

Germany had a real housing crisis after the Second World War, when many towns and cities lay in ruins. In the early 50s there were only 10 million dwellings available for just under 17 million households. Gradually, however, the crisis was overcome by means of a housing programme under which as many as 700,000 dwellings a year were built.

Today the main problems are in the metropolitan areas. Young couples, large families and foreigners have difficulty finding flats which meet their needs or which they can afford. There are many reasons for the housing shortage. Accommodation is being sought by people in the high-birthrate age groups and by others entering the country. And many Germans from the eastern states have moved to the west.

Between 1988 and 1993 the population increased by about four million. In 1988, after years of declining building activity, the situation changed and since 1989 house production has increased steadily. In 1993 probably more than 400,000 new dwellings will be built. Since 1990 about 1.1 million units have been modernized in the new states with funds from the Kreditanstalt für Wiederaufbau, a government loan agency. Indeed, repair and modernization is the main objective of government policy in the east, where much of the housing stock

is in a deplorable condition due to the failings of the former communist regime.

Public funding has been increased and in 1991 the Federal Government introduced another social

*Sun-collectors
provide energy*

housing scheme which provided a further boost.

■ ■ ■ **Housing quality.** There are still large differences in quality between accommodation in the old and the new federal states, and in the amount of living space available. In western Germany the average living space available for each in-

*Renovated old town-houses
in Wuppertal*

dividual is 35 sq m, which is more than twice as much as in 1950. In the east it is about 28 sq m. More than 95% of all flats have a bath and 75% central heating. The housing stock in the west is on the whole much younger than accommodation in the new federal states, where still about 55% of the houses were built before 1948. Many of them are in a poor state. They lack modern sanitary facilities and the heating systems are outmoded.

The communist regime in the former GDR kept rents extremely low. As a result, the local authorities, cooperatives and private owners had hardly any funds for maintenance and modernization. In the western states, on the other hand, quality has its price. Rents, that is, not counting incidental expenses and heating, account for about 20% of an average household's net income. In some cities the rents are even higher, in the countryside lower.

There remains a tremendous housing problem to be solved. In eastern Germany not only must new dwellings be built but millions of old ones renovated. The redevelopment programme is going very well. In 1991 and 1992 funds were earmarked for the renovation of some 30% of eastern Germany's housing stock. And in 1993 the Federal Government has provided another DM 31 billion.

Many houses owned by local authorities are being privatized. Private investors receive tax relief and grants for this purpose. The housing sector in the east is on the verge of a new "investment offensive" now that some of the major obstacles such as the old debts of building societies and the uneconomical system of rock-bottom rents have been removed.

But greater efforts were required in the western part of the country as well. The promotion of housing and the conditions for a well-functioning housing market have been continually developed. Federal funding for housing projects for low-income groups has been constantly increased, from DM 1.76 billion in 1991 to DM 2.7 billion in 1992 and in 1993.

■ ▨ ▨ **Housing allowance and tenants' rights.** Dwelling space is a basic human need, which is why in Germany everyone whose income is insufficient to meet the cost of adequate accommodation has a statutory right to housing allowance. It is paid as a grant towards the rent or as a subsidy towards the cost of home ownership, though subject to income limits.

At the end of 1991 more than three million households received housing allowances. The cost to the federal and state governments, who share the burden, in 1992 was about DM 6.8 billion. Since 1991 allowances have also been paid in the new federal states under legislation which allows for the special situation there and is more generous than in the west.

On the whole, housing allowance has proved to be an effective social measure. Tenancy law, which is based on freedom of contract, is aimed at establishing a fair balance of interests between landlords and tenants. No tenant need fear unjust and arbitrary eviction or excessive rent increases.

Thus a landlord can only give notice to a tenant who has met the requirements of his contract only if he can prove "justified interest" (that is to say, if he can show that he needs the accommodation for his own purposes). He may put up the rent provided he does not go beyond what is charged for comparable accommodation in the same area. Tenants in the new states receive special protection against rent increases for a transitional period.

■ ■ ■ **Home ownership.**
90% of all German families dream of owning a house or flat. This coincides with the Federal Government's aim of spreading assets as far as possible. People deciding to build or buy their own home can thus count on various state benefits such as grants, loans and tax concessions.

■ ■ ■ **Urban development.** The Federal Republic is one of the most densely populated countries in the world. Most people today live in cities,

Experimental architectue on the Fraenkelufer, Berlin

towns or sizeable communities which were quickly re-built after the war. Little consideration was given to tradi-tional structures. Rapid motorization led to a boom in road construction, even in residential areas. For a time the "town catering for the car" was the ideal. The price of land in urban areas shot up and it became more and more difficult to ensure sensible building for the good of society as a whole. Many people moved to the country-side and commuted to work. The towns became deserted in the evening.

This trend has meanwhile been reversed, however. Since 1970 there has been a growing tendency to mod-ernize old buildings and whole districts. Efforts are now made to preserve urban structures as they have evolved and to make the centres more attractive. Zoning plans give priority to housing projects. In many towns the bu-siest shopping areas have been turned into pedestrian precincts. Local transport services are being extended. There are car park information and guidance systems and better surveillance of stationary vehicles. In many built-up areas the speed limit has been lowered to 30 km/h (19 mph). The "Bremen Model" for urban planning would keep traffic out of housing estates. Local building regulations have been simplified and the community are brought into the planning process sooner, the aim being the "humane town".

Environmental protection

Protecting the environment and our natural resources is one of the biggest challenges facing government, industry and society. It is a source of much public concern and many people have, through their active commitment, highlighted the need for protective measures and helped considerably to improve the situation.

The business community, too, appreciate that ecology and economy do not have to be contradictory and that environmental protection is also necessary on economic grounds. The consistent safeguarding of the atmosphere, water and soil over time is essential for sound economic advancement. More than half a million people are directly or indirectly involved in preventing or reducing pollution. A modern environmental protection industry has thus evolved. German high-tech engineering products are much in demand and now account for more than 20% of world trade in this field.

■ ▒ ░ **Environment policy.** Responsibility for environmental matters at federal level lies with the Federal Ministry for Environmental Protection. One of its subsidiary agencies is the Federal Environmental Agency in Berlin. Each of the federal states, too, has an environmental department.

Government policy is based on three principles: - prevention, i.e. new projects are developed in such a way as to avoid pollution or damage, the polluter pays, i. e. it is not the public at large but those causing the damage or pollution who hear the responsibility and the cast of removal; and cooperation, i.e. government, industry and society join forces to combat environmental problems, since every individual has a duty towards the environment.

The government's task is to provide the framework for action by companies and individuals to preserve the natural environment. In recent years a broad range of legal instruments has been introduced and these are being constantly developed. The German Governments's aim is to ensure as soon as possible standards of environmental protection throughout the country. This requires investment running into billions, mainly for the rehabilitation of old industrial sites, waste disposal and new purification facilities. But national measures are not sufficient in themselves since polluted air knows no frontiers and contaminated rivers flow through many countries.

A major task is that of coping with such global problems as climate change, the ozone gap and the loss of biodiversity. This requires worldwide cooperation, which is why the German government pursues an active international policy, especially within the EC. The outstanding event of 1992 was the UN Conference on Environment and Development held in Rio de Janeiro. The government is making every effort to give early effect to that conference's resolutions and to ensure continuing international cooperation.

Its strategy is geared to self-sustaining, environment-friendly development and requires other policy areas to make greater allowance for the exigencies of environmental protection.

■ ■ ■ **Keeping the air clean.** The atmosphere in Germany, as in other industrial countries, is heavily polluted by emissions from power stations, factories, traffic and home-heating systems. This is particularly evident in the damage caused to forests. About 68% of tree stocks are slightly or severely damaged. Only 32% are healthy. Thus human health, the soil, lakes and rivers, buildings and architectural treasures must be protected from further air pollution.

A comprehensive clean-air programme has been introduced. The aim is to get to grips with pollution at source and reduce it drastically. Pollutants from power stations and district heating plants, for instance, as well as car exhaust fumes, are held back by filters and catalytic converters. Legislation on large furnaces compelled power station operators to quickly introduce modern technology.

Emissions of sulphur dioxide and nitrogen oxide from industry have already been reduced by 20/30% and a further reduction of 40% is hoped for by the mid-90s. Between 1983 and 1993 emissions of sulphur dioxide from power stations in western Germany were reduced by about 84%, those of nitrogen oxide by 74%.

As far as traffic is concerned, air pollution is being increasingly reduced through the introduction of catalytic

A stratospherie balloon for the collection of air samples

converters to remove nitrogen oxides from exhaust fumes. Now all new motor vehicles in the European Community must be equipped with them. Further reductions are achieved by the use of unleaded petrol, which is on sale at all German filling stations.

Ensuring clean air, too, is an international challenge. Half of the sulphur dioxide pollution comes from neighbouring countries, while half of the pollution emitted in Germany is carried by the wind to other countries. Thus the 1983 Geneva Convention on Long-Range Transboundary Air Pollution is of great importance in this respect.

Two of the biggest threats to the world's climate are carbon dioxide, which is one of the causes of the "greenhouse effect", and chlorofluorocarbons (CFCs) which are destroying the earth's ozone layer. Here Germany is playing a pioneering role by requiring the country's CFC production to be stopped altogether by 1995.

Carbon dioxide emissions are to be reduced by 25-30% by the year 2005 (based on 1987 figures). The government has adopted an ambitious comprehensive plan to achieve this goal. Between 1987 and 1992 CO_2 emissions had already been reduced by 14,5%.

■ ■ ■ **Noise abatement.** Noise, especially from traffic, has become a serious threat to health in densely populated areas. Noise abatement measures are therefore urgent. Many residential streets have been declared reduced-traffic zones and the noise levels for cars and aircraft. Sound barriers are erected along roads and railways or on adjacent buildings. Efforts are also being made in industry and in the building trade to reduce noise levels.

■ ■ ■ **Protection of rivers, lakes and seas.** Major improvements have also been achieved in protecting rivers, lakes and seas, but only through the introduction of tougher legislation and the construction of new, espe-

Emmission sensors monitor combustion in the cylinder

cially biological, sewage farms by industrial firms and municipalities. These regulations were designed to prevent organic pollution of surface water in particular.

In the early 70s heavily polluted rivers like the Rhine and the Main were, biologically, practically dead, but today they again have several species of fish. The rivers and lakes of the former GDR, however, still need a major cleansing operation. This is largely being done on the basis of the Effluent Act. Steps have also been taken, internationally, within the EC and at national level, to protect groundwater from toxic, non-biodegradable plant-protection agents. Increasingly heavy restrictions are placed on the use of such substances. In 1986 stricter limits were also introduced with regard to drinking water.

Many pollutants ultimately end up in the sea via the rivers and the atmosphere unless they are neutralized on land. But shipping and oil extraction, too, contribute to marine pollution. These problems can only be solved through joint action by all littoral states.

Steps to reduce pollution of the North Sea were introduced on Germany's initiative at the International North Sea Conferences of 1984, 1987 and 1990. As a result all countries have meanwhile stopped discharging pollutants and burning waste at sea. The dumping of dilute sulphuric acid, too, in the North Sea will be stopped by 1998.

The littoral states of the Baltic Sea formed in 1974 the Helsinki Commission for the protection of the Baltic Sea. In 1992 it adopted an international action programme aimed at removing the main sources of pollution within the next twenty years.

■ ■ ■ **Nature conservation and landscape management.** The proportion of land in the western part of Germany covered by buildings and roads increased from about 8% in the 50s to about 12% in the late 80s. Thus the proportion of natural landscapes was reduced accordingly, making the task of protecting flora and fauna increasingly more urgent.

The Federal Nature Conservation Act, which forms the basis for state laws on conservation and landscape planning, has been constantly improved, as have the regulations on protection of species.

Ten large regions in Germany requiring special protection have been declared national parks. There are also

Removing oil discharged into the sea

many nature reserves as well as 12 biosphere reserves recognized by UNESCO.

Germany is playing an active part in the elaboration and implementation of international agreements, for example:

- the Bonn Convention on the Conservation of migratory Species of Wild Animals;
- the Bern Convention on the Conservation of European Wildlife and Natural Habitats, which will assume increasing importance through cooperation between east and west European countries within the framework of the Concil of Europe;
- the Washington Convention on International Trade in Endangered Species of Wild Fauna and Flora and the Convention on Biological Diversity signed at the 1992 Conference on Environment and Development held in Rio de Janeiro.

Initiatives for nature protection measures at national level also come from cooperation among EC countries. The Community's directive for the protection of birds and its flora-fauna-habitat directive have been incorporated in German law. And both federal and state governments are deeply involved in the realization of the EC's biotope network NATURA 2000.

■ ■ ■ **Water management and soil protection.** The 1986 Waste Act introduced modern waste-disposal methods. This law gives the avoidance and recycling of waste priority over traditional methods of disposal. Waste that cannot be recycled must go to depots or incinerators. Strict regulations apply to the disposal of "special waste", i.e. toxic or otherwise dangerous waste, for which there are special facilities.

The government has meanwhile developed its waste management plans with the aim of creating a recycling system based on comprehensive product liability and the principles of the ecological and social market economy. Under this system producers and consumers will assume a far greater responsibility for a product's whole life cycle.

Recycling is very important to a country like Germany which has few raw materials. Some household waste destroyed by burning is used for distant-heating purposes.

In 1991 the government introduced regulations for the avoidance of packaging waste. This led to the creation of the private sector dual system (DSD) or "Green Dot" in 1992. Under this arrangement waste packaging material stamped with the green dot by the manufacturer is collected and recycled. The cost is included in the price of the product.

Germany produces about 13 million tonnes of packaging waste every year: 3.8 million tonnes of glass, 5.1 million tonnes of paper and cardboard, 1.4 million tonnes of synthetic materials, 703,000 tonnes of tin, 122,000 tonnes of aluminium and 407,000 tonnes of composite materials. This policy aimed at avoiding waste in the first place and then recycling the rest is already proving successful. In 1992, for instance, 15% less waste had to be taken to public depots, and this proportion is expected to quadruple by 1995.

The ground in many parts of the country has been contaminated with heavy metals. Intensive farming, too, has caused a serious deterioration of soil structure. The government is therefore drawing up comprehensive measures to conserve the soil as a storer and filter of water, but also as a biotope for plants and animals.

Umweltbundesamt (Federal Environmental Agency)
Bismarckplatz 1, 13585 Berlin

Sectors of the economy

· Industry · Technology · Crafts and trades
· Agriculture, forestry, fisheries · Commerce · Foreign trade
· Raw materials and energy · Money and banking
· Fairs and exhibitions · Transport
· Posts and telecommunications · Germany for the tourist

Industry

The mainstay of the German economy is industry. The approximately 52,000 industrial enterprises in united Germany employ more than 7.5 million people, more than any other sector of the economy. However, industry's importance has declined considerably as a result of structural change, its share of GNP having fallen from 51.7% in 1970 to 37.7% in 1992.

In the same period the public and private service sector increased their share considerably. Private services are now accounting for 32.4% of GNP, commerce and transport 14.4%. Rapidly expanding branches like data processing or the aerospace industry have failed to compensate for the decline of such traditional branches as textiles and steel.

Only about 2.5% of industrial enterprises are large companies with more than 1,000 employees, whereas about two thirds are small firms with less than 100 on the payroll. Thus the great majority of businesses are of medium size.

But in spite of the large number of successful companies in this category, the large industrial corporations are of increasing importance. Nearly 40% (3.5 million) of the total workforce in the industrial sector are employed by them. The Siemens Group alone, for instance, employs 413,000. Furthermore, the relatively small number of big companies account for just under half of industry's total turnover.

Many of these firms have international names and branches or research facilities overseas. They include Siemens the electronics firm, Volkswagen, BMW and Daimler Benz, the carmakers, Hoechst, Bayer and BASF the chemical corporations, Ruhrkohle AG, Siemens, VEBA and RWE the energy groups, and the Bosch group. Nearly all of them are corporations and are extremely important for a large variety of small and medium-sized suppliers.

After the Second World War industry played a crucial part in Germany's economic recovery. A decisive factor in this process was the transition from a controlled economy to a market economy in 1948. One of the basic principles of the social market economy is entrepreneurial responsibility. The businessman must himself see to his company's growth and ensure that it can adapt to changing circumstances. Government policy is mainly confined to creating favourable conditions for industry. In the Federal Government's view competition is the best way to keep German industry technologically and structurally competitive on world markets. It ensures the largest possible number of small and medium-sized firms and this is the reason why the government aims to improve conditions for the smaller industries. The following is an outline of the main branches.

■ ■ ■ **Vehicle manufacture.** One of the biggest branches of industry in Germany (14,6% of total industrial

The biggest industrial firms in the Federal Republic of Germany (1992)			
Company, domicile	Sector	Turnover (DM m.)	Workforce
1. Daimler-Benz AG, Stuttgart	automotive, electrical engineering, aerospace	98,550	376,500
2. Volkswagen AG, Wolfsburg	automotive	85,400	273,000
3. Siemens AG, Munich	electrical engineering	78,500	410,000
4. Veba AG, Düsseldorf	energy, chemicals	65,400	129,800
5. Bundespost Telekom, Bonn	telecommunications	52,500	232,000
6. RWE AG, Essen	energy, building	52,400	113,600
7. Hoechst AG, Frankfurt	chemicals, pharmaceuticals	45,500	117,700
8. BASF AG, Ludwigshafen	chemicals, energy	44,500	123,300
9. Bayer AG, Leverkusen	chemicals, pharmaceuticals	41,200	156,400
10. Thyssen AG, Duisburg	steel, machinery	35,800	147,300
11. Bosch GmbH, Stuttgart	electrical engineering	34,400	147,300
12. Bayerische Motorenwerke, Munich	automotive	31,200	73,600

turnover) is vehicle manufacture, mostly cars, in some 3,000 firms. The Federal Republic is the largest producer of automobiles in the world after Japan and the United States. In 1992 the West German automotive industry alone, with a workforce of some 758,000, registered a turnover of DM 233 billion. Roughly half of the 4-5 million vehicles produced in Germany every year are exported.

The car industry has a long tradition in the new federal states, too, but the models produced under the old communist regime had no chance when faced with international competition after the country was united. Their production has been phased out and several large West German companies have opened plants in Saxony and Thuringia.

West Germany's car makers will have invested about 10 billion marks in the eastern part of the country by the end of 1993. Once production is in full swing over 400,000 cars a year will leave the assembly lines - twice as many as in the former GDR.

■ ■ ■ **Mechanical engineering** embraces over 6,200 companies in West Germany and some 900 in the new federal states, the largest number of firms in any branch. Small firms have always predominated, and it is thanks to their flexibility and technological efficiency that Germany is among the world's leaders in this field. Only three per cent of companies have more than 1,000 em-

Fitting a dual tyre to a lorry

ployees. There are mainly firms who mass-produce or design and manufacture large, complex facilities. Over 90% of companies in this branch are small or medium-sized with less than 300 employees. They are specialists who play a key role as suppliers of high-quality plant and production equipment for industry. Hardly any country has a wider range - 17,000 products, from consoles via printing and agricultural machinery to machine tools. In 1992 this branch of industry (in east and west), with a total workforce of just under 1.2 million (the biggest in any branch), produced a turnover of DM 222 billion. Some 40% of the goods produced were sold abroad. This means that the Federal Republic accounted for one fifth of total exports of machinery among the western industrial countries.

The **chemical industry** is the most important branch of the basic materials and production goods industry in Germany. Its state-of-the-art technology has put it among the world's leaders. This applies especially to its three principal corporations (Bayer, BASF, Hoechst). There is also a large number of medium-sized companies. The total workforce is about 655,000, and turnover in 1992 was about DM 210 billion. Roughly 51% of the industry's output was exported.

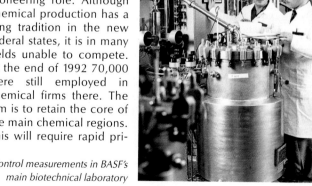

The chemical industry is making considerable efforts to improve environmental protection and has in some areas assumed a pioneering role. Although chemical production has a long tradition in the new federal states, it is in many fields unable to compete. At the end of 1992 70,000 were still employed in chemical firms there. The aim is to retain the core of the main chemical regions. This will require rapid pri-

Control measurements in BASF's main biotechnical laboratory

Production of chips

vatization and the establishment of new companies. Major investments have improved the prospects.

The **electrical engineering industry,** with a turnover of DM 225 billion (1992 in east and west) and 1.1 million employees, is likewise one of the main branches. As a result of the fall in production and turnover following unification, only about 80,000 were still employed in the electrical industry in the new federal states at the end of 1992.

Other important branches of industry are **food,** where in 1992 a workforce of around 575,000 produced a turnover of DM 219 billion (in east and west), and the **textile and clothing** industry (345,000 employees, turnover DM 70 billion (1992, east and west). In 1992 the **steel industry** in united Germany had a turnover of just under DM 43 billion (workforce 180,000). **Mining** had a turnover of DM 35 billion (east and west, workforce 225,000).

In the case of the **precision engineering and optical industry** (1,600 small and medium-sized companies employing about 145,000) the turnover was more than DM 20 billion in 1992. Many of these companies feature prominently in international trade.

The **aerospace industry** is comparatively small but from the technology point of view is of great importance. It demands the highest standards from suppliers and co-manufacturers and is thus in many fields a pioneer of modern technology. The development of civil aircraft has been subsidized by the Federal Government since 1963. This applies in particular to the Airbus models, which are an example of fruitful cooperation between European firms.

Bundesverband der Deutschen Industrie (BDI)
(Federation of German Industries)
Gustav-Heinemann-Ufer 84-88, 50968 Köln

Technology

Whether automobiles or pharmaceutical products, optical instruments, machine tools or whole power stations - the Federal Republic of Germany supplies the world market with high-quality products. She is one of the leaders in many branches of industry. In 1988 four German companies were among the world's top ten innovative enterprises. In the case of research-intensive products, Germany exported over a quarter more than she imported. In bilateral trade she has a negative balance with Japan and the United States only.

▪ ▪ ▪ **Competition.** It is crucial for German firms to keep abreast of international competition, which is increasingly becoming a high-tech race. Structural change is forcing many enterprises to concentrate on areas of technological and industrial growth. As a country with but few natural resources, Germany has always had to rely on exports of top quality, advanced products. Thus production methods have to be efficient and economical and based on state-of-the-art technology. This is the only way to achieve a high "exchangeable value" in international trade and thus safeguard jobs and incomes in Germany.

▪ ▪ ▪ **Promotion of technology.** Technological development and innovation are primarily the responsibility of companies themselves. The government only comes to their assistance if it is considered necessary in the national interest. It promotes cooperation between industry and research. This cooperation helps small and medium-sized enterprises cope with the challenges of new technology and creates favourable conditions for innovation.

The growing number of technology parks and the existence of 16 publicly financed big-science establishments which have contractual relations with more than 300 companies testify to this effort.

Every year the Federal Ministry for Research and Technology invests some DM 2.5 billion in big science. In 1992 it funded research projects by small companies to the tune of about DM 580 million. This enabled them to improve their production methods. They are also helped as regards "technology transfer", that is to say, the practical application of research findings.

Small companies can obtain information about the latest technological developments, for instance with regard to the use of computers for production purposes, in "demonstration centres" established by the ministry.

Research and development in the former GDR concentrate on much the same areas as in the Federal Republic: steel, mechanical engineering, automobiles, electrical engineering and chemicals. These are the focal points for the current restructuring of East Germany's economy. Many West German companies are cooperating with firms or research establishments in the new federal states on projects concerned with communica-

This turbine is intended for a waterworks

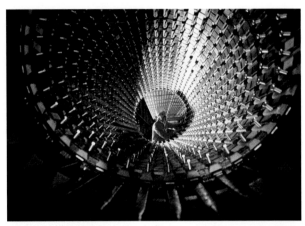

Installing the winding in a generator

tions technology, microelectronics, laser technology, environmental engineering and chemical technology.

■ ■ ■ **Strengths and weaknesses.** The significance of research-intensive products for Germany's international competitiveness is reflected in the industry's exports. In 1991 Germany accounted for 17% of world trade in manufactured industrial goods, the largest share among the OECD countries. Regarding R & D-intensive technology (18%) she was in 1991 on level with the United States and distinctly behind Japan, which accounted for 21%. In sophisticated technology German industry has been successful in such fields as pharmaceutical products, new organic chemicals and synthetics, plant protection agents, electronic systems in the field of medicine, advanced optical and measuring instruments, and of course cars and engineering.

It has been less successful in the fields of electronic data processing, microchips and consumer electronics. One area where Germany has done comparatively well is telecommunications. In the field of environmental protection technology, however, German companies are leading the way and have the largest share of world trade (20.5%). German enterprises are also actively engaged in biotechnology, which will be one of the key technologies in the next few decades. The United States and Japan hold the leading positions, however.

Crafts and trades

Although crafts and trades in the Federal Republic are smaller than the industrial sector they have a much longer tradition. They flourished particularly in the Middle Ages, as proved by the mighty cathedrals and elaborately ornamented guild houses throughout the country. But today still they are a considerable economic factor. In 1992 about 5 million people were employed in this branch, which had a turnover in 1992 of approximately DM 700 billion.

■ ■ ■ **Crafts in the industrial society.** Industry needs the small craft industries because they are very flexible suppliers of products and parts. But they are also the link between industry and the consumer since quality industrial products have to be serviced and repaired.

Craftsmen are also producers themselves. Bakers, confectioners and slaughterers provide a wide range of foodstuffs. Houses in Germany are still mostly produced by hand by builders, carpenters, plumbers and painters. And many trades, such as those of hair stylist, chimney sweep or contract cleaner, are indispensable.

But crafts and trades are of special importance for two other reasons. One is that they offer scope for a large number of self-employed people and are thus a kind of school for young entrepreneurs. The other is that they provide some of the most important training centres.

It is here that about 40% of all apprentices in the Federal Republic learn their trade. Germany's craft industries urgently require apprentices, especially in rural areas. Those who cannot be taken on after training are highly valued in other branches of industry.

In 1949 Germany had over 900,000 craft businesses. This number declined but the overall workforce increased. In 1993 there were some 650,000 such firms in the whole of Germany, employing eight people on average.

Crafts and trades are playing a very important role in the restructuring of East Germany's economy. They are providing the impetus for growth. Even in the days of communist central planning, some 82,000 small private firms were able to exist alongside the 2,700 production cooperatives. From the time of unification to the end of 1992, the number of small businesses in the new federal states had increased to about 117,000 and a workforce of more than 800,000.

Judging by the size of the workforce, the main trade is that of bricklayer or construction worker. The wide range of craft products is on display at the international craft trade fair held every spring in Munich.

■ ■ ■ **State support.** The Federal Government helps medium-sized and small enterprises to increase their competitiveness. Assistance covers tax relief, management consultancy and low-interest loans. The federal and state governments finance various programmes to help new firms.

■ ■ ■ **Organization.** In Germany only persons listed in the Crafts Register (a list of self-employed craftsmen in the district) are allowed to carry on a trade or provide apprenticeship training. The usual qualification is that of master craftsman.

Electrician testing switching equipment

Some special jobs have to be done by hand

Tradesmen are organized in guilds at town or county level and in regional guild associations. The guilds are responsible for vocational training and continuing education. They can also negotiate collective wage agreements and set up health insurance funds for their members. The craftsmen organize their own affairs and look after their interests through the chambers of handicrafts. The chambers maintain the Crafts Register and Apprentices Register. The guilds have an umbrella organization known as the Central Association of German Craft Industry and Trades, while the chambers belong to the German Association of Chambers of Crafts and Trades. The national organization for the regional and trade associations is the Federation of German Crafts and Trades.

Installing a switch cabinet

Zentralverband des Deutschen Handwerks
(Federation of German Crafts and Trades)
Johanniterstr. 1, 53113 Bonn

Agriculture, forestry and fisheries

Germany is not only a highly industrialized country but also has an efficient farming community who produce a broad range of high quality foodstuffs. About half of Germany's total area of just under 36 million hectares is given over to farming.

Agriculture also has responsibilities which assume increasing significance in a modern industrial society. It ensures that rural settlements can function efficiently and preserves farming landscapes that have developed over centuries. But like other sectors of the economy, agriculture has undergone radical changes in the past 40 years.

■ ■ ■ **Agriculture.** In West Germany the number of farms has decreased by about one million since 1950. Attracted by the prospect of better incomes, many farmers left the land to work in industry and service enterprises. Furthermore, increasing mechanization saved manpower: In 1950 there were some 1.6 million farms employing just under 3.9 million family workers full time.

In 1992, however, there were only about 580,000 farms with just less than 540,000 full-time family employees.

As the number of farms and workers dwindled, productivity increased. In 1950 one farm worker produced enough food for only ten people; in 1991 the number was 71. In spite of this huge growth in productivity, farm wages have not always kept pace with those in industry. True, the income gap had been reduced to just under 10% by the late 80s, but it has been widening again as a result of the unfavourable price situation.

Despite the changes family farms still predominate. More than 70% work less than 50 hectares (120 acres). In contrast to other West European countries, a good 40% are part-time farms, i.e. the main family income is from activities outside farming. Farmers must reckon with a slight drop in incomes in 1992/93, following a small increase the previous year. Germany's farmers earn about two thirds of their income from their livestock.

The chief crops in West Germany in terms of proceeds are milk, pork and beef, cereals and sugarbeet. In some

German bread in all its variety

regions wine, fruit and vegetables as well as other mar-
ket-garden products play an important role.

In West Germany livestock farms are generally small.
The factory-type holding is the exception. For instance,
just under 80% of milking cows are kept on farms with
less than 40 animals, and almost 80% of pig-fattening
farms have fewer than 600 animals.

In the eastern part of the country the pattern of farming is different. After the Second World War there were
about 600,000 holdings which were forced by the communist regime to give up their independence. They were
replaced by agricultural production cooperatives, large
holdings including people's cooperatives and farms,
which finally numbered about 5,100. The agricultural
production cooperatives specialized in the mass production of certain goods. They had on average 4,300 hectares (10,700 acres) under cultivation. Strictly separated
from these were the livestock farms with, on average,
over 1,650 cows, 11,000 pigs or 500,000 laying hens.

When the country was united in October 1990 farmland in the former GDR was returned to private ownership. Although there is still considerable uncertainty as
regards land and property ownership, some 14,000 farmers have decided to run their own farms. At the same
time, three quarters of the 4,500 or so production cooperatives have been transformed into registered co-

operative societies, partnerships or joint-stock companies.

The government provides support in order to ease the difficult process of integrating East Germany's farms into the European Community. Funds are also provided to help convert the former production cooperatives into competitive enterprises. This has proved successful in that many individual holdings have made considerable profit through cultivating large areas.

Apart from maintaining food supplies, farming in the densely populated, highly industrialized Federal Republic of Germany has other increasingly important functions, including
- nature conservation
- looking after the countryside to provide attractive leisure time
- and recreational areas, and ensuring a continuous supply of agricultural raw materials for industry.

The family farm is best suited to meeting these various requirements since it can adapt to new developments and ensure that foodstuff production is environment-friendly.

■ ■ ■ **The Common Agricultural Policy of the European Community.** With the introduction of the common agricultural market of the European Community in the 60s important areas of agricultural policy were transferred to European institutions. This applies in particular to market and price policy and, to an increasing extent, structural policy.

The Community's original objective was to increase agricultural productivity and thus farmers' incomes, to stabilize markets, and to maintain food supplies at reasonable prices. Much has been achieved in the intervening decades, especially as regards increasing production, with the result that supply of major products such as cereals and beef far exceeds demand.

Consequently, easing the strain on markets by restricting production has become an urgent priority. A number of such measures have already proved effective, such as quotas for milk and sugar, as well as compensation for farmers who take land out of production and go over to extensive farming.

But further measures were necessary and the EC agricultural reform of 1992 has laid the foundations. The market price support system is being superseded by more effective controls on quantity (e.g. set-aside arrangements) and direct assistance.

In spite of the growing difficulties encountered by importing countries Germany's exports of farm products reached a record level in 1992, i.e. DM 34 billion. Her imports, on the other hand, amounted to DM 67 billion.

Germany is the world's largest importer of agricultural products. Germany is the fourth largest exporter of farm products. A good thirds of her agricultural trade is with EC countries. One fifth of farm incomes is generated by exports.

■ ■ ■ **National farm policy.** Although many decisions on agricultural policy are today taken by the European Community, a few important matters are still in the hands of national governments. This applies in particular to structural policy. Although the Community sets the framework, the national parliament and government provide the substance. The German Government does so chiefly through its "joint responsibilities" with the states for improving agricultural structure and coastal preservation.

This includes water management, the construction of central water supply and sewage treatment facilities, country roads, reallocation of land and village development.

The central and regional governments also provide support for individual farmers who wish to rationalize production methods. In addition, funds are provided for underprivileged areas where agriculture is an important economic and social factor.

■ ■ ■ **Food.** Maintaining food supply, quality and variety at reasonable prices has always been the aim of the government and the European Community. That this has been achieved is shown by the fact that people have been spending an increasingly smaller proportion of their income on food. In the old western states in 1991 it was just under 16% (excluding spirits and tobacco etc.) compared with 23% in 1970.

The range of high-quality foodstuffs available in Germany was extended as a result of the gradual harmonization of food legislation in the Community even before the single market was launched on 1 January 1993. New laws that are constantly adapted in the light of scientific

Appreciated worldwide: German wine

knowledge protect the consumer from hazards to health and fraudulent products.

Consumers must be in a position to judge quality and price and possess the knowledge to choose a balanced diet and avoid food-related illness. The government provides the necessary information and advice through various agencies such as the Deutsche Gesellschaft für Ernährung (DGE, German Nutrition Society), the Auswertungs- und Informationsdienst für Ernährung, Landwirtschaft und Forsten (The Food, Agriculture and Forestry Information Service), as well as the regional consumer protection centres. They provide not only scientific facts about nutrition but also up-to-date information on products, prices and keeping private stocks of food.

The mobile information service (MOBI) in the new states has had a multiplier effect. The vehicles used for that purpose are now at the disposal of the five regional consumer safety centres.

Another important source of nutritional advice and information are the four-yearly reports prepared by the DGE on behalf of the Federal Government. According to the 1992 report there has been an improvement on 1988. Moreover, eating habits in eastern Germany are not much different from those in the west. As always the main problems are overeating and malnutrition.

■ ■ ■ **Forestry.** Almost a third of the Federal Republic's total area - 10.7 million hectares (4.13 million sq miles) - is covered by forest. The state with the largest forest area in proportion to its total size is Rhineland-Palatinate (about 41%), while the one with the least forest - apart from the city states - is Schleswig-Holstein (10%).

Between 30 and 40 million cubic metres of timber is felled in Germany every year. This meets about two thirds of domestic demand. Germany is one of the largest exporters of timber.

Forests are important not only as sources of timber but also as recreation areas for the inhabitants of industrial conurbations. Furthermore, they have a beneficial influence on soil, air and climate in that they retard water run off, weaken the impact of wind, clean the air and prevent erosion and landslides. In short, they are a very important environmental protection factor.

A Forest Preservation and Forestry Promotion Act was enacted in 1975. This stipulates that forest land can only be cleared for other uses with approval from the regional authority. The law obliges forest owners to reafforest harvested areas.

The foremost aim is to preserve or restore the natural appearance of the forests and ensure their proper management. Since the early 1980s there has been increasing forest depletion. The trees lose their needles or leaves, growth is retarded and they finally die.

There are various biotic and abiotic causes of this new type of damage, mainly air pollution. Although protective measures have been proved effective the state of the forests - according to a 1992 status report - has continued to deteriorate. According to statistics published by the German Nature Conservation League in 1993, one quarter of all trees are badly damaged. In the 32 European countries covered by the League's report, the area of forest damaged increased in 1992 from 53,8% to 57%. Further efforts at both national and international level are necessary in order to reduce air pollution from industry, traffic, households and agriculture.

■ ■ ■ **Fisheries.** The fishing industry, too, has undergone structural changes in recent decades. Coastal countries worldwide have extended their fishing zones to 200 sea miles, with the result that traditional stocks

Replenishing conifer stocks in the Fichtelgebirge

have been decimated by overfishing, chiefly because of the excessive use of modern catching methods. This has greatly reduced Germany's ocean fishing fleet. The fishing industry, which employs 48,000, had a turnover in 1992 of DM 11.3 billion.

Germany's principal fishing areas are the North Sea, the Baltic and the Atlantic off the British Isles and around Greenland. Her only chance of surviving the threat to her fishing industry resulting from the development of international maritime law was within the framework of the European Community, which introduced catch quotas in order to safeguard species. One of the species threatened with extinction is the red tuna. Catches are to be reduced to 50% within the next two years. As an experiment the activities of large ships will be monitored by satellite for twelve months in order to protect stocks and keep check on catches. The German government has also helped to keep the fishing fleet going by providing initial and bridging support.

The EC common fisheries policy was reviewed in 1992 after ten years and a new regulation adopted for the next decade. It is an extrapolation of the previous policy and focuses in particular on the principle of "relative stability" (i.e. fixed quotas for member states). The aim is to establish once and for all an economic and ecological balance between usable marine resources and fishing fleets by protecting stocks and reducing fishing capacities.

Herring catch off Rügen

Deutscher Bauernverband
(German Farmers' Association)
Godesberger Allee 142-148, 53175 Bonn

Commerce

For decades the commercial sector in Germany has accounted for about 10 per cent of GNP. Some four million people - one eighth of the total workforce - are now employed in approximately 600,000 commercial enterprises (wholesale and retail).

Although there has been a tendency for companies to merge, most are still in the small or medium-sized category. About half of them employ only one or two, and one tenth fewer than ten, usually including the owner and family members.

■ ▨ ▧ **Wholesale trade.** Wholesalers sell commercial goods from manufacturers or foreign markets to other traders, processors, industrial users and bulk consumers. They buy large quantities and sell them in smaller amounts. Retailers especially obtain consumer durables and other items from them. The wholesale trade's turnover in 1949 was about DM 50 billion, in 1992 just short of one trillion marks.

German unification and the opening of East European markets have provided fresh stimulus. In 1992 some 20,000 wholesalers were registered with the chambers of commerce in eastern Germany. The wholesale trade in the west employs 1.4 million people in about 126,000 enterprises.

All foodstuffs under one roof in the supermarket

■ ■   **Retail trade.** As the last link in the distribution system and in direct contact with consumers the retail trade has undergone a remarkable structural change in recent decades. The advancement of self-service especially, which began in grocery stores, opened the door to extensive rationalization. New types of operation, such as discount stores or hypermarkets, came into being.

Today the main characteristics of the retail trade are greater competition and smaller profit margins - all to the customer's advantage. In 1992 and 1993 retail prices increased at a noticeably slower rate than the general cost of living.

In 1949 turnover in the West German retail trade was DM 28 billion. This rose to over 667 billion in 1992, to which must be added roughly 120 billion in the new federal states. The greater proportion was accounted for by foodstuffs, spirits and tobacco (over 25%), then textiles and clothing (about 13%). West Germany's 400,000 retailers have a workforce of approximately 2.5 million.

Rationalization reduced manpower in the West German retail trade up to the late 80s, but from 1986 to 1993 there was an increase of 6.6%. Again, German unification was the reason. The downtrend in the east continues, however. The retail trade is subject to considerable seasonal change, with more than 30% of the workforce working only part-time. The number employed in the retail trade in east Germany in 1992 was 550,000,

Fresh vegetables from the market

Individual service in the corner shop

which explains why the poor selection of goods of communist times has given way to an extensive range.

According to the chambers of commerce, nearly 150,000 private firms between Rügen and the Erzgebirge were offering their wares. Wholesale and retail trade in the former GDR was almost entirely state-controlled. Only about 15,000 businesses, mostly very small, were still in private hands before the country was united.

Increasing motorization and the trend towards bulk buying have favoured the hypermarkets and self-service department stores. As a result, many small traders have not been able to compete. From 1962 to 1986 the number of retailers fell from 445,000 to 340,000. However, small and medium-size retailers have been able to compete with large enterprises by catering for individual tastes and offering expert advice and personalized service. The formation of purchasing associations has helped many of the smaller firms to hold their own.

Hauptverband des Deutschen Einzelhandels (German Retailers' Association) Sachsenring 89, 50677 Köln
Bundesverband des Deutschen Gross- und Aussenhandels (Federation of German Wholesale and Foreign Trade) Kaiser-Friedrich-Strasse 13, 53113 Bonn

Foreign Trade

International trade is crucial to the German economy. Germany has always sought close trade relations and upheld the principle of divided labour. This is consistent with her liberal trade policy based on the removal of customs and other barriers to trade. By consistently pursuing an outward-looking policy she has achieved the largest trade turnover next to that of the United States. The main principles of German trade are:

- international division of labour rather than self-sufficiency;
- global competition rather than trade restrictions;
- and reconciliation of interests rather than economic confrontation.

■ ■ ■ **External trade.** The total value of the old Federal Republic's imports and exports increased from DM 19.7 billion in 1950 to over DM 1,308 billion in 1992. Since 1952 exports have usually exceeded imports, and this in spite of several revaluations of the mark. In the 80s the export surplus rose sharply, reaching DM 134.5 billion in 1989, but after reunification it shrank, not surprisingly.

One of the reasons is that the heavy demand from the new federal states boosted the country's imports, making her a "locomotive" of world trade in a period of global recession. In 1992 Germany's imports were worth DM 637.8 billion compared with exports totalling DM 670.6 billion.

Nearly one in three gainfully employed persons works directly for export. Germany is one of the world's biggest suppliers of industrial equipment. The main exports are motor vehicles, machinery, chemical and electrical engineering products. German exporters are known for the quality of their products, service and delivery. As a country with high wages Germany has concentrated on high-tech products in order to make up for her disadvantage as regards costs.

The most important imports are farm and electrical products as well as textiles, goods with which especially developing or newly industrialized countries are forcing their way into world markets.

As a result of her extensive trade relations Germany is affected by disruptions of world trade since they have an impact on jobs, investments, profits and standards of living. Thus a stable world economy, free trade and a well-functioning monetary system are crucial to the German economy.

■ ■ ■ **Trading partners.** The progressive economic integration of the European Community has greatly increased intra-European trade. In 1992 some 54% of German exports went to EC countries.

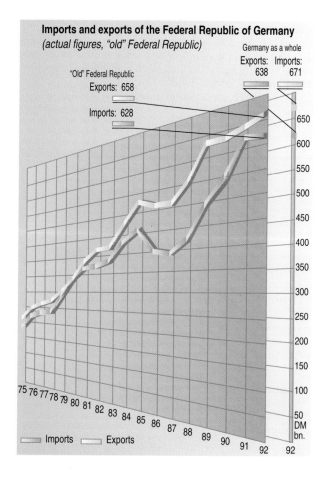

Imports and exports of the Federal Republic of Germany
(actual figures, "old" Federal Republic)

Germany as a whole
Exports: Imports:
638   671

"Old" Federal Republic
Exports: 658
Imports: 628

650
600
550
500
450
400
350
300
250
200
150
100
50
DM
bn.

75 76 77 78 79 80 81 82 83 84 85 86 87 88 89 90 91 92   92

▭ Imports   ▭ Exports

Germany's main trading partner is France. In 1992 she exported goods and services worth approximately DM 87 billion to that country, whereas imports were worth a good DM 76.4 billion. Other major importers of German products are Italy, the United Kingdom, the Netherlands and Belgium/Luxembourg. Next in line are the United States, which in 1992 spent roughly DM 42.6 billion on goods from Germany.

France also heads the list as far as Germany's imports are concerned, followed by the Netherlands, Italy, Belgium/Luxembourg, the United Kingdom and the United States. Germany does 70-75% of her trade with European countries, 10-15% with the Asia/Pacific region, about 7% with North America, and 2% each with Africa and Latin America. Her largest trade imbalance for many years has been with Japan. Whereas she imported goods worth DM 38 billion from that country in 1992, Japan spent only DM 14.6 billion in Germany.

Germany's principal trading partners 1992

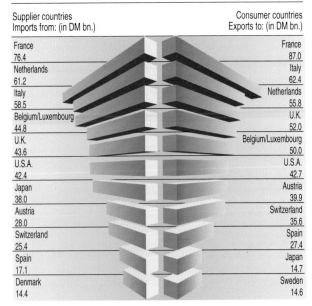

Supplier countries Imports from: (in DM bn.)	Consumer countries Exports to: (in DM bn.)
France 76.4	France 87.0
Netherlands 61.2	Italy 62.4
Italy 58.5	Netherlands 55.8
Belgium/Luxembourg 44.8	U.K. 52.0
U.K. 43.6	Belgium/Luxembourg 50.0
U.S.A. 42.4	U.S.A. 42.7
Japan 38.0	Austria 39.9
Austria 28.0	Switzerland 35.6
Switzerland 25.4	Spain 27.4
Spain 17.1	Japan 14.7
Denmark 14.4	Sweden 14.6

In 1990 the new federal states appeared in Germany's trade statistics for the first time. Trade relations of the former GDR were mainly focused on the state-trading countries of the former Eastern bloc. And in 1992 as well, half of the region's foreign trade turnover was with central and eastern Europe, the Soviet Union being the main partner. And the latter's successor states still play an important role, having in 1992 imported goods worth roughly DM 13.9 billion from Germany.

■ ▨ ▨ **Investment abroad.** After the Second World War the Germans had to start from scratch where foreign investment was concerned. Nearly all German assets abroad had been lost. But meanwhile the total invested abroad is worth approximately DM 250 billion. And other countries have undertaken to invest more than DM 50 billion in Germany. Easily Germany's most important partner for investment is the United States, followed by Switzerland, the United Kingdom, the Netherlands and France.

There are many reasons for investing overseas. Some companies switch production outside Germany because domestic wages are too high. Others have to secure their supplies of raw materials and therefore buy an interest in foreign suppliers.

In many cases the aim is to maintain and expand markets abroad. Where trade restrictions or unfavourable exchange rates prove to be a hindrance to direct exports, one way to solve the problem is to produce the goods where they are to be sold.

At any rate, investment abroad helps consolidate international trade. It is conducive to the international division of labour and to economic and industrial development in the Third World. They receive not only long-term capital but technology, know-how and business experience.

In order to offset possible economic and political risks attaching to investment in developing countries, the Federal Government has introduced special promotional instruments. For instance, it has concluded investment protection agreements with over 70 countries and nations in Central and Eastern Europe.

These accords provide national and most-favoured nation treatment, the free transfer of capital and profits, fair compensation in the event of expropriation, as well as independent international arbitration.

To guard against political risks the Federal Government also affords financial guarantees for investments it considers worth supporting. The German Finance Company for Investments in Developing Countries (DEG) promotes direct investment in the Third World. Medium-sized German companies receive low-interest loans and grants to help them finance branches in developing countries and the transfer of technology.

■ ■ ■ **Current account.** Germany's traditionally large export surpluses often drew criticism abroad, but the current account shows that the foreign trade surplus is offset by heavy deficits in the service sector. The huge amounts spent by German holiday makers abroad, remittances by foreign workers in Germany to their relatives at home, payments to the Soviet Union, development assistance, and the Federal Republic's contributions to the European Community and other international organizations erode most of that surplus from trade.

Indeed, Germany's current account has even slipped deeply into the red since unification. The credit side of DM 76.1 billion in 1990 has plunged into a deficit of DM 32.9 billion in the space of only one year. And in 1992 as well the debit side was DM 39.2 billion. Thus Germany is no longer the world's biggest exporter of capital. On the

German trade fairs attract many foreign exhibitors

Skipbuilding on the North Sea coast

contrary, she is having to borrow considerable foreign capital in order to finance eastern Germany's economic recovery.

Bundesverband des Deutschen Gross- und
Aussenhandels
(Federation of German Wholesale and Foreign Trade)
Kaiser-Friedrich-Strasse 13, 53113 Bonn

Energy and raw materials

As stated earlier, the Federal Republic has little in the way of raw materials and energy and is therefore largely dependent upon imports. She has to buy two thirds of her primary energy from other countries. Her dependence on minerals, too, is quite considerable. Germany has few deposits of iron ore and oil.

One quarter of the country's natural gas consumption can be met from local sources. There are large deposits of coal and salt, however, which will last for many decades. Geological and climatic factors limit the country's economically exploitable renewable sources of energy.

■ ▓ ▒ **Energy supply.** Having consumed 481 million tonnes (coal units) in 1992, Germany is one of the world's largest consumers of energy. Her efforts to conserve and make rational use of energy have proved successful. In the period 1973 to 1992 the domestic product in the old federal states grew by more than 50%, but energy consumption by only 7%.

Since unification lignite has become the principal domestic source of energy. The main deposits are in the Rhineland, Southern Brandenburg and Saxony as well as in Saxony-Anhalt and eastern Lower Saxony. Extractable resources total about 56 billion tonnes. Lignite was also the main source of energy in the former GDR, but energy supply there was one-sided and caused environmental pollution on a massive scale. Since the country was united production had declined by over 60% up to the end of 1992 on account of the restructuring of the economy and the diversification of energy supply in the new states. Lignite nonetheless remains one of the main sources of energy, although to a less extent than in the past. The cuts in production and the massive government programmes for rehabilitating the environment and modernizing power stations has reduced pollution considerably in recent years.

The main pitcoal deposits are in the Ruhr region (North-Rhine/Westphalia) and in the Saarland. The reserves there total about 24 billion tonnes.

In 1950 pitcoal accounted for 73% of the old Federal Republic's energy consumption. By 1992 it had fallen to just under 18%. But oil, too, lost ground to other sources of energy, largely on account of the oil-price explosions in the 70s. From 55% in 1973 (compared with just 5% in 1950) oil's contribution to energy supply fell to just under 41% in the late eighties. It has meanwhile risen again to 41.5% (1992). The crisis of the 70s in particular showed how much uninterrupted energy supplies mean to Germany.

Following new discoveries in the Emsland region and in the North Sea, Germany's natural gas reserves are estimated at about 350 billion m³. Gas is imported from several countries and supplies are secured until well into the next decade. In 1992 gas accounted for 17% of primary energy consumption in the western part of the country and approximately 18% in the east.

Germany has not produced any uranium since the late 80s. She imports the enriched uranium needed for the operation of nuclear power stations and she has adequate supplies through the foreign holdings of German mining companies. In 1992 nuclear energy still accounted for a substantial proportion of electricity generation (34%).

■ ■ ■ ■ **Energy policy.** Reliable energy supply is essential for a well-functioning, modern economy. This, as

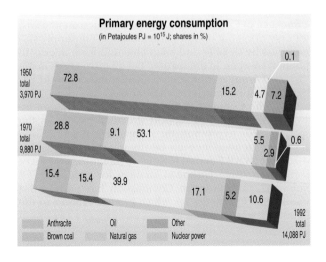

Primary energy consumption
(in Petajoules PJ = 10¹⁵ J; shares in %)

1950 total 3,970 PJ — 72.8   15.2   4.7   7.2   0.1
1970 total 9,880 PJ — 28.8   9.1   53.1   5.5   2.9   0.6
1992 total 14,088 PJ — 15.4   15.4   39.9   17.1   5.2   10.6

Anthracite   Oil   Other
Brown coal   Natural gas   Nuclear power

well as environmental and conservation factors, are the
principal objectives of the government's energy policy
as presented in its 1991 Energy Plan. This plan takes account of the changes in the energy sector following
Germany's reunification, the greenhouse effect, the
progress of European integration, and the transformations in central and eastern Europe and the former Soviet
Union.

Now market principles and laws apply throughout the
country. This includes stricter environmental legislation
which has resulted in the closure of some reactors.

The energy industry in Germany is mostly in private
hands. The government's task is to provide a suitable
framework, which includes an Energy Act and regulations for crisis prevention and the build-up of emergency
stocks, as well as laws to protect the environment.

Since 1973 conditions on international energy markets
have changed fundamentally several times. Two sharp
increases in the price of oil caused global recessions,
then the price dropped rapidly in late 1985. The transformation in central and eastern Europe and in the former
Soviet Union have given a new dimension to east-west
cooperation in the use of the energy resources of these
countries, especially Russia. These developments and
the Gulf war of 1990/91 have underlined the uncertainty
as to the price of what is still the most important source
of energy.

Because of Germany's heavy dependence on imports,
not only of oil but of other commodities, the supply system must be flexible and adaptable and have access to
different sources. In the wake of the oil price crises in the
70s, the European Community placed the common energy policy on a much broader basis.

Today the Community has a considerable array of instruments available to support structural change in the
energy sector, to promote the rational use of energy, and
to reduce dependence on oil (they include the THER-
MIE, SAVE, JOULE and ALTENER programmes). As part of
a comprehensive European strategy for reducing CO_2
emissions, the European Commission has proposed a
combined CO_2/energy tax which has the support of the
German government.

Owing to the rapidly increasing environmental pollution of recent years due to the production and consump-

Solar modules convert light energy into electricity

tion of energy, greater attention will have to be paid to more economical and rational methods. Both the German energy industry and consumers have already achieved considerable progress in conserving energy and ensuring its environment-friendly use. Government energy policy focuses on the following aspects:

- Efforts to reach a consensus on future energy policy, especially with the regard to the utilization of coal and nuclear energy, on energy conservation and the more intensive use of renewable sources of energy.

- Ensuring an environment-friendly energy supply, this being one of the main objectives. A focal point of government efforts in the 90s is the development and application of a comprehensive strategy for protecting the climate.

- A free market policy in order to ensure a reliable, economical, efficient and environment-friendly supply of energy.

- Continued efforts to economize on energy consumption and in the promotion of research on and use of long-term alternative sources of energy, especially those of the renewable kind.

- Further integration within the framework of the internal European market.

Owing to Germany's heavy dependency on imports, cooperation both with the other members of the European Community but also within the International Energy Agency and with the countries of central and eastern Europe and the successor states of the Soviet Union is of crucial importance.

Pitcoal and lignite will continue to help safeguard the nation's energy supply, but the contribution will be much smaller than it was in the late 80s. Pitcoal, however, will remain an important source of energy for the steel and electricity industries.

Unfavourable geological conditions mean that German coal is much more expensive to mine than imported coal. The Federal Government and the governments of the coalmining states of North-Rhine/Westphalia and the Saarland provide considerable public support for coalmining in order to maintain sales to these two coal-using industries.

The government still feels that it is right to continue to use nuclear energy until such time as other comparably safe, environment-friendly and cheap sources of energy are available. It helps keep CO_2 emissions down. In 1992, for instance, use of nuclear energy for the production of electricity prevented the emission of 150 million tonnes of CO_2. As always, safety has priority over profitability. Germany's nuclear reactors are known throughout the world to conform to the highest safety standards.

State-of-the-art coalmining equipment

■ ■ ■ **Raw materials.** Germany's supply of raw materials is at present secure. Imports consist of ores, concentrates and ferro-alloys from the commodity-producing countries and of supplies from west European countries who, though they have no raw materials of their own, have the necessary processing industries (foundries, refineries).

But apart from exploring new sources of energy at home and abroad the government is also trying to reduce raw material consumption. Growing importance attaches to the recycling of used materials (see chapter on environmental protection). The commodity-using industries maintain adequate reserves in case supply is disrupted.

A coal-Fired power plant at Werne-Stockum

In order to safeguard supplies of commodities Germany needs above all well-functioning markets. Her relations with the commodity-producing countries, many of whom are underdeveloped in industrial terms, are based on the following principles:
- maintaining world economic growth and efficiency,
- stabilizing commodity export earnings, especially in the least developed countries and ensuring continuous supplies,
- accelerating the industrialization process in the developing countries and facilitating the technology transfer from industrial countries,
- opening the markets of industrial countries to imports of manufactures and semi-manufactures from developing countries,
- promoting a steady flow of capital to the developing countries and protecting investors from expropriation,
- securing a larger transfer of resources to industrial nations for the benefit of the developing countries, and
- the general exploration of raw material deposits by means of cooperation projects with CIS countries.

Germany has always been able to rely on commodity imports and at present there is no sign of this situation changing. Maintaining supplies is primarily the responsibility of the private sector, who trade on the basis of long-term contracts with sources in as many different regions as possible, by obtaining holdings in producer companies and trading on their own behalf, as well as building up reserves, carrying out materials research and recycling waste materials.

The government can and should merely create the general market conditions and provide support only where this is necessary in the interest of the economy as a whole. Thus it is primarily concerned with ensuring that world commodity markets function properly because of their vital importance to Germany's industries.

It achieves this objective mainly by underwriting investment in developing countries against political risks, providing guarantees for untied loans, promoting exploration (as under the 1971-90 programme), and through the work of the Bundesanstalt für Geowissenschaften und Rohstoffe (Federal Institute for Geosciences and Natural Resources) in advance of commercial exploration.

Money and banking

The unit of currency in the Federal Republic of Germany is the Deutsche Mark (DM 1 = 100 Pfennigs). It is freely convertible, i.e. it can be exchanged for any other foreign currency at any time at the going rate. There are no restrictions on capital transactions with other countries. The deutschmark has for decades been one of the most stable currencies in the world, it is the anchor of the European Monetary System, and it is the second most important reserve currency after the American dollar.

■ ■ ■ **The Bundesbank.** The Federal Republic of Germany's central bank is the Bundesbank (German Federal Bank) in Frankfurt am Main (since 1957). It is headed by the Central Bank Council which draws up the guidelines for the country's monetary policy. It consists of the Bundesbank's directors and the presidents of the state central banks. According to law the Bundesbank is "independent of the Federal Government in exercising its powers".

Only the Bundesbank is empowered to issue banknotes. It is the "bank of banks", i.e. their last resort, and the country's "house bank". It also manages the currency reserves.

The Bundesbank's fundamental task is to safeguard the currency. Thus apart from fulfilling the traditional role of a central bank, maintaining the nation's monetary system, the Bundesbank has a special responsibility for maintaining economic stability. It must ensure the deutschmark's value both internally and externally. It is therefore commonly referred to as the "guardian of the currency".

By regulating the supply of money in circulation the Bundesbank keeps the mark stable while at the same time making available the necessary means to finance economic growth. To this end it relies on minimum reserves, refinancing and an open-market policy. The banks are required to keep a certain percentage of their liabilities (minimum reserve) with the Bundesbank, interest-free. By varying this percentage the central bank can influence the credit-creating scope of the banks.

With its refinancing policy it regulates the allocation of bank credit. It does so by buying bills of exchange and lending money on securities. The discount rate (for bills) and the Lombard rate (for loans on securities) are important regulatory factors.

The Bundesbank may engage in open-market transactions only to regulate the money market. By buying securities it allows money to flow into the economy, by selling them it withdraws money.

In accordance with the Treaty of 18 May 1990 on Economic, Monetary and Social Union the former east German currency was converted into deutschmarks as from 1 July 1990. At the same time all 572 banks in eastern Germany were subject to the Federal Republic's banking laws. Since that date the Bundesbank has regulated money supply and credit for industry in united Germany and handles the banking side of domestic and international payment transactions.

■ ■ ■ **The European Monetary System.** The purpose of the European Monetary System (EMS), which was established in 1979, is to stabilize exchange rates between the currencies of member states in the European Community. For a long time it ensured reliable exchange rates in Europe and had a favourable impact on member states' own efforts to maintain stability.

All Community members are in the EMS, and most of them are in the Exchange Rate Mechanism (ERM) as well. The ERM fixes the central rates for each currency. Currency market rates are allowed to fluctuate up to a maximum of 15% either side of the central rate. If major fluctuations are imminent the central banks are obliged to buy or sell the currencies affected and stabilize the exchange rates. If the economic trend so requires, the central rates can be adjusted by means of a unanimous decision of the EC finance ministers and central bank governors.

From 1979 to 1993 most EC currencies were subject to narrow band widths of plus or minus 2.25%, but they were widened to plus or minus 15% as from August 1993, although members hoped to move back within narrower margins. Obviously, the EMS binds only the exchange rates of the participating countries. The rate with other currencies, such as the dollar or the yen, fluctuate freely on the currency markets.

Within the EMS there is a European Currency Unit (ECU) which serves as a link and unit of account between member currencies. The ECU is not a currency in itself, however, but a "basket" of the twelve EC currencies containing, for instance, 62 Pfennigs, 1.33 French Francs, 152 Italian Lira. At present the DM contributes about 30% to the value of the ECU, the French Franc 20%, the Pound Sterling, the Dutch Guilder and the Italian Lira about 10% each.

Bundesbank headquarters in Frankfurt/Main

Under the Maastricht Treaty signed in December 1991 a common European currency is to be established by 1990 at the latest. Membership of the Monetary Union is subject to strict criteria, that is to say, member countries must have low inflation, interest rates and budget deficits. Participants in the Monetary Union have undertaken to transfer their monetary sovereignty to a politically independent European Central Bank, the foremost objective of which will be to maintain price stability.

European Monetary Union will have various advantages. Companies will have a reliable basis on which to plan, tourists will not have to exchange currency, which means their holidays will be cheaper, the European currency can become a world reserve currency, and increased competition will improve the efficiency of the European economies. This will make it possible to safeguard present jobs and create new ones.

■ ■ ■ **Credit institutions.** There is a large variety of financial institutions in Germany, ranging from public savings banks via cooperative (Volksbank, Raiffeisenbank) and private banks, to building societies, mortgage institutions, giro clearing banks, central depositaries for securities, and investment trusts. In the course of time a concentration process has taken place, however. Whereas there were just under 14,000 independent credit institutions in the 50s, by 1991 the number had shrunk to 4,453. And the trend continues, with about 100 cooperative banks merging into larger group institutions every year. At the same time the number of private banks is dwindling. In 1957 there were 245 of them, today only 80.

In spite of the extensive structural changes that have taken place the balance of power within the banking industry has hardly altered. The private commercial banks have consistently retained 30% of all banking business, the public institutions just under 50%, and the cooperatives about 20%.

There are 342 lending banks (including large ones like the Deutsche Bank, Dresdner Bank and Commerzbank), twelve giro clearing banks, 734 savings banks, four cooperative central banks, 3,392 credit cooperatives, 35 mortgage institutions and public mortgage banks, 16 banks with special functions, 34 building societies and 567 foreign banks.

The private banks include large ones that are joint-stock companies. Giro central banks are the central credit institutions of the public savings banks in the regions. As house banks of the states they are mainly concerned with regional financing. Most savings banks, which cater mainly for employees and the self-employed, are operated by the municipalities. They are autonomous public enterprises, the local authority being liable. The cooperative central banks are the principal regional institutions of Volksbanken and Raiffeisenkassen, i.e. the rural and commercial credit cooperatives. Well over 11 million people have shares in these cooperatives.

Mortgage banks are private real-estate credit institutions which give mortgages and local-authority loans and raise the necessary funds by issuing mortgage and local-authority bonds. Buildings societies accept the savings deposits of people who want to build or buy their own homes and give them loans for this purpose after a proportion of the total sum has been saved. Among the special credit institutions is the Kreditanstalt für Wiederaufbau (Development Loan Corporation). It provides investment loans, lends to developing countries, and helps finance exports.

Symbols of the trade in front of the Frankfurt Stock Exchange

The activities of all credit institutions in Germany are supervised by the Bundesaufsichtsamt für das Kreditwesen (Federal Banking Supervisory Office) in Berlin. If in spite of this control a credit institution gets into difficulties, so-called "fire brigade funds" of the banking trade compensate for savers' losses.

■ ■ ☐ **Financial markets.** Hardly any other sector of the German economy has grown so vigorously as the financial sector. The assets of Germany's banks increased from DM 3 trillion at the end of 1988 to DM 4.5 trillion at the end of 1992. Whether non-cash payments or savings, stocks and shares or loans - all have increased considerably in the last ten years.

In 1992 Germany's stock exchanges registered the record turnover of DM 4.6 trillion (compared with DM 3.4 trillion the previous year). Two thirds of this amount was accounted for by fixed interest rate securities, one third by shares. The huge demand for funds following the country's unification caused the net sale of domestic

German banknotes

pension securities to increase from DM 219 billion in 1991 to DM 284 billion in 1992.

Securities in Germany are traded on eight exchanges (Berlin, Bremen, Stuttgart, Frankfurt, Hamburg, Hanover and Munich). The Frankfurt exchange, however, is easily the largest and rivals London for third place in the world behind New York and Tokyo.

A new institution founded in 1992 was the "Deutsche Börse AG" in Frankfurt, a holding comprising the Kassen-verein (Clearing House), the Wertpapierdatenzentrale (Securities Data Centre), the Deutsche Terminbörse (DTB, German Futures Exchange) and the Frankfurter Wertpapierbörse (Frankfurt Securities Exchange). The Deutsche Börse AG is today a leading supplier of exchange services in Europe. The DTB especially has expanded considerably since its creation in 1989. In 1992 it handled over 34.8 million contracts, compared with 15.4 million in the previous year.

Frankfurt is also the headquarters of the Bundesbank,

many large banks and hundreds of credit institutions and brokering firms. About 90% of all financial transactions in Germany are managed in this metropolis on the river Main.

■ ■ ■ **Modes of payment.** These days nearly all financial transactions in Germany are handled via accounts. Cash transactions are being ousted by a highly-developed remittance system involving cheques, direct debit, credit cards and electronic payment systems. As late as the 60s some German workers were still receiving their wages in cash. Today nearly every employee has a giro or salary account. In addition, more than 35 million Germans use Eurocheques. Credit cards are becoming increasingly popular. In 1980 some 580,000 people were using them, today the number is about seven million.

Bundesverband Deutscher Banken
(Federation of Commercial Banks)
Mohrenstr. 35-51, 50670 Köln
Deutscher Sparkassen- und Giroverband
(Association of Public Savings and Girobanks)
Simrockstr. 4, 53113 Bonn
Bundesverband der Deutschen Volksbanken und
Raiffeisenbanken e.V.
(Federation of Cooperative Banks)
Heussallee 5, 53113 Bonn

Fairs and exhibitions

Germany's trade fairs have a long tradition. They developed in the early Middle Ages out of markets where people came to trade their wares. They were under the protection of the princes, who granted various towns the right to hold them. Thus the fair in Frankfurt on the Main was first mentioned in the privilege granted by Emperor Frederick II on 11 July 1240. Another from the Emperor Maximilian in 1507 established the Leipzig Fair, which acquired international fame.

In Germany the former comprehensive fair has been superseded by the specialized fair. Germany's importance as a location for international fairs is known throughout the world. At present, 116 of the 150 international specialized fairs are held in Germany. In 1992 they attracted more than 130,000 exhibitors, including 54,000 from abroad, and over nine million visitors. German industry as a whole spends in the region of DM six billion on fairs.

The sites for Germany's fairs are constantly being enlarged. There is considerable investment in new buildings, conversion, and innovative exhibition concepts. The proportion of foreign exhibitors at German fairs has increased steadily and in 1992 was about 41.5%. An expanding range of goods and services stimulates competition and makes for even greater international participation.

■ ■ ■ **Fairs and exhibitions in Germany.** Apart from the major events, some 130 regional and many small fairs take place every year in Germany. The main German venues are Berlin, Düsseldorf, Essen, Frankfurt am Main, Hamburg, Hanover, Cologne, Leipzig, Munich, Nuremberg and Stuttgart. Of special importance is the Hanover Fair, which has been held every spring since 1947. With some 6,000 exhibitors of capital goods and consumer durables in a display area of almost 500,000 square metres, it is the largest fair in the world.

Since 1986 Hanover has also been home to for a separate fair devoted to office, information and communications technology, known as "CEBIT", which in 1992 had 5,600 exhibitors from 45 countries and attracted a record 660,000 visitors. The spring and autumn consumer goods fairs in Frankfurt am Main focus on ceramics, glassware, china, arts and crafts, jewelry and stationery.

Frankfurt is also host to a number of major specialized fairs such as the international automobile show (IAA), the biennial sanitation, heating and air conditioning Fair (ISH), or the "interstoff" (clothing and textiles). And every autumn publishers and booksellers from all over the world meet at the Frankfurt Book Fair.

The 17 international fairs held in the city make it the principal venue in Germany and one of the most frequented fair centres in the world.

Cologne, too, is an important venue for such fairs as "ANUGA" (foodstuffs), "photokina" (photography), an international furniture fair, the "art-cologne" and various others for household goods, hardware, bicycles and motor-cycles. The main events in Berlin are the International Green Week (an agricultural and food exhibition), the International Tourism Exchange, the overseas imports fair known as "Partners for Progress", and the International Audiovisual Fair. In 1992, after a break of 60

Every year Cologne stages the ANUGA, the international food fair

years, the International Aerospace Exhibition (ILA) returned to Berlin.

Major fairs in Düsseldorf are "Drupa" (printing and paper), the "GIFA" (foundries), "INKAMA" (instrumentation and automation), "INTERPAK" (packaging machinery and materials) as well as the fashion fair "IGEDO" which takes place several times a year.

Outstanding events in Munich are the "BAUMA" (construction machinery), the International Light Industries and Handicrafts Fair, and "SYSTEMS" (computers and communictions). This and other fairs for the computer and electronic components industries are attracting increasing attention.

German unification has also merged two quite different types of trade fair: the decentralized, specialized type organized in cooperation with western firms, and the state-controlled type of the former GDR geared to Leipzig's comprehensive fair. Leipzig has in the meantime changed its concept so that now the traditional spring fair consists of several specialized exhibitions. It is banking on its experience in trade with eastern Europe and aims to stimulate economic recovery there. A number of the fairs held in the new states have meanwhile gained in stature and attractiveness.

■ ■ ■ **Fairs and exhibitions abroad.** The growing integration of the world economy makes it increasingly important for German industry to participate in foreign trade fairs in order to promote exports. For this purpose

Leipzig's industrial fair has a long tradition

Special-purpose vehicles at the IAA in Frankfurt/Main

it has information stands, displays goods, designs and models, or runs joint exhibitions with government agencies. In 1992 some 3,500 German firms participated in major fairs abroad with government support.

At regular intervals Germany organizes industrial exhibitions abroad, such as the 1991 "TECHNOGERMA" in Seoul. In 1992 she participated in the World Exhibition in Seville. Germany proposes to host the World Exhibition in Hanover in the year 2000. Its motto will be "Man, nature, technology".

Ausstellungs- und Messeausschuß der Deutschen Wirtschaft (AUMA)
(German Council of Trade Fairs and Exhibitions)
Lindenstrasse 8, 50674 Köln

Transport

A modern industrial society like the Federal Republic of Germany needs an advanced transport system. It gives people mobility, makes it easier for them to choose where to live and work, and also helps to equalize living conditions. Without a well-functioning transport system industry and commerce could not develop the necessary efficiency and flexibility. For a country as heavily dependent on foreign trade as Germany this is particularly important.

The government is confronted with major challenges due to the fact that the European single market launched at the beginning of 1993 and the opening up of Eastern Europe make Germany an even more important hub of trade and transport in the heart of Europe.

■ ■ ■ **"German Unity" transport scheme.** The old federal states have a good transport and communications network and the development of new systems in the eastern states is progressing rapidly. This infrastructure is crucial for the region's economic recovery. It has been estimated that this will require investment running into billions up to the year 2000.

Priority is being given to east-west transport links since they will play a key role in the process of merging the two parts of the country and promoting economic growth in the east. Already in 1991 the government selected 17 major road, waterway and rail projects, known as the "German Unity" transport scheme, which will largely be completed by 2000. It has set aside about DM 13.1 billion for this purpose in 1993.

■ ■ ■ **The Federal Transport Plan.** The first transport plan for the whole of Germany, adopted in June 1993, will cost approximately DM 453 billion. It will involve both the modernization and renewal of the rail, road and waterway networks up to the year 2012. 54% of this investment is earmarked for rail and waterway systems, so this is the first time road communications have received the smaller share.

In extending the federal highways network some 1,000 bypasses will be built. In order to expedite matters the Bundestag enacted a law in 1993 intended to simplify

and thus considerably shorten planning procedures
throughout the country.

■ ■ ■ **Means of transport.** Private cars are easily the
most popular means of transport in Germany. In 1992
buses and local railway systems accounted for 84 billion
passenger kilometres, the railways 63 billion and aircraft
18 billion. In the field of freight transport, trucks led the
way with 203 billion ton kilometres, followed by the railways (81) and inland shipping (55).

■ ■ ■ **Deutsche Bundesbahn and Deutsche Reichsbahn.** In February 1993 the cabinet adopted railway reform bills which focus on converting the two hitherto
public railway systems, Deutsche Bundesbahn (DB) and
Deutsche Reichsbahn (RB), into a private corporation as
from the beginning of 1994. The government hopes that
this structural reform will enable the railways to play bigger part in the growth of transport systems with only a
limited burden on the treasury.

Since they are a very environment-friendly means of
transport the railways will remain indispensable for the
movement of bulk goods and passengers. Modernizing
the railway network in the new states alone will cost
some 40 billion marks.

In 1991 the western DB introduced its first high-speed
services. The new ICE trains can travel at up to 250 kmh.
Other high-speed rail services are planned. The new
routes between Hanover and Würzburg and between
Mannheim and Stuttgart make the railways even more attractive, especially for businessmen.

The aim is to offer an attractive alternative to air and
car travel over distances of up to 500 km. DB was
operating Intercity expresses as early s 1971. Since 1991
more than 630 highly efficient long-distance trains have
been operating daily between more than 250 cities.

The railways perform an important function in providing local transport in densely populated industrial areas.
Attractive services are being introduced to induce motorists to switch over to public transport. This would also
help ease the burden on the environment.

Over the years billions have been spent on modernizing fast metropolitan railway networks (S-Bahn) in Berlin
and Hamburg, in the Ruhr district, Frankfurt am Main,
Cologne, Nuremberg, Stuttgart and Munich. They have
been linked with underground, trams and bus systems to

The ICE - progress in rail transport

Looking onto the Avus expressway from Berlin's radio tower

form "transport grids" in nearly all densely populated areas. Passengers may switch from one system to the other using the same ticket. However, local public transport is still a declining percentage of transport overall.

State governments and town councils are trying to reverse this trend, especially as the centres of large towns are becoming increasingly congested by cars.

■ ■ ■ **Roads.** There are more cars on Germany's roads than ever. In 1992 there were approximately 45 million registered vehicles, including 39 million cars (1950, in the old Federal Republic, only 1.9 million, 1986 approx. 31.7 million).

The network of trunk roads has a total length of 226,000 km (1992), including more than 11,000 km of autobahns (motorways). In size, therefore, it is second only to that of the United States. Leaving aside the situation in the new federal states, the main concern at present is not so much to build new roads as to remove bottlenecks and accident black spots, and to provide more links with regions with little transport infrastructure.

On nearly all of Germany's roads there is a graduated speed limit. On national highways, for instance, it is usually 100 kmh, in built-up areas 50 kmh and in some cases only 30 kmh. Only parts of the autobahns have no speed limit, except for certain types of heavy vehicles (trucks, coaches, etc.).

To many people the car remains an indispensable means of getting to and from work and of enjoying leisure-time pursuits. Rapid goods transport from door to door would not be possible without the use of trucks. The motor vehicle will therefore remain one of the principal means of transport.

In some areas, however, road and rail transport do not compete but rather complement each other. One example of this is the "pick-a-back" system by which trucks are transported over long distances on special railway wagons. In container traffic, too, in which the railways are an important link in the transport chain, road and rail work together. This also applies to car-carrying trains.

Although the motor-car means a lot to the individual in terms of mobility and quality of life, it also has its negative aspects. Together with industry and private households, cars are one of the main sources of air pollution.

For several years now buyers of low-pollution cars have enjoyed tax concessions.

Road safety is constantly being improved, mainly through modern roads, traffic education in schools, the advance of traffic technology and the construction of increasingly safer cars. In spite of increasing mobility and traffic density in the west, the number of road fatalities in 1992 was the lowest on record. In the east, too, the negative trend has been broken, but improving road safety remains a permanent task.

The most popular means of local transport is the bike

■ ■ ■ **Shipping.** As a large exporting and importing country, Germany has a merchant fleet of her own. In 1992 it comprised 916 vessels with a gross registered tonnage of 5.10 million and is one of the most modern and safest in the world. Two thirds of the ships are at the most ten years old. Germany is one of the leaders in the field of container and roll-on, roll-off traffic.

Her seaports (the largest being Hamburg, Bremen/Bremerhaven, Wilhelmshaven, Lübeck and Rostock) have been able to hold their own in international competition. Although foreign North Sea ports such as Rotterdam are closer to the industrial centres of Western Europe, the German ports have made up for this disadvantage by investing heavily in infrastructure and port facilities. They are now "fast ports" which can turn even large vessels around in a short time. The Baltic Sea ports in Mecklenburg-Western Pomerania expect to benefit from increased traffic with eastern Europe.

■ ■ ■ **Inland shipping** has an efficient waterways network at its disposal in the west. Duisburg has the largest inland port in the world. The main international artery is the Rhine, which accounts for two thirds of goods transported by inland waterway. Some 3,900

The intersection of the Weser and the Mittellandkanal

freight vessels ply the country's rivers and canals, which have a total length of 6,900 km. This network has been enlarged by the completion of the Main-Danube Canal, which has provided the missing link between the Rhine and the Danube. The main task in coming years will be to enlarge eastern Germany's waterways, which have remained largely unaltered since pre-war days.

■ ■ **Air transport.** The strong growth of interna-

Frankfurt Airport

tional air traffic is making heavy demands on Germany's airports and air traffic control systems. In 1992, more than 88 million passengers were registered at Germany's airports, plus nearly 1.5 million tonnes of air freight. The largest airport is Frankfurt am Main; indeed it is one of the principal airports in Europe. Other German airports are Berlin-Tegel, Berlin-Schönefeld, Bremen, Cologne/Bonn, Dresden, Düseldorf, Erfurt, Hamburg, Hanover, Leipzig, Munich, Nuremberg, Saarbrücken and Stuttgart. Berlin's airports in particular are to be enlarged. Deutsche Lufthansa is one of the leading international airlines. In 1992 it carried about 26.9 million passengers using a fleet of about 220 airliners. Every year over 15 million holidaymakers fly by Condor, LTU, Hapag-Lloyd, Aero-Lloyd, Germania and other smaller companies. Some 100 international airlines maintain regular flights to German airports, from where there are direct flights to roughly 200 destinations in more than 90 countries.

German airports are operated as private companies but are under public control. Since 1993 air traffic control has been the responsibility of the Deutsche Flugsicherungs GmbH (German Air Traffic Control Co.). Airport and air safety standards are constantly updated in order to cope with the heavy congestion in Germany's airspace.

■ ■ ■ **Prospects.** Experts predict a continuing growth of transport in Germany. They say, for instance, that passenger transport on the roads will increase by about 30% by the year 2010, rail traffic by roughly 40%, while air traffic might even double. As regards freight traffic, the increases will be even greater. Road haulage, for instance, is expected to grow by 95%, rail freight and waterway traffic each by 55%. All the more important to make transport systems as environment-friendly and as safe as possible and to make the best possible use of their capacities by using state-of-the- art information and communications systems.

Posts and telecommunications

In 1490 the first teams of horsemen were relaying mail between Innsbruck in Austria and Mechelen in what is now Belgium. That was the birth of the postal service in Germany. The 500th anniversary of that event was celebrated in 1990. Almost at the same time, the postal and telecommunications system in Germany was completely reorganized. Three services formerly controlled by the Federal Ministry of Posts and Telecommunications were transferred to three newly formed public enterprises:
- Deutsche Bundespost POSTDIENST (postal services)
- Deutsche Bundespost POSTBANK (banking services)
- Deutsche Bundespost TELEKOM (telecommunications).

A central administration, the Bundespost, was retained for the 700,000 workforce, but the three new undertakings have a certain amount of independence and much greater entrepreneurial scope. None the less, privatization is under way. In a second reform phase TELEKOM, POSTDIENST and POSTBANK are to be converted into corporations, and TELEKOM shares will be traded on the stock exchange as from 1996.

The public interest in the entire sector of postal and telecommunications will still be safeguarded by the federal ministry. Legislation introduced on the basis of a constitutional amendment as well as government policy ensure that postal services will continue to serve the community as a whole. The ministry's main task will be to provide the legal and technical framework for the entire postal and telecommunications market. The three undertakings are being operated alongside private companies in accordance with business principles in order to provide efficient postal, banking and telecommunication services for the public. The system has been restructured in order to keep postal services competitive in a fast-growing European market. This applies especially to telecommunications, where new technology is being introduced at ever shorter intervals and services have to cater for customer demand.

■ ■ ▧ **TELEKOM.** This enterprise builds and operates all telecommunication facilities for the exchange of news and data. It includes the mobile and stationary telephone network and global satellite communications. Whereas the telephone network as such is under the sole responsibility of TELEKOM, the latter has to compete with private firms in the field of mobile and satellite communications and as regards the sale of equipment and systems to subscribers. Thus the consumer has a wide choice, from the various types of telephone via mobile means of communication to satellite data communications.

All telephone calls in Germany can be dialled by the subscriber direct. This also applies to telephone calls made to 215 countries. A rapidly growing service is telefax. In 1992 some 1.1 million fax machines were in operation, and the number is increasing at the rate of 20,000 a month. TELEKOM's telex network, with 70,000 terminals, gives increasing prominence to new text and data services (about 105,000 terminals). A fibre-optics network for video conferences, picture telephone and high-speed data transmission is being rapidly extended. In 1994 500,000 households are to be linked up to the system in the new states alone.

Cable television has become the second largest telecommunications service. So far about 63% of households in the east and a good 59% in the west can now receive public and private cable television and radio programmes. In 1991 about nine million households were connected to the cable network. TELEKOM is faced with the huge task of replacing the obsolete telephone net-

Leipzig: connecting up to modern telecommunications network

work in the former GDR. In 1990 and 1991 large sections of a completely new digital overlay network were installed and put into operation. The network uses fibre optics, relay systems and state-of-the-art digitalized switching technology. It links the telecommunication centres in the new states among themselves and with the old states in the west. By the end of 1992 1.3 million new connections had been installed in the new states, and 850,000 more in 1993. The total number of terminals in Germany in 1992 was 35 million. They carry about 45 billion telephone calls a year.

Card telephones are supplanting the coin variety

Telephone cards were introduced in 1989. This non-cash means of telephoning is becoming increasingly popular and, like postage stamps, is coveted by collectors.

■ ■ ■ **POSTDIENST.**

With a staff of about 380,000 the POSTDIENST of the German Bundespost is one of the largest service enterprises in Europe. It is required to carry letters and freight at a standard price for all. This service is extremely cost-intensive. At present the POSTDIENST depends on grants from TELEKOM and hopes to be showing a profit by about 1996. It meets private competition partly by means of international cooperative agreements and intends to introduce a completely new freight plan in order to compete its private sector rivals for parcel services.

As regards letter services, the POSTDIENST aims to ensure that 90 out of every 100 letters mailed reach their destination the next day.

The unification of Germany confronted the postal services with the historic task of introducing a new postal code system for the whole country. The new system became effective on 1 July 1993, so now there is no postal division into east and west. Previously there had been two separate systems, each using four digits, which meant that about 800 towns in east and west had the same code numbers. The new system has five digits and makes for quicker delivery.

■ ■ ■ **POSTBANK.** The German POSTBANK maintains a comprehensive banking service even though it is not permitted, on legal grounds, to offer credit or investment services. None the less, nearly a third of the population have a post office savings account. Money can be paid in or withdrawn at any post office counter. There is also a POSTBANK giro service which is used for a great many non-cash payments.

The POSTBANK is trying to attract new customers by improving and extending its services. Since 1991, for instance, it has been possible to use a POSTBANK card to obtain money from all post offices and cash dispensers. The POSTBANK also intends to join the market for fixed-term deposits, federal treasury bonds and life assurance savings. The POSTBANK is already Germany's largest institution specializing in deposits and payments, managing more than five million post office giro accounts and nearly 24 million savings accounts.

Federal Post Office in figures (1992)

	Postdienst	Telekom	Postbank
Staff	390,000	256,000	23,000
Letters	15,56 bn. p. a.		
Goods consignments	640,0 m. p. a.		
Telephone connections		33.6 m.	
Radio telephones		0.5 m.	
Telefax		0.3 m.	
Cable connections		7.9 m.	
Postal savings accounts			24 m.
Postal giro accounts			5 m.

Germany for the tourist

Germany has a remarkable variety of beautiful towns and landscapes in a comparatively small area. The Federal Republic is also popular with the Germans themselves, as shown by the fact that nearly half of them spend their holidays in their own country. Only 12% of overnight stays are by foreigners (for comparison, in Austria the number is over two thirds). Nevertheless, those foreign visitors spent about DM 17 billion in 1992.

■ ■ ■ **German attractions.** For centuries the German-speaking regions of Europe were a loose association of many sovereign states with lots of small and large "residencies" or capitals. Nearly all of them had a long and individualistic cultural tradition, as shown by the numerous cathedrals, palaces, castles, libraries, museums, art collections, gardens and theatres all over the country which are ever popular with art connoisseurs and art lovers.

But visitors are also attracted by the variety of the landscape. In the north they are drawn by the coasts and islands and the sea climate. Tourists also flock to the lakeland areas in Holstein and Mecklenburg, to the Central Uplands and the Alps for hiking, or to Lake Constance and the Bavarian lakes in the south for water sports. Those looking for romantic scenery choose the Rhine, Main, Moselle, Neckar, Danube and Elbe valleys.

There are nearly 90 "tourist routes" which take visitors away from the major traffic arteries, such as the "Fairy Tale Route" or the "German Wine Route" opening up the country's traditional landscapes and providing access to a great variety of attractions in idyllic old towns and villages. They lead through regions with breath-taking scenery. The best known among them is the "Romantic Route", which brings to life the Middle Ages, especially in Rothenburg ob der Tauber, Dinkelsbühl and Nördlingen.

The tourist picks up the tracks of the country's long history even in places that are not mentioned in travel guides. In Bavaria he is enveloped by the gaiety of baroque architecture, in the north he encounters the severity of brick gothic buildings. In some places time ap-

The Lautersee near Mittenwald with the alpine backdrop

pears to have stood still. The visitor can expect hospitality and the famous "Gemütlichkeit", a word that is difficult to translate but expresses the idea of warmth and friendliness, the "good feeling". There are plenty of opportunities to meet local people at the countless regional and town fairs and traditional festivals.

■ ■ ■ **Food and wine.** Cuisine and accommodation are of a a high standard, ranging from cheap rooms on a farm or at a guesthouse to the luxury holiday parks and top-class international hotels. Tourist services are still underdeveloped in some parts of the new federal states but the problems are gradually being solved.

In the restaurant trade experts now speak of the new "German culinary miracle". Contrary to the popular belief, German cuisine does not consist solely of knuckle of pork and sauerkraut. For the gourmet there are increasingly more restaurants which compare with their French or Italian rivals. This is borne out by the ratings to be found in the leading international restaurant guides. There is also a wide range of regional specialities. German wines have an excellent reputation, and the fact that the Germans know a thing or two about beer brewing hardly needs mentioning.

The Germans themselves also appreciate foreign food

"Little Venice": row of houses along the Regnitz in Bamberg

The lighthouse on the Baltic Sea island of Hiddensee

and the visitor will find Italian or Chinese restaurants, to name only a few, in even small towns and villages.

■ ■ ■ **Tourist routes.** Apart from the excellent autobahns there is also a dense network of national highways and local roads. Long-distance rail travel is provided by comfortable trains, all of which have a dining car, and most of the night trains also have a sleeping car. Those who wish can also reserve a seat on car trains. All through the year the Federal Railways offer cheap city tours and other special offers for young people, the elderly and organized groups. In September 1992 they introduced a cheap "rail card" which can be used on all routes for a whole year to obtain tickets at half price.

For ramblers there are routes of all lengths to choose from, but Germany is also easily accessible to the cyclist. The formalities for foreign visitors are straight-forward. Citizens of many countries can enter Germany as tourists for up to three months without a visa. And there are no restrictions on the amount of foreign exchange which may be brought into or taken out of the country.

■ ■ ■ **Protecting the environment.** Like everywhere else in the world, mass tourism is proving harmful to the environment in some regions. One need only mention the burden of traffic, urban sprawl caused by colonies of holiday chalets, or air and water pollution. The government has been taking stronger measures to contain ecological damage. Resorts are increasingly encouraging the kind of tourism that is less of a burden on the environment. For instance, they are trying to halt the spread of tourist facilities and hotels in country areas.

■ ■ ■ **The German Central Tourist Board.** Apart from the commercial travel operators there is the German Central Tourist Board (DZT). The DZT is a member of international organizations such as the European Travel Commission. It publishes a wide range of information brochures about the Federal Republic in many languages

Deutsche Zentrale für Tourismus
(German Central Tourist Board)
Beethovenstrasse 69, 60325 Frankfurt am Main
Deutscher Fremdenverkehrsverband e.V.
(Tourist Industry Association)
Niebuhrstrasse 16 b, 53113 Bonn

Structures of the social market economy

· Industrial relations · Codetermination
· Social security · Health

Industrial relations

The great majority of the 35.5 million workforce (29.7 mill. in the old, 7.8 mill. in the new, states) are wage and salary earners, i.e. employees, civil servants and trainees or apprentices. In addition there are about 3 million self-employed, most of whom also have others on the pay-roll, apart from to 600,000 helping family members. Employers include private companies, federal, state and local government authorities, and other public institutions. Employers and employees cooperate with each other, as they must, but their interests sometimes clash. They then have the right to negotiate collective agreements without interference from the government. The state sets the general conditions by legislation but it does not lay down how much workers should be paid. This and many other matters - for example holidays - is left to the "social partners", i.e. the trade unions and employers' associations, to negotiate themselves.

■ ■ ■ **Trade unions.** The biggest labour organization is the Deutscher Gewerkschaftsbund, DGB (German Trade Union Federation) with about 11 million members in 16 unions (as at end 1992). DGB unions are based on the principle of "one union, one industry", that is to say they enroll workers of an entire industry regardless of the kind of work they do. Thus a chauffeur and a bookkeeper working in a printing plant would be in the same Printing and Paper Workers' Union (IG Druck und Papier).

Apart from the DGB there are a number of other trade union rganizations. Only the three largest are named here. The Deutsche Angestellten-Gewerkschaft, DAG (German Union of Salaried Employees) with around 578,000 members. Its members are salaried staff from practically all sectos of the economy. The Deutscher Beamtenbund, DBB (German Civil Servants' Federation), with about a million members, is the main organization of permanent civil servants which, on account of civil service law, is not involved in collective bargaining and cannot call members out on strike. Otherwise it has all the characteristics of a trade union and has considerable influence. There is also the Christlicher Gewerkschaftsbund Deutschlands, CGB (Christian Trade Union Federation of Germany) which, with its affiliated unions, numbers 316,000 members.

The German trade unions are not connected with any particular party or church. No one can be forced to join a union. The closed shop system (which, according to agreements between employers and unions, allows only union members to be employed) is alien to Germany. The degree of unionization, i.e. the proportion of workers who are members of unions in certain industries, varies greatly but averages less than 50%. The unions maintain many colleges and training centres for their members. The DGB sponsors the annual "Ruhrfestspiele" arts festival at Recklinghausen, and awards a cultural prize of considerable standing.

■ ■ ■ **Employers' associations.** The central organization of the many employers' associations is the Bundesvereinigung der Deutschen Arbeitgeberverbände, BDA (Confederation of German Employers' Associations). The BDA covers all branches of business - industry, crafts, commerce, banking, insurance, agriculture and transport.

About 90% of entrepreneurs are members of an association - a much larger proportion than in the case of

The member unions of the DGB (21 Dec. 1992)

Industrial unions/ trade unions	Members (in thousands)	Share in DGB (%)
Non - metallic minerals	695.7	6.3
Mining and energy	457.2	4.2
Chemicals - paper - ceramics	818.8	7.4
Railway	474.5	4.3
Educations and science	346.0	3.1
Gartening, acriculture and forestry	120.2	1.1
Trade, banks and insurance	629.7	5.7
Wood and plastics	204.8	1.9
Leather	31.9	0.3
Media	236.3	2.1
Metalworkers	3,394.3	30.8
Food, drink and tobacco - gastronomy	394.7	3.6
Police	197.5	1.8
Postal	611.2	5.6
Textiles - clothing	288.2	2.6
Public sector, transportation and traffic	2,114.5	19.2
German Trade Union Federation	11,015.5	100

employees. The BDA represents them only in their role as employers, i.e. as negotiating partners of the trade unions. It does not sign pay agreements itself. All other interests - e.g. taxation or economic policy - are taken care of by other business organizations, such as the Bundesverband der Deutschen Industrie, BDI (Federation of German Industries), the Zentralverband des Deutschen Handwerks (Central Association of German Crafts and Trades) and the Bundesverband des Deutschen Gross- und Aussenhandels (Federation of German Wholesalers and Exporters).

■ ■ ▨ **Collective agreements.** A distinction is made between two types of collective agreement. The wage or salary agreement regulates pay and in most cases is agreed for a year at a time. The framework or general agreement regulates conditions of employment such as working hours, holidays, minimum notice, overtime rates, bonuses, etc., and often runs for several years. But there are often agreements for special types of work. Labour and management can negotiate freely provided they meet certain minimum requirements prescribed by law. In actual fact, however, most collective agreements go far beyond these. For instance, although the statutory maximum weekly number of working hours is still 48, practically all Germans work less than 40 hours a week, some only 35. Similarly, nearly all workers have a contractually guaranteed paid holiday of six weeks or more

Changing shifts in a large car factory

Steelworkers demonstrating in Bonn's Hofgarten

while the law prescribes a minimum of 18 days. More-over, nearly all workers receive additional holiday money and a Christmas bonus on the basis of collective agreements. In many cases actual wages, salaries and other payments are considerably above agreed rates.

■ ■ ■ **Industrial action.** In Germany industrial action may only be taken in connection with collective wage agreements. It is therefore restricted to the parties to those agreements. A strike may not be called on matters covered by agreements still in force.

For these and other reasons industrial action has al-ways been moderate compared with other industrial countries. Furthermore, in many cases provision has been made for arbitration if the two sides cannot agree. Under the rules of most unions the members have to be balloted. Only if a qualified majority are in favour may a strike be called.

The workers' right to strike is counterbalanced by the employers' right to lock them out. Within certain limits, lockouts have been upheld by the Federal Labour Court and the Federal Constitutional Court, but the issue is still controversial. As the state remains neutral in labour dis-putes, neither strikers nor locked-out workers receive unemployment benefit. Union members receive strike pay for loss of earnings, but non-members get nothing. During a strike they must either live on their savings or apply for national assistance.

■ ■ ■ **Cooperation.** Workers and entrepreneurs are not in opposition to one another all the time, however. They also cooperate in many ways. This is most apparent on the shop floor, but the representatives of both sides' organizations also meet on many other occasions, for example on apprentice examination committees. In the labour courts which rule on employment disputes there are lay judges at all levels from both sides. And the leaders of various organizations meet frequently when politicians seek their views. These and other forms of co-operation help to foster mutual understanding without blurring the differences between their respective interests.

Codetermination

In the 19th century Germany changed from an agricultural into an industrial society with considerable social upheaval. The rapidly growing new class of industrial workers initially lived in abject misery, almost totally without protection or rights. The nascent labour movement formed its own organizations which enabled the workers gradually to improve their situation and their social security, though sometimes only after a tenacious struggle.

But the workers continued to be totally dependent on their companies until well into the 20th century. The power of the owners was almost limitless. Today labour rights in Germany are protected by works constitution and codetermination laws.

■ ■ ■ **Works constitution.** The Works Constitution Act of 1952 governs industrial relations at the workplace. This applies to social welfare and personnel matters, but especially the right of employees, works councils and unions to have a say in practically all areas of company decision-making.

■ ■ ■ **Rights of individual workers.** Employees have specifically defined rights. They include the right to be informed and to express opinions on matters relating directly to their job. For instance, they can ask to be informed about the effects of new technology on their work, inspect their personal file, and ask for explanations of assessments of their performance or their payslip.

■ ■ ■ **The works council.** The works council represents employees in relation to their employers. A works council may be elected in all private companies employing at least five people. Employees under 18 as well as apprentices under 25 may elect representatives of their own. All can vote from the age of 18, but only those who have worked for the firm for at least six months are eligible for election to the council. This also includes periods in another branch of the same company. Foreigners, too, are entitled to vote and hold office. Members of the works council normally perform their duties in addition to their normal work. Large firms, however, must release one or several members of the works council from their jobs to do council work full-time. In a single company a general works council may be established, at group level a group works council. In government authorities at all levels and other public institutions the equivalent employees' organization is the staff council, which is elected in accordance with the Staff Representation Act.

Managerial personnel are not represented by the works council. They include, for instance, a firm's fully authorized officer or comparable staff in senior positions. In firms with at least ten managerial staff a committee of spokesmen may be elected.

As in the case of a works council, such spokesmen's committees may also be formed at company and group level but only if on the first ballot the majority of the managerial staff are in favour.

■ ■ ■ **Responsibilities and composition of the works council.** The works council must, among other things, ensure that the laws and regulations, accident prevention rules, collective wage agreements and company arrangements applying to employees are observed. It must arrange a shop-floor meeting every three months and report on its activities. Employees attending the meeting may comment on the council's decisions and make proposals of their own.

The composition of the works council depends on the size and nature of the workforce. Thus in a company with 5 to 20 voting employees it consists of one person, in companies with 21 to 50 three, and in companies with between 51 and 150 employees it has five members. The larger the company, the larger the works council.

Where a corporation has several works councils a general works council has to be elected. The same applies to the representative committees of young employees and apprentices.

In companies with more than 100 employees an economic affairs committee must be formed. It is a consultative body whose members are nominated by the works council.

If the works council has at least three members the firm's workers and salaried employees must be represented in proportion to their numerical strength. If it has nine or more members it forms a works council committee which handles day-to-day business. On certain

Codetermination at work creates a good climate

conditions union representatives may also attend council meetings.

Codetermination rights cover such matters as company organization, working hours, including the introduction of short time or overtime, holidays, social
facilities confined to the department, company or group,
technical monitoring of conduct or performance,
accident prevention rules, occupational diseases and
health protection regulations, allocation of company-
owned housing or termination of tenancy, as well as
pay structures, piecework payment and bonus schemes,
etc.

The works council also has a considerable say in job
descriptions, work processes and the working environment, personnel planning and vocational training.
Where a company proposes to introduce changes (e.g.
to reduce operations, close down or move to a different
location) the works council may under certain conditions draw up a "social plan" which cushions the economic effects on those affected.

On all matters concerning personnel, such as appointments, classifications and transfers, the employer must
obtain the approval of the works council. This it may refuse to give in certain circumstances governed by law. If

the employer intends to carry out the proposed measures nevertheless he must seek a decision from the labour court.

The employer must also consult the works council before any dismissal. If he fails to do so the dismissal has no effect. Where a person is to be properly dismissed the works council may lodge a protest. In this case the employer must continue to employ the person dismissed at his request if the works council has objected on grounds covered by law and the employee has taken the matter to the labour court. The employer must await the court's decision. In such proceedings a justified complaint by the works council considerably strengthens the employee's position.

The Works Constitution Act and the rules governing elections to works councils also apply in the new federal states. The same holds true for the Spokesmen's Committee Act, which covers the codetermination rights of managerial staff.

■ ■ ■ **Codetermination.** Worker participation in company affairs is one of the mainstays of the social system. It is based on the conviction that democratic legitimation cannot be confined to government but must apply in all sectors of society.

Nearly every company decision has an effect on its employees, irrespective of whether it concerns marketing, product development, investment, rationalization, etc. Hence employees should have a say in company decision-making through their representatives.

The willingness of employees to assume a share of responsibility through their unions has been an important social factor in the Federal Republic's old states. The workforce in medium-sized or large companies (corporations, joint-stock companies, partnerships limited by shares, cooperatives or friendly insurance companies) can influence company policy through their representatives on the supervisory boards. This codetermination is not confined to social affairs but extends to all company activities.

Thus the supervisory board may, for instance, appoint and dismiss the management (board of directors), demand information on all company matters, and have the last word on major decisions, e.g. with regard to investment or rationalization measures.

Codetermination in large mining and steel companies is governed by legislation enacted in 1951 and 1956. Worker participation in the running of large firms in other branches is covered by the Codetermination Act of 1976. Germany's four codetermination laws have been applicable in the new federal states as well since 1 July 1990.

■ ■ ■ **Codetermination in large enterprises.** Enterprises other than mining and steel companies which either alone or together with their subsidiaries have a workforce of more than 2,000 are governed by the 1976 act, which requires the supervisory board to be made up of equal numbers of representatives of shareholders and employees.

However, the shareholders have a slight advantage in the event of a stalemate in that the chairman of the board, who is always a representative of the shareholders, has a second, casting vote. In the appointment of a labour director the employees' representatives have no veto.

■ ■ ■ **Composition of the supervisory board.** The supervisory board consists of equal numbers of shareholder and labour representatives. In enterprises with a workforce of up to 10,000 the board has 12 members (i.e. 6:6), and this increases to 16 (workforce 10,000-20,000) or 20 (workforce over 20,000).

The firm's articles may provide that the minimum board size as prescribed by law, i.e. 12 members, be increased to 16 or 20 members, and one consisting of 16 increased to 20. Some of the labour seats on the supervisory board are allocated to union representatives (two in the case of a 12- or 16-member board, three in the case of a 20-member board).

■ ■ ■ **Election of labour representatives on the supervisory board.** All labour members on the supervisory board, i.e. those on the company's payroll and the union representatives, are elected by direct ballot or by delegates.

In companies with up to 8,000 employees the law prescribes a ballot, but employees may, with a majority vote, opt to be represented by delegates.

In the case of enterprises with a workforce of more than 8,000 the law prescribes elections through delegates. The employees may, however, reverse this procedure, that is to say they can choose by a majority vote to have a direct ballot.

■ ■ ■ **Election of shareholder representatives.** Shareholder representatives on the supervisory board are elected at the company's annual meeting.

■ ■ ■ **Election of the chairman.** The members of the supervisory board elect the chairman and vice-chairman at their constituent meeting. A two-thirds majority is required. Failing this a second vote is taken in which the shareholder representatives elect the chairman and the labour representatives the vice-chairman.

■ ■ ■ **The board of directors.** The supervisory board appoints and dismisses members of the board of directors. Here too a two-thirds majority is necessary, otherwise a mediation committee is appointed. Should this too fail to produce an absolute majority a second ballot is taken in which the chairman of the supervisory board has a casting vote.

A labour director with equal rights is chosen according to the same procedure. The labour director is chiefly concerned with personnel and social affairs.

■ ■ ■ **Codetermination in the coal and steel industry.** Codetermination in the coal and steel industry is the oldest and most extensive form of worker participation. It applies to companies with a workforce of more than 1,000.

■ ■ ■ **The supervisory board.** The supervisory board consists of an equal number of shareholder and workers' representatives and a "neutral" member.

In firms covered by the Codetermination Act the board consists of 11 members (in larger companies it may be increased to 15 or 21).

Two of the five labour representatives must work for the company, and three must be proposed by the unions represented in the company (i.e. external members). All workers' representatives are first selected by the works council and proposed for election at the general meeting. The election is only a formality since the meeting cannot reject the nominees. The supervisory board then proposes a neutral member, the eleventh, who, in the event of a stalemate, has the casting vote.

■ ■ ■ **Board of directors, labour director.** The members of the board of directors are appointed and dismissed by the supervisory board. One of the members

Voting by show of hands at a works council meeting

must be a labour director who cannot be appointed or dismissed against the wish of the majority of workers' representatives on the supervisory board. Thus labour directors are in a way the exponents of codetermination at management level.

■ ■ ■ **Codetermination in small enterprises.** In companies with 500-2,000 employees a third of the members of the supervisory board must be representatives of the workforce. Although they have hardly any say in decision-making they do have access to important information.

Deutscher Gewerkschaftsbund
(German Trade Union Federation)
Hans-Böckler-Strasse 39 40476 Düsseldorf
Deutsche Angestelltengewerkschaft
(German Union of Salaried Employees)
Karl-Muck-Platz 1 20355 Hamburg
Deutscher Beamtenbund

(German Civil Servants' Federation)
Dreizehnmorgenweg 36 53179 Bonn
Christlicher Gewerkschaftsbund Deutschlands
(Christian Trade Union Federation)
Konstantinstrasse 13 53179 Bonn

Bundesvereinigung der Deutschen Arbeitgeberverbände
(Confederation of German Employers' Associations)
Gustav-Heinemann-Ufer 72 50968 Köln

Social security

Germany's social security system has a long history and its efficiency is legend. Social benefits and services account for nearly 30% of the gross national product and in 1992 exceeded DM 900 billion. Nearly a third of this was accounted for by pensions insurance and over a fifth by statutory health insurance.

The state thus meets the requirements of article 20 of the constitution (Basic Law), which says that the Federal Republic is a democratic and social federal state. Its purpose is not to meet all the citizen's needs but rather to provide for them on the basis of their entitlements. It does so by enacting extensive legislation on sickness, accident and old-age insurance, as well as child benefit, rent subsidies, unemployment benefits, etc. It also makes provision for social assistance (i.e. minimum living allowances).

■ ■ ■ **The history of social insurance.** Social insurance in Germany dates from the Middle Ages when miners first set up joint funds to support needy colleagues after accidents at work. But it was not until the late 19th century that a comprehensive social insurance scheme emerged. It was triggered by Germany's industrial revolution which had greatly increased the number of industrial workers, who had practically nothing and no protection against illness or accident.

This became a domestic issue and the Reich Chancellor, Otto von Bismarck, introduced progressive social welfare legislation. Although his motives were partly political since he wanted to take the wind out of the sails of a growing labour movement, that legislation is generally recognized as the foundation for a social insurance scheme which also served as a model for other industrial countries.

Laws enacted in 1883, 1884 and 1889 established three branches of insurance which are still the nucleus of the German system: health, accident, invalidity and old age. Pensioners had to be 70 and the maximum annual pension was 190.40 marks. In 1911 these schemes were merged in the still valid Reich Insurance System, which added pensions for widows and orphans. Invalidity and old age insurance was extended to all salaried employees. A separate insurance system was introduced for miners in 1923. Unemployment insurance was established in 1927, and as from 1938 craftsmen, to the extent that they were not privately ensured, were covered by the social insurance scheme.

After the Second World War the system was greatly extended and improved. In 1957, for instance, a statutory old age insurance scheme for farmers was introduced, and in that same year pensions in general were indexed, i.e. adjusted in line with the average increase in incomes. Further reforms were introduced in 1972 and 1992.

Since 1990 the social security system has also benefited pensioners, war victims and physically handicapped persons in the former GDR. The treaties on economic, monetary and social union and on national unification signed in that year provided that all citizens in united Germany should have the same benefits after a transitional period.

■ ■ ■ **Pensions insurance.** The statutory pensions insurance scheme is one of the pillars of the country's social security system. It ensures that workers will not suffer financial need and are able to maintain an adequate standard of living in retirement.

All wage and salary earners are required by law to be in the scheme. Self-employed persons who are not com-

In many occupations physical handicaps are no disavantage

pulsorily insured by virtue of their membership of certain trades can join voluntarily.

Contributions (currently 17.5% of gross earnings) are levied up to a certain income level (at present DM 7,200 monthly). Worker and employer contribute half each. The scheme pays old-age and invalidity pensions. After the death of an insured person the dependants receive a proportion of the pension. There is a „waiting period" for pensions, i.e. a minimum membership of the insurance scheme. As a rule the old-age pension is payable at the age of 65, but under certain conditions it can be drawn at 63 or 60. Women can claim a pension when they are 60.

The size of the pension depends on the amount of insured income from employment. The 1992 reform gave older employees a more flexible choice of retirement age. They can now opt for a part-pension, part-work arrangement. The system has been adjusted in the light of changes in demographic and economic conditions and secures the financial basis of pensions beyond the year 2000.

Social security (1992, in DM bn.)

	3
Education allowances	7
Rent allowances	17
Accident insurance	18
War pensions	21
Child and youth services	30
Child and child-raising allowances	44
Social assistance	71
Civil servants' pensions and allowances	89
Employers' contributions	111
Work promotion, unemployment insurance	111
Health insurance	210
Retirement pensions	291

The main objective was to keep pensions related to incomes and contributions, to maintain living standards, and to enable pensioners, too, to benefit from the country's economic progress. For the great majority of employees the statutory pension is the only old-age security. It must therefore maintain the standard of living they have been accustomed to during the many years when they have paid insurance contributions.

Since the 1957 reform, the average pension in the west after 45 years is about 70% of the average net income. Thus in 1992 it was approximately DM 1850, for women on average DM 1150. And since 1 July 1990 average pensions in the new federal states have been 70% of average incomes in eastern Germany after 45 insured years. Pensions in the new states increase on an annual basis in line with the wages of the working population there. The aim, therefore, is to bring east German pensions up to the level of West German pensions as soon as possible. As from 1 January 1992 pensions legislation applies to the whole of Germany without distinction. Paying pensions is not the only purpose of the pensions insurance scheme. It also helps to maintain a person's capacity for work or to improve or restore that capacity. Thus it covers the cost of curative treatment and provides support for people who have to undergo retraining for health reasons.

■ ■ ■ **Company pensions.** Company pensions are a valuable supplement to the statutory scheme. Many companies provide them on a voluntary basis. Under the Company Pensions Act of 1974, employees retain their claim to a company pension even if they leave before retirement age, provided they are at least 35 years old and their entitlement is ten years old or at least three years if they have worked for the company for 12 years. Even if the employer becomes insolvent the works pension is still not lost. In such cases it is paid out of a fund established for this purpose.

■ ■ ■ **Health insurance.** Nearly everyone has health insurance, whether as compulsory or voluntary members of the statutory health insurance scheme (90%) or through private insurance. Under the state scheme insurance is compulsory for all workers, salaried employees and several other categories up to a certain income level. In some cases voluntary insurance is possible. The state system also covers pensioners, the unemployed, apprentices and students. Employees pay their contributions into their respective health insurance fund (e.g. the district, company or guild fund, the merchant seamen's, miners' or farmers' fund). All insured persons have a free choice of panel doctors and dentists. They pay half of the contributions, their employers the other half. In 1993 the average contribution rate was 13.4% in the west, 12,5% in the east, of the proportion of income on which contributions are based.

The health insurance fund pays the cost of medical and dental treatment, drugs and medicines, etc. as well as hospitalization. It pays all or part of the cost of any necessary curative treatment. There are also maternity, family and home-nursing grants. In the event of sickness employees receive their full wages for up to six weeks, in some cases more. After that period the statutory fund provides sick pay, which amounts to 80% of the regular wage, for up to 78 weeks. The annual cost of health insurance is staggering. Some services and items paid for by the health insurance fund were restricted in 1991 and people are required to meet a larger proportion of the cost and therefore bear more of the responsibility themselves.

■ ■ ■ **Accident insurance.** Protection and support after accidents at work and in the case of occupational diseases is provided by the statutory accident insurance scheme.

In Germany all employees and farmers are insured by law against accident. Other self-employed people can join the insurance scheme voluntarily. Students and school children are also covered.

The main providers of accident insurance are the district professional and trade associations. The funds come from contributions paid only by employers. Claims arise from bodily injury or death resulting from an accident at work or illness or death caused by an occupational disease. Accidents which occur on the way to and from the place of work also fall into this category.

In the event of injury the insurance fund bears the full cost of treatment. Benefits are also paid if the person is unable to work. If he is incapable of earning a living or dies as a result of an accident or occupational disease the insurance pays a pension or death grant and pension for dependents, as the case may be. Like other pensions they are increased in line with general incomes.

Vocational assistance under the accident insurance scheme covers rehabilitation training and help in obtaining employment. The professional and trade associations are also required to issue regulations on prevention of accidents and control of occupational diseases, and to monitor their observance.

■ ■ ■ **Child benefit.** The upbringing and education of children is a considerable financial burden on the family. A Child Benefit Act was passed to help ease that burden. Parents or guardians are paid benefit for each child up to the age of 16, for those at school or undergoing vocational training up to the age of 27. The benefit is DM 70 for the first child, DM 130 for the second, 220 for the third, and DM 240 for each additional one. Parents in the higher income brackets receive less child benefit from the second child onwards.

Parents also enjoy tax relief in the form of an annual child allowance (DM 4,104). Since 1986 a child-raising allowance of DM 600 per month has been paid for the first six months. After that the allowance depends on the parents' income. In addition, mothers or fathers wishing to look after their children themselves can claim up to three years leave from work during which they cannot be dismissed.

■ ■ ■ **War victim's benefits.** The purpose of the war victims' aid scheme is to compensate, at least financially, the war- disabled, servicemen's widows and war orphans. They are paid index-linked pensions. In addition, the war-disabled can receive ther-

An accident victim being rescued

apy and support in starting work and a career. Members of the armed forces who suffer damage to their health and the victims tims of violence, as well as their dependents, are taken care of in the same way.

■ ■ ■ **Social Assistance.** Social assistance is provided for people who cannot help themselves and receive no help from others. Under the law everybody living in Germany - native or foreign - is entitled to social assistance in times of hardship in the form of maintenance grants covering disability, illness or home care. Most of this assistance is provided by the states and local authorities. In 1992 the total cost was DM 42.5 billion. Since 1991 the Social Assistance Act has also been applicable in the new federal states.

Health

The Federal Republic of Germany has a ramified system of health care backed up by appropriate social services. Although health care is basically the individual's own responsibility, it is also the concern of society as a whole. All people, regardless of their financial or social situation, should have the same chance to maintain or restore their health. Health care in Germany is a decentralized, pluralist and self-governing system.

The average life expectancy in the Federal Republic has increased steadily over the past 40 years. It is currently 72 for men and 79 for women. This trend is chiefly the result of medical care. The aim is to increase life expectancy further still by reducing the incidence of „civilization" illnesses.

More attention will therefore be concentrated on preventive medicine, which includes better health education, regular precautionary check-ups, as well as information on healthy living.

The biggest threats to health in Germany, as in all highly developed industrial countries, come from the modern way of life. Half of all deaths are the result of cardiovascular diseases, followed by cancer. Allergies are becoming increasingly prominent, but also conditions typical of old age such as those affecting the central nervous system. The infectious diseases of earlier generations, such as tuberculosis, cholera, diphtheria and pneumonia, are no longer the threat they once were, thanks to modern medicine. But a new big challenge is AIDS.

■ ■ ■ **Doctors and hospitals.** In 1991 there were about 202,000 doctors in Germany's old states, compared with some 42,200 in the new. Medically, therefore, the Germans are among the best cared-for nations in the world. Less than half of the nation's doctors are independent. The others work in hospitals or administration or they are engaged in research. There are about 665,000 beds available in roughly 2,400 hospitals, as well as some 1,200 preventive care or rehabilitation centres.

Hospitals are maintained by the state and local authorities (more than half of the beds), charity (mostly church) organizations (more than 40% of the beds) and private enterprises.

■ ■ ■ **Drugs and medicines.** The safety of medicines receives high priority. The Pharmaceuticals Act stipulates that medicines may be passed on to consumers only after their quality, effectiveness and harmlessness have been tested and confirmed by a government agency. Even after approval they are kept under constant observation so that dangers are quickly recognized and remedial action can be taken.

The act also sets out detailed safety regulations for the production of pharmaceuticals, and it determines which substances may be sold only in pharmacies and which only on a doctor's prescription. Monitoring is the responsibility of the Federal Health Office and the corresponding state agencies.

■ ■ ■ **Preventive health care.** The old saying that prevention is better than cure is assuming increasing importance. Government policy is to encourage everyone to look after their health and by avoiding risks.

Preventive examinations have been introduced in many fields. Various federal and state institutions as well as private non-profit organizations provide information, courses and advice on such matters as

- care during pregnancy, health education for young children
- hazards to health such as alcohol, nicotine and drug abuse, overeating, malnutrition, lack of exercise - the well-known causes of cardiovascular diseases which are also a contributory factor in cancer and other frequent diseases
- programmes to help people who are chronically sick or disabled, and their relatives, to live with their illness or disablement.

Examinations are offered for the early detection of disease, such as those for cancer which were introduced in 1971. The fight against AIDS (acquired immune deficiency syndrome) demands the greatest possible effort. The government, in collaboration with the World Health Organization and the members of the European Community, is carrying out a programme to protect people from HIV infection and at the same time provide comprehensive advice and care for those infected or showing symptoms.

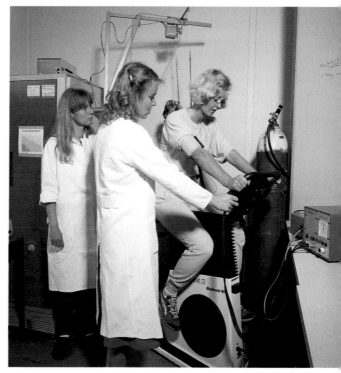

Measuring blood pressure under stress

In this respect it is important not to isolate or discriminate against those affected. Until such time as an effective vaccine and treatment are available, education and advice are the best way of preventing this disease from spreading. This programme encourages and helps those concerned to behave responsibly in order to protect themselves and others.

Sick people and their families often need medical care over and above that provided by the medical profession and hospitals. For them there is comprehensive counselling as well as the opportunity to discuss their problems with people suffering from the same disease. Opportunities of this kind are afforded by numerous self-help groups which today have an established place in the nation's health system. They include:

- Deutsche AIDS-Hilfe (German AIDS Support)
- Deutsche Multiple-Sklerose- Gesellschaft (German Multiple Sclerosis Society)
- Deutsche Rheuma-Liga (German Rheumatism League)
- Frauenselbsthilfe nach Krebs e.V. (Women's Post-Cancer Self-Help Group)
- Angehörigenvereine psychisch Kranker (groups of family members of persons suffering from psychic disorders, e.g. drug-dependent persons)
- Anonyme Alkoholiker (Alcoholics Anonymous).

■ ■ ■ **International activities.** Germany plays an active part in the work of international organizations concerned with health. No country can cope alone with the challenges of modern diseases such as AIDS or the health hazards of environmental pollution. Efforts to combat them, as well as research activities, call for international cooperation. Germany also feels obliged to give the developing countries professional advice and financial assistance in developing their public health system.

As a member of the World Health Organization (WHO) the Federal Republic is represented on several important bodies. Every year it organizes more than 35 international meetings on matters of topical interest in collaboration with WHO.

More than 30 scientific institutions have been named as centres for cooperation with this international organization. The Federal Republic is the fourth largest contributor to WHO. Within the European Community Germany is actively involved in the development of community health policy. One of the EC's main objectives is to maintain high health standards in member countries.

Examples of these joint activities are „Europe Against Cancer", a research programme, the proposed European identity card for emergencies, an action programme involving an exchange of information on detoxification centres, and cooperation on measures to combat AIDS, alcohol abuse and drug addiction. This cooperation will be greatly intensified as the Community assumes responsibility for health within the framework of the European Political Union.

■ ■ ■ **The cost of health care.** After establishing an efficient public health system in the new states the government had to address the difficult and perennial problem of financing health services on a national scale. The re form programme initiated in 1989, and particularly the Health Reform Act which became effective at the beginning of 1993, helped to stabilize expenditure on health services.

Furthermore, the efficiency of the statutory health insurance system, which covers about 90% of the population, has been considerably improved. In 1992 the system cost DM 210 billion - about half of total expenditure on public health.

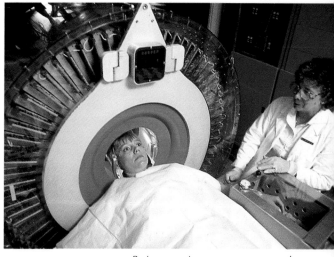

Brain scan using computer tomography

Life in the community

· Woman and society · Youth · Sport
· Leisure and holidays
· Clubs, associations and citizen's action groups
· Churches an religions communications
· Mass media and public opinion
· The press · Radio and television

Woman and society

According to the Basic Law, men and women have equal rights. This constitutional rule is absolutely clear, but in practice it is more a wish than a reality. Now, therefore, the constitutional committee appointed by parliament has decided that another clause should be added to the effect that the government will take steps to ensure equality and seek to remove the disadvantages suffered by women.

Old preconceived notions of what women are and what they are not „entitled to" die hard. Women still do not have the same opportunities as men in society, politics and at work. Many of them are subject to heavy stress through family and work. Nonetheless, their status has gradually improved over the years. And they are in the majority: In Germany there are nearly three million more women than men.

■ ■ ■ **Equality before the law.** The principle of equality has only gradually been applied. In 1957 a law was introduced which gave women equal rights where matrimonial property was concerned. Then in 1977 their position with regard to marriage, divorce and family were improved so that, for instance, the question of guilt in divorce cases no longer applied. Now the only criterion is whether the marriage has irreparably broken down. In addition, divorcees now share pension entitlements.

■ ■ ■ **Women in employment.** In order to give greater effect to the equality principle at work the government has passed another law which covers such matters as the advancement of women in federal authorities by allocating more women to posts in public agencies, banning discrimination of women at work, and prevents sexual harassment at the workplace. Under a 1980 law requiring men and women to be given equal treatment at work, women may no longer be discriminated against on grounds of sex. Other laws protect pregnant women and do not allow them to be given heavy manual work.

There has been a marked improvement in vocational training for girls and women, who can now attend any school or training establishment. Just under half of all who have obtained university entrance qualifications so far in the 90s are women. Over 40% of all students are women. And the number of women who have completed a course of vocational training has increased significantly since the 50s.

Every second woman (55%) between the ages of 15 and 65 is in employment. Women have become indispensable in industry, the health system and education. But there is discrimination: They tend to lose their jobs faster than men and find new ones less quickly, and they are offered fewer apprenticeships. Male employees still receive distinctly higher wages than their female counterparts.

Women who do the same or similar work to that of men can assert their claim to equal pay in court. Discrimination occurs nonetheless in the differing assessments of the types of work. „Women's" work pays less than „men's" work.

In the public service, on the other hand, the law has given women better opportunities for employment and promotion. Discrimination against women at work occurs largely because their working life shows a different pattern. In former times women often went into less demanding trades because they regarded employment merely as an interim occupation before starting a family. But today

A broker on the Frankfurt Stock Exchange

ever more women want to return to work after a period of child-raising. There are government reintegration programmes to help them. Many choose part-time work and this too is promoted by the government on economic and social grounds. At present, however, there are far too few part-time jobs available.

In the new states the situation is different. In the former GDR 90% of the women went out to work and were enabled, with public assistance, to combine work and family chores. As a result of the restructuring process, however, women in those regions are losing their jobs at twice the rate of men.

In addition to the various assistance programmes offered by the federal and state governments and local authorities to cope with these changes, various initiatives have been launched and associations established.

■ ■ ■ **Women and family.** In Germany 8.4 million out of 19.5 million couples have no children in the household or are childless. The birthrate is declining. The number of families with three or more children is decreasing while the number with one or two is growing.

The doctor's assistant, a job much in demand

The government is aware of the importance of Family promotion, as manifest in its legislation providing for child-raising allowances and leave. Where one of the parents stays at home to raise a child the state pays DM 600 a month (for each child) for 18 months. In addition, that parent is entitled to child-raising leave (since 1992 three years). During this period the parent cannot be given notice. Another advantage is that child-raising periods (three years for each child born in 1992 or later) count towards the parent's pension claim. And since 1992 the same applies to time spent taking care of sick family members. This is an important step towards a fair assessment of work in the family compared with gainful activity.

■ ▥ ▥ **Women in politics.** Women have enjoyed the suffrage and the right to stand for election in Germany since 1918. Although the number of politically active women is increasing it is still much smaller than that of men. Some of the political parties have introduced quotas to increase the number of female representatives on executive committees.

There has been at least one women minister in every Federal Government since 1961. In the present administration there are four. There have been two female presidents (speakers) of the Federal Parliament. Now there is also a separate Federal Ministry for Women and Youth which was established in 1991. All regional governments have women ministers or ombudswomen. More than 1,250 municipalities have created „equality posts" specially for women.

The government, in cooperation with its EC partners, champions equal rights for women in various institutions of the United Nations, the European Community and the OECD. Parallel to the statutory measures to establish equality of the sexes, a strong women's movement has developed in Germany. It vehemently opposes discrimination against women. It has emerged outside the existing women's organizations and has been the driving force in setting up centres for battered wives and their children which now number 324 throughout the country.

In legal terms equality has almost been achieved 40 years after this principle was incorporated in Germany's Basic Law. There are no longer laws which discriminate directly against women or prescribe a certain role for

Rita Süßmuth, President of the Bundestag, delivering a speech

them, but in some cases they are still disadvantaged socially, largely on account of the way the working world and society are structured. There is therefore still some leeway to be made up in securing equality.

The „women's lobby" is the Women's Council, the central organization of women's associations. It represents 47 associations with some eleven million members.

Deutscher Frauenrat (German Women's Council)
Simrockstrasse 5, 53113 Bonn

Youth

Nearly one in five inhabitant of the Federal Republic of Germany is under 18 years of age. They number well over 15.5 million and about 10% of them are of foreign nationality. Roughly one third of the total population (over 26 million) are under 27. For the great majority of them opportunities in life and future prospects have increased considerably over the past ten years. This applies to the eastern as well as the western part of the country.

In the west especially most young people are comfortably off in material terms. Their financial prospects have never been better and they are well supplied with consumer goods.

Never before have so many young people travelled as much as they do at present, both at home and abroad. Thus 95% in the west and 83% in the east are satisfied with life. And 72% look confidently into the future, indeed those in the east are even a little more optimistic than their west German counterparts. This confident mood cannot by any means be taken for granted. Only ten years ago nearly 60% of the 15-24 year-old group of west Germans were rather pessimistic about the future.

■ ■ ■ **Different expectations?** For the young generation in the east the collapse of the communist system first meant the end of a dictatorship which had ruled their lives and tried to rule their minds. They perceive the social upheaval and reunification as both an opportunity and a source of confusion. Having been released without preparation from a command society and doctrine that had been imposed from above they understandably have difficulty coming to terms with the wide range of influences and possibilities of a free society.

They are expected to start afresh in nearly all spheres of life. This process of orientation and the problems confronting young people in a pluralistic society in any case adds to the difficulty of this period of transformation. The individuals and groups with whom they identify themselves, as well as the schools, churches and other institutions providing education, have lost much of their credibility and authority.

When asked in the spring of 1993 about the changes that have taken place in Germany's since unification, 71% of young people in the east said the decision to adopt the western political system was the right one. Sixty per cent felt there were now more opportunities for self-fulfilment, 26% saw no change, while only 30% felt that the situation had deteriorated. Taking a realistic view of the problems, the optimists were in the majority.

In spite of the different living standards in east and west, there are hardly any significant differences in the assessment of personal problems or the major political issues in Germany. The biggest personal problems are jobs, training and education. The dominant theme in eastern Germany is unemployment.

■ ■ ■ **The problem of orientation.** As the influence of family, church and neighbourhood has declined, the freedom of young people to take matters into their own hands has increased accordingly. This is indicated by longer periods of study and the widening generation gap due to the fact that young people take their bearings from the standards set by their peers, the growing significance of leisure and consumption, and the effects of the mass media.

But although this increases the pressure to be more in-dependent, 83% of the young people interviewed in western Germany and 89% of those interviewed in the east said that if they had personal problems their first source of help was their parents. This is proof that young people are looking for clear guidance and role models.

Not all young people meet with understanding for their problems at home or in school, of course. In many cases their links with other persons of responsibility or social groups have been weakened, and very often these groups are rejected by isolated young people. In this situation they may easily succumb to modes of beha-viour which pose a danger to them and the community.

It is compounded by the lack of job prospects, which is part of the reason for social and political radicalism that has of late been manipulated and exploited by the leaders of extremist right-wing groups for their criminal objectives.

This problem is by no means confined to the new Ger-man states, although the after-effects of the communist dictatorship and the uncertainty resulting from the social

Light, music and movement: the disco scene

upheaval there have produced particularly volatile chemistry. Attacks by young people on foreigners, especially in the east, have highlighted the situation of the people there. Whereas the culprits from the extreme right are being pursued with the full force of the law, the government are trying to identify the causes.

■ ■ ■ **Youth violence and animosity towards foreigners.** Recent xenophobic violence in Germany has alarmed and mobilized the public at large and caused outrage and justified criticism abroad. Most of those who have been called to account are young people.

First there was much speculation about the social and psychological reasons for this spate of violence, but the first substantial results were published in a 1993 study commissioned by the Federal Ministry for Women and Youth. It reveals that over 70% of the perpetrators are between 15 and 20 and only 5% older than 30. The great majority are male (only 4% female) and of low educational standard. 18% of them are unemployed, well above the average.

The unemployed percentage of suspects in eastern Germany is 20%, significantly higher than the 12% in the west. The proportion of those suspected of being members of right-wing extremist groups is also significantly higher in the east (37%) than in the west (19%). Again, the 64% of offences against foreigners that are the result of mass activities is also much larger than in the west

(21%), where there is a larger incidence of offences by groups of less than ten persons or individuals.

The study concludes that offenders do not mainly have the same background or biographical characteristics. Also striking is the fact that they do not have a common motive or political convictions. They are rather driven to their crimes by „if anything diffuse feelings and ideas about Germans being threatened by foreigners, especially asylum-seekers, or suffering discrimination because of them". Nonetheless, the results of the study show that offenders belong to extremist right-wing and xenophobic and skinhead groups. According to police statistics 38% belong to skinhead groups, 25% to right-wing extremist and 19% to xenophobic groups.

■ ■ ■ **Measures to stamp out violence.** Representative opinion polls show that the overwhelming majority of young people in Germany have no sympathy for those who attack foreigners. Nor can young offenders and their political leaders expect any lenience from the police and judicial authorities.

The federal and state governments have demonstrated their resolve to pursue suspects with all democratic means and bring them to account. But political and other leaders realize that in the long run the police and prosecuting authorities are not the only answer to politically motivated acts of violence. Equally important are education and information, especially in view of the age of the culprits.

Since 1991, therefore, the Federal Government has launched several programmes designed to eradicate xenophobic attitudes among young people. They include projects at the main centres of violence and measures to promote the youth work of voluntary organizations in the new states.

Since the beginning of 1993 it has together with the state interior ministers been running a massive publicity campaign against extremism and animosity towards foreigners. It includes the use of posters, advertisements in youth and illustrated magazines, schools and public buildings, as well as constant appeals at major public events for fairness towards foreigners. Multiplier workshops are held for teachers, journalists and representatives of youth magazines and publications, and special press kits are distributed in schools to help children

Licht-Blicke!

FAIRSTÄNDNIS

Menschenwürde achten – Gegen Fremdenhaß

Ob mit kleinen Gesten oder großen Lichterketten: Immer mehr Bürger demonstrieren gegen den Fremdenhaß, den Rechtsextremisten schüren. Das sind Licht-Blicke, die Täter und Hintermänner ins Abseits stellen.

Gewalt gegen Fremde ist mit Verboten und Strafen allein nicht zu überwinden. Ebenso notwendig sind

Verständnis für die Fremden, ihre Sitten und Lebensweisen und Fairneß im Umgang miteinander.

Jetzt sind alle gefordert. Jeder einzelne kann sich im Betrieb oder in der Schule, in der Clique oder im Verein durch Wort und Tat für mehr Toleranz und Fairständnis gegenüber Fremden einsetzen. So machen wir aus Fremdenhaß ein Fremdwort.

Die Innenminister von Bund und Ländern

*"Fairständnis" – a "fairness towards foreigners" campaign
sponsored by the federal and state interior ministries*

promote mutual tolerance among Germans and foreigners.

■ ■ ■ **Organizations and groups.** Young people in west Germany are far more apt to be members of a group than their counterparts in the east. This applies both to formal youth organizations and clubs and to cliques. 37% of youths and young adults in west Germany are members of a youth organization, in the east only 19%. The proportion of these who are members of sports clubs is 62% in both east and west. 68% of the young west Germans interviewed said they belonged to a clique, compared with only 31% in the east. This is partly due to the fact that there is still no adequate network of independent youth organizations in the new states, a situation which is compounded by an acute shortage of buildings, centres or sports facilities for spontaneous or organized youth contacts. This is also reflected in leisure-time activities. Whereas in the west sport is well and away the most popular form of leisure-time occupation, in the east it is listening to music and reading.

In Germany there are about 80 supraregional youth organizations catering for about a quarter of all under 18-year-olds in Germany. Most of the national associations are affiliated to the Deutscher Bundesjugendring (German Federal Youth Council) and include the Arbeitsgemeinschaft der Evangelischen Jugend (Young Protestants Association), the Bund der Deutschen Katholischen Jugend (Federation of German Catholic Youth Associations), the trade union youth associations, the state youth associations and the Ring Deutscher Pfadfinder (German Boy Scouts Association).

The one with the largest membership is the Deutsche Sportjugend (Federation of German Youth Sports Associations). There are also youth political organizations. Most of the parties in the German Bundestag have youth organizations under their wings. They belong to the Ring Politischer Jugend (Council of Political Youth Associations).

■ ■ ■ **Government policy.** The upbringing of children is primarily the responsibility of parents or guardians. The state helps in their personal and social development so that they are responsible for themselves and find their proper place at work and in society. It cares of young people by legislating for their protection and by providing them with social assistance and opportunities for voluntary activities. It purposely allows the various organizations, including the churches and other independent institutions, to take the lead in providing such assistance.

There thus emerges a range of services which reflect the currents of society and provide a genuine choice for young people and their parents. Germany's federal system, by which responsibilities are delegated as largely as possible to local institutions close to the people is also manifest in government youth assistance programmes. The greater proportion of the funds required are provided by the state and local authorities.

The government's main channel for implementing its youth policy and promoting youth work is the Bundesjugendplan (Federal Youth Plan), under which DM 225 million a year is spent on out-of-school youth activities. This plan has existed for 40 years and is used to finance political, social and cultural youth work as well as international youth exchanges.

Increasingly more funds are being provided to promote children's activities outside the family. The greater part of these resources is used to finance youth associations. Their work has concentrated in recent years on foreign children and the problem of right-wing extremism and violence.

International youth contacts are a bridge of understanding. Consequently, more than 150,000 young Germans and Frenchmen take part in about 4,000 events every year sponsored by the Franco-German Youth Organization. In the 30 years since that organization was formed there have been more than 4.5 million participants in 154,000 programmes.

Another youth organization of this kind, the German-Polish Youth Organization, was founded in July 1992. Since the beginning of 1993 it has been able to dispose of its own fund for the promotion of German-Polish youth movements which is fed by both governments.

Deutsch-Französisches Jugendwerk
(Franco-German Youth Organization)
Rhöndorfer Strasse 23, 53604 Bad Honnef
Deutsch-Polnisches Jugendwerk
(German-Polish Youth Organization)
Friedhofsgasse 2, 14473 Potsdam
Deutscher Bundesjugendring
(German Federal Youth Council)
Haager Weg 44, 53127 Bonn
Deutsche Sportjugend
(Federation of German Youth Sports Associations)
Otto-Fleck-Schneise 12, 60528 Frankfurt
Bundesvereinigung Kulturelle Jugendbildung
(Federation of Youth Cultural Associations)

Küppelstein 34, 42857 Remscheid
Arbeitsgemeinschaft für Jugendhilfe
(Youth Assistance Association)
Haager Weg 44, 53127 Bonn
Bundesarbeitsgemeinschaft Jugendaufbauwerk
(Federal Association for the Development of
Youth Organizations)
Haager Weg 44, 53127 Bonn
Youth associations of parties represented
in the German Bundestag:
Junge Union Deutschlands
(Young Union of Germany)
Annaberger Str. 283, 53175 Bonn
Arbeitsgemeinschaft der Jungsozialistinnen und
Jungsozialisten in der SPD
(Association of Young Socialists in the SPD)
Ollenhauerstr. 1, 53113 Bonn
Junge Liberale
(Young Liberals)
Lennéstr. 30, 53113 Bonn
Internationaler Jugendaustausch und Besucherdienst der
Bundesrepublik Deutschland e.V.
(International Youth Exchange and Visitor Service of the
Federal Republic of Germany)
Hochkreuzallee 20, 53175 Bonn

Sport

Sport is a favourite leisure-time activity in Germany. This is reflected not only in the popularity of television broadcasts but also in the fact that there are more than 75,000 clubs affiliated to the Deutscher Sportbund (German Sports Federation). More than 21 million people are members of sports clubs, and another 12 million „do their own thing".

Sports organizations in Germany are self-governing. They receive support from the state only where they lack the necessary funds. Government policy on sport is based on cooperation. This also applies in the new federal states, where independent organizations have meanwhile been created. There, too, fair play and partnership come before victory at any price, and the focus is now on popular sport through clubs and associations as the foundation for the development of top-level sport.

■ ■ ■ **The German Sports Federation.** The central sports organization in Germany is the German Sports Federation (DSB), which embraces 16 regional federations and many individual sports associations. In all the various branches there are over two million people working in an honorary capacity as coaches or officials. The western part of the country has a large network of facilities for mass and competitive sport. There are, for instance, about 50,000 school and club sports grounds, nearly 30,000 gyms, and 7,700 indoor and outdoor swimming-pools. In the new states, however, there is still a great shortage of facilities for mass sport, due to the fact that for decades all the effort went into competition at the highest level.

■ ■ ■ **Popular sports.** The German Football Federation (DFB) is by far the biggest sports organization in Germany, having more than 5.25 million members. Soccer is played at thousands of amateur clubs. It is also a spectator sport, attracting hundreds of thousands to professional games every week. This popularity has increased since the 1990 World Cup in Italy, when the German team won for the third time. Sports like tennis, golf and horse-riding are enjoying increasing popularity.

The international success of stars like Steffi Graf, Boris Becker and Michael Stich has made tennis a national sport. Mass sport is largely influenced by the professionals, particularly in soccer, tennis and horse-riding.

■ ■ ■   **Sport in the service of people.** Most people who indulge in sport do so not because they want to reach the pinnacle but for the exercise and the pleasure of taking part in a group activity. Sport is good for one's health and makes up for the lack of exercise in an increasingly technological world. Year by year more and more people are attracted to sport, and organized sport is providing even greater opportunities. At the average club these days one can play soccer, handball, volleyball, basketball, tennis and table-tennis, or take part in track and field events. Water sports, too, are very popular, and there are various possibilities for physically handicapped and elderly people, and for mothers and small children. Popular and leisure-time sports are also promoted by the DSB programmes „Trimm dich" (Get Fit) and „Sport für alle" (Sport for All) which include open competitions in running, swimming, cycling, skiing and hiking. Every year millions of people take part. About 700,000 people a year have their performance in various sports tested in order to qualify for a „Sports Badge" which is awarded by the DSB. There is a gold, silver and bronze standard.

■ ■ ■   **Top-level sport.** Germany has 41 national sports centres and 22 Olympic training facilities as well as many regional centres. The armed services, too, develop tal-

The German eight winning gold at the 1993 World Championchips

Franziska van Almsick, the most succesful German swimmer

ent in their own facilities. Top sportsmen must these days undergo intensive training with full health care and a certain measure of financial security. These responsibilities are shared by the associations and the „Stiftung Deutsche Sporthilfe" (Sports Aid Foundation) which was established in 1967. It regards itself as a welfare organization and tries to ensure that sportsmen can at least devote themselves to training without having to worry about the cost.

But it also helps them obtain qualifications for the time when they leave competitive sport. The foundation is not a governmental organization. Its funds come from private donors, the sale of special postage stamps on sporting themes, and from a television lottery („Glücksspirale").

■ ■ ■ **Government promotion.** Sports organizations in Germany are supported by the state in many ways. The Federal Government mainly promotes competitive sport. It provides funds for training and competitions, medical care for top athletes, the training and employment of coaches, the construction of sports facilities and for scientific research. Sports for the disabled as well as international events by the various sports organizations also qualify for public support.

Government money is likewise spent on sending

*Top of the women's world
tennis rankings: Steffi Graf*

coaches and advisers to Third World countries. Since 1962 nearly DM 190 million has been set aside for the promotion of sport in more than 130 countries. Top competitive sport is promoted in order to develop sport in general, but also to enable leading sportsmen and sportswomen to be able to participate on an equal footing with their rivals in European and world championships and in the Olympic Games. Support for popular sport is mainly the responsibility of the regional and local authorities. It focuses on facilities, as well as school, university and club sport.

Deutscher Sportbund
(The German Sports Federation)
Otto-Fleck-Schneise 12, 60528 Frankfurt/Main

Leisure and holidays

Travel is one of the most popular leisure-time activities in Germany. In 1992 about 70% of those over the age of 14 took a holiday of at least five days away from home. The proportion was even greater in the new eastern states who, after all, had a lot of catching up to do in this respect. For decades they were confined to Eastern bloc countries, only being allowed to travel to the west in very exceptional cases.

Growing prosperity and shorter working hours mean more leisure-time and holidays. In 1992 the average annual number of working hours in the western states was only 1,519.

It was not always like that. At the turn of the century few workers were given holidays. The first steps in this direction came in 1903 in the metal and brewing industries, when workers were allowed three days annual holiday. By 1930 the average annual holiday was between three and fifteen days. Not until 1974 was the statutory minimum holiday of 18 working days introduced in the old Federal Republic. Today most collective wage agreements provide for holidays of six weeks and more, and most employers pay holiday money as well.

■ ■ ■ **Destinations.** Many Germans spend their holidays in their own country, but most prefer the warmer climate of the south. In 1991 they spent over 50 billion marks abroad, compared with the 18 billion which foreigners brought to Germany. The most popular countries for German tourists are Italy, Spain, Austria, France, Switzerland and the United States. They can call on the services of growing numbers of travel operators.

Holiday habits have changed. In former times the emphasis was on rest and sun-bathing, but these days many people prefer an active holiday. They like unspoilt nature, away from environmental pollution. This also applies to weekend leisure-time activities. Numerous clubs and associations, the churches and local authorities offer leisure-time programmes at sports grounds, indoor and outdoor public baths, libraries, hobby courses at evening classes, as well as art, science, literature and music groups, etc.

Mountain hiking opens up glorious landscapes

Germany's many lakes are ideal for windsurfing

According to opinion surveys, the ordinary German family spends about one fifth of its income on leisure-time activities and this proportion is increasing. Commerce has recognized this trend and a thriving „leisure industry" has grown up. The Deutsche Gesellschaft für Freizeit (German Leisure Association) was established in 1971. It researches leisure-time behaviour and provides information and advice. It has 30 member associations.

Deutsche Gesellschaft für Freizeit
(German Leisure Association)
Bahnstrasse 4, 40699 Erkrath

Clubs, associations and citizens' action groups

■ ■ ■ **Clubs.** There are few Germans who do not belong to at least one of the country's 300,000 or so clubs or associations. Nearly one in four is a member of a sports club, and over two million are members of choral societies. There are associations of marksmen, stamp collectors, dog breeders and local culture, carnivalists, allotment holders and amateur wireless operators, and not forgetting youth and women's groups. Members pursue their hobbies but socialize as well.

Some of these associations also play a role in local politics. People with different party affiliation come together in the marksmen's club or the local historical association, for instance, where they make informal contacts that can affect the life of the community. These associations do not have a defined political role, however.

■ ■ ■ **Associations.** It is different with groups which represent specific material interests of their members. These comprise above all the big labour and employers' associations. In addition to these there are many other organizations which pursue certain professional, business, social or other objectives. Thus house owners, tenants, motorists, for example, have associations, some with very big memberships. There are organizations of minorities, too.

These common-interest organizations engage in public relations to win sympathy for their causes. Their expertise can also be called upon in the preparation of legislation. Their influence is considerable, but it would be an exaggeration to say Germany is ruled by associations.

■ ■ ■ **Citizens' action groups.** A fairly new type of association is the citizens' action group, many of which have been formed since the early 70s. Citizens get together, usually spontaneously, to try and remedy a grievance where they feel a matter has been neglected by the authorities or the council. In most cases local issues are at stake, for example the preservation of old trees due to be felled to make way for a road, a child-

Lively discussion in citizens' action groups is a part of democracy

ren's playground or efforts to prevent the extension of an airport.

Sometimes action groups pursue contradictory aims, e.g. campaigning for a bypass road to reduce traffic in a residential area, or against such a road for ecological reasons. They have achieved many objectives, especially at local level, putting forward new ideas and being ready to compromise. Action groups are operating all over the country, the best known being the peace movement. The government welcomes and supports groups who draw attention to social problems and play a constructive part in their solution.

It is a basic right of all Germans to organize and take part in peaceful demonstrations. However, the final decision on controversial matters lies with the democratically elected governments and parliaments. They are bound to take the decisions that are best for the community as a whole. This makes it important for individuals and citizens' action groups to become involved as soon as possible in the preparation of government decisions, especially in the planning stage. Some legislation, for instance the Federal Building Act, already provides for such civic participation.

Churches and religious communities

"Freedom of faith and conscience as well as freedom of religious or other belief shall be inviolable. The undisturbed practice of religion shall be guaranteed." Everyone in the Federal Republic takes this provision of the Basic Law (article 4) for granted as a fundamental right. Over 58 million people in Germany belong to a Christian church. 29.5 million are Protestants, over 28 million Roman Catholics, and a minority belong to other Christian denominations. The 1919 Weimar constitution separated church and state without, however, completely removing historicalities. The legal situation thus created is by and large the one which obtains today, corresponding provisions of the Weimar constitution having been incorporated in the Basic Law adopted after the Second World War.

There is no state church in Germany. The state is neutral vis-à-vis religions and creeds. The churches have a special status as independent public corporations, so that their relationship with the state is often described as a partnership. Apart from the Basic Law, that relationship is regulated by concordats and agreements. The churches' property rights are guaranteed. They have a claim to grants from the state which, for example, contributes towards the salaries of clergy and assumes, in whole or in part, the cost of certain church establishments, such as kindergartens and schools. The churches are empowered to levy taxes on their members, which as a rule are collected by the state. The clergy are trained mainly at state universities, and the churches have a say in appointments to chairs of theology. The work of the churches in running hospitals, old people's and nursing homes, consulting and caring services, schools and training centres is an indispensable charitable and social commitment.

■ ■ ■ **The Protestant Church.** The Protestant Church in Germany (EKD) is an alliance of 24 mostly independent Lutheran, reformed and united churches. Following the country's unification it once again represents the national Protestant Church. Church administrative regions are not identical with the territories of the federal states.

The 1992 Protestant Church Convention held in Munich

The EKD's main legislative body is the Synod, its chief executive body the Council. The Church Office in Hanover is the central administrative department. The Protestant Churches are members of the World Council of Churches and they cooperate closely with the Roman Catholic Church.

■ ■ ■ **The Catholic Church.** The Catholic Church in Germany consists of five provinces with 22 bishoprics. Following the country's reunification the church began reorganizing the areas which previously were under the jurisdiction of the Bishops Conference (founded in 1976). Two offices of bishops and an apostolic administratorship are to be raised to the status of dioceses and a new bishopric is to be formed in Hamburg. Germany's archbishops and bishops, seventy in all, consult together at the spring and autumn assemblies of the German Bishops Conference, which has a secretariat in Bonn.

The impetus from the Second Vatican Council for the involvement of the Catholic laity in church affairs is translated into action by elected lay representatives. Together with the 100 or more Catholic associations they form the Central Committee of German Catholics. The visits of Pope John Paul II in 1980 and 1987 evoked a tremendous response and stimulated the ecumenical movement and dialogue between state and church.

■ ■ ■ **Other religious communities.** Other religious communities include in particular the free churches. Two

Processions take place on the Corpus Christi Day

of the largest Protestant free churches, the Methodists and the Protestant Community (Evangelische Gemeinschaft) joined together in 1968 to form the Protestant Methodist Church (Evangelisch-Methodistische Kirche). In addition there are the Baptists. The Old Catholic Church came into being as a breakaway from the Roman Catholic Church in the 1870s after the First Vatican Council. The Mennonite congregations, the Society of Friends (Quakers) and the Salvation Army are known for their social activities.

In 1933 about 530,000 Jews lived in the German Reich. Following the nazi genocide the Jewish communities now have about 40,000 members. The largest community is in Berlin (nearly 10,000) and Frankfurt am Main (just under 5,000). The national organization is the Central Council of Jews in Germany. In 1979 a College of Jewish Studies was established in Heidelberg which has won international recognition. The presence of many foreign workers and their families has greatly increased the importance of religious communities which previously were hardly represented in Germany. This is the case with the Greek Orthodox Church and especially Islam. Today, more than 1.7 million Moslems, mostly Turks, live in the Federal Republic of Germany.

■ ■ ■ **Joint action.** In the period from 1933 to 1945 many Protestant and Catholic Christians fought against National Socialism. Two of them were Pastor Martin Niemöller on the Protestant and Bishop Clemens August Count von Galen on the Catholic side. Their cooperation in this struggle strengthened interdenominational understanding and awareness of the common political responsibility. The churches also played an important part in the peaceful revolution in the GDR. The churches address the public in many ways, for example by publishing comments on topical issues and other information. Worthy of special mention are the two lay movements, the German Catholic Convention and the German Protestant Convention, which meet every two years but alternately. Charitable works are carried out by the German Caritas Association (Deutscher Caritasverband) on the Catholic side and the Diaconal Service (Diakonisches Werk) on the Protestant side. Both churches are involved in overseas development aid. The major church aid organizations are funded by voluntary donations. Thus the Protestant "Bread for the World" and the Catholic "Misereor" and "Adveniat" have together collected billions of marks for emergency relief and especially for long-term development measures. "Renovabis" is a new Catholic charity formed in the spring of 1993. Its motto is "partnership and solidarity" with central, eastern and south-eastern Europe. The Synod of the EDK has for its part decided to organize a national collection from 1994 for emergency measures and reconstruction in eastern and south-eastern Europe as part of its programme "Churches help Churches". In recent times, the Christian churches have stated their views - often critical - on such public issues as peace and disarmament, foreigners and political asylum, employment, the environment and family.

Protestant:
Kirchenamt der Evangelischen Kirche in Deutschland
Herrenhäuser Strasse 12, 30419 Hannover
Catholic:
Sekretariat der Deutschen Bischofskonferenz
Kaiserstrasse 163, 53113 Bonn
Jewish:
Zentralrat der Juden in Deutschland
Rüngsdorfer Strasse 6, 53173 Bonn

Mass media and public opinion

Article 5 of the Basic Law guarantees freedom of opinion
and freedom of the press and also the right to obtain information from generally accessible sources. There is no
censorship. The International Press Institute in London
describes the Federal Republic as one of the few countries where the state respects the strong position of a free
press.

■ ■ ■ **Function of the mass media.** The press, and in
the broader sense all mass media, has been referred to
as the "fourth estate" next to the legislature, the executive and the judiciary. And it is true that all mass media
play an important role in the modern society. With their
wide range of news and opinion they help the people
understand and keep check on parliament, government
and public administration. They thus have considerable
responsibility.

The Federal Constitutional Court noted that "a free
press which is not controlled by the state and not subject
to censorship is an essential element of a free country"
and that in particular "regular press publications are indispensable to the modern democracy. If the people are
to be able to make decisions they must be supplied with
the information with which to assess opinions."

■ ■ ■ **Diversity of the media.** The people have a
choice of many different and competing media. The
daily papers alone in the western part of Germany sold
about 30.5 million copies a day (end of 1992).

At present upwards of 25 million television sets and
over 28 million radios are officially registered. On average Germans over 14 devote nearly five hours a day to
media products, i. e. newspapers (half an hour), the
radio (2.5 hours) and television (two hours). And supply
is increasing constantly. Only about 5% of the population are not reached by the media at all.

The great majority, however, use two or more sources.
Most turn to television first for political information and
then read a newspaper for greater detail. For news of
events near home people usually consult the local
newspaper. Young people read newspapers less frequently. But television, too, is losing some of its public

appeal, in spite of the increasing number of programmes available.

■ ■ ■ **Sources of news.** The mass media obtain their material from news agencies at home and abroad, from their own correspondents, and from direct research. Radio and television stations have offices in all major cities around the world, as do the big newspapers.

The leading domestic news agency is the Deutsche Presse-Agentur (dpa), then the Deutscher Depeschen-dienst (ddp; which merged with the former East German Allgemeine Deutsche Nachrichtenagentur, ADN), Associated Press (AP), Reuters (rtr) and Agence France Press (AFP). dpa supplies nearly all German dailies. AP, rtr and AFP can base their German language services on the global networks of their parent companies in the United States, the United Kingdom and France respectively. Good newspapers buy their material from at least two of these services, broadcasting networks up to five. Apart from the general agencies there are various others which specialize. They include the Protestant Press Service (epd), the Catholic News Agency (KNA) and the Sports Information Service (sid). Agencies like the Vereinigte Wirtschaftsdienste (vwd) also provide information for private companies and business organizations.

A press conference in Bonn

Various private organizations, public authorities, parties, companies, etc. have their own press departments which, like outside agencies, keep information flowing to the mass media. This is done by means of news conferences, press releases, mailings, picture services and briefings for journalists.

It is part of the journalist's daily routine to research topics of his own choosing. Public authorities in Germany are required to provide journalists with information within the framework of the law. In Bonn alone there are nearly 1,000 accredited correspondents. The 550 Germans among them are members of the Federal Press Conference, and the more than 400 journalists belong to the Foreign Press Association. Both are entirely independent of the authorities.

■ ■ ■ **The Press and Information Office of the Federal Government (BPA)** acts as a mediator between government and public. The head of this public authority is at the same time the government spokesman.

The system differs from that of some other countries in that the government spokesman always attends the Federal Press Conference to brief Bonn's journalists. He goes to the press, not vice versa. This also applies to news conferences given by the Federal Chancellor and ministers in conjunction with the Federal Press Conference. The BPA is also responsible for keeping the Federal President, the Federal Government and the Bundestag informed about "published opinion" in Germany and abroad. In order to provide this service the BPA evaluates 27 news agencies and monitors more than 100 radio and 25 television programmes in German and 22 foreign languages.

■ ■ ■ **Public opinion research.** "Published opinion" does not always tally with public opinion at large. In some cases they are very far apart. Demoscopic institutes scientifically study public opinion on the basis of representative samples, i.e. the opinions of usually 1,000-2,000 people.

The private institutes concerned with political opinion research attract considerable public attention. The large German newspapers and periodicals as well as television corporations regularly publish the results of such surveys of the nation's political mood, the standing of parties and leading politicians, and of topics of current interest such as nuclear energy, unemployment, political asylum. The federal and state governments as well as the political parties use the results of these surveys to keep abreast of changes of opinion for medium and long-term planning, and as a means of assessing the impact of political measures.

Interest is particularly keen prior to elections, when the parties size up their chances and the demoscopic organizations put their finger on the nation's pulse. Although opinion polls are now very reliable, they are still only "snapshots", as it were. Election-day polls are generally the most accurate. Computer calculations on election night, however, are based on results from selected districts. With their analysis of changes in these election results according to regions, party strongholds and population groups, the researchers complement the data resulting from their surveys and can thus help explain the situation to the public.

The demoscopic know-how acquired over the past quarter of a century is not only reflected in detailed reports, which are required reading for the politician, but also used by observers in neighbouring countries.

The Press

Newspapers enjoy increasing popularity in Germany. They have more than held their own despite the advance of television. In terms of the number of newspapers per 1,000 inhabitants, Germany is in fourth place behind Japan, the United Kingdom and Switzerland.

■ ■ ■ **Newspapers.** Local and regional dailies predominate. On workdays about 410 newspapers appear in the old and new federal states. They publish nearly 1,650 local and regional editions in more than 140 offices. The total circulation is about 32 million. Small papers, too, keep their readers informed about the national and international political, economic, cultural, sporting and local events.

More than two thirds of all newspapers are bought on subscription, the rest are sold on the streets. One of the tabloids is the "Bildzeitung" which has the biggest circulation (4.4 million a day). The biggest selling subscription paper is the "Westdeutsche Allgemeine Zeitung" (circulation about 650,000). The large national newspapers have smaller circulations but considerable influence on political and business leaders. These are the "Frankfurter Allgemeine Zeitung" and "Die Welt", the "Süddeutsche Zeitung" and the "Frankfurter Rundschau".

Other important national opinion leaders are the weeklies "Die Zeit", "Die Woche", "Rheinischer Merkur" and "Deutsches Allgemeines Sonntagsblatt". They offer background information, analysis and reports. There are also Sunday newspapers such as "Bild am Sonntag", "Welt am Sonntag" and "Frankfurter Allgemeine Sonntagszeitung". In recent years more and more regional papers have been publishing Sunday editions as well. Many foreign newspapers also print special editions for foreigners living in Germany.

■ ■ ■ **Periodicals.** More than 8,000 periodicals are published in Germany. The best-known internationally is the news magazine "Der Spiegel", with a circulation exceeding one million. Another news magazine "Focus" was launched in 1993.

There is a large group of about 1,500 popular periodicals with a total circulation of over 117.4 million. These include illustrated magazines such as "Stern" and "Bunte", as well as specialized periodicals with radio and television programmes. Special-interest publications are also becoming increasingly popular. They deal with one particular subject comprehensively, whether it be tennis or yachting, computers or electronic instruments.

There are also many technical journals, though with only a moderate circulation. Others include the political weeklies, church newspapers, customer periodicals, freesheets and official announcements. One third of the periodicals market is accounted for by various organizations and associations. The motoring magazine "ADAC-Motorwelt" published by the Allgemeiner Deutscher Automobilclub has a circulation of nine million, the lar-

Circulation figures for leading newspaper and magazines

Daily newspapers (1993, in some cases with associated papers)	
Bild (Hamburg)	4,404,900
Westdeutsche Allgemeine (Essen)	1,205,600
Hannoversche Allgemeine (Hanover)	554,600
Sächsische Zeitung (Dresden)	447,100
Süddeutsche Zeitung (Munich)	404,700
Rheinische Post (Düsseldorf)	396,300
Frankfurter Allgemeine (Frankfurt)	394,800
Augsburger Allgemeine (Augsburg)	366,000
Südwestpresse (Ulm)	363,100
B.Z. (Berlin)	324,500
Hessische/Niedersächsische Allgemeine (Kassel)	323,700
Kölner Stadtanzeiger (Cologne)	287,600
Berliner Zeitung (Berlin)	258,100
Rheinpfalz (Ludwigshafen)	246,000
Märkische Allgemeine (Potsdam)	241,800
Westdeutsche Zeitung (Düsseldorf)	241,500
Braunschweiger Zeitung (Braunschweig)	223,700
Ostsee-Zeitung (Rostock)	223,000
Ruhr-Nachrichten (Dortmund)	222,000
Die Welt (Berlin)	220,300
Lausitzer Rundschau (Cottbus)	211,600
Frankfurter Rundschau (Frankfurt)	189,700
Berliner Morgenpost (Berlin)	180,200
Die Tageszeitung (Berlin)	61,700
Weeklies and Sunday newspapers	
Bild am Sonntag (Hamburg)	2,649,900
Die Zeit (Hamburg)	493,300
Welt am Sonntag (Hamburg)	423,400
Bayernkurier (Munich)	153,600
Rheinischer Merkur (Bonn)	110,900
Deutsches Allg. Sonntagsblatt (Hamburg)	90,700
Newsmagazines	
Der Spiegel (Hamburg)	1,073,100
Focus (Munich)	477,900

The wealth of information available at a newspaper stand

gest in Germany. This range of information is rounded off by local free-sheets and newspapers published by alternative groups. Also on sale in the cities are foreign newspapers and periodicals.

■ ■ ■ **Press concentration.** The number of independent newspapers in Germany has fallen steadily since the mid-50s. The publishers with the greater financial and technical resources have been able to dominate various regional markets. As a result, many towns no longer have two or more local papers to choose from. And many of those still in publication do not have "full news rooms", that is, editorial offices which produce their newspapers completely independently. They obtain a substantial proportion of their material from another newspaper or newspaper group.

Restructuring has gone hand in hand with technical change due to the introduction of computers and state-of-the-art printing technology. Although this has reduced production costs, newspapers, like nearly all print media, depend on advertising for their economic survival.

Advertising covers a large part of the cost. It is debatable whether the loss of diversity and independence resulting from press mergers jeopardizes press freedom.

■ ■ ■ **The major publishing companies.** Economic developments have led to the formation of large publishing houses. In the daily press sector the biggest conglomerate is the Axel Springer AG, although its 20% share of the newspaper market is largely due to the high circulation of "Bild".

As regards Sunday papers, Axel Springer AG is almost without competition with "Welt am Sonntag" and "Bild am Sonntag".

Economic and journalistic power is also concentrated in the publishing groups of the "Westdeutsche Allgemeine Zeitung", Süddeutscher Verlag, Verlag DuMont Schauberg and the FAZ group. Much more important in terms of economic power and journalistic effectiveness are the publishers of periodicals, especially the generale interest ones. Leaders in this sector are Bauer Verlag and the Burda group as well as Axel Springer AG.

The media corporation with the largest turnover, and in fact the second largest in the world, is Bertelsmann AG, which has global interests and covers book and record clubs, book and periodical publishing, music production, films, radio and television, and printing.

■ ■ ■ **Press rights.** Press rights are covered by state legislation, which is consistent on the basic issues, which include the right of journalists to refuse to disclose their sources of information, as well as the right of others who have been the subject of newspaper reporting to have a counter-statement published. Print media are required to indicate the title and address of the publication, the date of issue, names of owners and editors, etc. ("masthead requirement"), and to exercise due care.

Publishers and journalists exercise self-control through the German Press Council, which looks into charges of negligence and unethical behaviour. Its views are not binding, however.

Bundesverband Deutscher Zeitungsverleger
(Federation of German Newspaper Publishers)
Riemenschneiderstrasse 10, 53175 Bonn
Deutscher Journalistenverband
(German Journalists Association)
Bennauerstrasse 60, 53115 Bonn
Verband Deutscher Zeitschriftenverleger
(Association of German Periodical Publishers)
Winterstrasse 50, 53177 Bonn
IG Medien (Print Media Union)
Friedrichstrasse 15, 70174 Stuttgart

Radio and television

The broadcasting media, i.e. radio and television, in Germany are not state-controlled. The system, as well as the freedom of broadcasting, are governed by law. The Federal Parliament legislates on posts and telecommunications and is therefore responsible for the technical aspects of broadcasting. The networks themselves, however, are under state jurisdiction.

Germany has a dual system, that is to say public and commercial systems exist side by side. It is based largely on a 1986 ruling by the Federal Constitutional Court that the public corporations should meet the public's general broadcasting requirements, with the private companies playing a supplementary role.

For many years Germany had only public corporations, but this changed in 1984 when private television and radio broadcasters were allowed to compete for the first time.

■ ■ ■ **The public corporations.** In 1991 Germany had 11 regional broadcasting corporations, two organized under federal law, and a second national television network (Zweites Deutsches Fernsehen, ZDF) based on an agreement between all the federal states. The largest broadcasting station is the Westdeutscher Rundfunk (Cologne) with 4,400 staff, while the smallest is Radio Bremen with about 650.

The others are Bayerischer Rundfunk (Munich), Hessischer Rundfunk (Frankfurt am Main), Norddeutscher Rundfunk (Hamburg), Saarländischer Rundfunk (Saarbrücken), Sender Freies Berlin (Berlin), Süddeutscher Rundfunk (Stuttgart), Südwestfunk (Baden-Baden), Ostdeutscher Rundfunk Brandenburg (Potsdam) and Mitteldeutscher Rundfunk (Leipzig). They cater more or less for the regions where they are located, although some supply programmes for several regions.

Each broadcasts several radio programmes and the regional corporations form a Standing Conference of Public Broadcasting Corporations (Arbeitsgemeinschaft der Öffentlich-rechtlichen Rundfunkanstalten Deutschlands, ARD). Together they operate a nationally transmitted television programme officially called "German Television" but generally referred to as "Channel One", for which they all provide material. In addition, they produce regional "Third" TV programmes. The Mainz-based Zweites Deutsches Fernsehen is a television-only station which transmits the "Channel Two" programme nationwide. It is the largest in Europe.

There are two radio stations with special responsibilities, the Deutschlandfunk (DLF) and Deutsche Welle (DW), both located in Cologne. The DLF is financed by the Federal Government together with the regional broadcasting corporations, whereas the DW is funded entirely by the Federal Government.

Prior to the country's unification both stations broadcast Germany-oriented programmes for domestic and foreign consumption. They transmit in German and many foreign languages. Deutsche Welle (Voice of Germany) will continue in this role, though it now incorporates the foreign language departments of the DLF and RIAS television. RIAS used to operate as the "Radio in the American Sector" of Berlin. Although it was under the responsibility of the United States Information Service, it had a German director-general. A new system, "Deutschlandradio", will begin broadcasting on 1 January 1994. It is a merger of DL, RIAS and the cultural affairs station of the former GDR. Its organizational framework will be the ARD and ZDF and it will broadcast from Berlin and Cologne.

■ ■ ■ **Self-government and broadcasting freedom.** The public corporations are in general controlled by three bodies: the Broadcasting Council, the Administrative Council and the Director-General.

The members of the Broadcasting Council are representatives of the main political and social groups. They are elected by the state parliaments or nominated by the political parties, religious communities and business and cultural organizations.

The Council advises the Director-General on programming and ensures that basic principles are observed. The Administrative Council draws up the corporation's budget, watches over day-to-day management, and comments on technical aspects. Its members are elected by the Broadcasting Council and they for their part elect the Director-General, subject to confirmation by the Council. The Director-General runs the corporation in accordance with the decisions of the Broadcasting and Administrative Councils. He is responsible for programme content and represents the corporation in its external relations.

This system guarantees the broadcasting corporations' independence from the state. It does not, however, exclude all political influence. Although the party representatives do not hold a majority on the supervisory board, a kind of power-sharing arrangement has developed. This is particularly evident when appointments are made to top posts and draws much public criticism.

The corporations may not favour any side and must maintain editorial balance. This does not prejudice the "freedom of broadcasting", that is, the right to express decided points of view. On the other hand, the corporations are required by law to provide equal opportunities for the expression of opinions.

■ ■ ■ **Radio and television programmes.** Each regional corporation broadcasts up to five radio programmes. They provide a broad variety of entertainment, music, current affairs, sport, regional affairs, drama, opera, and so on. Most networks run scientific and literary series, and special programmes for foreign workers are provided in their own languages. Their orchestras, choirs and ballet ensembles enrich the cultural landscape of many cities.

In the nationally transmitted ARD and ZDF television programmes political reporting, home and foreign affairs documentation, television plays, films and entertainment play a big part. German TV networks have long been buying and selling programmes abroad. For their foreign coverage both ARD and ZDF have extensive correspondent networks and their own studios in many countries all over the world.

ARD and ZDF participate in Eurovision's international exchange, mostly for sporting events. They also contribute to the news pool of the European Broadcasting Union. The ZDF and six other European networks commission films through the European Film Production Community.

ARD and ZDF are also involved in the Franco-German TV cultural programme "ARTE" and "3sat", a cooperative network sponsored by Austria, Germany and Switzerland.

Production control room in a news studio

Channel Three television programmes are transmitted by the ARD corporations. They focus on regional affairs ranging from politics to culture, and they broadcast television for schools and further education courses at various levels.

Television in the Federal Republic went colour in 1967, using the German PAL system. More than 80% of registered sets are for colour.

■ ■ ■ **Finance.** The public broadcasting corporations obtain most of their funds in the form of licence fees. Television licence revenue is split 70:30 between ARD and ZDF. Both also depend on income from commercial advertising. They have much less time for commercial spots than private companies, with whom they now have to compete for advertising.

Television rights, especially for major football and tennis events, have become much more expensive, yet the public corporations cannot increase license fees to cover the cost without the approval of the regional parliaments.

■ ■ ■ **Commercial broadcasting.** The public corporations first had to contend with competition in 1985 when

"SAT.1" began operating from Mainz as the first commercial television broadcasting company. It was followed in 1986 by "RTL plus Deutschland" (now "RTL", Cologne). Both have meanwhile become very popular. At the beginning of 1991 "RTL plus" reached two thirds of all households and "SAT.1" a little more than 62%. Other private broadcasters are "Pro 7" and "Deutsches Sportfernsehen" (DSF). "RTL" and "SAT.1" are mainly concerned with sport, entertainment and feature films but also offer good political programmes. "Pro 7" concentrates mainly on films, whereas "DSF" specializes in sport.

Commercial programmes are transmitted via satellite and cable and can also be received via terrestrial frequencies. A number of foreign TV programmes are offered in the same way. The commercial stations are operated by consortia, mostly of media companies. In contrast to the public corporations, their only source of revenue is advertising.

In 1991 there were already about 100 private radio stations, although only a few of them offer a full programme catering for a whole state. The law requires radio stations to cater for wide-ranging public tastes. The Federal Constitutional Court has ruled, that private broadcasters, like the public corporations, may not influence public opinion one-sidley. Their programmes must reflect to a certain extent diversity of opinion.

■ ■ ■ **Broadcasting innovation.** New technology has considerably changed the broadcasting landscape in Germany. In 1992 some 19 million households were linked up to the broadband cable network which the Post Office has been laying since 1982. Nearly half of them receive both radio and television programmes. The aim in the 90s is to make cabled programmes available to 80% of all 30 million households.

Direct satellite broadcasting (DSB) has meanwhile become a serious rival to cable. It is an economically viable alternative for everyone, not only those not yet linked up to the cable network. Satellite programmes can be received directly by anyone with a dish antenna.

DSB raises the question of boundary limitations. It is not yet certain whether national, European, or global concepts will prevail. In 1992 two supranational public

At ZDF headquarters, Mainz

and one private organization were operating most of the 15 satellites which supply Europe with about 70 television and radio programmes.

One of the satellite programmes is "3sat", a joint undertaking by the ZDF, the Austrian Broadcasting Corporation and the Swiss Radio and Television Company. There are also "1Plus", "ARTE", "VOX", "Kabelkanal" and other programmes.

Viewers and listeners in Germany now have a wide range of programmes to choose from. Among the new media which are available via television are Btx, the Post Office's viewdata system. It enables subscribers to conduct a dialogue with suppliers via telephone. The possibilities range from stock exchange reports to bank account transactions.

The public corporations offer videotex, a service using the normal television signal. Videotex appears on the screen on call and offers news, weather reports, tips for consumers, and much more.

Arbeitsgemeinschaft der öffentlich-rechtlichen
Rundfunkanstalten Deutschlands (ARD)
(Association of Public Broadcasting Corporations)
Arnulfplatz 42, 80335 München
Zweites Deutsches Fernsehen (ZDF)
(German Television Channel Two)
P.O. Box 4040, 55100 Mainz
RTL
Aachener Str. 1036, 50858 Köln
SAT.1
Otto-Schott-Str. 13, 55127 Mainz

Education and science

· Cultural diversity · Schools
· Vocational education · Higher education
· Adult education · Scholarship and research

Cultural diversity

Nowhere is the country's federal structure more apparent than in the cultural sphere. Germany never had a cultural metropolis like France's Paris or Britain's London. The considerable cultural autonomy of the regions has led to the formation of small and large cultural centres with different points of emphasis. Thus cultural activity is to be found in even the smallest towns and communities.

Berlin, as capital and future seat of government of united Germany, will also play an important cultural role, but the other cities will retain their standing as cultural centres. The country's federal structure ensures that its cultural diversity will be preserved and that there will be an intensive exchange between east and west which was lacking prior to unification.

This diversity is apparent from the spread of cultural institutions and activities. The Deutsche Bibliothek (German Library), which is directly sponsored by the Federal Government, is located in Frankfurt on the Main, with branches in Leipzig and Berlin. The national archives of the Federal Republic are in Koblenz and there are branches in Berlin, Potsdam, Freiburg im Breisgau and Bayreuth, among others. Hamburg has the largest concentration of newspaper publishing. Cologne and Düsseldorf are centres of modern art. Berlin has the most theatres. There are scientific academies in Berlin, Düsseldorf, Darmstadt, Göttingen, Halle, Heidelberg, Leipzig, Mainz and Munich. The principal museums are in Berlin, Munich, Nuremberg, Cologne and Stuttgart. The most important literary archives are in the small Württemberg town of Marbach and in Weimar (Thuringia).

It is due to such cultural polycentrism that there are no remote, desolate "provinces" in Germany. One need not travel hundreds of miles to see good theatre or hear good music. Even in some small towns one finds valuable libraries or interesting art collections. This goes back to the days when Germany consisted of many principalities whose rulers wanted to make their residences centres of culture, and when a self-assured middle class patronized the arts and sciences in their towns.

Premiere of the opera "Eréndira" in Stuttgart's Staatstheater

The establishment and maintenance of most cultural facilities in the Federal Republic of Germany is the responsibility of local government. Legislation on cultural matters - with few exceptions - is the prerogative of the federal states. Each has a large measure of autonomy in organizing its schools system. Here it becomes apparent that there are also negative aspects to cultural federalism. Since school curricula and examination standards often vary from state to state, problems can arise when families move and the children have trouble adjusting.

But the state governments are cooperating with each other where possible through their Standing Conference of Ministers of Education and Cultural Affairs. The federal and state governments cooperate in planning and financing university building. They also have a joint commission for educational planning and research promotion. Within this framework they support pilot projects in all fields of education.

The purpose of these bodies is to ensure the degree of standardization necessary for a modern, efficient education system without abandoning the rich diversity of German cultural life.

Schools

Germany's 41,000 schools have 9.2 million pupils and roughly 587,000 full-time teachers. The Basic Law guarantees everyone's right to self-fulfilment and to choose his place of education and profession or occupation. As a result, the government is required to provide all citizens with the best possible opportunities to receive the kind of education that is commensurate with their abilities and interests. Such educational opportunities should be available throughout life so that young people will become emancipated and able to play their part in the country's democratic system. As an industrial country short of raw materials, Germany largely depends on her skilled labour and therefore invests heavily in education. In 1991 the federal and state governments and local authorities, together with industry, spent about DM 95 billion on education in the western part of the country.

■ ■ ■ **Statutory basis.** According to article 7 of the Basic Law the whole school system in Germany is the responsibility of the state. On account of the country's federal structure, that responsibility is shared by the central and state governments. General and vocational, continuing and higher education, as well as kindergartens, fall within the purview of the states. Thus there are different systems and types of schools in the 16 states. A common basic structure exists, however, in the form of an inter-state agreement signed on 14 October 1971, which covers such matters as compulsory schooling, organization, recognition of certificates, etc. The necessary degree of uniformity and comparability of the systems is also ensured by other agreements among the states (through the Standing Conference of Ministers of Education and Cultural Affairs of the Länder, KMK) on, for instance, the restructuring of the upper level of the grammar school, university entrance qualification standards and the mutual recognition of comprehensive school certificates.

Following the country's unification the new states have introduced new schools legislation geared to the value-concepts of the Basic Law, the inter-state agreement of 1971, and the various KMK accords.

A school playground during the main break

■ ■ ■ **Compulsory schooling.** School attendance is compulsory from the ages of six to 18, i.e. for 12 years, during which full-time attendance is required for nine (in some states ten) years, followed by part-time attendance at a vocational school or additional full-time schooling. Attendance at all state schools is free. Materials, in particular textbooks, are also provided, some of them free of charge.

The Basic Law requires that religious instruction be included in the curriculum, except in non-denominational schools. From the age of 14 pupils may drop the subject if they wish. Parents have the right to decide whether their children are to be taught religion. The significance of denominational schools has decreased. Most states have "interdenominational schools oriented to Christian principles" in which only religious instruction is given in denominationally separate classes. As a rule girls and boys are in mixed classes. There are also various private schools which, if they are alternatives to state schools, are subject to government approval. They receive state grants.

■ ■ ■ **Kindergartens.** The kindergarten is a German institution adopted by many countries. It develops the ability of children to express themselves fluently, usually at play, teaching them to become useful members of society. Some children spend only the morning in kindergarten, but there are also many all-day kindergartens.

The kindergartens are not part of the state school system but come under child and youth services. Most of them are run by the churches, charity organizations and local authorities, some by firms or associations.

About 80% of all three to six-year-olds attend kindergartens. In four states children have a statutory right to a kindergarten place. This will apply throughout the country as from 1996, but attendance will still be voluntary. Parents usually have to contribute to the cost.

■ ■ ■ **The school system.** At the age of six children enter the primary school (Grundschule). In general it lasts four years, in Berlin and Brandenburg six. In most states children's work in the first two years at school is not graded but assessed. After primary school they attend one of the other schools available to them according to their ability. The fifth and sixth school years are known as the "orientation phase" when children and their parents can revise their choice of school, except in Bavaria.

About one third of the children pass from the primary school to the junior secondary school (Hauptschule). Most then (at the age of 15 or 16) take a course of vocational training, which includes attendance at a vocational school until the age of 18. The Hauptschule opens the way to many occupations for which formal training is required.

The range of subjects taught there has been steadily broadenedy. For example, nowadays almost every pupil is instructed in a foreign language, mostly English, and given vocational orientation to ease the transition from school to working life.

Intermediate school (Realschule) as a rule takes six years (age 10 to 16). It leads to a graduating certificate qualifying for continuing education at a technical school (Fachschule or Fachoberschule, which are specialized schools offering vocational training at upper secondary level). The intermediate certificate is also regarded as a prerequisite for a medium-level career in business or administration. A third of all pupils achieve this qualification.

The nine-year Gymnasium (5th to 13th school years, in the new states except Brandenburg only up to the 12th year at present) is the traditional grammar or senior high school in Germany. The former classification into ancient language, modern language and natural sciences Gymnasium is now rare. Today the so-called "reformed upper phase" (11th to 13th years) is the rule. Under this system courses have replaced the conventional classes. In these courses, alongside certain compulsory elements, students concentrate on the subjects they are most interested in. This is intended to facilitate the transition to higher education. Some Gymnasiums specialize in business or technical studies. A current topic of debate is whether the years spent at school leading to higher education should be reduced to 12 nationwide. The conference of ministers-president will decide in 1994.

German educational system in diagram form

Further training
(general/vocational further training in diverse forms)

Graduate-level vocational qualification

Vocational qualification	General higher education qualification	**University/technical university**
		Teacher training college
		Polytechnic
		Administrative college
Technical school	**Evening grammar school/college**	**Art college**
		Comprehensive university

	Vocational training qualification				General higher education qualification	
13	Intermediate vocational qualification			Polytechnic qualification	**Higher grammar school level**	13
12	Vocational training in firm and vocational school (dual system)	Vocational extension school	Full-time vocational school	Technical secondary school	(grammar school, vocational grammar school, comprehensive school)	12
11						11
10	Basic vocational training year					10

Elementary school qualifications after 9 or 10 years/secondary school qualification

10		10th school year					10
9							9
8	Special school	Elementary school	Secondary school	Grammar school	Comprehensive school	8
7						7
6		Orientation level					6
5		(dependent on/independent of type of school)					5

4				4
3	Special school	Primary school		3
2				2
1				1

School year	Special kinder-garten	Kindergarten

Graduation from the Gymnasium, the so-called "maturity certificate" ("Reifezeugnis" or "Abitur") is the prerequisite for study at a university. However, the number of Gymnasium graduates has increased to such an extent that certain restrictions have had to be introduced (numerus clausus), with university places being awarded on the basis of grades and aptitude tests.

Another model is the comprehensive school (5th to 10th school year), which incorporates the hitherto separate traditional types of school. Some comprehensive schools have their own senior grades akin to those of the Gymnasium. According to ability, pupils have the option of taking courses with higher or lower standards. Vocational familiarization is part of the syllabus. Comprehensive school certificates are recognized throughout the country. This type of school has followed the tradition of the old Volksschule (elementary school) and become the second pillar of school education alongside the Gymnasium. The Hauptschule and Realschule, on the other hand, have become less popular.

The new states have other types of schools such as the "Regelschule" or regular school (Thuringia), the "Mittelschule" or middle school (Saxony) and the "Sekundarschule" or secondary school (Saxony-Anhalt). They have merged the courses of the Hauptschule and the Realschule and from the 7th school year (i.e. the age of 13) courses are geared to the leaving certificate, which is equivalent to those awarded in western Germany.

A "cornet" filled with sweets - a German tradition on the first day at school

Physically or mentally handicapped children whose needs are not adequately catered for at general education schools attend special schools.

Anyone who for any reason has missed out on educational opportunities can catch up via the "second route". Evening colleges give working people the chance to prepare for Gymnasium graduation in courses lasting three to six years. Hauptschule or Realschule certificates can be obtained in the same way. This second route is hard going, if only because of the time factor, and students have to make considerable sacrifices.

▪ ▪ ▪ **Teachers.** For every type of school there are specially trained teachers. All must have completed a course of higher education but the contents and duration of such courses vary. Courses for Grundschule and Hauptschule teachers usually last six semesters (three years). Longer courses are required for Realschule, Sonderschule, Gymnasium and vocational school teachers. All applicants for the teaching profession have to pass an examination. This is followed by a period of practical training and a second examination. Teachers are generally made permanent civil servants. Transitional rules still apply to teachers in the new states.

Vocational education

The number of school leavers qualifying and opting for higher education is increasing while the proportion signing up for apprenticeships is on the decline. Those who do not reach university entrance standard usually take a course of vocational training, but so do many of the higher education qualifiers. Most of them are trained within the "dual system". This comprises practical, on-the-job learning with theoretical instruction at vocational school. Thus the private and public sector are jointly responsible. Government draws up the training regulations while the state governments oversee the vocational schools.

More than 1.7 million young people are receiving training in the 370 or so recognized trades for which formal training is required. Their popularity varies, however. Almost 40% of the male trainees are concentrated in 10 preferred vocations, while the proportion in the case of females is 55%. The occupations which most attract boys are motor mechanic, electrician, industrial mechanic and wholesale or import/export clerk; the girls' favourites are doctor's assistant, sales assistant, hair stylist, and office clerk. Greater efforts are being made to provide training for young people who have not served an apprenticeship.

■ ■ ■ **Vocational schools.** Apart from learning on the job the trainee has to attend vocational school on one or two days a week for three years. The schools teach general subjects and the theory which apprentices are better able to learn at school than at work. Courses lead to a final examination and certificate. Vocational schools are also obligatory for all under the age of 18 who attend no other type of school. These students do a "vocational preparation year" in which they are taught the theory which eases their choice of training.

■ ■ ■ **Other forms of vocational training.** Apart from apprenticeship and vocational school there are a number of other training systems. There is the full-time specialized vocational school (Berufsschule) whose courses last one to three years. They can be counted as an apprenticeship or part of it.

The specialized secondary school (Fachoberschule) admits pupils with an intermediate certificate. The courses last two years (for those who have completed an apprenticeship, one year) and qualify participants for the Fachhochschule, which is a polytechnic-type of college. Courses cover theory as well as workshop and on-the-job training. The Vocational Promotion Agency provides DM 4.3 million a year for the rehabilitation of handicapped young people. Under this scheme employers are required to reserve at least six per cent of total jobs for the handicapped. Fines are imposed on those who do not comply.

■ ■ ■ **On-the-job training.** Practical on-the-job training, usually called apprenticeship, takes from two to three and a half years, depending on the occupation, but in most cases three years. Only state-approved trades are covered. For participants who have a university entrance qualification the apprenticeship may be shortened by six months, and by another half-year if they perform exceptionally well.

Instruction in the use of electronic controls

Instructor and apprentices engaged in gas welding

The apprentice is paid a "training wage" which increases annually. What has to be learned, and finally tested, for a trade is set out in training regulations. These are issued by the responsible federal ministries and are based on proposals from the business associations, employers' organizations and trade unions.

The training concludes with an examination held by the self-governing business organizations, such as a chamber of industry and commerce or crafts or other institutions. On the examination board are representatives of the employers and unions as well as vocational schools teachers.

Over 500,000 firms in all branches of the economy, including the free professions and the public service, provide vocational training. Large enterprises have their own training workshops, but small firms train newcomers on the job. Where firms are too specialized to be able to impart all the necessary knowledge they can send their apprentices to inter-company training centres in order to broaden their vocational skills.

■ ■ ■ **Training for all.** In principle, no young person in Germany should begin working life without a vocational training. The number of unskilled workers is declining. Here the dual system has proved its worth, which is why some parts of it are being adopted by other countries.

In the 80s, for demographic reasons, demand for training places was very heavy but in recent years it has been outpaced by supply. In 1992, for instance, there were 623,000 places available in the west (98,000 in the east) for 512,000 (96,00 in the east) young people seeking an apprenticeship. This has been made possible by massive efforts on the part of all concerned - industry, the federal and state governments, the Federal Institute for Employment, and the Trust Agency (Treuhandanstalt). Inter-company training centres are now available in the new states as well. Under the Unification Treaty, vocational training qualifications were recognized in both parts of the country. This makes for greater mobility among young people.

Higher education

The Federal Republic's oldest university, at Heidelberg, was founded in 1386. Several others have had 500-year jubilees, including Leipzig (founded 1409) and Rostock (1419). But apart from these venerable institutions there are very young universities, more than 20 having been founded since 1960.

In the 19th century and in the first half of the 20th the educational ideal of German universities was the one pursued by Wilhelm von Humboldt at the Berlin University founded in 1810. The Humboldt type of university was conceived for a relatively small number of students. It was to be a place of pure science where research was done for research's sake and students were not taught primarily with a view to their future professions. This ideal clashed increasingly with the requirements of a modern industrial society. Alongside the traditional universities there emerged technical universities, teacher-training colleges and specialized colleges, the latter especially in the 70s and 80s. Education policy also changed. The demand for the best possible educational opportunities for all young people found general recognition.

Whereas in 1960 only 8% of each age group took up academic studies, nowadays nearly one in three seeks a university place. The number of students rose to about 1,800,000 in 1992/93. In that year alone there were more than 290,000 freshmen, continuing the slightly downward trend of recent years. The state tried to meet growth in demand since the 60s by expanding existing universities and building new ones, and by increasing teaching staff and university funding. New courses were focused more on professional requirements. However, expansion could not keep pace with the growth of the student community so that the situation has deteriorated in recent years. As the average length of time spent at university is too long the government are working on a structural reform programme to improve the efficiency of higher education.

■ ■ ■ **University organization.** The institutions of higher education in the Federal Republic of Germany (apart from church-owned colleges and universities of the armed forces and the National College of Public Administration) belong to the states. The federal government lays down the general principles of the university system and helps finance building and research.

The universities are self-governing. Within the framework of the law, each institution draws up its own constitution. It is headed by a full-time rector or president elected for several years. All groups - professors, academic staff, students and employees - play their part. In most states the student community manage their own affairs.

■ ■ ■ **Types of universities.** The mainstay of the tertiary education system are the academic universities and equivalent institutions. Courses culminate in a Master's degree ("Magister"), a "Diplom" or a public-service degree ("Staatsexamen"). After that, further qualification is possible up to doctorate level or a second degree. Some courses lead only to a Master's degree or a doctorate. Another, the most recent but increasingly attractive type of tertiary college is the "Fachhochschule", a specialized higher technical college or polytechnic. It provides a more practical education, especially in engineering, business administration, social science, design and agriculture, leading to a "Diplom". Today nearly every third new student enrols at a Fachhochschule, whose courses are shorter than those of universities.

In two states comprehensive universities (Gesamthochschulen) were established in the early 1970s. They combine the various tertiary forms under one roof and offer corresponding integrated courses.

Also new in the Federal Republic is the distance-learning university in Hagen, Westphalia, which opened in 1976. It now has nearly 49,000 students who, in addition to their correspondence courses, also attend regional centres.

■ ■ ■ **Courses and students.** Government policy has opened higher education study to all strata of the population. In the 1952/53 winter semester 4% of the freshmen came from wage-earner families, compared with about 19% today. In 1952 one fifth of students were women, today the figure is just under 40% in the western part of the country and over 45% in the east. The federal and state governments also want foreigners to study in Germany. In 1990 the number was over 100,000.

Students have extensive freedom in shaping their courses of study. Although for many courses curricula are recommended and interim examinations obligatory, in many others students can choose between certain subjects and lectures.

No fees are charged for the first course of study. If neither the student nor the parents are able to meet living expenses the state helps. Financial assistance can be obtained under the Federal Education Promotion Act (BAFöG). Half the amount is a grant, the other half a loan which usually has to be repaid within five years after the expiry of the maximum period for loans.

In 1992 about 90% of students in East Germany and roughly 33% in the west claimed BAFöG loans. The universities have student welfare organizations which, with state subsidies, finance refectories and hostels.

In the west about 10% of students live relatively cheaply in hostels, in the new federal states just under 70%. Some 40% of all freshmen are still living with their parents. Rents on the open market are a serious problem for many students. But at least there is cheap insurance. All students have statutory accident insurance cover and pay reduced contributions towards the health insurance scheme.

■ ■ ■ **The problem of student numbers.** Despite the considerable expansion of the university system the enormous growth in the number of people wanting to study has led to admission restrictions (numerus clausus) having to be introduced for an increasing number of subjects. Where restrictions are local university places are awarded by the university direct, but where they are national places are allocated by a central agency in Dortmund (Zentralstelle für die Vergabe von Studienplätzen), usually on the basis of average marks in final school exams and the length of time applicants have been waiting. This applies particularly to medicine, dentistry and veterinary science. There are also tests and interviews. Special consideration is given to hardship cases.

Reforms have been under discussion for some time, principally with a view to reducing the length of courses. Today students spend on average 14 semesters (seven years) at university, much longer than in other countries. Many of them have even completed an apprenticeship or compulsory military or civilian service before going to

A typical lecture-hall scene

university. The fact that they begin earning their living comparatively late in life is a serious disadvantage, also in view of the increasing international mobility, as for instance in the European internal market.

Polytechnic students are generally more optimistic than their counterparts at university about their future prospects. In 1993 just under 60% thought they could find places in industry and business after completing their course.

■ ■ ■ **The situation in the new federal states.** The reform of higher education in eastern Germany, partly under a programme costing DM 2.4 billion, has improved the academic range and regional distribution of institutions. Now there are 15 universities, 12 art and music colleges and 21 polytechnics, the latter having been unknown in the former GDR. The polytechnics have been established on the recommendation of the Science Council and 15,000 students had already enrolled in them for the 1992/93 winter semester. The number of students in eastern Germany in 1992 was 266,000.

Some of the research carried out at academies is being reintegrated into the universities and some transferred to extramural research establishments financed jointly by the federal and the state governments. Suitable professors and lecturers with an untainted political past are being incorporated in the public service. Many university teachers have come from the west and joined in particular law, economics and arts departments. Cooperation between universities and industry is developing in this new landscape.

Hochschulrektorenkonferenz
(The University Rectors' Conference)
Ahrstrasse 395, 53175 Bonn
Deutscher Akademischer Austauschdienst (DAAD)
(German Academic Exchange Service)
Kennedyallee 50, 53175 Bonn

Adult education

Every year ten million people in Germany take advantage of the many opportunities for further education.
Continuing education is necessary in a modern industrial
society in view of the fact that the demands of work are
increasing and changing all the time. Many people have
to change occupations several times in their life. But further education is also an important leisure-time factor. It
has a political function as well since the individual can
only have a say in matters if he is capable of making his
own judgement in various fields.

■ ■ ■ **Adult education centres.** Adult education centres were introduced towards the end of the 19th century, based on the Scandinavian model. They impart
mainly practical but also theoretical knowledge. Today
the subjects range from astronomy via language courses
to Zen meditation. There are some 1500 such centres in
the Federal Republic and numerous sub-centres. They
are generally run by local authorities or registered associations.

Funds are contributed by the state governments. Adult
education centres are non-political and non-denominational. Most of them take the form of evening classes, but
there are also residential centres which offer courses
lasting several days or weeks.

In 1991 alone, they ran nearly 450,000 courses which
were attended by about six million people (in 1965 there
were 78,000 courses and 1.7 million participants). Three
million took part in 80,000 individual events. Most popular are language, health education and crafts courses.

For a number of years certificates have been awarded
in various subjects such as languages, mathematics,
science and technology. Many participants make up for
opportunities lost at school: in 1991 nearly 4,300 obtained a junior secondary, 3,000 an intermediate school,
and well over 2,700 a university entrance qualification.
This widely varying tuition is provided by some 5,600
full-time teachers and nearly 130,000 part-time course
leaders.

■ ■ ■ **Continuing vocational training.** There has been
a remarkable increase in continuing education courses.

An adult education centre

Last year a third of the country's employees participated, and in the new states the proportion is over 40%. Industry spends more than DM 10 billion every year on further training for the labour force. There are 11 supraregional training institutes run by industry and 30 continuing education institutes. Large enterprises additionally run courses for their own employees. The participants are meant either to achieve a higher vocational qualification, refresh their skills in their own occupation or learn a completely new job.

There is a growing willingness to retrain for a different occupation, especially in the computer sector. Courses generally last two years in which full-time tuition alternates with practical training. Three out of four participants in further-training schemes report that they obtained better jobs.

The state provides roughly DM 5.5 billion a year for such training. During the course trainees receive grants or loans. The cost of tuition and teaching materials can be wholly or partly borne by the state.

Unemployed people in particular are resorting increasingly to continuing education to improve their employment prospects. Three quarters of unemployed participants who complete courses successfully find work within six months. The employment agencies pay a grant for up to 12 months to companies who give permanent employment to retrainees. The armed forces provide further training for servicemen in their own technical schools. There they can work for all school certificates up to the university entrance qualification (Abitur). The services, too, have their own establishments providing courses leading to various school certificates (see chapter on "Schools"). Their trades promotion service organizes initial courses, retraining and continuing training.

■ ■ ■ **Wide selection of courses.** The trade unions also have a large continuing education programme. The Volkshochschulen and the German Trade Union Federation (Deutscher Gewerkschaftsbund, DGB) are linked in a working group called "Arbeit und Leben" (Work and Life). This provides workers with courses in economic and social affairs, works constitution, insurance and labour law and much more. Works council members and other labour representatives can take courses at special DGB academies.

The churches, too, are active in the field of adult education. The Protestant Church maintains 15 academies where it holds seminars on topical issues. In the foreground of Catholic continuing education work are family and marriage problems and theological and cultural subjects.

Foundations closely allied to the political parties also have continuing education programmes: Friedrich-Ebert-Stiftung (SPD), Friedrich-Naumann-Stiftung (FDP), Konrad-Adenauer-Stiftung (CDU), Hanns-Seidel-Stiftung (CSU), and Heinrich-Böll-Stiftung (The Greens). Private distance-learning organizations also offer about 1,000 continuing education courses. In 1992 there were 180,000 participants, including 26,000 from the new states, there the process of developing continuing education is in full swing.

Deutscher Volkshochschulverband e.V.
(German Adult Education Federation)
Rheinallee 1, 53173 Bonn

Scholarship and research

In recent years the Nobel Prize winners for chemistry, physics and medicine have included Germans. The 1991 prize for medicine was awarded to Erwin Neher and Bert Sakmann for their work in the field of cellular biology. In 1989 the prize for physics was shared by Wolfgang Paul and two American colleagues, and in 1988 the prize for chemistry was shared by Johann Deisenhofer, Robert Huber and Hartmut Michel. Thus if one takes Nobel Prizes as the yardstick, Germany is holding its own in fields of advanced research.

Germany used to be known as the "land of science". Her universities led the world in many areas of scholarship. Up to the Second World War ten out of 45 Nobel Prizes for physics and 16 out of 44 for chemistry went to Germans.

But after 1933 the nazis drove many of the country's best brains abroad. A good number of them went to the United States, where they were of inestimable value to the country's scientific institutions. Germany had a hard task making up for this brain drain after 1945 and it was a long time before she caught up with the world's leaders.

Today there is a problem of a different kind but one which also holds out good opportunities: how to integrate the scientists and research institutions of the former GDR into an efficient research organization spanning the whole country. Up to 1992 more than a hundred non-university research institutes had been established in the new states, with employment for 12,500. They are a valuable complement to the world of research in Germany.

The structural changes have been drastic, especially in the field of higher education and research, but the process has largely been completed in terms of both subject-matter and personnel. None the less the government realizes that further efforts are necessary in order to unify research. It has for instance financed innovative, inter-university and inter-departmental research projects which also bring in external specialists, some from industry. A joint initiative for "product renewal" is intended to close the gap between investment promotion and manufacture of marketable products and thus help industry in the new states sustain development.

■ ■ ■ **Research establishments.** Research in the Federal Republic is done by the universities, public and private non-university and non-industry institutes, and industry itself.

Research by university teachers has a long tradition in Germany. "The unity of research and teaching" has been a pillar of German academic life since Wilhelm von Humboldt reformed the Prussian universities in the early 19th century.

The universities are the bedrock of German research. They are the only institutions whose research embraces all scientific disciplines. Most basic research is done there and they produce successive generations of scientists and thus ensure continuity. Non-university research is primarily an extension of the work done at the universities.

For instance, major research projects, especially in the natural sciences, can only be managed by big teams using expensive technology and with heavy financial backing.

Such large-scale research is best done in the government-funded centres for new sources of energy (e.g. nuclear fusion), aerospace, medicine, molecular biology, environmental and polar research.

The established system of joint promotion of research by the central and state governments proved to be a stabilizing factor precisely after the peaceful revolution in the former GDR when the country sought to unify re-

Spending on research and development
(old federal states, in billions of DM)

Researching sector	1971	1981	1991
Non-university research institutions	3.01	5.78	9.00
Universities and colleges	4.27	5.87	10.56
Private industry	10.70	26.60	49.42
Total	18.77	39.32	68.98

search as well. In Germany some 475,000 people have jobs connected with science and research - roughly one third scientists, one third technical and one third other personnel.

In 1990 the country spent DM 80.7 billion (about 2.6% of the gross domestic product) on research and development. The biggest contribution comes from industry (just under DM 48 billion), the Federal Government DM 18 billion and the states DM 13 billion. This puts Germany in third place behind Japan (over 3% GDP) and the United States (just short of 2.8%).

■ ■ ■ **Sponsors of research.** The universities are in many areas, especially big science and the arts, the most important sponsors of research and often the source of innovation. In fields of applied research and development they cooperate with other establishments and industrial laboratories. This speeds up the practical application of their theoretical findings. The polytechnics, too, play an important role in this regard and are particularly useful contacts and intermediaries for small firms.

Closely linked with the universities are the seven academies of science in Düsseldorf, Göttingen, Heidelberg, Leipzig, Mainz and Munich, and the recently founded Berlin-Brandenburg academy. They are centres of scien-

Phytogenetic research at the Max Planck Institute

Adjusting a cloud-monitoring radar installation

tific communication and mainly support long-term scholarly projects such as the publication of encyclopaedias, etc. Crucial support for university research comes from the German Research Foundation, the largest sponsor after the federal and state governments.

In 1992 alone it dealt with a record 12,000 applications for research funds, a fact which reflects the creativity and innovative energy of Germany's universities. The foundation receives its funds from the federal and state governments (in 1992 approx. DM 1.6 billion).

The Max Planck Society for the Promotion of the Sciences is the largest research organization outside the universities and its 60 or so facilities in the west are financed from public funds. It is developing further establishments in the east. The Max Planck Society engages in basic research which is either not done by the universities or requires particularly large equipment.

The 16 big-science institutions are another important instrument of government research policy. They receive 90% of their funds from the Federal Ministry for Research and Technology and 10% from the government of the state where they are located. Their research ranges from microparticles via aerospace to cancer, environmental and climate research.

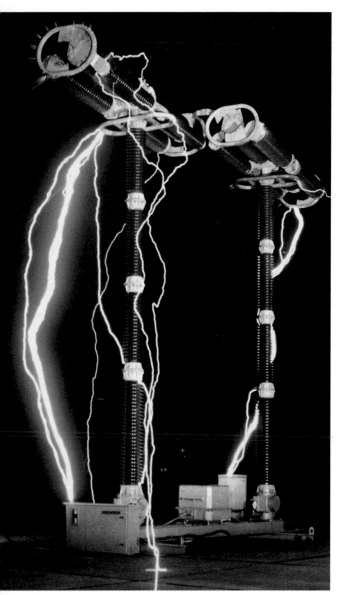

Insulation test on a high-voltage power switch

An important link between research and its practical application is the Fraunhofer Society for the Advancement of Applied Research. In its 50 or so institutes it carries out commissioned projects, mainly for industry. It already has 10 facilities and 12 branches in the new states.

Other significant contributions are made by the Fritz Thyssen and Volkswagen Foundations. They and the Donors Association for German Science (Stifterverband für die Deutsche Wissenschaft) are much in demand for research projects, especially in collaboration with the universities.

The Alexander von Humboldt Foundation, which receives financial support from the government, enables foreign scientists to do research in Germany and, vice versa, German scientists to work on similar projects abroad, and pays for research trips by outstanding foreign scientists.

Many of the tasks facing the government today cannot be accomplished without scientific preliminary work and consultation. Such activities are the responsibility of the many research institutions of the federal and state governments, such as the Federal Health Office (Bundesgesundheitsamt) or the Federal Environmental Agency (Umweltbundesamt).

■ ■ ■ **International cooperation.** The promotion of international cooperation in the field of research is a major aspect of government policy. There are various forms of cooperation apart from the promotion of exchanges and direct cooperation between German foreign scientists, for instance via the DAAD (German Academic Exchange Service) or the Alexander von Humboldt Foundation.

Germany has concluded agreements on scientific and technological cooperation with over 30 countries. Within the European Community it plays an active part in joint research and technology programmes. Cooperation also extends beyond the Community, as reflected in the COST (cooperation with third countries on applied research), JET and ITER (European and worldwide research on nuclear fusion) programmes, the EC's participation in the EUREKA and ESA projects, and the more recently EC-EFTA cooperation under the European Economic Area agreement.

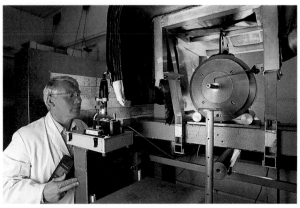

Fibre-optic testing at the Fraunhofer Institute, Euskirchen

Some of this work is carried out by institutions with large-scale facilities beyond the means of individual countries. They include the high energy accelerator of the European nuclear research organization (CERN) in Geneva, the very high flux reactor of the Max von Laue-Paul Langevin Institute (ILL) in Grenoble, or the European Molecular Biology Laboratory (EMBL) in Heidelberg.

The aim of all these programmes is to coordinate national research, to pool resources in joint projects and hence increase Europe's competitiveness.

■ ■ ■ **Research policy.** Research in Germany is determined by the freedom of teaching and research as anchored in the Basic Law, by the country's federal structure which divides responsibility between the federal and state governments, and by the demands of industry. Primarily it is the scientific institutions themselves who decide what research to undertake and assess the results, especially in the field of basic research.

Every four years the Federal Government submits a research report (the most recent one in 1993) in which it informs the public and parliament about the aims and focus of financial support for research and development.

Although private companies choose their own research projects, the government can provide incentives in the form of tax concessions or grants on the basis of subsidiarity, i.e. it can, for instance, promote large-scale projects which are in the public interest but are too costly for an individual company.

In the years ahead government policy will focus on the technologies of the 21st century, especially in the fields of transport, health and environment, and on support for small and medium-sized enterprises.

D 2 Mission: work in the materials lab

Culture

· Literature · The book trade and libraries · Art
· Architecture · Museums, collections, exhibitions · Music
· Theatre · Cinema · Festivals

Literature

The oldest testimony to German literature is the Song of Hildebrand, a story about how Hildebrand has to fight and kill his son Hadubrand for honour's sake. The Song of Hildebrand was sung at court by wandering minstrels. The names of German authors began to emerge in the 12th century. They included Wolfram von Eschenbach, Walther von der Vogelweide and Gottfried von Strassburg who wrote poems and epic stories, often in the French style.

German literature has always borrowed from abroad. The humanists of the Renaissance discovered Greek and Roman literature. Martin Luther translated the Bible into the vernacular and made it accessible to all German-speaking people. He thus laid the foundation for common high German. Not until the 17th century did writers like Martin Opitz start creating a German national literature. But it could not be kept within national confines. Its medium, the German language, was never limited by natural boundaries. Whether someone writing in German is an Austrian, Swiss or German usually is of little concern to the reader. It is the native language of Swiss, Austrians and Germans alike. The poets Rainer Maria Rilke, who was born in Prague, and Hugo von Hofmannsthal, born in Vienna, are just as much a part of German literature as the writers Robert Musil from Klagenfurt, Thomas Mann from Lübeck and Franz Kafka from Prague. And what would German literature be without the Swiss Gottfried Keller or Max Frisch, the Austrians Adalbert Stifter or Thomas Bernhard, the poet Paul Celan, who was born in Romania, or the Bulgarian Elias Canetti? The works of all these authors are contributions to German literature. However, the following brief survey will largely be confined to the literature of eastern and western Germany.

■ ■ ▢ **Highlights of the past.** In the 18th century, the Age of Enlightenment, Storm and Stress and Classicism, writers and philosophers were primarily concerned with the struggle of ideas. Later, against the backdrop of wars of liberation, they were also concerned with developing a German or cosmopolitan literature.

Gotthold Ephraim Lessing was the first to have commoners appear in a tragedy and to extol humanistic ideals. In Riga, Johann Gottfried Herder developed concepts of a new national German literature and made Shakespeare, among others, his model. Not long afterwards the "Storm and Stress" writers gathered around Johann Wolfgang von Goethe.

Goethe and Friedrich Schiller are Germany's classical writers. For half a century their ideal, a harmony of self and world, sentiment and reason, bound by a strict form, dominated German literature. The French Revolution of 1789 was a break in that very fruitful period.

The romantic poets strived after quite different ideals. Many of them were driven by patriotic sentiments. The romantics of Jena and Heidelberg renounced the visions of the Enlightenment. They wanted not to improve the world but to spiritualize, to poeticize it. Introspection, the reverse glorification of the Middle Ages, as well as the romantic longing for national heritage, competed with the desire to open up new worlds, new vistas.

Thus emerged collections of folklore in the form of songs, fairy-tales and sagas by Clemens Brentano, Achim von Arnim and the brothers Grimm. The response was considerable and long-lasting. Georg Büchner incorporated fairy-tales in his ironic, realistic dramas, and Heinrich Heine's "Lorelei", the most frequently quoted German poem, is a saga of the Rhine.

But this was also the time when great works of international renown were translated into German. The translations by Ludwig Tieck and the Schlegel brothers of Shakespeare and Cervantes became very famous and provided the stimulus for many more translations of great works, from the Romance and old Nordic languages, and later from Oriental and Indian literature.

The great 19th century German writers are still widely read today: Adalbert Stifter, Theodor Storm, Wilhelm Raabe, Theodor Fontane. Thomas and Heinrich Mann count among this century's greats, and works by Rainer Maria Rilke, Gottfried Benn, Hermann Hesse and Bertolt Brecht rank among the leading authors of that era.

During the twelve-year nazi dictatorship many German writers went into exile. Whilst in Marseilles, Anna Seghers described in "Transit" how people persecuted by the nazi regime desperately tried to flee Europe. In

Denmark Bertolt Brecht complained about the "Finstere Zeiten" (Dark Times), and Thomas Mann wrote his "Doktor Faustus" in the United States. Only a few writers (including Gottfried Benn, Hans Carossa, Ernst and Friedrich Georg Jünger, Erich Kästner and Ernst Wiechert) stuck it out in the "Internal Emigration", some of them being banned from writing or producing material that was non-committal.

■ ▦ **The new beginning after 1945.** After the Second World War German writers made a fresh start. They first tried to fill the vacuum with works in the foreign mould. They tried Hemingway's neo-realism and Jean Paul Sartre's existentialism. One spoke of "Trümmerliteratur" (literature of the ruins) and of "Zero Hour" literature.

The most radical example is "Draussen vor der Tür" (Outside the Door) which the author himself, Wolfgang Borchert, described as "a play which no theatre wants to stage and no public wants to see". This, like other works of that period, reflects the author's strong political commitment. Writers like Günter Eich, Peter Huchel or Hans Erich Nossack considered it their task to influence politics by literary means.

In the 50s and early 60s this attitude largely gave way to a different approach. Some authors criticized society on moral grounds. Their uneasiness about the negative aspects of the economic upswing, about the egotism and materialism of the affluent society, found articulation, for example, in novels like "Das Treibhaus" (The Greenhouse) by Wolfgang Koeppen or "Billard um halb zehn" (Billiards at Nine-thirty) by Heinrich Böll, whose short stories, too, deal with the legacy of National Socialism, a theme which dominated German literature in the 50s and 60s, as in Alfred Andersch's "Sansibar oder der letzte Grund" (Zanzibar or the Abyss) or the "Blechtrommel" (The Tin Drum) by Günter Grass. Many writers made the medium itself, language, the subject of literature (Uwe Johnson, Peter Härtling). They spoke of the "reprivatization" of literature. The most prominent German playwrights of that era were the Swiss Friedrich Dürrenmatt ("Der Besuch der alten Dame" [Visit from an Old Lady], "Die Physiker" [The Physicists]) and Max Frisch ("Andorra").

■ ▦ **The 68ers.** The new turning-point came in the late 60s. Literature focused on its social function. The

Günter Grass

stimulus was provided above all by the student movement of that period (the "68ers"). Literature was to serve
the political cause. Poets (F. C. Delius, Erich Fried, Yaak
Karsunke) and playwrights (Rolf Hochhuth: "Der Stellver-
treter" [The Deputy]), Heinar Kipphardt: "In der Sache J.
Robert Oppenheimer" [Re. J. Robert Oppenheimer]) and
Peter Weiss: "Die Ermittlung" [The Investigation]) deal
with contemporary topics or bring day-to-day happen-
ings onto the stage (Martin Sperr: "Jagdszenen aus
Niederbayern" [Hunting Scenes from Lower Bavaria]),
(Franz Xaver Kroetz: "Wildwechsel" [Watch Out for
Game]).

Many writers of the 60s, too, saw themselves as political authors, especially Heinrich Böll ("Ansichten eines
Clowns" [Opinions of a Clown]), "Gruppenbild mit
Dame" [Group Picture with Lady]); Günter Grass ("Hun-
dejahre" [Dog Years]); Martin Walser ("Halbzeit" [Half
Time]); Siegfried Lenz ("Deutschstunde" [German Les-
son]), all of them members of Group 47, a fluctuating
group of writers formed by Hans Werner Richter with the
aim of "bringing together and encouraging young writers".

Uwe Johnson was the one to concern himself most
with the division of Germany ("Mutmassungen über

Jakob" [Conjecture about James]). Group 61, on the other hand, depicted the working world (Max von der Grün: "Irrlicht und Feuer" [Will- o'-the-Wisp and Fire]); Günter Wallraff: ("Wir brauchen dich" [We Need You]). Yet another group focus on the old principle of "concrete poetry" as a question of language per se. Prominent among them are Ernst Jandl, Friederike Mayröcker, Helmut Heisenbüttel and Franz Mon. In 1968 the "Kursbuch" (The Time-table), a literary magazine by Hans Magnus Enzensberger, proclaimed the "death of literature".

■■■ **The rediscovery of the self.** In the 70s many German-language authors made their personal feelings the subject of their works (Max Frisch: "Tagebuch" (Diary); Wolfgang Koeppen: "Jugend" (Youth); Thomas Bernhard: "Die Ursache" (The Cause), "Der Atem" (Breath), "Die Kälte" (The Cold); Elias Canetti: "Die gerettete Zunge" (The Rescued Tongue)). Since the mid-70s there has been a separate body of women's literature (Carin Struck: "Klassenliebe" [Classroom Love]; Verena Stephan: "Häutungen" [Skinnings]; Brigitte Schwaiger: "Wie kommt das Salz ins Meer" [How does

the Salt get into the Sea]), which is still trying to establish itself. In the field of documentary literature there is a mixture of political pretentiousness and self-reflection (Uwe Johnson: "Jahrestage" [Anniversaries]); Walter Kempowski: "Tadellöser & Wolf"; Günter Wallraff: "Ganz unten" [Right Down at the Bottom]).

Ordinary, day-to-day events are reflected more strongly in the lyricism (Wolf Wondratschek, Nicolas Born, Ulla Hahn) and drama of those years (Botho Strauss: "Trilogie

Martin Walser

Gabriele Wohmann

des Wiedersehens" [The Wiedersehen Trilogy]) than in novels. But again and again there is the "flight into poetry".

In the late 80s works by the "old masters" were a pleasant change from the "production literature" of this period (newspaper articles, reviews and other ways of making a living by the pen). Heinrich Böll, who won the 1972 Nobel Prize for Literature, wrote "Frauen vor Flusslandschaft" (Women against a River Landscape) in 1988 and Grass "Die Rättin" (The Female Rat) in 1986. Patrick Süskind's 1985 "Das Parfüm" (The Perfume) is still on the bestseller lists. "Ohne einander" (Without One Another) is Martin Walser's latest novel.

■ ■ ■ **Production literature.** Johannes Mario Simmel, whose topical novel about asylum-seekers and foreigners "Auch wenn ich lache, muß ich weinen" (Even When I Laugh I Have To Cry) appeared in 1993, Willi Heinrich, Heinz G. Konsalik and Utta Danella - the number of writers of light literature in Germany is legion. The same is true of the authors of screenplays, stories for periodicals and novelettes. A man who reviews literary works with "papal authority" is Marcel Reich-Ranicki, almost a household name and a controversial figure. His reviews have "made" many of today's authors, and much of his criticism is itself literature. For in the process of distributing modern literature discussion groups on books often made up of writers reviewing the works of colleagues are still a path to literary success, although they are constantly losing ground on account of the financial power of the big publishing monopolies as reflected in their massive advertising of current books in the media.

■ ■ ■ **Children's literature.** Children's literature very soon became a branch of its own in Germany. "Struwwelpeter", which Heinrich Hoffmann, a doctor, wrote for his three-year- old son as a Christmas present in 1845, became world famous. "Max und Moritz", the two mischievous boys from the pen of Wilhelm Busch, have taught many generations of children. The adventures of "Heidi" by Johanna Spyri has been filmed several times. Still a great favourite is "Das doppelte Lottchen" (Double Lottie), "Das fliegende Klassenzimmer" (The Flying Classroom) and other youth novels by Erich Kästner. Ottfried Preussler: "Das kleine Gespenst" (The Little Ghost) and James Krüss: "Tim Thaler" have a huge readership.

But books for the young also deal with serious subjects. Michael Ende tells in "Momo" the story of the

"graue Herren" (Grey Gentlemen), who steel people's time and make them dependent on them. Peter Härtling, too, has written some outstanding children's books. Since the 70s Christine Nöstlinger has realistically looked into the every-day problems of young people. Her book "Nagle einen Pudding an die Wand" (Nail a Pudding to the Wall) was awarded the "Preis der Leseratten" (the Bookworms' Prize) in 1991. The prize was initiated by the "Stiftung Lesen" in Mainz and the winners are chosen by a

Siegfried Lenz

jury of children. Picture books by Janosh: "Oh wie schön ist Panama" (How Beautiful Panama Is) and Helmar Heine: "Freunde" (Friends) are popular with adults as well.

■ ■ ■ **Separate trend in the east.** In the former GDR post-1945 writers were required to extol Soviet-style "socialist realism". Most of the works produced in the 50s were later described as "construction" literature. The subjects were land reform, distribution of large estates to refugees and farm workers, or the redevelopment of farm holdings. The enemy-image was obvious. The good people,

Sarah Kirsch

including the party secretary, take up the struggle with the bad people, the big landowners, the "bourgeois scholars", the disguised western agents. And of course everyone knew who was going to win.

In the 60s most authors still believed they could improve the political system. A kind of critical, subjective writing emerged. "Construction" literature was superseded by "arrival" literature. Novels such as Jurek Becker's "Jakob der Lügner" (James the Liar) and Hermann Kant: "Die Aula" (The Hall), the prose and poems of Johannes Bobrowski: "Levins Mühle" (Levin's Mill) and "Litauische Claviere" (Lithuanian Pianos), the stories of Franz Fühmann: "Das Judenauto" (The Jew's Car), and the plays of Peter Hack, Heiner Müller and Volker Braun caused a stir in the Federal Republic at that time. Many of them were first or only published in the Federal Republic and were instrumental in gaining recognition for the GDR as a "cultural state". Many authors returning from exile (e.g. Anna Seghers, Arnold Zweig, Johannes R. Becher) wrote books that were in line with the communist system or wrote very little at all. Soon more or less concealed rejections of "socialist realism" began to appear. Christa Wolf coined the term "subjective authenticity" ("Nachdenken über Christa T." [Reflections on Christa T.]). In the 70s Wolf Biermann, the singer/songwriter who had been critical of the system, was banned from appearing on stage and in 1976 deprived of his citizenship and forced to leave the country. His courageous example was followed by others. Stefan Heym: "Der König- David-Bericht" (The King David Report), Ulrich Plenzdorf: "Die neuen Leiden des jungen W." (The New Suffering of Young W.), Franz Fühmann: "22 Tage oder Die Hälfte des Lebens" (22 Days or Half a Life), Reiner Kunze: "Die wunderbaren Jahre" (The Wonderful Years) and Günter de Bruyn: "Märkische Forschungen" (Studies in the March), criticized the GDR and its system of informers which they themselves could hardly escape.

East German literature faced a crisis and turned to subjects that had hitherto been taboo, such as utopian literature and women's topics. Indeed, some even looked at the darker side of socialist society, such as those who had built a career out of the system (Günter de Bruyn: "Neue Herrlichkeit" [New Glory]), conformists (Christoph Hein: "Der fremde Freund/Drachenblut" [The Alien Friend/Dragon's Blood]), the contradictions between rulers and ruled (Volker Braun: "Hinze-Kunze-Roman" [Tom, Dick and Harry Novel]), and real life in the GDR (Wolfgang Hilbig: "Die Weiber" [The Womenfolk]), "Alte Abdeckerei" [The Old Flaying House]).

■ ▓ ▒ **Post-unification literature.** Germany's unification has greatly enhanced the literary scene in the new German states. Both that had been previously censored became bestsellers in eastern Germany's bookshops which, immediately after the Berlin wall was opened were selling 25% more books than before. Authors from the former GDR, who were often enough caught up in the power system, are having difficulty coming to terms with the past.

Writers need time to digest reality and reproduce it in their art. It remains to be seen which authors from the former GDR will continue to write and how they go about it. But it will also be seen how the changed political circumstances are mirrored by West German authors as well. The reading public are full of expectancy.

The book trade and libraries

The first book to be printed with movable type was published in Mainz in 1455. The inventor, Johannes Gutenberg, was printer and publisher in one. Thus the birth of the new technology coincided with the beginning of German book publishing and selling. Frankfurt am Main had been the leading publishing centre since the late 15th century. In the 18th century, because of restrictions imposed by the emperor, it was surpassed by Leipzig. After the Second World War, Frankfurt regained its preeminence as a result of the country's division. Now several cities are major publishing centres in Germany: Munich, Berlin, Hamburg, Stuttgart, Frankfurt, Cologne and Leipzig.

In terms of book production Germany comes second to the United States. In 1990 there were almost 70,000 first and new editions. More than 600,000 titles were available in German bookshops.

There are over 2,000 publishers in the Federal Republic. About 80 of them have an annual turnover of DM 25 million or more, but none of them dominates the market. There are also many small companies who contribute to the variety of literature available to the public. After the war book clubs attracted a wider readership. They derived their origin from the idea of "national education". One of them, the Büchergilde Gutenberg (Gutenberg Book Guild) was founded by the trade unions. Today there are ten book clubs with about six million members. Subscription on this scale makes books cheaper.

In 1992 the total turnover of books and journals came to about DM 14.8 billion, a record which was chiefly due to heavy demand from the new federal states. In statistical terms, the average price of a hardback in 1992 was about DM 37.45, considerably less than in the previous year. Paperbacks are much cheaper. The book trade is the only branch of commerce in Germany still permitted to dictate retail prices. Bookshops have to sell every book at the price set by the publisher, on the ground that prices have to be maintained in order to ensure that small bookshops too can make a living.

Mergers have taken place in the book trade as well. In the 70s the smaller shops with sales space of up to 500 sq m were in the majority. Now the larger bookstores are taking over, especially in city centres. Wholesale chains from France and the United Kingdom are also acquiring a larger share of the market. The 577 bookshops in the former GDR, which in the old days were run as "people's enterprises", have meanwhile been privatized. Two thirds of them have been sold in eastern Germany, the rest to buyers in the west. Many famous publishing houses who opened new establishments in the west when Germany was divided have since been reunited with their parent companies in eastern Germany, one of these being the Reclam-Verlag.

■ ■ ■ **Book Trade Association and Book Fair.** The professional organization of publishers and sellers is the Börsenverein des Deutschen Buchhandels (Book Trade Association) in Frankfurt. This organization launched the Frankfurt Book Fair, which is held every autumn. Apart from the commercial side, it is also the book trade's "window on the world" and a major cultural event. Every year it has a different theme. In 1992 it was Mexico, 1993 Flanders and the Netherlands, while in 1994 the focus will be on Brazil. In 1992 more than 8,000 publishers from 95 countries exhibited their products.

The fair culminates in the award of the Peace Prize of the German Book Trade Association. Recent prize winners have been Léopold Sédar Senghor, Max Frisch, Yehudi Menuhin, Teddy Kollek, Vladislav Bartoszewski,

Book production by field
(first and new editions 1991)

Titles	Area	%
5,647	General	8.3
3,173	Philosophy, psychology	4.7
3,350	Religion, theology	4.9
14,820	Social sciences	21.8
4,132	Mathematics, natural sciences	6.1
9,397	Applied sciences, medicine, technology	13.8
5,293	Art, art and crafts, photography, sport, games	7.8
12,953	Linguistics and literature, fiction	19.1
9,125	Geography, history	13.5

The Cusanus Library, Bernkastel on the Mosel

Hans Jonas, Václav Havel, György Konrád and Amos Oz. Germany's second most important book exhibition is the spring fair in Leipzig, which, on account of its location, sees its role partly as that of intermediary with the countries of eastern Europe.

■ ■ ■ **Libraries.** Unlike other countries Germany has no ancient national library. It was not until 1913 that the new German Library in Leipzig brought together all German-language literature under one roof. Today that library holds some 7.2 million volumes. The division of Germany after the Second World War led to the foundation of the German Library in Frankfurt am Main in 1947. It had the same function in the west as the Leipzig library in the east. It was founded by the book trade and since 1969 has been a federal institution. In addition to all German language literature published since 1945, it collects the "exile literature", that is, works produced between 1933 and 1945 by German writers who fled the country to escape the nazi regime. It contains about 5.3 million volumes. Plans are being made to fuse these two principle libraries.

One of the country's main public libraries is the Bayerische Staatsbibliothek in Munich (more than six million books), another the Staatsbibliothek Preussischer Kulturbesitz in Berlin (about four million). In addition to the general libraries (mostly state and university libraries)

Browsers' corner in a large bookshop

there are specialized libraries such as the Central Medical Library in Cologne. A library with an outstanding reputation is the Herzog-August-Bibliothek in Wolfenbüttel, which has over 660,000 volumes, including 12,000 priceless medieval handwritten books.

In western Germany there are also some 15,000 public libraries with more than 30 million volumes. Most of them are owned by the local authorities and churches. In the former GDR there were about 9,500 public and union libraries. When the unions were disbanded in 1990 their libraries became public property.

Börsenverein des Deutschen Buchhandels
(The German Book Trade Association)
Grosser Hirschgraben 17-21, 60311 Frankfurt am Main

Art

When, in 1947, one of the first post-war art exhibitions opened in Augsburg under the motto "Extreme Art", it evoked little enthusiasm. The public weren't used to abstract art. Under National Socialism most schools of modern art had been declared "degenerate". This was the regime's catchword for a campaign to destroy everything in art that was too critical or too abstract. Thus the German expressionists and abstract painters were affected. Great contemporary painters such as Oskar Kokoschka (1886-1980), Max Beckmann (1884-1950) or Vassily Kandinsky (1866-1944) were taboo. In 1937 alone, 1,052 paintings were confiscated from German galleries. As a result, German artists lost touch with international trends.

■ ■ ■ **Developments since 1945.** After the Second World War the gap was closed with remarkable speed. Painting followed pre-war trends and owed much to Paul Klee (1879-1940) and Vassily Kandinsky, who had already moved towards abstract art before the First World War. Also still alive were the great "degenerate" artists Oskar Kokoschka, Max Beckmann, Max Pechstein (1881-1955), Emil Nolde (1876-1956), Erich Heckel (1883-1970) and Karl Schmidt-Rottluff (1884-1976). Their task was to bring back the modern art that already seemed almost history. The abstract expressionism which evolved in France under the influence of the Germans Wols (Wolfgang Schulze, 1913-51) and Hans Hartung (1904-67) established itself. Its main exponents were Willi Baumeister (1889- 1955), Ernst Wilhelm Nay (1902-68) and Fritz Winter (1905-76).

In the early 60s the Düsseldorf group "Zero" proclaimed a new beginning. It was in the Op-Art category, which had its roots in, among other things, the experimental tradition of the Bauhaus. The best-known members of this group are Otto Piene (born 1928), Günther Uecker (born 1930) and Heinz Mack (born 1931). They did not regard art as a platform of pathetic humanity but turned to natural phenomena: light, movement and space. They directed attention to the objective, technologically influenced environment and its significance to mankind. This aim is apparent in the fire and smoke pictures of Piene, Uecker's nail pictures and Mack's light steles and dynamos. In Op(tical)-Art the specific facets of visual perception, including the optical illusion, become the focal point.

Pop-Art did not evoke the same response in Germany as in the United Kingdom and the United States, whereas Signal Art and Hard Edge painting were taken up by Günter Fruhtrunk (1923-1982), Karl Georg Pfahler (born 1926) and Winfred Gaul (born 1928) and became very popular.

Thus whereas artists in the Federal Republic were able to follow existing traditions and draw on new currents flowing from western Europe and the United States, their colleagues in the former GDR were tied to the "socialist realism" prescribed for them. They were permitted to do nothing more than portray a favourable picture of the socialist society and its kind of people. Until the late 60s the artistic creation promoted by the regime's functionaries was predominantly a description of working life under the socialist system.

New trends in painting came mainly from the Leipzig Academy of Art. Among its best-known artists were Werner Tübke (born 1929) and Bernhard Heisig (born 1925), whose monumental paintings, though still tied to historical or social themes, shed the sterility of the 50s and 60s. Wolfgang Mattheuer (born 1927), also a member of the Leipzig Academy, went much further in his efforts to derive more out of realistic painting. His pictures, such as Snow White as the Statue of Liberty, are more a synthesis of post-expressionist new objectivity and "magic realism" than a testimony to socialist realism. A. R. Penck (born 1939), who left the GDR in 1980 and achieved fame in the west, chose as his theme idols of the Stone Age. The works of these painters were very much in demand by western galleries in the late 70s.

■ ■ ■ **The artists of today.** "Informel", a post-war form of abstract painting, is still not yet outmoded. It turned visual art into action, used new, unusual materials. Paint was applied thickly, and sometimes the artist departed from the traditional rectangular shape. The result was "happenings", "critical realism", the "New Wild Ones" who lived life to the full in neo-expressionism. There were also light displays, rotating elements, collages, pos-

Markus Lüpertz: "Der Regen", 1978

ters, and above all action art, which usually takes place outside the artist's studio.

Joseph Beuys (1921-1986) set the trend. He no longer attached importance to "immortal" works but staged art as action. For instance, he had himself taken across the river Rhine in a dugout. He spared no expense to "bring art to society". HA Schult, too, has a liking for the spectacular. His action theme is "Fetish Car", to the amusement of the general public. In Cologne, for instance, he had his car monument raised onto a medieval tower.

Action of this kind is also appreciated by the American Jonathan Borofsky, who in Germany likes to decorate the "city as an artistic space" with moving objects. One of his works is the "Hammering Man", a black giant with a slow hammering motion, to be seen in front of the exhibition hall in Frankfurt on the Main. On the occasion of "documenta 1992" in Kassel Borofsky integrated another provocative object, the "Himmelsstürmer" (The Idealist) into the city landscape.

At present there is a trend towards mammoth objects, though there is still considerable variety. Anselm Kiefer (born 1945) shapes massive works of art in his studios, which are like shop floors in factories. They are made mostly of lead but also include aircraft in their original size.

"Zweistromland" (Two-stream Country) is the name of a 32-ton sculpture consisting of 200 books made of lead on shelves eight metres long. He calls his pictures, many of which are inspired by mythology, "picture bodies" because he attaches various materials to them such as dust, flower petals, ash or roots. Kiefer, who has frequently taken as his subject the burdens of Germany's recent past, presents with his monumental works the magnitude and misery of a culture-oriented world.

But between action art, the giant silhouettes in the townscape, and Kiefer's lead objects there are in Germany countless types of artistic experiment in which the artists are prepared to try any form, any material. There is much *arte povera* as well as realistic, surrealistic or expressionistic elements. Rebecca Horn (born 1944) presents sculptures as "performances" and uses them in her own films.

Gerhard Richter (born 1932) is a master of ambiguity on the border between abstract and non-abstract art, often changing his style. He categorically rejects interpretations of his work. Georg Baselitz (born 1938), who has won many awards and gained an international reputation, expresses in his upside-down pictures the misery of the human creature. What matters to him is not that which is portrayed but the actual doing and artistic freedom.

Markus Lüpertz, currently director of Düsseldorf's Kunstakademie, gives us with his "dithyrambic painting" a "drunken, rapturous" feeling of life. He is one of the "fathers" of the new materialistic art in western Germany, although he has always avoided wild gestures and splurges of colour. Sigmar Polke (born 1941) represents the occult trend but also enjoys practical jokes. "Dürer will be here in a moment", is the name of one of his objects. With the help of photochemicals he makes his works constantly change. A. R. Penck seeks through his pictures, whose matchstalk figures recall archaic symbols, to create a universal language which all can directly understand.

Huge dolomite blocks and the Heinrich Heine monument in Bonn bear the signature of Ulrich Rückriem (born 1938). Günter Uecker today celebrates the "poetry of destruction". Jörg Immendorf (born 1945) is a kind of modern historical painter. In his picture "Café Deutschland" the storm of history blows the Berlin wall away. Vi-

Anselm Kiefer: "Adelaide"

deos, computers and telecommunications are also used for artistic purposes. Karlsruhe's "Centre for Art and Media Technology", opened in 1992, and the "Institute for New Media" of Frankfurt's Städelschule perceive the electronic media as forms of expression which complement traditional painting and sculpture. The focus is on videoart and the interaction of computer and observer. Holographic art, which has gained ground in the United States in particular has found notable creative representatives in Germany, too, one being the Berlin painter and graphic artist Dieter Jung. His hologram- light pictures in virtual light, such as "Into the Rainbow", "Motion in Space" and "Sonnenwind" make him the poet of this art form.

■ ■ ■ **Galleries and exhibitions.** Most works of art are to be found in the museums and galleries of the big cities. Painters like Max Ernst, Otto Dix, Chagall, Picasso, Dalí and other "classical artists" still draw visitors in their thousands. Avant-garde works are particularly prominent in Cologne and Düsseldorf, home to artists most con-

Ulrich Rückriem: No Title

cerned with experimentation. In Berlin the Grisebach
auction centre is on the way to becoming as famous as
Sotheby's in London. The most spectacular exhibition is
the "documenta" which takes place in Kassel every five
years. At this "international exhibition of contemporary
art" the avant-garde are on display for 100 days, shocking, provoking or amusing, bringing the whole city into
the picture, so to speak. In 1992 the exhibition drew a
record 600,000 visitors.

■ ■ ■ **Art promotion.** Few painters and sculptors can
live on the proceeds from the sale of their works. They
receive government grants and assistance from private
companies. The "Kunstfonds e.V.", founded in 1980,
helps recognized artists finance ambitious projects. The
fund has DM 1.7 million a year for artistic purposes. Of
this amount DM 1.3 million is provided by the Federal
Government, the other DM 400,000 coming from publications on contemporary art.

Well-known places of cultural activity are the artists
colony at Worpswede in northern Germany, the Villa
Massimo and the Villa Romana in Italy. At these centres
scholarship holders can work without disturbande and
free from financial worry. Industry, too, promotes art. For
over 40 years the cultural section of the Federation of
German Industry, for instance, has been awarding prizes
to painters and sculptors.

"Art on buildings" is also encouraged. It is now normal
for companies to set aside one per cent of their building
costs for artistic decoration. As a result, one sees paintings in the corridors of high-rise buildings of large banks,
and action artists leave their mark in front of the buildings of government departments or private companies.

Architecture

Twentieth century German architects have been trend-setters. The strongest influences came from Weimar and Dessau, where the Bauhaus school was formed in the 20s. This applies especially to Walter Gropius (1883-1969) and Ludwig Mies van der Rohe (1886-1969), two of the leading figures of the Bauhaus style, whose functional approach won worldwide recognition. Masterpieces of this synthesis of art and technology are to be seen on all continents.

For a long time the situation after 1945 was a great disadvantage. The destroyed towns and cities had to be redeveloped and cheap housing was needed for millions of people. In those days little consideration could be given to architectural quality. In later years there were bitter complaints about the monotonous architecture of satellite townships and the dull fronts of department stores and office buildings. This was particularly true of the former GDR. There valuable old buildings were destroyed and scarce resources used to build massive housing estates, all constructed in the same prefabricated mould.

Today architects are experimenting more and more but at the same time providing buildings that meet human needs. While the success of many projects is still attributable to the Bauhaus style and philosophy, new trends, such as the post-modern, have produced some remarkable buildings. German architects are also gaining prominence abroad with their bold designs, for instance Helmut Jahn, who is based in Chicago, a city of modern, high-rise buildings. He built the 256-metre high tower at Frankfurt's exhibition site, the highest office block in Europe.

In the winter of 1993 Joseph Paul Kleihues is designing Chicago's new Museum for Contemporary Arts. He attracted attention with his work on the Tempelhof Stadtreinigungswerk and the Neukölln Krankenhaus, both in Berlin, and as director of planning for the International Building Exhibition. Other leading German architects are Gottfried Böhm, who in 1986 became the first German to win the Pritzker Architecture Prize, Günter Behnisch and Oswald Mathias Ungers, who has a preference for geometric forms.

■ ■ ■ **Outstanding structures.** Germany has some fine representative building. The skeleton high-rise, all-glass type, as exemplified by Mies van der Rohe's Seagram Building in New York, has an interesting variant in the Federal Republic in the three-sectional Thyssen House in Düsseldorf (built by Helmut Hentrich in 1960) and the office building of Hamburg's Elektrizitätswerke (Arne Jacobsen and Otto Weitling, 1969).

An example of unconventional, dynamic architecture is the central office of the BMW car-making firm in Munich, with its striking cylindrical form (Karl Schwanzer, 1972), or the Bahlsen building in Hanover with its interlocking cubist forms (Dieter Bahlo, Jörn Köhnke, Klaus Stosberg, 1974).

Another striking landmark is Stuttgart's television tower with restaurant and observation platform (Fritz Leonhardt, 1956). The tent-like structures (Günter Behnisch, 1972) designed for the 1972 Olympic Games in Munich are world famous. The sports facilities are situated in a park which continues to be a popular area for leisure pursuits.

Architectural fantasy also finds expression in concert halls, opera houses, theatres and museums. World fa-

Underground station entrance at Reinoldikirchplatz, Dortmund (W. v. Lom)

Nikko Hotel and sculpture, Düsseldorf

mous are Berlin's neue Philharmonie by Hans Scharoun
(1964) with its vineyard-like terraced auditorium constructed around the orchestra. By contrast, Münster's
Stadttheater incorporates a classical ruin. Stuttgart's
Liederhalle and Mannheim's multi-purpose hall at Her-
zogenriedpark are fine examples of assembly hall architecture. Museums which integrate well into the local
townscape were built by Hans Hollein in Mönchen-
gladbach (1982) and Gottfried Haberer, who created
Cologne's Wallraf-Richartz-Museum/Museum Ludwig
(1986). James Stirling's Neue Staatsgalerie in Stuttgart
was also received with much acclaim (1983).

Another outstanding piece of architecture is the new
Museum für Kunsthandwerk (Arts and Crafts Museum) in
Frankfurt am Main, which was designed by Richard
Meier (1985). Bonn's Bundeskunsthalle designed by the
Viennese architect Gustav Peichl, was completed in
1992. University buildings, too, reveal some interesting
examples, for instance the University of Constance,

Ludwig- und Wallraf-Richartz Museum, Cologne (Busmann & Haberer)

The fire department, Weil am Rhein (Z. M. Hadid)

whose buildings fit asymmetrically into the terrain. And the Filderklinik in Filderstadt near Stuttgart demonstrates how a hospital can be organically merged with the landscape.

Many churches, too, have been built in Germany since the Second World War. The architects had plenty of scope for experimentation. Worthy of mention are Berlin's Memorial Church (Gedächtniskirche), which had been destroyed during the war. Egon Eiermann fused the old ruin with a new steel construction with large glass sections (1963). Other noteworthy structures are the fortress-like pilgrimage church at Neviges by Gottfried Böhm (1967) and the Hopfenstangenkirche built by Wolfgang Gsanger in Forchheim (central Franconia).

■ ■ ■ **Urban planning.** Present-day architecture must also make allowance for the needs of urban planning. During the reconstruction phase in Germany much historical substance was sacrificed. Old residential buildings, from the late 19th century, for instance, were not considered worth preserving. But in the meantime people's attitudes have changed. The historical value of buildings is now appreciated. New buildings are integrated as far as possible into the local environment, the utility structures of department stores built in the 50s and 60s are no longer wanted.

A greater awareness of the natural growth of town centres is reflected, for instance, in the Schneider department store in Freiburg (Heinz Mohl, 1976) or Würzburg's Kaufhaus by Alexander von Branca. The "Alte Oper" in Frankfurt on the Main is a magnificent building from the late 19th century. Its exterior was completely reconstructed in 1981 and it now houses an ultra-modern concert hall and congress centre.

More and more houses and groups of old or historical buildings as well as entire streets are being listed as protected objects. This also applies to industrial buildings such as the foundry in Bendorf on the Rhine or the pithead tower of the German Mining Museum in Bochum. The city has begun renovating the old houses in the centre. This will provide additional accommodation and is in keeping with the current trend of encouraging people from the outskirts back into the city.

The task of urban redevelopment will continue for a long time, especially in town centres in the former GDR, and has to be seen in the context of housing demand (see chapter on "housing and urban development").

Museums, collections, exhibitions

The broad range of museums in Germany reflects the nation's social and cultural developments. There are more than 3,000 museums in the Federal Republic of Germany: state, municipal, association and private museums, museums of church and cathedral treasures, residential, castle, palace and outdoor museums. They have grown up over the centuries out of royal, church, and later civic collections.

Princely collections were, of course, not intended for the erudition of the general public. Their owners wanted to show admiring visitors all their wonderful possessions. In Munich, for instance, which was an international art centre as early as the 16th century, Bavarian dukes collected not only works of art but also machinery, craftsmen's tools, musical instruments, minerals and exotic objects from distant lands.

The "Grünes Gewölbe" of the Saxon electors of Dresden was probably the largest treasure house in Europe in the 17th century. It eventually became an art gallery, but also a mathematics and physics museum and a mineralogy museum.

Not only rulers but many wealthy citizens had private collections. As a result, there was a museum in Germany for every field of art, all types of activity. Especially the large museums tried to display as much as possible and in many cases there was fruitful competition. Nearly everything was exhibited: from Rembrandt and Picasso to tapestries (Kassel), from wine-making equipment (Koblenz) to meteorites (Marburg), from mummies from the moors (Schleswig) to optical instruments (Oberkochen) or the oldest boat in the world reconstructed from original parts (Bremerhaven).

■ ■ ▨ **Art lovers and patrons.** Today, Germany's museums, both traditional and modern, try to appeal to all sections of the population. They now offer the "living experience", which includes video equipment, cafeterias and very light rooms. The museum becomes a place of contact and discussion and the exhibits are related to the present. The result is that Germans today visit the museum as casually as they used to go to the cinema.

The Museum of Modern Art ("slice of gateau"), Frankfurt/Main

Year in, year out over 100 million people visit Germany's museums, which in some cities occupy a whole district. Examples are the embankment in Frankfurt, or Berlin, where the Stiftung Preussischer Kulturbesitz (Foundation for Prussian Cultural Property), established in 1951, can fill whole museums with its collections from Prussian days. As in former times, wealthy private citizens are partly responsible for the museum boom through their sponsorship.

Peter Ludwig, a businessman in the Rhineland, is one of the best-known. He supports mainly modern art galleries up and down the country. The latest to receive his help is the "Ludwig-Forum" in Aachen, a former umbrella factory, which also puts on exhibitions of art from the former GDR. Bonn's "Haus der Geschichte" (Art and Exhibition Hall of the Federal Republic of Germany) was opened in 1992, and the Haus der Geschichte der Bundesrepublik Deutschland (Centre for the History of the Federal Republic of Germany), likewise in Bonn, is under construction, while in Berlin the Deutsches Historisches Museum (German Historical Museum) presents German history in its entirety right up to the present time.

An important role is played by art and anthropological museums on account of the broad range of their displays. The Deutsches Museum in Munich, for instance, has originals and models depicting the development of technology and science, while the Germanisches Nationalmuseum in Nuremberg has the largest collection on the history of German art and culture from prehistory to the 20th century. Also unique is the large number of ethnological museums in a country which was only briefly a colonial power but nevertheless produced many outstanding discoverers and scholars who were concerned with foreign cultures. In addition to the Berlin museums, the Linden Museum in Stuttgart deserves special mention in this respect.

There is a growing demand for special exhibitions. On such occasions the museums and galleries can draw on their extensive stocks. Historical exhibitions such as "Die Welt der Staufer" commemorating the medieval imperial Hohenstaufen dynasty, held in Stuttgart in 1977, or

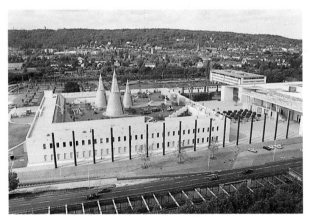

The Federal Art and Exhibition Hall, Bonn

*From the 1993 exhibition "Bernward of Hildesheim
and the age of the Ottonians", Hildesheim*

"Preussen - Versuch einer Bilanz" (Prussia - An Appraisal)
and "Jüdische Lebenswelten" (Jewish Life), both which
took place in Berlin in 1981 and 1991 respectively,
aroused considerable interest. Also extremely popular
were comprehensive retrospectives such as the Darmstadt Jugendstil (Art Nouveau) exhibition "Ein Dokument
deutscher Kunst" (1976).

It has also been possible to bring major international
itinerant exhibitions to Germany, such as the Tutencha-
mun exhibition and a display of treasures from San
Marco in Venice. And the biggest Cézanne exhibition to

date, held in Tübingen's Kunsthalle, in 1993, was a large success. Art from non-European countries attracts considerable interest in Germany. The exhibition "Die Frau im alten Ägypten" (Women of Ancient Egypt) attracted 250,000 visitors to Cologne. The city of Aachen presented "Vergessene Städte am Indus" (Forgotten Cities on the Indus), and Munich staged an exhibition of Mongolian culture.

The largest festival of modern art in the world is Kassel's "documenta", which takes place every five years and draws many visitors - in 1992 a record of more than 600,000.

■ ■ ■ **Museum variety.** The broad regional distribution of Germany's museums makes them accessible to large numbers of people. There is no central government "museum policy", but museums cooperate with one another in many fields, such as restoration and security, central documentation and research. Such activities are coordinated by the Deutscher Museumsbund (German Museums Association), which was established in 1917. A similar task is performed by the Institut für Museumskunde of the State Museums of Prussian Cultural Property in Berlin.

Museum architecture, too, shows great variety, ranging from the 19th century art "temples" to such ultra-modern buildings as the Neue Staatsgalerie in Stuttgart or the Architekturmuseum (Museum of Architecture) and the Museum of Modern Art in Frankfurt am Main. Many museums were destroyed during the Second World War, but their collections were stored in safe places. There are still traces of war damage. It took over 30 years to rebuild Munich's Neue Pinakothek. Museums in the west are again working in partnership with those in the eastern part of the country. In March 1993, for example, some 150 works of art, including drawings by Dürer, Delacroix, Toulouse-Lautrec and Manet, which had been carried off during the Second World War, were returned to Bremen's Kunsthalle.

Principal museums
Art
Aachen: Domschatzkammer, Neue Galerie
Berlin: Staatliche Museen Preussischer Kulturbesitz, including the Gemäldegalerie and the Nationalgalerie

Bonn: Städtische Kunstsammlungen, Kunst- und Aus-
stellungshalle der Bundesrepublik Deutschland
Braunschweig: Herzog-Anton-Ulrich-Museum
Dessau: Bauhaus-Archiv
Dresden: Gemäldegalerie Alte und Neue Meister,
"Grünes Gewölbe"
Essen: Museum Folkwang
Frankfurt am Main: Städelsches Kunstinstitut, Museum
für moderne Kunst
Hamburg: Kunsthalle
Hanover: Niedersächsisches Landesmuseum, Kestner-
Museum
Hildesheim: Roemer-Pelizaeus-Museum
Karlsruhe: Staatliche Kunstsammlungen
Kassel: Staatliche Kunstsammlungen
Cologne: Wallraf-Richartz-Museum/Museum Ludwig
Leipzig: Museum der Bildenden Künste
Munich: Alte Pinakothek, Neue Pinakothek
Regensburg: Museum Ostdeutsche Galerie
Stuttgart: Staatsgalerie
Cultural history
Bonn: Rheinisches Landesmuseum
Cologne: Römisch-Germanisches Museum
Mainz: Gutenberg-Museum; Römisch-Germanisches
Zentralmuseum
Munich: Bayerisches Nationalmuseum
Nuremberg: Germanisches Nationalmuseum
Würzburg: Mainfränkisches Museum
Science and technology
Berlin: Museum für Technik und Verkehr
Bochum: Deutsches Bergbau-Museum
Bonn: Zoologisches Forschungsinstitut und Museum
Alexander Koenig
Braunschweig: Staatliches Naturhistorisches Museum
Bremerhaven: Deutsches Schiffahrtsmuseum
Dortmund: Museum für Naturkunde
Frankfurt am Main: Naturmuseum und Forschungsinsti-
tut Senckenberg
Mannheim: Museum für Technik und Arbeit
Munich: Deutsches Museum
Stuttgart: Staatliches Museum für Naturkunde
Anthropology
Berlin, Frankfurt, Göttingen, Hamburg, Kiel, Cologne,
Lübeck, Munich and Stuttgart.

Music

From Beethoven to Stockhausen, from Claudio Abbado to Marius Müller-Westernhagen, from the Magic Flute to Cats, from the huge concert hall to concerts in the barn - music is always in the air and always on offer all over Germany. Many cities have orchestras and opera houses of their own. Over 100 local and regional music festivals are held on a regular, usually annual, basis. Conductors, orchestras and soloists from all over the world appreciate the music scene in Germany, and not only on account of its propensity for experimentation.

■ ■ ■ **Opera houses and orchestras.** In united Germany there are 95 government-subsidized opera houses and concert halls and 195 professional orchestras, some with a very long tradition. The country's oldest opera house is in Hamburg, having been built in 1678. The most modern are in Cologne and Frankfurt am Main. Berlin has three opera houses. Among the most beautiful are the Nationaltheater in Munich and the Semper-Oper in Dresden, both of which were built in the Italian renaissance style.

The leading orchestra is the Berlin Philharmonic Orchestra, the "masters of perfect sound". But others with international names are the Munich Philharmonic Orchestra, the Bamberg Symphony Orchestra, the Leipzig Gewandhaus Orchestra, Dresden's Staatskapelle, and several radio symphony orchestras.

■ ■ ■ **Conductors and soloists.** In Germany there is a regular exchange of international artists and promising new names. The Berlin Philharmonic Orchestra is conducted by the Italian Claudio Abbado, successor to Herbert von Karajan, who died in 1989, while many German conductors are under contract abroad. Kurt Masur, for instance, is conductor of the New York Philharmonic Orchestra, while Christoph von Dohnányi is chief conductor of the Cleveland Orchestra. German soloists such as the violinist Anne-Sophie Mutter, the trumpeter Ludwig Güttler, and singers such as Hildegard Behrens, Dietrich Fischer-Dieskau, Peter Hofmann, René Kollo, Peter Schreier, Hermann Prey and Edda Moser count among the best in the world.

Symphony concert in the palace, Mannheim

■ ■ ■ **The repertoire.** The great classical works are popular in many parts of the country. There are also traditional festivals (see chapter on "festivals") devoted to the works of individual composers, such as the International Beethoven Festival in Bonn (Beethoven's birthplace in Bonn attracts visitors from all over the world) or those devoted to Georg Friedrich Händel in Göttingen and Halle. The Wagner Festival in Bayreuth is still a major attraction. Helmut Rilling, founder and director of the Gäching Choir and of the "International Bach Academy", as well as several ensembles in Leipzig and Dresden, specialize in the works of Johann Sebastian Bach.

The most popular opera is Mozart's Magic Flute (audiences totalling over half a million), while among operettas Strauß's The Bat is the main attraction.

The world of ballet in Germany experienced a "miracle" in the 60s. This was mostly due to the outstanding work of the South African John Cranko with the Stuttgart State Ballet, which was continued by the Brazilian Marcia Haydée. The innovative productions of Pina Bausch and her Wuppertal Tanztheater, too, have been widely acclaimed by critics and public alike.

One of the traditional music theatres is the Friedrichstadtpalast in Berlin. The musical "Cats" has been running in Hamburg for years.

There are also regular programmes of works by modern classical composers such as Paul Hindemith, Igor Stravinsky, Arnold Schönberg and Béla Bartók, as well as Boris Blacher, Wolfgang Fortner, Werner Egk and Carl Orff who, with his world-famous "Schulwerk", encouraged children to take up music. Bernd Alois Zimmermann, an audacious avant-gardist, very soon established his place in musical history with his opera "Die Soldaten" (The Soldiers).

Today's composers try to win public support for music outside the realm of familiar harmony by using the most unusual effects in large theatres. In 1990, Hans Werner Henze offered a kind of wild action theatre with his opera "Das verratene Meer" (The Betrayed Sea) based on the novel by the Japanese writer Yukio Mishima. Aribert Reimann, who experiments with cords of 20, 30 and more notes, presented his opera "Lear" in Munich as a ghastly psychodrama. Karlheinz Stockhausen stages visionary opera in Wagnerian dimensions. Mauricio Kagel, an Argentinian living in Cologne and for many years a leading composer in Germany, regards himself as a "complete art maker" in that he uses his body as a musical instrument. The American John Cage obtained his music from computers, and Wolfgang Rihm used sheet metal and drums in his "Oedipus".

The fact that less spectacular contemporary music has also received attention is mainly attributable to the

Anne Sophie Mutter, the violoin virtuoso

The Philharmonic Orchestra performing on the Waldbühne, Berlin

broadcasting networks, who play and commission works by modern composers. Workshop performances, too, have helped to promote modern music. The best known among them are the "Donaueschinger Musiktage" and the "Internationale Ferienkurse für Neue Musik" in Darmstadt.

■ ■ ■ **Jazz, Rock and Pop.** Little interest was shown in German pop music until the "New German Wave" emerged with often scurrilous songs in German. Nina Hagen, the punk singer with the shrill voice, and Udo Lindenberg with his "Panic Orchestra", attracted a considerable following. The German jazz scene, which in the 50s was more of a protest movement, now has musicians of stature: the trombonist Albert Mangelsdorff is one of the best exponents of Free Jazz. Klaus Doldinger tries to link up rock and jazz with his group known as "Passport". And the Cologne group BAP are conspicuous for their dialect songs.

By comparison, the catchy German pop song popular in the 50s and 60s is almost non-existent. Dance orchestras like those of Bert Kaempfert, James Last, Max Greger and Paul Kuhn, on the other hand, won international fame. Other singers who have gained prominence are Peter Maffay, Marius Müller-Westernhagen and Nena. Well known groups today are "The Scorpions" and "Die Prinzen". Then there are the singer-songwriters Franz Joseph Degenhardt, Wolf Biermann, Reinhard

The Scorpions, the internationally famous German rock band

Mey and Hannes Wader, each with his own original style.

■ ■ ■ **Music for all.** There are various competitions to promote young talented musicians. The best-known among them is "Jugend musiziert" (Youngsters Make Music). Music is also greatly encouraged at school. In western Germany alone there are over 700 public music schools as well as about 15,000 choirs. Instrument making has a long tradition in Germany. Violins from Mittenwald, for instance, are world famous. Nearly half of Germany's school children play a musical instrument, the principal ones being the flute and guitar. Listening to music is still much more popular with the younger generation than watching television. The music branch is flourishing. Every year over 200 million German and foreign records, cassettes and CDs are sold in Germany.

Deutscher Musikrat (German Music Council)
Am Michaelshof 4a, 53113 Bonn

Theatre

Berlin, Munich and Hamburg especially are cities which haven't been "seen" unless one has been to the theatre. Berlin alone has over 150 of them, including the "Deutsches Theater" and the "Schaubühne am Lehniner Platz". But other cities too have remarkable repertoires. Bochum and Essen are good addresses for those who prefer the unusual, and Mannheim comes to mind because it produces the most plays.

Germany has no "theatre capital" which attracts all the best talents. This makes for a highly varied theatrical landscape. There is plenty of theatre in the provinces, too: in Veitshöchheim or Memmingen in Bavaria, in Massbach (Franconia) or Meiningen in Thuringia. This variety is traditional. In the 17th and 18th centuries many of the German princes set up splendid court theatres in their capitals. In the 19th century many towns and cities, having acquired more civic rights, made the theatre a public institution.

■ ■ ■ **The theatres.** Every season Germany's theatres are subsidized to the tune of over two billion marks or the equivalent of about DM 100 for each ticket. Public support is provided for the state or municipal theatres, but most private ensembles, too, can expect some financial help. Very few of the 420 German theatre companies could survive without subsidies. Public funding is meeting with growing criticism, however, on account of the great cost of rebuilding eastern Germany's economy. Most of the theatres in the former GDR are in a poor state and badly equipped.

Drastic economies and closures can hardly be avoided. Even famous houses are threatened with closure. Whereas in the past art and commerce were strictly separated, theatre directors now court industrial sponsors - as indeed do those responsible for production in other branches of art.

■ ■ ■ **Theatre-goers.** The theatre is extremly popular in Germany, especially among the older generation. In the 1989/90 season some 34 million people attended plays and festivals. These include six million who attended non-subsidized musical productions in Bochum

The theatre at Düsseldorf

and Hamburg. The theatres have a subscription system which enables theatre-goers to buy tickets for ten or twelve plays, operas or concerts etc. in advance.

■ ■ ■ **Dramatists.** German theatres have a preference for classical works, often in bold modern or politicized productions. Extremly popular are Schiller's "Kabale und

The stage of the Cuvilliéstheater in the Residenz, Munich

Liebe", Lessing's "Nathan der Weise" and Kleist's "Der zerbrochene Krug". In the 1991/92 season Shakespeare's works were the most popular, followed by Brecht's, whose "Dreigroschenoper" attracted more than 184,000 visitors.

Contemporary playwrights are not nearly so popular, but some have been very provocative. One of them, Rolf Hochhuth, has dealt with controversial subjects in such plays as "Der Stellvertreter" (The Deputy) written in 1964. And Harald Mueller, with his "Totenfloss" (Raft of Death), written after the Chernobyl disaster of 1986, develops a daunting apocalyptical scenario. Tankred Dorst, who in 1990 was awarded the Georg Büchner Prize (one of the most highly esteemed literary prizes in Germany), wrote a psychological narrative play with his "Deutsche Trilogie" (German Trilogy). Heiner Müller takes his themes from historical disasters. Botho Strauss depicts the upper middle class, often with a mythical strangeness. Klaus Pohl, on the other hand, has supplied the theatre with murder stories. Franz Xaver Kroetz, author, director and actor, has been the most popular German dramatist worldwide since Brecht. He has written about 40 plays, most of which take a critical look at society. They have been translated into more than 40 languages.

"Lady Macbeth von Mzensk", staged by the Staatsoper, Stuttgart

"The Landuage of Angels - Easy to love",
produced by Pina Bausch

■ ■ ■ **The producers.** In many cases the real theatre stars are the producers. Many of them seek to provoke the public. They leave hardly any classical play as the author wrote it. Some of them claim that their productions are their own work, which led someone to coin the term "producer theatre". Names like Jürgen Flimm, Claus Peymann, Peter Zadek, Luc Bondy and Robert Wilson fall into this category. Peter Stein is the man who invented "thinking in pictures". The suggestive imagery of his productions have been impressing critics and audiences alike since the early 80s. Indeed, his production of Anton Chekov's "Drei Schwestern" (Three Sisters) was shown in Moscow. Today Stein is director of the Salzburg Festial. In 1993 he received the Erasmus Prize in Holland.

Deutscher Bühnenverein
(German Theatre Association)
Quatermarkt 5, 50667 Köln

Cinema

German films once enjoyed world fame. That was mainly in the 20s and 30s when Fritz Lang, Ernst Lubitsch and Friedrich Wilhelm Murnau were at their best. In those days half the world loved Marlene Dietrich and the "Blue Angel". But the nazi regime ended it all. Most of the great directors and many actors went into exile. The legendary Ufa film company lost its artistic vitality and was eventually reduced to the level of making nazi propaganda films.

After the war German film-makers had difficulty catching up with the rest of the world. And today they are also having to struggle in the face of powerful competition in the form of television, which is siphoning off not only cinema-goers but also directors and actors. Expensive Hollywood films dominate most cinema programmes. Foreign productions also benefit from the fact that they are nearly always dubbed in German.

This makes life difficult for the German film industry. Doris Dörrie's "Männer" (Men) and Wolfgang Petersen's war film "Das Boot" (The Boat) are notable exceptions. But films of high artistic standard are appearing regularly, largely due to heavy government subsidies and support from television, which frequently cofinances feature films.

■ ■ ■ **Cinemas and cinema-goers.** Germany's cinemas were most popular in the 50s when television was still in its infancy. In those days over 800 million people a year went to the cinema, compared with hardly 106 million in 1992. Yet more is being invested in the German cinemas than ever before, to meet the growing demand for comfort and technical sophistication. In the first quarter of 1993 alone, the Film Promotion Institute received applications for financial support worth DM 80 million. The biggest attractions are the mammoth Hollywood productions, which have cornered 82% of the German market. The German film industry increased its share to just over 10% in 1992.

Germany's 3,670 cinemas are still in a highly competitive market. In the second half of the 80s alone, 450 independent cinemas went bankrupt. Competition in the field of entertainment is growing constantly. Ever more feature films are being televized, chiefly owing to the huge expansion of cable, satellite, video and pay-TV. One of the aims of government promotion is to give cinemas a fair crack of the whip in this highly competitive branch of industry.

Since 1990 media corporations and international cinema groups have been investing in German cinemas, reversing the trend towards the small studio and building the huge palaces of former times. Warner, for instance, has mega-cinemas in Mühlheim on the Ruhr and Gelsenkirchen. Multiplex cinemas with as many as 18 screens and more than 5,000 seats have already been opened in Bochum, Essen, Hanover and Leipzig, and others are under construction or scheduled for Berlin, Frankfurt am Main and Dresden.

■ ■ ■ **Germany's young film makers.** In the 60s and 70s the film industry in West Germany experienced a revival. Directors in the former GDR were forced by the regime to glorify life under socialism. Despite this some of them produced interesting films. Young directors in the Federal Republic had a much easier time. Having tired of the timid comedies and folklore films, they produced a series of remarkable and widely varying films with financial support from the Federal Ministry of the Interior.

Alexander Kluge, for instance, in his film "Abschied von gestern" (Farewell to Yesterday), skilfully fused fiction with documentary material. Werner Herzog, with his "Jeder für sich, Gott gegen alle" (Everyone for Themselves, God against All), sensitively depicted the life and suffering of the enigmatic foundling Kaspar Hauser. Bernhard Sinkel and Alf Brustellin directed "Lina Braake", perhaps the best comedy among the new German films. Rainer Werner Fassbinder provided impressive insights into German society with films like "Katzelmacher", "Die Ehe der Maria Braun" (The Marriage of Maria Braun) and that Berlin epic "Berlin Alexanderplatz". In only 13 years Fassbinder, who died in 1982, produced 41 television series and films, including "Die Sehnsucht der Veronika Voss" (The Yearning of Veronika Voss), for which he received the Golden Bear at the 1982 Berlin Film Festival. Fassbinder is the only post-war German director to have had a festival in New York devoted

A scene from "Rosenemil" (Dana Vavrova, Werner Stocker)

entirely to his works. This was a tribute to his innovative and courageous films of the 70s which has given lasting stimulus to the German cinema.

Ulrich Edel's film "Christiane F. - Wir Kinder vom Bahnhof Zoo" (Christiane F. - We Children from the Zoo Station), a provocative study of life in Berlin, became internationally popular.

These early commercial successes inspired unusual productions. Wim Wenders (born 1945) described taciturn heroes in films like "Paris, Texas" or "Der Stand der Dinge" (The State of Things), for which he was awarded the Golden Palm at the 1982 Cannes Film Festival and the 1983 Federal Film Prize. In 1988 he surprised the film world with his "Der Himmel über Berlin" (Heaven over Berlin), in which an angel in Berlin falls in love with a trapeze artist. This film, which won the Federal Film Prize and then the prize for best director at the Cannes Festival, was also a success abroad.

The actress Margarethe von Trotta attracted attention through her portrayals of famous women. "Rosa Luxemburg" is regarded as her best film. "Die bleierne Zeit" (The Leaden Epoch), made in 1981 was a successful critical and empathetic comment on the situation in the Federal Republic. Werner Herzog (born 1942) offered exciting action films with unusual heroes, subjects and locations. At the Cannes festival he won the prize for best director for his film "Fitzcarraldo", starring Klaus Kinsky, the story of a fanatic opera fan bent on building an opera house in the jungle.

■ ■ ■ **Filmed literature.** German directors have shown themselves to be particularly ambitious and often successful as well when it comes to filming major literary works. The best among them is Volker Schlöndorff (born 1939). He filmed Robert Musil's "Der junge Törless" (Young Törless) and Heinrich Böll's "Die verlorene Ehre der Katharina Blum" (The Lost Honour of Katharina Blum). For his adaptation of Günter Grass's bestseller "Die Blechtrommel" (The Tin Drum) Schlöndorff was awarded the Golden Palm at the 1979 Cannes Film Festival. And in 1980 the Blechtrommel won an Oscar as the best foreign film.

Novels are still greatly valued as material for films. Petersen's world success "Das Boot" (1981) was based on the novel of the same name by Lothar Günther Buchheim. Doris Dörrie, currently Germany's best-known woman director, based her 1988 film "Ich und Er" (Me and Him) on Alberto Moravia's novel, whereas Schlöndorff brought Arthur Miller's "Death of a Salesman" (1985) and Margaret Atwood's "The Story of a Servant" (1990) to the big screen. His adaptation of Max Frisch's novel "Homo Faber" with Sam Shepard in the main role was particularly successful. For this film he received the Silver Film Band in Berlin.

The Golden Film Band went to another literary film in the same year: "Malina" by Werner Schroeter. Starring French actress Isabelle Huppert, it is a story of self-destruction and is based on a coded autobiography by the Austrian writer Ingeborg Bachmann. A perfect example of the new-realism local culture film is "Herbstmilch" (Autumn Milk) directed in 1988 by Joseph Vilsmaier. This film, of the bestselling autobiography of the same name by a woman from the Bavarian countryside, Anna Wimschneider, was one of the most successful German productions of recent years.

German film-makers are increasingly prepared to try their hand at the difficult art of comedy and satire. Loriot, Germany's most satirical humorist, brings out the comedy of every-day situations in his films "Ödipussi" and "Pappa ante portas". And director Michael Schaack, in his cartoon "Werner Beinhart" presents us with a

A scene from "Der Sandmann" (Director: Eckhart Schmidt)

comic hero. Otto Waalkes appears in his films as a shrill-voiced comic. His 1992 "Otto - der Liebesfilm" was the box-office hit of 1992 followed by Helmut Dietl's "Schtonk", a farce about Hitler's ostensibly discovered diaries.

Sönke Wortmann had two successes in 1992 - "Allein unter Frauen" (Alone among Women) and "Kleine Haie" (Little Sharks) and shows much promise. Outsiders like Christof Schlingensief, too, are attracting attention with their realism. His "Das Kettensägenmassaker" (The Chainsaw Massacre) and "Terror 2000", both made in 1992, explore with seemingly anarchistic intent the contradictions and problems of German unification.

■ ■ ■ **Financial support.** New creative films have emerged chiefly as a result of support from the federal and state governments (the total amount in 1992 being DM 180 million, most of it going to Bavaria, Berlin and North-Rhine/Westphalia) and from the "Kuratorium junger deutscher Film", which awards prizes for first films (in the case of newcomers also second films) of artistic value. The curatorium is an agency of the federal states and has an annual budget of about two million marks.

There is also a general agreement between the film industry and the television corporations under which the latter provide considerable funds for coproductions. Under this arrangement such jointly produced films may not be broadcast on television until at least two years have lapsed. The Film Promotion Act of 1968 provides for financial assistance not only for film production but also for cinemas which specialize in films of artistic value. The funds are obtained by means of a levy on all cinemas and the video industry. The Federal Ministry of the Interior makes annual awards to these "programme cinemas".

In 1951 the ministry began awarding an annual German Film Prize. Its categories are the Golden Bowl, which is worth one million marks, and "film bands" in gold and silver with prizes of up to DM 900,000. The ministry also awards prizes to help cover production and distribution costs.

A Film Assessment Agency, which was established in 1951 by agreement among the federal states, issues ratings for feature and short films: "wertvoll" (valuable) and "besonders wertvoll" (especially valuable). These ratings translate into tax exemptions or reductions, as well as subsidies under the Film Promotion Act. They also provide guidance for the public.

Arbeitsgemeinschaft Neuer Deutscher Film
(New German Films Association)
Agnersstr. 14, 80789 Munich
Spitzenorganisation der Filmwirtschaft
(Central Organization of the Film Industry)
Langenbeckstrasse 9, 65205 Wiesbaden

Festivals

In Germany festivals are not the prerogative of the big cities. They are also staged by charming small towns, with their own particular atmosphere like Schwetzingen and its rococo theatre.

There are more than 100 music festivals alone. Every three years in September Bonn stages its International Beethoven Festival, while in August and September Augsburg stages Mozart concerts in a rococo ambience. Eutin celebrates the opera composer Carl Maria von Weber, who was born there, whilst Halle and Göttingen focus their festival on Georg Friedrich Händel. Munich and Garmisch-Partenkirchen, on the other hand, have a festival devoted to Richard Strauss. The Richard Wagner Festival in Bayreuth has been an annual event since 1876. For Wagner fans this festival is like a magnet for nowhere else can they see such unusual productions.

There is hardly a city without a music festival. Munich has its Opera Festival (July), Frankfurt am Main the Frankfurt Festival (September), Stuttgart the European Music Festival (August and September), and Berlin the Jazz Festival (November). Every year in August Heidelberg offers its romantic Castle Festival. The Schleswig-Holstein Festi-

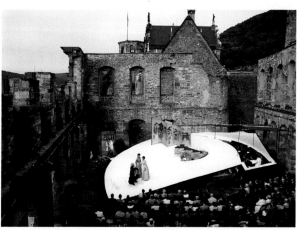

"Così fan tutte": Mozart at Heidelberg's Castle Festival

val founded by the pianist Justus Frantz in 1986 brings internationally famous musicians to this northern-most state of the Federal Republic and has become extremely popular - a big musical event in a provincial setting.

Those more interested in the theatre can enjoy Berlin's Theatre Festival, which every May produces the best German language plays. The Ruhr Festival in Recklinghausen, likewise in May, tailors its classical and modern repertoire mainly to a working-class public in the heart of the Ruhr district. Then there are numerous towns like Bad Hersfeld, Schwetzingen, Schwäbisch Hall or Jagsthausen, whose historical castles, palaces and churches provide a charming backdrop for productions of mainly classical works.

The oldest festival the form of the Passion Plays at Oberammergau (Upper Bavaria), which are staged every ten yeears in fulfilment of a pledge to God by the people of the village for delivering them from the plague in 1634.

Berlin hosts the country's top film festival. The International Film Festival takes place there in February and the Golden and Silver Bears are awarded. Other interesting events are the Nordic Film Festival held every November in Lübeck, and Mannheim's International Film Week in October, which has become a major forum for short films.

Germany's festival organizers like their events to have an international flair. Bayreuth, for instance, in addition

*Heiner Müller directed "Tristan und Isolde"
at the 1993 Richard Wagner Festival, Bayreuth*

to staging ist famous Wagner Festival, has also been staging the International Youth Festival since 1950. And Berlin has its "Horizonte", a festival of world cultures.

Index

(D) = diagram; (P) = picture; (T) = table

Richard Hoyt was born in Hermiston, Oregon, and now lives in Portland. He received a journalism degree from the University of Oregon and a doctorate in American Studies from the University of Hawaii, spent two years as a special agent with US Army Intelligence, five years as a newspaper reporter, and ten years as a college professor. He now writes fiction full-time.

By the same author

Trotsky's Run
The Manna Enzyme
Cool Runnings

RICHARD HOYT

Head of State

PLEASE RETURN ME

GRAFTON BOOKS
A Division of the Collins Publishing Group

LONDON GLASGOW
TORONTO SYDNEY AUCKLAND

Grafton Books
A Division of the Collins Publishing Group
8 Grafton Street, London W1X 3LA

Published by Grafton Books 1987

First published in Great Britain by
Severn House Publishers Ltd 1986

ISBN 0-586-07050-8

Printed and bound in Great Britain by
Collins, Glasgow

Set in Times

For Jacques de Spoelberch

The fact is that a smell of decomposition began to come from the coffin, growing gradually more marked, and by three o'clock was quite unmistakable. In all the past history of our monastery, no such scandal could be recalled, and in no other circumstances could such a scandal have been possible, as showed itself in unseemly disorder immediately after this discovery among the very monks themselves. Afterward, even many years afterward, some sensible monks were amazed and horrified, when they recalled that day, that the scandal could have reached such proportions. For in the past, monks of very holy life had died, God-fearing old men, whose saintliness was acknowledged by all, yet from their humble coffins, too, the breath of corruption had come, naturally, as from all dead bodies, but that had caused no scandal nor even the slightest excitement.

– *The Brothers Karamazov*, Fyodor Dostoyevsky

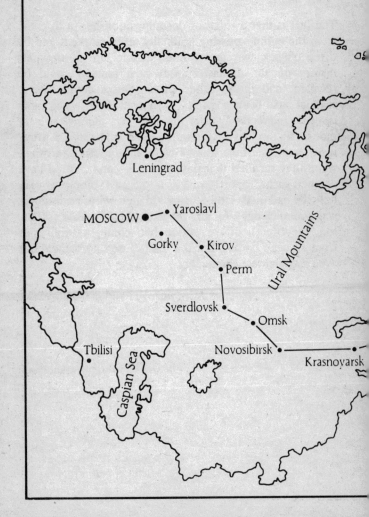

THE TRANS-SIBERIAN EXPRESS

Leningrad

Yaroslavl

MOSCOW

Gorky

Kirov

Perm

Ural Mountains

Sverdlovsk

Omsk

Tbilisi

Novosibirsk

Krasnoyarsk

Caspian Sea

Arctic Ocean

SOVIET UNION

Sea of Okhotsk

Vanino

Lake Baikal

Komsomolsk-on-Amur

Chegdomyn

Khabarovsk

Irkutsk

Chita

Zima

Dalnerechensk

VLADIVOSTOK

Nakhodka

Sea of Japan

Book One

1

The January temperature plunged to twenty degrees
below zero on that sad day in 1924. But the bitter wind in
Gorky was of no consequence to those hardy Russians as
they set about to bury the one who had led them in those
first historic, exhilarating hours, and in whose shadows
the world was destined to live. The bearers were rotated
so that more might share the honor of feeling his weight.
As they were replaced, they fell in among the mourners
who followed silently behind. They carried him along a
snow-packed trail through a forest of birch and aspen.

The Russians had a four-hour walk ahead of them, yet
they did not cover their faces. They were carrying the
weight of history. They were determined to shoulder it
proudly. They breathed in great clouds of white. They
bore the crimson coffin slowly along the trail. A terrible
wind lowed among the birches as dark clouds gathered in
the northwest; it would snow later in the day. They did
not wince, did not falter. Their eyes were sad. They
believed he had been a messiah and so was immortal, yet
they had not imagined his coffin could be so heavy.

The mourners did not feel the cold working its way up
through the soles of their boots; they were Russians and
so knew the cold. Their solemn countrymen gathered
among the trees to see the beginning of the melancholy
journey.

Three windows had been cut in the coffin so his head
could be seen lying in calm repose. He had a high,
intelligent forehead. His cheekbones had a hint of Asia
about them. His jaw was defiant, unyielding, his mouth

unforgiving. His hard, furious eyes were closed. He looked calm, at peace in the end.

He had redeemed them and imprisoned them at one and the same time, although they did not believe that, would not believe it; such treachery was too outrageous for them to comprehend, they even who had known the czars. He had given them deliverance, and their bodies and souls were his. Their children would be his as well, and their children's children; such were the consequences of his remorseless passion.

The bearers heard the steam engine well before they got to the Gorky station. Out there, alone in the forest, with the windowed, crimson coffin on their shoulders, they heard the engine up ahead, waiting. The engine inhaled with a high-pitched wheeze and exhaled heavily: sssssh, WHUH! Ssssssh, WHUH! Ssssssh, WHUH! Scoop of frigid air, release of spent steam. Scoop of frigid air, release of spent steam. Ssssssssh, WHUH! Ssssssh, WHUH! Tiny at first, muffled by the snow, the sluggish rhythm got louder and more insistent as the bearers approached the station.

Thus it was that Vladimir Ilyich Ulyanov – known as V. I. Lenin – was being taken to his rest.

One of the men at the station waiting to say good-bye was named Salomon Ginsburg. He wore a Russian-style fur hat – a *papakha* – pulled down over his ears and a heavy woolen scarf pulled up over his mouth and nose. He wore a heavy blue overcoat and shifted from foot to foot to keep his feet warm. He wore spectacles in the manner of intellectuals and in fact was one, a historian. When Ginsburg saw the peasants waiting for Lenin, he saw poetry. Ilyich himself had disdained peasants; to him, they were ignorant cattle.

For keeping Lenin's company and for being Lenin's friend, for standing by Lenin's side and fighting Lenin's fights, Salomon Ginsburg had toiled for three years in one of the czar's lumber camps east of the Urals. Ginsburg had surrendered one of his little toes and part of one ear to frostbite, and his kidneys, pummeled for the pleasure of one of the czar's guards, had never recovered.

Ginsburg was a passionate revolutionary but did not himself want to rule. He was like their friend Trotsky in that regard. Ginsburg had not taken part in Lenin's government, although he remained close to Lenin. A week before he died, Lenin had confided in Ginsburg that the great experiment had gone wrong. They had ignited a revolution to free peasants from oppression and had themselves turned to the same old despotism. Lenin told Ginsburg he wanted Trotsky to be his successor and had put that on paper. Lenin had said he didn't trust Stalin: 'He loves power for the sake of power, Ginsburg. You've seen him. You know. Turn the country over to him and you'll lose everything. Everything, Ginsburg.'

Ginsburg put his gloved hands under his armpits and shifted from foot to foot to keep warm. He saw the red coffin emerge from the woods, riding the shoulders of the solemn bearers.

At last the bearers approached the station, a small building made of uneven white bricks that looked as though they had been laid by drunks or jokesters. The engine seemed even more loud and demanding. A billow of white steam rose above the red station roof with every sighing WHUH! of the awaiting engine.

The mourners on the platform parted respectfully as the coffin approached. As the coffin passed, however, they pressed forward, leaned to get a better look. They wanted to be able to tell their grandchildren: I was there. I saw.

Ginsburg coughed slightly and said, 'Good-bye, Ilyich,' as the coffin passed by. Without another word, he turned

13

his back on the gathering and walked alone into the trees, thinking about his son Avraam. Ginsburg thought about Stalin and a rush of fear coursed through his body, swept across his face.

Eighteen months later, Salomon Ginsburg, on a walk along the shores of the Gulf of Finland, was taken into custody by Stalin's secret police. He was taken into a bare room and beaten until his face was a bulbous potato, purple with bruises. Ginsburg signed a paper that he could not read because he had been blinded during the beating. Then he was dumped into the river Neva, where he drowned.

The bearers slowed on the icy platform. Nobody spoke. Nobody fussed or argued.

A single red railroad car awaited to carry the coffin to Moscow. The passenger car was attached to an enormous black steam engine. The engine had been cleaned for the occasion, and its blackness stood in startling contrast to the white of the snow and the red of the car. *Sssssh, WHUH! Sssssh, WHUH!* The steam rushed forth, billowing white in the frigid air.

The engineer of the steam engine had never met Lenin, but he loved him still. He was a Ukrainian and his name was Yuri Korenkho. He had been chosen for Ilyich's last ride – sent out from Moscow – because he had been Trotsky's engineer in 1919 and 1920, when Trotsky beat off the White Russians and foreign mercenaries who threatened to topple the Bolshevik government. Korenkho believed. Sure, the Bolsheviks were brutal, but that was the way of life in Russia. The czars had been worse. And now that the foreigners were driven out and the Bolsheviks were secure, Korenkho was certain life would

14

get better – better for his little son, Serafim, better for everybody. Lenin had made it all possible.

Korenkho leaned out in the cold air and watched for the wave of the hand signaling that Ilyich's coffin was aboard and secure. There it was, a wave of the hand. Korenkho turned and pulled on a lever that released the brakes with a great savage gust of steam that made people step back on the platform.

Yuri Korenkho pulled the throttle out one notch, and the engine began to move slowly. Take your time, the party officials had told him. Let the people see. Korenkho felt proud and honored to be the engineer on this run. It would be a lovely story for little Serafim when he was older.

Korenkho saw to it that the engine moved slowly, slowly down the tracks. *FOO! WHAH!* the engine said. *FOO! WHAH!* The great iron wheels moved on heavy thighs. *FOO! WHAH! FOO! WHAH!* Oh, the pain, the pain. Outside, young workers with shovels ran alongside throwing sand onto the rails in front of the locomotive's great iron wheels. They wanted to be able to tell people they had sanded the rails for the locomotive that took Comrade Lenin to Moscow and to posterity.

When the young workers fell behind, exhausted, running awkwardly in their heavy boots, the funeral train came upon an icy stretch of tracks, and as the wheels of the engine spun momentarily, the *FOO! WHAH!* speeded to a sudden *Fffffffffhhhhhhhhhffffffffhhhh!* then, on dry steel, slowed to the *FOO! WHAH!* dirge.

Salomon Ginsburg had reason to fear the consequences of Lenin's death that day. Yuri Korenkho did not, yet he too paid for Stalin's insecurity. Four years later, Korenkho was summarily pulled from his family in Odessa – he had a wife and three small children – and sent to the railyards

15

at Krasnoyarsk in Siberia. Korenkho was one of twenty thousand Ukrainians sent to Siberia in one forced move. The Bolsheviks told the Ukrainians the people needed railroad workers in Siberia and put Korenkho to work sledging spikes into ties on roadbeds that took a terrible beating from the weather.

Korenkho eventually contracted a savage case of dysentery that would not go away. Rather than fuss with such a bothersome wretch, the Bolsheviks simply shot him.

Up ahead, peasants bundled in coats, with woolen scarves wrapped round their faces, closed in by the tracks to say good-bye to Ilyich.

So it was that Ilyich was taken to Moscow. The outpouring of emotion in Red Square during the next few days startled even the Bolsheviks.

The Soviets built a platform in the House of Trade Unions – which later became the State Historical Museum – at the north end of Red Square. The temperature plunged to twenty below zero, and a snowstorm pushed through Moscow, as uncounted thousands of Russians gathered to pass by Lenin's body. Hour after hour after hour they filed wordlessly by his coffin and saw Ilyich lying there, one hand closed, one open, his head on a white pillow. At the end of three days and three nights, the Soviets, feeling they were called upon to do something dramatic, hastily dug a vault under the Kremlin wall facing Red Square.

On the morning of Sunday, January 27, 1924, Lenin's red-draped coffin was placed by the vault as the Russian people gathered in the huge square, waving red handkerchiefs and wearing black armbands trimmed with red. They laid scarlet funeral wreaths by the coffin. Bands played mournful dirges. Minor officials, railway workers, factory workers, and union men made passionate

16

speeches glorifying Lenin and extolling his virtues and character.

The noise began at exactly four o'clock that day. Naval guns opened up, firing salvo after salvo. The army turned its seige guns loose: boom after boom erupted from Red Army bases across the country. Sirens wailed in the factories and on the streets. Foghorns boomed. Steam whistles screamed on locomotives and aboard ships. People rattled cans and shook bells and kicked barrels. The din reverberated in every village and city in Russia and across that hodgepodge of annexed, captured, or stolen lands and territories known collectively as the Union of Soviet Socialist Republics.

The demonstration continued unabated for three shocking, elemental, emotional minutes, and at the end of it grown men wept.

2

The arctic air was numbing cold that Sunday night, and if logic had prevailed, the eight pallbearers would have ridden in two cards and shared body heat. But no, there were four cars assembled for the ride out the main gate of the Kremlin to Red Square. Joseph Stalin, the general secretary of the party, would have preferred eight cars with himself riding last, but that would have violated the collective sense of propriety. Stalin assumed the responsibility for determining the order of departure and arrival. He had decided that he and Felix Dzerzhinsky, who controlled the secret police, would arrive last. Lenin had hated pomp and ceremony. Stalin rather liked it, in fact insisted on it.

Stalin scrawled the order on a piece of paper and gave it to his driver, who was chief driver. None of the others said anything. Grigory Zinoviev made a snuffling sound. Stalin and Dzerzhinsky had the secret police; what could Zinoviev do? What could any of them do?

It was less than a kilometer from inside the Kremlin to the place by the wall where they would carry Lenin's frozen body. Stalin settled in on the seat of his limousine and waited for his car to join the procession. He folded his hands neatly on his lap.

Stalin knew there would have to be an autopsy. But he wasn't worried. He would shoot any physician who didn't agree with his decision that Lenin had been felled by a stroke. Stalin had thought this over since he had learned that Lenin was losing his grip and telling people Stalin loved power too much. When Lenin had begun saying

18

that Leon Trotsky, a Jew, should inherit the leadership, Stalin had decided it was necessary to put a quick end to Lenin's illness. Lenin had to die someday – everybody died someday. Stalin had seen no reason why he shouldn't hurry things up a little.

A majority of the members of the central committee were Jews. Stalin didn't like Jews. If they gave him trouble, he'd have them shot.

The heavy cars entered from the north end of Red Square, moving slowly down a roped-off passage through the mass of bundled Russians. Soldiers with megaphones shouted at the mourners to stand back. Other soldiers blew whistles at anybody who touched the ropes. The soldiers outside the vault had moved the crowd back to accommodate the automobiles. Lenin's bearers were to arrive in a fashion later made famous in America by movie actors on Oscar night. The workers and peasants watched the heavy cars moving slowly over the ice. Each of them wondered: Which one is Stalin? Which one is Dzerzhinsky? Stalin ordered men flayed. Dzerzhinsky did the flaying.

As they turned right on Manyejhnaya Square, Stalin and his comrades could see a sea of mourners coming up Volkhonka Avenue from the west, down Kalinina Prospekt, Gertsena Avenue, and Gorky Street from the north, and Karl Marx Prospekt from the east. The white city was given color by the browns and grays of their winter coats.

Mikhail Bakunin, Lev Kamenev, V. M. Molotov, Mikhail Thomsky, and Zinoviev were bearers because they were Lenin's revolutionary comrades. Ianis Rudzutak was a union official; his only reason for being there was that he was favored by Stalin. Felix Dzerzhinsky, the head of Cheka, Stalin's secret police, rode with Stalin. But Dzerzhinsky opened his door just a fraction before

19

Stalin. This was not an accidental gesture; they arrived together but everybody knew they were not equals.

The bearers wore impeccably tailored black winter coats and sable *papakhas*. They stood silent for a moment, humble but proud.

The very last to step out into the terrible cold was Joseph Stalin. As he did so, the clouds parted briefly to reveal a pale white half moon. Stalin was not a man who could bring himself to bow his head in mourning – even as one of Lenin's pallbearers. He stood tall. The awe and fear in the peasants' eyes was a radiant glow to him, a charming warmth. While others' bones were cold that night, Stalin felt nothing.

Stalin looked at the sea of faces before him and could hardly believe their affection for Lenin. The problem was that they were religious. The Bolsheviks did not want competition from gods and so had banned religion. So now this: the peasants had seized upon Lenin. This upwelling of emotion had shocked Stalin. He couldn't send all these people to Siberia; that would be an inauspicious beginning for his rule. What would he do?

Stalin hadn't pursued power over the Kremlin so assiduously without knowing something of its history. He knew, for example, that Lenin's tomb was not far from Lobnoye Mesto – the Place of the Skull – a stone mound from which the heralds of the medieval Muscovites had read the laws. The Muscovites believed their city would one day become the Third Rome and inherit the earth. Then, they believed, the laws of Russia and its conquered territories, of the entire earth in fact, would be read from that mound. They believed Lobnoye Mesto was the center of the earth, and would radiate a secret power for eternity.

There was a skull within this mound, they said. This skull was the source of the secret power. Protect it and the power was theirs. Lose it and their power was gone. The skull was priceless beyond imagination.

Lobnoye Mesto was just off the southeast corner of Red Square – a matter of yards away from the base of St Basil's Cathedral. The czar's men had beheaded state criminals at Lobnoye Mesto. The czars – Ivan the Terrible, Peter the Great if he was in the mood – had watched from a high tower. Stenka Razin, the Cossack chief who had led the peasants of the Volga in revolt, had been beheaded at the mound.

Joseph Stalin, thinking of Lobnoye Mesto, gathered with the other bearers. Stalin had received ecclesiastical training as a young man and so knew the power of myth and symbol. Outwardly – as many people later recalled – he was somber that night; his face was properly melancholy. Inwardly he felt a strange, wonderful mixture of joy and expectation.

Quickly and confidently, Stalin assumed the head position at the right-hand, forward side of the red coffin. He would enter Lenin's vault as Lenin's right-hand man, Lenin's trusted lieutenant and disciple – the man who would assume the responsibility of Lenin's socialist vision. The eight men bent as one and hoisted the coffin shoulder high. Joseph Stalin could hardly feel the weight. Lenin's corpse was no burden at all.

Joseph Stalin studied the report on his desk before he addressed the small man in the neat jacket. His name was Dr Leonid Ilyich Latsis. He had been trained in Paris and until the Revolution had lived in Petrograd. He had embalmed royalty. He was the best available in Moscow.

'I want you to tell me about Lenin's body,' Stalin said. 'What will happen to it when it thaws out?'

'The bacteria will take over and the corpse will begin to decompose,' Latsis said. When he had visited the

21

Winter Palace he had worn a tie. He wondered if he should have worn a tie for Stalin. Was a tie too pretentious for a member of the proletariat?

Stalin said, 'How long does this take? Tell me exactly what happens.'

'In a few hours there's apt to be a greenish tinge here,' Latsis said. He put his hand on the lower part of his abdomen. 'By the second day dehydration sets in. The green skin spreads from the abdomen. Is Comrade Lenin on ice?' Latsis wondered if it was proper for him to ask questions. He didn't want to be shot for some violation he knew nothing about.

Stalin seemed not to mind. 'Yes, he is. Tell me, can you stop this process by embalming?'

'Embalming?'

'Yes.'

Leonid Latsis sensed danger. What was he being asked to do? One did not fail Joseph Stalin.

'Well, it can't, not really,' Latsis said. 'The embalming we do, with formaldehyde, is only intended for a couple of days, until the bereaved have a chance to see the body, no more. We make the corpse look nice. We put color on its face. Then we bury it, and nature takes its course.'

'I was thinking of something more permanent,' Stalin said.

Latsis knew he was in trouble. 'Well, I suppose we could do the body in sections, put the formaldehyde in the femorals and brachials as well as the carotids.'

'Explain that,' Stalin said.

'The carotids are arteries on your neck – here, under your jaw. You pump a formaldehyde solution in the arteries and blood comes out the veins. You do it up, then down.' Latsis raised his chin up and, using his forefingers as needles, pointed first up, then down, on

22

either side of his chin. 'The brachials are under your arm, here, and the femorals are on the inside of your thigh.' Latsis showed Stalin the location of his own brachials and femorals. He paused. 'We can put lanolin in the solution and that'll help some. The best way to preserve him for a long time is to keep him cold enough so the bacteria can't live.'

'On ice?'

'Yes. You could freeze him. We have found mastodon flesh preserved in the permafrost.'

Stalin didn't like that idea. 'How about a vacuum? Couldn't we put him in a vacuum? Do bacteria live in vacuums?'

'Some of the worst kinds,' Latsis said.

Stalin was not pleased by the drift of the conversation. He'd been expecting something better. This was the twentieth century, after all. There were submarines, radios, and airplanes. Stalin didn't think it would do to have people parading through an ice room to see Lenin lying there like a side of venison. Stalin said, 'I want you to pump him full of the most effective solution possible and do whatever you do to make his face look normal. Then I want you to go back to your laboratory and find out how to make it permanent. I'll see to it that you get all the dead bodies and assistants you need.'

Latsis was trapped. 'Yes, sir . . .' He cleared his throat and opened his mouth but said nothing else. Latsis read the journals in French and German. There had been no advances that would accommodate Joseph Stalin. This was 1924, sure, but to do that, preserve Lenin perfectly, permanently, why there was just no way. None.

As the undertaker left, Stalin made a note that viewing Lenin should be done by permit only, so that the viewers' body heat might not encourage bacteria.

Latsis and his fellow doctors did their best with Lenin's

23

body, but changes in the corpse followed inevitably according to the laws of nature. Deterioration set in. To call attention to a need for progress, Latsis was summarily shot. His colleagues were removed from the project and exiled from Moscow. More doctors were brought in. For two years Russian physicians tried to do something to Lenin's face, which was now wrinkled from dehydration.

In 1926, Stalin brought another man of science before him, Dr Ilya Zbarsky. Stalin said, 'Lenin looks like an old man. He looks like he's scowling. I want this stopped.'

Zbarsky said nothing. Everybody knew what had happened to Latsis and his associates. Lenin looked like he was scowling because his skin had dehydrated and shrunk. That had happened to King Tut, and it had happened to V. I. Lenin. It was impossible to boil Lenin in water and plump him up like a raisin.

'I know they make wax figures that look like real people,' Stalin said. 'There's a museum in London. I want you to get an artist and have the artist give him a proper face.'

Zbarsky was relieved. Stalin was making a little sense for once. 'It could be done,' Zbarsky said. 'We can have Lenin's skull, Lenin's skin, but with a thin wax overlay. Wax his face, his neck, and his hands. That's all that anybody can see. We can put a red light on him. Red will give him a youthful appearance.'

Stalin smiled. 'There's no real difference between makeup and wax if you get right down to it; wax is thicker and looks better, is all. I want you to have it done quietly and announce that you have discovered the secrets the Egyptians used to embalm the pharaohs. Announce that Lenin's body will last for eternity.'

Thus it was that Lenin's face regained its middle-aged appearance in 1926. Joseph Stalin, without anybody being the wiser, had shifted the location of Lobnoye Mesto as casually as a carny shifting a pea under a walnut shell.

In 1930, a mausoleum of red Ukrainian granite and Karelian porphyry was built over Lenin's vault. Then Lenin's body disappeared from sight for a few months. It was announced that the Kremlin's sewers had overflowed, and the mausoleum would be closed while these repairs were undertaken. When the mausoleum was opened a few months later, Lenin's body – defying all the laws of nature – had entered an even younger incarnation. Lenin's fierce, resolute middle-aged face was gone. He had become a young man, calm, contemplative, remote from the struggle that had raged in the wake of his death.

A left-wing German physician was given a quickie tour of the tomb to inspect V. I. Lenin. The secret police ensured Stalin's pleasure by threatening to shoot the doctor for the wrong answer.

Premier Stalin shook his head in amazement: the dumb kraut – the Fritz – had proclaimed Lenin authentic without even touching him. Stalin was so amused by the success of his nonsense of Egyptian embalming that he decided that the USSR needed its own pyramid. He proposed that the country build a thousand-foot pyramid in Moscow, and top it with a dramatic statue of V. I. Lenin.

This was the first of a series of proposals for a Lenin monument that eventually ended up with Ivan Dmitrov's celebrated statue of Lenin in Oktyabrskaya Square.

3

Sixty-three years later, a smuggler crossed into eastern Turkey from Soviet Georgia with Contact David's proposition for the Central Intelligence Agency.

4

Just as it was a note that drew the Americans into the story, three years earlier a note had instructed Isaak Ginsburg to appear at 2 Dzerzhinsky Square for a 'preliminary interview' so that his request to emigrate from the USSR might be processed by Soviet authorities.

The notice was so designed as to allow for an individual's name and the government's particular concern. It began with a blank space. Here someone had typed 'Isaak Avraamovich Ginsburg.' The text of the form followed: 'Your presence is required at 2 Dzerzhinsky Square.' There was another blank space where someone had typed '2 P.M., 26 February.' The form continued, 'for the purpose of.' A typist had completed the blank line that followed with 'preliminary review of your application to emigrate to Palestine.'

There was another blank line, a short one, where the typist had entered 'I. Podoprigora.'

Below I. Podoprigora, the form read 'Committee for State Security.'

The form did not say that Irina Podoprigora was the personal secretary of Colonel Felix Jin of the Jewish Department of the Fifth Chief Directorate of the KGB. The Fifth Chief Directorate was responsible for the internal control of the Soviet population. There were separate departments for the control of troublesome nationalists in Latvia, Estonia, Lithuania, Georgia, and Armenia as well as separate departments to deal with Moslems, practicing Christians, and intellectual malcontents. All these except for the Jewish Department were

27

handled on a regional basis. There was a central control for these regional units that reported to a party committee and the Secretariat.

Such was the importance of the Jewish Department that it was national rather than regional in organization.

For years the Soviet Union had attempted to rid itself of Jews by systematically repressing the Jewish culture – chiefly by prohibiting the use of the Yiddish language. Ginsburg himself knew only isolated phrases. The government had also imposed an impossible tax on Jews who wished to emigrate, but had eventually removed that obstacle on the grounds that it was too obvious.

The government's stated concern was the loss of scientists and engineers who had been educated at state expense. The Soviets did not like it when one of their botanists turned up at Oxford University. They were furious when a Jewish émigré – working on a computer that enabled him to beam paragraphs around like Captain Kirk on *Star Trek* – wrote a novel excoriating communism as it was practiced in the Soviet Union.

Sometimes the Kremlin assented to pressure from the Europeans and let a few Jews out. The way Ginsburg saw it, if he were lucky enough to be on the list at the time, he might get to go. If not, he knew, he risked an asylum or the gulag.

Two young military officers – an older and a younger lieutenant – these were ranks having nothing to do with age – sat next to Isaak Ginsburg in the metro as he rode toward the old KGB headquarters at Dzerzhinsky Square. They had an animated conversation about Soviet preparations for the Seoul Olympic games. The officers agreed that the Americans had made fools out of themselves in the last Olympics, strutting gold medals won against no competition. The Soviets had done the same thing in Moscow, but that was different. Things would be different in Seoul as well. The East Germans would unleash their swimmers. Bulgarian weight lifters would show their power. Russian boxers and gymnasts would clean up.

The younger lieutenant said that if the Americans didn't have black athletes, they'd lose to Albania.

The older lieutenant wondered if a Zionist athlete had ever won a medal. He couldn't think of any.

Ginsburg emerged from the train at the metro stop opposite the Moscow Hotel and found his way to the sidewalk above – on the north side of Karl Marx Prospekt. There was a metro stop just down the street on Dzerzhinsky Square, but he wanted a few minutes to think about possible answers to inevitable questions. It was a cold day with a pale blue sky. He had been over the details of his situation several times, each time flopping his adversary's logic.

As Ginsburg saw it, if they were going to send him to a camp, they'd have sent soldiers, not a request for a preliminary interview. The KGB probably interviewed everybody who applied for permission to emigrate.

Across Ploschad Pyatidesyatiletye Oktyabrya – Square of the Fiftieth Anniversary of the October Revolution – formerly Ploschad Manyejhnaya, pilgrims to Lenin's tomb spilled from old buses parked there as Soviet security officers went through the morning ritual of forming them into a double line.

One after another the buses unloaded: peasant women in head scarves, children in uniforms, old men. They were herded through the gate into the park area to form a queue that in another hour would be moved along a white line on the bricks of Red Square. This line led to Lenin's tomb at the base of the Kremlin wall. A man with a battery-operated loudspeaker shouted, and the people who had gotten off the buses did as they were told, moving in groups this way and that.

Ginsburg walked east on Karl Marx toward the Bolshoi, where by night the most beautiful ballerinas in the world danced on long legs, small backs arched, their wrists and arms of willow.

A long block west of the Bolshoi – two long blocks from the Kremlin itself – lay Dzerzhinsky Square. All Soviet citizens knew that it was at Dzerzhinsky where – as medieval cartographers said of unknown, and therefore feared, territory – dragons lay. The old KGB headquarters was on the one side of Dzerzhinsky; adjoining it on the right was Lubyanka Prison, built by German slave labor.

Number 2 Dzerzhinsky, which had been erected by the czars, was a high, romantic clutter of arched, barred windows and decorative columns. The main KGB headquarters was no longer at Number 2. It had been moved to the outskirts of Moscow, to a curved building in the International Style of architecture that resembled nothing so much as the CIA's headquarters in Langley, Virginia. In fact, it sat outside Moscow's outer ring road much as the CIA's headquarters sat just off Washington's Beltway.

The halls of power were in the new KGB building. Ginsburg assumed the officers at Dzerzhinsky would be young, enthusiastic, and on their way up, or old, embittered, and on their way down. Ginsburg could be impaled by either horn: ambition or indifference.

Ginsburg descended a short flight of stairs to the pedestrian passageway under Karl Marx and came up on the other side. There were several hard-faced young men on the broad sidewalk in front of the gray stone building. The young men were athletic inside their well-cut suits. They had necks as hard as wood.

Two men closed in around Isaak Ginsburg as he approached the main entrance to the storied building, the original Moscow Center. Ginsburg felt a flutter of anxiety and pushed open the revolving door. He immediately faced a woman behind a desk. The woman, whose reddish-purple hair had been colored by henna, motioned with her hand for Ginsburg to stop.

A man at her side said, 'Raise your hands.'

Ginsburg did as he was told, and one of the young men who had followed him inside frisked him for weapons. He stepped back.

Ginsburg hesitated, then lowered his hands. He looked down at the parquet floor, then up at a large oil of Lenin that dominated a pale green wall.

The man snapped his fingers impatiently, and Ginsburg dug the envelope with the summons from his jacket.

The red-haired woman held out her hand for the summons and studied it momentarily. She opened a desk drawer and took out a form with a small photograph clipped to one corner. The photograph, Ginsburg saw, was a copy of one that had been part of his file at Moscow University. She looked at Ginsburg, then at the photo, then at Ginsburg, then at the photo. She did not want to lose her KGB perks through carelessness. She was thick of body, serious of expression. She reread Ginsburg's summons.

'Jin,' she said. She looked up at Ginsburg; she picked up the receiver of her desk telephone and dialed a number. 'One for Comrade Jin,' she said.

Fifteen seconds later, a tall, serious man in a brown suit appeared. His shoes echoed *click, clack, click, clack* on the parquet floor. He took the summons, read it, looked at Ginsburg, and said, 'Jin?'

'Yes,' the woman said. Ginsburg followed the man to an elevator, which they took to the third floor.

The man walked down the hallway, motioned Ginsburg to stop, and knocked softly on an office door. When the door buzzed, he opened it. 'Comrade Jin,' he said.

31

Ginsburg heard a voice say, 'Yes?'

'Citizen Isaak Ginsburg, comrade.'

'Send him in and wait outside,' the voice said.

Ginsburg stepped inside, knowing – as he saw Felix Jin – that his life would never be the same.

Jin was small and dark-complexioned. He had a high forehead and intelligent eyes that had a suggestion of an eye fold. His black hair was neatly parted. He was slender, fastidious in his manner but not effeminate. He was young for a colonel – in his early thirties.

Colonel Felix Jin said, 'Go ahead, you can sit.' There was a single chair opposite his desk.

Ginsburg sat.

'Would you like a cigarette?'

Ginsburg shook his head no.

Jin said, 'You're wondering, so I'll tell you. My great-grandfather was Mongolian. My father was a mathematician. My mother was Russian, a ballerina at the Kirov. A man named Jin cannot afford mistakes.' He paused and added, 'And you are a Jew.'

Ginsburg said nothing.

'Far better to have a one-syllable surname,' Jin said. He removed a file from a metal cabinet as Ginsburg stared out the barred window at barred windows on the other side of the building's central courtyard. The office was smaller than he had expected. It was the same green as the entrance hallway and was lit by a single, large white globe on the ceiling.

Jin opened the file on his desk and began reading. 'A good dossier,' Jin said. He looked at Ginsburg, looked at a photo in the file, looked back up at Ginsburg. 'You want to emigrate to Palestine?'

Israel, Ginsburg thought. He said, 'Yes.'

'I thought you called it Israel.'

Ginsburg cleared his throat.

Jin smirked. 'A poet, it says here. It says your grand-father was a poet.' He looked at the folder. 'Salomon Ginsburg. Drowned in the Neva River.'

'Yes.'

Jin said, 'Allegedly a friend of Lenin's. Is that true?'

'That's what my father said.'

'Tell me about your poetry, comrade. What kind of poetry do you write?'

'Lyric poetry, I guess you would call it. I write about small moments.'

Jin read more of the file, the KGB's assembled life of Isaak Ginsburg. 'This says the Writers Union doesn't like your work.'

'I think I am a good poet,' Ginsburg said.

'Ahh, pride,' Jin said. 'You were denied membership in the Writers Union. Therefore you are not a poet, comrade. Writers are members of the Writers Union.'

Ginsburg didn't know what to say.

'They cite this,' Jin said. He held up a chapbook of Ginsburg's poems that had been circulated in manuscript at Moscow University. 'You play a stupid game, Gins-burg. "Journey to Lobnoye Mesto." You think we can't read. Poems about blighted trees that are not trees. Do you think we are so stupid that we can't understand parable and metaphor?' He flopped the chapbook back into the folder.

'I don't think you have thought this over sufficiently, Ginsburg. You're a university graduate, qualified to teach the English language. We educate you, then you want to go to Palestine. Do you think that's fair?'

'I think I would be better off there,' Ginsburg said.

'You are an arrogant Jew, Ginsburg. A parasite. If you are Salomon Ginsburg's grandson, you've slandered and denigrated everything that he stood for. I think what you

33

need is a chance to learn how to love your country. What do you think?'

Ginsburg didn't answer. He wasn't meant to answer.

Felix Jin said, 'Two years in a camp, then. For parasitism. This will give you time to think about your pretensions, Ginsburg. No poetry. You will not write poetry while you are confined. Is that understood?' He made an entry on Ginsburg's file. 'There,' he said, 'this will make clear what I have in mind. Your camp commandant will see that my wishes are carried out.'

Ginsburg was stunned. 'I thought this was to be a preliminary interview.'

'Preliminary to your being sent to a camp. Do you expect us to waste the people's time when we have everything we need in your file here?' Comrade Jin punched a button, and the door to his office opened instantly. Jin said, 'Lock this man up. He is to be sent to Siberia as soon as it can be arranged.'

Ginsburg felt the guard take him by his arm. He was to be taken now. A camp! Both Ginsburg's parents and his younger brother had been killed in a train derailment, so it wasn't as though he had a family to say good-bye to. Still, it was a shock. He had come believing this was to be a first step. Numb, disbelieving, he allowed himself to be led down the hall.

5

The Russian winter made a final rush on Moscow the first week of March; the snowflakes rushed hypnotically against the windshield as Leonid Akimovich Kropotkin negotiated the center of the tracks that were developing on Kalinina Prospekt. The Kropotkins lived close to the Kremlin in one of Moscow's finest apartment houses. This was owing to Kropotkin's position in the foreign ministry. Kropotkin refused to use the metro like other people. He owned a Volga and liked to be seen in it.

It was part of the emotional minuet of their married lives – the steps rehearsed and familiar after six years of marriage – that Leonid and Natalia Serafimovna said little on their way home from the party. Natalia waited for the alcohol to fuel her husband's suspicions of her infidelity. He would begin with the accusations. If she said nothing he would take it as an admission of guilt. If she tried to defend herself, he would become enraged. This opening movement was inevitable. It was always the same. Always. It never varied.

Thus began marital violence as the Kropotkins practiced it. Doomed couples the world over have their own dances, played to different tunes and themes.

Kropotkin seemed more drunk than usual, so Natalia, who knew well the pain of his temper, vowed silence in response to his lead.

'I see you found young Korzov charming company tonight, Natasha.' Kropotkin geared down carefully to avoid swerving on the hard-packed snow. When the Volga had been slowed safely, he glanced at her.

Natalia said nothing. The folds of his broad face made him seem suddenly older to her, drunker, meaner.

'If it weren't for me, you'd probably be in a camp like your father. You certainly wouldn't be the most favored *znachok* designer in Moscow. Speak to me.'

'Oh, Lyonya.' Natalia wanted him to please, please stop. Why couldn't he get horny like other men? Sonia Akimova said her husband got amorous when he was loaded. Sometimes he had a hard time getting it up, Sonia said, but he was always game to try. Not Leonid, Leonid turned mean.

'You shop the best shops because of me. You travel to the Netherlands and the United States because you're married to me. And how do you behave?' He paused. 'How?'

Natalia said nothing. Leonid's speech was slurred, a sign he was entering the final stages, teetering above the terrible abyss of mad rage.

'Like a slut is how. A cunt.'

'Lyonya.' Her voice was small. She was frightened. She had reason to be.

Kropotkin was suddenly calm as they neared their apartment. He parked the car, saying nothing. She followed him inside, still frightened but hoping that the music of paranoia had somehow subsided.

It hadn't. In the elevator he said, 'Korzov's an insipid adolescent. Why you're attracted to them is beyond me.' By 'them,' Kropotkin meant younger men. He was twenty-two years older than Natalia and felt his added years gave him character that all younger men, by definition, somehow lacked. It never occurred to him that while some men gain character with age, others lose it – or never had any.

The truth was, Ivan Korzov was forty-four years old and apparently so ambitious as to be indifferent to women; Natalia Kropotkina's women friends suspected him of being a homosexual. Natalia knew her husband: an insecure, flaccid, fifty-four-year-old party suck who had risen above the destroyed careers of competents who favored a more flexible Soviet foreign policy. 'We talked about the American elections,' she said.

'With Korzov?' Kropotkin was disbelieving, derisive. He unlocked the door of their apartment. He turned, laughing, showing the gold caps on his teeth. 'What does Ivan Korzov know about the Americans? Does he shave yet, could you tell?'

'Korzov says the reactionaries will win the presidency again because the American public doesn't trust the Democrats with the economy.'

Kropotkin said, 'The reactionaries will win again because American companies will see to it that they win. They'll buy the election.' That was the correct answer. Korzov had sounded soft. Kropotkin was curious. 'Korzov said the Americans don't trust the Democrats? Really?'

Natalia was suddenly concerned that she might inadvertently get Korzov in trouble. 'Someone said that. Maybe it wasn't Korzov. Someone said the American public doesn't trust the Democrats. What does it matter who said it? I wasn't interested in Ivan Korzov.'

'No? You don't know who said something like that? How could you forget?'

'I talked to a lot of people tonight, Leonid.'

'Sure you remember; it was either Korzov or it wasn't. If it wasn't him, who was it? It was Korzov.'

'I didn't say that.'

'And you wanted to go to bed with him.'

'No, Leonid.'

'Sure, you did.' Kropotkin went into the kitchen and returned with a bottle of vodka and a glass. He poured the glass half full of vodka and took a hit. 'I think we should talk, you and me.'

'No, please.'

Kropotkin finished the glass of vodka and dragged her into the bedroom by the elbow. 'Take your clothes off,' he said.

Natalia Kropotkina sat on the bed and bent to begin with her boots. She braced herself for the first blow. It came hard, alongside her ear. She cried softly and the next blow came – this one from the other side.

Kropotkin said, 'No yelling or you'll regret it.'

Natalia said, 'Please, Lyonya, not the face this time. I've got a show coming up next weekend.'

'Take them off.'

As she removed her boots, Kropotkin again struck her on the sides of her head. He threw her against the wall as she pulled her sweater over her head. This was not any kind of agreed-upon sexual drama or mutual exploring of fantasies. In fact, it was not sexual at all. It was Leonid Kropotkin's madness and his wife's pain. He enjoyed it for reasons that were perverse and deviant, not ideological or institutional. Leonid Kropotkin's demons were private and Freudian, found among unfortunate, unacceptable men in all cultures.

Either way, Natalia suffered.

In the end, Natalia Kropotkina was naked and bruised. Her nose was bloody, but she had not suffered the black eye that was her worry, and which was almost impossible to hide with cosmetics. She winced with every breath from a broken rib. This was the eighth or ninth rib that had been fractured from having been slammed against the edge of a dresser. She had lost track of the broken bones.

Kropotkin said, 'Now put your clothes on and get out.'

Natalia, wincing each time she had to bend or twist her

torso, dressed herself and left the apartment to spend the night with her friend Sonia Akimova. Kropotkin's penis was limp on these occasions, paralyzed by vodka; he liked to be left alone to curse women and nurse his hatreds in private.

On the way down the hall to the wing where Sonia and her husband lived, Natalia wondered suddenly what it would be like to shoot Leonid. She hated him. Wanted him dead. Wanted to kill him, although this shocked her because she had always accepted domination. She saw him yelling at her, pushing her. Then she pulled a pistol out of her handbag and shot Leonid and watched him die with a surprised look on his face.

That was what Natalia thought about on her way to Sonia Akimova's.

The Akimovs lived in a hideously cramped, one-bedroom apartment. The Kropotkins had three bedrooms, due to Leonid's influence – he 'needed' a study at home.

Sonia Akimova opened the door, knowing who it was because of the time of night. She knew the reason as well. This was not the first of Natalia's early-morning visits. Sonia went to get cigarettes and a bottle of Ukrainian brandy while Natalia curled up on the sofa and wept softly. Neither woman said a word. The only light was the glow of cigarettes. Natalia told Sonia what had happened, what Leonid had done.

Sonia inhaled slowly so that she wouldn't have to say anything. Natalia's stories and questions were always the same. What could she say?

Natalia wiped away her tears with the back of her arm. 'It's sick, I know. But there's nothing I can do, nothing. I can't leave him – he'd destroy me with a snap of his fingers.'

'You'll have to get your rib taped so you can stand to be on your feet at the showing,' Sonia said.

'Ribs heal.'

'Yes, Natasha, but the scars remain.' Sonia Akimova embraced her friend to help the mending begin yet one more time.

6

Isaak Avraamovich Ginsburg and the other *zeks* rode like cattle in the empty boxcar that left Moscow the fourth of March. Except for a crack where the edge of the metal door had been twisted in a derailing, the *zeks* could not see the Russian landscape. They didn't care especially. With few exceptions, they knew, the Soviet landscape varied little from Vladivostok on the Sea of Japan to Vyborg on the Finnish border.

Once in a while a bored, doomed *zek* peered through the crack at the forests of white-barked birch trees and the snow. There were aspens, too, with their pale, off-green bark. And spruce.

Isaak Ginsburg met the coughing *zek* on that terrible run to Zima. The train rattled east from Moscow, headed for the Urals, then Siberia: Sverdlovsk, Novosibirsk, and beyond. Zima itself – two hundred miles north of Mongolia – was just west of Irkutsk on the shores of Lake Baikal.

There were forty-two prisoners in the car. Some were first-timers like Ginsburg. Others, like the coughing *zek*, were veterans of the Gulag Archipelago. They knew all about the islands of suffering. They knew Zima would be a dunghill: it was intended as their purgatory.

The coughing *zek* kept to himself yet never strayed far from the largest group in the boxcar. The cougher was a veteran. He coughed until he was weak, then coughed more. It was as though he were trying to turn his torso inside out. He could not stop. Could not. His face went

41

tight with each spasm. His rheumy eyes appeared to see nothing, yet Ginsburg sensed they saw everything.

The boxcar had once carried used tractors, and there were tire prints of black grease on the splintered floor. The veteran *zeks* knew that if they arrived at Zima with black smears on their blue-gray trousers, they would have to answer for it. And it was likely, they knew, they would have to serve their entire sentences with the same annoying grease smears.

There was a crude stove made from a barrel in the center of the boxcar, but it was not used for the first two days. The *zeks* avoided the greasy tire prints, huddling together in the corners to conserve body heat. They cupped their balls with their hands to keep thier hands warm. They massaged the toes of one foot with the heel of the other.

The second morning out, Ginsburg took a turn at the door crack, peering out at a frigid Russian morning. Smoke rolled from the chimneys of unpainted peasant huts with roofs of tarpaper or corrugated tin.

Before the *zeks* were shipped from Moscow, a barber had shorn their heads with an enormous pair of Polish-made shears. This was so their heads could be painted with an insecticide to rid them of parasites. They were not bald in the sense of being properly shaven. They simply ended up stupid-looking; scraps of hair stuck up here and there like weeds. Their ears stuck out. They pulled their caps down over their ears, both to keep their heads warm and because they were doing their best to remain dignified in the face of routine humiliation. The *zeks* knew they looked pathetic and so were embarrassed. Except for their memories they owned nothing at all, not even a head of hair.

When he returned from watching the Siberian winter through the crack in the door, Ginsburg knew what he had to do. He had to remember what was being done to him. He would be a witness. He wouldn't have access to pen and paper; he knew that. He had to endure a two-year sentence; Jews had suffered far worse for trying to emigrate. He would need a device of some kind. He began, saying the words softly, turning them over so he could hear their sounds, as a cabinetmaker notes the grain of wood:

> Strangely, there were no tears
> as we stood before the shears.
> On the terrible train I sucked frozen bread.
> It was an awful dread.

Ginsburg repeated the lines three times. He would memorize quatrains. Ginsburg was a modernist – a style possible only for underground poets in the Soviet Union – and considered rhyming poems old-fashioned at best, doggerel at worst. He didn't care. The point was solely to help him remember. The rhyming would do that.

Late into the third night, the coughing *zek* said the temperature had dropped to twenty degrees below zero. He said he could calculate the temperature from how long it took spit to freeze. He spat and watched it freeze, counting:

'*Oh-deen, dvah, tree, cheh-tee-reh, p'yaht*' – one, two, three, four, five.

When the spit had frozen, the *zek* fell into another spell of coughing. An hour later the train stopped, and they were given firewood and coals for the stove.

When the train began moving again, the coughing *zek* eased toward Ginsburg and said softly, 'We would have frozen to death if they hadn't given us some wood. After all the work it took them to shear us, they didn't want us to freeze to death. They're efficient that way. We're

43

cheap labor. You'll get just enough of what it takes to live, no more. You'll see.'

The *zeks* formed a line that snaked its way around the stove, into a frigid corner, then back around the stove again. The first rule of the cold was to keep moving. Ginsburg followed the coughing *zek*, who walked with an odd, shuffling, flat-footed gait. As Ginsburg approached the stove the second time, he tried another quatrain:

We warmed ourselves on imagined fire,
 the raw edge of desire,
until our piss splattered like yellow glass and we were given
 birch to burn,
Russian style, we lined up for the heat. Each *zek* got a turn.

They stayed awake that night. Those who slept would sleep forever. The train stopped several times. At each stop the *zeks* heard the voices of women traffic controllers giving instructions to engineers and workers in the rail yards over huge loudspeakers. They were wonderful voices, still soft while giving instructions. Ginsburg tried to imagine a woman to match each of the voices.

The fire was cold by dawn, and they knew there would be no heat from the rising sun, a pale orange as it rose through the gloomy industrial haze above a Siberian town up ahead. The sky was a dry, frigid blue above the pall.

Five of the *zeks* had fallen asleep by the time the Soviets gave them more wood. When the fire got going again, the sleeping *zeks* didn't bother to wake up. The other *zeks* stepped over the frozen bodies as though they didn't exist.

They were given their food for that day late in the afternoon – a tepid, cloudy soup that featured small bits of fat. Ginsburg drank his gratefully. The coughing *zek* consumed his soup quickly, dining by the feet of one of the dead men. The workers who delivered the soup noted the bodies when they collected the bowls and the huge pot.

When the soup people had gone, the coughing *zek* – sensing it was safe because the bodies had been left behind – began quickly stripping the frozen corpse of its clothes. The other experienced *zeks* did the same thing; they were upon the frozen *zeks* with ferral quickness. Now dressed in an extra layer of clothing, the veterans dragged the pathetic bodies to one corner of the car and stored them with their spines and wood-hard buttocks towards the center of the boxcar. Nobody wanted to look at their faces.

At the next stop the train halted again, and they were given more wood. The men who delivered wood pretended they didn't see the frozen, naked bodies in the corner of the boxcar.

When the fire was going again and the temperature in the boxcar was bearable, the coughing *zek* took Isaak Ginsburg aside. 'You should not memorize your poetry out loud where other *zeks* can hear. There are people who would use it against you. It's bad enough on the outside; in the camps it's worse.'

Ginsburg knew the *zek* was right.

'You don't know these men,' the *zek* said. He was scolding Ginsburg, master to apprentice. Ginsburg had a lot to learn if he were to survive.

Ginsburg said, 'I wasn't thinking.'

'You're a Jew, aren't you?' The *zek* coughed.

Ginsburg nodded yes.

The *zek* said, 'Trust no one. Be invisible.'

The clanging and banging of metal on metal got louder as the train hit a rough stretch of track. The *zek* seemed lost in thought as they both considered the racket. He was overcome by another attack of coughing. Ginsburg knew he wanted to say something more.

'Go ahead, tell me,' Ginsburg said.

The *zek* coughed. 'Those poems . . . they're so you can remember, am I right?'

'Yes, they are.'

The cougher lowered his voice to a bare whisper. He looked at Ginsburg with his sad eyes. 'If I make it to Zima, I'm going to kill myself, first chance I get. I've been in one or another of these camps for sixteen years. When you've been gone that long, there's no reason for them to send you back. Everybody's forgotten by now. I'm tired of coughing. I'm dying. It hurts too much to continue.' He coughed again. Ginsburg started to object, but the *zek* took him by the arm. 'This is best for me, believe me. What are you here for?'

Ginsburg smiled. 'Parasitism.'

'You're here for being Jewish and a writer.'

'Yes.'

'For how long?'

'Two years.'

The cougher considered that. 'That's not bad. I'd count on more time than that if I were you.'

'How much more time?'

'You can always figure on a couple more years. They'll get you for something. They'll do something to you. It's usually more time.' The *zek* fell silent. 'But not always,' he said. 'It could be something else. Sometimes more time is preferable.'

The cougher looked around to see if they were clear of eavesdroppers. 'I had a friend once in one of these camps. His name was Dr Serafim Korenkho and he shared a potato with me when we were both starving.' The *zek* paused. 'Later they sent him to one of their extermination camps. I promised him when I got out that I'd tell his daughter what happened to him.'

'His daughter?'

'Natalia. The last Serafim heard she was married to a man named Kropotkin who's in the foreign service. She's an artist. She designs *znachki*.'

'*Znachki!*' The ubiquitous *znachki* were patriotic lapel pins that featured Lenin's head or commemorated socialist accomplishments.

'Serafim said some artists are good at doing horses or dancers; his daughter is good at doing Lenin. He said Natalia's designs must be approved by a committee of party members. The Kropotkins live in Moscow, although they have lived overseas, in New York, Serafim said, and Holland. She would be about your age.'

'What happened to Korenkho? I want to hear the rest of it.' Ginsburg was curious about Natalia Kropotkina.

The melancholy cougher considered that. He looked around. 'After a while ears get curious.' He walked away, flat-footed.

Later he returned to finish his story.

The coughing *zek* removed the second layer of clothing that he had stolen earlier from the frozen corpse. He held the clothing out to Ginsburg. 'Put this on.'

Ginsburg said, 'No.'

'I said to put it on,' the cougher said. 'This is my choice. It is what separates men from dogs, I think. I may have forgotten the difference.' The cougher smiled sadly. 'I still have this right.' When Ginsburg took the clothing, the cougher squatted and removed his shoes. He gave Ginsburg both pairs of socks, pulling them off two at a time. 'See, no toes,' he said. 'Lost 'em two years ago. Socks don't do me much good.' He embraced Ginsburg, then lay down on the icy floor of the boxcar. Without looking up, he said, 'Believe me, I'm tired. I want to go to sleep.' The *zek* repressed a cough.

47

Ginsburg knew the cougher had decided. There was no turning back.

The *zek* said, 'I ask a favor.'

'Certainly.'

'I want you to keep my promise to Serafim Korenkho.'

'Done.'

The cougher sighed. 'Thank you, my friend. Best to stay well clear of me so as not to remind the others that you have three pairs of socks.'

Ginsburg did as he was told, and after a while the coughing *zek* stopped coughing, and his body was stripped by one of the living, a younger *zek* who had watched in frustration as the veterans beat him to the corpses the first time around. This time he was ready. He worked quickly, and when he came to the cougher's toeless, bare feet, he cursed and glared at Ginsburg; his eyes were furious.

The *zeks* arrived at Zima in the midmorning with a pale sun providing no heat at all. A terrible wind buffeted the train while they waited at the siding. Finally a truck backed up to the door of the boxcar. Two workers wearing heavy coats and breathing in great, frosty puffs stepped inside the boxcar and set about collecting seventeen frozen, nude corpses, including the one who had coughed his last the night before. The workers, who had Asian faces, seemed not to care that they were dealing with human beings. They slung the Leninist jetsam into the back of the truck, where the corpses hit with a hollow thump and tumbled to rest, arms and legs sticking this way and that.

The workers were in a hurry to get in out of the cold. When the bodies were on board, they slammed the rear door shut and raced for the shelter of the cab. The truck departed for the camp furnaces with an impatient grinding of gears and plunged across frozen potholes at high speed, the driver seemingly oblivious to the damage he was causing the truck. In the back, the frozen corpses banged and rattled like wooden chairs.

The twenty-five remaining *zeks*, grateful to be alive, were loaded onto a second truck.

Isaak Ginsburg had not only arrived at Zima alive, but with all his toes as well. He was the only *zek* from his car who could say that. Ginsburg almost wished he had lost at least one toe. He was too lucky. Something awful would happen to make up for his intact feet. Since religion was officially prohibited in the USSR, the Russians were given to superstition. Ginsburg was no different. He had a sinking feeling in his stomach.

Just what would the punishment be? he wondered as he bounced along in the back of the truck. What would make up for his having arrived at Zima with toes that would still move the next day?

A corporal with an AK-47 slung over his shoulder flung open the truck door and shouted, 'Out, out, out!' He had an unemotional peasant's face. He watched them with the indifference of a sated lizard. Two privates watched, also with reptilian eyes and AK-47s. The stiff, shivering *zeks* began to climb slowly off the back of the truck. The terrible wind knifed through them. They were weak. Their joints ached.

Standing on the back of the truck, waiting for his turn to lower himself to the ground, Ginsburg saw they were only a couple of miles east of Zima; the camp was on the edge of the sprawl of peasant huts that led to all Siberian towns. Ginsburg could see the train station from the back of the truck. As he lowered himself to the frozen earth, he heard the horn of a train just south of the camp. In fact, he saw it.

It was red with a yellow stripe down its side. The air horn of the Trans-Siberian Express went *hnnnnnnaaaaaa* as the train passed the camp, slowing for the white station house up ahead. There would be a fifteen-minute stop at Zima while the brakes were checked with the thump of a carman's hammer and the diesel was replenished.

'Form a line! Form a line or you'll be shot!' the corporal shouted.

The *zeks* quickly formed a line.

7

Captain Yevgenni Mikheyev, Commandant of the people's lumber camp at Zima, watched the *zeks* as they were unloaded from the truck. Mikheyev wore polished black boots. The hem of his immaculately tailored gray officer's coat fell to the middle of his calves – a design for Siberian winters. His aide had treated his *papakha* with lanolin, and it glistened in the cold morning light.

It was the misfortune of Captain Mikheyev's *zeks* that their commander had succumbed completely to the warming succor of the Leninist vision, thus relieving himself of the burden of conscience. Mikheyev was numbed beyond recovery by the coarseness of his profession. He was insensitive to irony and contradiction. Having lost whatever it is that separates men from beasts, Mikheyev ended up a casual brute, pathetic in his way, different from gorillas and baboons mainly in that he had larger genitalia.

Ordinarily Mikheyev preferred to sleep in on Saturday mornings and rub his face against Anna's soft, flubbery white breasts. When she was in the mood she let Mikheyev twist her nipples while she made horny little noises in her throat. Unfortunately, regulations required that a camp commandant meet each shipment of *zeks* personally, in immaculate military dress. Mikheyev expected his career to rise without a hitch; he followed regulations.

The corporal gave the truckdriver the information he needed to complete the forms necessary to conclude the transaction. When the corporal got the *zeks* squared away into a line of lonely, cold, and frightened men, he said, 'Captain Commandant Yevgenni Mikheyev will have a word with you.'

Captain Mikheyev lit a cigarette, inhaled, and took two steps forward. He spoke so quietly, his prisoners could hardly hear him.

'My name is Mikheyev. I own you while you are here. You have work to do and you will do it. You will work twelve hours a day, seven days a week with the logs there.' Mikheyev gestured at the logs. 'On the seventh day you will work longer so that the camp may be kept clean.'

Mikheyev smoked. He took his time, making the shivering *zeks* wait. 'If you disobey the rules, you will be flogged, put into solitary confinement, shot, or whatever other punishment occurs to me. You'll find that this punishment varies according to the severity of the infraction and according to my mood. You may be assured that I can be quite imaginative.'

8

The Company representative who received Contact David's message, Rennie Kriss, was allegedly an agent of Trans-Global Enterprises Ltd., a British importer of Middle Eastern handicrafts. Kriss, who grew up in Australia, had what could be palmed off on nonnative speakers of English as a British accent. Kriss insisted that the message be sent to Company headquarters in Langley, Virginia, via courier rather than coded cable.

9

Natalia Kropotkina's friend Sonia Akimova was in a contemplative mood when she swung her green Lada into the parking space to the rear of St Basil's Cathedral. The warming May sun shone on the cathedral's colorful domes and made Moscow almost balmy. The two women walked to the southern end of Red Square and made their way through the visitors toward GUM, the Queen Mother of Soviet department stores.

Natalia had good reason to be in bad spirits. The selection committee had awarded her the pin commemorating Ivan Dmitrov's monumental Lenin statue in Oktyabrskaya Square, only to overturn the award for reasons that were obscure. Those who claimed to know said Natalia was becoming an individualist and so needed taking down a notch.

The reason for Sonia's moodiness was less clear.

GUM formed the eastern boundary of Red Square, and sat almost opposite Lenin's mausoleum. This was the heart of Moscow – right in the middle of Intourist hotel country – and so foreign visitors mingled among Russians. Intourist guides told the foreigners that a visit to GUM was a must, like the V. I. Lenin Museum, the State Historical Museum, the Pushkin Fine Arts Museum, the Bolshoi, and so on; GUM was a Soviet showcase.

At GUM, Soviet citizens were treated to the cornucopia of Leninist economics.

Because of her marriage to Leonid Kropotkin, Natalia had a card that admitted her to the privileged sanctuary of reserved shops in GUM. These shops for the extra-equal comrades were on the third floor, past a long bank of shops that were empty and closed. Natalia was able to take one guest with her – in this case Sonia. Sonia couldn't buy anything, however; Natalia had to do that.

For her part, Sonia had a friend, Ekaterina, who had a contact inside GUM; the contact knew about the arrival of decent items that were scarce even for the party elite.

'Katya's never been wrong yet, has she, Natalia? Not once.' Sonia had access to theater tickets that Ekaterina did not have, and so was the frequent recipient of Ekaterina's GUM tips, this one for wool sweaters. 'Irish wool,' Sonia said. 'Polish at worst. A lot of sizes, Katya says.'

'Maybe you'll find something,' Natalia said. Sonia was slender but large busted, and a Russian sweater in combination with a Russian bra made her look like a 1950s American movie starlet.

Sonia hated having her breasts stick out like the ends of rockets. 'Well, maybe this time. I'd like something handsome and a bit loose, you know. Maybe something like those sweaters we saw in the Finnish magazine.' Sonia had cooled on the shopping trip at the last minute, and Natalia had had to talk her into coming. Now Sonia was cheering up again.

'After we shop, what do you say we have a drink at the National? I got my card renewed.' This was a treat for Sonia, Natalia knew. Every time they went to GUM, they visited the bar in the National, where it was possible to have an Old Crow. Sonia loved American whiskey and the intimacy of the bar where foreign guests had a drink after a day of sightseeing.

'Let's try something different this time – the Rossiya. We're in a rut, don't you think?'

Natalia was surprised but tried not to show it. Sonia

professed to dislike the Rossiya. 'Sure. Wherever you like.'

'You have a card for the Rossiya too, don't you?'

'I've got a Rossiya card.'

Sonia looked pleased. 'Good, then the Rossiya it is.' She followed Natalia through the entrance of GUM and under a net hung to catch plaster that was crumbling from a decorative arch.

Sonia said, 'You want to look at the *znachki* before we go upstairs?' She knew Natalia would be eager to look at the largest collection of commemorative pins for sale in the Soviet Union. This shop, in the southeast corner of the courtyard nearest Red Square, had 350 numbered pins mounted on a wall behind glass.

'Oh, sure,' Natalia said. Seventeen of the pins that featured Lenin were hers, including the top two bestsellers in the Soviet Union for three years running. The *znachok* shop in GUM always made Natalia feel wonderful. It wasn't hard to spot Natalia's pins: they were the class of the lot.

Natalia Kropotkina found it impossible to go shopping at GUM without remembering the department stores in the Netherlands and the United States where her husband had been posted – first at The Hague, then at the United Nations. Having had a bite of that wonderful capitalist apple, she wanted more. When Natalia returned to the Soviet Union, she had been appalled at the lines and deprivation she had formerly taken for granted.

Natalia's only hope of going back to the West was through Leonid, and she knew it.

Natalia Kropotkina had shopped in Bloomingdale's, and so no longer believed the Soviets' claim that GUM was the best department store in the world.

56

If the Soviets had claimed GUM was the grandest-looking, or had the most curious architecture, they would have had an argument. On the outside, the store looked like a gilded warehouse of industrial charm. On the inside, however, GUM was lovely. Tiers of classic Roman columns rose impressively – if decoratively – around two long rectangular courtyards that formed the dramatic center of the GUM architecture. Between the columns were the facades of small shops, three floors of them.

Shoppers strolled along elegant Victorian balconies overlooking the ground floor. It was possible to lean against the black iron rail and watch shoppers queuing up at the wine shop, the ice cream stall, and the bakery near the entrance. High above the hubbub of shoppers there was a vast rounded skylight made of hundreds of small panes of glass. Thus shoppers enjoyed the sunshine that suffused the civilized courtyards with a natural, warming glow. The shops beneath the skylights were painted pale blues and greens. Cooling colors for the long waits, went a Moscow joke.

Natalia Kropotkina knew that American entrepreneurs would have turned the lovely GUM building into a truly fabulous store – fashionable, possibly filled with trendy eateries. In New York, Natalia had been in stores with fashion shows, stores with disco music and flashing lights to add a festive, gay atmosphere.

The Leninists would say this was extravagant, she knew, wasteful. Still, it was wonderful to watch people have a good time and to shop free from want. It was almost as though the Russians were closet masochists, preferring sacrifice and deprivation to laughter and joy.

The shops in the lovely GUM building were determinedly, steadfastly utilitarian. A state monopoly had no reason to charm or please its customers, and so each shop had the decor and warmth of a garage sale. Each little cell, whether it offered blouses or underwear, was seemingly indifferent to quality and fashion. There were four walls, a ceiling, tables for display – that was it. If you wanted a coat, there was a coat shop, drab wraps hung on metal racks. A customer looked at herself or himself in a plain mirror and either bought or chose not to buy; the state didn't care. If you wanted shoes, there were bins of shoes. In GUM you waited in line always. There was an unsmiling clerk to take your order. There was an unsmiling clerk to total the bill on an abacus.

Following Sonia into an underwear shop, Natalia remembered the fabulous lingerie for sale in Dutch and American stores. Natalia hadn't been able to believe it at first. She had bought everything she could get her hands on. Provocative panties with strings that untied at the hip. Translucent panties to please imaginative capitalist men. Little shifts that didn't cover enough of your breasts. Bras that didn't feel as if you were wearing birdcages or chain mail on your chest.

None of this did any good with Leonid, however, Natalia only succeeded in arousing him to anger, not passion. He could only worry that some other man might have seen her looking this splendid or would in the future. It apparently never occurred to him to give the strings a pull and see what would happen. Natalia Kropotkina had a fabulous figure and knew it. She dreamed of meeting a man who would pull the strings unabashedly and enjoy. She could give him a little show. Turn him on. Why not? Was this a decadent, Western fantasy? she wondered. Was there something wrong with her? She thought about this at night, her hand at her crotch, middle finger moving, while her fantasy lover watched, pleased, encouraging her, making outrageous suggestions. All this while Leonid – his suspicions drowned by sleep – lay snoring heavily, dreaming what?

Last week Leonid had caught Natalia, dressed in a pair of her American panties, admiring the curve of her hip in her dressing mirror. He had thrown her against the wall so hard it knocked the wind out of her and brought a retaliatory thump from the apartment next door.

Natalia Kropotkina was curious about Sonia's sudden preference for the Rossiya over the National and was somehow disturbed by it. They had just stepped outside GUM, by the gray juice machines, when Natalia said, 'I say we have our drink at the National, Sonia. I hate the Rossiya.' Natalia had the entrance permit; there was nothing Sonia could do.

Sonia looked stricken. 'I thought we had already decided.'

'I don't like the Rossiya,' Natalia said. She turned in the direction of the National and began walking with a stride that said she had made up her mind.

Sonia was suddenly agitated. She glanced at her wristwatch. 'If you insist,' she said.

Natalia led the way into the National through the revolving door, past the doorman who checked pass cards, and up a short flight of broad, carpeted stairs. At the top of the stairs, turning right toward the bar, she saw the reason for Sonia's nervousness.

Straight in front of the open door, at a window table overlooking the Square of the Fiftieth Anniversary of the October Revolution, Leonid Kropotkin sat, looking south toward Lenin's tomb. He was holding the hand of a slender, blond woman.

Natalia pretended that she had seen nothing. She was furious. At Leonid. At Sonia. After they were seated, she drank her Pernod in thoughtful, stony silence.

Later, as they walked across Red Square to Sonia's

car, Natalia exploded, 'How could you have, Sonia? How could you?'

'You saw him, then?'

'Yes, I saw him! How long have you been working for him? Just what is it he wants to know?'

'He wants to know if you're seeing another man. He says he's certain you've been seeing another man. He wants to know who. Today, he wanted me to keep you out of the National.'

'You knew why, I take it.'

'I guessed it, Natalia. I didn't have any choice. Your husband doesn't leave people choices.'

'I know that,' Natalia said, 'Who is the woman?'

'If you could get tickets to the Bolshoi this weekend, you could see her dance.'

What Sonia said was true; no doubt she hadn't had a choice in the matter. Natalia didn't want to know the form of coercion, whether it was a threat of punishment or promise of reward. What did that matter now? She knew, as a Russian, that friends were often required to spy on friends. Some of the stories of treachery were awful. Still, Natalia had not expected it to happen to her. Not her.

Her husband beat her and she was unable to fight back. Now this! Finding out that the jealous Leonid was himself an adulterer was nothing compared to the outrage of losing Sonia as a friend. Why did Leonid feel it was necessary to use Sonia? There had to have been a way that would have been just as efficient and caused less misery.

On the way back they saw a line suddenly gather on the sidewalk outside of a small food market. 'Cucumbers, do you think?' Sonia asked. She pulled quickly to the curb.

Natalia joined the line without seeing what it led to.

Sonia checked up ahead and came back to join Natalia, grinning. 'Even better. Green beans. They're beautiful!'

'Green beans!' Natalia spoke with self-conscious gaiety. There was no reversing the clock for herself and Sonia.

10

It was Isaak Ginsburg's misfortune, when he was called before the commandant, that the May 9 anniversary of the Soviet Union's victory in the Great Patriotic War of 1941–45 was just three days away and Anna Mikheyev was entering the first day of her period. During the prior ill-tempered week, Anna's hormones had made her so jittery and tense that she couldn't stand to be touched. Mikheyev's hand on her breast felt like squeaky chalk on a blackboard. Anna's jumpiness had put Mikheyev in a foul mood.

No good could come from a meeting with a camp commandant. All *zeks* knew that. For a commandant to call a prisoner to his office and then not punish him was unthinkable; it invited unrest. A conscientious commandant, to insure a sufficient level of intimidation, always made a prisoner's humiliation public. This insured a smooth-running camp at a minimum of expense to the government.

Ginsburg was escorted to Mikheyev's office by two privates with AK-47s slung over their shoulders, and was ushered into the office without a word being spoken. Yevgenni Mikheyev looked up at a portrait of Lenin on the wall and made a sucking sound with his lips.

This was the first time Ginsburg had seen Mikheyev close up. Owing to a wide jaw and broad forehead, Mikheyev's face was shaped something like the figure eight with a blunted middle. His nose was both wide and short, but turned up slightly at the end. He had huge dirty blond eyebrows that needed plucking; an abundance of hair grew out of the bottoms of his ears. He had long, slack hair, also a dirty blond, that he habitually combed back with his fingers – a nervous tic of long standing.

Mikheyev's military tunic was covered with heavy campaign medals and bright ribbons. He seemed to have one of everything the Red Army had ever awarded, but he didn't look like the kind of man who would rise to command anything. Ginsburg wondered if he might not be the grandson of General Yuri Mikheyev, a hero of the siege of Leningrad.

The commandant looked down at Ginsburg's file on his desk. Ginsburg saw it was identical to the one Felix Jin had consulted – complete with his University of Moscow photo and the Writers Union objections to his poetry – and wondered if this rap sheet of his life, the summary of the party's complaints against Citizen Isaak Ginsburg, a slandering, possibly psychopathic Jew, an individualist, might not follow him for the rest of his days.

Mikheyev made a great show of comparing the photo in the file with the dark-eyed man standing before him. When he was satisfied they were the same, he said, 'Prisoner Ginsburg.' This statement set out the nature of their relationship. 'I am the grandson of General Yuri Mikheyev, but I suppose you've been told that.'

'Yes,' Ginsburg lied. He wanted to say his grandfather was Salomon Ginsburg, who had been there with Lenin, but he held his tongue. Intellectuals like his grandfather had brought about a successful revolution against the czar. Joseph Stalin did not trust independent imaginations, which was why he had murdered just about every one he could find. This fear, still prevalent at the Kremlin, was the reason Ginsburg was at Mikheyev's office in Zima.

'So you know I do my duty. My grandfather did his duty. I do mine. Your file says you are a parasite. You

63

libeled your country with your scribbling. What do you have to say for yourself? Answer now, don't just stand there.'

'I wrote about small moments, comrade, not politics.'

'That's not what the president of the Writers Union says. It's right here, Ginsburg. Do you mean to argue with the president of the Writers Union? Are you saying he doesn't know how to read poetry?'

'I don't mean to say that at all – '

'Well, then?' Mikheyev interrupted.

'I – '

'Felix Jin says you are not to write poetry during your sentence, Ginsburg. Right here, he says it: "This man is not to write or recite poetry during his incarceration."' Mikheyev tapped his finger on the line where Jin had made his notation. 'I know of Felix Jin,' he lied. 'A thoughtful man. Have you been writing poetry, Prisoner Ginsburg?'

Isaak Ginsburg knew he was about to pay for having arrived at Zima with ten toes. 'No, comrade,' he said.

'You're a liar. You were overheard reciting it aloud on the train coming here. Do you deny it?'

Ginsburg said nothing.

'Answer me, *zek*.'

'I was remembering old poems, not writing new ones,' Ginsburg said.

'Well, you're a liar, Ginsburg. You were overheard reciting poetry on the train from Moscow.' The commandant ran his fingers through his blond hair, then opened a pack of Russian cigarettes. He lit one, watching the *zek* in front of him. Mikheyev was suddenly furious.

'Twenty million people died for our country in the Great Patriotic War.' Mikheyev had been watching heroic war movies and patriotic documentaries all week on television. 'Twenty million!'

'I was given to understand I was not to compose.'

'Twenty million!' Mikheyev shouted. 'Lying parasite! And you criticize!'

The commandant scribbled a note in Ginsburg's dossier.

Mikheyev took a handkerchief from his pocket and blew his nose. 'The problem is you think too much, Ginsburg. We need to give you something to think about other than poetry,' he said. He mopped up the moist leavings at the bottom of his nose.

Mikheyev pondered, and then his face brightened. He looked pleased. 'Let's see, I'll give you a week to heal before you ride the train back. That ought to do it. You need to be up and around if you expect to ride the train to the relocation center at Gorky, eh, Prisoner Ginsburg?

'Two weeks in solitary confinement. One week before you leave, you'll be made to pay for libeling your country and ignoring the conditions of your sentence. It will be done at the dispensary by Dr Aleshkin. An imaginative cut – Aleshkin has the skill, I'm sure. You should be well enough to travel in a week.' Mikheyev did not want questions. 'If I catch you writing poetry again, I'll have your fingers smashed. What I am going to have done to you will make you understand that the knife is more powerful than the word, just as the state is superior to the individual.'

While Ginsburg watched, aghast, Captain Mikheyev picked up a ball-point pen and detailed the sentence in Ginsburg's file so that the camp surgeon might perform the unspecified surgical punishment two years hence.

'You'll be a far different man when you leave than when you arrived, Ginsburg. I guarantee. Now leave.'

The *zeks* at Zima were housed in a low building with a corrugated tin roof. The building had four wings, one of

65

them longer than the others, so that it was shaped like a crucifix. The compound was surrounded by a fifteen-foot-high barbed-wire fence. Ten yards beyond that there was an even higher wooden fence; the outer fence was topped by three strands of barbed wire. There were towers on all four corners of the compound and a tower in the center. The central tower contained a huge searchlight.

There was a storage area for great piles of logs to the west of the fence – toward Zima. To Ginsburg this was a mountain of logs. The logs were guarded by yet another barbed-wire fence.

Ginsburg had two years to consider Mikheyev's sentence. He could not write; that was out of the question, he knew. Ginsburg was determined that Mikheyev would not rob him of his passion and imagination. The question was, what would he become on his release? How would he live each day?

There were no trees inside the compound and the twenty-foot high wooden fence blocked out the leafing birches in the spring. The lovely images and moments of truth that had been the pleasure of Ginsburg's life were gone. He didn't try to recover the loss. It didn't occur to him even to try in his colorless world.

Ginsburg's unspecified surgery triggered endless speculation and macabre jokes among the *zeks*: just what would happen to Ginsburg? The punishment would require a week's time for Ginsburg to heal – enough to travel, however much the pain.

Aleshkin, the doctor, would do what had to be done. Just what could that be? What? The worst was unthinkable.

Ginsburg plunged himself into his work in order to forget and so that the time would pass more quickly. Work hard and the time would go faster, he believed. The *zeks* worked twelve hours a day, seven days a week.

Ginsburg hooked a chain around a log so that a boom might swing it into a new pile. He did this wearing bulky gloves in the bitter winter and shirtless in the summer.

If the wind was right, the *zeks* could hear the women giving instructions to engineers and brakemen over the loudspeakers at the Zima railroad station.

The *zeks* memorized the voices of those who worked the various shifts and gave them names: Sasha, Anna, Olga. Olga worked graveyard and had a warm, soft voice. Ginsburg thought Olga's instructions were wonderful as they rode gentle breezes, floating across shacks and mud in the spring and summer, across the snow and ice in the winter.

Ginsburg wasn't Olga's only admirer among the prisoners at Zima. Olga's soft voice was, by common agreement of the *zeks*, far superior to those of Sasha, who worked days, and Anna, who worked swing. Anna had a harsh voice. She would be heavy-hipped, the *zeks* reckoned: she would trudge when she walked.

The *zeks* survived off a chunk of bread and a cup of water in the morning, some rice with a chunk of fat at noon, and a watery gruel at night that was supposed to be borscht. The borscht featured a hunk of fat on Tuesday and one thin slice of sausage on Thursday. One *zek* was detailed to ration the slices. On Sunday the *zeks* got a cup of tea and that was wonderful, a treat. Sometimes, in late fall and early winter, they got crumbs of potato or bits of beet in their borscht. Their only utensils were their fingers.

In two years Ginsburg had fresh vegetables just twice: two slices of cucumber on May Day. This bounty was to celebrate the working people of the world, and was observed, as were all their meals, by a six-foot-high portrait of Lenin on one wall of the mess hall. Ginsburg weighed 170 pounds when he began. At the end he weighed 118 pounds and had loose teeth.

Ginsburg shared a six-foot-by-five-foot wooden cell with a squat Georgian named Lado Kabakhidze, a widower whose daughter Nina was a conductress on the Trans-Siberian Express. Kabakhidze was serving time at Zima for black-market activities. He had gotten caught, he said, for swapping the people's cheese for Greek shoes smuggled across the Black Sea in a Turkish fishing boat.

Kabakhidze said he had originally been sentenced to four years, but this had been extended two years by Mikheyev, who, in a fit of rage at the camp's mediocre production, claimed that Kabakhidze, among others, was a lazy shirker of his duties as a prisoner.

Ginsburg and Kabakhidze passed their few leisure hours playing chess on a board scratched onto the wooden floor of their tiny cell. They used scraps of wood for their men. They used their thumbnails to mark their wins, losses, and draws on the wall. They took turns cleaning the tin can that was their toilet. And they talked.

One night when they were alone, and cold, and listening to the silence of the Siberian winter, Ginsburg told Kabakhidze of his promise to the coughing *zek*. He told Kabakhidze how the cougher had given him his second layer of clothing and both pairs of socks and had curled up to sleep his last.

'It was on our last night on the train, Lado. The cougher sought me out and put his arms around me and told me to keep moving; we would share our heat. We were on the edge. I thought I would die that night.'

'You're still alive.' Kabakhidze said.

Ginsburg smiled, remembering. 'Because of him. And he was alive, he said, because of a physician named Serafim Korenkho, who shared a potato with him when they were both starving. In saving the cougher's life, Korenkho saved mine.'

'That's something you don't forget, Isaak.'

'The cougher told me Korenkho was sent to Slansky because he refused to experiment on human subjects. There's a slate mine there, and that's where the cougher knew him. About three years ago, Korenkho was transferred to an underground uranium mine at Asht, in the Tadzhik Republic. The cougher said they make no effort to protect the *zeks* from radiation in the uranium mines, in the uranium enrichment plants, or when they clean the nozzles of atomic submarines.'

'You come out with cancer,' Kabakhidze said. 'Those are death camps, Isaak.' He adjusted himself under his blanket. 'I had a friend once, Isaak. But that's a long story.'

'The cougher wanted me to know so I could remember.'

'What happened to Korenkho?'

'A *zek* who knew him at Slansky told the cougher he saw Korenkho a couple of years ago. This *zek* was pulled off his train to help load and unload supplies that had arrived on the same train. The supplies turned out to be medical equipment destined for a clinic that was surrounded by dormitories.'

'At Perm, this was?' Kabakhidze asked.

Ginsburg studied Lado's profile in the near darkness. 'Yes. How did you know?'

'It's one of those stories you hear if you spend enough time in the camps. My friend may have ended up there. The story is they do research on cancer victims. They don't need rats or monkeys. They have all the real people they need to test their drugs and operations.'

'The *zek* told the cougher he saw Korenkho sitting in a room watching television with some other patients. He was pale and was sitting with a tube draining black fluid from his lungs into a bottle on the floor. After the trucks were unloaded, the *zek* was taken back to the station and put into another carload of prisoners.'

Kabakhidze said, 'That's the place. Has to be.'

'The cougher's friend said the clinic is located on the east side of Perm, that is east of the Kama River. He said there's a huge bluff north of the railway tracks with apartment buildings on top of the bluff and a valley of log huts below. That's where the clinic is, at the northern end of the valley. The cougher wanted Korenkho's daughter to know about the potato. He wanted her to know the kind of man her father was. The cougher was starving and Korenkho shared.'

'You don't forget somebody like that.'

'The cougher said Natalia Serafimovna is married to a man named Kropotkin. She designs commemorative *znachki*. Can you believe that? After what they did to her father?'

'People do what they must do, Isaak.'

'She's about my age and has a Moscow residence permit.'

'If Mikheyev doesn't extend your sentence, you'll be getting out of here before me. You should look up my daughter, Nina.' Lado Kabakhidze fell silent, then he said, 'I hate this fucking cold, Isaak. If Mikheyev extends my sentence again, I'll die here. It was warm in Georgia; they grow lemons there. Nina looks like her mother did when she was young. Did I tell you that?'

11

Isaak Ginsburg's scheduled March 4 release date came and went with no word from the camp administration. Each day Ginsburg awoke, wondering if that was to be his day. When the guard unlocked the cell door for breakfast and work on March 12, he said, 'No breakfast for you this morning, Ginsburg. You are to report to the infirmary at three o'clock today. Where are you scheduled to work?'

'Helping unload the train.' Ginsburg swallowed. A wave of anxiety washed through his body and he felt giddy.

The sergeant wrote a note on a small pad and gave it to him. 'Give this to your shift foreman. You're to remain in the yards today. We'll send someone for you.'

Within a half hour all the *zeks* and guards at the Zima lumber camp knew this was Isaak Ginsburg's day. The other prisoners watched Ginsburg out of the corners of their eyes.

Isaak Ginsburg walked to the infirmary in the company of two young men carrying AK-47s. He wondered, as he made his way along the muddy trail, if he shouldn't make a break for it – try for a burst of 7.76mm slugs in his back.

Ginsburg didn't run. He was taken to the infirmary, which was in a short wing of the compound. The commandant's office was just down the hall together with the offices of his chief administrators. The infirmary people ordinarily had little to do except amputate frozen fingers

71

and toes and dispose of dead *zeks*. Ginsburg was a special case.

The chief medical officer at the infirmary was named Fyodr Dmitrevich Aleshkin. The onerous task of carrying out the commandant's instructions had fallen upon him. He hated it, but it was either do this or face similar treatment himself. While poor red-headed Aleshkin had never been what you would call the model of the healing physician, he was nonetheless a civilized human being and did his best for the *zeks* at Zima.

Aleshkin's hand trembled visibly and he cleared his throat as he ushered Isaak Ginsburg into the barren room where operations were performed. The operating table, Ginsburg saw, had wheels on it. It was portable, 'Ginsburg, is it?' Aleshkin asked.

'Yes,' Ginsburg said. He could hardly breathe. He hoped he wasn't going to faint. He willed himself to stay on his feet. Get it over with. 'What are you going to do?'

Aleshkin ignored the question. 'If, uh, you'll take off your clothes, please.'

Do what you have to do, Aleshkin, Ginsburg thought. He put his cap on a nearby chair and bent to remove his shoes, wondering if he could straighten up again or if he would fall flat on his face. He began unbuttoning his shirt.

Aleshkin said, 'We'll knock you out. You won't feel anything when you wake up because of the drug. When you wake up, Captain Mikheyev wishes to talk to you. After a couple of hours, there'll be quite a lot of pain. You'll be very sore.'

Ginsburg's mouth was dry.

'I'll try to do a good job,' Aleshkin said. 'In time you'll heal. I'll give you some medicine.'

Good job? Heal? There was no sense pestering Aleshkin with questions, he knew. Aleshkin had his orders. 'Please get on with it,' Ginsburg said.

Aleshkin said, 'Yes.'

Ginsburg climbed up on the table, which had a pad on it, covered with a sheet. That was the first time he had been on a sheet in two years. He lay back as if he were in a dream. Someone took his forearm, and Ginsburg felt a needle. A warm wave flushed across his face. He hadn't felt this good in two years, warm, drifty, ethereal.

All this for the offense of having memorized doggerel in a freezing boxcar.

Ginsburg realized this barbarity was part of the discipline his well-intentioned grandfather Salomon had helped bring about. Ginsburg felt his arms being tied down. He saw that Aleshkin had another hypodermic.

He heard Aleshkin saying, 'I don't have any choice in this matter, Ginsburg.'

Ginsburg said, 'Without choice we are dogs, Aleshkin. Without choice we bark at the moon. When it sets, we bark even louder. Do what you think you have to do. Get it over with.' He watched as Aleshkin slid a second needle into his arm.

Isaak Ginsburg awoke in Captain Mikheyev's office. He was still on his back, his arms still strapped to the table. There was a huge poster of Lenin on the wall. This wasn't the usual hard-jawed, determined Lenin. This was a casual Lenin wearing a blue cap with a small bill. Ginsburg was still drifty, confused. He looked at the portrait.

The cloudy figures and figureless voices in the rising fog rolled something else into the room. Another table? Ginsburg turned his head to the side. There was a cloth draped over something small in the middle of the table. He heard a voice. Aleshkin? 'He'll be clearing in a few minutes,' the voice said. Yes, Aleshkin. Someone else spoke. Mikheyev? Isaak Ginsburg saw the commandant standing there in his trim officer's tunic.

'Well, Ginsburg, how does it feel?' Mikheyev asked.

Ginsburg felt no pain or discomfort anywhere, and said so. He was still woozy from the drug.

Aleshkin said, 'I told you. It's the Sodium Pentothal.'

Ginsburg could still see and hear. He could talk. He had his tongue. So much for one fear that had plagued his nightmares for months. He clenched his fists. His fingers were present. He moved his ankles; he still had feet.

'Are you clear now?' Mikheyev bent over the operating table.

'I'm clear,' Ginsburg said.

'Good,' Mikheyev said. 'Show him, Aleshkin. He'll want to see.'

Aleshkin removed the cloth from the center of the second table, uncovering what was there, staining the sheet with blood.

Isaak Ginsburg looked and started retching.

Mikheyev stepped back. 'Yes, Ginsburg. They're yours. Say good-bye to your balls, poet.'

Ginsburg retched and gasped, turning his head so his throat would clear. It was ghastly. He couldn't move. He closed his eyes, refused to open them.

Aleshkin said, 'We'd better unstrap his arms or he'll choke.'

'Sure, sure.' Mikheyev stepped aside so Aleshkin could free Ginsburg's arms.

Ginsburg grabbed for his genitals. They were bound in bulky surgical dressing.

Mikheyev said, 'You'll heal, Ginsburg.'

Ginsburg turned on his side and continued retching. He was at once exhausted and filled with horror and rage. He vomited until there was nothing left in his stomach to come up. He continued to retch, caught in

74

painful spasms. He could hardly breathe. Ginsburg started easing his hand back toward the bulky dressing.

'There'll be some discomfort when the anesthetic wears off,' Aleshkin said.

To that Mikheyev added, 'You'll have to clean up after yourself, you know.'

Ginsburg glared at him in rage. His mouth moved but he was unable to speak. He refused to look at the other table.

'Yes, those are your balls, Prisoner Ginsburg. You've probably never seen them from this angle. Maybe we'll feed them to your fellow *zeks*. Siberian oysters.'

'I . . .' Ginsburg's wit failed him.

'Would you like a bullet?'

Isaak Ginsburg wiped his mouth with the back of his arm. He started crying suddenly, bawling. He couldn't help it. He looked pathetic and knew it. 'Yes,' he said.

'Well, ask him.' Mikheyev gestured at the portrait of Lenin. 'Say, please, Comrade Lenin.'

Ginsburg looked at the poster. What did it matter? Everything would be over in a few minutes anyway. He said, 'Please, Comrade Lenin.' Ginsburg wanted to die very badly.

Mikheyev said, 'Well, good. Here, how would you like it? In your mouth? I can blow your brains out if you'd like. All you have to do is open your mouth.'

Mikheyev removed the revolver from the holster on his hip and put the muzzle into Ginsburg's open mouth.

Ginsburg could feel the barrel against his teeth, could taste the metal.

'Now?'

'Yes.' Ginsburg could hardly say the word around the metal barrel.

When the hammer slammed down on an empty chamber, Isaak Ginsburg jerked rigid.

75

Yevgenni Mikheyev burst out laughing. He laughed and laughed until he was weak and had to lean against his desk. 'Wasn't that wonderful, Aleshkin? Wasn't it wonderful? Did you see the look on his face?'

Ginsburg stared at Mikheyev.

Mikheyev said, 'It was a joke, Ginsburg. A joke. Tell him, Aleshkin.'

'Those balls belong to poor Susley, who died of pneumonia last night. We would have done this earlier, but we didn't have a body.'

Ginsburg grabbed for his bandaged crotch.

'Everything's there,' Aleshkin said. 'Numb, but there. I deadened them with a shot.' Aleshkin looked as if he, too, were about to be sick.

'They could have been yours, couldn't they, Ginsburg?' Mikheyev was still amused. He picked up Ginsburg's file from his desk. He would use his adjutant's office to detail the punishment as was required by regulation. Mikheyev had a spotless dossier. He followed instructions to the letter. This would be a wonderful entry. He couldn't wait.

Yevgenni Mikheyev hoped that his record of efficient and imaginative punishment would be noticed by his superiors and he would be rewarded with a posting in European Russia.

Isaak Ginsburg momentarily forgot about revenge. There was no matching Mikheyev's barbarity. All Ginsburg wanted to do was get the fuck out of the Soviet Union.

12

Isaak Ginsburg and the other *zeks* recently released from the gulag were returned to civilian life by a Soviet administrative unit in Gorky. The prisoners waited in line in a low, white-brick building dated 1972 in red brick. The party insisted that buildings be dated in the Soviet Union so that the progress of Leninism might be noted. According to the plaque next to the main entrance, the relocation center stood beside the path down which bearers had carried Comrade Lenin's coffin in the bitter cold of January 1924.

Ginsburg was now officially cured of parasitism, having spent two years at Zima. What he would do and where he would live was at the leisure of the state. Ginsburg was at the mercy of the St Peter of Gorky; he or she, a bureaucrat, would decide whether or not Ginsburg would return to Siberia or be sent to warmer climes.

Captain Mikheyev's damnable joke had made him even more resolved to get out of the country. Ginsburg stood. He stared. He moved one foot forward. He stood. He stared. He stood on one foot, then the other. He contemplated the path worn in the linoleum by countless *zeks* who had shuffled down this queue before him, each one, like himself, awaiting the decision of another government bureaucrat. He took another small step.

In the Soviet Union everybody learned to wait in line. Ginsburg reflected on this fact. This was a form of socialist training: everybody was equal in a line. Mothers waited in line to deliver babies. Wives waited in line for cucumbers. Children waited in line to kick a ball or to receive a test

77

score. Men waited in line to buy vodka so they could forget about waiting in line.

Ginsburg waited for more than three hours before he reached the woman in a gray uniform sitting at a large table surrounded by stacks of folders. St Peter was a woman. The name K. Trofimova was stenciled onto a rectangular piece of cardboard tacked onto the front of the table. Comrade Trofimova, who wore a Lenin pin on her lapel, waited to pass judgment on the next sinner against the people.

Trofimova took her time with her paperwork on the *zek* before Ginsburg. She stacked the file in the proper stack. She made a neat little check on a list of names. She put the notebook in its proper place. She made a quick notation in a larger notebook. She had bright blond hair with brown roots. Her large breasts pushed at the front of her gray uniform. She seemed pleased with her decision. She looked up at Ginsburg.

'Ginsburg, Isaak Avraamovich,' he said. He wondered if K. Trofimova's Lenin pin had been designed by Natalia Serafimovna.

Trofimova regarded the tall, dark-eyed man. He had an intelligent face and had somehow maintained his dignity through whatever it was he had experienced. His hair, just growing out after a recent hacking with crude shears, looked ridiculous, worse than a soldier's if that were possible. Trofimova found it hard not to smile. She turned to the list of names and found his. Without looking at him, she said, 'A Jew. I make the decisions. If you protest, I'll send you above the Arctic Circle. Is that understood?'

Ginsburg said, 'Yes.' If he were a gymnast, or a hockey player, or a chess master, he'd have a chance.

Trofimova retrieved Ginsburg's file and opened it on the desk before her. Even upside down, Ginsburg could

78

read the summary of Mikheyev's awful joke. Trofimova hadn't gotten that far when she glanced up at Ginsburg. 'You have a university education?'

'Yes.' Foreign service officers traveled abroad; that was out. A KGB agent. Ginsburg repressed a smile.

'And you wanted to be a poet.'

'Yes.' Like Osip Mandelstam, he thought.

'You are a Jew.'

'Yes.' The Soviets didn't want Jews, didn't like them, yet wouldn't let them leave.

'You Jews think too much.'

We Jews replaced the czars with Jins and Mikheyevs, Ginsburg thought. 'Yes,' he said.

'You wanted to emigrate to Palestine.'

Ginsburg said, 'I'll gladly go wherever you send me.'

It was only then that Trofimova came across Mikheyev's final punishment. She cleared her throat and kept reading.

Mikheyev had printed his summary in neat letters so Ginsburg was able to read it easily, even upside down, Mikheyev had included everything in his description of the '"castration" of the prisoner, I. Ginsburg.' Aleshkin had used an injection of novocaine to deaden Ginsburg's genitals. Ginsburg's vomiting was recorded in one neat sentence. His plea to be shot was noted. At the end, Mikheyev said, 'The punishment was one-hundred-percent effective. Under its threat the prisoner ceased slandering the state; he did not, to my knowledge, write or recite poetry in his two years at Zima. Prisoner Ginsburg was returned to civilian life unharmed, ready to resume a useful and productive life.'

Ginsburg read the last sentence and shook his head.

Trofimova reread Mikheyev's description of Ginsburg's special punishment twice through, then turned the book slightly on the table. She pointed at the long paragraph. 'Is this true?' she asked. She looked at the form again.

'Yes,' Ginsburg said.

'Is this exactly what happened? Tell me.' She turned the folder so he could read it better. This was a violation of regulations, but she didn't care.

'Yes, what it says is true. That's exactly what happened.'

Comrade Trofimova started to speak, then closed her mouth.

The men in the line waited patiently. If they complained, they risked return to a camp.

Ginsburg waited, outwardly patient. He thought of Yevgeny Yevtushenko. In the early 1960s, when Nikita Khrushchev was pushing de-Stalinization, had not Yevtushenko been allowed to read his poetry in New York?

Trofimova said, 'All these men in this line today are being assigned as laborers. Because of your education there is a need for you in several cities. None of these are in Europe. They are in Siberia or the Urals.' She unfolded a map. 'There are possibilities in these cities.' She pointed to several cities on the map.

Ginsburg hesitated. He studied the map. Sverdlovsk at the eastern foothills of the Urals was the closest to Moscow. He couldn't imagine there were many writers in Sverdlovsk.

Trofimova said, 'You must choose, comrade. I am doing you a favor.'

There was an opening in Novosibirsk – New Siberia – the largest city east of the Urals. The Soviets called it the Chicago of Siberia, but there was a nearby community of academics. 'Novosibirsk, please,' Ginsburg said.

'Novosibirsk?'

'Yes.'

Trofimova removed an assignment sheet from a neat stack of forms and began filling it out in a small, neat hand. She made out a travel order. She filled in a form that told him where to report in Novosibirsk. 'They'll tell you what you'll be doing when you arrive,' she said without looking up. When she was finished she said, 'Why did you choose Novosibirsk?'

'They say Novosibirsk has a wonderful opera house,' Ginsburg said. 'And a lovely circus too.'

She glanced up at Ginsburg and caught his dark eyes straight on. 'Do you like the circus?'

'The Soviet Union has entertainment for everybody: doves, ice-skating bears, clowns.'

Comrade Trofimova looked at the *zek* behind Ginsburg. She said, 'Next.'

Isaak Ginsburg arrived in Novosibirsk the second week of April, twenty-six months after he had been summoned to Felix Jin's office. Ginsburg had to go through four lines in Novosibirsk: the first to register with the police; the second to find the location of his work; the third to decide where he would live; a fourth for a physical examination.

The first two lines went relatively fast. All the police bureaucrat did was compare the photo in the file with the man before the table. In the second, Ginsburg waited thirty minutes to receive a paper saying he was to be a bookkeeper in a grocery store. The female clerk said, 'Report to work at eight o'clock Monday morning. Take this to the housing line. The woman there will have to know where you'll be working.'

The keeper of housing in Novosibirsk was another woman, K. Krupskaya. Ginsburg waited in line, clutching six different papers, all required for housing. The first form gave him permission to travel to Novosibirsk. The second was a canceled travel voucher. The third said yes, he had checked in with the Novosibirsk militia. The fourth confirmed his employment as a bookkeeper in a grocery store. The fifth gave the location of the grocery store and said he was to be assigned housing. The sixth listed biographical information including his age, the fact that he was a Jew, and his education.

When K. Krupskaya saw Ginsburg's occupation, she hesitated. She wet her lips. 'Housing is very crowded in Novosibirsk,' she said. 'We are working very hard to correct this, but now space is limited.' She studied his job assignment again. 'Downtown apartments, of course, are out of the question. They aren't to be had.' She considered the employment form again.

She said, 'We are building a major subway station near the opera house here in Novosibirsk. The construction people have taken over a small building that they use for office space and a place where they can weld and do light repairs. There is one small room left in that building, Ginsburg. It's very close to where you work.'

'Anything's fine by me,' Ginsburg said.

K. Krupskaya said, 'The man in charge of the construction is an acquaintance of mine. He's a very congenial man. Thoughtful.' She studied Ginsburg.

Ginsburg grinned. His assignment to a grocery store was a wonderful bit of luck. 'I always help my friends,' he said.

'His name is Georgi Kashva. If he doesn't like you, he'll send you back.'

'Kashva.'

'The foreman. He'll want to talk to you. The room is very tiny, but I'm sure you'll make do. You'll share a kitchen and a bathroom with the construction workers. You'll be moved within a year and a half; the building will be torn down.'

'Yes.'

K. Krupskaya said, 'You will then be reassigned at our leisure, comrade.'

'Yes,' Ginsburg said.

'It won't be downtown next time,' she added.

'I understand,' Ginsburg said. He had lost four teeth to the miserable diet at Zima, and explored the vacant holes with his tongue. He joined the line for his physical examination.

Isaak Ginsburg had to ease his way across a wallow of mud to get to the apartment building, which had metal scaffolding and planks leaning against the front wall. There was a pile of buff-colored bricks on one side of the main door. Someone had emptied his sinuses at the sill of the front door, and it was apparently the practice to tromp mud inside.

The crews had gone home for the day and there remained a single man, sitting alone with his muddy feet sprawled wide on the linoleum floor. He leaned against a desk on which there was a pile of papers, a yellow hard hat, and a crumpled paper bag.

'Kashva?'

'Yes.' Georgi Kashva stood.

Ginsburg said, 'My name is Isaak Ginsburg. I'm told that I should talk to you about living here.'

Kashva pulled a pocket watch out of his pocket and checked the time. 'My wife's expecting me. Listen, let me get to the point. This is a nice location and private, but I was kind of hoping Katerina would send someone who might be willing to help me out a bit. I've been using this room in the afternoons sometimes.' Kashva twisted his wedding band. 'Her name's Irina. She has kind of red hair.'

'I can go for a walk or something.'

'I really would appreciate it.'

'I'll be working as a clerk in that grocery store down the street there.' Ginsburg pointed with his head. 'If I see

83

something . . .' He left the second half of the sentence unstated.

'Really! That's the choicest grocery store in Novosibirsk. Isn't this a wonderful country? I give Katerina paint so she and her husband can redecorate their apartment. In return she sends me you. What do you want? I can get you anything.'

'For now, nothing. Maybe one day.'

'Ask when you're ready,' Kashva said. 'I know people.' He opened the bottom drawer of the desk and removed a liter bottle of vodka and two water glasses that he proceeded to fill a quarter full.

'Here's to friends,' Kashva said. 'Call me Georgi.'

'Friends,' Ginsburg said. 'Isaak.'

They both emptied their glasses Russian style, tossing the vodka back in one gulp.

'That tastes like two more, Isaak,' Kashva said. He poured another round.

'To fresh green peppers!' Ginsburg said.

'Certainly.' Kashva drank to fresh green peppers. They drank another round. They were both a little tipsy when Kashva took Ginsburg to his diminutive room. Ginsburg stashed his paper sack of belongings and walked outside with Kashva. On the way out Kashva said, 'None of my construction people are to know about this. No one.'

'I understand,' Ginsburg said. He parted with Kashva and, still drunk, went for a walk in the direction of the opera. Once he looked back and there was a man who seemed to be watching him. Was this man following him? Ginsburg could see the dome several blocks away in the late afternoon sun. The weather was balmy. A huge, dramatic statue of Lenin with others stood in front of the opera. There were three determined soldiers at Lenin's right hand, a robust young man and wholesome young woman on his left, signifying industry and agriculture.

Ginsburg watched an exuberant pair of newlyweds climb out of the back seat of a well-used Lada and start running toward the statue. Their friend took a picture of the couple placing flowers at Lenin's feet.

13

When James Burlane finished the story about Isaak Ginsburg in *Newsweek*, he sailed the magazine across the room where it landed in a heap to join *Time*. Burlane was incensed. He couldn't see how magazine editors could stomach giving Ginsburg one line of copy, much less running spreads with his picture and quoting his bullshit poetry.

Burlane got up to go play hackey-sack and breakdance with the kids down the street. He did this to maintain his coordination lest he come up against a Russian with quick feet. As a breakdancer, he was something to behold: his gangly arms yanking quickly, smoothly into odd contortions. He did this pretending he was gouging Libyan eyeballs or snapping Iranian necks. Burlane had had to move once when reporters from a local television station showed up to videotape him winning a neighborhood hackey-sack competition.

Later, he'd go for a drive to his special place in Virginia and practice keeping cans hopping in the air with his silenced .22 machine pistol. He'd have liked to have taken little Emilio, the local hackey-sack champ, who'd be thrilled to watch the cans jump, but that was out of the question. Today, Burlane decided, he'd pretend the cans were Isaak Ginsburg's forehead.

14

The grocery store was a few doors away from the fanciest department store in town. There, a man could buy a pocket watch that had a sailing ship molded into the pot metal back and a red CCCP beneath the six on the face, or a woman might choose an almost stylish Yugoslavian lamp or a Hungarian vacuum cleaner that worked.

The ballet dancers who worked in the opera house lived in nearby apartments. The dancers received special treatment because they were proof to the world of superior socialist accomplishments. They were athletes as well as artists, and their vigorous training required a special diet: chocolate sometimes, or Western European beer. This food was obtained through Ginsburg's grocery store; it was handiest to the opera house. When the dancers wanted some black caviar and decent wine to toast the opening of a performance, that's where they ordered it.

The grocery store might have been fashionable, but it had a musty, pungent odor, the smell of earth. The smell was caused by cabbages in the summer, dirt-encrusted beets and potatoes in the fall, and stumpy, unwashed carrots on into the winter. There were seldom vegetables in the spring – occasionally an extra ration of green onions – but the odor continued, dank and acrid.

The manager, Anatoli Fedorov, was watching for Ginsburg and introduced himself as Ginsburg leaned over the vegetable bins, inhaling the aroma of dried mud. 'Smells like Russia, doesn't it?' Fedorov said. 'I take it you're

Isaak Ginsburg.' He shook Ginsburg's hand and took him back into his little office to talk.

Fedorov read from a folder with Ginsburg's name on it. This folder was similar to the file the housing woman had studied – a censored version of the file studied by Comrade K. Trofimova in Gorky and of the master file presumably stored in a KGB facility.

Fedorov said, 'You graduated from Moscow University. Very impressive.' He stopped.

'I've always been good at exams.'

'It's a knack, they tell me.'

'If you learn the subject, you'll do well on the exams. Learning the subject takes hard work.'

Fedorov said, 'I think I'm doing this backward. Maybe I should show you how the store works first, then get into the details of what you'll be doing. Have you ever kept books before?'

'No,' Ginsburg said. 'But I'm a quick learner.'

'I think it's better to start out front. You'll need to know the clerks' records so you can keep a clean tally.' With Ginsburg's file in his hands, Federov led his new bookkeeper on a tour of the small sales room. 'The apartment houses are smaller in this area, so we aren't packed all the time. You will see some lines when we get hothouse cucumbers or onions in from Leningrad.' Fedorov didn't say the cucumber lines sometimes turned the corner of the block outside.

'There seems to be enough frozen hake to satisfy everyone,' Fedorov said. Because of its fishy taste and mushy texture, a little hake could satisfy a lot of people. The government could afford to buy it because the Americans and Japanese scorned it.

Ginsburg wondered if Fedorov was working with the people who were following him. 'Wonderful fish,' Ginsburg said.

'And of course we're one of the few stores with a good supply of socialist sausages.'

The sausages looked like bloated, bulbous turds. Ginsburg hesitated, with a pause that Fedorov would note were he working for the KGB's Jewish Department. 'They look delicious.'

'You spent some time in a camp, didn't you, Ginsburg? That's why you're here in Novosibirsk.'

'Yes,' Ginsburg said.

'What for, do you mind my asking?'

'I asked to emigrate to Israel. I spent two years in a lumber camp at Zima for parasitism.'

'Did I tell you that my son, Yuri, and his cousin, Aleksei, are facing the university examinations next year?'

'Could you use a tutor? I can help.'

Fedorov smiled. 'There are ways I can return the favor.'

A few days after he had settled in, Isaak Ginsburg became a tutor to Yuri and Aleksei, going to his supervisor's home every day to instruct the young men in approved Leninist explanations of history and economics.

Fedorov kept Ginsburg well supplied with vodka while he, Fedorov, read the newspaper in the next room. Fedorov grinned and got a little loaded himself. Ginsburg occasionally stayed on afterward to drink more vodka; he and Fedorov talked about Dostoyevsky and Turgenev, whom they each admired for different reasons.

A week after Ginsburg began his tutoring duties, Fedorov gave him a half-dozen beautiful yellow squashes from a small lot that had arrived unexpectedly from west of the Urals. The squashes were treasures.

Ginsburg gave them to Georgi Kashva.

A fortnight later, Ginsburg was able to pass along two bottles of special vodka to Kashva. These were shipped from Khabarovsk in the Far East and contained ginseng, which was said to improve a man's potency. 'For you and Irina!'

The flow of gifts from Ginsburg to Kashva inevitably wound up in Irina's hands. Ginsburg never asked for anything in return. Irina was able to swap the good food for perfume, clothes, jewelry even. Kashva told Isaak that Irina got hornier and hornier with each gift. He'd never seen anything like it. He wanted to know if Ginsburg could get him some more vodka with ginseng in it. Kashva said he'd used up the last of his ginseng vodka to prepare himself for Irina's reaction to the American pantyhose she had scored with an earlier gift from Ginsburg.

Georgi Kashva felt indebted to Ginsburg for this bounty and one night, loaded on vodka, guilty, told him about his prized connection, a Georgian named Abu Ali. He said if Ginsburg ever got his hands on some extra rubles and wanted something really special, Abu Ali was the man. Abu Ali could get Isaak Ginsburg anything his heart desired.

15

Isaak Ginsburg didn't think it took a genius to read between the lines of Soviet literary journals. The Soviets were once again under international pressure for being anti-Semitic and for refusing to let Jews emigrate to Israel; the Moscow Writers Union was in the market for a house Jew to show the world. The road to freedom ran through Moscow; the road to Moscow was paved with obeisance.

The KGB would watch him constantly, he knew, just as someone was watching him now. Let them.

Ginsburg made a list of the most likely hangouts for approved writers in Novosibirsk, and began prowling libraries and bookstores each night after he finished tutoring Yuri and Aleksei. He spent as many nights at a place as it took to know its clientele. He browsed. He circulated. He checked the bulletin boards. He stayed each night until closing. He read everything he could find by popular, currently approved Russian poets. He read everything he could find about Lenin – and that, on a Soviet bookshelf, was a lot of books.

In the end, the place he wanted was only twenty minutes away, walking at a good clip. It was an establishment library and so not infected by intellectual malcontents. Plus that, it offered something special: a small room with a samovar so readers could step in out of the quiet of the stacks and talk about books over a cup of tea. It was the gathering place for the approved Novosibirsk literati.

The library was run by an enthusiastic old Communist

named Arkady, who was nosy and who immediately set about to learn Isaak Ginsburg's reading habits. Comrade Arkady kept lists of books everyone read in case there was a deviant lurking undetected. Arkady thought he did this on the sly, but all his regulars knew it and assumed their reading habits were passed on to the KGB. Ginsburg detected Comrade Arkady's curiosity on his third visit and knew this was his place.

Moreover, once a month, on a Saturday night, the members of the Novosibirsk Writers Union met there to read poetry and talk about books. This session was for members only.

Learning this, Isaak Ginsburg made himself a regular at Comrade Arkady's library. One night, Ginsburg felt Arkady's presence over his shoulder as he squatted near the shelves reading a book of poems by Dmitri Lagunin, who was a current Moscow favorite and much published in Soviet literary journals.

'Isn't Lagunin wonderful?' Arkady whispered. He had a red face and tiny little lines on his nose. His front teeth had been recapped, and his mouth flashed gold as he talked.

Ginsburg nodded gravely. 'He has a wonderful ability to get to the heart of the communal spirit. You'll notice he doesn't waste words. He gets it down there.' Ginsburg held his thumb and forefinger apart about the distance of a small berry. 'Like that. Like so,' he whispered. He thought, *That's the size of Lagunin's brain*. Ginsburg held up Lagunin's book. 'He's fabulous. Say, earlier I looked for Kuharin's biography of Lenin, but I see you don't have it.' If Lagunin was an asshole, Ginsburg wondered what Kuharin must be. Kuharin was even worse.

'Ahh, you're a man who knows your Lenin,' Arkady said. 'You want Kuharin, I'll get you Kuharin.' He grinned. 'It may take a while, but I'll get you one. My name is Arkady Nikitovich Zhelanov, but around here they call me Comrade Arkady.'

'Isaak Avraamovich Ginsburg.'

Comrade Arkady's face changed almost imperceptibly. 'It may take a while,' Arkady said. He squatted beside Ginsburg and ran his fingers across the spines of several Lagunin titles. '"The mother ties the sheaves with loving hands . . ."'

Ginsburg finished the line: '"Sings the song of Lenin's land.' A wonderful poem.'

Arkady pulled at his red-veined nose. 'Say, you do know Lagunin!' Arkady seemed amazed.

'Isn't he wonderful? Gripping language,' Ginsburg lied. 'Special stuff.'

'I'm getting a volume of Svetaylo in tomorrow. Do you know her work?'

Ginsburg, to Arkady's surprise and delight, recited one of Tanya Svetaylo's poems. 'Isn't she nice? She knows her peasants, doesn't she?'

Tanya Svetaylo wrote about simple, happy peasants, and the joys of living in permafrost country. The party called her a socialist Rousseau although she wasn't anything of the sort. She was yet another slavish adherent to approved socialist dogma and everybody knew it. Ginsburg felt it was all but impossible for a stylish writer to be a party favorite; felicity of style generally went hand in hand with felicity of thought. Svetaylo avoided grace at all costs. She was about as elegant a writer as one of those ice-skating bears in the Novosibirsk circus.

Nevertheless, Svetaylo was declared a master stylist and so she officially was. The members of Ginsburg's old Moscow circle of friends used to speculate on the number of party dicks she must have sucked. Ginsburg masked his rage with a contemplative, thoughtful face.

Isaak Ginsburg began work on his new oeuvre in

Comrade Arkady's library. He worked every night, carefully rewriting and polishing his work. Each page of his tablet was a maze of circled and crossed-out words, arrows, and carets.

One Saturday afternoon, Ginsburg again felt Arkady's presence over his shoulder.

'Oh, a poet!' Arkady said.

Ginsburg looked embarrassed. 'I was once, but not anymore.'

'What do you mean, not anymore?'

Ginsburg knew Arkady was straining his nearsighted eyes trying to make sense of Ginsburg's illegible scrawl and the confusion of copy marks on the page. 'I write only for myself.' Ginsburg did his best to look caught.

'Nonsense. When people write, they write for other people to read. You will read before the Writers Union. A word from me is all it takes.'

'Well, I don't think so, thank you,' Ginsburg said.

'Nonsense. Done!' Arkady said, and it was so: Ginsburg had no choice but to read before the group. 'Most of the local writers will be there,' Arkady said. 'We'll drink some vodka. Maybe talk about books. There's some people I'd like you to meet.'

'Certainly, then, if you think it would be all right.'

'What do you mean, is it all right? Nonsense,' Arkady said. 'You come, Comrade Ginsburg. You finished with the Chaychev title?'

Ginsburg nodded. 'I think Chaychev's a good judge of character. He's right: Lenin was a gentle man, not at all given to violence. The costs of the Revolution must have been hard on him.' Ginsburg looked solemn.

16

*Contact David's request and the accompanying report by
Rennie Kriss were forwarded to Ara Schott, deputy director
of the CIA. Schott took Kriss's report to the office of the
Director of Central Intelligence, Peter Neely – also known
as the DCI. This was done in accordance with Neely's
standing instruction; the President had a keen interest in
rumors of discontent in the Soviet Union.*

*The DCI adjusted the cuff of his jacket and considered
the note. He turned soundlessly, effortlessly in his swivel
chair, a chair so splendid as to elevate him from the
mundane world of his underlings. Neely's subordinates
called this chair Cloud Nine, but never to his face.*

*Neely was DCI because he was a friend of the President
and made slick, sincere appearances before committees of
Congress. Power was to his taste, but he was insecure in
the nether regions of the cold war. 'What do you think,
Ara?'*

*Ara Schott had been chief of counterintelligence during
the Townes affair. He was chief of covert operations now.
After Schott had mastered the art of defending, Neely had
put him on the attack. Schott was given neither to hyperbole
nor to panic. 'Heavens, I don't know,' he said. 'I think
this is one for Burlane.'*

17

Comrade Arkady closed the library at nine, and the writers adjourned to the tea room. The Novosibirsk Writers Union had provided buckets of iced vodka, crackers, and red salmon caviar. The writers at the party didn't spend a whole lot of time talking about writing or about books. They speculated about the tastes of the new president of the Moscow Writers Union. They complained about the Novosibirsk allocation for the coming year; the previous year they'd been treated to Polish beer at their monthly gatherings. They gossiped about one of their colleagues, a novelist, who had been given a Moscow residence permit.

Anatoli Stalnov was president of the Novosibirsk chapter of the Writers Union. Ginsburg sensed that Arkady secretly hated Stalnov. Arkady doubtless wanted to be president of the Novosibirsk writers himself. Arkady had done the boring detail work for years – including organizing these readings – tirelessly and apparently enthusiastically.

Stalnov was a slender man, in his late forties, with thinning black hair that he combed straight over his head. He had heavy black eyebrows and intense, aloof brown eyes. His administrative duties had all but eliminated his time to write, although he still referred to himself as a writer. None of those who knew him dared suggest otherwise.

Isaak Ginsburg had done a little research on Stalnov.

Stalnov's reputation as a writer dated to the late 1970s. He had published three slender novels, one of them mentioned by Leonid Brezhnev in a discussion of a 'socialist renaissance' in Soviet literature that was published verbatim in *Pravda*. Brezhnev said the novel, *Mushroom Country*, was a Leninist 'lightning rod.' Stalnov was the object of attention for more than a year, but the excitement stopped abruptly when Brezhnev died. Stalnov was unable to get his stories published – lest fashion be changed by the followers of Yuri Andropov. Andropov's reign was short-lived, but it was too late for Stalnov. He was destroyed as a writer.

Comrade Arkady introduced Isaak Ginsburg to Anatoli Stalnov.

Ginsburg looked impressed on hearing Stalnov's name. 'You're not the author of *Mushroom Country*, are you?'

Although every aspiring writer in Novosibirsk had read *Mushroom Country*, Stalnov acknowledged the authorship with a grin. He was an official of the Writers Union, so he did not have to admit it was his last published story.

'It's a lovely little novel,' Ginsburg said. 'I like your description of the taiga birch – "ghosts of Russian past standing at our side." That says something to us all, I think.' This was like spreading warm manure on moldy bread, Ginsburg thought.

'Really?' Stalnov said.

'The ambiguity was wonderful,' Ginsburg said.

'Well, thank you, Comrade Gendorov. Gendorov is it?'

'Ginsburg.'

Stalnov hesitated. He looked surprised. 'A Jew, then.'

'Yes.'

Arkady said, 'Isaak is going to read some of his poetry tonight.' Ordinarily Stalnov would have picked the reader, But Stalnov had been away at his dacha in the Urals.

'I'll be looking forward to it,' Stalnov said. It was obvious that he didn't look forward to it and wouldn't have said so if Ginsburg hadn't been a Jew who liked *Mushroom Country*.

Comrade Arkady was in high spirits. He was going to catch himself a libelous Jew.

Isaak Ginsburg looked confidently out at the writers who breathed salty fish-egg breath and whose eyes were reddened by vodka. He said clearly:

> 'I am a Jew,
> And once complained,
> But I learned to love at Zima.'

Comrade Arkady looked confused. What was this? Anatoli Stalnov paid attention.

> 'Worked in the woods,
> Worked at the mill;
> Learned that forests matter more
> Than individual trees. Trees grow back.'

Comrade Arkady watched the listening writers out of the corner of his eye as Ginsburg read on from the messy pad.

Anatoli Stalnov listened.

Isaak Ginsburg read four poems, pausing between each. Each poem was more intense than the one before. In the end, Arkady moved quickly forward, prepared to throw Ginsburg out on his ear. He would have, too, had Stalnov not gotten there first.

Stalnov embraced Ginsburg. 'Wonderful stuff, Isaak! Wonderful! Is this true? Are you a Jew? Did this happen to you?'

'Yes.'

'You!' Stalnov laughed. 'I wouldn't have thought you were a Jew. A person can hardly tell these days.' Stalnov could hardly believe his good fortune. He was glad he had gotten to Ginsburg before that stupid little asshole. Without asking, Stalnov took Ginsburg's manuscript. He looked at the title: *A Second Journey to Lobnoye Mesta: Afterthoughts*.

'In this case the source of the secret, eternal power is love of the socialist vision,' Ginsburg said. 'That's our invaluable treasure at the Kremlin. The journey is what I went through in understanding that truth.'

'You're a Jew?' Stalnov asked again.

Ginsburg said, 'Yes, a Jew.'

'I would like to read the whole manuscript if I may,' Stalnov said.

Ginsburg hesitated. 'I don't want to get into any trouble. I didn't ask to read tonight.'

Anatoli Stalnov said it was his duty as the president of the Novosibirsk Writers Union to read Ginsburg's new oeuvre. Whereupon he tucked the manuscript under his arm. There would be no argument.

Stalnov read *Second Journey* when he got home from the gathering. He did not stop until he had read the poems twice through. The poetry was good enough that the intrusion of Leninism didn't make any appreciable difference. Ginsburg had all the correct opinions, but before the reader got too bored, Ginsburg had something interesting to say. It was a wonderful skill to be able to bloat a poem with ideology and still not have the reader gag. Stalnov admired Ginsburg's talent. Used properly, Isaak Ginsburg could make the Americans and Israelis choke on their words, Stalnov knew. The worst were the goody-goody Dutch. Ginsburg would shut them up.

Stalnov finished his chore in the early hours of the morning and went to sleep a happy man; although Irma

Stalnov's gelatinous buttocks felt extra comfortable resting against his hip, his final thoughts were of Moscow women.

Three months later, Isaak Ginsburg received a letter from the president of the Writers Union in Moscow, the same organization that had declared him unacceptable and turned his samizdat manuscripts over to the KGB. Would Isaak Ginsburg like to read his poetry in the Bolshoi Theater? That could be arranged. There would be a reception in the Metropole Hotel afterward.

The letter said that Ginsburg should contact Anatoli Stalnov, who was to be Ginsburg's sponsor.

Colonel Felix Jin took a sip of tea and for the second time read the report from Novosibirsk on the poet Isaak Ginsburg. The file on Ginsburg had taken an unusual turn, two unusual turns as a matter of fact – although the first had no apparent relationship to the second. Jin couldn't remember a more interesting case, certainly not one more provocative in its possibilities.

The first item was that Ginsburg's name had turned up in the KGB investigation of black-market activities. Ginsburg was living in a building taken over by a construction crew working on the new underground in Novosibirsk. The foreman of the crew was Georgi Kashva, who was on the KGB's list of possible black marketeers. The matter of housing could be innocent enough, Jin knew: Ginsburg had had no choice in the matter.

The second twist, reported by a librarian in Novosibirsk, struck Jin as curious in the extreme. The librarian had included some of Isaak Ginsburg's poems. Jin contrasted the poems with Ginsburg's dossier spread on the desk before him. At the bottom of this dossier, the camp commandant at Zima, a Captain Yevgenni Mikheyev, had proudly detailed a bizarre joke he had pulled on

Ginsburg. Even Jin was taken aback by the bogus castration, although he was an experienced KGB officer and thought he had heard everything.

Felix Jin wondered if it were possible for Ginsburg to write poems like these after Mikheyev's joke. Jin studied Mikheyev's notation and didn't think he himself could have done it. Had Ginsburg done some kind of psychological flip-flop? If he had, this was one for the textbooks.

The Novosibirsk KGB rated the librarian highly, but Jin wasn't so sure; the librarian was obviously anti-Semitic. Jin had no way of knowing how personality tics and jealousies might have skewed the librarian's judgment.

Colonel Jin knew he had to be judicious. The party was in the market for someone like Isaak Ginsburg. It would be suicidal for Jin to make any kind of allegation before he was sure of his facts.

18

Isaak Ginsburg and his compartment-mate Ivan Shepelev talked about wild mushrooms – Shepelev loved to gather big Urals *beliyes* – until eleven when they turned out the lights, pulled the shade on the window of their soft-class berth, and rolled over to sleep. Isaak Ginsburg lay there in the darkness listening to the rattling and banging of steel on steel. When he got to Moscow he would have to cut himself off from his former friends. If he was to turn himself over to the Soviets, he would have to be theirs completely. He twisted and turned and did not fall asleep for another two hours.

The next morning brought a humid, Continental day. This was the time of year Soviet photographers made shots for postcards and for magazines that circulated in the West: shots of buildings, bridges, monuments, and pretty girls. The summer leaves softened the hardship and poverty – like gauze or Vaseline over a lens.

Ginsburg shaved and stood in the aisle, watching the birches slide by. He didn't want to get involved with Shepelev. He paced the aisle and sat on one of the small seats that folded down under every other window. When there was a stop at a small town, he joined the others on the platform. After a while his feet began to tire; boredom closed in on him. He returned to the compartment and told Shepelev he was going to take a nap.

'The birches are so beautiful. I can't get enough of them,' he said. It felt good to get off his feet. He closed his eyes and lay on his berth. The hot August sun felt good on his body.

Shepelev watched his sleeping companion.

Later, Ginsburg awakened to see Shepelev returning from the aisle. 'Perm coming up,' he said.

Ginsburg sat up and looked outside and there it was: the bluff of people's apartment buildings overlooking an awesome valley of shacks. It was just as the coughing *zek* had described. The apartments were great, featureless, prefabricated concrete obelisks, hives of tiny cells for those Perm workers lucky enough to escape the isbas – the log shantytown.

Ginsburg began gathering his things: a light bag with clothing in it, and a heavy bag with a strap that cut into his shoulder. 'Good hunting, Ivan,' Ginsburg said.

'And a good visit to you too, Isaak,' Shepelev said. He gathered his two small bags and followed Ginsburg out of the train.

The train station at Perm was painted white, like that at Zima. The inside of the station was muddy, and echoed, and smelled like a root cellar. Isaak Ginsburg strode past soldiers in rumpled uniforms and peasants with medieval faces. The soldiers and peasants sat on old benches amid a clutter of bags, sacks, and baskets. and watched him. They were neither curious nor cautious. They waited for whatever was going to happen to them to happen.

Ginsburg strode past a group of oxenlike women wearing dark blue head scarves and Day-Glow orange vests over their dark blue blouses. They walked on heavy, slow thighs, looking down at their coarse brown shoes. They carried the crude birch brooms they had used to sweep the railbed and station yards. Ginsburg wondered what they thought of when they went to sleep at night.

Isaak Ginsburg knew that he had been followed in Novosibirsk. He wanted to look back to see if Shepelev or anyone else were there now, but he didn't.

The Lenin Hotel was less than a half-mile from the railway station. It had been a sweltering, humid summer afternoon. Black clouds gathered to the west as he walked up the street.

At the hotel, Ginsburg changed his clothes. He walked down the hall to the bathroom. There was no hot water. Ginsburg brushed his teeth. Back in his room, he took a pint flask from the smaller of the two bags and had a slug of vodka as the first lightning popped over the river to the west. In a few minutes a wind kicked up and pushed rain against the window.

Ginsburg poured himself another drink as the thunder rumbled and gurgled, then crackled and popped. A startling bolt of lightning lit the street outside, followed by a booming crack overhead that sent Ginsburg out of his chair. In twenty minutes it was over, and Ginsburg went out to do what he had to do, wearing old trousers and a casual jacket with the heavy bag slung over one shoulder. The air was made fresh by the rain; it smelled good.

Ginsburg passed the railroad station and turned east on Brezhnev Prospekt, paralleling the tracks that ran east to west across the river. Brezhnev Prospekt was paved, but it was so dirty it was hard to tell, and the rain had turned the dirt to slime. Ginsburg stopped occasionally to rest and also to check the street behind him. He saw no one. Once he hung his heavy bag on the stub of a broken aspen branch and rested his shoulder, swinging his arm to get the blood circulating again.

Walk east, the cougher had said; stay north of the railroad tracks. Soon, unmistakably, Ginsburg was upon the valley of huts.

The pavement of Brezhnev Prospekt ended abruptly. Ginsburg made his way down a road that was a wallow of mud. The screeching of crickets replaced the sounds of city buses. He passed a maze of prefabricated metal garages that stored Ladas for the people lucky enough to own them. By some quirk of central planning, the garages in Perm were either purple or green. Judging from the muddy trails leading up the bluff, these cars belonged to people who lived on the top.

Just beyond the garages was a city of root cellars, mounds of earth, each with a small door and two vents on top. If the Americans should ever attack, the citizens of Perm were supposed to dart into a root cellar and settle in among the bags of beets and potatoes.

Ginsburg's feet were soon sticky balls of mud. After a couple of kilometers, he paused and whacked his foot against the white bark of a birch. As he cleaned his shoes, it occurred to him that each hut, no matter how dilapidated or pathetic, was surrounded by a fence. Each tiny garden plot, each crumbling isba was somehow staked out. In Russia, where everybody owned everything or nobody owned anything – depending on how you looked at it – everybody had a fence. Ginsburg remembered a line from the American poet, Robert Frost: 'Something there is that doesn't love a wall.'

Ginsburg smiled to himself and walked on with lightened shoes, the bag still cutting into his shoulder – although not as heavily as his determination to honor his word to the coughing *zek*. Ginsburg owed it to the cougher to see the Perm cancer clinic for himself before he told Serafim Korenkho's daughter, Natalia Serafimovna Kropotkina.

Isaak Ginsburg chose each step carefully. It was possible, in Perm, to drown in Russian mud.

19

Isaak Ginsburg found the cancer clinic at the far end of
the valley of isbas, as the coughing *zek* had said. The
administrative offices and laboratories were in a low,
white-brick building. The bricks were of various sizes,
and rose and fell like slow swells on a lazy sea. Maybe
the bricklayers had been hitting the vodka. The clinic was
in a lovely area, the center of a parklike woods of birch
and aspen.

While the Americans argued the efficiency and morality
of using laboratory animals, Soviet researchers – having
the advantage of working with human animals – pushed
hard for the great socialist breakthrough in cancer.

The research subjects lived in smaller buildings made
of the same white brick. The dormitories were fenced,
but the gates were open. and Ginsburg saw men in *zek*-
like uniforms sitting on benches under the trees. Ginsburg
found an empty bench, relieved his shoulder of the heavy
bag, and watched the patients.

The patients didn't seem to regard Ginsburg's presence
as unusual; no doubt residents of Perm strayed onto the
benches to contemplate the fluttering of leaves in a light
wind. The patients were younger men, most in their
twenties through early forties. Some were pallid, more
sick than others. A few hardly looked ill at all.

A man with an athletic build walked toward Ginsburg.
He walked alone, enjoying the leaden stillness of the
cooling, wet air. He whacked the ground with a stick. He
had an intelligent, alert face. He looked at Ginsburg,
wondering who he was. 'Hello, there,' he said.

'Good afternoon. I'm told that you're all dying here. Of cancer.'

The man looked surprised at Ginsburg's casual honesty. 'Yes, we are. I got mine at Sovetabad. See what's happening.' He lifted his cap. His head was bald.

Ginsburg shook his head slowly. 'Did the cancer do that, or drugs?'

'Experimental drugs,' the man said. 'Some of us can't shit. Some shake. Some puke. Others are going blind, I lost my hair, although my leukemia seems to have steadied. I have leukemia. Jaan Birk is my name. I'm an Estonian.'

'Isaak Ginsburg. Would you like some vodka?'

'Of course,' Birk said.

Ginsburg took a flask from his jacket pocket and gave it to Birk who unscrewed it and took a hard jolt. Ginsburg said, 'So, tell me. How did you get sent to Sovetabad?'

Jaan Birk took three small balls from the pocket of his crude hospital trousers and began juggling them with his left hand. 'I was athletic when I was younger. Do you really want to know?'

'Sure.'

Birk put the balls back in his pocket. 'I was sent to Sovetabad because of a woman and a Russian. My father was an army sergeant who was killed in Hungary in 1956. My mother died of pneumonia the next year, and I was taken in by her brother – my uncle Viktor Konnen – who was an animal trainer for the circus in Tallinn. I went into the Red Army like my father.' He took another blast of vodka. 'It was very rare for an Estonian to be made an officer. My uncle Viktor was proud of me. I thought it was the best thing that had ever happened to me until I met Nadia.'

'Nadia?'

'Nadia was also the worst thing ever to happen to me.

107

She was a gymnast at the Institute of Physical Culture in Leningrad where I was assigned. I was a younger lieutenant. We fell in love and I asked her to marry me, but she said no, she wanted to see if she could qualify for international competition. It was her dream to travel to foreign countries. The next world championships were scheduled for Lisbon, then Munich after that. She had been invited to train in Moscow.'

'Did she get to travel?'

Birk shook his head. 'No, she didn't, and two years later she said yes, she wanted to marry me. She had given it her best, but she wasn't good enough. She was grateful that I waited while she tried. She returned to Leningrad and we were married. Then, it turned out, there was this problem.'

'There always is,' Ginsburg said.

'It turned out that in Moscow, Nadia had gotten cut from the competition early on. She also caught the eye of the first cousin of the director of the Institute of Physical Culture. He intervened and she was allowed to continue training. She said that at the time going to bed with the Russian seemed a small enough price to pay.'

Ginsburg dug a bottle out of the heavy bag and opened it.

'The Russian showed up a year after we got married. He said he had arranged for her to be a trainer in Moscow. She was to return to Moscow. She said no. A month later I was arrested for "libeling the Soviet people" and sent to Sovetabad.'

'And Nadia?'

'Nadia killed herself. As you see, I'm here waiting to die. Before, I thought of myself as an Estonian who was also a citizen of the Soviet Union. I will die an Estonian only.'

'You will die then.'

'We all die someday,' Birk said. 'I'm part of what the Russians call an experimental group. I live in a barracks full of ex-*zeks* who worked with uranium and plutonium. We've all got the same form of leukemia and they've got us on a drug that keeps it in remission. We spend our days cleaning, sweeping, raking, shoveling, pruning, and puking. Actually we're given quite a lot of freedom; we're allowed to visit our families on furloughs.'

'I see.'

'It's for our morale, they say. All that puking. They're going to take us off the drug in a year. This is so they can see how fast we deteriorate. The Russians are a wonderful people, Ginsburg.'

'What?'

'Just like pulling the plug on a bathtub to see how fast it drains. We know a guy who's screwing one of the secretaries who works in the administration. She says our group's scheduled to be taken off the drug next summer – part of their research. We've got one more year of puking before they turn us over to the disease again. You were a *zek* too, weren't you. What happened?'

Ginsburg said, 'I spent two years at a lumber camp in Siberia. At Zima.' Ginsburg told Birk what Yevgenni Mikheyev had done to him at Zima. When he had finished, Birk said nothing. Both Ginsburg and Birk remained silent for a full two minutes. A slight breeze kicked up, stirring the leaves on the birches.

'Well, they got us both, then,' Birk said. He took a heavy slug of vodka. 'You know, a man in my position spends a lot of time drunk. There's not a lot else to do except puke. A person gets to thinking of ways to get even. Do you do that?'

'Every day at Zima. When I got out, though, all I wanted to do is get out. What are you going to do to them? Nothing.'

109

'I've been thinking it would be fun to steal Lenin's head from the tomb,' Birk said casually. He laughed and gave Ginsburg a crooked grin. 'Wouldn't that be a kick in the nuts? Swap it for a year of open emigration, say.'

'Steal Lenin's head?' Ginsburg was disbelieving.

'Sure,' Birk said. 'I used to be an army officer. I could do it. A little parting gesture from a comrade with leukemia. Keep in mind, Isaak, that these are Russians we're dealing with, not humans in the ordinary sense.'

Ginsburg could only grin and shake his head. The proposition was so obscene as to be humorous. In fact, a few years earlier a satirical samizdat had circulated in Moscow in which a man hid himself in Lenin's tomb after closing and stole Lenin's head – which turned out to be stuffed with straw. Ginsburg remembered some lines written by the American poet, T. S. Eliot:

> We are the hollow men
> We are the stuffed men
> Leaning together
> Headpiece filled with straw. Alas!

This was a far more outrageous proposal than merely stealing a head. This was the Leninists' secret of secrets – the new heart of Lobnoye Mesto, the skull that radiated a secret power for eternity. The arrogance and conceit of Russian destiny had not changed since the medieval Muscovites, through all the czars, through Ivan the Terrible, through Joseph Stalin.

If Jaan Birk stole Lenin's head, he would castrate the Communists; there was no word more accurate than the naked truth. Captain Mikheyev had stolen Isaak Ginsburg's poetry, and having thus neutered him, gave Ginsburg one final lesson in the horror of impotence.

Ginsburg said, 'Say, do you have a place to store a

110

little something?' He opened his bag wide enough for Birk to see.

Birk was amazed.

There were a half-dozen bottles in the bag: Old Crow, Old Granddad, Bombay gin, and three bottles of Johnnie Walker Black Label scotch.

'Maybe this'll help you figure out a way to steal Lenin's head.'

Jaan Birk said, 'You don't think it could be done? I could do it. I may be a little drunk now, but there has to be a way. You figure out a way to get me some weapons and get the head out of the country, and I'll come up with a way to get it out of the tomb. Where did you get this stuff?'

'From a special store in Novosibirsk,' Ginsburg said. 'If the comrades in the Politburo drink well, I don't see why we shouldn't also. Everybody is equal in the Soviet Union, as we all know.'

'I could figure out a way.'

Ginsburg said, 'I told you I shared a cell with a man named Lado Kabakhidze.'

'With the conductress daughter.'

'With the conductress daughter. If she carries my letter, it'll arrive unread.'

Jaan Birk was amazed. 'I think you're drunker than I am, Isaak Ginsburg.'

20

In his new role as Moscow's resident Jewish Poet, Isaak Ginsburg received invitations to an unending round of readings, openings, and parties. He was introduced to visiting French and Italian Communists eager for reassurance that the Soviet Union was the object of libel and was not, in fact, as coarse as it appeared in the bourgeois Western press. When a group of Marxist officials arrived from Liverpool, Ginsburg was summoned forth to read poems extolling the beauty and glory of the universal city. When journalists arrived from New York, Ginsburg read poems filled with Yiddish allusions and references to the Old Testament.

Ginsburg knew he would eventually meet the designer Natalia Serafimovna Kropotkina in the course of his social life. Dr Serafim Korenkho's daughter had married well. Leonid Kropotkin was powerful and respected in the Communist party.

In late September, Ginsburg first saw Natalia at an exhibition of her lapel pins in the Hotel Rossiya, just south of Red Square and overlooking the Moscow River. Kropotkina had designed the fifteen-kopek pin Premier Spishkin had worn on his lapel when he spoke before the United Nations General Assembly. A rectangular pin, red bordered by gold, it was now on lapels all over the Soviet Union.

Paintings of Natalia Kropotkina's pins – the originals of her work – were mounted on portable panels that partitioned a conference hall into smaller, more dramatic viewing spaces. Spotlights mounted above the panels dramatized the pins on display.

At one side of the hall stood a long table with bread, caviar, vodka, and bottles of beer in buckets of ice. Natalia herself was surrounded by men with serious faces who nodded heavily, jowls waggling, as she gestured with a slender hand toward first one, then another of her works.

A sign by the entrance said N. Kropotkina's Lenin pins were wonderful examples of socialist commemorative art, art that brought people together. In a lapel pin, the sign said, art and pride in the great socialist accomplishments were one. The biography on the wall said N. Kropotkina had been compared to Rodin and Diego Rivera. By whom wasn't made clear.

Natalia was a small woman with long, jet-black hair that had been brushed to a luster. She was fine-boned, petite, with a pale complexion, green eyes, and heavy eyebrows. Ginsburg spent a lot of time looking at the *znachki* but did not approach the artist herself. It would be coarse to tell Natalia about her father at an exhibition of her commemorative pins. He decided to wait.

If Ginsburg thought he was anonymous, he was mistaken. Natalia Kropotkina saw him and was furious. Her father had died in a slate mine at Slansky and here this odious suck had intruded on her exhibit. Jews of her acquaintance had more pride than Ginsburg. Natalia wanted the slime out of the hall, out of the building. She wanted to scream at him, wanted to grab him by the arm and shake him, but restrained herself. Ginsburg was an official hero. To make a scene would call attention to her father and would be the end of her pin designing. Even Leonid wouldn't be able to save her.

Ginsburg was tall and slender with curly hair and brown eyes that caught her own momentarily. There was something about his eyes, a calm. Presence. But there was more than that. Guilt? No. Resolve? Perhaps. What? No matter. When Ginsburg left the room, Natalia Kropotkina stared at him in barely disguised hatred.

Isaak Ginsburg thought Natalia was beautiful. He had never seen such striking green eyes. He went back to his apartment and drank vodka and thought about Natalia Kropotkina and her father and the coughing *zek* and Mikheyev and Jaan Birk's outrageous proposal.

Natalia Kropotkina was torn between hatred born of loyalty to her father's sacrifice and the memory of the complex brown eyes that had briefly held her own at her exhibition in the Rossiya. In spite of herself, Natalia was curious about Ginsburg. She met him again, as she had known she would, in the second week of October at a party given by a director of the Bolshoi. It was a gathering of artists and writers and those party officials – including her husband, Leonid – who enjoyed the company of artists and writers. When she saw Ginsburg, he was alone, having himself some French brandy and pickled mushrooms.

Serafim Korenkho had died in a camp because he had opposed medical experiments on human beings. Isaak Ginsburg, apparently without pride, had become a party suck on a level to rival Leonid. Natalia wondered how Ginsburg could spend two years in a camp only to turn around and abase himself, so assiduously and blatantly toadying up to the worst party creeps.

Ginsburg had a wonderful feel for the Russian language. Not even Natalia could fail to appreciate that. But just how he was able to be such a worm was beyond her.

Natalia looked Ginsburg's way, then returned to her conversation with two officials of the Artists Union. She wanted to ask Ginsburg flat out why he was such a jerk.

114

She didn't care about the consequences, the consequences be damned. The problem was how to quietly tell the bastard off without incurring Leonid's suspicion.

Leonid was drinking hard. Natalia knew she should be careful, stay among women, chat with men only briefly. Leonid kept his eye on her, and now there was no Sonia for comfort and support in the early hours of the morning. Leonid had successfully destroyed that. There was only the couch, cigarettes, vodka, and the companionship of her refrigerator, which had been making a humming sound lately.

Later, on her way back from the toilet, Natalia angled in Ginsburg's direction. She wanted to spit in his face.

Ginsburg disarmed her with his eyes and said, 'I know what happened to your father, Mrs Kropotkina. A *zek* told me on the train to Zima.'

Natalia wanted to swear at him, even slap his attractive face; she could hardly believe this. 'You what?' she whispered savagely.

'I know what happened to Dr Serafim Korenkho. My name is – '

'Isaak Ginsburg, I know. My father died of a heart attack in a labor camp in Slansky. He died honorably, comrade.' Her use of 'comrade' was a bullet. Natalia glared at him, hating him, wanting to tell him what she thought of him. Her father was dead, Ginsburg lived, a roach.

Ginsburg was calm. 'He died honorably, yes, but not at Slansky. He died as the subject of experimental drugs at a cancer research clinic in Perm. The very thing he opposed, I'm told.'

'He what?' Was Ginsburg a liar on top of everything else?

'Your father was sent to Slansky, then to a uranium mine. The *zek* on my train and your father were starving in an earlier camp and your father shared a potato with him. Your father saved the *zek's* life, the *zek* saved mine – a chain of humanity so that we may remain civilized and never forget, Mrs Kropotkina. Your father wanted you to know what happened to him at Perm.'

Natalia Kropotkina was stunned, yet she believed Ginsburg; the Communists were capable of anything. She glanced at her Leonid. He was looking at her. 'My husband, you see. I want very much to know about my father, but – '

'Would you like to talk later, then? Your father would understand that this is a matter of honor for me as well as the man whose life he saved. Perhaps I am not so terrible as you might think. Sometimes we do what we have to do.'

Natalia didn't know what to say. She wanted to know about her father. Now she wanted to know Ginsburg's story as well.

'Believe me, I understand your rage, Mrs Kropotkina, but I would like a chance to explain myself. Please.'

Natalia believed what Isaak Ginsburg had said about her father. She wanted to know the rest of the story, all of it. She was also transfixed by Ginsburg's physical presence. The possibility that Ginsburg was working for the KGB did not occur to her. For reasons that were elemental and primal, she knew he was telling the truth. 'Let me give you the number at my studio,' she said. 'I'm generally there in the afternoons.'

21

Comrade Sergei Pavlichenko was an impressive figure on the stage of the small auditorium. Pavlichenko had all the trappings of a poet: a gray beard, a corduroy jacket with leather elbow patches – French-made and therefore stylish, but well worn and therefore Bohemian – and an English cigarette that he waved passionately. The party leaders wanted their poets to look like poets.

'We ask ourselves who we are, we Russians . . .' Pavlichenko stroked his beard thoughtfully.

'We have magpie souls, black and white. Magpie hearts. Who
   are we?'

Pavlichenko's voice rose angrily until he shouted the question again. 'Who are we?' The Soviets encouraged the clichéd angry-artist notion on condition that the anger be directed according to their instructions. Pavlichenko, who liked shopping in privileged sections of GUM, did his best to make the polemics colorful.

Isaak Ginsburg, who sat near the front of the hall with the other writers and editors of the Writers Union, nodded in agreement at the correct places. Pavlichenko's dramatic reading was a pathetic spectacle; everybody had to agree with him or risk being sent to a camp.

Pavlichenko started to sweat. Before the reading, he'd slugged down a quarter of a liter of vodka with friends. He squeegeed his forehead with the palm of his hand and flipped the sweat onto the stage with a gesture that said he was a worker's poet and this was honest worker's

117

sweat. He ended his poem with his arms outspread, palms
open, embracing all: 'The taiga is of us. For us. Ours.'
He took a deep drag on his cigarette, closed his eyes and
exhaled slowly.

Isaak Ginsburg applauded enthusiastically and said,
'Wonderful! Wonderful!' *Bullshit! Bullshit!* Pavlichenko
was a raging asshole. Ginsburg had a fleeting vision of
himself smashing a surprised Pavlichenko in the face with
his fist. Ginsburg turned to the jowly man on his left
and said, 'Powerful material, don't you think? Powerful.
Pavlichenko knows how to read.'

'It's a pleasure to hear him,' the jowly man said.

Isaak Ginsburg said, 'Incomparable.' He followed the
jowly man down the aisle and onto the stage to congratu-
late Pavlichenko on his performance. The jowly man
walked like a huge, obese goose. Ginsburg remembered
his grandmother's wonderful pâté.

Pavlichenko was glad Ginsburg had attended the reading. 'Comrade Ginsburg! What do you think?'

'I think you were wonderful, comrade. Your best work,
I think.' Could anything be worse than having to listen to
Pavlichenko? Ginsburg embraced Sergei Pavlichenko.
'Congratulations,' he said. 'Beautiful work.'

Pavlichenko, pleased, said, 'You will stay to drink a
little vodka, won't you, comrade? Selyutin's throwing a
party.'

Ginsburg said, 'Ordinarily I would, but I've been
working on an epic poem and it's coming for me. Nights
are my best time, as you know. When it's coming, it's
foolish for me not to get it on paper. You know how it
is.'

'I understand, Isaak. Believe me, I understand. Thank
you for coming to the reading.'

Isaak Ginsburg went to retrieve his coat from the

cloakroom and froze. Up ahead, Felix Jin, coatless, waited by the entrance to the lobby.

When Ginsburg got near, Jin said, 'Comrade Ginsburg! Good that you came. Are you going to Selyutin's gathering?'

'No, I think I'll go on home tonight, Comrade Jin.'

'Me too,' Jin said.

'I'm working on an epic poem commemorating the completion of the BAM.' The BAM was a rail line in the Soviet Far East that looped north of the old Trans-Siberian tracks. It was intended to help develop the interior as well as provide tracks farther away from the Chinese border.

'Up all night, eh?'

Ginsburg said, 'Yes, comrade.'

'Writing poetry?'

'Writing poetry is hard work. Even reading it can be work. Did you see Pavlichenko sweat? That sweat is from his heart, believe me.'

Jin said, 'You don't seem to have come with anyone in particular, Comrade Ginsburg. Are you alone? Do you mind if I join you on the ride back into town?'

'Join me, certainly.'

Ginsburg and Jin waited their turns at the cloakroom. They put on their heavy coats and *papakhas* and wrapped woolen scarves around their throats. They waited patiently for their turn through the heavy revolving door at the main entrance. There were policemen at the door to prevent the importation of knowledge.

Outside, snow twisted and whirled in the gusting wind. Ginsburg and Jin walked along a path that curved through a narrow parklike strip that bordered the main street in front of Moscow University. Ginsburg liked to walk among the wintry ghosts of white-barked birches. In the spring and summer huge fat-bodied Russian magpies watched the sidewalks from the birches. These magpies, the ones that had apparently inspired Pavlichenko, were big as crows or ravens. Behind the two men, the spires of the university loomed high, cathedral-like.

'A wonderful Russian experience to walk among birch on a snowy night,' Ginsburg said.

'Yes, it is. Cleans the lungs.'

'We come and we go, but the birch remain, and the snow returns every fall. Where would we be without the birch?'

Jin looked up at Ginsburg's face. 'Did it seem to you that Pavlichenko might have engaged in parody as some kind of prank tonight?'

Ginsburg looked surprised. 'Why, no. I'm sure he was sincere.'

'When they defect, you know, the defectors tell the British and the Americans that they survived on irony, survived laughing at their countrymen.'

'I can't believe that of Pavlichenko,' Ginsburg said.

Jin nodded his head in agreement. 'I can't either.'

Ginsburg's heart fluttered and a sickening wave of anxiety coursed through his stomach. His face flushed momentarily. Ahead, in the huge expanse of an empty parking lot, he saw a crowd surging toward them. He was saved. 'Look there!' he said. 'The circus is letting out.'

Hundreds of bundled Russians were moving rapidly in the direction of the metro stop, preparing for a wild scramble for seats on the underground trains.

Unless they hurried, Ginsburg and Jin had a wait ahead of them. Either way, they would have to ride packed into the metro car like oily, smoked sprat.

They joined a huge knot of people surging into the station, then waited while those ahead of them were sucked quickly downward by a metro escalator. The escalators on the Moscow metro were said to be the

120

fastest in the world, a claim that went unchallenged by visitors who rode them. The deeper the escalator, the faster it seemed to hurtle. The escalator at University Station slung the line of people down, down, down. The platform was twenty-five yards below, a precaution against American rockets.

The wooden steps of the escalator whipped *zip, zip, zip* as they emerged from the top. Passengers descended at a dizzying rate, stomachs aloft, as on a swiftly descending Ferris wheel. At the bottom of the escalator the stairs disappeared *zip, zip, zip*, at the same startling speed.

A woman in a blue uniform watched at the bottom lest a child or confused older citizen get sucked, screaming, into one of the quarter-inch spaces that were grinning jaws on either side of the descending stairs.

Jin was quick and aggressive. He pushed his way to the front of the platform and they were able to board the first train back into town. They both stood, holding on to a stainless steel post, listening to children talk about bears that roller-skated, about the 'American rodeo' that was part of the show. There had been bucking broncos and lassos. Ginsburg wondered if Russian cowboys could ride and rope better than American cowboys.

The train rumbled into the darkness of the tunnel and after a couple of stops emerged onto a bridge. The Moscow River below them was frozen and white. The V. I. Lenin Central Stadium, also under a mantle of snow, was to their left. It was dramatic and beautiful to ride over the Moscow River in a snowstorm. The heart of Moscow was up ahead.

The snow twisted and swirled above the city. The young couple next to Ginsburg and Jin had been most impressed by an acrobat who had been catapulted from a seesaw onto the top of ten men standing feet on shoulders. It had been a seemingly impossible feat. The young

121

woman said Russian circuses were the best circuses in the world.

The metro entered a tunnel again. Ginsburg said, 'Perhaps you would like to come up to my apartment, Comrade Jin. Have a little vodka.'

'Do you mean that?' Jin sounded surprised and pleased by the invitation.

'Certainly, comrade. If you like, I'll show you the poems I'm working on. They're some of my best. I think.'

Jin knew Ginsburg was up to something. Ginsburg secretly hated Jin, had to. 'Yes, that would be nice,' Jin said amiably. 'Maybe for a few minutes.'

Isaak Ginsburg wondered if Colonel Jin knew that he had been seeing Natalia Kropotkina.

22

Anatoli Stalnov had been summoned from Novosibirsk to function as Ginsburg's officially approved mentor – an honor bearing with it a Moscow residence permit; the Soviet Union had put an eight-million cap on Moscow's population and so extruded unhappy exiles from the city at the same pace as it received delighted new residents.

No Muscovite mentioned Stalnov's professional exile in Novosibirsk. He once had been of no use and was sent away; he was now useful and so was returned. His duty was to screen invitations and requests extended to Isaak Ginsburg. The official reason for this romantic but absurd chore was that Ginsburg needed privacy for the arduous hours he put in at the typewriter.

In the second week of December, Anatoli Stalnov told Isaak Ginsburg the two of them had to talk. Saying no more, he led the way to the Moscow River. The awful Russian winter was upon the city. This was one of those evenings when Moscow took on an eerie calm, sitting alone out on the edge of Asia. Ginsburg and Stalnov, breathing frigid air that seared their lungs, strolled along an icy path beaten in the snow along the eastern bank. The northern lights unfolded overhead, celestial curtains of greens and yellows and reds.

'Moscow is a beautiful city,' Stalnov said.

'You can smell the cold.'

'It's like this all winter long in Novosibirsk,' Stalnov said. His breath came in frosty puffs that hesitated an instant in the wind, like delicate crystal, then disappeared.

'The avenues look like canals iced in.'

Stalnov said, 'No traffic and the snow muffles everything else.'

Did the snow muffle even the screams in Lubyanka Prison? 'It's lovely,' Ginsburg said.

Stalnov said, 'We could be walking alone by a river in Siberia. Just us.'

The two men walked, listening to the crunch of their boots on the frozen crusts of footprints. 'Listen, Isaak, it hasn't been announced yet and won't be for a couple of weeks, but Comrade Zhukov has negotiated a resumption of the Geneva arms talks.'

'Really?'

'You're part of the bargain, Isaak Avraamovich. You'll read a commemorative poem at the signing of the resumption agreement, which will be held at Vladivostok during the first week of May.'

Ginsburg was confused. 'Vladivostok?'

'At the airport there. We want to remind the world that the last agreement we signed with the Americans – at Vladivostok – was never approved by the US Senate. Zhukov will give Secretary of State Kaplan a bust of Lenin. Kaplan will give Zhukov a carved eagle. You'll read your poem. I tell you this so you'll have time to do your best work.' Stalnov paused. 'Anything less than your best would be an embarrassment to us both, comrade.'

'Thank you. I won't let you down, believe me.'

Stalnov checked his wristwatch. 'I suppose we should be heading home.' He led the way up the long trail to Red Square. At the top of the slope and on their left, the heavy, gloomy south wall of the Kremlin overlooked the river. Stalnov's star rose with Ginsburg's, but if Ginsburg turned out wrong, then Stalnov would pay.

Stalnov said, 'It has been suggested that you ride a train across the Soviet Union so as to impress the foreign reporters with your love of country. You could read a poem somewhere in between, Irkutsk say. By the way, Isaak, I think it would be wise of you to consider carefully some of the people you meet in these gatherings. I'm thinking of the matter of ladies.'

'Ladies?'

'You've been observed with Natalia Kropotkina. Natalia's an attractive woman, I know, and intelligent too.'

Ginsburg looked surprised, but wasn't. He assumed that Anatoli Stalnov was working for the KGB.

'You should listen to me, Isaak. I don't want you to get into trouble, or her . . .' Stalnov's voice trailed off. 'Isaak, you should know something about Leonid Kropotkin. He's insanely jealous of his wife. People know that here. You have to keep your distance.'

Isaak Ginsburg had one of those wonderful moments of inspiration that had once gone into his poetry, an unexpected coming together of associations: the talk of presenting a bust of Lenin to Stuart Kaplan; Stalnov's suggestion of a trans-Siberian train ride; the mention of Natalia.

It was time to write Jaan Birk.

Isaak Ginsburg took the subway to the edge of the city and back. He rode to the southwest, got off, blended in with the crowds, and rode to Nogina Plaze, where he changed for a third and final run. He had gotten a lot of practice in the routine in the weeks since he had met Natalia; one of her artist friends had an apartment near the Kosmos Hotel and the Monument to the Conquerors of Outer Space.

This area was far north of Red Square – near the edge of the city. The monument and the hotel were dwarfed by the nearby Ostankino television tower, 536 meters high, which looked like a bizarre metal Tinker Toy anchored by guy wires.

Ginsburg was happy to take whatever precautions were necessary for his meetings with Natalia.

When they were finished with their coming together and lay side by side, sweaty, enjoying one another's smell, Ginsburg said. 'I talked to the conductress today, Lado Kabakhidze's daughter. She got in from a run from Novosibirsk yesterday afternoon.'

Natalia sat up in bed. 'Will she do it?'

Ginsburg was still surprised by the vehemence of Natalia's desire to steal the head. Defecting was one thing; stealing Lenin's head was quite another. In addition to her good looks and intelligence, Natalia Kropotkina was a gutsy woman. Ginsburg admired her nerve. 'Lado's dead.'

'What?'

'They extended his sentence again, Nina said. He died three weeks later. Of a heart attack, they told her.' Ginsburg sighed at the memory of Lado Kabakhidze.

'I'm sorry to hear that, Isaak.'

'Lado was my friend.' Ginsburg fell silent, then said, 'Nina's with us. For her father. She's Lado's daughter, all right. She'll take a letter to Jaan Birk. When we find out what Jaan needs, she'll get one to Kashva. If Kashva agrees to pass Birk's list on to Abu Ali, we'll see – that's all we can do. It's up to the Americans then. If the Americans say yes, I'll figure out a way to retrieve Birk's equipment. The hard question is, can you get the commission for the Vladivostok pin?'

'Listen, Isaak, Ivan Dmitrov wanted me to have the pin commemorating his Gorky Park statue, but I was screwed out of it by some damned bureaucrat on the committee. Dmitrov would have gotten a better-looking pin from me, and he knows it. So now he sculpts the bust Zhukov gives Kaplan. Believe me, he'll want me even more for this one.'

'More than ever?'

Natalia studied the tip of her finger. 'Oh, I might have to talk sweet, but I think he'll come around.'

'Then you know him well enough?'

'I know him, and they won't turn him down twice.' Natalia put her cigarette out in the ashtray on the floor by the bed. 'Vladivostok in May sounds fun. They have a beach there, don't they?'

'Stalnov knows we've been seeing each other, so I suppose Jin does too.'

Natalia looked startled. 'He doesn't know about our meetings here, does he?'

'I've been careful,' Ginsburg said. 'Say, Tashenka, I loved those sexy panties you were wearing today. Where did you get those anyway?'

Natalia Kropotkina smiled. 'At Bloomingdale's in New York. When we get there, I'll wear them for you all the time if you want.' Natalia reached over and slid her soft hand onto Isaak's thigh. 'Why, just look at that thing! Standing right up there, and so soon after last time. Lucky for me your Captain Mikheyev was just having himself a little fun.'

23

James Burlane was the Company's randy genius and Bohemian spy – the man, it was said, who got things done. The gangling Burlane ambled on alone, a paperback in his hip pocket. He combed his hair with his fingers. He dug at his crotch if it itched. He laughed out loud if something struck him as funny, which was often.

Burlane was long of face and long of nose, which turned slightly to one side. He was irreverent of authority, indifferent to fashion, and disdainful of possessions, saying he doubted if anyone on his deathbed ever remembered owning a Ford. Women found him attractive for reasons that were obscure and infuriating to serious men who wore neckties and drove washed BMWs.

More than one Company official – wondering about Burlane's background – had pulled his dossier for a quick peek. To their amazement, they learned that he was the son of a railroad worker and had grown up in the unlikely town of Umatilla, in the desert country of north-eastern Oregon. Burlane had no power at the CIA; in fact, he scorned it. Everybody knew it would be stupid to put a man of his imagination in charge of anything. Burlane cheerfully agreed. He didn't give a damn about power.

At the bottom of his dossier, a Company psychologist had noted: 'Subject J. Burlane apparently regards the world as some kind of interesting zoo or menagerie. We see no reason to believe this mild neurosis should be incompatible with his present duties.'

Burlane preferred penguins and lazy cats to pit bulls and Dobermans. He entered battle on behalf of the former.

He was the Company's ace, and everybody knew it, which is why the director and deputy director of the CIA summoned him to consider Contact David's proposal.

24

The enormous red wall that defended the Kremlin, citadel of the Soviets, built on the banks of the Moscow River, was in fact an isosceles triangle with a blunt tip that faced the southwest. The northern wall of the triangle – which actually ran to the northeast, reckoning from the apex of the triangle – faced Volkhonka Avenue and the Square of the Fiftieth Anniversary of the October Revolution.

The base of the triangle faced Red Square and ran just slightly to the southeast – reckoning from the Square of the Fiftieth Anniversary of the October Revolution. The southern wall curved inward slightly. This was to accommodate a bend of the Moscow River.

In front of the Northern Wall there was a narrow garden with sidewalks – a promenade of sorts – where pilgrims and tourists strolled among lovely birches. There were five towers on this stretch of the wall, including the two at the corners; the tower in the center was replete with turrets and cupolas, and marked the main entrance to the Kremlin. Just behind the main entrance was the tallest of the onion-shaped domes of the Russian Orthodox church that rose, golden, dazzling, on the inside of this most secular of secular capitals.

The promenade in front of the northern wall was bordered by a high black fence of heavy metal pickets. There was a gate at the eastern end of the park. Just inside this gate – facing the Square of the Fiftieth Anniversary of the October Revolution – lay the entombed body of the Soviet Union's Unknown Soldier.

Two soldiers wearing stainless-steel helmets and white

gloves, with chromium bayonets on their rifles, guarded the eternal flame at the gravesite.

Just in front of the grave began a four-inch-wide white line that led to Lenin's tomb. The line went east, then turned an oblique right and entered Red Square.

Inside the square, the line made a second oblique right and ran parallel to the eastern stretch of the Kremlin wall.

There was a broad sidewalk along the base of the wall, then a row of small trees, then the mausoleum that contained the tomb of V. I. Lenin – and Joseph Stalin too, until he was evicted by followers of Nikita Khrushchev. There were concrete bleachers on either side of the mausoleum, where members of the Politburo and other Soviet officials watched the May Day demonstrations and various military parades.

The mausoleum, made of granite and porphyry – a hard, purplish-red stone containing small crystals of feldspar – was a terraced, four-sided pyramid some forty feet on each side. This pallid, purplish-red porphyry was as close as the Soviet architects could come to the symbolic socialist red. Although the mausoleum was built some forty feet in front of the Kremlin wall, when viewed from the front – from Red Square – it looked as though it projected directly from the wall itself.

Visitors filed into the mausoleum and past the body in a steady line from 11 A.M. to 1 P.M. daily – Tuesdays and Fridays excepted.

Jaan Birk used the first three days of his ten-day New Year's furlough studying the tomb. He waited patiently in line each time through. He timed each trip with the second hand of his watch, and after the fourth trip through knew exactly how long it took.

The line entered the main entrance of the mausoleum,

turned left, and went down a dimly lit flight of stairs. There was a guard at the bottom where the corridor turned right. Then a second flight of stairs, shorter this time, with a guard at the bottom. The corridor went left again, down a longer flight of stairs. Another guard, a turn to the right, more stairs.

There was a guard.

More stairs. Steeper this time. To the right again.

And there was a guard, and heavy metal doors opened for visitors.

The room was small and dark.

The coffin was in the middle. It sat atop a raised rectangular pedestal so that Lenin himself lay roughly at eye level. Visitors entered from the southwest corner of the room, parallel with Lenin's shoulders, and circled against the walls to the northwest corner where they exited. This was a U-shaped tour. It was done quickly and silently, with no lingering: other citizens waited their turn.

There was a moat between the visitors and the coffin, far too great a distance for even a champion athlete to clear from a standing start. There was no water in the moat, but rather soldiers – five of them. Two stood on each side of the coffin, at Lenin's shoulders and feet. The fifth soldier stood above Lenin's head at the open end of the U-shaped promenade.

The coffin itself was enclosed in glass. There was a black blanket folded to Lenin's waist. One hand was slightly open, the other slightly closed. Lenin's head rested on a red pillow. The room was black save for a soft red light that bathed Lenin's face from above.

The guards, Birk noted, were stiff from standing at attention.

The Soviets were understandably careful to preserve their embalmed icon underneath the Kremlin wall. The troops housed at the base of Spasskaya Tower carried loaded AK-47s. The guards carried loaded weapons. When the inevitable alarm went off, more soldiers would appear from Spasskaya at once.

Jaan Birk considered the vast size of Red Square. He held out the palm of his left hand: Red Square. He put his right hand in front of his eyes. He couldn't see his left hand anymore. Birk considered that and opened a pack of cigarettes. He took a drag of hot air and eased the smoke onto his hand and grinned.

He remembered a yellow mongrel named Boris, and grinned even more. Birk thought of Viktor Konnen, the animal trainer who had reared him, and of his aunt, Greta, whom he loved dearly.

Birk decided to go to Tallinn on the Gulf of Finland. Perhaps, once he had been there, he would have a plan ready for Ginsburg.

In Tallinn, Viktor and Greta Konnen lived in retirement from the circus. Birk looked forward to juggling brown eggs tossed to him by Viktor. He looked forward to Greta's borscht. Greta put an extra splash of vinegar into her borscht, which Birk thought had to be the best in Estonia.

Jaan Birk sat backward, watching Leningrad Station, then Moscow, slide away from him. He rode backward because the railroad hadn't bothered to turn the day car around. Travelers going to the capital were somehow favored over those leaving. Sit forward entering, backward leaving: this saved labor, no doubt. Whether or not it was political, even the cynical Birk was uncertain. Anything was possible with Russians.

The train passed the Ostankino television tower on Birk's left, then a large labor camp downhill on the same side. The Kryukovo labor camp. Officially the camps did not exist. Nevertheless, the Soviets had attempted to block the train passengers' view of the camp by erecting a solid wooden fence on stilts. The bottom of the fence began twenty feet off the ground.

Almost all the isbas had painted shutters and many were painted all over. Birk assumed the peasants here had gotten extra rations of paint because their isbas were built alongside the main run from Moscow to Leningrad.

The far end of Birk's car was filled with uniformed soldiers. Enlisted men, they had crude haircuts and drank vodka from bottles in paper bags. They were drunk and getting drunker, loud and getting louder. Russians! Birk despised them.

Boris was not a fancy breed of dog. He was a cur, a yellowish-brown mongrel so nondescript and totally dog-like as to be almost an abstraction of a dog, suitable for an illustration in a children's book. He was part terrier possibly, part hound of some kind. He had a short coat, and his ears hung rather than perked. He had friendly brown eyes, and his tongue was given to good-natured flopping.

Boris had one distinction: he had been retired from the circus for political reasons. In what had started out to be a comradely joke among circus people, Victor Konnen had trained four dogs – a center forward, two wingers, and a goalie – to ice-skate and play hockey. The Soviet Union had a famous hockey team of ice-skating bears that played at state circuses. Konnen's dogs had beaten the bears nine to four in Novosibirsk, and destroyed them by an eye-popping eleven to two in Moscow.

Nine of these eleven goals were scored by Boris. He was too quick for the bears, who were intense and determined, but awkward on the ice. Both Boris and his Estonian master were summarily retired on the orders of an unnamed Kremlin official who was enraged at the debacle.

Viktor Konnen petted Boris's head. 'Poor Boris.' Boris had once been a lively dog, but he was bored now. He missed the circus life.

Birk couldn't wait until Greta got back from the communal kitchen with the borscht. When she did, it would be like old times.

'Sure. He's a friendly old guy. He likes a little affection. Isn't that right, Boris?'

Konnen massaged the back of Boris's neck. Boris gave a contented sigh. He just loved it when Konnen gave him a little massage. Boris had worked harder for Konnen than for the other trainers at the circus because Konnen liked him. Konnen respected him. Konnen saw to it that he got everything he wanted to eat. Konnen did special little things for him.

Birk fondled Boris's ear and thought surely he saw the dog smile.

'He hasn't been feeling well, I don't think.'

Birk stroked Boris's ear. 'Good old Boris.' Boris looked extra contented. All the attention was wonderful.

'He's not old. For a dog he's middle-aged. It isn't age that slows him down. He's bored not having anything to do. He misses the circus.'

Boris stretched out on the floor, receiving one hand each from Birk and Konnen. It was splendid. Ahhh!

Birk told Viktor Konnen what Birk and Ginsburg had in mind and why. He told Konnen how it was he proposed to get Lenin's head out of Red Square. Konnen was an Estonian too and hated Russians.

When he had finished, Konnen said, 'I can do that. You'll have to get me the silent whistles. Boris should be able to hear one a quarter of a mile away.'

'Boris will have to take his chances when it's over.'

'We all die someday, Jaan. Some sooner than others.'

'Some sooner than others,' Birk agreed. 'How long will it take you to train him?'

'Two or three weeks if I work at it every day. He's the kind of dog who's not afraid of anything, so the smoke shouldn't bother him. But I should run him through it with the smoke the last three times.' Viktor Konnen knew his nephew and his dog were going to die soon anyway. Boris had spirit. If Boris could talk, Konnen was certain, he would volunteer just as the dying Jaan had volunteered. 'I can practice in the taiga. I know of a place,' Konnen said.

The door opened and Greta was back, pot of borscht in one hand, jar of vinegar in the other, and a smile on her face. She had a liter bottle of vodka tucked under one arm.

25

On the last day of his New Year's furlough, on his return to Moscow from Tallinn, Jaan Birk gave Isaak Ginsburg his shopping list. They met in a snack shop on Gorky Street where a few pastries were sold, along with slices of bland cheese and small sausages. Patrons ate standing at narrow tables. The tables were chest high so they could be leaned on – elbow high if the customer was short, elbow low if he was tall. Ginsburg and Birk sipped tea that the counterwoman had ladled out of a large stainless-steel pot.

Ginsburg and Birk had to hunker slightly, elbows low. There were two women workers in the snack bar and three customers: an old man and two young women. Ginsburg and Birk were pensive as they watched the traffic on Gorky Street outside. The small Ladas on Gorky suddenly began pulling to the side of the road. People outside the snack bar stopped to watch.

A heavy, black formation of shiny Volgas appeared with a surreal quickness. The Volgas, said by tourists to look like 1955 Chryslers, had curtained windows and small red flags flying from staffs mounted on the fenders just above the headlights.

Three cars in the middle of the phalanx carried members of the ruling elite of the Communist party. They were on their way to the Kremlin. To the Politburo.

'Look at them go,' Birk said. 'Another day of hard work saving us from the Americans.' Birk opened a blue-and-white pack of TU–134s, Bulgarian cigarettes. An

Aeroflot TU–134 was on the front of the package. Both Ginsburg and Birk lit up, thinking.

'They say TU–134s are the best cigarettes in the world,' Ginsburg said. Hot air. Ginsburg knew that. Everybody knew it. Inhale a Russian cigarette, and you got hot air. The current joke in Moscow was that the Soviet Union made the biggest microchips in the world.

'Wonderful cigarettes,' Birk said. Birk knew that if he inhaled a French Gauloise, or an American Marlboro, he'd get a rush of nicotine. That's what cigarette smoking was all about; that's why people smoked cigarettes. They liked the nicotine. They got hooked on it. Birk had long ago wearied of hot air.

Birk would have preferred catching his cancer from cigarettes rather than a uranium pit. That, at least, would have been his choice. His risk. There was no doubt that it would have been more fun. Birk said, 'I love the taste.'

Ginsburg looked south down Gorky Street where the black Volgas had disappeared. 'Well, Jaan, let's go for a stroll. I want to see your list.'

Birk shrugged. 'Let's go.' And so they walked south on Gorky toward the Kremlin. Moscow's layout resembled the cross-section of a felled tree, with concentric rings intersected by spokes fanning out from the center. Gorky ran north to south, where it ended at the entrance of the red-bricked State Historical Museum. The other side of the museum was the northern end of Red Square.

The Kremlin and the districts adjacent to it were encircled by the Boulevard Ring and the Sadovoye Ring. A third ring, the Moscow Circular Road, marked the city limits. Gorky was one of the wide avenues or 'prospekts' – Leninsky, Kutuzovsky, Mir, Leningradsky, and others – that radiated from the center of the city. These prospekts were far too wide for pedestrians to negotiate above ground, so there were subterranean sidewalks at the intersections of streets.

Isaak Ginsburg and Jaan Birk walked south on Gorky, past the Museum of the Revolution, past the Moscow City Soviet, past Central Telegraph, past the Hotel Intourist to the wide Square of the Fiftieth Anniversary of the October Revolution just north of Red Square.

It took Ginsburg and Birk two underground hikes to emerge at the southern end of the Hotel Moscow, which itself was the eastern border of the Square of the Fiftieth Anniversary of the October Revolution. They walked south, the State Historical Museum on their right and the Central V. I. Lenin Museum on their left. Then they were into it, into the northeastern corner of Red Square.

They walked south in front of the huge GUM department store, which was the eastern edge of Red Square and the chief obstacle to their plan.

Ginsburg angled to his right, toward the center of the square. 'Natalia wanted to come. She wanted to meet you, but she couldn't get away from her husband.'

'I would have liked to have met her also. Please tell her that I'm doing my part for her father as well as myself. Tell her he'll be with us in spirit.' He handed Ginsburg the list, which Ginsburg studied.

'Can you get them, do you think?'

'I hope so. If I can, I'll have them for you on March sixteenth, when I get back from a reading in Tbilisi. The question is, is that time enough?'

'It should be. Later, a dog will have to be delivered from Tallinn to Moscow.'

Ginsburg looked at the list again. 'A dog?'

'Can it be done?'

'It can be done.' A dog?'

'I'll send you an order of battle in which everybody's responsibilities will be clearly specified.'

Ginsburg cleared his throat. 'I want to tell you, Jaan, that if Natalia and I make it out and ever have a son, we will name him for you. He'll be yours as well as ours.'

Jaan Birk embraced his friend. 'We'll see what happens, Isaak.'

26

Natalia Kropotkina slung her Japanese camera over her shoulder and locked the door to her Lada. She'd never been able to get within a yard of Ivan Dmitrov without him somehow pawing her. He'd insisted on showing her the working model of the monumental Oktyabrskaya Square statue, the Dmitrov masterwork begun twenty years earlier – Natalia was then just thirteen years old – and still unfinished. Natalia knew perfectly well that the socialist Michelangelo had something more interesting in mind than talking about the difficulties of completing the Oktyabrskaya monument. So did she.

The Kremlin had decided that if Comrade Grigori Zhukov gave a bust of Lenin to the American secretary of state at Vladivostok, then the statue ought to be something special. Thus the Soviets had instructed Ivan Dmitrov to sculpt a Lenin bust for the occasion – something special, just for the Americans. This bust – a thoughtful, contemplative Lenin for the American barbarians – was displayed at the Hotel Rossiya, and would remain there until Zhukov took it to Vladivostok. In the Rossiya, European visitors to Moscow could appreciate the man of peace, whose journey to America would commemorate the reopening of the Geneva arms talks.

Natalia knew Dmitrov was worried that whoever designed the Vladivostok pin wouldn't get every nuance of his Lenin just right, precisely the way Dmitrov had rendered the bust – or worse, choose not to include Lenin on the Vladivostok pin at all. That was possible.

141

Dmitrov's Oktyabrskaya sculpture had a long and complicated history. Joseph Stalin's original proposal for a thousand-foot pyramid topped with an immense statue of Lenin had failed because of the cost involved. Another suggestion was to sculpt a huge Lenin to overlook Moscow from the Lenin Hills. That was rejected as being too far away from the center of the city. Following Nikita Khrushchev's visit to New York City in 1959, the Soviets set about to strip the old-world charm of Oktyabrskaya Square – at the eastern tip of Gorky Park – and replace it with a modern look. This was to provide an appropriately grand setting for the long-absent Lenin monument in the capital city.

Ivan Dmitrov, who, it was said, drew his first portrait of Lenin when he was six years old, had spent a lifetime given over to the glorification of communism through monumental sculpture. He was given the task of creating this, his masterwork.

The Oktyabrskaya statue would stand on elevated ground in the center of the square, almost within sight of the Ferris wheel in Gorky Park; to the north across the Moscow River lay the golden domes of the Kremlin. The chief architect of Moscow and one of the planners of the monument told *The New York Times* that this location – on the route taken by dignitaries from the airport to the Kremlin – was 'an important, prestigious place.'

There were those who thought that if Natalia Kropotkina had been allowed to develop as a sculptor, she would have been Ivan Dmitrov's equal. Natalia herself found it hard to imagine the Soviets giving a woman a chance at sculpting the grandiose Lenin that was Dmitrov's chief claim to immortality.

Dmitrov was supposed to be Natalia's colleague. The truth was, Dmitrov did not consider her any sort of colleague at all. Dmitrov sculpted celebrated monuments to Communist heroes; he was the Rodin of the USSR. Brezhnev had sat for him, so had Andropov and Konstantin Chernenko and Petr Spishkin. Natalia Kropotkina merely designed lapel pins.

So Ivan Dmitrov talked down to her, which she accepted without apparent resentment. The truth was, Dmitrov made her furious. On top of that, Dmitrov apparently thought his status as celebrity gave him the right to rest his hand on her rump whenever he felt like it. His hand roamed casually, with professional aplomb – as though he were contemplating curve and line for a statue of Aphrodite.

Ivan Dmitrov opened the door to his studio, tilted his face to one side, and grinned broadly, 'Tasha! How good to see you!' He removed his thick-rimmed glasses and there – with busts of Karl Marx, Yuri Gagarin, and Fidel Castro looking on – gave her an embrace that lasted five or six counts more than a little bit too long.

'You're so kind, Comrade Dmitrov,' Natalia said. She successfully broke from his grip and ran for the model of Dmitrov's monumental Lenin at the far end of the room. The model, four-feet-three-inches tall, sat atop a revolving pedestal beneath the skylight. 'Oh, Ivan Yevgennivich, tell me all about it! I want to hear it from you. A treat! How is it coming?' She laid her camera and handbag on one of Dmitrov's workbenches.

'Let me take your coat.' Dmitrov was a slow-talking man who took his Lenin seriously. He knew that Natalia Kropotkina felt bad about having had the Oktyabrskaya pin taken from her. 'Do you like it?'

Natalia walked slowly around the model of the Oktyabrskaya monument. The tail of Lenin's heavy coat furled dramatically in the wind; at Lenin's feet, a heroic group of comrades strode into the future. It was in fact, a thing of beauty in its way – somehow blending the imaginations of Diego Rivera, Norman Rockwell, Che Guevara, Shostakovich, and Yevgeni Yevtushenko. 'I think it's beautiful, Ivan Yevgennivich. How much longer before it's finished?'

'A year, eighteen months possibly. Here, let me show you the model. My pleasure.' Dmitrov put his glasses back on and took her confidently by the elbow. 'The real statue will sit on a two-hundred-ton pedestal of Ukrainian granite. This model's on a revolving pedestal, you see, so I can see what it looks like from various angles. Here, let me show you.' Dmitrov turned the statue slowly with his hand, then stopped it. 'This is how it will look from the entrance of the subway exit.' He turned it again. 'This from Leninsky Prospekt. See?'

'Yes, the profiles are most dramatic, you're right.'

Dmitrov was pleased. 'Let me tell you about the smaller figures at Lenin's feet. I wanted them to dramatize the essential Lenin: striving toward the future of peaceful coexistence, a future without the exploitation of man by man.' Dmitrov gave Natalia a little hug to punctuate the sentence, and continued his explanation. 'The woman above them, you see, is the symbol of the victory. She's calling them all forward under the direction of Lenin. I finished her left shoulder last month. Then we have a peasant soldier here. A commissar. A young woman from the intelligentsia. You see, here, the newspaperboy has news of Lenin's revolutionary decrees. See, a warrior from the Caucasus here, and beside him a Kirghiz tribesman.'

Here, Dmitrov's hand strayed to her hip, then on to the curve of her behind, where it remained. 'We have representatives of oppressed people of Asia. All these are symbols of the individuality of nationalities living together in harmony in communism.' He moved his hand slightly on Natalia Kropotkina's flank. A reassuring touch.

Dmitrov turned the pedestal. 'Now, on the back here, facing Leninsky Prospekt, is the figure of a woman, symbolizing motherhood and womanhood. The child is the future, you see.' Dmitrov's hand gripped Natalia's rump, sharing with her his commitment to the future.

'It's wonderful, Ivan Yevgennivich.'

Dmitrov stepped back and admired Natalia's figure. He slipped his arm around her again. 'The model I had for the victory woman had a fabulous body – much like your own figure as a matter of fact. Isn't she heroic? She was proud of herself, felt good about herself. She wasn't afraid to show me. I said, "Galya, be dramatic. I want passion. Drama."'

'Very dramatic,' Natalia said.

'Tasha, have you ever modeled? Have you? You should, you know. You have a wonderful body. I suspect better than Galya's even. You know that, of course. You can't hide it. Men can't hide their imagination. It's natural to seek beauty, you know, to have it. I'm no different than other men. By the way, Natasha, I'm sorry you didn't get the commission for the Oktyabrskaya *znachok*. I recommended you for it.'

Both Natalia and Dmitrov knew Natalia had lost the Oktyabrskaya pin because she hadn't protected her flanks in the party. In fact, she had lost it out of envy. There was always that risk when one seemed to outshine the group in the Soviet Union. Ivan Dmitrov had escaped that quicksand years earlier, but he was one of the exceptional and fortunate few.

She said, 'Well, it's done. There's nothing we can do about it. But they are going to do a pin commemorating the Vladivostok signing, aren't they? There was an article in *Pravda* the other day.'

Ivan Dmitrov had not escaped the quicksand without being able to perceive an exchange in the making. Dmitrov said, 'Why, yes, they are going to commission a Vladivostok. I have a friend who's on the committee.'

'Do they want something special or just another lump of pot metal? They'll put your Vladivostok Lenin on it, surely – you sculpted it specially for the Americans.'

Dmitrov smiled. 'I believe they have something unusual and dramatic in mind.'

'The designer who gets the pin would have to go to Vladivostok to witness the signing, wouldn't she? If I did that pin, I could guarantee to put your bust on the front and do it right.'

Dmitrov smiled. 'Would you like a trip to Vladivostok, Natalia Serafimovna?'

'I don't mind travel. I like it, in fact. Especially trains. I'd like to go on the Trans-Siberian. They wouldn't have any objection to that, would they, Comrade Dmitrov? Maybe I could design a train *znachok*. I've always wanted to do a train *znachok*.'

'I can't imagine they'd have any objections,' Dmitrov said. 'As a matter of fact, it would probably be impossible for you to get a spot on an airplane if you wanted one. Aeroflot will be overwhelmed with journalists and officials on their way to the signing.' Dmitrov drew Natalia closer.

Natalia said, 'You can be sure I understand the unusual and dramatic, Ivan Yevgennivich. I'd probably need to study the bust for many hours. That will be difficult in the Rossiya lobby.'

'But you can borrow my copy – it's impossible to tell it from the original. And don't worry about the pin, Natalia. I'll talk to people.'

'I probably won't be able to get the copy back until after Vladivostok. Would that be a problem for you, comrade?'

Comrade Dmitrov was getting an erection. 'No, no, that's fine, Natalia. It's a copy. What do I need with the copy?'

'They couldn't very well overturn your recommendation twice in a row, could they?'

'You may rest assured they won't overturn it twice, Natalia Serafimovna.' Ivan Dmitrov was eager to unwrap his prize.

Natalia Kropotkina felt Dmitrov's hand at the zipper of her skirt. She undid the two buttons in front and slipped the skirt down. Natalia hated this business, but she didn't have any choice. At least Dmitrov was excited by her and that was affection of sorts, she supposed. That was better than Leonid, who only wanted to beat her – but certainly nothing compared to the joy of being with Isaak; she hoped Isaak would never know what she had to do to guarantee the Vladivostok pin.

Natalia turned and raised her leg, showing Dmitrov a triangular patch of jet-black public hair through sexy American panties. She figured if Dmitrov wanted drama, drama he'd get. She arched her back and gave him the profile he had wanted. She took off her sweater, and turned as she removed her bra. If she had to perform, she was determined that it be a winning performance. Second place was no place.

Dmitrov led Natalia Kropotkina onto a bed in the next room where he sometimes took a nap after a hard day in the studio.

Natalia settled on the bed thinking of the cafés in Greenwich Village where she'd hung out with young artists. Sure, some of them, the most ambitious, made whores of themselves to get what they wanted. Others didn't have to. Others sculpted, painted, or wrote whatever they wanted to. Maybe they weren't rich, but they followed their imaginations.

Natalia decided that if she and Isaak got caught, they got caught.

She turned, giving Dmitrov a dramatic angle of her hip. Dmitrov, down to his socks and shorts, looked beside himself with anticipation. However much Comrade Kropotkina wanted to ride the Trans-Siberian Railroad with Isaak Ginsburg, she had to resist the urge to vomit.

27

None of the staff at the Perm Cancer Clinic knew what to think of the remarkable upsurge in morale among the twelve bald subjects in the leukemia experimental group. In early January, they seemed to perk up for no discernible reason.

Then, in March, came the odd request. The subjects' spokesman, Jaan Birk, asked if it might not be possible for them to join one of the periodic trips to Moscow to visit Red Square and the Kremlin. These bus trips were made possible by the Komsomol, the Communist Youth League, as a reward for deserving comrades.

The commandant of the Perm Cancer Clinic hesitated. It was one thing to inflict upon the patients boring, repetitive lectures about the Leninist dream. But this? Were they laughing at him? he wondered. There was no printed directive or regulation for something like this. On the other hand, the researchers monitoring the group said to let them have an occasional trip or furlough if they wanted; it was good for morale.

The commandant signed the form authorizing the trip. The baldies were going to get their plugs pulled in July anyway. What difference did it make?

As an investigator, Colonel Felix Jin was grateful for the mountain of forms, receipts, dockets, and ledgers that paralyzed the country. There were residence permits, travel permits, work permits. Receipts were piled upon receipts. There were cynical comrades who considered this love of documents a cultural disease, a form of Soviet arthritis. The purpose of the paper was not so much to accomplish anything – nobody nourished hopes of that – but rather to record error and deviance from already lethargic norms. Just to be sure that no comrade got away with anything, the Soviets saved just about everything.

Colonel Jin thought it was a good thing the USSR had plenty of trees for paper.

When a cultural administrator in a provincial city asked for a local appearance by a Moscow writer, the request was forwarded through the Moscow Writers Union. The request was recorded – a figurative gold star for initiative. The writer's excuse for saying no – few writers wanted to leave Moscow for even a day, unless it was to go to a Black Sea resort – was recorded as well. If the writer was a Jew, the request was forwarded to Jin. Jin was amused to see that Isaak Ginsburg, who had recently had a poem published about noble peasants thriving in the heart of Siberian winters, had himself wangled a reading in Tbilisi, capital of the Soviet Georgian Republic.

Book Two

1

James Burlane sat, or rather sprawled, on his chair looking as though he were waiting for a movie to start. Neely and Schott were behaving like they had on the final night of the Townes affair. That time, Burlane had effectively taken charge, much to the relief of the two men who reported to Congress and the President. Here they were again, licking their lips and clearing their throats, loving the power but not wanting to make hard decisions.

Peter Neely said, 'I assure you this is an interesting one, Mr Burlane. I don't think we've had anything like this since that business with Philby and Derek Townes. Would you like to tell him, Ara?'

Schott considered the problem of Contact David with his finger resting thoughtfully on the cleft of his chin. 'This one's right up there, Jimmy.'

'We need your advice, Mr Burlane.'

Schott said, 'You remember Rennie Kriss, Jimmy? The guy who grew up in Australia. Well, we've been working him out of Turkey as an exporter of cottage-industry stuff. Kriss has offices in Istanbul and Ankara, but he spends most of his time posing as a buyer in eastern Turkey near the Georgian and Armenian borders. We got him a British passport so he can cross the Iranian border if he wants. He's supposed to help monitor the flow of heroin from Turkey, to watch black-market activities in the area, and to help our people in Iran.'

'Poor bastard.'

'Yes, well, here, let me show you.' Schott slid back the

153

cover from a white screen at one end of Neely's office and flipped the switch of a projector that had been wheeled into the room for the briefing. The map on the screen was of the Caucasus – that narrow area of the Soviet Union west of the Caspian Sea, east of the Black Sea, and south of the Caucasus Mountains. This area included the Soviet republics of Abkhaz, Georgia, Armenia, and Azerbaijan. 'Kriss spends most of his time here, in Turkey – Erzurum is the place – and it was here a couple of years ago that he made contact with a Georgian black marketeer who calls himself Abu Ali.'

'Black market in what?'

'Consumer items that are hard to get in the Soviet Union – video-tape recorders, jazz tapes, blue jeans, electric shavers, whatever. The Georgians are notorious entrepreneurs. There are Georgian lemon barons, millionaires from smuggling citrus to Moscow.'

'God, does Kriss go across that fucking border?' Burlane dug contemplatively at his armpit. He did his best to stay the hell away from the Soviet Union. He couldn't understand guys like Kriss.

Schott said, 'Yes, he has on occasion. Late at night always, and blindfolded. Abu Ali takes care of the rendezvous and makes the guarantees. He usually takes the buyer into Turkey. He arranges the border crossing. He guarantees buyer and seller. The buyer gets what he wants. The seller gets a fair price. Abu Ali takes his forty percent and everybody's happy.'

'Has Kriss ever talked to Abu Ali in person?'

'No,' Schott said. 'They always deal through intermediaries.'

'It's not like there's an interstate highway across the Turkish border. Ali's gotta be scrounging for the local cheese and free-lancing for himself. Kriss's gotta be off his hinge.'

'Kriss knows that, Jimmy. Now then, Abu Ali recently gave Kriss a letter, ostensibly an inquiry as to sensitive goods available on the outside, prices and so on. On the inside, Kriss found a letter addressed to the American ambassador at Ankara. Well, the ambassador read the letter and found out it was really for us. It was a shopping list, that's true.' Schott leaned forward intently. 'Listen to this, Jim. The sender wants twelve silenced automatic pistols. He wants twelve digital wristwatches with stopwatch and alarm. He wants smoke grenades capable of laying a quick, heavy pall over an oversize soccer field. He wants enough smoke bombs to do that four times. He also wants a flare gun – one that can be concealed in a coat pocket – and eight flares, four green and four red. Yes, and two silent dog whistles. That and fifty thousand American dollars.'

'Oh! A mere fifty K. Does he want benefits too? Free dental care? Paid vacation? Little cottage in Florida? All the vodka he can drink?'

Schott grinned. 'No, Jimmy, no paid vacation.'

'I don't suppose he said what we'd be getting for all this.'

'Yes, he did. He said the money was to pay two middlemen – Abu Ali and one other. He said he would use the pistols and the rest of it to bring the Soviet Union to its knees.' Ara Schott lit himself a cigarette.

'I see,' Burlane said. 'An overachiever.'

'Yes, it's beginning to look that way,' Schott said. 'Would you like to tell us what you make of all this?'

James Burlane said, 'The buyer wants four lots because he wants to practice three times. It'd take balls to practice with smoke bombs. He gets caught and he'll wind up as a slave laborer north of the Arctic Circle drinking boiled pine needles for vitamin C.' Burlane licked his lips and made smacking sounds. '*Zek* tea. Mmmmmmm! He isn't

155

asking for any specific model of automatic pistol. The Soviets only go on the market for something they can copy; that would mean a specific model. The same thing for the smoke bombs. In addition to that, the buyer's unfamiliar with what's available on foreign markets – or wants us to think he is.'

'That's possible.'

'Or Abu Ali could be KGB. Maybe they're funning us a little, haw-hawing us. Bringing the Soviet Union to its knees. Would the CIA be able to resist a hook like that? Hey, the KGB pockets a neat fifty and a good time was had by all.'

'Does it sound like that to you?'

'No. Abu Ali could be going for the entire fifty for himself, but that'd queer his connection with Kriss.'

'In which case the dissident could be . . .?'

'A loon. A dreamer. Vladimir Mitty. Nobody brings the fucking Rooskies to their knees with twelve pistols.'

Schott said, 'That's what Kriss thinks.'

'If he was an Albanian or somebody, I'd say give him the stuff, no harm done, except what if he's planning on assassinating somebody? Premier Spishkin, say. Do you really want that?'

Peter Neely spoke up for the first time. 'We most assuredly do not want that, Mr Burlane. Absolutely not.'

'If his idea of bringing down the Soviet Union is to assassinate someone, he's dreaming. But if he is a loon and can't get what he wants from us, he'll get it somewhere else. You have to consider that.'

'Exactly,' Schott said. 'Either way we get blamed if someone gets shot.'

'I say we talk to him. That way, at least we can see who he is. He probably has to train his dog; that's what the whistles are for. If he's going to practice with the smoke bombs and flares, he'll need privacy out in the taiga somewhere. All that'll take a little time.'

Ara Schott said, 'If we think he's going to assassinate someone, we tip off the KGB.'

'Exactly. If he has something more imaginative in mind, we sit back with popcorn and a six-pack. We'll give them nine-millimeter Marakovs. More fun if they get shot with their own pistols.'

'Peter and I would like you to talk to him, Jimmy.'

'Me? Yalta was the last time, Ara. You promised. No more Rooskies. I want to travel to Rangoon while I can still get it up. Mmmmmmmm, those brown-bodied little lovelies!' Burlane pretended to straighten his underwear.

Schott said, 'You won't have to cross the border, Kriss says. Abu Ali will bring the buyer to you.'

Peter Neely spoke up again. 'The President wants us to keep a close watch on this kind of thing, Jimmy.'

'Hey, there're other people. This is the storied Central Intelligence Agency. You've got marksmen, linguists, pole vaulters, whatever you want. Get one of them. Rendezvous with this guy and you risk having KGB agents ride down on you like wild Indians. I told you no after Yalta. Spiriting Kim Philby from Yalta! Jesus!' Burlane shook his head at the memory of that one. 'I caught some kind of fungus in Istanbul that I've never been able to get rid of. Hey, did the President give me a medal? Did you even give me a raise? If I get pranged, will you erect a Tomb of the Unknown Burlane? I hate those fucking Russians as much as you, but give a guy a break, Ara.'

Ara Schott said, 'Jimmy, you have to listen to reason now. You have to look at it our way.'

'You want to look at the fungus I picked up on my way to the Philby grab? Your main man, Mr Get-Things-Done. Here, let me show you.' Burlane started to unbuckle his trousers.

157

Peter Neely said, 'That won't be necessary, Mr Burlane.' Neely believed in neatness and hard work. He'd risen up the corporate ladder at IBM where neat, efficient managers and engineers dominated the computer market. Since his appointment as DCI, everyone at Langley, it seemed, was a little neater, a little more serious. Yet the truth was that Burlane, this gangly, grinning man with hair that spiraled up in a rooster tail in the back, was the best man they had. 'You work out the details with Ara, Mr Burlane. Do what you have to do.'

Burlane gave a tug at his prominent, slightly crooked nose, and laughed. 'Well, in that case.' He blew Ara Schott an obscene, sucking kiss. He started to give Peter Neely one too, then, out of deference to authority, left the director alone. 'I get another fungus, I'm gonna be pissed.'

Peter Neely smiled a nervous smile, as though he were an embarrassed parent whose child had just disrobed in public. Neely said, 'Just the other day I was telling the President that morale's never been higher.'

2

'What the fff . . .' James Burlane sat up startled, and peered out of the window into the blackness. The voice on the loudspeaker, which had started high and wavering, a tenor at the Met, plunged into a low vibrato that sounded like a man gargling or maybe gagging. The gargling rose, hovered, rasping – Louis Armstrong maybe – then went loony, manic – a frenzied Mick Jagger working up a sweat. Burlane sat up and looked out the window to see if he could locate the source of the a capella jamming. He saw the mosque silhouetted against the blue-black sky. The muezzin went into a riff of crazy *woo-woos*, Cochise on the warpath, that reverberated down the narrow streets of Erzurum.

Burlane got up to take a leak. If he'd seen the Islamic cuckoo's nest the night before, he would have gone to another hotel. He had had to put up with Islam before. The Iranian holy men were the worst, Burlane thought. Righteous zealots. Ayahtollah Assholas. When the muezzin had finished with his dawn call to prayer, Burlane returned to the warmth of the bed, his bladder pleasantly emptied, and thought about the sweet peppermint tea he would have for breakfast.

Later, after he had checked out and retrieved his passport, Burlane had his peppermint tea with Turks on rickety chairs at rickety tables that sprawled out onto the yellow brick street. The Turks watched him out of the corners of their eyes. He was an obvious European. They knew about Europeans in Erzurum. Europeans in

Erzurum were drug dealers, spies, or losers of one sort or another.

Burlane assumed he wouldn't be able to buy the *International Herald-Tribune* in Erzurum, so he had bought a *Conan the Barbarian* paperback at Kennedy – this because of the wonderful cover that depicted the musclebound Conan rescuing an eminently porkable lovely who was chained to a tree. *Get me in the mood for dealing with Russians*, he had thought. Now Burlane sipped the sweet tea and wondered about the loon who wrote the Conan books; Burlane tried to imagine himself sitting at a word processor all day pretending to be a barbarian.

Burlane lingered over his tea. At exactly ten o'clock he left and strolled down the narrow street that emptied into a bazaar assembled around a fountain that didn't work. Vendors in the market sold fruit, vegetables, and virtually any kind of trinket or doodad imaginable. Burlane bought a hashish pipe and walked along admiring it until a young man fell into step beside him.

'Hashi?' the young man said.

'How much?'

'Very cheap.'

Burlane said, 'I think I'll pass today.' He put the pipe away and kept walking. He bought a fig and walked along eating until a second young man fell in beside him. This one was sixteen or seventeen years old with the beginnings of a mustache on his upper lip.

'Hashi?'

Burlane said, 'How much?'

'Special deal today for long-legged men.'

That completed the sequence. 'Hah!' Burlane said.

The young man slipped him a hunk of hashish. Burlane followed him to a room that was bare save for a weathered carpet upon which the bearded Rennie Kriss squatted by

160

the four neatly stacked wooden boxes that contained Burlane's merchandise. Burlane did not ask how Kriss had gotten the boxes by Turkish customs at Ankara. That was none of Burlane's business.

Kriss said something to the young man in Turkish and the boy left them alone. 'My boy says you weren't followed. He's a good boy. Smart.'

'There was a fucking muezzin jamming outside my bedroom window this morning,' Burlane said. Burlane made a wobbling, guttural sound in the back of his throat in imitation of the crier. 'Why can't they just set an alarm like everybody else? All that yammering.'

'They take turns, you know. I think they try to outdo one another.' Kriss nudged the boxes with his knee. 'Whoever wants this stuff has to have real hair, trying to pull a hit inside there.' Kriss motioned his head north, in the direction of the Soviet Union. 'Can you imagine?'

'If I had my druthers, I'd stay at home and watch a ball game.'

'You won't have to cross the border. That's how Abu Ali earns his fee. You drive east toward Kars and the Russian border. About twenty miles out, something like that, the road will flatten out in some crappy-looking country, desolate. Go until you come to an abandoned mud hut by what looks like a dry lake. The hut'll be on your right, and there's an upside-down abandoned car outside that's been stripped of everything except the paint and the bullet holes in the fender. Park your car and wait. The buyer speaks English.'

'What will happen?'

Kriss told him. Burlane repeated the routine word for word. 'That's it. You got it,' Kriss said.

Burlane rose and took the bag. 'In lieu of flowers send donations to the Portland Trail Blazers.'

Kriss laughed. 'Abu Ali's interested in bucks, not corpses. You'll be okay.'

161

3

James Burlane rented a Ford Escort with a caved-in fender. He had to pump the brakes furiously to make them work and the steering wheel wobbled, but he had driven worse. It was a balmy day. He loaded his hash pipe and drove along nursing a glowing ball in the bowl, his arm hanging out of the window, which wouldn't roll up. Burlane thought about all the American men driving air-conditioned Hondas to work that morning, puffing sweet tobacco in pipes intended to make them look serious and thoughtful, successful – contemplative if not intellectual.

Rennie Kriss's directions were accurate enough, and by three o'clock James Burlane was sitting in the shadow of the mud hut waiting, a tall paper bag at his side. It was his job, given him by Peter Neely and Ara Schott, to talk to the Russian buyer and to make the decision, yea or nay. If Burlane thought the buyer was a genuine nutter, bent on assassination of a Soviet Leader, then Burlane was to waste him. If he had something else in mind, then Burlane could give him the goods – that was if Burlane felt like it.

Thus it was, finally, that not Neely, not the President, not the Joint Chiefs of Staff, would make this decision. It was James Burlane's alone.

Two, then three, cars passed without slowing. Then an old Renault slowed and Burlane double-checked the settings of the camera in the bag. The car stopped, and when a slender, dark-haired man got out of the Renault, Burlane tilted the paper bag as if he were taking a drink

162

and flipped the switch that activated the shutter *clack, clack, clack* of the Nikon behind a two-hundred-millimeter lens. Burlane wasn't Ansel Adams; the pictures would be grainy, but that wasn't the point.

When the dark-haired man got out of the car, Burlane could tell by the look on his face that he was the buyer and that he was an amateur. Burlane opened the trunk of his Escort and swapped the bag with the camera for a bag with a bottle of Greek brandy that Kriss had included with the two boxes of pistols, smoke bombs, and flares.

'I was wondering which way it is to Erzurum? I'm going to the market,' the dark-haired man said in good English.

James Burlane smiled. He'd seen this man before. Where? 'Well, you're in luck,' he said. Burlane handed the dark-haired man the bottle of brandy. Then he took a pistol out of his pocket and said, 'I'm a professional and good at my work. If I don't believe your story, I just might kill you. Do you understand?'

'I understand.'

'I think we should sit in the shade, then. I take it you have a few minutes to talk.'

'I have a few minutes.'

James Burlane followed the dark-haired man to the lengthening shadow of the mud hut. When they were both sitting, he said, 'When I travel in the Middle East, I always smoke hashish. Do as the Romans do, I always say. Better than pickling your liver in alcohol the way you Russians do. Christ!' Burlane held the hash pipe and his silenced .22 with his right hand and loaded the pipe with his left hand.

The dark-haired man started to say something, then changed his mind.

'What is it you want to do with these pistols and stuff there, Dave? You don't mind me calling you Dave, do

163

you? Our man christened you David after he read your little note. Bringing down Goliath and all that. What is your real name, by the way?'

Contact David smiled and handed Burlane a European edition of *Time* magazine.

Burlane laughed. 'Supersuck! I read that story.' He glanced at the article, which included Ginsburg's picture. There hadn't been such a fuss over a Soviet writer in the United States in years. Ginsburg was an especially bizarre case; he was the literary darling of Moscow, writing lyric poems about the beauty of peasants and the spirit of sacrifice. 'You don't mind if I keep calling you Dave for now, do you?'

Ginsburg smiled. 'Of course not. I've been sucking, as you put it, for a reason.'

'You want to give me the reason?'

'At first, I did it because I wanted an opportunity for foreign travel. I wanted to defect. Then I met a man who had a better idea, and I did it so I could meet you here.'

'Fifty thousand dollars is a few bucks there, Dave. I suppose we can spring for that easily enough, but it's the risk that gives us the trots. Do you want to assassinate somebody or what? Is there somebody who doesn't like your poetry? We have to know these things.'

'No assassination.'

'Good. There's no point in them. You shoot one asshole and another pops up in his place. After each of your premiers dies we have to go through a period of uncertainty, not knowing who is speaking with authority and what the new government intends to do. We won't help you shoot somebody for the hell of it.'

'No assassination.'

'Now, exactly what is this nonsense about bringing the Soviet Union to its knees?'

'If it works, we will do just that,' Ginsburg said.

'We? Dave! Dave! You have to be more specific than that. We? Are you pregnant or do you have a turd in your pocket?'

'I'm working with someone. He . . . he says the fewer people know what we plan, the better. Including you, he says.'

Burlane considered that; it was a proper answer. 'You can understand our concern, can't you? We can't risk having any of this blamed on the United States. Those people have ICBMs and submarines with rockets parked off our coast.'

'I can't imagine that the United States would be involved in any way.'

'Other than my giving you this stuff – if I do – is there any way at all, even remotely, that the United States might be mixed up in it? I have to know that.'

'No.'

'Where did you learn your English?' Burlane glanced at the magazine article.

'University of Moscow.'

Burlane motioned with his head. 'Why didn't you work through the Israelis? Mossad would have helped you any way you wanted.'

'My Tbilisi connection said he had had problems with Mossad in the past. He recommended your Rennie Kriss instead.'

Burlane shook his head. 'You know, you could have your freedom now. Just go with me. Forget the sling-shot crap. You've made it across. Forget it. There's nothing you can do that'll really hurt those people. Nothing. I can get you to Israel or the United States, whichever.'

'I . . . No.'

'Hey, No reason to worry because your life's in my hands. I'm a reasonable man.' Burlane gave the hash pipe to the dark-haired man who took a drag, doing as

165

Burlane had done. Burlane said, 'If I give you these boxes and you hit someone, I swear to Yahweh, I'll beat the KGB to you and shove ham sandwiches up your ass.'

'I understand your concerns and I assure you, you have no worry, none at all. What I plan on doing is outrageous, yes, but I guarantee that other than yourself no Americans are involved, and the United States will be safely out of harm's way. You may regard the Soviets as an American problem, but they're *our* problem. I do this for reasons that are both personal and public. They're mine, Russian, and not just Jewish.'

'What personal reasons?' Burlane understood personal reasons. If Ginsburg had maintained that he was doing this solely for altruistic reasons, Burlane would have shot him.

'They did something to me personally, and to the man I mentioned.'

'They? There you go again.' Burlane thought, *Christ, I'm sounding like Ronald Reagan.*

'The commandant in the camp mentioned in the magazine there. His name is Mikheyev. I took everything the Soviets did to me until then. That's when I decided to do something. The people helping me all have reasons of their own.'

'What did Mikheyev do to you?'

'You wouldn't believe me if I told you.' Ginsburg swallowed at the memory. 'Americans have nothing to do with what I want to do. I don't especially admire or hate Americans. I haven't been allowed to learn a whole lot about them.'

James Burlane took a hit on the hash pipe. 'I'm typical. We Americans are violent as hell, just like they're always telling you. We walk around with hard-ons and guns blazing. I would have wasted you if I thought you were

166

lying, just bored a hole through your heart or taken half your face.' Burlane couldn't help but grin at that line.

'I just want my country back. I'm asking for your help. That's it and nothing more, I assure you.'

'How did you get in touch with Abu Ali?'

'Through a black marketeer in Novosibirsk, a friend.'

'Are you going to steal something?'

'Yes.'

'From the Red Army?'

'No.'

Burlane thought Ginsburg was telling the truth, at least most of the truth. He believed something terrible had happened to Ginsburg. He wanted to give the Russian a shot at whatever it was he had in mind. He liked the idea of a poet and his pals going out in a blaze of glory like Butch Cassidy and the Sundance Kid. 'Aw, fuck, that's good enough for the assholes I hang out with,' he said. He retrieved a diminutive Czechoslovakian tape recorder from his pocket. 'If you want to communicate with me again, you should use this. Do you know what a one-time pad is?'

'No.'

'Okay, Dave, I want you to listen now and understand this. The one-time pad was invented by an American cryptanalyst named Joseph O. Mauborgne in 1918. It requires each of us to have an identical key and it is good for one message, one time only. It is foolproof as long as each party keeps his copy of the key secure. What I did was sit down at a word processor and filled a page with numbers at random. Just punched away like a monkey. Here.' Burlane gave the dark-haired man a sheet of paper covered with numbers.

'This is the key. I have one identical to it. I've given you forty-eight lines with eighty numbers in each line. You can send me one message with as many letters as the numbers on this page will let you. To send the message you need to assign numbers for letters. The easiest way is to go from A to Z. A is oh-one because it is the first of the alphabet; T is twenty because it's the twentieth letter. That's what we'll use. You write the numbers of your text under the numbers of the key. Do you understand so far? Here, let me show you.' Burlane took his copy of the key and began writing numbers under the key. 'See how that's done?'

'I see.'

'Now you add the numbers of your message to the key above it. You send me the total. I subtract the key and come up with the numbers that tell me your message. Forget about punctuation, spaces, and all that. I'll figure it out.'

'But what about the Soviet computers? Surely – '

'Fuck the Soviet computers. They can run this through their computers as much as they want. The key is pattern-less. They can come up with words okay, but they'll be all possible words in all possible languages. This is used for messages that must be absolutely secret. The problem is that there has to be a new key for each message. Governments have to communicate quickly with agents and military units. It's logistically impractical for all but rare cases.'

'Like this one.'

'Like this one. Keep your key secret and burn it when you're finished with it. Pour water on the ashes and mix it up a little. You send your one message with this. Send it to me, J.B.' He held up the small recorder again. 'You figure your message out carefully – add the numbers of your text to the key above it – then turn this on to "record." An American female voice will say hello and give a name, then you simply list your numbers – run them together without a pause from beginning to end.

Take your time; there's no need to hurry. Dial the American embassy in Moscow. When the other person answers, you turn this on to "play." The woman will say hello and identify herself, then the recorder will speed up and deliver the entire sequence of numbers in a matter of two or three seconds. The Soviets will be recording the call. Hang up and get out of there.'

Ginsburg considered that. 'I assume the Soviets are clever enough to slow down their tape of the call.'

'Sure they are. Let them have the numbers. We just don't want them to have time enough to trace the call. The tape will distort the numbers so the KGB won't have a voice print on you. When you're free, destroy the machine. The bottom of the Moscow River wouldn't be bad. Any more questions, Dave?'

'I'm grateful.'

'Do what you have to do, but keep the United States out of it.' Burlane put away his pistol. He helped Ginsburg pack the wooden boxes in the trunk of the Renault. Then he went back to his car and retrieved a liter of Canadian whiskey and a flight bag loaded with Japanese digital watches, German cigarette lighters, and small automatic cameras. 'This stuff's for your friends,' Burlane said.

Ginsburg raised the bottle and said, '*L'chayim*, friend.'

Burlane took a snort too. 'Mud in your eye, Dave.'

James Burlane couldn't help but laugh on the way back to Erzurum. The poet's chutzpah was too delicious. Wait until he told Neely and Schott about this one: the guy was literally right out of the pages of *Time* magazine!

The Company trio monitoring the activities of Isaak Ginsburg were having yet another breakfast meeting when James Burlane spotted the story in *The New York Times* about the May signing in Vladivostok of the agreement to resume the stalled Geneva arms talks. On page five there was a sidebar reporting a curious addition to the Vladivostok ceremony, insisted upon by the Soviets.

Isaak Ginsburg, the Soviet Union's famous Jewish poet, would read a commemorative poem at the signing.

Peter Neely barely masked his irritation at Burlane, however much a genius, who was so rude as to read a newspaper when the DCI was talking to him. 'So now what, Mr Burlane?' Neely's voice almost seemed not to rise.

Schott too was becoming impatient. He echoed Neely: 'So now what, Jimmy?'

Burlane looked up from the paper with an expansive grin. Then he gave way to a Burlane giggle. 'Hey, Ginsburg is my kind of man. Yessireee! Would you look at this!' He handed Neely the *Times* and pointed to the paragraph that said it all.

Neely read the paper, and even he couldn't suppress a smile.

Schott read the story over Neely's shoulder. 'A commemorative poem in Vladivostok?'

Burlane said, 'Isaak Ginsburg. Our man! The problem with you guys is you think small.' Burlane rubbed his hands together and giggled. 'Sweet! Sweet!'

Burlane said, 'Remember, I told Ginsburg that if he needed any help, he should let us know. I taught him how to use a one-time pad. If he sends a message to us through the American embassy, we'll know I'm right.'

Ara Schott, 'Do you think he'll call, Jimmy?'

'Sure. He'll call. He'll want to get whatever he's going to steal out of the Soviet Union.'

4

The ladies from Perm knew about the research being conducted at the cancer clinic and would have preferred other companions for their outing to Moscow, but it would have been pointless to complain. The Perm ladies did their best to accept their bald companions despite the fact that the men had gotten drunk on the bus. The research subjects were singing romantic, sad songs.

They had left Perm early Wednesday morning and had spent the night sleeping upright in their seats. The women did, that is. The bald men continued their drinking, until, one by one, they too had fallen asleep in the early hours of the morning. As they approached Moscow they started drinking again. When the bus entered the city, the bald men resumed their songs.

The bus crossed the Moscow River on the suspension bridge and turned right on Komsomolsky Prospekt, which was nearly empty of traffic. They passed a busload of football players and a mechanical sweeper scouring the gutters. Mechanical sweepers kept the streets clean in this part of the city; the Soviets did not want foreign visitors to contemplate women in babushkas sweeping streets with twig brooms.

The bus slowed and entered the Square of the Fiftieth Anniversary of the October Revolution. The bald men fell silent. Two men coughed. Birk was suddenly afflicted with a sleepy, sluggish feeling. He sat, becalmed in the final minutes, as the bus joined a queue of blue buses waiting to unload passengers. He watched the emptied

171

buses join a line waiting to be parked in the neat formation of blue buses in the square. Birk wondered if Russian
minds, like Russian buses, did not spend a lot of time
idling.

Birk remembered his dead wife, Nadia. His lids were
heavy at the memory.

The bus turned right, around the corner of the black
iron fence, and came to a halt near a restraining rope
strung between the tops of movable stanchions. Behind
this rope, unsmiling young army officers, bearing electric
megaphones, paced with serious eyes and an air of self-
importance. The gray of the megaphones matched the
gray of the officers' uniforms, and the gray of the overcast
sky.

Jaan Birk felt a shiver of anticipation. He wondered if
the Bolsheviks had felt like this when they turned the
guns of the Aurora on the czar's Winter Palace in St
Petersburg.

Four eighteen-man squads of Kremlin guards were
detailed to guard the Lenin mausoleum. These squads,
rotated every eight hours, were trained to form a perimeter around the mausoleum in the event of a
disturbance.

The two South units – South One and South Two –
were responsible for blocking access to the open area
along the banks of the Moscow River. The northern edge
of the square, which led to the heart of the city, was
defended by North One and North Two.

South One and North One were lead units, which
meant they were the first soldiers onto the square in case
of an emergency. South One was housed in the base of
Spasskaya Tower, to the left rear of the mausoleum; and
North One in the base of Nikolskaya Tower, to the right

rear of the mausoleum. South Two and North Two were quartered inside the Kremlin.

In the event of an alarm, the seventy-two soldiers were given eighteen seconds to surround the mausoleum. This included a thirteen-second hundred-meter sprint by lead soldiers carrying AK-47s. These soldiers were handpicked and disciplined – the best the Red Army had to offer.

Older Lieutenant Vladimir Petrovich Zaytsev, commander of South One, spent his time sketching on a small pad in the CO's diminutive, bare office.

While Zaytsev sketched, his men watched a Soviet Union vs. Bulgaria weight-lifting competition on television or played a card game called Fools in which, one by one, players left the game until only one was left, the loser. The fool. The winners laughed at the fool and made little devil's horns with their forefingers sticking out above their ears.

Because of the architecture of the mausoleum – the steps and corners – the Soviets were convinced it was physically impossible for anybody to do harm to Lenin's body and escape from the mausoleum alive, much less Red Square. It couldn't be done. Could not. Even sprinters from the Red Army track squad couldn't do it.

The first pilgrim out of the Perm bus was a tall bald man with a cap on his head, the first of twelve becapped bald men to leave the bus. He took one step forward and was waved to a halt by a soldier. He looked up at the corner of the Kremlin wall. An officer with a megaphone said, 'Stay clear of the ropes.'

The bald man did as he was told. He gripped the pistol in his coat pocket.

A second man joined the first and a third joined the second. The bald men banded together out of training, out of the need for support, out of a kind of vague fear.

They shivered both from the chill in the air and the realization that they were about to die.

Birk was the seventh of the bald men out of the bus. He stood with the others in the tailings of the white cloud that issued from the bus's throbbing exhaust. The ladies from Perm tightened the knots of their flowered scarves. Jaan Birk found himself remembering the soft down on his young wife's stomach. She had been an athlete, a gymnast, and had a hard, muscular body from years of training. But when she was on her back, smiling, her stomach slack, the downy hair on her body was soft beyond description.

A stout young woman, one of Natasha Kropotkina's Lenin pins on her lapel, read their names from a sheet of paper. The Perm women and the bald men answered when their names were called.

In addition to Jaan Birk the bald men were:

Aleksei Ivanovich Avdeyev, thirty-one, originally sentenced to five years' imprisonment for his belief in God. Avdeyev contracted his cancer cleaning the nozzles of atomic submarines at Paldiski Bay, Estonia, on the Gulf of Finland.

Konstantin Davidovich Arlovsky, twenty-seven, originally sentenced to an indeterminate sentence in a psychiatric hospital for 'failing to appreciate reality' after he requested permission to emigrate to Israel. Arlovsky contracted his cancer mining uranium underground at Cholovka, in the Ukraine.

Yuri Yevgennevich Chernetsov, forty-three, originally sentenced to eight years' imprisonment for his work for Amnesty International. Chernetsov contracted his cancer at Chelyabinsk-40, a nuclear warhead plant in the Urals.

Mikhail Aleksandrovich Denisenko, thirty-six, originally sentenced to ten years' imprisonment for advocating Ukrainian independence. Denisenko developed cancer at

174

the uranium enrichment facility at Mangyshlak, on the Caspian Sea.

Jaan Gennadevich Fedoseev, thirty-two, originally sentenced to five years' imprisonment for baptizing his son. Fedoseev became ill working in the open pit mine at Kavalerovo, in the Soviet Far East.

Vladimir Anatolevich Kesamidze, twenty-five, originally sentenced to seven years' imprisonment for advocating the maintenance of the Georgian language. Kesamidze developed cancer working in high-level radiation at the underground uranium mine at Asht, just north of the Afghanistan border.

Mark Iosevovich Ivashov, forty, originally sentenced to ten years' imprisonment for teaching the Yiddish language. Ivashov developed his symptoms while working in a nuclear enrichment facility on Vaigach Island in the Arctic Ocean.

Nikolai Prochorevich Karpekov, thirty-seven, originally sentenced to six years in a strict regimen camp for 'denigrating the Russian past' in an article on czarist secret police published in a British magazine. Karpekov contracted his cancer in the mine at Cholovka, in the Ukraine.

Boris Samuilovich Lieberman, thirty, originally sentenced to seven years in prison for asking permission to emigrate to Israel. Lieberman developed cancer while working in the uranium enrichment facility at Shamor Bay, opposite the northern end of Sakhalin Island.

Oleg Simeonovich Mayeseen, thirty-four, originally sentenced to ten years in a strict regime camp for asking permission to emigrate to Israel. Mayeseen developed cancer in a nuclear enrichment facility at Kyshtym in the Urals.

Ivan Vladimirovich Bychkov, twenty-nine, originally

sentenced to four years in a strict regime camp for staging an unauthorized production of Samuel Beckett's 'Waiting for Godot.' Developed cancer in a uranium mine at Omutninsk near Leningrad.

The stout young woman who had checked their names said, 'You will stay together and do as you are told until it is your turn to join the line to begin the walk to the mausoleum. Knives and other weapons are not allowed inside. Cameras are forbidden. You will stay on the white line. You will walk in pairs. You will walk rapidly. There are many people who would like to see the body today. You will not talk or linger once you are in the tomb. Is that understood?'

The question was not asked in the manner that encouraged response.

Several hundred people milled about the ropes outside the gate, trying to figure out where the line would be formed. How long would they have to wait? Would they get to see Lenin that day? People wanted to know. Rumors and guesses were cheap.

The Komsomol leader of the Perm group showed the officer a form that had been signed by the stout young woman, and the officer unsnapped the rope.

'Make sure you have them all,' he said.

The leader checked their names on a piece of paper – they each answered as before – and the Perm visitors were taken to a slowly forming queue that led to the beginning of the official line to Lenin's tomb. The official line began at the center of the promenade in front of the Tomb of the Unknown Soldier.

When the Perm group formed their section of the line, the bald men pushed their way into the positions assigned to them ahead of time by Birk. Each man had a place. The women weren't given a chance to protest.

After a twenty-minute wait, the line, moving two by two, moved through the gates at the end of the park. Jaan Birk's squad of bald men were on their way to Lenin's tomb.

5

The hushed, contemplative pilgrims, walking steadily along the white line, advanced two by two by two by two into the vast space that was Red Square, the official parade ground of the Soviet Empire. There was room enough in Red Square to accommodate scores of companies of goose-stepping soldiers, squadrons of tanks and armored personnel carriers, dozens of sophisticated rockets poised skyward on mobile launch pads – whatever it took to properly commemorate the anniversaries of socialist accomplishments.

The Soviets used portable rope barriers to keep Red Square empty as visitors filed into the mausoleum and out again. The bald men kept their eyes on the Lenin mausoleum as they walked; it was forward and to their right. The Kremlin wall rose behind the mausoleum. There was a large tower to the left of the mausoleum – Spasskaya Tower – topped by a red star, and one to the right – Nikolskaya Tower – also with a star.

Jaan Birk had taken the outside of the double line – the Red Square side – so that as the line snaked through the mausoleum itself he would be closest to the guards standing at Lenin's feet.

Birk rubbed his thumb against the 9mm Makarova in his coat pocket. The piece of meat felt cool and dry in its plastic bag. Birk's adrenaline surged. His body felt wired, alive. He could do anything, he believed. Anything. Steal Lenin's head from the tomb. Anything.

He moved the pad of his thumb up and down, up and

down, on the barrel of the pistol. He put the palm of his hand against the cool of the meat.

The turn toward the mausoleum's entrance came as the pilgrims were almost directly in the middle of Red Square. Birk's breathing quickened and his mouth felt cottony as he approached the point that was directly in front of both the Red Square entrance of the State Historical Museum and Lenin's mausoleum. There, abruptly, the white line made a hard right and the pilgrims followed.

Birk walked straight toward the entrance. He glanced at the empty concrete bleachers on either side of the mausoleum where Kremlin officials sat to review ceremonial and commemorative parades in the square. Birk glanced up at the Kremlin wall behind the mausoleum. The red flag with the hammer and sickle flopped lazily on the mast atop the massive green-roofed dome inside the Kremlin.

Birk swallowed. Lenin's body was the most sacred of sacred relics in the Soviet Union. It was also a festering, vile pox in whose name the Russians ruled, Birk was convinced, without any vision except the maintenance of absolute, unyielding power.

The double file kept a brisk pace.

Each bald man from the Perm bus punched a control on his digital wristwatch as he crossed the threshold of the mausoleum and turned left to descend the first flight of stairs. The alarm on each of these watches was carefully set to match the wearer's place in line. Birk had had a time working out the schedule.

They stepped into the main entrance.

There was a left turn.

The bald men went down the stairs.

There was a right turn.

More stairs.

A last right brought the pilgrims into the chamber where the coffin lay bathed in red light.

The bald men looked ahead for their assigned guards. Lenin's face was serene under the red.

Birk came to the end of the tomb. He was at the foot of the embalmed god.

The alarm sounded simultaneously on the wrists of twelve bald men entering, leaving, and spaced throughout the mausoleum. The bald men drew their pistols and fired point-blank at their assigned soldiers. The soldiers had been standing at attention for forty minutes and were rigid as boards.

The soldiers saw pistols being pointed in their direction as slugs thumped *plup! plup! plup!* into their chests and torsos.

In less than four seconds, twelve soldiers lay dead or dying inside the mausoleum – a perfectly timed ambush.

Jaan Birk leaped into the space around the pedestal and pushed the coffin hard, sending it crashing onto the other side.

The glass top shattered. Birk was upon the body.

At the main entrance to the mausoleum, a bald man who had brought up the rear waited for the Perm ladies and others to get clear, then shouted, 'For Russia!' He sprinted toward the middle of Red Square, throwing smoke bombs as he ran.

Inside, Birk grabbed Lenin's head. There was no need for him to twist. The head was not fastened to the torso. Because it was dehydrated and hollow, the head was surprisingly light.

Older Lieutenant Zaytsev was sketching in the shoulder of a young girl when the alarm went off in the bottom of Spasskaya Tower.

The soldiers were on the move, running, falling into place.

Lieutenant Zaytsev was the first one out the door. 'Go! Go! Go!' he yelled.

Within five seconds the soldiers of Zaytsev's South One squad were sprinting into Red Square, looping wide in the direction of St Basil's Cathedral, then north. South Two followed Zaytsev's unit. North One emerged, sprinting, from the base of Nikolskaya Tower.

The point soldiers of the lead units, sprinters, raced to complete the encircling movement that arced toward the middle of GUM.

The only sound was the rapid clump, clump, clump of their boots as they triple-timed across the square.

The perimeter was not yet completed and there still were no police sirens when the soldiers saw the first figure running for the center of the square.

The figure was throwing objects.

'Fire!' Zaytsev shouted.

The objects burst into smoke as the chatter of AK-47s reverberated against the Kremlin wall and echoed off GUM.

The runner's body straightened. The upper half of his torso toppled onto the square, but a final smoke grenade tumbled from his hand onto the pavement in front of him and exploded. The smoke spilled onto the square, rolled forward toward GUM, rolled backward toward the mausoleum.

The soldiers had been trained to respond to terrorists and smoke bombs, but nobody really believed they would ever have anything to do. In Moscow? In Red Square?

Lieutenant Zaytsev said, 'Hold your places. Shoot them when you see them.'

Another figure emerged from the smoke, throwing. He

181

died as the first man had. His final smoke grenade exploded at the very feet of Zaytsev's soldiers.

Zaytsev realized what was happening, understood the terrorists' strategy. Another of them must be running through the smoke to spread the perimeter. The terrorists were attempting to fill the space that was their enemy.

'Fall back!' he shouted. 'Fall back!' That was what the contingency plan said to do.

There was another burst of machine-gun fire. Another explosion. More smoke. A pall hung over Red Square. The open space that had been an impossible barrier thirty seconds earlier was suddenly eliminated.

The terrorists would try their rush next, Zaytsev knew. Correctly, he shouted, 'They'll be coming. Back! Back! Back!'

The troopers knew the contingency plan as well as Zaytsev. They backpedaled, eyes on the murk, fingers on the triggers of their weapons. The seventy-two-soldier perimeter gave and stretched. The firing lanes widened, then narrowed again at the five entrances to Red Square.

The soldiers knew the rush was next. The terrorists would be upon them at nearly point-blank range.

Jaan Birk opened the mausoleum door wide enough to fire the flare pistol. When the flare had burst green over the white haze. Birk took out a silent whistle and began blowing.

Isaak Ginsburg saw the spectacular burst of green above the smoke. He fondled Boris's ears and released the eager dog.

Boris raced into the smoke. There had been meat at the other end when he had practiced with Viktor Konnen in the taiga.

Ginsburg squatted against the curving eastern base of St Basil's Cathedral and waited . . .

6

Older Lieutenant Zaytsev stared hard into the murk,
looking for movement. His life depended on his being
able to see the enemy first. Zaytsev held his AK-47 waist
high, lest the enemy come from the smoke without
warning. He checked his men, checked the murk again.
It hung, scarcely thinning.

'Back! Back! Back!' He trotted backward, groping for
the edge of the cloud.

One of his soldiers fired into the murk, but not before
another bomb exploded, enveloping St Basil's in thick
smoke.

Zaytsev shouted, 'Four! Four! Four! Four! Stand fast!'
He raced along his line as his troops retreated quickly
and set themselves into Perimeter Four, which was the
rope barrier between St Basil's and GUM. The firing
lanes had closed.

Then it came, bursting high above the smoke: a green
flare.

A signal. Intended for whom? Somebody beyond the
smoke, obviously. Nobody could enter or leave the perimeter without being wasted by AK-47s. Still, Zaytsev's
initial confidence that he had been trained to handle
anything, could handle anything, softened slightly. The
contingency plan said the rush was next. The rush hadn't
come.

The lack of a rush was illogical, suicidal. It was madness. Zaytsev was worried. He didn't understand what
his enemy was up to.

Lieutenant Zaytsev had so many responsibilities and

183

worries that he didn't see the mongrel dog loping happily through the smoke dragging a bag behind it.

The Kremlin was surrounded by the wailing of police sirens. The police would form a perimeter well back, on the streets and avenues leading to Red Square. The encircling perimeter of Kremlin guards was secure. Nobody could take it from the rear; the police would see to that. If the perimeter failed for any reason, the police were there as a backup.

No one talked on the perimeter. The soldiers – alert, mouths dry, hearts pumping – reloaded their AK-47s.

Jaan Birk blew his silent dog whistle at the door of Lenin's mausoleum wondering if his plan would work. How could it not work? Boris had been through this routine literally dozens of times. How could it not work now? Birk was certain his Red Army instructors would have approved.

Then, suddenly, there was Boris standing in front of him. While Boris gobbled his meat, Birk put the head in the bag and tied it to Boris's collar, lest he get hurt and had to travel wounded. He put the heavy cotton drawstrings into Boris's teeth.

Birk reloaded the flare pistol. He kneeled and embraced the dog, then straightened and fired the red flare. He felt Boris tighten under his hand.

Then Boris was gone, disappearing into the smoke, following the sound of the whistle Jaan Birk could not hear. Birk shut the door and checked his watch. He opened the door slightly. He unscrewed the silencer and fired four blind shots into the murk in the general direction of the soldiers that were out there. Birk hoped he didn't. hit anyone. He didn't want to hurt some poor soldier doing his duty.

Lieutenant Zaytsev couldn't conceive of what his enemy might be up to. First a green flare, now a red. To what point? Why? When Jaan Birk fired the shots, Lieutenant Zaytsev was loping along his perimeter, asking each of his men in turn, 'Have you been breached?' Have you been breached? Have you been breached?'

The answer, around Zaytsev's portion of the defensive half-circle, was '*Nyet. Nyet. Nyet.*'

After Birk's shots, Red Square was eerily silent; a lazy pall of smoke hung low in the midday air. Higher up, the green and red flares drifted and thinned above the unfolding drama.

Zaytsev's walkie-talkie crackled. Colonel Igor Ivanovich Stargov said, 'Situation, South One. Report.'

The smoke didn't bother Boris. His master had taken him deep into the taiga where there was nobody to see the smoke.

Boris was having a good time. He could hear the whistle more clearly as he made his way back to the southeast corner of St Basil's Cathedral. When he found the man with the whistle, he would be given more meat.

Boris was a smart dog and strong, but basic just the same. When he was hungry, he wanted to eat. He was still hungry. He couldn't wait for the meat.

On the walkie-talkie, Lieutenant Zaytsev said, 'South One reporting. We are established at Perimeter Four. We have not been breached, repeat, have not been breached. Visibility zero.' Zaytsev wanted to ask his commander why the rush had not come, but he said nothing.

Colonel Igor Stargov said, 'Stand fast and await further instructions, South One. If they rush you, shoot them.'

Stargov paused. 'Lieutenant, have your men shoot them in the legs. I want prisoners.'

'Yes, sir,' Zaytsev said. When the colonel was off the air, Zaytsev toured his area of the perimeter again. 'If they rush you, take their legs,' he said. 'If they rush you, take their legs.'

Zaytsev returned to his post at the Red Square side of St Basil's, and allowed himself a sigh of relief. The flares had popped, and nothing had happened. The enemy had not tried to breach the perimeter; now he was trapped. The haze was still thick, but clearly Zaytsev's men had done their job. They had not been breached. All they had to do was wait for the smoke to thin. There would be medals when this was over, a promotion.

The smoke thinned more rapidly now. Zaytsev counted seven dead bomb throwers.

A half minute passed. Zaytsev wondered if there were any terrorists alive other than the man with the pistol. No sooner had he thought this than from the direction of the pausoleum two or three pistol shots were fired at the perimeter, a pointless gesture at that range.

Why hadn't the terrorists made their final rush when they still had cover from the smoke? Surely the terrorists would be better off taking their chances with the perimeter than facing captivity in Lubyanka Prison after having defiled Lenin's tomb. Zaytsev hesitated to imagine the tortures they would endure. Their timidity in rushing the perimeter was insane, mad. Now they were doomed.

The thinning smoke looked romantic. *Later*, Zaytsev thought, *I'll tell people I felt like an artillery captain in the Crimean War*. He would be on television on every conceivable Leninist anniversary until his dying day. Zaytsev smiled.

The outline of the mausoleum became clear. Zaytsev saw the front door open and shut quickly. There were more terrorists inside the building. *Why* hadn't they taken advantage of the smoke when they had it? Had they simply panicked and lost their nerve?

And why the flares?

One of the terrorists opened the door quickly and fired a shot at the perimeter, hurting nobody.

One of the soldiers on the northern rim of the perimeter returned the fire.

This was followed immediately by Colonel Stargov on the walkie-talkie. 'Hold your fire! Hold your fire!'

Lieutenant Zaytsev was glad it wasn't one of his men who had returned the fire. He wondered if they might not have to storm the mausoleum. He was not permitted to issue an assault order on his own. He waited, listening to his walkie-talkie for instructions . . .

Isaak Ginsburg blew on the silent whistle. Would Birk's plan really work? Could a dog really hear this whistle that he himself couldn't hear? Ginsburg was standing beside the curved base of St Basil's, not fifteen yards behind Zaytsev. In fact, he could hear Zaytsev's conversations with his commander and knew that so far Birk's scheme was working.

Suddenly the cheerful Boris was standing at Ginsburg's feet looking up at him.

Ginsburg handed Boris his second hunk of raw meat and grabbed the bag. He didn't look at Lenin inside with his flattened nose and battered eyebrows. Ginsburg dumped the bag into a larger plastic shopping bag.

Ginsburg put his hand on Boris's neck. 'Stay,' he said. He strode off in the direction of the Hotel Rossiya, leaving Boris behind, wolfing down his meat, which was delicious, well worth the effort of dragging the bag through the smoke.

The mausoleum was clearly visible now. Lieutenant Zaytsev awaited word. Then Colonel Stargov spoke on the walkie-talkie: 'Hold your present position, Lieutenant. Your instructions remain the same.'

A minute later, with the mausoleum even more clearly visible in the dissipating haze, Colonel Stargov appeared in person at Lieutenant Zaytsev's post.

It was Stargov who first saw Boris, sitting where he had been told to sit, with a happy look on his face, his tongue lolling.

Boris knew he had done a good job. He had followed the two whistles as he was supposed to do. He had devoured two wonderful chunks of meat, and now the show was over. It was his time to be praised and played with. Would these nice men pat him on the head and ruffle the fur behind his ears? That's what his master always did. He tried a wag of his tail.

'Lieutenant, how long has that dog been there?'

The door to the mausoleum opened and someone took some more wild shots at the perimeter.

Zaytsev turned back to St Basil's. A dog! Zaytsev was amazed. 'Why, I don't know, sir! We've been expecting a rush from the smoke.'

Colonel Stargov had seen trained dogs before. This one looked for all the world as though it had been trained to stay. Stargov beckoned to Boris. 'Come,' he said.

That was the magic word. Even the magic gesture. The affectionate Boris came happily, tongue flopping, expecting some attention.

Colonel Stargov couldn't help but give the dog a friendly pat. The dog's tail went *flop, flop, flop*.

A green flare, a red flare, now a trained dog. What was going on? Colonel Stargov thought he'd seen everything in his days of commanding nigger guerrillas, but this one was a real puzzler. Stargov said, 'We have decided to take our time, Lieutenant. We have decided on Potemkin Three.'

'Yes, sir.' Potemkin Three meant that South One and North One would surround the mausoleum while South Two and North Two stormed the interior. Zaytsev and his North One counterpart were being relieved of the primary responsibility. Zaytsev was relieved but didn't show it. Zaytsev pitied the prisoners. Colonel Stargov had served in Angola, Somalia, and Afghanistan. He was said to have bragged of hammering men's testicles to putty, of skinning women alive.

Boris thought Stargov was wonderful. He slurped happily at Stargov's hand.

Stargov was equally taken by Boris. Somebody had to take the dog, why not him? He said, 'What do you say, boy? Would you like to come with me? Huh, boy? I've got a dacha on the Volga. You can romp around in the summer and chase squirrels.'

Boris knew a friend when he saw one. His tail flopped furiously. He grinned a dog's grin, drooling slightly.

7

Isaak Ginsburg was not the only Russian or foreign visitor to retreat from the smoke and shooting at Red Square. The streets of central Moscow quickly emptied as people ran from the danger. Ginsburg himself walked, he didn't run to the Hotel Rossiya. He did not want to attract attention, although it was impossible for anyone to attract attention away from the shocking drama unfolding behind him.

Ginsburg slipped unnoticed into the hotel entrance facing the Moscow River and so away from the square. The hotel guests were gathered around the windows at the western side of the hotel, watching the smoke spilling around St Basil's at the top of the slope.

Natalia Kropotkina waited.

She said quickly, 'I've cut the patch out of the duct. It won't take but a minute.'

Ginsburg handed the bag with Lenin's head to Natalia. 'Work quickly, but be steady with the torch. They'll take this hotel apart board by board, brick by brick.'

Isaak made his way to the bar where he had been when the shooting had begun; he'd been chatting with the bartender ten minutes earlier. Ginsburg said, 'I thought I could see better from higher up.' He gestured, meaning one of the upper floors of the Rossiya.

The bartender said, 'What did you see up there?'

'Nothing. Just smoke. Thought I might as well come back here and have another drink.'

'What do you think's happening, Comrade Ginsburg?'

'Terrorists of some kind. I never thought I'd see that in the Soviet Union. Never.' Ginsburg shook his head.

'A guy over there thinks somebody stormed Lenin's tomb. Can you imagine?'

Ginsburg shook his head no. 'It's beyond me.'

'CIA,' the bartender said.

'That or Estonians. Americans are animals. Estonians are fanatics. Take your pick. I wouldn't want to be them.' He thought of the strange American he had met in Turkey, and of Birk and his bald suicide squad in the mausoleum, holding the soldiers off to give him time to establish an alibi and Natalia Kropotkina time to weld.

The bartender poured himself and Ginsburg each a full three-quarters of a water glass of cold vodka. He said, 'This'll be something to tell our kids.'

Twenty minutes later Ginsburg was joined by Natalia Kropotkina.

The bartender said, 'Ahh, Mrs Kropotkina. A little interruption from your sketching, eh?'

'A double vodka, please,' Natalia said.

The bartender said, 'You'd better get your sketching done in the next few days, Mrs Kropotkina. They're going to pack that bust for Zhukov to take with him to Vladivostok.'

Outside, guards were being posted at the doors of the Rossiya.

In the heat of action, Colonel Igor Ivanovich Stargov had concentrated on the immediate military problem: establishing and maintaining a perimeter so as to prevent the escape of whoever it was who had stormed the mausoleum. It was only afterward, with the smoke thinned to nothing and the cold sun at one o'clock, that he had an opportunity to consider his burden of responsibility.

This was not any mausoleum; it contained the earthly remains of Lenin.

The command of the security forces at the Kremlin was largely an honorary assignment, but it was not taken lightly. In order to show their zeal, commanders of the Kremlin guard had a history of drilling their soldiers mercilessly so that in the event of an emergency, absolutely nothing could go wrong.

Igor Ivanovich could not make a wrong decision. He was not entitled to one mistake. He had to do everything right, and he knew it.

The mausoleum was now surrounded by an enormous semicircle of kneeling soldiers, ready to fire. A helicopter circled lazily overhead. Colonel Stargov approached the mausoleum from the rear and summoned the two older lieutenants who were commanders of North Two and South Two.

'We won't assault it. I don't want them accidentally shot. I want them alive. We'll use gas to knock them out. I'll go in first.'

The two lieutenants were disappointed they weren't going to storm the mausoleum, but they did as they were told. They sent for the gas, which was kept in the Kremlin in the unlikely event that there should ever be some unpleasantness in Red Square. In five minutes they had gas grenades that could be fired from rifles.

Colonel Stargov donned a gas mask. He threw open the door, met no resistance, and fired a grenade down the stairs. The rifle bucked against his shoulder once, twice, three, four times as he reloaded grenades and fired. He then retreated to the square and removed his mask. He glanced at his wristwatch.

'They can close the doors if they want.' Stargov said. 'That'll get to them in a couple of minutes. It only takes a whiff. They won't even be able to see it.' Stargov checked his watch again. After twenty minutes, oxygen in the air would neutralize the gas and it would be safe to enter without a mask. The men inside, however, would stay unconscious for another hour – more than enough time to take them over to Lubyanka. Stargov waited. He received a report: there was no unauthorized use of radio bands. All streets were blocked off, and the militia was awaiting further instructions.

No radio communication. Stargov considered the smoke. Considered the two flares. Considered the dog. So far the heroics belonged to Stargov and his men. But if something went wrong! Well, then, that was a different story. Stargov was amused that his seniors were keeping their distance from this one. Let Stargov have it. The bastards.

It was time to go inside.

'I want you all to remain up here, Lieutenant. I'll go down alone. I want no one, I repeat *no one* inside until I give a specific order.' If the terrorists had somehow mutilated Lenin's body, there should be no witnesses. It would be easy enough to repair the corpse, Stargov knew. No problem.

Leaving his unit commanders guarding the main entrance, Colonel Stargov entered the mausoleum and pulled the wick out of a metal tube. If the wick was yellow, there was gas lingering in the air. When the yellow turned blue, the air was clear. The wick was blue, and Stargov took off his gas mask. He went down the stairs, stepping over the bodies of Lenin's honor guards. The door to the tomb was open. He stepped inside.

The small room was dark as it was before, but the soft red light shone on the pedestal where the coffin had lain. Stargov saw the terrorists, five of them, lying arm in arm against the wall, knocked out.

V. I. Lenin's body was at the bottom of the moat. The

193

coffin was on its side. Stargov quickly knelt to check the body.

There was no head.

Lenin's head was gone.

Missing.

No head.

Stargov's blood turned sweet; his face warmed from a flush of adrenaline.

There was no head.

Lenin's head was missing.

Stargov looked around the tomb. Bodies, yes. Nothing else. He checked the stairs descending from the entrance. No head there.

He checked the stairs ascending to the exit. No head.

Stargov went back to the tomb. Perhaps he had overlooked it. How large was a human head, after all? He was just confused, was all. Excited. He searched the coffin again. Looked around the pedestal. It wasn't there. He walked over to the inert terrorists who lay openmouthed, clutching their pistols.

Stargov first saw the pinkish-white splatters on the wall. Five of them. Then he pulled a bald head forward and saw the cavity in the back. Each of them had sat, an arm linked with a comrade's, and put a bullet through the top of his mouth and out the back of his head.

Colonel Stargov had fired knockout gas at dead men. And there was no head by the corpses.

Lenin's head was missing, gone.

Stolen from the tomb.

He picked up a stainless steel whistle in front of the dead men. He blew on the whistle. No sound.

Stargov suddenly understood why there had been a dog at the edge of the smoke. The dog had retrieved the head in the smoke. The flares were signals. Stargov put the whistle in his pocket.

194

Who could know where Lenin's head might be by now? Stargov knew his career was ended, possibly his life as well, but he had to do the best he could. He had to work fast, because the premier would be clamoring for an answer. The Politburo. Everybody. He knelt by the dead terrorists.

He pulled off their caps. They were bald, all five of them.

Four of them had stars of David painted on the tops of their bald domes.

He straightened the man in the middle, who had died slumped over. This man was bald like the others but did not have a star of David.

Instead he had an Estonian flag on his lap, together with a photograph of himself with his arm around a smiling young woman, and an ordinary sheet of typing paper folded once and containing one neatly typed paragraph:

We love our country, but not what it has become. The oppression of the czars has become our national way of life – this in the name of Lenin. We are loath to do it, but we will begin taping a protracted mutilation of Lenin's head in a month or less. We will mail copies of these tapes to television stations around the world unless you announce, publicly, that for one year, any resident of the USSR and its satellite countries in the Warsaw Pact, Cuba, or Vietnam may emigrate for any reason whatsoever. This is to include Jews, Estonians and other regional nationalities, political dissidents, artists, writers, scientists – anybody! This emigration will be supervised by Amnesty International and officials of the World Court at The Hague. If you announce your blessing of emigration before we begin, then we will return Lenin's head to you, one section each month, for you to reassemble in secret. At the end of the twelfth month we'll send you the last section, Lenin's teeth. Nobody will have to know we took the head in the first place. We do this to reclaim Comrade Lenin's honor. We are certain that if he knew of the atrocities committed in his name – worse

195

than under the czars – he would not only approve of what we are doing, but he would do his best to help us.

Colonel Stargov read the paper three times through, considering the consequences of that single paragraph.

He put the paper in his pocket, took a deep breath, and walked up the stairs of the mausoleum to begin the horror of telling the Politburo what had happened. He told Zaytsev and the other commanders of the guard that the terrorists had committed suicide. Comrade Lenin's body was in perfect condition. The terrorists had damaged the inside of the tomb but had not harmed the body.

'Establish a tight perimeter around the mausoleum and shoot anybody who tries to enter. Nobody is to enter. Nobody. This desecration of Comrade Lenin's tomb is an ugly thing. Until my personal, explicit order to the contrary, the only visitors are to be accompanied by me or by Premier Spishkin.

Stargov issued orders that the area surrounding Red Square, which had been sealed off as part of the response to the attack, remain closed. In addition to closing Red Square, Stargov took the precaution of ordering the evacuation and closure of the State Historical Museum, the Central V. I. Lenin Museum, GUM, and St Basil's Cathedral. He also ordered that guests be confined to their rooms in the National, Intourist, Moscow, Metropole, and Rossiya hotels.

That done, Stargov got into the black Volga waiting to spirit him to the inside of the Kremlin; the Communist leadership would be assembling to find out what had happened to Comrade Lenin's tomb. It was Stargov's bad luck to be the bearer of some very bad news indeed. Boris curled up at the feet of his new master, offering such comfort as he was able.

8

The Soviet Union was just four weeks away from the scheduled Vladivostok agreement to resume the arms talks at Geneva, and the American Secretary of State had even agreed to accept a bust of Lenin from Soviet Foreign Minister Grigori Mikhailovich Zhukov. It was a period of euphoria for the Politburo. The Soviets could hardly believe that the idiotic Americans would so humiliate themselves. And now this: an assault on Lenin's tomb!

There were those who said they hadn't seen senior Kremlin officials move so quickly since the Cuban missile crisis a quarter of a century earlier.

Those yearning for economic and foreign policy reforms were optimistic when Premier Petr Spishkin was chosen as the Party's general secretary. The old-guard of aged Stalinist warriors, hardened by the trials of the Great Patriotic War 1941–45, had refused to relinquish power, until one by one – Leonid Brezhnev, Yuri Andropov, and Konstantin Chernenko – they were dead. Spishkin looked good on television, but that was about it. Soviet bureaucrats, zealous in defense of their power, refused to yield.

Nine of the thirteen Politburo members were in Moscow that day, including Foreign Minister Zhukov and Spishkin's two principal rivals – Defense Minister Gennadi Stepanovich Vorobiev and the chief of the KGB, Valery Nikolaevich Karpov.

Spishkin's resolve was essential to the Russian reopening of the arms limitation talks with the Americans and everybody knew it. The Soviet economy was nearly exhausted from years of military competition with the United States. The Pentagon continued to demand and receive arms and rockets at a punishing pace. Then Ronald Reagan had proposed the prohibitively expensive 'Star Wars' gambit aimed at screwing up Soviet rockets at launch.

Something had to be done.

The competition between Vorobiev and Karpov was now on hold pending the signing of the Vladivostok agreement.

Colonel Stargov entered the meeting at three o'clock.

The nine Russians had gathered in a small, windowless room, furnished with a lush red carpet, a large cherry table, and chairs covered with Armenian leather. There was a silver samovar in one corner where the comrades might make themselves a cup of tea.

Foreign Minister Zhukov, sensing that his agreement with the Americans somehow hung in the balance, watched with darkened eyes.

Premier Spishkin's hand was steady as he settled into his chair and lit a cigarette. 'Colonel Stargov.'

Stargov began by informing the Politburo of the security measures he had put in place. He then described, as best he could, the ambush inside the mausoleum, the directives and contingency plans in effect at the time, the actions of the terrorists, and the response of his officers and men. He detailed the smoke bombs, the flares, the dog, and the dead men inside. Then he dropped the shocker.

'The head is missing from Comrade Lenin's body,' he said. 'It is nowhere in the mausoleum, I assure you. It is gone, stolen.' Stargov then read the typewritten paragraph that offered to swap Lenin's head for one year of open emigration from Warsaw Pact countries, Cuba and

Vietnam. When he had finished, he read the paragraph again. Then he gave the piece of paper to Premier Spishkin.

Premier Petr Spishkin hesitated. He read the paper, his hand on his chin. He hadn't felt like this since he'd commanded a tank in Poland in 1944. 'The head is missing! You're sure, Colonel?'

'I checked the mausoleum carefully. That includes the tomb itself, and both the entrance and exit stairs, the bleachers, and the trees between the mausoleum and the wall.'

'It was smart of you to keep the square cleared, Colonel. Tell me, what do you think happened to the head?'

'I think the dog we found carried it out under cover of the smoke,' Stargov said. He hoped they didn't confiscate the dog, whom he had already decided to name Vladimir. 'I think he was sent in and out again.'

'Under cover of the smoke,' Vorobiev repeated. 'This could be done, do you think, Colonel Stargov?'

'Yes, sir. I think the colored flares were used to send signals to someone handling the dog outside the smoke. They would guess that we jam radio signals immediately in a case like this. One of the dead men had what I take to be a silent dog whistle.'

'And the men – who are they?'

'I don't know, sir. They ranged in age from their mid-twenties to early forties, I would say. They're all bald, as I said. They burned their papers before they killed themselves. We'll be able to trace them through their fingerprints, but that will take time. Four of them, they . . .' Stargov cleared his throat. 'Four of them – they were inside the mausoleum – four of them had the Star of David painted on the tops of their bald heads.'

Spishkin looked stunned. 'Zionists!'

199

Stargov said, 'The man with the note had an Estonian flag in his lap. And a small photograph of himself with his arm around a young woman.'

'Jews and Estonians!' KGB chief Karpov was enraged.

Premier Spishkin said, 'The decision we have to make, quickly, is whether or not to search for the head. The sooner we act, the better our chances for getting it back, whoever they are. On the other hand, we can hardly conduct an adequate search without telling our people what they're looking for.'

Vorobiev said, 'That's one course, immediate action. Close the city and turn it upside down. But if we fail . . .' Vorobiev saw no need to complete the thought. 'I think that we should continue Colonel Stargov's story that the body is intact. We can always make another head.'

Karpov said, 'I can see to that and personally guarantee the maker remains forever silent. If an innocent finds the skull, we simply confiscate it and announce that it is bogus. We can turn GUM and the museums and hotels upside down looking for other conspirators. Colonel Stargov and I could head the search. If a head is found, we should be able to neutralize the finders.'

Thus did the members of the Soviet Politburo quickly coalesce around a plan: they would announce that the tomb was desecrated, but Lenin's body was unscathed. The attack had been perpetrated by Romanians (the Politburo was currently angered at the introduction of private enterprise in the Romanian economy and had been thinking of invading Bucharest). Karpov would conduct an immediate, intensive search of the area surrounding Red Square looking for unspecified 'evidence' left by the terrorists.

Vorobiev said, 'If you need any help at all, Comrade Karpov . . .'

Premier Spishkin coughed and took a sip of tea. 'Which

brings us to Colonel Stargov's note. I'm afraid that's your problem as well, Valery Nikolaevich. I want every KGB agent in the country put to work finding out who these people are. Find their co-conspirators and we just might have a chance. Perhaps you can help there, Gennadi Stepanovich.'

'Certainly,' Vorobiev said.

'I don't think we can overestimate the importance of finding Comrade Lenin's skull. Spishkin passed the terrorists' sheet of paper down the table.

'We have some time. They have to get the head out of the country,' Spishkin said. 'I think it makes sense to put Comrade Karpov and Comrade Vorobiev in charge, to be assisted by Colonel Stargov. I think the rest of us should wait as patiently as we can, ready to help if called upon. Other than the conspirators, we in this room are the only ones who know Lenin's head is missing. If word gets out, the one responsible will be found out and shot. I don't think that's unfair. We cannot fail. Cannot.'

The other members of the Politburo assented by their silence. It was just possible, if their plan failed, to put the entire blame on Spishkin, Vorobiev, and Karpov. If that happened, any one of them might have a chance to become premier, and they all craved power as others craved chocolate, alcohol, and sex.

Later that day, Foreign Minister Grigori Zhukov, who kept a personal journal for most of his adult life – smuggled to the West before his later imprisonment – entered his thoughts during that historic meeting:

'Nowhere in the mausoleum,' Colonel Stargov told us. Lenin's head was missing. Words fail me. I cannot describe the terrified silence that followed. Yes, terrified rather than melancholy, because survival is the most powerful of human instincts. We all wondered: How much more could our scaffold bear? The Politburo was torn by dissension which had seemed to worsen over the years. The Eastern Europeans were pressuring us for more freedom. The arms race was consuming forty to fifty percent of our gross national product. The agricultural collectives, which had cost us millions of lives during the Stalin years, had never worked, and we couldn't feed ourselves. We were falling dangerously behind the West in high technology. Under Lenin's banner and in Lenin's name, we had persevered.

We had used Lenin as the Christians used Jesus. 'Yes,' we told them, 'it is true you may do without now, but stay with us, believe, and we will deliver you to Comrade Lenin's promised land.' If Marx was right that religion is the opiate of the masses, had we not used the same drug? After all these years of attempting to suppress Christians, stubborn believers persevered. We sent them to camps and psychiatric wards and still they persisted in their superstitions, still passed their Bibles from hand to hand. Was there really any qualitative difference between Christianity and the secular religion we built around Lenin? Had we not replaced Christian icons with our own?

There was a stubborn will to believe among the Russian peasants; we all knew that. Until we were vouchsafed the return of Lenin's head, we were vulnerable to a passion that the KGB might not be able to control.

We had always portrayed ourselves as mere caretakers of Lenin's vision. We did Ilyich's work for him. Now his head was gone. True, the head had been a joke to anybody of intelligence. We had insisted against common sense that we had miraculously preserved Lenin against the bacteria that level us all. Stalin had had the idea that the peasants would see an eternal body as proof of a messiah, and he had been right. The head was symbolic of our trust.

Now, after all our talk, we had managed to let bald-headed thieves steal Lenin's head. What if it were true, as we secretly suspected, that Russians loved Lenin but only suffered us because we gave them no choice? In the terrifying emotion of the moment would they, in loyalty to the desecrated Lenin, hold us responsible for all that had gone wrong? Would we be trusted with anything?

For more than sixty years we had conducted a secular version of the Moslem jihad, or holy war; now it was coming back on us. Surely not all my comrades would agree with this analysis, but we all knew our decisions tonight were fraught with uncommon danger. Even Vorobiev and Karpov, who were probably planning on assassinating or imprisoning one another, put aside their differences. When one spoke, the other, for once, listened. It would have been amusing had it not been so tragic. As I pen these words I can hardly believe it yet.

9

The Kremlin watchers in Langley and at the State Department didn't know what to make of the Politburo's reaction to the assault on Lenin's tomb. The watchers had really been through it in the last months of Brezhnev, Andropov, and Chernenko. But even the most veteran and perceptive of the experts had never seen anything like this. Kremlin spokesmen were releasing all manner of contradictory statements. Lights were on all night at the White House and the Executive Office Building.

Nobody knew if Premier Petr Spishkin still ran the Kremlin or not. There had been one rumor that Gennadi Vorobiev, the minister of defense, was in charge; another theory was that Valery Karpov was in charge.

The President and the secretary of state demanded that the Company tell them what the hell was going on in the Kremlin. The signing of the agreement to renew negotiations for arms limitation was to take place on May 5 – twenty-three days away. Would it be aborted after all that hard work?

'We need answers, and we need them now, Peter,' the President had said. 'This is top priority, urgent.' The President didn't believe the arms talks would do any good, but he needed them so that his defense budget would survive intact. The generals and defense contractors were counting on him.

Schott and Burlane went to Peter Neely's office the day after the assault. Schott seemed slightly apologetic about having gotten the Company into such a mess. Burlane seemed unconcerned, if not actually amused.

Peter Neely's face tightened and the muscles of his jaw tensed. A goddamned poet! Who would have believed? Smoke bombs and flares in Red Square. Why did this have to happen on his watch? When Burlane had reported back from Turkey, the DCI had been convinced his man had done the correct thing. Now he wasn't so sure. Was he wrong to trust someone who was so different from himself as James Burlane? Neely looked first at Schott, then at Burlane.

'Well, now,' Neely said. 'What do we make of all this? Jesus Christ! Smoke bombs! Flares!' Neely's voice rose. The tension in the room hung like that brief lethal millisecond before lightning strikes. Neely slammed the *Washington Post* and *The New York Times* on his desk. He was furious.

Schott said, 'Our Moscow people say there've been rumors of a dog. That would fit with Ginsburg's request for silent whistles.'

Peter Neely didn't need the Company's Moscow people to tell him the obvious. Burlane had given Ginsburg green and red flares, hadn't he? And smoke bombs. He glared at Burlane. 'Mr Burlane?'

'He told me he was going to steal something. I believed him.' Burlane grinned.

Schott said, 'From Lenin's tomb? Jimmy, dammit, this is serious business! We're set to sign an agreement to resume the Geneva talks.'

'They probably did find a dog,' Burlane said. 'I can't imagine even Ginsburg would try to smuggle a dog out of there in that confusion.'

Schott said, 'Peter, our people tell us the Soviets sealed off the blocks surrounding the Kremlin almost immediately. Only the people at the fringes who heard the shooting were able to get out. The Soviet press says Vorobiev and Karpov are leading the search personally, along with Colonel Igor Stargov, commander of the Kremlin security forces.'

'Looking for the rest of the Romanians, *Pravda* says.'

Burlane said, 'Hey, it's ridiculous for those guys to search those hotels room by room themselves. If they're after clues, they've got professionals who know how to look for clues. They're looking for something else, I say.'

Peter Neely said, 'Like what, Mr Burlane, please?' Neely had an edge to his voice, having seen that Burlane was wearing off-brown socks with his unpolished black shoes. This was the man who had given Ginsburg what he needed to attack the mausoleum. If the goddamned newspapers ever found out what they'd done, Neely'd have to roast the Company's best agent in public.

Burlane said, 'The Kremlin damn well wants to find out whatever it was the dog carried out of the mausoleum under the cover of the smoke. It was easy enough to do, if you think about it. Someone carried one of the silent whistles into the mausoleum. Someone had one at the edge of Red Square. If the Soviets know about the dog, which they probably do, then Stargov will figure out what happened.'

'Exactly *what* was easy enough, Jimmy? We can hardly wait, Jimmy.' Like Neely, Ara Schott was most comfortable with serious and orderly people.

'The Soviets say they'll open the mausoleum when it's repaired,' Burlane said. 'They have to show folks there is nothing wrong with Lenin's body, just like they said. Only the deal is, Lenin's head is missing and the new one's going to be a complete as opposed to a partial fabrication.'

'Be serious, Jim.'

'A dog could do it. Under cover of a bank of smoke, he could do it. I checked on that this morning. I didn't tell the animal people what I was talking about. You wouldn't even have to have that large a dog. Ginsburg got away with it, too, or they wouldn't be conducting this incredible search. The wristwatches were needed for timing. It was apparently perfectly executed, a quick surprise hit. Boom! A quick layer of smoke. The dog in. The dog out. The guys in the mausoleum don't make it, but Ginsburg – or the other guy – does.'

Schott said, 'The Russians say it was a suicide squad. They could be telling the truth, I suppose. But where do you get warriors like that?'

Burlane looked thoughtful. 'You've got a point there. Yes, probably a suicide squad. Ginsburg couldn't possibly risk having one of them live.' Burlane slouched further down in his chair. 'I don't know where he got them, but I'd make book he did it. This guy had a certain kind of lethal calm about him. He's a smart son of a bitch. I don't think he did anything by accident.'

Neely said, 'Why not Lenin's hand? Wouldn't that be easier? And it'd have his fingerprints, wouldn't it? Or wouldn't they still be good?'

Burlane said, 'Take Lenin's hand when you can have his head? Come on, now. That'd be like snatching a wristwatch when you can have the money belt. Ginsburg's got Lenin's teeth along with the skull, hasn't he? You can identify the skull by the teeth. At the risk of coming off like Sherlock, I think that's it. Ginsburg's clever, and he hates the fuckers. He figures out how to make the grab and pulls it off. He got the head past the search. Now he has to get it out of the country to do anything with it. How? Notice how he's anticipated success.'

At the end of the meeting, Peter Neely directed that any one-time pad received by the American embassy in Moscow addressed to J. B. be treated as Priority One. Peter Neely was to be beeped or called immediately in the event of a Priority One.

10

The call came at 3:24 A.M., Wednesday, April 14, two
days after the assault on the mausoleum. Peter Neely
turned from beneath his sleeping wife's leg and answered
the phone.

A woman said, 'Jackie?'

Neely said, 'You have the wrong number,' and hung
up. Neely left his warm bed, put his clothes on, and
drove his Mercedes to Langley – followed at a discreet
distance by a black Trans-Am containing the two men
who were there for his protection.

This was the message to J. B. in Langley, Virginia:

Have Lenin's head. Being followed. Riding the Trans-Siberian
Express from Moscow to Vladivostok, 10 A.M. Moscow time, 28
April, with 1 May stopover for reading at Irkutsk. Traveling
with accomplice Natalia Kropotkina. We seek one-year open
emigration from USSR and Soviet bloc countries, Cuba, and
Vietnam in return for the head. Can you ride this train also, J.
B.? I have a need for your services that I will make clear at an
appropriate time. We wish we could do this alone but we
cannot. If you are honorable men and value freedom as you say
you do, you will do this. Isaak Avraamovich Ginsburg.

Neely, stunned, reread the message. James Burlane
was right. Isaak Ginsburg had stolen the head from
Lenin's corpse with the help of the Central Intelligence
Agency. Ginsburg was going to ride the Trans-Siberian
to Vladivostok to read a commemorative poem at the
signing, and he wanted Burlane with him. Dammit!

Peter Neely now knew why the Kremlin had gone off

its nut. No wonder! If Petr Spishkin found out the Company was involved in a scheme to steal Lenin's head from the tomb, Spishkin would probably launch the goddamned rockets.

In Moscow that day, Felix Jin and the other colonels of the KGB's Jewish Department were called before their chief, Valery Karpov. Comrade Karpov's comings and goings were mysterious to all but a handful of his subordinates, but everybody knew that he had virtually gone without sleep in the two days that had passed since the raid on Lenin's tomb. Karpov and Defense Minister Gennadi Vorobiev had personally led the day-and-night search of the area surrounding Red Square.

Karpov ordinarily kept himself aloof from mundane labor, preferring instead the pleasures of conniving. His desires were made known by memo, and failure to meet them was dealt with harshly. Jin and his fellow officers knew that for Karpov to call a personal meeting after two sleepless days of hard work meant something very serious indeed.

The assembled officers were those who monitored lists of Jews considered to represent the greatest potential threat to the state. One colonel oversaw a list of outspoken scientists and engineers. A second watched Jews who attempted to contact the world outside the Soviet Union. The third, Colonel Jin, followed the activities of writers.

Felix Jin had spent most of his adult life learning how to read opaque, ambiguous statements. An aptitude for separating the truth from outright lies was the secret of success for Russian bureaucrats, but Karpov's performance was so fraught with possibilities that Jin was stunned.

Karpov told the officers of the Jewish Department that the Romanian terrorists who trashed Lenin's tomb had connections to Zionists, and possibly to Estonians. That fact was to be kept secret.

Karpov then said there was reason to believe that one or more Zionists who were part of the plot had traveled to Perm within the previous year. That fact also was to be kept secret. Karpov did not specify the connection between Zionists and Perm.

Karpov told the colonels they were to personally review their respective lists for any Jew who had been to Perm in the last year. If any of the officers had such a Jew on his list, he was to personally supervise a total surveillance of that Jew.

'Comrade Colonels, we are looking for specific physical evidence. This is not in microdot or microfilm. To give you a rough idea, it is as large as this perhaps.' Karpov held his palm out and weighed whatever it was he was looking for. 'You'll know it when you find it. This is to be top secret among us. If you find it, immediately isolate everyone involved. They are to talk to no one.' Karpov reviewed a note he had made to himself.

'I hope you have all followed the personal computer memorandum and have learned how to operate the portable American computers we stole for you. That's what we got them for, so we can work quickly and efficiently in an emergency. I assume you've all learned your' – he glanced at his card – 'your "software," it says here.'

Only Felix Jin said, 'Yes, sir.'

Karpov stared balefully at the other two officers. 'What this means, comrades, is that you're going to have to use a KGB operator and shoot him for security when you're finished with this. You're to shoot him – or her – yourself. When this is finished, I want you to learn how to use those computers. Now, I have these.' He held up a small box containing floppy disks.

'These contain the names and data from all the people

that were interviewed in the Red Square area for the past two days. This includes individuals on the streets, in the subway, in the museums, GUM, and hotels.' Karpov held up a second box of floppies. 'These contain the names and identifying data of all visitors to Perm hotels in the previous year.'

Colonel Felix Jin and his colleagues wondered just what evidence it was that was so sensitive that Comrade Karpov felt obliged to keep it secret. *Sure, comrades, find this thing on penalty of your careers, but I can't let you know what it is.*

The colonels walked out of the new KGB headquarters as though such bizarre instructions were commonplace. They couldn't complain or speculate lest word get back to Comrade Karpov.

Felix Jin, feeling good that he alone had followed Karpov's orders and learned how to work his brand-new Kaypro, happily took his disks to his office at Dzerzhinsky Square. To have scored like that in such an emergency was a political coup in KGB politics, and was good for Jin's career.

Jin slipped into the chair, turned on the machine, punched the reset button, and slipped his Perfect Writer disk in Drive A and the disk with the interview data in Drive B. The prompt came up, and Jin typed 'MENU' and hit the return bar.

The menu appeared and Jin typed D, B, to see exactly what was on the disk. Nothing happened. He tried again. Jin was puzzled. He removed the disk in Drive B and slipped in one he'd been using to write reports. This time the disk directory appeared as requested.

Something was wrong with Karpov's disk. Jin called the new KGB headquarters and got through to Karpov. 'They've sent me faulty disks, Comrade Karpov. I'll have to have good ones to do my job.'

Karpov swore. 'Good that you called me personally, Colonel. Send them back. I'll get you new ones.'

Felix Jin did as he was told and waited, impatient to get on with the investigation. He smoked a cigarette, bewildered at the number of fuck-ups in the KGB.

A half-hour later Karpov called back, an edge to his voice. He said, 'I'm afraid I have some bad news for you, Felix.'

'Yes, comrade?' Jin wondered what could possibly have happened.

'It seems there was a disagreement over what kind of computers we should buy. Some of your colleagues, Felix, said we should buy IBMs because they're more famous. Others said Kaypros are the better deal because they're cheaper and will do everything we need. In the end there was a compromise; we decided to buy IBMs for the officers here at Moscow Center and Kaypros for those of you still at Dzerzhinsky.'

'What?' Another decision by committee. Jin had read the computer manuals and guessed what the screw-up was. He was furious.

'The codes used to operate those machines are different, Felix.'

'I could have told you that, Comrade Karpov.'

'I'm sorry, Felix. Who would have thought they don't use a common code? You can have somebody else shoot the operator if you'd like. It's not your fault and I understand that.'

'I'd prefer to isolate the operator until this matter is finished.' Jin remained calm with effort.

'Of course, Felix.' Valery Karpov hung up.

The computer specialist, a personable young woman named Vera, used an IBM PC. The computer singled out one name, which appeared in neat green letters:

Isaak Avraamovich Ginsburg.

Comrade Ginsburg had been in the Hotel Rossiya at the time of the assault on Lenin's tomb, and he had spent one night in Perm the previous August.

Jin sat back in his chair and considered the stunning connection.

He pulled Ginsburg's file. The stop at Perm had apparently been made en route to Moscow from Novosibirsk. Jin had the operator input all names mentioned by KGB agents who had been following the poet. These were people Ginsburg had known from school and in his days as an underground poet as well as his most recent past in Novosibirsk and Moscow. With growing excitement, Jin watched the operator key in the names. Jin instructed the operator to find out if any of these names were on Karpov's Red Square or Perm list.

One was: Natalia Serafimovna Kropotkina. Comrade Kropotkina, like Ginsburg, had been in the Hotel Rossiya at the time of the affair on Red Square.

Jin reread Ginsburg's dossier. There was evidence to suggest that Ginsburg was having an affair with Natalia Kropotkina, the *znachok* designer who was married to the foreign service officer, Leonid Kropotkin. Comrade Jin picked up the phone and ordered a full KGB report on Natalia Kropotkina.

It was only then that Jin saw a one-line reference to something that had no meaning before and which he had forgotten: from March 12 through March 15, Ginsburg had been to the Georgian Republic to read his poetry. Tbilisi was just fourteen hundred kilometers from Tel Aviv. This was interesting because Ginsburg's landlord in Novosibirsk, Georgi Kashva, was believed to have contacts with smugglers operating out of Georgia.

11

James Burlane knew it was coming, that predictable old dumbshit mental constipation of bureaucrats faced with danger. It was choke time. Be careful time. Protect your ass time. Burlane was different. Burlane had been a fan of the Green Bay Packers when he was a kid. He remembered two things clearly: Bart Starr, faced with third and short, throwing long to Boyd Dowler or Max McGee, and Starr, money on the line, turning automatically to Paul Hornung.

Lenin's head! This Isaak Ginsburg affair was real money time. Burlane was the Company's main man, dammit, the Paul Hornung of the Central Intelligence Agency. He wanted that ball.

Burlane said, 'Listen, Mr Neely, you cannot, just *cannot* leave that man hanging out there alone. He's asking for our help. He's not asking anything impossible. He's not saying they have to hold free elections or let people own property or anything like that.'

Ara Schott said, 'We have to be very, very careful, Jimmy.'

'Bullshit!'

Schott was surprised by Burlane's vehemence. 'You have to consider the consequences of something like this, Jimmy.'

Burlane looked disgusted. 'So tell me about the consequences.'

'Well, for one thing,' Neely said, 'how could we conceivably handle all those people, assuming the Russians

214

would let them go? That may seem coarse to you, but it's something we have to consider.'

'You could pull a Franklin Roosevelt, I guess. Leave them there to get crapped on and thrown in camps. I don't know about you, but that does strike me as a trifle coarse.'

'Roosevelt had a war to fight, Mr Burlane,' Neely said.

Burlane did his best not to glare at the DCI. 'If we don't do this, to what end did we fight that war? Ask yourself that. We must do this. We must.'

Ara Schott said, 'The European economies are running twelve to eighteen percent unemployment as it is. How are they going to handle a flood of Poles and Czechs?'

'And Jews?' Burlane put in.

'And Jews,' Schott said. 'I'll be honest and tell you I'm not certain Israel would be too excited about this.'

Burlane shook his head.

Neely said, 'You've got education to think about, language problems.'

'Not to mention the risk of having the Soviets find out we helped Ginsburg out.' Schott doodled on a piece of paper.

Burlane leaned forward, serious as he rarely appeared to be. 'As civilized men, we have a moral obligation here and we all know it. There are some things we do because they must be done. This is one of them.'

Ara Schott looked surprised. 'A what, Mr Burlane? Moral obligation? Civilized men? This is the Central Intelligence Agency. We're responsible for the security of the United States and nothing more. You know that, man!'

'We have to help him. I say again, this is an opportunity that transcends politics. We do what we have to do and the devil take the hindmost. What follows, follows.'

'Just how would you propose to get on that particular

train, Mr Burlane?' In order to protect his reputation as a civilized man and an executive who considered all possibilities, Neely felt he should hear Burlane out. Neely jotted a note on a classified pad on his desk.

'He's given us everything we need, a setup. He's their wonder-boy poet, the house Jew. The Soviets aren't just tolerating attention for Ginsburg, they're inviting it with this commemorative poem business. We choose an influential left-wing magazine of politics and the arts. We tell the editor that the President of the United States would like a few words with him. A little tête-à-tête over breakfast, say.'

Schott said, 'And the President would do what?'

'The President would ask the editor to make an urgent request to the Soviets. The editor wants one of his magazine's cultural reporters to accompany Ginsburg on the ride to Vladivostok. Me.'

Neely took another note. 'Have you forgotten, Mr Burlane, that we solemnly promised a committee of the United States Senate that we would forever cease and desist using journalists as cover for our covert operations?'

'Screw the Senate! Thomas Jefferson bought the Louisiana Territory without asking Congress like he was supposed to. That was unconstitutional, but you didn't hear anybody complaining.'

Neely looked surprised. 'I thought you didn't want anything to do with going inside the Soviet Union ever again.'

'Changed my mind. I ski. I shoot. I read. They say Nelson won the battle of Trafalgar because he let his commanders do what they had to do in the heat of battle. For God's sake, please, please let me do this.'

216

Three days later, the editor of the liberal political magazine *New Democrat* – still glowing from the pleasure of having eggs Benedict and melon balls with the President of the United States, an affable man who had called the editor by his first name – gave the Company a list of writers. These were men and women who had written for his magazine in the past and who might very well be hired to write a story about Isaak Ginsburg's trip across the Soviet Union to the Vladivostok signing. The editor did this despite having written in his magazine – just two weeks earlier – that the affable President was an ignorant, bigoted, right-wing ideologue, an incompetent whose refusal to confront the deficit threatened the country with economic chaos.

Ara Schott and James Burlane wanted a writer whose known personality and temperament were a rough match for Burlane. Their ideal candidate, they agreed, would be well enough known for the Soviets to assemble his dossier quickly, but would have an unknown face. He could not be a columnist or public personality.

James Burlane received the list of names on April 17. He ran his finger down the list, and when he reached Quint, James Allen, he burst out laughing.

Jim Quint – who grew up in western Montana – did magazine work and, under the pseudonym of Nicholas Orr, wrote a series of paperback adventures featuring a hero with the unlikely name of Humper Staab, so called because if he wasn't humping somebody, he was stabbing them. Two years earlier, a boxed feature accompanying a *Newsweek* magazine cover story on the Company described the adventures of an unnamed superspy who was, in fact, James Burlane. The joke at Langley, *Newsweek* said, was that this superspy was the real-life model for 'Humper Staab.' Alas, poor Quint was later sued for libel by Humperdinck Staab, a minor OSS agent in World War II. Burlane claimed to be disappointed.

Burlane, originally from eastern Oregon, responded easily and naturally to James, Jim, or Jimmy. Under the circumstances, this was as good a match as the Company could hope for.

Jim Quint agreed to get lost for a while. He wrote a quickie autobiography for James Burlane to memorize and bought himself a ticket to Jamaica; he said he'd once had a helluva time there.

The Russian embassy in Washington, eager to please the editors of the *New Democrat*, quickly approved Jim Quint's application for a visa; Quint's passport now contained Burlane's picture. Yes, Burlane could accompany Isaak Ginsburg on his trip across the USSR on the Trans-Siberian Express.

Felix Jin studied the incomplete first report on Natalia Kropotkina on April 18; this was preliminary to the definitive dossier that Jin had requested. Although sketchy, it was suggestive.

Natalia Kropotkina had been a leading candidate to design the pin honoring Ivan Dmitrov's monumental Lenin statue but had not received the commission, allegedly because of her ambition for personal attention. Then Dmitrov himself had apparently intervened to recommend that Natalia design the pin commemorating the Vladivostok signing.

In order to design the Vladivostok pin, Natalia Kropotkina said, she had to witness the signing. Comrade Kropotkina had requested space, subsequently approved, on the same train as Isaak Ginsburg.

Jin requested the engineer's drawings of the East German cars used on the railroad. He also ordered a search of railroad records to find Ginsburg's compartment-mate or mates on his way from Novosibirsk to Moscow when he had stopped to spend a night at Perm. He called Tbilisi and asked for a report on Ginsburg's visit there.

The railroad drawings were flown in from East Berlin on April 19. There were far higher priorities for stolen American computers than for railway passengers, so the search for Ginsburg's traveling companion would take longer, perhaps weeks. Tbilisi said there was nothing unusual about Ginsburg's visit except that he was missing for a nine-hour period on a Sunday, March 15 – the day before his return to Moscow. Tbilisi believed the missing hours were benign. The agents responsible for the lapse in surveillance had been disciplined.

Jin studied the drawings of the railroad cars. There were ten two-person compartments on a soft-class car. There were toilets at each end. There was a small compartment for bed linen next to one toilet, followed by the conductress's compartment, which contained one seat that served as a bed at night. The remaining compartments had two seats, one on each wall. The space under each was divided into an open and a closed baggage area. The seats, which were hinged on the wall, folded up for access to the closed areas. There was a loft for luggage above the door and the ceiling of the aisle.

In order to isolate and control Ginsburg and Kropotkina – and to find whatever it was Karpov was looking for – Jin ordered that the couple be berthed in a railway car placed at the tail end of the Trans-Siberian Express. He ordered them assigned to Compartment One, next to the conductress. If they were screwing now, they would be screwing on the train. Jin reserved the next compartment for the technicians needed to tape conversations and videotape their sex life.

12

From the moment James Burlane laid eyes on the Intourist guide who was to accompany him on the Trans-Siberian Express, he knew she was a honeypot. Whether the KGB was on to him, he did not know. If it were, KGB officers would know from his dossier that he had a hyperactive sex drive, something the Company tolerated because of his skills as an agent. Whatever. If the KGB had assembled a file on Jim Quint, they'd have found that the writer from Bison, Montana, was likewise damned with too much testosterone.

The Soviets knew how to break a man. The blonde who waited for Burlane/Quint at the main desk in the lobby of the National Hotel had a body upon which clothes were obscene.

The Americans called these women honeypots because men, drawn to the nectar of sex, become stuck like wriggling flies, susceptible to KGB blackmail. The KGB called them swallows, as in pretty birds, although Company men alleged the term was used in a sexual context.

The honeypot had watched Burlane from the moment he reached the foot of the stairs. She had a folder tucked under her arm; Burlane noticed that the folder flattened the side of her enviable breast. 'Mr Jim Quint? My name is Ludmilla Kormakova and I'll be your guide on the way to Vladivostok.'

Burlane shook her hand and said, 'Pleased to meet you, Ms Kormakova.' He thought, *Good Christ!* and followed her outside to the waiting Volga taxi, his eyes somewhere below her waist. The odds of his accidentally drawing an Intourist guide who looked like Ludmilla were statistically negligible. Burlane threw his one bag into the trunk and joined Ludmilla in the back seat, where he was overwhelmed by the French perfume she was wearing. He wanted to dive into her lap sniffing like a hog after truffles.

As the taxi pulled into the traffic, Burlane's guide said, 'You must call me Ludmilla. You are doing articles on the Trans-Siberian Railroad and Comrade Ginsburg. I'm told the *New Democrat* is one of the better American magazines. Very influential.'

'Please call me Jim,' Burlane said. Nobody had accused the *New Democrat* of being influential since Franklin Roosevelt's first term. 'We try to be the conscience of progressives in America.' The truth was that the *New Democrat* was too New Deal-Old Democrat for Burlane's taste. He hadn't read it on his own for years, and had had to OD on recent issues to prepare for this trip. Ludmilla's perfume made him giddy.

'We are, of course, making the longest train ride in the world. We will be crossing almost one hundred degrees of longitude in Europe and Asia. We will be crossing seven time zones, although we will be observing Moscow time throughout.'

Ludmilla made Burlane want to lick his lips. He was thinking this when he realized he should be taking notes. He scrambled for his notebook and began scribbling as the Volga wheeled through sparse traffic. 'Seven time zones,' he said. 'That's really something.'

Ludmilla paused so Burlane could record the number of degrees longitude to be crossed. She said, 'Yes. It is fifty-eight hundred and ten miles from Moscow to Vladivostok on the Sea of Japan. This trip will take us a full seven days, or one hundred seventy hours, on the train. There will be four days to Irkutsk, which is north of the Gobi Desert, and three more days to Vladivostok. Because of Comrade Ginsburg's reading in Irkutsk on May Day, we will be arriving on the morning of the eighth day.'

'I see,' Burlane said.

'It will be Moscow to Perm the first day, Perm to Omsk the second, Omsk to Krasnoyarsk the third, and Krasnoyarsk to Irkutsk the fourth. We will arrive in Irkutsk the morning of May first and leave that night. We will have a room in the Intourist Hotel in Irkutsk so that you might rest if you like. It is a long ride on the Trans-Siberian Express.'

'And we'll be arriving in Vladivostok . . .?'

'The morning of May fifth, Jim, because of the delay at Irkutsk. As to time on the move, it will be Irkutsk to Mogocha the fifth day, Mogocha to Khabarovsk the sixth, and Khabarovsk to Vladivostok the seventh. Ordinarily, foreigners are not allowed in Vladivostok, and must go instead to Nakhodka. Foreigners are allowed to stop at Novosibirsk, Irkutsk, and Khabarovsk. That trip is longer – fifty-nine hundred miles – a trip of almost eight days or one hundred ninety-two hours and thirty minutes. This is because travelers must stop over for one day in Khabarovsk.'

'Why is that?' Burlane said.

'It is done that way, Jim.'

Burlane retrieved his map of the Soviet Union and found Khabarovsk by way of showing his interest. 'I see. Well. Here it is: Khabarovsk.'

'The Paris of the Soviet Far East,' Ludmilla said.

'On the Amur River.'

'The Amur River has one of the highest volumes of water of any river in the world.'

Burlane wondered if a legit journalist would give a damn. He decided the safest course was to come on red

222

hot. He scribbled 'Amur River, much water' in an illegible scrawl.

Ludmilla said, 'If you took the train from New York to Los Angeles via New Orleans, you would cover just thirty-four hundred and twenty miles.'

Burlane was starting to get an erection watching Ludmilla rattle off facts and numbers. He'd have to tell that to Schott if he made it out alive.

'And you have to understand that if you go west from Moscow, it's another four hundred and eighty miles to the Finnish border. Incidentally, Yaraslavsky Station is so named because Yaraslav on the Volga was the original terminal point of the rail line that eventually spanned our country.'

Their driver pulled to a stop at the bizarre Victorian building that was Yaraslavsky Station. Ludmilla brushed against him as she retrieved her bag from the trunk of the Volga. Burlane knew that to keep his hands off her would be a sacrifice of a magnitude rarely endured by soldiers of the cold war.

James Burlane and his guide strode quickly through a huge room with a high ceiling from which hung ornate electrical chandeliers. Black granite columns braced the ceiling. Burlane walked with the loose, confident stride of a man who had been in a lot of train stations in the Third World and so was familiar with the resigned faces and rancid odor of poverty. As far as Burlane was concerned, the only difference between the residents of the Soviet Union and those of Timor or Mozambique was that the Russians had ICBMs, and travelers there didn't have to worry about getting ripped off because the state had a monopoly on violence along with everything else.

The travelers in Yaraslavsky Station were encamped like refugees from a war zone, sitting upon or beside all

223

manner of cardboard boxes and bags wrapped in newspaper and tied with string or hemp. Some smoked cigarettes; others took quick hits of vodka so as to remain oblivious. The women guarded the food: bags of cabbage, small apples, loaves of coarse bread, balls of butter wrapped in greasy paper, and bits and pieces of fat and hunks of smelly sausage rolled in paper cones.

Burlane stepped over the mud-encrusted boots of a soldier sprawled in an alcoholic stupor. A man with a crude haircut observed him idly, wondering, Burlane supposed, where he was from. Patches of white from the man's skull showed through where the shears had strayed too close. A small boy in a coat so heavy the sleeves would not bend at the elbows stared at him. Ludmilla was a Russian, easily identified as a privileged Intourist guide. Burlane was different. He was not a Russian.

The watchful travelers didn't know Burlane was an American; he could have been Belgian or Spanish for all they knew. It was enough that he was from someplace that was not the USSR. In the Soviet Union a foreigner was a possible source of a watch that worked or blue jeans that didn't come apart at the seams, but other than that he was something to be avoided.

Burlane followed Ludmilla down the platform to Train No. 1, which left Moscow for Vladivostok at 10 A.M. Train No. 1 was called the Rossiya – the Russia – and was red with a yellow stripe down its sides. Burlane counted twenty passenger cars – ten on either side of two dining cars – plus an enormous East German engine up front. They walked to the very end of the train, where the car that contained their soft-class compartment waited.

It did not surprise Burlane – as he and Ludmilla moved down the aisle in search of their compartment – to see Isaak Ginsburg waiting to enter his compartment two doors down. Ginsburg was with a dark-haired woman who would have attracted Burlane's attention by virtue of her figure, but the fact that she carried a bronze bust of Lenin under her arm was a showstopper. Burlane found it difficult not to stare.

Burlane and Ginsburg glanced at one another in a quick moment of mutual sharing and responsibility. Burlane and Ginsburg had a pact. The trust was theirs, and the danger.

James Burlane and Ludmilla Kormakova stored their bags under the seats. Burlane, followed closely by Ludmilla, returned to the aisle to watch the activity on the platform; he had a long ride ahead of him, and there was no reason to sit down too soon. Just as he did not believe it was an accident that he had drawn an Intourist guide of Ludmilla's remarkable beauty, Burlane knew it was not the luck of the draw that he and Isaak Ginsburg were assigned a car at the extreme rear of the train.

Burlane assumed that the dark-haired woman was Natalia Kropotkina, the accomplice of Ginsburg's message. Burlane wondered why she would want to lug a heavy bust of Lenin across the Soviet Union.

As the train began its journey, the conductress came in to sweep the carpet. She was a small woman in her early thirties. Her duties included taking care of the huge stainless electric samovar just opposite her compartment. The samovar looked to Burlane like a coffee maker in an American cafeteria. The conductress made and delivered tea, swept the carpets, stocked the toilets with paper, and made sure the passengers in her car were back on board after each stop. She performed these duties so quietly and unobtrusively as to be chameleonlike.

The conductress said something to Ludmilla, and watched Burlane as Ludmilla translated.

'She says her name is Nina Kabakhidze, Jim. She is originally from the Autonomous Republic of Georgia, which has some of the most productive citrus groves in the Middle East. She is a senior conductress. She will be with us all the way to Vladivostok. If you need help, you are to ask her.'

Burlane nodded his head in acknowledgment, then promptly forgot Nina Kabakhidze's name. Kabakhidze was hard to remember.

Ludmilla said, 'We'll have all the hot water we need for our tea, Jim. I brought us some special tea. From GUM. The very finest tea in the world is available at GUM.'

13

They were no sooner out of Yaraslavsky Station than the conductress, wearing a dark gray skirt and a light gray blouse, served *chai*, Russian tea, to the passengers in her car, drawing piping hot water from the enormous samovar. Even Burlane had to admit that Russian tea and bread were some of the best he'd ever had, and the idea of having a generous samovar of hot water on each car was civilized.

'Your Russian tea is wonderful,' he said. 'And your bread too. I like that.' The truth was he'd had better Russian tea than this.

Ludmilla said, 'Our Russian bread is the best in the world, Jim. This is because it contains no additives and is baked according to national standards. The only bread that can compare with it is the bread of Canada, which costs almost twice as much.'

Burlane hadn't meant to provoke a lecture. 'It is good.'

'It is very important in our socialist way of life that such things as tea and bread be the best and available to everybody at a price they can afford. Which do you like the best, Jim, the dark bread or the light bread?'

'The dark, I think. Maybe we should have some tea in our compartment.' Burlane hoped to end the discussion of Russian bread. He went back into the compartment thinking that socialist travelers must be a thirsty group; the samovar looked like it held three or four gallons of water.

Later, Burlane stepped into the aisle to stretch his legs, and met Isaak Ginsburg. It was time, Burlane knew, for

Jim Quint to introduce himself. 'My name is Jim Quint, Mr Ginsburg. I don't know if you've been told, but I'm an American journalist assigned to do a story about the trip across the Soviet Union and your poems at Irkutsk and Vladivostok.' The dark-haired woman in Ginsburg's car was sketching; her bust of Lenin sat on the fold-down table below the compartment window.

'Yes, for the *New Democrat*,' Ginsburg said.

Burlane said, 'A poetry reading in Irkutsk on May Day. That ought to be wonderful stuff for my readers.' His eyes asked: *Is Lenin's head on this railroad car? Is that why you wanted me on this train?*

Ginsburg's eyes replied yes to both questions. He said, 'We Russians are passionate people, Mr Quint. We love poetry and language. Poets are valued in the Soviet Union.'

Burlane said, 'Most Americans want to learn, they really do. The problem is that the owners of most magazines won't let them print the truth. The *New Democrat* has a special empathy for working people.'

'The truth is all we Russians ask.'

'I assure you, I'm not a propagandist. I write what I see, and the *New Democrat* will print what I write; it's that kind of magazine.' Burlane wondered where in hell Ginsburg could stash a human head on a train with the KGB watching over his shoulder.

'I'm living proof there is no repression against Jews in the Soviet Union, Mr Quint. Poets of quality are published. There are no obstacles to getting good work published.'

'Are you telling me you can write what you want? There is no censorship in the USSR?'

'None,' Ginsburg said. 'We're encouraged to write the truth. Contrary to what you're led to believe in the West, the Soviet Union is a wonderful place for a writer.'

'I assure you, I'm after the truth, not rehashed propaganda.' Burlane was outwardly sincere, serious. He thought, *Bullshit too, bub!* He said, 'I should be getting back to my compartment. My guide is waiting. Perhaps we could have a chat sometime before Irkutsk.' The dark-haired woman had put down her pad and was listening to their conversation.

Isaak Ginsburg said, 'Certainly.' Ginsburg glanced at the woman. 'Mr Quint, I'd like you to meet Natalia Kropotkina. Natalia Serafimovna is one of the most famous designers of commemorative pins in the Soviet Union. You know what they are, don't you?' Ginsburg showed Burlane the small red pin on his lapel. 'This is one of Natasha's most popular.'

Burlane looked at the pin. 'Very nice.' He shook Natalia's hand. He envied Ginsburg.

Ginsburg said, 'She's been commissioned to do a pin commemorating the Vladivostok signing.'

'I see.'

Burlane inspected the pin on Ginsburg's lapel. 'Very nice,' he said. 'I saw you sketching your bust of Lenin there.'

'This is a copy of the bust Comrade Zhukov will give to Stuart Kaplan – it's identical, in fact. I need to study it for my Vladivostok assignment; it'll help pass the time on the train.'

'Six thousand miles is a long way,' Burlane said.

Ginsburg said, 'Mrs Kropotkina's husband, Leonid, is a foreign service officer. He's at The Hague this week. The Americans are being tried for war crimes in Central America.'

'Ahh, I see,' Burlane said.

Natalia said, 'Would you like to take a closer look at the bust, Mr Quint? The sculptor, Ivan Dmitrov, is an acknowledged master.'

Burlane stepped into the compartment and squatted by the table to examine the bust, which was slightly larger than a real head. As far as he was concerned, Dmitrov's Lenin looked like all the others he had seen in the Soviet Union, but he suspected that Natalia Kropotkina was telling him something.

'It's lovely, lovely,' Burlane said. 'May I pick it up?'

'Why, of course.' Natalia Kropotkina's English was even better than Ginsburg's.

Burlane held the bust in both hands. 'It's heavy.'

'That's because it's bronze!' Natalia laughed easily.

He knew he should not talk too long with Ginsburg and Natalia. Too much talk invited error. 'I'd better get back to my compartment,' he said. 'My guide will be wondering what happened to me.'

Burlane had hardly turned around when he was confronted by a group of Western European men gesturing, laughing, and talking in English with varying accents. One of them, a pot-bellied Englishman in a vested suit, spotted Burlane as a foreigner – and a likely English-speaker. 'Hello, there. My name's Bob Steele.'

'Jim,' Burlane said.

'Some ride, eh, Jim? My friends and I are journalists on our way to Vladivostok. They've got us all berthed in one car. I'm with *The Daily Telegraph* in London.'

'I see.'

'Quite a bunch, actually. We're having fun. Stocked in a good supply of vodka for the trip. We've got a couple of matched sets, British and Dutch, plus a German, a Frenchman, and a Dane. Drinkers and talkers. Good group. Even our Intourist guide's a nice guy, a bit serious maybe, but he likes his vodka too.

'What is it you do, Jim?'

Burlane thought, *Oh shit!* He said, 'Well, as a matter

230

of fact, I'm a journalist too.' He thought, *Drop it, Bob, will you?*

Bob Steele looked puzzled. 'What are you covering?'

'I'm doing a story for the *New Democrat* on the poet Isaak Ginsburg. That's why they've got me in this car instead of with the rest of you.'

Steele grinned. 'Ahh. I see.'

Burlane felt relieved; he seemed to have made it.

Then Steele said, 'Say what's your last name? Maybe I've read some of your stuff.'

Burlane's heart sank, but he remained cheerful on the exterior. 'Jim Quint.'

Steele looked startled. 'Jim Quint?'

Burlane laughed. 'That's it, fresh out of Bison, Montana.'

Steele glanced at his colleagues. He seemed not to know what to say next. Finally he said, 'Pleased to have met you, Jim. It looks like my group's heading on back.'

Burlane watched them leave the car. Bob Steele, the last one out, glanced back at Burlane. Steele obviously knew the real Jim Quint. Damn!

When James Burlane returned to the compartment he found it suffused with Ludmilla Kormakova's marvelous odor. Its effect on Burlane was nothing short of aphrodisiac. He was in for a long, long ride across the Soviet Union.

'There are ninety-three assigned stops between Moscow and Vladivostok,' Ludmilla said as they settled in with their tea. Over the edge of her teacup, she looked into Burlane's eyes and gave him a warm smile.

Decent photography required light, not darkness. That first night Ludmilla Kormakova established precedent by leaving the reading light on above her bunk when she undressed. Burlane, in boxer shorts that featured tiny

231

strawberries with little green leaves, lay back under his blanket and watched the show with much appreciation.

Ludmilla, naked, was fabulous – sleek of flank and brown of nipple. Her pubic hair, blue-black and shiny, stood in sharp contrast to the white of her thighs.

Ludmilla had remarkable nipples. When Burlane saw them, he wanted to attack them, chewing.

Ludmilla turned out the reading light and slipped into the berth opposite Burlane's and said, 'I can't stand clothes when I sleep.'

'A person's skin needs to breathe at night.' Burlane wondered where she had been trained. At Verkhonoye? Probably. The KGB's Verkhonoye sex school was located between Kazan and the Urals in the Tatar Autonomous Soviet Socialist Republic. Stories of the outrageous training given swallows there were legendary at Langley. Burlane had often speculated about what he would do if he ever crossed paths with one. Now that had happened, and he could do nothing. He hoped she didn't think he was gay, or else she might be replaced by some jerk in tight pants.

James Burlane lay back, incapacitated by a throbbing erection that gripped his crotch like a pair of pliers. KGB bastards. Burlane was infuriated. His taut muscle did not relax, stayed tight, demanded action. Discipline, he told himself. Discipline. It wasn't until 1 A.M. that James Burlane was at last released from the Ludmilla-induced priapism and fell asleep to the clanging, banging lullaby of the Trans-Siberian Express.

14

James Burlane awoke the next morning wondering where the train was. He fished his wristwatch from the heel of his shoe: 7 A.M. of his second day on the train. Ludmilla Kormakova had prepared for his arising and was now sleeping, or pretending to sleep, with one breast casually exposed for Burlane's pleasure. The morning light suffused Ludmilla's wonderful prominence with an erotic alpenglow. Burlane considered this bounty for a moment, then raised the sliding green shade above the window.

The train passed some isolated peasant huts – a shanty here, a shack there, a pathetic hut, each one fenced. They came upon an impoverished hamlet, then taiga and birch, a shallow swamp of mud, a river, and another squalid village.

Burlane was contemplating the morning sun when Ludmilla said, 'Good morning, Jim.'

'Well, good morning, Ludmilla!' Burlane said heartily. Burlane was thankful that Quint's name was Jim. Burlane could react quickly to Jim. Burlane could never react to a Russian word or phrase. If he did, any pretense of cover was finished; the real Quint did not speak Russian. Burlane was curious about what Siberia looked like, but he did not want to spend the rest of his life there. Burlane wondered if Ludmilla would give him an inadvertent little show when she got up.

The answer was yes. Given the one hundred and eighty degrees in which Ludmilla could have exposed her lower charms, she chose to aim her stern directly at Burlane as she bent to retrieve her clothes from under the bunk.

Burlane, still under the covers, stared in appreciation. It was hard not to be moved by the nutty juxtaposition of ball-stirring physical beauty with the banging and clattering of the Trans-Siberian Express.

'You Russians are physically very similar to Scandinavians aren't you?' Burlane said. 'Lovely!' His peers would have said that James Burlane was one of a select few agents in the world capable of deadpanning that line knowing he was being videotaped by a KGB camera.

As Ludmilla slipped on her clothes, the train hit a storm front and the sky turned suddenly dark. 'We will enter the Urals later today, Jim. The Urals divide Europe and Asia. The USSR is both the largest European and the largest Asian country. Shall we go to breakfast, do you think?'

The first day out, the indifferent waiter had brought them an elaborate menu listing chicken Kiev, sturgeon, baked desserts and other delicacies, as well as beluga, sevruga, and malossol caviars, aged cheeses, and fresh fruit. As the Russians on the train understood perfectly, the menu had nothing to do with what was available; it was for show only. For breakfast the chef offered fried eggs served in a metal dish and floating in tepid yellow oil, plus a thin slice of cheese; rice and boiled meat was the treat at lunch; mashed potatoes and borscht were served for supper.

Breakfast was different the second morning. The eggs were served with more oil, and the slice of cheese had been replaced by an emaciated weiner.

Another gloom descended after breakfast, and the sleet returned. Then the sleet turned to a dry snow that came down furiously. The snow stopped twenty minutes later, and they were into sun again with a bank of black clouds to one side of the train.

Ludmilla Kormakova drew hot water from the samovar

for some tea. The Russian tea was served in clear glass cups held in silver-plated holders that had a handle. They were lovely cups. Ludmilla, in the manner of Russians everywhere, loaded her *chai* with several lumps of Cuban sugar.

Borscht was available for lunch. This version contained slices of sausages along with hunks of unidentifiable fat that floated in the reddish-purple grease on top. The reddish-purple borscht reminded Burlane of warm vegetable oil colored with Kool-Aid.

The train passed through more sleet, more snow, and into the sun again.

Late that afternoon, Burlane saw the Urals up ahead. There were places in the United States where the lowest Rockies rose like this, suddenly, up from the plains.

The Urals were low and rounded, much like the Appalachians, and forested largely by conifers that crowded out the ubiquitous birch of the taiga. The mountains looked to Burlane like the coast range of Oregon and Washington or the Rockies at their lowest. Rounded folds rose to higher ridges, the easternmost edge of Europe, beyond which a pale orange orb rose above the distant tridges.

Ludmilla curled up her legs, sipped her tea, and read an English-language edition of William Faulkner's *As I Lay Dying*.

Burlane nursed his tea and watched the Urals. An hour later the train was in a pass of sorts, high up, on a roadbed carved out of the mountains. Once, Burlane saw a derailed train at the bottom of a canyon. The train, far away and tiny, looked like a discarded toy.

Ludmilla looked up from her book and said, 'I would like to go to the United States sometime. Just to see what it's like.' She turned a page. 'I like John Steinbeck too – *The Grapes of Wrath*.'

'Have you read *Uncle Tom's Cabin*?' Burlane asked.

'Oh, yes, Jim. That one was required in school. Jim, did you ever read *As I Lay Dying*?'

'A long time ago.'

'One of Addie Bundren's sons accidentally bored a hole in her forehead while she was in her coffin. I can't figure out which one of the sons it was. I've read it and reread it. My English is not so good, I think.'

Burlane said, 'The mountains where the Bundrens lived are very much like the Urals. Do you like to camp?' Burlane hated camping. Hated the sand and discomfort and bugs.

'Oh, I love to camp, Jim.'

'I think I'm getting hungry again,' Burlane said. In spite of the awful food, Burlane looked forward to mealtime because meals were a break from the monotony of sitting, staring at birch or more birch, sleeping, or standing in the aisle with the other inmates of the railway carriage, carefully ignoring Ginsburg.

When James Burlane and Ludmilla Kormakova entered the diner, Burlane saw they were watched by a black-haired, dapper man. The dapper man sat alone in the crowded car, sipping his tea with contentment while others waited for a seat. He wore brown slacks and a gray sweater. He had large brown eyes. He parted his black hair neatly on one side.

The foreign travelers ate in the second dining car. The travelers in the lead cars were entirely Russian and had the first dining car to themselves. The slightly built Russian man must have eaten in the other diner on the first day. Burlane wondered why he had switched dining cars.

After Burlane and Ludmilla had finished their dinner of mashed potatoes, two small pieces of boiled meat, and

236

a small salad of pickled vegetables, they sat sipping Bulgar, a thick brown drink that tasted like yeasty cider, and that Ludmilla said was made from fermented bread. Then Ludmilla ordered a bottle of sweet, fortified red wine from the Georgian Republic.

No sooner had Ludmilla poured herself half a water glass of wine than she put her hand over the glass and said, 'I'm suddenly not feeling well, Jim. Do you think you could finish this for me: You can join me in a few minutes.'

Burlane said, 'You should never leave a writer alone with a bottle of good wine.' The wine was awful.

When Ludmilla was gone , the black-haired man rose and walked to Burlane's table. He said, 'My name is Felix Jin. Do you suppose I could join you for a few minutes? I see that you are a foreigner, and among other things I collect foreign coins.'

I'll bet, Burlane thought. He said, 'My name is Jim Quint. I'm an American.' Burlane shook Jin's hand, then started digging in his pockets for coins.

'I am a railway official, which is why I speak English.'

'A railway official?' Burlane gave Felix a small handful of change.

'I'm on my way to Nakhodka for a meeting, but I go to Vladivostok first. And you?'

'I'm a journalist. The poet Isaak Ginsburg is in the end car there, the same as me. I'm going to write an article about him.'

'I see. Very interesting. Isaak Ginsburg is very well known in the Soviet Union. Is he well known in America?'

'There've been some articles about him in the maga-zines. Americans want to know all about him.'

'He is very good.'

'I also write adventure novels, spy books. I have this character named Humper Staab. If he's not humping a

237

lady, he's stabbing a bad guy. Americans like that kind of stuff. Sex and violence.' Burlane gave Felix Jin a goofy grin. 'But this is strictly *New Democrat* work. I have to take a break from the fiction once in a while or it gets to me.'

'And you are from where in America?'

'Bison, Montana. Mmmmmm. This is wonderful wine you folks have.'

'Ahh, Montana. That's in the west, isn't it? Cowboys. The pretty lady with you is Russian, is she not?'

'She's my guide. She's with Intourist. A real professional, very helpful,' Burlane said.

Suddenly Bob Steele was standing at Burlane's side. 'Well, Jim Quint!'

Burlane put his foot on Steele's toe and pushed hard. 'Bob, good to see you again.'

Steele removed his foot. 'You should come up and chat, Jim. We've got ourselves a couple of cribbage boards.'

'Hey, thanks for asking. If I get bored later on, I just might do that.' Burlane was affable. He hoped he'd broken Steele's fucking toe.

Bob Steele said good-bye and left the diner, trying not to limp.

After he had gone, Felix Jin said, 'Mr Steele and his friends are having a good time.' He stood. 'It was very pleasant meeting you, Mr Quint. By the way, do you play chess?'

'I used to play a little years ago. I'm not any good.'

'No matter. you'll find that your conductress will have a chess set for you to use. Chess is the national game of the Soviet Union. Perhaps we can play tomorrow. It will give us something to do.' Jin left, heading toward the front of the train.

Ludmilla Kormakova had set Burlane up for a conversation with the charming Comrade Felix Jin. Comrade Jin was KGB. Burlane decided just for the fun of it to let the good comrade wait one more night before he let himself be taped *in flagrante delicto* with Ludmilla.

15

James Burlane's wretched little bladder started complaining an hour after his hormones finally let him fall asleep. He awoke to a high-decibel din of booming and clacking, thundering and banging. Burlane wondered why it was he had had the misfortune to have been born with a little bladder and a big nose. People like Neely and Schott got to sleep all night and shave beneath okay noses in the morning.

How could anybody sleep in this din? Burlane sighed and let his eyes adjust to the darkness. Ludmilla had wrapped the blanket around her, cocoonlike, to keep warm. She was sound asleep, her blanketed form jerking and pitching to the lurching of the train. Burlane put his clothes on and, keeping his eye on Ludmilla, felt along the top of the sliding door of the compartment. Nothing.

Burlane felt along the bottom runner. Oops! There it was, a small switch screwed onto the center of the track. This told the next compartment when somebody opened or closed the door. The KGB had put them near the end of the train so it would be easier to monitor their movements. Burlane assumed one of the compartments would be loaded with cameras to record Ludmilla's seduction of himself. That would no doubt be Compartment Two, between himself and Ginsburg and Natalia Kropotkina.

Burlane slipped his shoes off and got back into bed. His bladder would have to wait. There were some questions he had to consider.

Had Ludmilla been instructed to seduce a writer for

240

the *New Democrat*, or was she stalking James Burlane, agent of the Central Intelligence Agency? The first was probably routine – get pictures for the possibility of blackmail in the future – but the second was malignant. If his cover had somehow been blown, did the KGB know about Isaak Ginsburg? Did the Soviets know Ginsburg had Lenin's head on this railroad car?

Burlane was sure Jin was the chief KGB officer on board. It was very possible that the KGB routinely followed the USSR's famous Jewish poet and were merely uncertain about Burlane – and curious. They would naturally expect spies to slip into Vladivostok for the signing; the city was ordinarily off limits to foreigners. Although the Company had publicly disavowed the use of journalists as cover, the KGB didn't believe that for a moment. Burlane probably wasn't the only journalist the KGB chose to offer a swallow that week.

Burlane slipped his silenced .22 pistol into his pocket – this lethal little weapon designed to Burlane's specifications by a Langley gunsmith. He rose quietly, put his shoes back on, slid the door open, and stepped into the aisle.

Burlane closed the door carefully and grabbed the handrail while he adjusted to the rhythm of the train. This was a hard, quick beat – one-two-three-four, one-two-three-four – like a rhythm set by gorillas pounding metal drums and sledgehammers. It was occasioned by wheels striking rail joints that were slightly askew from the spring thaw and by the hard pounding of traffic. Above the insistent beat was a rhythm brought about by the yanking and jerking of the metal couplers between the cars. This was a rattling THUMP *boom-boom-boom, THUMP boom-boom-boom*.

Burlane made his way to the conductress's end of the car. He stopped beside the huge samovar, which radiated

241

heat in the darkness, and considered the passing taiga. He stepped into the john and was almost overcome by the odor of piss before he could find the light switch. The floor was slimy with urine. The lid was up on the toilet itself and Burlane relieved himself.

Burlane hit the center of the toilet okay. He wondered why Russian men apparently let fly at random, not giving a damn about the poor bastard who came next. Maybe it was because Russian underwear didn't have flies, so Russian men had to pull down the waistband or aim it out the leg. Burlane stepped on the toilet's flush lever and saw that the waste emptied directly onto the tracks below.

Burlane stepped into the aisle again and said 'Jesus Christ!' out loud. He sucked in a welcome lungful of fresh air. He supposed the smelly mess was the result of too damned much vodka. If the soldiers with their fingers on the rocket buttons couldn't shoot any straighter than Russian men could piss, the USSR was in deep, deep trouble.

Colonel Felix Jin turned on the little color television set to review the tapes of Ginsburg and Natalia's evening performance. It was one of the perks of his rank to personally review sex tapes. These tapes gave the KGB blackmail material. The library at Moscow Center had tens of thousands of them.

Natalia Kropotkina was an especially attractive woman, so Jin looked forward to the tape. He turned it on and there was Natalia, modeling a G-string of translucent white nylon for Ginsburg. Jin inadvertently sucked in his breath when he saw her black pubic hair through the nylon.

Ginsburg was on the berth on the camera side of the compartment, and so out of sight of the camera. The effective result was a private performance for Jin as well as the poet; in seconds Jin had an erection. Natalia removed the wispy underpants. Jin made a small, inadvertent sound.

Natalia put on a pair of red bikini panties that had little strings on the hips. Felix Jin got out a bottle of vodka and poured himself a tall drink. He wondered where she got those things. In New York probably; he remembered that her diplomat husband had had a United Nations posting.

Natalia turned her back to Ginsburg and shifted her weight from one hip to the other, then untied a string.

Jin swallowed. The bikini fell. Jin poured himself another hit.

The next panties were black.

A receiver on the floor went *beep! beep! beep!* Jin slammed his hand on a small bar on top. The beeping stopped. 'Yes?' Jin shouted angrily. He punched the hold button on the video.

'Quint has stepped into the hall, Comrade Jin. He is standing in the aisle by the samovar.'

'The alarm functioned properly, I take it?' Jin found it hard to take his eyes off Natalia, frozen on the screen in her black panties. He reversed the tape as he talked to his subordinate.

'Yes, sir, it did.'

'Beep me if the door to Ginsburg's compartment opens or if you hear any kind of tapping going on. Turn your instruments up.' Jin had some more vodka. He punched the control on the recorder again, and Natalia Kropotkina began her strip all over again.

'Comrade Jin, the door to the lead toilet has opened.'

'Call me when he's finished and back in bed, comrade.' Jin went back to Natalia Kropotkina. Then he thought better of it, and turned the machine off. He began pacing in his compartment. He smoked another cigarette, wondering why other men always wound up with the Natalias of the world.

Five minutes later the beeping started again. He was still tense. 'Yes, comrade?'

'He's back in bed, Comrade Jin. One strange thing happened. After he stepped out of the toilet he said, "Jesus Christ."'

'"Jesus Christ"?'

'Yes, comrade.'

'That's all?'

'Yes, comrade. "Jesus Christ."'

'Thank you, comrade. Your instructions remain the same. If anyone moves in that car, I'm to be notified immediately.'

'Yes, Comrade Jin.'

Felix Jin lay back down and adjusted his blankets to preserve the warmth. He listened for a while to the rattling and banging of the train. This was curious indeed. Jim Quint had said 'Jesus Christ.' Was that a Christian prayer of some kind? Was that all there was to it? Why would anybody pray after taking a leak? Pray for what? More than that, was it possible that the author of the Humper Staab books, a reported chaser of women, could be a Christian?

Americans were notorious hypocrites, Jin knew. The Protestants had ignored the slavery in the United States and were currently the most diehard defenders of Pentagon budget requests. Jin was convinced any kind of aberrant behavior was possible from believers in deities; the Poles were a case in point. But what did Christians say in their prayers? Jin didn't know and couldn't remember from his courses on American social customs.

Jin had just reviewed the quickie KGB report on Jim Quint. The report hadn't mentioned Quint being a

Christian, and it was difficult to believe he was one. Was Montana Christian country? No, Christian country was in the American South and the state of Utah. Would a Christian write thrillers? Yes, if it made money. Jin had read stories about Christian ministers who made fortunes with their radio and television programs.

Jim Quint should be taught a lesson or two. Jin would pass word on to Ludmilla to turn on the charm. He wanted her to lure the good Christian into a performance that would really make him pray, although he doubted if Quint and Ludmilla could top Natalia's stunning fashion show.

Jin decided he ought to visit Ginsburg and Natalia the next day. He and Ginsburg knew one another, after all. He was curious about Natalia. It wasn't just that he admired her sexy underpants. He wanted to know why she chose to lug a heavy bronze bust across the Soviet Union. The truth was, all Lenin busts looked the same after a while and everybody knew it.

He should also get to know Jim Quint better, too.

Felix Jin decided he should review the Natalia Kropotkina tape one more time.

16

On the third day out of Moscow and with the Taiga of Omsk somewhere behind them (the encyclopedic Ludmilla Kormakova was not sure if Omsk was east of Eden), James Burlane decided it was time to interview Isaak Ginsburg. Burlane assumed the interview would be recorded by the KGB – or even visited by the dapper little Russian who wanted to play chess.

Late that day – well east of Novosibirsk and with the sun setting behind the train – Burlane stepped into the aisle and rapped on Ginsburg's cabin.

Isaak Ginsburg opened the sliding door. 'Yes?' he asked.

'Mr Ginsburg, I wonder if I might ask for a few minutes of your time this evening. My readers will be curious about a lot of things.'

'I see.' Ginsburg glanced at Natalia.

'They'll want to know about your camp experience and your poetry.' Burlane unfolded his notebook.

'Certainly,' Ginsburg said. He seemed uncertain what to do next.

'We could do it in my compartment if you like.'

Ginsburg said, 'No, no. We can talk here. Won't you come in, Mr Quint?'

It didn't take Robby Burns to tell James Burlane that the best-laid plans of mice and men aft gang agley. Burlane had no sooner stepped into the compartment than he heard Bob Steele yelling cheerfully after him, 'Jim, old man! Quint!'

Burlane turned and leaned into the aisle. 'Yes, Bob?'

'Say, if you're going to interview Comrade Ginsburg, I wonder if I might listen in? You can have all the directs. I'm doing Grigori the Terrible versus Noble Kaplan, but I can use a little color.'

Burlane wondered how it would feel to grab Bob Steele by the throat and shake him a little.

Steele continued blithely on, 'The *Telegraph* likes poets, proper stuff. Be a chap, Jim.'

'If it would be okay with Mr Ginsburg . . . ?'

Isaak Ginsburg said, 'No reason why not.'

Steele shook Ginsburg's hand. 'Bob Steele of *The Daily Telegraph*. Rhyming's quite popular in London. "There once was a man from Khartoum. He took a dyke up to his room. They spent the whole night, arguing who had the right . . ."' He grinned mischievously. He wasn't going to finish the limerick.

Burlane thought, *You son of a bitch*. He said, 'Sit down, Bob.'

Steele stared at Natalia, who wore a dress she had bought in New York. This dress – it was light gray – hung properly, which is to say clung lazily and sensuously, to the curves of Natalia's figure.

Steele stood transfixed, staring, his hand resting on his round belly.

Burlane grabbed him by the shoulder, squeezing as he did, and pulled him to the berth offered by Ginsburg. Steele licked his lips and fumbled for his notebook.

Burlane ignored Steele's attraction to Natalia. He said, 'Mr Ginsburg, my readers will be wanting to know about your experience in a labor camp – how you got there, how it changed you, and so on.'

Ginsburg said, 'It was an education, Mr Quint.' He started to speak again but stopped to acknowledge the entrance of Colonel Felix Jin, who looked neat and dapper in a business suit.

Jin said, 'I see you're having an interview, Mr Quint.'

'It's kind of cramped, but you're welcome as far as I'm concerned. This is Felix Jin, Mr Ginsburg. He's a railway official.' Burlane thought, *Why not? Might as well invite the whole train into the compartment.*

Isaak Ginsburg said, 'Comrade Jin and I have met before.'

Burlane thought, *I'll bet you have, Isaak.*

'I can stand,' Jin said.

'I was telling Mr Quint that my experience at the labor camp at Zima was an education for me, an awakening. I was an egoist when I went in. I wrote poetry for the wrong reasons. A man has no true peace unless he puts the group before himself. The group matters, not individuals.'

'The group?' Jin asked.

'The larger whole, comrade.'

Burlane nudged Steele, who was beginning to embarrass him in his admiration for Natalia Kropotkina.

Jin said, 'What do you think, Mr Steele?'

Steele looked distracted. He struggled to remember the conversation. 'Soup? Large bowl. Perhaps later.'

Oh, shit! Burlane thought. He said, 'Pay attention, Bob, or you won't get any color.'

Both Jin and Natalia grinned. Isaak Ginsburg pretended Steele had said nothing unusual. Burlane thought he'd better let the interview peter out. He said, 'I understand you're designing a pin to commemorate the signing, Mrs Kropotkina.'

'Why, yes, I am,' Natalia said.

Steele was moved to animation by the turn of the conversation. He found Natalia Kropotkina more interesting than a bleeding rhymer. Sod the Russians. 'Yes, I'd like to know about that,' he said.

Natalia put her hand on the bust of Lenin on the table

in front of the window. 'I'll very likely feature this bust, a copy of the one our Comrade Zhukov will give your Secretary of State Kaplan. This is by Ivan Dmitrov, who is doing a monumental Lenin in Moscow. Lovely, is it not, Comrade Jin?'

'Dmitrov is a skilled sculptor,' Jin said.

'Very skilled,' Natalia said. 'There are vastly different problems dealing with a bust this size, and the head of a monument.'

'Or with one of your commemorative pins,' Burlane said.

Natalia laughed. 'Thank you, Mr Quint. But it takes a great deal of courage to tackle a monument. A monument is dramatic and the stakes are high.'

Jin said, 'And the details, Mrs Kropotkina? I was wondering where the details matter the most, in the small or the large – the commemorative pin or the monumental statue?'

Natalia laughed. 'They're most important in a bust this size, life-size. In a monument, you're dealing with broad planes and dramatic light. In a pin, the figures are too small for details.' She put her thumb under the *znachok* on the collar of her dress and pushed it out for Jin to see. 'The cuts are few and subtle, yet this is clearly Lenin, as you can see.' She looked at Burlane with her green eyes.

Burlane said, 'It gets so cold back in Montana that a guy with a real full bladder can piss at a moose and bring it down with icicles. Does it get that bad in this country?'

Jin said, 'Where was it you said you were from in Montana, Mr Quint?'

'Bison,' Burlane said. 'Bison, Montana.'

When they were back in the hall, Bob Steele said, '"And they spent the whole night, arguing who had the right, to do what, with which, and to whom."' He giggled, and leered over his shoulder at Ludmilla, who waited for

Burlane in their compartment. 'Lucky you, Jim. They're giving you the treatment. We get a flatulent male.'

'Ludmilla's real laughs.'

'You have to remember they're taping everything. Still . . .' Steele looked at Ludmilla again. 'If you ever get tired of fucking, you can come on up to our car and drink a little vodka.' He sounded wistful. 'We stocked up when we left Moscow so we could get loaded every night. When in Rome, do as the Romans and all that. Relieves the boredom.' Then he perked up: 'Say, that Comrade Kropotkina's something, isn't she? How'd you like to attack that dress? Pull it right on off. Wasn't that something?'

'Lucky Ginsburg,' Burlane said. Beyond a doubt, somehow, Bob Steele was going to get in his way and cause a whole lot of grief. There wasn't a whole lot Burlane could do about this. He had learned the footprint rule as a rookie, an axiom of his clandestine calling: the best-laid plans of mice and men are almost always covered with the footprints of well-meaning assholes.

Bob Steele said, 'Pecker up, Jim,' and wandered up the aisle towards his own car.

Writers were well known for being loons; craziness was their muse. They were drunks and cockhounds. This was expected of them. The author of the Humper Staab novels would hardly be constantly shy or retiring when presented with a swallow like Ludmilla Kormakova. In order to establish his bona fides as Jim Quint, Burlane knew he would have to give a convincing show of eccentricity. A businessman or a family man might be shy or retiring, but not Quint.

It was time to protect Jim's good name.

Burlane wondered if Ludmilla Kormakova would give him a dissertation on the magnificent length and breadth

250

of Soviet penises. Did Soviet women tilt the Richter scale when they had an orgasm?

Burlane was certain he'd learn all that and more in the night ahead. He stepped inside the compartment.

17

James Burlane slid the door shut. At the click of the latch, his pants began to bulge; he couldn't help it. Burlane wondered what a swallow thought about at a time like this. The weather? How to keep her pussy in the best light for the cameras? What? Did Ludmilla think only of statistics, even now? One more capitalist male seduced and photographed for future blackmail.

Burlane dropped his hand to his belt buckle.

Before he got to the brass button of his Levi's, Ludmilla Kormakova had her sweater off.

The suspected Christian advanced toward Ludmilla. He lurched as the train entered a curve. His engorged member shivered like a Douglas fir in a stiff wind. The KGB swallow stretched out on the narrow berth for his pleasure, her eyes closed.

Burlane turned his swollen unit in the direction of Ludmilla Kormakova's Slavic face. The unit, excited, twitched in anticipation. Burlane slipped it into the softness of Ludmilla's mouth where it shuddered gratefully at the lovely warmth.

Ludmilla's mouth churned, a wonderful washing machine. She paused and looked up, catching Burlane's eyes straight on. 'Do American men like this?' she asked.

'Oh, that's quite charming,' Burlane said. He wondered if he could hold off for the kind of show he wanted to give the comrade photographers in the next compartment.

'Just you and me, Jim.'

'Just you and me, Ludmilla.'

James Burlane thought Ludmilla smelled wonderful.

Her body was extra warm. Her hands and mouth moved lightly over his body pausing here and there, teasing.

Burlane wondered if it might not be possible, during the fun, to aim his behind at one of the KGB lenses close up, so that the Russian on the other side might get to see a vision of himself as in a mirror unadorned by anything except the truth. Burlane could give the Russian a little wink with his buns.

Burlane accepted Ludmilla as a challenge. Did he have it in him to keep up with a KGB sparrow, taking into account his biological handicap in the matter of endurance?

Ludmilla seemed willing to subject herself to anything to make the exhibition more outrageous. Burlane found it hard not to smile when the flushed and sweaty Ludmilla produced bonds and suggested that she be spread-eagled on the floor of the train, which had hit a hard stretch of rail and was jerking wildly to and fro, hammering and banging, hammering and banging. Burlane, brandishing a stuporous but functional third erection of the night, complied with apparent gusto, although he was in fact exhausted and wanted to go to sleep.

Ludmilla Kormakova was unwilling to show mercy until Burlane's game but tuckered unit hung like old glory on a rainy morning – limp, unable to stir. Burlane was pleased by his performance. He had provided Jim Quint with suitably eccentric persona. In fact, he had given the author of the Humper Staab paperbacks a sexual appetite worthy of Harold Robbins or Danielle Steele – Henry Miller even. Quint's fictional Humper Staab would have been hard pressed to keep up.

A few minutes before dawn, exhausted, smelling of Ludmilla, giddy with the memory of her mouth and crotch, James Burlane fell asleep to a *whack, bang! whack, bang!* stretch of tracks.

253

18

Late the next afternoon, James Burlane looked up to see Felix Jin standing at their door. He had a bottle of Stolichnaya vodka in one hand and a chess set in the other. 'Would you like to play a game, Mr Quint? It helps pass the time.'

'Sure,' Burlane said. 'Won't you come in? You can play in here.'

'Well, thank you,' Jin said. He sat on one end of Burlane's small berth and Burlane sat at the other. Ludmilla went to make herself a cup of tea, then returned to watch the game from her berth.

Felix Jin drew white and moved first, leading with his king's pawn.

Burlane blocked him with a pawn.

The nature of the game was established almost immediately. Jin moved quickly to control the center of the board and thus dominate the game. Then he built up the strength and power of his pieces. He did this with ease and efficiency. He was patient. He did not waste moves. He was technically far the better player and soon had both position and strength on Burlane.

Jin poured the vodka. He matched Burlane glass for glass. When a glass was empty, Jin refilled it.

'How long have you been a writer, Mr Quint?'

'Oh, about sixteen years.' That was the correct answer. Burlane wondered how specific a file on Jim Quint the Soviets had been able to gather.

'I see.' Jin moved a knight. 'Did you learn your skills

in college, or do writers and journalists serve some sort of apprenticeship in the United States?'

Burlane considered the board. 'I was a history major at the University of Montana.' Quint had been. Burlane moved. He was impressed by the brutal efficiency of Jin's game. Burlane moved the best he could, striking here, retreating there. He had the saving ability to be able to anticipate Jin's build-up. When Jin took a piece, Burlane was able to retaliate. Burlane did not yield without striking in return.

Felix Jin was calm. He believed Russians could do anything if they put their minds to it and amassed their resources. They had done this in space, athletics, the ballet, the military, the intelligence business. In the first three of these efforts they had, respectively, demonstrated their superior minds, bodies, and culture. In the Red Army and KGB they had demonstrated their power and determination.

James Burlane seemed unperturbable. He didn't make mistakes, even as Jin's development slowly enveloped his king. He moved a rook onto a square that commanded both a critical rank and a critical file and refused to move it. Jin offered him a couple of cripples. Burlane refused to budge.

Jin threatened the rook.

Burlane shifted it slightly but retained its advantage.

Jin decided to go around the rook. Jin had superior power; it could be done. Jin circled the rook and bore down on Burlane's king.

Burlane defended his king, but his position was weakened with each move.

Jin was one move away from mate . . .

. . . when James Burlane casually pushed his rook the length of the board and grinned at Ludmilla.

Jin looked stunned. 'Why, that's mate!' All of Jin's

careful development of power and position had been in vain. His jaw fell. He'd been beaten. How could that have happened?

Isaak Ginsburg was restless. He lay on his bunk wide awake, unable to sleep. He turned onto his right side, then his left, then onto his back, even onto his stomach, which he ordinarily never did. He wanted to see Zima. What if he should miss Zima? What if he should let it go by? Ginsburg could not sleep. He spent the night counting off the stops.

There were small reading lights mounted above the berths, but they were on the window side. By putting his pillow at the other end, Ginsburg could see the leafless tops of the birch at least. After a while he gave up trying to rest and propped his head up. The green fabric roll-up shape on the window of his compartment was stuck in the up position, so he could watch all night long if he wished.

Natalia slept on the other berth, the moonlight shining off her black hair.

Ginsburg could see the front of the train up ahead in the moonlight that lit the Soviet Union from Severnya Zemlya in the north to the Gobi Desert in the south. It was a Russian moon; the hollow eyes and wide face were clearly Slavic, Ginsburg saw. The night was ablaze with stars and there was a circle around the moon. Beside the train, white-barked birches were ghostlike going by, going by, going by.

Boom whacka boom whacka boom! Boom whacka boom whacka boom! Ginsburg lurched against the wall of the compartment as the train hit a rough stretch of track.

The run from Kansk to Tayshet was an eternity of scattered, stunted trees. There was more of the same, if that were possible, from Tayshet to Nizhneudinsk. They

256

reentered the taiga at Tulan on the Iya River. Ginsburg looked at his watch. It was four in the morning; Ginsburg had been staring at the moonlit landscape for six hours. In a half-hour there would be a stop at Kuytun, then two hours later, Zima, on the Oka River.

Ginsburg stood up. He would watch the taiga from the aisle and get some exercise; the station and the lumber camp were both on the aisle side of the train. The big diesels up front were pulling twenty passenger cars and nobody had bothered to line up the cars so the aisles were on the same side. The aisle was on the south side of one car, the north side of the next.

He slipped into his shoes and stepped into the aisle.

Where Felix Jin waited, smoking a cigarette. 'Pleasant night, Comrade Ginsburg.' Jin looked at his watch. 'Or should I have said morning?'

'I shouldn't have drunk all that vodka with Natalia Serafimovna. Makes me pee all night.' The train hit a rough spot as Ginsburg headed for the toilet, and he had to brace his hand against the window. He killed some time in the toilet, cursing Felix Jin.

When Ginsburg got back, Jin took a drag on his cigarette and said, 'I knew you'd want to see when we went past.'

'Zima?'

'What else, a man spends two years in a place like that. He has something happen to him like happened to you. He wants to see what it looks like.'

'I want to see, yes,' Ginsburg admitted. There seemed no point in lying. 'I used to lie awake at night listening to the trains pass.'

'You want to see what the camp looks like from the train. I would, too.'

The engine was momentarily visible in the moonlight,

257

then disappeared around a curve, pulling the necklace of red cars deeper into the maw of the taiga.

Jin said, 'Looks like a mechanical dragon, doesn't it, with the yellow stripe and all.'

A red denizen of Russia, Ginsburg thought, forged by the hammer, carrying tractors to fields where peasants still harvested by sickle. That and soldiers to watch the restless Chinese. He said, 'Roaring dragon.'

Felix Jin unfolded the small seat under the window and sat, his shoulder against the glass. He looked up ahead, at the front of the train. 'So many birch, Ginsburg. Hour after hour after hour we travel. The birch never seem to stop. Have you ever wondered how many there are? As many birch as Russians who died in the Great Patriotic War, do you suppose?'

'The birch are survivors,' Ginsburg said.

'As were the residents of Leningrad. We have a hard life in the Soviet Union, Ginsburg. We know the cold. Napoleon did his best to conquer us. The Germans tried twice. We stood fast each time. We know hardship. We work together.'

The train entered another wide curve. The track did not run flat out, straight and true, as do the Union Pacific and Burlington Northern on their way across the prairies and farmlands of North America. The Trans-Siberian meandered through the taiga en route to isolated towns on the banks of cold, slow rivers.

Jin said, 'I grew up in Irkutsk, you know. But of course you would have no way of knowing that. My paternal great-grandfather was Mongolian, which is how I came by my surname.'

'You told me.'

'Being a Jin can be a burden, as you can imagine.' As they were approaching the stop at Kuytun, Jin said, 'After that business in Red Square, the KGB checked the hotel records in Perm. They wondered who might have been visiting the cancer clinic, you know. I see you spent a night there on your way to Moscow from Novosibirsk.'

'I was working on an epic poem about the spirit of transformation. There is a dramatic valley of isbas to the east of Perm overlooked by a ridge of progressive communal apartments.'

'I read the poem in *Novy Mir*. Very clever. By the way, Ivan Shepelev, the man who rode with you from Moscow, remembered you clearly. He said you were carrying a bag that was so heavy the straps dug into your shoulders. What was in that bag, Comrade Ginsburg?'

'Some Ukrainian wine for literary colleagues in Perm, comrade.'

The train slowed for the five-minute stop at Kuytun. The platform was nearly empty. Some men whose breath came in frosty puffs unloaded some boxes from one of the cars down the line. A woman gave instructions over a loudspeaker. Ginsburg wondered if Olga would be working the night shift at Zima.

Ginsburg remembered talking to Lado Kabakhidze in their cell at Zima. Neither Ginsburg nor Kabakhidze had any responsibility while they were imprisoned in the camp. They did as they were told. Their only goal was to survive. They worked as little as they could get away with. They chiseled, hoarded, swapped, or stole what they could. Some of them snitched on their friends to please the guards.

Life was hard. The *zeks* made do.

The train left Kuytun.

The system at the Zima lumber camp was so designed as to encourage and reward the worst behavior both by prisoners and their guards, thus insuring Captain Mikheyev's authority and power. Ginsburg wanted to tell Felix Jin that in those essentials, Zima was the Soviet

Union in miniature, a prison inside a prison. Ginsburg wanted to tell Jin that all he was trying to do was give the Russian people the Lenin they had been promised and denied. They had been promised their humanity. They had received Jins and Mikheyevs.

If Lado Kabakhidze were still alive, Ginsburg knew, he would be proud of his daughter, Nina. Nina was fighting back.

Outside, the Siberian landscape rushed by.

Felix Jin said, 'I was wondering why Mrs Kropotkina is lugging that heavy Lenin bust across the Soviet Union.'

Ginsburg looked surprised. 'She's to do a Vladivostok commemorative pin. That's the copy of Ivan Dmitrov's bust.'

'Does she really need that? For a little pin?' Jin was not convinced.

'She is proud of doing good work. When she does a *znachok*, she wants to do it exactly right,' Ginsburg said.

'I see.'

In time the Trans-Siberian Express was upon Zima and pulled into the dimly lit station. A lone man bundled in a heavy coat stood on the platform. Felix Jin smoked and said nothing. The dispatcher's office summoned carman Rosnoveyev to the brakeman's shack. A woman's amplified voice echoed among the buildings.

Olga. Nothing had changed.

If his plan worked, if Ginsburg got Lenin's head out of the Soviet Union and somehow escaped himself, he would find a way to smuggle a pretty Western dress to Olga. He didn't want to meet Olga especially, didn't care to know what she looked like. He liked her the way she was, an abstraction and so without flaws, a reminder of the Russian warmth and compassion that endured in spite of all the hard times and suffering.

The train began moving, began rolling. The whacking

260

and banging gained momentum. The station gave way to the sprawl of peasants' isbas. The camp was at the edge of the wretched shacks; the cutting whorl of the barbed wire looped atop the outer wooden fence was clearly visible in the Siberian moonlight.

Jin lit another cigarette. 'There it is, Comrade Ginsburg.'

'Yes, there it is.' Zima. Ginsburg thought:

> The Möbius strip of barbed wire
> Had two sides that were one,
> Had no beginning, no end.
> Circled all of Russia.
> Truth cut.
> Truth went
> Snip-snip,
> Snip-snip,
> Snip-snip,
> At the bloody snarl
> That seemed to have no end.

19

A blonde without a hint of smile lines was to take
them from the Irkutsk Intourist Hotel to the May Day
demonstrations in Lenin Square. James Burlane had
joined Bob Steele and the other journalists, and they
were chatting among themselves when the blonde, who
had been eavesdropping, said, 'A parade? Who told you
that?' Then, with tourists looking on in amusement, if
not amazement, the journalists were singled out for
special attention:

'You are to understand that this is not a parade,' she
said. 'These are spontaneous public demonstrations. The
citizens of Irkutsk themselves do this to show their
support for workers of the world. Is that understood? Is
that clear? We have a parade in November to celebrate
the Revolution.'

'I see,' Steele said on behalf of the contingent of
journalists.'

'There will be no tanks or rockets today. Come back in
November for that.'

Steele, amused, dutifully noted: 'Demonstrations, not
a parade.' He had been given to understand that the May
Day celebrants would follow one another through the
streets of Irkutsk, which was his definition of a parade.

The guide turned and pushed her way through the
heavy glass doors of the hotel, and began walking north –
downstream as the Angara flowed – followed by the
journalists, then the tourists. The Englishman from the
London *Times* gave Bob Steele a nudge with his elbow.
'Stout show, Bob!'

Burlane noted that Felix Jin had chosen not to attend the demonstrations.

They walked along the sidewalk; the Angara was on their left. It was a swift, broad river. The roofs of the deteriorating shacks and decaying warehouses and leafless trees etched the skyline on the ridge beyond the river. The journalists and tourists walked into a steady, cold wind.

There seemed to be militiamen and soldiers and roadblocks everywhere, but the contingent from Irkutsk Intourist Hotel was allowed by without a fuss.

The tourists were taken to a roped-off area on the sidewalk at one end of the large Lenin Square. The Intourist guide took the journalists, Isaak Ginsburg, and Natalia Kropotkina to the bleachers where local and regional officials were gathered.

The journalists waited in the bleachers. There was a Russian Orthodox church to their left, and an impressive fountain straight ahead. When they sat, Bob Steele managed to plant himself beside Burlane.

'So how's your story coming, Jim?'

'Ginsburg's a wonderful poet, he really is. You have to give it to him.' Burlane's face told Steele nothing.

Steele winked at Burlane. 'Remember the time I took you down to Soho and we got pissed on scotch and watched chaps with earrings and green hair?'

Burlane wished Steele wasn't quite so eager to participate in his Jim Quint cover. Unfortunately, Steele was both human and a newspaperman. Burlane knew he wasn't about to drop his curiosity. Burlane could hardly blame him; in Steele's shoes, Burlane would want to know also. Burlane said, 'You drank scotch, Bob. I smoked a joint.'

When the group of visitors and foreign journalists left the hotel – Ginsburg, Natalia Kropotkina, and Jim Quint among them – Felix Jin knew it was time. He checked his wristwatch. He would have at least an hour, even if they decided to return early from the demonstrations. That was unlikely, Jin knew. Ginsburg would be reading a commemorative poem from the people's dais and so would have to sit with the officials until the very end. The same was true of Quint, who would be obliged to stay with the press corps.

Colonel Jin dialed a number on the room phone and said, 'Now, please.' He hung up and took an elevator to the fifth floor, where four men waited with heavy leather briefcases. Jin and two of the men went into Isaak and Natalia's room. The other two went to Jim Quint's room.

Jin settled into a chair and smoked a cigarette while the two men began the search of Isaak and Natalia's room. The other two went to Jim Quint's room.

Jin settled into a chair and smoked a cigarette while the two men began the search of Isaak and Natalia's room. He said, 'If they're smuggling something and you don't find it, we'll send you to mine gold at Kolmya.'

The two KGB technical men set to work with Jin's admonition ringing in their ears.

Jin smoked and watched the search, wondering again if Natalia Kropotkina really needed to drag that heavy bronze bust all the way to Vladivostok and back. He snubbed out one cigarette and lit another as a tech man examined colored pencils under a microscope that he had unpacked from his briefcase. Another man, using a slender wire, checked the interior of tubes of watercolor. They checked the soles of shoes. They checked the seams of clothing with an electromagnet plugged into the wall.

The technician who found Natalia Kropotkina's collection of sexy underwear held up a pair of transparent red panties. He grinned. 'Artistic decadence!'

Jin and the other technician laughed.

Colonel Jin called for tea and lit a third cigarette. Jin began to sweat. He stood and paced. He sat when the tea arrived. 'We'll save this for last,' he said. He put the heavy Ivan Dmitrov sculpture in his lap. The larger-than-life size of the bust increased its impressiveness correspondingly. Jin looked at his wristwatch. 'Better hurry, comrades,' he said.

Jin decided that when he left, he'd send the technicians on ahead and pocket Natalia's sexy underwear for the computer specialist in seclusion. Vera would appreciate panties like that. Natalia Kropotkina was married to a foreign service officer; she could always get more.

Finally Jin could stand the suspense no longer. 'Would you give me one of your hammers, please? Thank you.' The bottom of the bust was fitted into a wooden base. Jin turned the bust upside down and held it with his arm. He began tapping at the wood. The base popped off.

Nothing!

Jin slumped in his chair. He'd allowed himself to become convinced the heavy bust was the answer to the mystery. Jin picked up the telephone and dialed a number. He said, 'I will remind you again that I want the transcript of the Quint-Steele conversation as soon as it's ready. I want to know everything they said.'

20

The local party chief, Ivan Zlokazov, arrived at last, and officials began a series of speeches. They were pleased, they said, that Irkutsk was in the world spotlight that day; they were pleased that so many foreign journalists were there to witness the demonstrations. They were especially pleased to have as their guest Isaak Ginsburg, who would be reading a commemorative poem in Vladivostok. The peace-loving people of Irkurtsk were proud to stand side by side with the working people of the world.

While the spontaneous demonstration was being organized stage left, down a boulevard that led into the square, Zlokazov, a small man in a bulky blue coat loaded with colorful ribbons and medals, began a small dissertation on the wonders of Lake Baikal obviously intended for the visiting journalists.

Zlokazov began by stating that Lake Baikal, the deepest lake in the world, contained one-sixth of the world's supply of fresh water, and had more fresh water than any other lake in the world, including all of the American Great Lakes combined. This was the third or fourth time Burlane had heard that statement, or variations of it. Burlane wondered what foreigners were supposed to make of it. Were the Soviets going to poison everybody's water and demand that thirsty people pledge their allegiance to Lenin? Were the Soviets now able to halt the rain? Who gave a damn?

Comrade Zlokazov talked about the special meaning Lake Baikal had to the people of Irkutsk. There were

1200 species of animals in the lake that were found nowhere else in the world. Lake Baikal contained the world's only fresh-water seal. The sturgeon in Lake Baikal grew to be 500 pounds. Lake Baikal contained the unique gwyniad, *Coregonus omul*, a white relative of the salmon. Zlokazov told of the lake's 280 varieties of shrimplike crustaceans, of strange worms, of the millions of flightless, waterborne insects called *rucheiniki*. The *rucheiniki* remained in the larval state for two or three years before they embarked on their two- to three-hour life span – that is, assuming they weren't eaten by an *omul* their first minute out. He told about *bikerit*, a kind of inflammable wax that floated on the water. Zlokazov said there was a fish in the lake so transparent that one could read *Pravda* through its slender body. Lake Baikal contained four kinds of emerald-colored sponges. The finest sables in Siberia roamed its shores.

Bob Steele mumbled, 'So what's the bloody point, comrade?'

The man from the London *Times* said, 'The sod's giving us a biology lecture.' He put down his ball-point pen.

Zlokazov told about pop-eyed fish with eyes like giant bugs that lived between seven hundred and sixteen hundred feet below the surface of Lake Baikal where the temperature was a comforting thirty-eight degrees Fahrenheit. The females gave birth to two thousand live offspring. When all these fish eventually died, they sank to the bottom of Lake Baikal, adding to the silt that was five thousand feet deep in places. Zlakozov paused for the kicker to the story of the deep-living, pop-eyed fish. 'This silt has allowed socialist scientists to calculate that Lake Baikal was formed twenty-five million years ago in the Tertiary Period, making it the oldest lake in the world.'

Comrade Zlokazov finally wound down:

'The workers of Irkutsk have a special mission to preserve this most beautiful and unique lake in the world. We hold that trust dear.'

This recitation of facts – humbling both the Galápagos Islands and the Great Lakes – was intended to give the foreign journalists a biggest-and-best Irkutsk peg for their stories. The assembled Russian guests applauded warmly, if not overenthusiastically; the bizarre facts of Lake Baikal were always recited when foreigners were present.

Ginsburg was now escorted to the microphone and introduced as 'a modern Russian master.'

James Burlane scribbled notes with professional aplomb.

At the speaker's dais, Ginsburg stood before the microphone to address the empty square before him; the residents of Irkutsk were either assembling for the demonstration, or humble spectators gathered along Karl Marx Prospekt a half-mile away. Ginsburg's reading was for the comrades and their guests in the bleachers.

Isaak Ginsburg recited a long, passionate poem about Lake Baikal. When Ginsburg had finished, and the applause had abated, the unsmiling Intourist guide handed each writer a copy of the text – translated into English, French, and German – together with explanations of various allusions.

Finally the band began playing stirring music. Nine young people entered the square carrying enormous photographs of local party officials and an even larger photograph of V.I. Lenin.

This was followed by a series of young people in bright costumes of primary colors: yellow, red, green, blue. They held color-coordinated flags, cards, plastic balls, or hula hoops. Once assembled before the bleachers, they did synchronized routines with the flags, cards, balls, or hula hoops. They waved their arms and kicked their legs high and did calisthenics in choreographed unison.

'I like the spontaneity,' Steele said.

Burlane said, 'It's the spirit of community.'

The young men did enthusiastic push-ups, squat-jumps, and jumping-jacks to music played over the loudspeaker. They ran in place, kicking their legs high, moving as one. A man on the loudspeaker told about their schools, how old they were, and how pleased they were to demonstrate their solidarity with the working people of the world.

Comrade Zlokazov and those assembled in the bleachers applauded politely.

When each group finished its routine it continued around the square and left, heading for Karl Marx Avenue, a half-mile away, where the local residents waited to see some of the color.

After nearly an hour, a mass of Irkutsk citizens brought up the rear. They were dressed in red, most of them, and waved enormous red flags and banners that proclaimed peace. The silken flags and banners furled dramatically in the cold wind.

Burlane said, 'A nice break from riding the train, eh, Bob?'

'This is precisely the kind of stuff I was after. I was impressed by the spontaneity.'

'I was impressed by the drama,' Burlane said.

After they were released from the demonstrations, Isaak Ginsburg and Natalia Kropotkina joined the citizens of Irkutsk on the parklike promenade beside the Angara River. The cold wind that had cut through Irkutsk earlier had subsided; the sun was warming, and the local residents, having a day off, were out for a stroll. The promenade was nicely landscaped, but the trees had not yet begun to leaf out.

Ginsburg and Natalia passed three couples out together, drunk; the men carried the vodka in paper bags. Two of the young women were drunker than the rest. The couples talked loudly, the young women giggling nonstop. They staggered, laughing, tripping, bumping into one another. One of the young men, Ginsburg thought, looked ill and lagged behind momentarily, apparently to calm alcohol-induced nausea.

Ginsburg and Natalia, accompanied by the screeching of sea gulls that floated over the river, walked down one of the concrete stairways that led to the rocky shore. These stairs were spaced about every hundred yards along the promenade. To their left, upstream of the Intourist Hotel, a mob of people waited in line for an open-topped boat that took short tours on the river.

Below them, halfway to the tour boat landing, a small boy squatted by the side of the river. He was imitating the screech of sea gulls. Ginsburg and Natalia sat at the base of the stairs, not wanting to disturb him. He was no more than ten or twelve years old and cupped his hands around his mouth as he made the call.

A white gull, aloft above the water, gave a poignant cry in return.

The boy called. The Angara rushed swiftly by, deep and frigid.

The gull answered, the water far below it.

'Maybe he'll be a naturalist,' Natalia said of the boy.

'Maybe he'll have a gull act in the circus,' Ginsburg said. No Soviet circus was complete without a dove act. These were always performed by pretty girls, who pulled white doves out of hats, bags, boxes, whatever, and threw them into the air. These doves, joined by more birds pitched into the air from the wings, nearly always settled on the pretty girls' shoulders and extended arms while sweet music played and the accompanying narration over

270

the loudspeaker talked about peace and the peace-loving Soviet Union.

Natalia looked up at the retaining wall at the edge of the promenade. The man they had noticed earlier was sitting on the wall looking down on them.

Ginsburg and Natalia returned to the promenade and continued downstream, followed by the man who had watched them from above. They were about to take another flight of stairs to the shore, when another drunk stumbled up onto the sidewalk from the river. He lurched this way and that. His face was a horror. He had pitched forward onto the shore and the right side of his face was bloody, a shredded mass of raw flesh. The blood was mixed with dirt and gravel. His right eye was closed. He had not been mugged or beaten. He had simply tripped. He grinned crookedly, using only the good side of his mouth.

A group of five May Day celebrants, themselves inebriated, parted to avoid the lurching drunk. Other than stepping lightly aside, they seemed not to have noticed him. It was as though he were invisible and the blood and raw flesh didn't exist. Only one young man looked back. He took a bottle of vodka from his jacket and took a long, hard drink.

21

The temperature plunged quickly after dark, and by the time they were taken to the Irkutsk station at nine o'clock, it was downright cold. As before, Burlane and Ludmilla, and Ginsburg and Natalia were placed in the end car. Like the train they had ridden from Moscow, this version of the Trans-Siberian Express was also called the Rossiya. When Burlane and his guide entered their compartment, Burlane saw the familiar camera hole in the wall. It was the same car.

After he and Ludmilla had settled into their compartment, Burlane checked his map and saw that Irkutsk was located 50 miles northwest of the southern tip of Lake Baikal – the Angara being a north-flowing Siberian river. The lake itself – from 25 to 50 miles wide and 350 miles long – ran from southwest to northwest. Burlane wanted to watch the passing of Lake Baikal, but it was more than an hour before the train reached the southern tip of the lake.

When the train turned east and the pine forests of the Khamar Daban Ridge rose steeply outside the compartment, Burlane knew they had reached the shore of Lake Baikal.

'Are you going to look at the lake, Jim?' Ludmilla asked.

'I think so. Give me a chance to stretch my legs.' Burlane stepped into the aisle and there, below him, was the frozen surface of Lake Baikal, a great calm under the moonlight. Burlane stood, turning his map toward the light, while Ludmilla sat on one of the fold-down seats.

The train went in and out of a tunnel, one of a series of tunnels through the steep ridges that bordered the lake. These tunnels were guarded at both ends by barbed wire and soldiers with machine guns – standard security, Burlane knew, for Soviet tunnels.

'Lake Baikal is the deepest lake in the world,' Ludmilla said as they looked at the expanse of ice in the moonlight.

Burlane wondered if he was condemned to a repetition of the impressive facts of Lake Baikal. He was.

Ludmilla said, 'This lake holds one-fifth of the world's supply of fresh water. That has been established. It is the oldest lake in the world.'

'The speaker at the demonstration today told us it was one-sixth.'

'Yes, Jim, one-sixth. He was right.'

'He told us all about the wonderful biology of the lake,' Burlane said.

'The white-fleshed *omul* lives here. It is a relative of the salmon. One of the most delicious fish in the world. Lake Baikal has four kinds of emerald-colored sponges and the world's only fresh-water seal,' she said.

Ludmilla's recitation of Soviet onlys and bests was pushing Burlane to the edge. 'Do you understand the English word lobotomy?' he asked.

Ludmilla considered the question. 'No, I don't believe I do, Jim. English vocabulary is very hard to learn. Is it a kind of drink?'

'Makes you sleepy, they say,' Burlane said.

'In Khabarovsk there is a kind of vodka that has ginseng in it. It – what is the American expression? – yes, it will put lead in your pencil, Jim.' Ludmilla brushed her breast lightly against Burlane's arm, then again. The second time she let it linger.

This casual gesture and others like it, at first provocative in the extreme, had become annoying as the birch

273

trees and hours and firsts and biggests passed. Burlane had thought Texas bragging was a bore. Texans were modest, retiring, in comparison with the Russians. If Ludmilla would include more claims like the aphrodisiac Khabarovsk vodka, her patter might be tolerable.

For example, Burlane, who had studied the history of the railroad for his assignment, knew that Lake Baikal was the last link finished in the trans-Siberian run. In 1904, with Russian forces under siege by the Japanese at Port Arthur in Manchuria, the czar's engineers laid extra-wide ties across the ice and tried to get an engine across. The resulting hole in the ice was five feet wide and fourteen miles long. Burlane smiled at the idea of the Russians cursing in frustration as their train sank slowly under the ice.

The train left Lake Baikal in the early hours of the morning and entered into a forest of fir, pine, and larch. The passing of the wonderful lake brought with it two bounties: the end of Ludmilla's regurgitation of Baikal facts and the end of the taiga. The day turned out to be the most beautiful stretch of the six-thousand-mile trip.

As they passed Petrovsk-Zabaykal'skiy, Burlane asked the ever ready Ludmilla about the telephone poles sitting atop metal stakes driven into the ground. He assumed it had to do with permafrost, and he was right.

Ludmilla looked serious indeed. 'This is because of permafrost, Jim. When there is permafrost we cannot bury a telephone pole in the ground. In winter, the top of the ground freezes down to the permafrost and increases in volume at the same time. The surface lifts, Jim, ten centimeters, sometimes twenty. A pole would lift with the ground and a what-do-you-call-it would form beneath it.'

'A cavity.'

'That's the word, Jim. Cavity. In the summer, when

the ground thaws, the pole can't settle because dirt will have filled the cavity. After a few years the pole would pop out of the ground.'

'You have problems with roads and railway tracks, I assume.'

'Yes, Jim. The bed is soft in the springtime. It gives.'

And so it did. The intensity of the whacking, banging, and jerking of the Trans-Siberian increased as it plunged farther into Siberia.

The train reached Chita shortly after noon and followed along the Shilka River, a tributary of the Amur. The river was a dramatic steamy haze, beneath which great blocks of ice crunched and bumped their way downstream – to the northeast – moving more quickly at the center than at the shores. Low hills on the sides of the river were topped by Korean pines turned white from a hoary frost. Everything was white: the sparse grass, fence posts, raised telephone posts. A warming morning sun shone from the pale blue sky. Burlane squinted at the wonderful white of the lovely valley.

Even the hoary frost of the Shilka River got boring. Burlane took naps and tried not to think about the fried eggs. Burlane was sick of eggs, sick of the hot little metal thingies they came in, sick of the yolks looking up at him, sick of the tepid yellow oil. He wondered how the Russians tolerated all that oil. The borscht had come more and more to resemble dishwater. How could the Soviets endure eating everything canned or pickled? Burlane thought of the vegetable section of an American supermarket. He longed for fresh fruit and vegetables. He thought of pears. Burlane loved pears.

Late in the afternoon, the train slowed for a bend and came suddenly upon yet another desolate town that did not qualify for mention on all maps, much less rate a stop on the run from Moscow to Vladivostok. The rough-cut, unpainted isbas each had its fence, its pile of birch firewood, its diminutive garden plot. Thin wisps of smoke trailed up from the metal chimneys.

Then, suddenly, Him, Lenin, on the side of a building. The red background of the portrait shimmered, luminous, bloodlike, a rose of communism against the dreary ochres and umbers of mud and winter swamps and leafless trees and weathered shacks.

Burlane didn't feel like giving the KGB another memorable performance with the perfect socialist woman. As the evening wore on, Burlane wondered what he should do. At last it came to him. 'My newspaper friend, Bob Steele, has invited me to drink vodka with him and his journalist friends tonight. I think I'll take them up on it.

'Oh, Jim, I got us some vodka today. We have plenty of vodka right here.' Ludmilla lifted her hinged berth and dug a bottle from the luggage stored below. 'Stolichnaya vodka is the most famous in the world. The Soviet Union makes the best vodka in the world, also the most millions of liters, did you know that? We have more kinds as well. Some of them are named for animals. We have what you would call grouse vodka. We even have a bison vodka, Jim. We have brown vodka and yellow vodka. There is a proper kind of vodka to drink with each kind of wild mushroom.'

Burlane had heard Russians were bonkers about wild mushrooms. He didn't want to trigger a dissertation about fungi in the Soviet Union. He said, 'I wouldn't want to disappoint Bob. I told him I'd join them tonight.'

Although James Burlane knew his conversations with Ludmilla Kormakova were taped, he was still surprised to find Felix Jin waiting in Bob Steele's compartment along with Steele and a tall, blond man with thick eyeglasses and a bemused look on his long face.

276

Steele was pleased to see Burlane. 'Are you joining us tonight, Jim? Good. Good. Mr Jin dropped by for a chat and I invited him to join us. The others are up front somewhere. I think they met some women.'

'Having their pictures taken perhaps,' said the man with the eyeglasses. He grinned at Jin.

Steele said, 'This is Wim Brouwer, Jim. Wim likes to kid. He's with *de Telegraaf* in Amsterdam.'

'Pleased to meet you, Wim.' Burlane shook hands and accepted a glass of vodka from Bob Steele.

Steele said, 'Mr Jin, you told us you work for the railroad, but you didn't say what you do.'

'Do tell us you're not with SMERSH, comrade,' said Brouwer.

Felix Jin laughed. 'You've been reading too much James Bond, Mr Brouwer. Although it is true that I am a detective, of sorts. I work with contraband smuggling on trains. We have a very low rate of crime in the Soviet Union, as you know, but we have an occasional problem the same as everyone else.'

Brouwer said, 'The Soviet crime rate is far lower than Europe's, our guide told us.'

'So it is reported,' Jin said.

'Is somebody smuggling something on this train?' Steele asked.

Jin said, 'As a matter of fact, there is.'

'A mystery!' Burlane said.

'On the Trans-Siberian Express!' Wim Brouwer poured himself some more vodka.

'Indeed,' Jin said.

Bob Steele refilled Jin's glass and his own. 'What is it you're looking for, Mr Jin?'

Jin looked embarrassed. 'I shouldn't have mentioned it in the first place.'

'Surely you won't care if we speculate,' Steele said.

Wim Brouwer rubbed his large hands together. 'Good idea, Bob.'

'As you like,' Jin said.

Steele said, 'Let's start with Wim, then. What are you smuggling, Wim? You look guilty to me. Look at those glasses and the size of your hands.'

'My shaving cream can is filled with cocaine. I say Mr Jin is after drug smugglers. Is that what you're after, meneer?'

Jin smiled. 'We rarely encounter drug smugglers in the Soviet Union.'

'All you Amsterdamers are druggers. Jim Quint? Your turn, Mr Author.' Steele pinned Burlane with his eyes and grinned mischievously. 'Surely you can come up with something good.'

'Look at him sweat.' Brouwer was having fun. He said, 'Everybody knows Americans are guilty as hell. Just look at him.'

Burlane put his finger on his lip and considered the question. 'I'm smuggling microfilms of the Russian SS-twenty rocket. They're hidden inside hollow buttons on my shirts. Humper Staab has a shirt with buttons like that.'

'You shouldn't read your own books, Mr Quint,' Jin said. 'And how about yourself, Mr Steele? Do you have a confession?'

Bob Steele said, 'You know that bust of Lenin Mrs Kropotkina is carrying with her? I'll bet you thought that was cast bronze. Well, it isn't. It's pure Russian gold. I'll be doing much in-out with Natalia after we get the bust out of the country.'

Wim Brouwer said, 'Meneer Quint doesn't have to rely on fantasy, judging from the looks of his Intourist guide. You must have contacts we don't, meneer.'

'I was fortunate. Ludmilla's quite professional,' Burlane said. He grinned at Jin.

'She seems to be,' Jin said.

Brouwer said, 'Looks like talent to me.'

'Quite a little performer, I'll bet,' said Bob Steele.

When his head threatened to spin a half hour later, James Burlane decided it was time to go to bed. He said his good-byes and started down the aisle, holding on to the rail for help. Behind him, he heard Felix Jin, who was in his cups, ask, in his heavily accented English, 'Why is not a woman like a man?'

Bob Steele and Wim Brouwer were still laughing when Burlane closed the door that led to the next car. His trip was a success; he was so loaded from his night with the boys that he wouldn't be able to perform for Comrade Number Cruncher.

22

The next morning, Ludmilla Kormakova entered her sixth day of reciting unknown facts of Siberia. As far as the hungover Burlane could see, Ludmilla was encyclopedic; she had lost no momentum. Her commentary continued without mercy: X thousands of sable pelts were produced annually in this region; Y millions of cubic yards of coal were mined in that area. The Soviets weighed gold by metric tons. They milled lumber by the trillions of board-meters.

There seemed to be a prestigious research laboratory every mile of the trip. Burlane was told the advances made by the Zabaykal'skiy Combined Scientific Research Institute in Chita, as well as the Forest Economy Laboratory of the Siberian Department of the Academy of Sciences.

'Oh, well, that's very interesting,' Burlane said, looking out at wretched shacks that would have embarrassed a dog in Appalachia.

'Darasun is famed for its mineral springs, Jim. It is said to be one of the best treatments in the world for abdominal, intestinal, and cardiovascular ailments. This water has been exported to China and Korea since ancient times.'

Burlane made a note. 'Oh, heavens!' He learned about gold in Vershino-Darasunskoye, about fluoric spar in the village of Usugli, about molybdenum ore deposits at Busheley. Except for gold, Burlane had no idea what these minerals were.

'Despite this great wealth, there are some drawbacks

to Siberia, Jim. In winter the temperature can drop to minus sixty of your American degrees Fahrenheit. When you exhale, the air crackles because your breath turns into ice crystals that explode with a snapping sound. In the summer the sun turns wood to charcoal and burns off grasslands.' Ludmilla paused in her commentary. 'Yes, here we are passing the village of Skovorodino, Jim. This was named in memory of A.N. Skovorodin, who was the first president of the village council of workers' deputies.'

At the impoverished sprawl of shacks called Blagoveshchensk, Ludmilla said, 'Here we have medical, agricultural, and pedagogic institutions.' Ludmilla consulted a small booklet. 'There is a polytechnical and an agricultural college, a financial-technical college, a teachers' college, and a college of civil engineering. We have the Far Eastern Branch of the Siberian Department of the Academy of Sciences, the Blagoveshchensk Latitude Laboratory of the Principal Astronomic Observatory of the Academy of Sciences, and the Far Eastern Zonal Veterinary Institute.'

That such a wretched hole should have such grand institutions seemed pathetic and ludicrous to Burlane. He nodded gravely and took notes on the confusing jumble of Russian words.

'You see the bog outside. This is a *bolotnaya tryassina*, Jim. This means marshy swamp. The grass and shrubs form a thick, elastic carpet. You can walk on this and it won't break through; it gives, then comes back again, so that it's like walking on green waves.'

'I bet that's a first. To be honest, I never did believe that business about the Red Sea,' Burlane said. 'If you don't mind, Ludmilla, I think I should go to bed early tonight. I have a headache.'

Burlane saved his smile until he had turned under his blanket and was facing away from Ludmilla. He wondered if he might not have nightmares of copulating with a woman who turned out to be a computer. He did not dream that. Worse, he dreamed of a naked blonde on a scarlet bed. Her smile was for Burlane alone. She beckoned with a languid hand. She called, softly:

'First! Biggest! Longest! Tallest! Widest! Oldest! Best! Only! World famous! Acclaimed! Fastest! Most accurate! Most unusual! Finest! Most beautiful!'

Burlane awoke with a start, sweating.

The train was stopped at a station.

A woman was giving workers their instructions over a loudspeaker. The sound of her loudspeaker voice with Russian v's and z's echoed off a building.

In a few hours it would be daylight again, then only one night before Vladivostok. Colonel Felix Jin sipped his tea and considered the hunks of ice in the Amur River floating under moonlight, floating northwest toward the Sea of Okhotsk and the Pacific Ocean. He took another sip. He was down to the dregs. Jin gave the buzzer two quick stabs, a signal to his aide that he would like another cup.

Moments later there was a respectful knock on the compartment door; Colonel Jin rose to accept the tea. He settled back with it as the train entered a small forest of Korean pine. Jin unfolded the East German drawings of the soft-class car and for what seemed like the thousandth time considered the interior design.

Isaak Ginsburg's compartment had been disassembled and put back together at the May Day stop in Irkutsk. KGB technicians had done the same with the compartment occupied by whoever it was who was calling himself Jim Quint. The technicians found nothing. They had disassembled and reassembled the conductress's compartment. Nothing. In fact, Jin had ordered railway workers

282

to disassemble the underside of the car and the roof, looking for . . .

What? Jin held out the palm of his hand and weighed the imaginary object just as Valery Karpov had done that day.

If Jin retrieved whatever had been removed from the tomb, well then . . . Felix Jin had always wanted a nice dacha on the Volga where he could fish in July, forage for wild mushrooms in September, possibly, or hunt deer in October. Jin had always wanted to travel in the West to see what it was like. That too was possible with success. On the other hand, if he failed – even if he didn't know what he was looking for – Jin was doomed.

Colonel Jin would not lose this contest as he had lost the chess match with Jim Quint. Jin had position and strength; the train and everybody in it were his. As a matter of fact, Jin had Ginsburg in check. Ginsburg was trapped. At Vladivostok, he would be vulnerable. He would have to try to escape with whatever it was he was concealing.

Jin folded the East German drawings and turned his attention to the transcripts of the conversations between Isaak Ginsburg and Natalia Kropotkina and between Jim Quint and Ludmilla Kormakova. He finished his tea.

Felix Jin put down his eyeglasses and massaged his eyes. He looked at the ice on the Amur. He put his glasses on and read some more. He ordered more tea. He read some more. The tea came. He sipped it and rang for his aide.

Jin said, 'Pavel, how long has the conductress been boiling this water? It tastes like yak piss.'

23

The next morning Burlane lingered under his blanket pretending to sleep so as not to endure Ludmilla's jabber. At eleven o'clock he could stand it no longer and got up. The train was passing yet another Siberian swamp. Shallow lakes had formed on both sides of the railbed as the spring thaw tried to work its way through the ice beneath the ground.

Burlane said, 'We need a change of pace. I'd like to buy our lunch from one of those peddlers on the station platforms. Will you help me?'

Ludmilla hesitated. 'Wouldn't you rather eat in the dining car? It's much nicer.'

'The Russians buy their food on the platforms. My editor wouldn't want me to be any different from the people.'

Ludmilla got up and took a walk. She came back later and continued her book. Then she said, 'Make sure you don't miss the train, Jim. Some of these stops are quite short.' Ludmilla lifted her feet as the conductress vacuumed the carpet on the floor of the compartment.

Burlane was surprised Ludmilla did not insist on accompanying him onto the platform when the train stopped. He scrambled down the aisle where the conductress held up five fingers, telling him five minutes. He was too slow for the quick Russians who were grouped around several peasant women wearing dark blue babushkas. The women, among the few entrepreneurs openly tolerated in the Soviet Union, were selling loaves of bread, small jars of jam, boiled potatoes, and pickled cabbage. Burlane could not use his Russian, and so couldn't compete with the other travelers. He checked on the two small shops on the platform. One sold Russian publications. The other had food, including cold fried fish.

Burlane, intent on some fried fish, got into line. Maybe there was time.

Behind him a man addressed him in Russian, 'Perhaps I could help you?' The man waited, then repeated the question in English.

Burlane – who had understood the question in Russian – turned, surprised, and said, 'Why, yes, thank you. I'm interested in a couple of those fish there, but I'm at a bit of a disadvantage.'

The man said, 'Comrade Kormakova thought you might need some help.' He ordered Burlane's fish for him, conducting the transaction with a stolid, unemotional face. He'd tried to trap Burlane and had failed.

James Burlane resisted the urge to give the Russian the finger and strode back to the car door where the conductress waited, waving her flock back with her hand.

The Trans-Siberian Express entered another wide curve and straightened out for the run to the next town and the next artery of the massive system of rivers that flowed northward to the Kara Sea and the Laptev Sea just below the Arctic Ocean. Burlane got his map out and studied the amazing river system.

In Europe – where the rivers flowed south to the Black Sea or the Caspian Sea – there was Yaroslavl' on the Volga, Shar'ya on the Vetluga, Kirov on the Vratka, and Perm on the Kama. The rivers flowed to the north on the Asian side of the Urals. The names of the cities and the rivers from which they drew their sustenance were as euphonious as those in Europe:

There was Yahutorovsk on the Tobol, Omsk on the Irtysh, Novosibirsk on the Ob', Krasnoyarsk on the

285

Yenisey, Nizhneudinsk on the Chuna, Tulun on the Iya, Zima on the Oka, Irkutsk on the Angara, Ulan-Ude on the Selenga, Chita on the Shilka, Tygda on the Zeya, Harbin on the Songhua, and Khabarovsk on the Amur.

These were not puny or tiny rivers lost on an endless continent; Burlane had found that out. They were neither large creeks nor small streams wistfully called rivers by people who don't know any better. They were heavy, stolid rivers – rivers that demanded fat lines and heavy type on atlases and maps. They collected runoff from an incredible landmass. They were not picturesque rivers: there were no canyons or vistas or waterfalls. They were broad continental rivers like the Mississippi or the Missouri. They were working men's rivers with the utilitarian cut of working men's coarse cottons and woolens.

The rivers wound their way through the taiga until they came to the tundra and slipped quietly under the polar ice cap. When winter ice gave way in May, the slate-gray rivers moved through a taiga muddy from the thaw. Peasants with eyes the color of the water fished the rivers in the summer.

Ludmilla said, 'Jim, in a few hours we will be entering the Jewish Autonomous Republic. In 1928 the Presidium of the Central Executive Committee of the USSR decided to turn this unoccupied territory over to settlement by Jewish workers. Settlers from the Ukraine and Byelorussia reached the Far East in July. They stopped here in the warm pine forests and established the village of Waldheim.'

Burlane knew the settlement was forced by Joseph Stalin at the point of a bayonet and was a favorite recruiting ground for slaves to work the Kolyma gold mines, where three million slaves died between 1936 and 1950. 'This is predominantly Jewish, then,' Burlane said, knowing that less than seven percent of the population was still Jewish.

'Oh, yes, Jim. This would be the Jewish Autonomous region. It is too bad it will be dark and you will not get to see it.'

At Khabarovsk the train turned south for the run to Vladivostok on the Sea of Japan. This was the last night on the train. At 11 P.M. the buzzer sounded in Felix Jin's compartment. Jin was wide awake. He could not sleep.
'Yes?' he said.

'Ginsburg went to the toilet, comrade.'

'So?'

'Comrade Jin, when Ginsburg returned to his compartment the sound to our microphone stopped for twenty minutes. The lens to our camera was also blocked.'

'Slow down, Pavel. First things first. How long did it take him to go to the toilet?'

'No longer than usual. A few minutes. Do you want the numbers?'

'No need,' Jin said. 'Did you check the toilet after he left?'

'I didn't have a chance, comrade. The conductress got up to lock the toilet for the stop at Dolnerechensk. She unlocked it after Dolnerechensk and put another roll of toilet paper inside.'

'And the other compartments?'

'No activity. The doors remained closed.'

'Did you get the markers?' A white stake marked every meter of the ten thousand meters from Moscow to Vladivostok. Jin had ordered the windows locked on the end car. Since it was possible to dump something onto the tracks through the toilet, Jin had ordered the nearest meter marked every time Ginsburg, Kropotkina, or Jim Quint went to the toilet.

287

'Yes, comrade. I radioed the marker number. That stretch of tracks will be searched within a few minutes.'

Jin sighed. 'Tell me about the missing twenty minutes.'

'Either Ginsburg or Natalia Kropotkina was leaning against our lens during that time. Or it could have been taped. We can't be sure which. We got our picture and our sound back at the same time, and they were drinking vodka and wondering if they couldn't see the Chinese border from the train.'

'Is there any possibility that the break was accidental?'

'That's always possible. The microphones could have developed a short with all this jerking and lurching, comrade. But the accidental loss of both the microphone *and* camera is unlikely.'

'What do you think they did in there?'

'I think they found our mike and lens opening and wanted to call off the nightly show. By the way, Comrade Jin, the journalists are at it again in Steele's compartment. They're really throwing one tonight, celebrating their last night on the train together. I don't know how they do it. Capitalists are such drunks.'

'We were right to separate them from Ginsburg and Quint. That would have been too much activity.'

'All that vodka!'

Jin said, 'I want a guard posted outside Ginsburg's door; if either Ginsburg or Natalia get up again, follow them to the toilet.'

'Yes, comrade.'

'Go inside the toilet with them. Watch them pee. Follow them back to their compartment. Stay right behind them.'

'Yes.'

Felix Jin suddenly thought of something. 'Stand by, Pavel. There's something I want to check.' Jin hung up and began pawing through the transcripts of the various conversations his agents had recorded. Yes, there it was:

On the first day out, the British journalist, Bob Steele, had introduced himself to Jim Quint; Steele had said he was pleased to meet Quint. A couple of days later, when Steele and Quint were waiting for the May Day demonstrations to begin at Irkutsk, Steele had mentioned drinking with Quint in London. The Intourist guide had reported it.

Colonel Jin called his subordinate. 'If Jim Quint leaves his compartment tonight, kill him, please, and store his body somewhere out of sight. Also, I will remind you that Ginsburg and Natalia Kropotkina are to be strip searched before they are allowed off the train in the morning. See that their luggage is X-rayed. There will be equipment waiting at the station.'

Having one's word obeyed and one's needs taken care of was one of the perquisites of rank in the KGB. Felix Jin was tired and wanted to sleep. He needed to be fresh in the morning. He said, 'I'm going to bed now, Pavel. I need to rest. I'm not to be disturbed until morning. Is that understood?'

Ludmilla Kormakova, bored with useless bits of Siberiana, gave up on Burlane at midnight and went to bed. That was a couple of hours later than Burlane would have liked, but he was alone at last to watch the taiga in the moonlight they'd had for the entire trip. Burlane chose to sleep fully clothed that last night. At one in the morning a hint of pain flickered through his inefficient bladder. He put on his shoes and stepped into the aisle.

There was a guard in front of Ginsburg's compartment, so Burlane turned left to use the toilet at the forward end of the car. He would have preferred the toilet at the conductress's end because it was cleaner.

The guard followed Burlane down the aisle.

There was another man waiting in front of the toilet.

Burlane slipped his hand into his pocket and slid the safety off his silenced .22. This was Paul Hornung time:

Money time.

Truth time.

The man by the toilet had a silenced pistol in his hand.

The door opened behind the man with the pistol.

Bob Steele.

The Russian started to turn. . . .

James Burlane pulled his pistol and snapped four quick shots at the Russian's torso and dived, rolling, toward his target. Burlane came up snapping shots at the man behind him.

When the second Russian accepted Burlane's .22 slugs in his heart – *plup! plup! plup! plup!* – he was on his knee, holding the wrist of his gun hand for support, aiming. Those steps were required by the KGB manual. He had executed them almost simultaneously. This too was as he had been trained.

Next, he was to have pulled the trigger.

'Dumb Slavs,' Burlane muttered. Although the racket of the train had muffled the reports of his silenced .22, the odds were none to worse that he would ever again get to drive to Annapolis for beer and soft-shell crabs. He turned to the shocked Steele, who was holding on to the door handle and staring at the bodies.

Burlane grabbed the feet of the corpse nearest to him and began dragging him toward the corpse at Steele's feet. 'Dammit, Bob, help me out!'

'Is this the way to the diner?' Steele said.

'Grab his feet, Bob.'

'We'd been drinking vodka and I went to bed with the spins. Poor Wim passed out, I think.'

Burlane glared at Steele. 'First, my friend, the diner is

the other direction; you're going the wrong way. Second, this is the Soviet Union, not British Rail; there's nobody there at this time of night.'

Bob Steele tentatively nudged the dead Russian with his foot. 'Bloody sods. What do they do for aspirin?'

'They're Russians. There's nothing in there to ache. I said, grab his legs.'

Steele did as he was told. 'I was wondering how they drink like that. Jim Quint is an old friend of mine.'

Burlane opened the door of the train and pushed the first dead Russian into the cold night.

Steele offered Burlane the arm of the second corpse. 'Who are you?'

Burlane pulled the body into position and shoved it off the train with his foot. He turned and looked Steele in the eye and whispered, 'I'm an ugly American.'

Steele swallowed. 'What do we do now?'

'We go back to our respective compartments and hope we get out of this country alive. If you're religious, pray.' Burlane stepped into the toilet to finish what he'd started out to do. This was the first time anybody had tried to kill him for wanting to take a leak. When he came out, Bob Steele was wiping vomit off his mouth with the back of his arm.

'Too damned much vodka,' Steele said.

James Burlane returned to his compartment. He reloaded his pistol and sat facing the door. If he could make it to dawn, he had a chance; it would be unseemly for the KGB to murder a foreign journalist on the day of the Vladivostok signing.

If they came before dawn, Burlane would take as many with him as he could and save the last shot for himself. He thought about his brother in Denver. His brother would be in bed with his wife at this hour of night. In the

291

morning he would shower, eat a decent breakfast, and drive to work listening to the traffic report on the radio.

James Burlane waited with great moons of sweat spreading from his armpits. He remembered his first kiss. He'd been fourteen years old at the time and it was like being very softly electrocuted. He remembered being an end on the high school football team in Umatilla, Oregon, and running out for a pass at a place called Fossil. The game was played on dirt in a rodeo arena, and the dim lights were all at one end of the field. The pass arced up in the yellow, spiraling, heading Jimmy Burlane's way. Then it entered the darkness and Jimmy couldn't see it . . .

Coming his way . . .

Running as hard as he could but not being able to see it . . .

Then striding into the mud wallow in front of the goal line where an underground waterpipe had burst . . .

Couldn't see the ball. . . .

A kiss and an invisible football were what James Burlane remembered as he waited, considering the darkness.

24

Ludmilla Kormakova awoke cheerfully the next morning and went into the aisle for hot water. 'There's nothing like hot Russian tea in the morning, Jim,' she said. 'I am to tell you it is forbidden to take pictures in Vladivostok. Mmmmm. The tea is nice.'

'It's delicious. Thank you. It tastes extra good this morning.'

'The conductress took on fresh water in Khabarovsk. They have one of the world's best drinking waters in Khabarovsk, Jim. It is very soft. There are no minerals. This peninsula is named for the nineteeth-century Russian navigator, Nikolai Mouraviov-Amursky. Vladivostok is built around a series of bays that are surrounded by a series of steep volcanic mounds.'

Burlane saw a tower on a high hill above the city.

'Do you see a tower, Jim?'

'Yes, I do.'

'That is a one-hundred-eighty-meter television tower. It sits on the highest volcanic mound on the peninsula. That would be called the Eagle's Nest, Jim. These are resort suburbs we are passing here. They are Sad-Gorod, Okeanskaya, and Sedanka. The seawater is very salty here; a warm current flows counterclockwise from the Sea of Japan. The climate is mild, and there are mud baths and beaches in addition to the forests. This is a favorite holiday spot for Soviet citizens in Siberia and the Far East.'

Burlane refused to jot this down in his notebook. He was tiring of the charade. All he saw was another ugly

Soviet industrial town, only different in that these unpainted, deteriorating buildings had been erected in a shabby helter-skelter on narrow terraces and along steep streets that ascended the hills from the water. Here and there a modern high-rise building rose from the rubble like a mushroom on a pile of dung. A harborfront of docks, shipyards, and workshops seemed to run for miles on a shoreline that twisted in and out of the series of bays. It was positively unreal. Burlane had never seen anything like it; all the unloading cranes on the planet seemed to have been assembled on Vladivostok's harborfront. How many were there? One hundred? Two hundred? Easily that many, Burlane felt. The bays were populated by tankers, freighters, and seagoing tugs suffering from various degrees of rust.

Ludmilla said, 'This is the busiest port in the Soviet Union, Jim. It is one of the busiest in the world. More than half a million people live here.'

Burlane thought, *It's also the only ice-free Soviet naval base in the Pacific, luv.* The sleek vessels of the Russian Navy were on maneuvers in the Sea of Japan, out of range of spies among the journalists and officials in Vladivostok for the signing. 'It certainly does look busy.'

'The large bay in the center there is Zolotoy Rog Cove. We will be taking Lenin Prospekt to the signings, Jim.' Here Ludmilla consulted a small booklet. 'Yes, on Lenin Prospekt is the Palace of Culture, the Drama Theater, the Far Eastern Polytechnic Institute, the Institute of Fishing Culture, and the Theater of the Young Spectator. This is a regional scientific and cultural center.'

I bet the bread here is the best in the world, too, Burlane thought. He said, 'It's nice to see such a robust city.' James Burlane smiled to himself. He hadn't given up hope; there was still a chance. But he was an American spy, and for an American spy to disappear on the shores

294

of Zolotoy Rog was like a cowboy dying with his boots on.

Later, out in the aisle to stretch his legs, he met Isaak Ginsburg.

'Wonderful weather, don't you think?' Ginsburg said. He shook Burlane's hand and left a small note there.

'It's positively balmy. For some reason, I'd expected more ice and snow, this being Siberia and all.' Burlane glanced at the note:

I did not want to give you details in case you got caught. So far, so good. The head is safe. Natalia and I wish to defect to the West. Can you help us? We will have the conductress, Nina Kabakhidze, with us at the airport signing. She has been indispensable; we cannot leave her to the Soviets. I cannot tell you how grateful I am for all that you have done.

James Burlane put the note in his mouth and masticated it, cudlike; he was as content as a Guernsey cow at milking time.

25

James Burlane was relieved to join the still shaken Bob Steele and his hungover colleagues for a tour of Vladivostok before the signing. The writers were stuffed into a large van, with Ludmilla Kormakova doing the honors of reciting local facts and numbers, biggests and bests.

The journalists were taken on a four-mile drive along Lenin Prospekt, which flanked Zolotoy Rog. They were shown a soccer stadium and a sandy beach. Ludmilla described the beach as 'the most beautiful in the Soviet Far East,' although it looked damned cold and bleak to Burlane. Did Russians on vacation in Vladivostok sun themselves in wet suits? Burlane wondered. Terraced gardens, overlooks, and residential blocks descended from the avenue to the water.

The journalists endured explanations of monuments for Sergei Lazo, a hero of the Revolution, for Admiral G. Nevelskiy, and for merchant seamen who died in the Great Patriotic War of 1941–1945, and for the sailing vessel *Manchur* that had brought the first settlers to the area in 1840. A model of the *Manchur* sat atop a column upon which Vladivostok was written vertically. Beneath that was a marble tablet with more Russian.

'On here is repeated the words of V. I. Lenin,' Ludmilla said solemnly. 'This says, 'Vladivostok is far away, but it is our city.'

'In the United States we say that about Cleveland,' Burlane said.

'Is Cleveland a beautiful city too, Jim?'

'Cleveland is a grand place.'

Bob Steele said, 'In England we say that about Liverpool, although some argue.'

After that the journalists were driven to yet another monument – also for Soviet soldiers dead in the Revolution – this one erected at the central city square. The Soviets had flown in veterans of the Great Patriotic War of 1941–45 to be interviewed by *Tass* reporters and photographed for Soviet television.

'These men are being interviewed because May ninth is the anniversary of the USSR's victory in the Great Patriotic War. We call this Victory Day,' Ludmilla said, although May 9 was four days away.

Burlane and the others got off the van. The journalists weren't certain what they were supposed to do with all this – European readers didn't care about Russian war stories – but allowed themselves to be herded from one hero to the next.

The veterans had so many medals on their jackets – chain-mail vests of patriotic armor – that they clanked when they walked. They were aged knights, arthritic, some of them, but still fighting the glorious fight. Here and there a rheumy-eyed veteran used a cane or was guided patiently by the elbow. They walked stiffly, clanking. The heroes were living reminders of the sacrifices of the Great Patriotic War.

Ludmilla said, 'We honor these men so that such an awful tragedy might never happen again.'

The veterans spoke straight into microphones thrust toward their sincere, old-men's faces. Soviet television cameras recorded every word, every gesture. If their memories had become fuzzy with time, nobody cared. If the stories of deprivation and valor became a little more dramatic over the years, that was beside the point. One particular hero – a former colonel, to judge by his decorations – reminded Burlane of a venerated old bird.

The heads of the colonel's solemn flock nodded in sorrow that such terrible things could have happened.

Ludmilla provided a running translation of what the colonel was saying. 'He says the Red Army has to remain second to none.'

The heads of the colonel-bird's rapt listeners bob-bobbed yes-yes in agreement.

'The colonel says the awful tragedy of invasion will never happen again. We negotiate in good faith, but we stand in the world second to no one.'

Heads waggled no-no. No more invasions. No second best.

The colonel recalled the details of battles fought more than forty years ago. Ludmilla said, 'He says the spirit of sacrifice has to continue. The younger generation has to carry on, has to be unselfish for the good of all. The old soldiers will be dead one day; then it is up to us, the younger generation.'

At this, there was a vigorous nodding of heads.

Ludmilla said, 'He says that in the end we can never trust treaties. We can never turn our future over to a piece of paper, never. We have to remember these stories and tell them to our children and our children's children.'

Another hero: a former sergeant with a broad, sad face.

'He's telling what it was like to eat bugs in a German prison camp. He says all prisoners had a moral duty to do everything they could to inflict the maximum harm on the people's enemies and to escape at the earliest opportunity.'

'They do have that duty. I agree,' Burlane said.

Bob Steele raised an eyebrow. 'They do indeed. Say,

Jim, you won't forget to pop over next time you're in London. I'll take you to my club.'

Felix Jin was still furious when he arrived at the Vladivostok airport at 2:30 P.M. Jin had given Pavel two simple instructions: first, if Jim Quint left his compartment in the night, he was to be wasted; and second, Colonel Jin needed his rest and was not to be disturbed for the rest of the night.

Pavel, having lost his two best agents to Jim Quint – by then an obvious American spy – remained calm and obeyed order number two.

Followed the second order to the fucking letter! The damned fool! Not a word until Jin got out of bed just outside Vladivostok. Jin knew Pavel had done this to postpone admitting that his men had gone two-on-one against Jim Quint, and wound up dead. Jin lit a cigarette and puffed quickly, inhaling deeply. Sometimes he felt sorry for his people.

On top of that, the X-rays of the luggage and the strip search of Ginsburg and Kropotkina had revealed nothing but a pair of green lace panties. Nothing at all.

Jin got out of the Volga lighting yet another cigarette. He glanced at his wristwatch. Thirty minutes before the ceremony. Had it just happened that Ginsburg's trip to relieve himself and the blackout came just before the stop at Dolnerechensk, where the conductress was required to lock the toilet? Jin's mind raced like an Afghani in a tank sight. The toilet. The aisle. The compartment. The aisle. The conductress's cabin. The samovar.

The toilet.

The samovar.

The samovar!

Jin leaped back into the car and ordered his driver to

299

take him to the train station. 'You will drive this car as fast as you can, comrade.'

The driver, who loved to hurtle through Vladivostok, was pleased to comply.

Colonel Jin lit a cigarette and held fast to the armrest. He checked his watch again.

Several travelers on the end car had commented on the improvement in the tea this morning.

Jin checked his watch: 2:35 P.M.

The samovars on the Trans-Siberian held a lot of water. Jin himself had taken the top off the samovar in the end car – just in case – but he had just glanced in.

Isaak Ginsburg could very well have fished something out of the samovar and stashed it in the toilet for the conductress to pick up a few minutes later – or could have put something into the samovar after he left the toilet.

Had Ginsburg and Natalia blocked the camera and cut the microphone to divert suspicion from the conductress?

Had the conductress made a pickup when she left off the toilet paper after Dolnerechensk?

Jin sprinted into the railroad station shouting demands. Accompanied by a railroad official, he cantered down the siding.

He got to the end car and scrambled up the steps.

Inside, Jin pushed the samovar over and leaped back to avoid the hot water. Yes, he was right. There it was.

Using his handkerchief as a pot holder, Felix Jin looked inside. Someone had put a false bottom into the samovar. The false bottom contained a single small metal loop in the exact center so the bottom, and whatever was hidden under it, could be removed by a long wire with a hook on the end. This was good work on somebody's part. At a casual glance, the bottom looked normal. The six neat holes that allowed water into the bottom chamber were drilled along the near edge and so were invisible to anyone not tall enough to look straight down.

Isaak Ginsburg had smuggled something across the USSR in the bottom of a samovar!

Without a word, Colonel Jin, checking his wristwatch, leaped off the train and began galloping back to his Volga. The ceremony would begin in twelve minutes.

Felix Jin jumped into the back of the Volga, yelling, 'Airport! Airport! Airport! Speed! Speed! Speed!'

Whatever had been smuggled in the space in the bottom of the samovar had to have been fairly substantial. But what?

Colonel Felix Jin thought an unthinkable thought, one that he most definitely could not phone ahead lest his conclusion be accurate and it was too late.

He shouted, 'More speed, driver, or I'll have you shot! Drive this car hard!'

The driver thrust the accelerator to the floorboard.

26

A half-hour before the signing, James Burlane and the journalists who had ridden the Trans-Siberian Express were taken to the airport to join the more numerous journalists who had taken Aeroflot flights from Moscow or entered via Tokyo from the south. There were more than a hundred print journalists, but the stars of the show were the television people.

The writers, including Burlane and Bob Steele, were roped off to one side of the concrete apron so they wouldn't get in the way of the people who needed to check the light, proper angles, and electrical connections. The Soviets favored television because photo opportunities could be controlled; writers often thought for themselves. The print journalists, pariahs, could do nothing but clutch their pathetic notebooks and mumble oaths in various languages.

A third, smaller group, also roped off, included various diplomatic aides of the two countries, plus Isaak Ginsburg, who carried a large, loaded shopping bag, Natalia Kropotkina, and the conductress, Nina Kabakhidze. Burlane did not see Felix Jin.

A battery of microphones was arranged on the apron at the Vladivostok airport. The agreed-upon document setting forth rules for the arms talks, bound in the specially tanned hide of Russian reindeer, awaited on a small table, along with a carved wooden eagle and Ivan Dmitrov's bust of Lenin.

In order that all the participants might understand their place, there were security guards everywhere. The print journalists and the Soviet and American aides were honored with the most guards. Only the television people were given any freedom to move about, but they too were guarded by solemn-faced soldiers in immaculate gray uniforms with red trim. Burlane noticed that they had been given decent haircuts for the occasion.

The party had obviously stressed the importance of the guards maintaining an appearance of civility and decency before the world's press. There were no crass megaphones in evidence; there was no pushing people around. The despicable American secretary of state was to come, sign the document, and leave with his tail tucked between his legs like the cur he was.

Stuart Kaplan, a slender, neat man with jet-black hair and square jaw, waited patiently with his aides for Foreign Minister Zhukov to arrive. The agreed-upon, published script called for both men to arrive at the same time, but it was obvious that Zhukov had chosen to make Kaplan wait.

'It looks like they're going to make your man wait,' Bob Steele said.

'They piss on people for the same reason we drink coffee or smoke cigarettes. Gives 'em a little kick.'

'The only reason they insisted on Vladivostok was to remind everybody that your Senate refused to ratify the agreement Gerald Ford signed here.'

Burlane shrugged. 'Everybody knows they're assholes.'

Kaplan looked elegant, a consummate statesman in his pin-striped blue suit. Kaplan smiled. He chatted pleasantly with his assistants. He did not look at his wristwatch.

The television cameramen, bored, took shots of Kaplan waiting patiently. The Soviets who were helping the cameramen looked pleased. Russian technicians – under orders from above – scurried to make sure the foreign cameramen got good shots of Kaplan being humiliated.

Steele said, 'The pathetic bugger looks like Oliver Twist standing there with his cup in his hand.'

'Pricks,' Burlane said of the Russians.

At twenty minutes past three, a convoy of eight or ten black Volgas escorted by motorcycles could be seen in the distance. The Volgas had red flags flying on the front fenders.

Grigori Zhukov emerged from his Volga and began walking toward the designated spot for the handshake, a small circle painted in front of the table. The two men were to stand in this circle; this was to assist television cameramen.

The conversation between Kaplan and Zhukov was amplified by loudspeaker. Zhukov's Russian was translated into English by a man with a British accent.

Stuart Kaplan, suddenly awash with television lights, strode to the table with his hand outstretched. 'Did you have a good rest, Grigori Mikhailovich!'

Burlane said, 'He's thinking Zhukov's an asshole.'

Steele pretended to be surprised at Burlane's ignorance. 'Zhukov's a sodding Russian. What do you expect?'

'Did you enjoy the sights this morning, Stuart?'

'Fine, fine,' said Kaplan.

Stuart Kaplan gestured for the bald eagle. Zhukov waved for Ivan Dmitrov's bust of Lenin.

Kaplan said, 'I give you this American bald eagle, a symbol of our dedication to peace and freedom. It is carved from myrtle wood, found only in southwestern Oregon and in the Holy Land.' He gave the eagle to Zhukov.

Zhukov smiled broadly and held the eagle out so the cameramen could get a close-up. 'It's lovely, lovely.' Zhukov put the eagle on the table and took Dmitrov's bust from his aide and handed it to Kaplan. 'You may rest assured, Mr Secretary Kaplan, that you Americans need Comrade Lenin more than we do.'

'Up yours, fuckhead,' Burlane muttered.

One of the Russian guards, an officer who obviously understood English, turned and stared at Burlane.

Burlane formed a V with his forefinger and middle finger, and put this to his mouth and quickly ran his tongue in and out, in and out between the fingers.

The officer glared.

James Burlane giggled and ran his tongue in and out two more times.

'Your fallen comrade was a man of peace and so honors us all,' Kaplan said.

There followed two long speeches, one by Comrade Zhukov, who called for peace and justice, and one by Secretary Kaplan, who asked for peace and freedom. Burlane regarded these speeches as hardly more pleasant than having a tooth pulled or his prostate checked.

Speechifying completed, the two men signed the document and stepped back with their gifts, so that Comrade Isaak Avraamovich Ginsburg might read his poem.

As Ginsburg started forwrard, he gave the heavy shopping bag to Natalia.

Then Felix Jin appeared at Natalia's right shoulder.

Natalia gave the shopping bag to Nina Kabakhidze.

Burlane said, 'When Ginsburg finishes his poem, there's gonna be some action, Bob, so stay alert.'

'Why, thanks.' Steele, pleased at his good fortune at falling into a story about an American spy at the Vladivostok signing, started edging his way closer to the retaining rope. He stopped after a couple of steps and said, 'Good luck, Yank.'

Burlane gave Steele a thumbs up.

Isaak Ginsburg arrived at the microphones on the small table to begin his committee-approved poem.

'You see him in the Urals, foraging for berries, or loping
  through the taiga.
In Alaska, he pauses outside a gas station;
He paws through garbage down in Yellowstone while people
  take his picture, click, click.
That old bear's grown shaggy looking for a full belly
And a good night's sleep . . .'

James Burlane did not watch television. With rare
exceptions he found television boring, intended for people
whose interests and passions were less active and imaginative than his own. He did not begrudge watchers their
pleasure, but rather wondered how they did it. How
could they sit there with their brain cells in a state of
suspended animation? Yet on this occasion, standing
there on the Vladivostok airport, Burlane was never more
relieved in his life than at the comforting whirring of
television cameras.

The Soviets ruled by controlling everything: what their
people saw and read; what they were allowed to feel and
say; where they were allowed to travel. This control was
insured by the barbed wire at their borders. But at
Vladivostok, in their rush to score a propaganda victory
over the Americans – Premier Spishkin wanted the world
to see every detail – the Soviets had turned over a small
bit of territory to the sovereignty of foreign television
cameras. Aided by Soviet technicians and American satellites, the pictures of the exchange of gifts and Isaak
Ginsburg's poem were being beamed, live, to an international audience.

All this was calculated so that everyone might enjoy
the humbling of Stuart Kaplan and the inferior American
war machine.

When Ginsburg finished, Burlane said, loudly, 'I think
I'll go for a scoop, Bob. Cheerio!'

James Burlane casually lifted the rope barrier that held

306

the print journalists in their assigned place and strode easily in Kaplan's direction. He walked with his hands well free of his body so everybody could see that he was unarmed. He was immediately the center of attention of the television cameras.

'I wonder if I might have a word with you, Stuart. You remember me, Jim Quint, of the *New Democrat*.' Burlane grinned hugely, expansively.

No soviet citizen would have dared be so outrageous. The Soviet security guards were momentarily confused. Should they shoot this man with the world watching on television?

Burlane turned and called back to the print journalists who stared at him in disbelief. 'Hey, he promised me an exclusive on this one. I'm calling him on it.'

The guards hadn't been told what to do if a Western journalist got this aggressive. No Russian journalist would dare be this brazen. Burlane's behavior was unthinkable.

Burlane said, 'Stuart, you'll be pleased to know I had a wonderful train ride from Moscow. A perfectly wonderful ride. All those lovely trees.'

Both Kaplan and Zhukov, stunned, stared at the large-nosed man in amazement.

'You said to look you up next time we were both in Vladivostok.'

Burlane walked right up to Kaplan with the cameras recording every detail. He lowered his voice and leaned down to the shorter man. He said, 'My name is James Burlane. I'm a Company man. I have three Soviet citizens who want to defect to the United States.' He turned to Zhukov and whispered, 'You keep your nose out of this, you miserable prick.' To Kaplan, he continued, 'You should consider this a direct order from the President of the United States. If you don't agree, I'll split your nuts with the arch of my foot right here in front of God and television. I did that to an Arab terrorist once, and to a bandit in Colombia. It works.' Burlane smiled graciously.

Stuart Kaplan hesitated.

'Believe me, I don't have anything to lose,' Burlane said. 'If you want to end up talking like Minnie Mouse, try me. This is utmost, extreme, urgent priority, Mr Secretary.'

The American secretary of state said quietly to the Soviet foreign minister, 'If you have the chutzpah to deviate from our agreement with peace on the line, I suppose I can too, Comrade Zhukov. where are your companions, Mr Burlane?'

Burlane grinned. 'Yes! My main man!' He lowered his voice. 'Hang in there.' He shouted, 'Isaak Avraamovich! Mrs Kropotkina! Nina!'

Burlane saw that Felix Jin was gone. So was the loaded shopping bag.

Colonel Felix Jin couldn't stop his hands from shaking. He was trembling like a reindeer with a belly full of fur balls. Lighting a cigarette was a major undertaking. He'd figured out Ginsburg's clever smuggling scheme at the very last second. Valery Karpov wasn't joking when he'd told the colonels they'd know what they were looking for when they found it.

There, on a table, was the head. The wax nose and lips and ears had taken a beating, had been battered and flattened, had been somewhat melted by hot water, but the face was unmistakable: V. I. Lenin.

Lenin's head had ridden across Russia in the bottom of a samovar. The conductress must have retrieved it from the toilet and smuggled it off the train.

Looking out the window, Jin saw that the American party was being loaded onto the plane – along with

Ginsburg, Kropotkina, the railroad conductress, and the American spy who called himself Jim Quint.

Jin picked up the phone and called the colonel in charge of security. 'I want the American plane held on the ground until further instructions. Do not give the Americans permission to depart until you hear from me. Is that understood? Do I make myself clear?'

Then Jin phoned Valery Karpov's emergency number in Moscow Central and identified himself.

Karpov, who had been watching the signing and the Burlane episode on live television, said, 'What's going on out there?'

'Very quickly, I will tell you I have what you are looking for on a table in front of me.'

'Describe it.'

'It has a goatee. High cheekbones.'

'Lenin's head.'

'Yes, Comrade Karpov.'

'Who knows about this, Comrade Jin?'

'Only me. Isaak Ginsburg, a woman *znachok* designer, and a railway conductress are involved. An alleged writer who is an American spy helped them defect. You probably saw that on television. They are now on the plane with the American secretary of state. I have the plane's departure on momentary hold.'

'It's all there? Everything? The teeth?'

'It's all here, comrade. It's been battered around a little, and it rode across Russia in the bottom of a samovar so the wax is quite melted, but it's all here. The features are recognizable. With a little work we can have it restored and back where it belongs.'

There was a silence on the other end.

Jin could hear Valery Karpov take a deep breath and exhale between clenched teeth as he considered his options.

27

The pilot of the Air Force jet seemed calm enough. He said, 'We are told there will be a slight delay before takeoff. We should receive permission any moment now.' That was easy for the pilot to say, but the secretary of state and his party could see clearly that there was no congestion at Vladivostok. This wasn't like waiting your turn at Kennedy or La Guardia. There wasn't anything but the unpredictable Russians keeping them on the ground.

There was an uneasy, jittery calm aboard the airliner. The lanky American with the uncombed hair and the three Russians sat in isolation at the front of the cabin. If anything went wrong, it was their fault and everybody knew it. Nobody on board seriously thought the Soviets would try to force their way into the plane – not with the scene being recorded on television. The Soviets could not, would not. Would they?

The secretary of state and his aides watched in silent resentment. Their plan had been to fly from Vladivostok to the Honolulu Airport. The President would meet them in Honolulu and there would be a parade down Kalakaua Avenue. They would live it up, heroes, in the Kahala Hilton. There would be rum punch to drink, Maui Wowie to smoke. There would be brown-skinned girls of fabulous racial combinations. The Americans waited, making light jokes, trying to act calm, but hearts fluttered. Were they being held captive by the Russians because of the defection business?

For the Soviets to hold an American secretary of state

hostage was tantamount to an act of war. Stuart Kaplan couldn't imagine that a defection of three citizens could cause the Soviets to risk nuclear war. That was absurd. Preposterous.

Kaplan, who had acted out of intuition earlier, now regretted that he had not been able to ask the Company's point man what this was all about.

James Burlane accepted defeat philosophically. He had been defeated before. At least his Russian accomplices would win their freedom.

Ginsburg sat in a dazed, stunned silence. Natalia wept quietly. Nina licked her lips nervously and looked at the planeload of frightened Americans.

Burlane said, 'You tried. It didn't work. Those things happen. Have you ever been out of the Soviet Union before, except for Turkey, I mean?'

'That was the only time.'

'After a while, you'll forget all about Russia. Drink a little good beer, maybe. Write whatever you want to write.'

'It's my home. I'll always miss it some,' Ginsburg said. 'Will they let us go?'

'They got what they were after, didn't they?'

'They got it.'

'Then they'll let us go. What are they going to do to us with all those cameras out there?' Burlane sighed. He'd have to remember to send a first-rate case of gin to Bob Steele for keeping his mouth shut and perhaps saving Burlane's life. Burlane hoped there was plenty of booze on board. He felt like drinking himself to sleep.

Moments later the pilot said, 'Well, we've been given permission to depart. Looks like they were having a little fun with us there. No problem.'

Nervous laughter fluttered down the cabin. The folks from State were clearly relieved. They had even received

311

a bonus – the defection and the uncertain minutes waiting for permission to take off would make a wonderful story when they got back. They would be heroes.

Twenty minutes later, when they were well over the Sea of Japan, Isaak Ginsburg said, 'Mr Quint?'

'My real name's James Burlane, Isaak. Jim to you. I'm very, very sorry you didn't make it. I think I have an idea of what your plan meant to you. You came close. You did your best.'

'Mr Burlane . . . Jim. Lenin's head is inside the bust Grigori Zhukov gave to your Mr Kaplan in the ceremony.'

'What?' Burlane twisted in his seat.

Natalia Kropotkina said, 'Ivan Dmitrov's bust was on display in the Hotel Rossiya at the time of the theft. I hid the head behind a patch in an air duct of the hotel that day, and we ripped it out after they had finished searching. I split my copy of the bust, put Lenin's head inside, and refinished the outside. Then I switched it with the bust on display at the Rossiya.'

Burlane was amazed. 'So what does Jin have down there?'

Natalia said, 'We needed a diversion. What Jin has is a fake Lenin I made out of a human skull, human hair, and wax. It looks like the real thing. I made a false bottom for the samovar on the train. The fake head was under that.'

'A little battered and worse for the hot water, but no doubt convincing,' Ginsburg said.

'Do you mean to tell me the Soviets have had Lenin's head for three weeks, waiting to give it to Kaplan?'

'How could we possibly smuggle the head out of the country ourselves? We decided to let Comrade Zhukov do it for us. The party was eager for Zhukov to give you Americans a Lenin.'

'Natalia, you had the tools and skill to make it work.'

312

Natalia grinned mischievously, thinking of Ivan Dmitrov's studio. 'Exactly.'

'And you needed me to draw their attention the fake head on the train.'

'Yes. We also needed you to help us defect,' Ginsburg said. 'In that, you succeeded imaginatively, I must say. But it is the head that counts, not us. We got the head out. That's all that matters.'

'Just how is this extortion plan going to work, Isaak?'

Ginsburg told him the details.

'Oh, I like that. Humiliation. Public spectacle. Wonderful! Did you tell the Soviets what you have in mind?'

'In a note our friend, Jaan Birk, left in the mausoleum.'

Burlane glanced at Kaplan, who was receiving congratulations from his advisors. 'Natalia, Isaak, you must pay attention now. Bureaucrats are the same everywhere – in Russia, the United States, Morocco, Singapore, Bolivia – it doesn't make any difference. If you ask bureaucrats for help, I guarantee they'll find a way to screw everything up. They'll steal your head, is what they'll do – with much noble sentiment – and everything you've done will have been in vain.

'What do we do, then?' Natalia asked.

'We tell my superiors that the Russians retrieved the head at the last second. Then I get us what we'll need to extract the year of open emigration. It won't be easy; the KGB will be scouring the planet.'

Ginsburg looked at Burlane, thinking. He started to speak, then stopped.

Burlane said, 'You're wondering how I can deceive my superiors.'

'Yes, Mr Burlane, I was.'

'They expect me to. You look surprised, Isaak. This way they can take credit later if everything works out right. If anything goes wrong, they can blame it on me, a

313

renegade. That's understood. We'll need a whole bunch of money, by the way.'

Isaak Ginsburg marveled at James Burlane. 'I was wondering about that,' he said.

'Defense contractors charge the Pentagon fifteen dollars for a nickle screw and six hundred dollars for a plastic toilet seat. I'll get what we need from them, no problem. They owe the public one.'

'You will?'

'To cut the Russians' balls off? Hell, yes!'

Ginsburg grinned. 'Yes, Mr Burlane. Exactly that. Later, I'll tell you the story of Lobnoye Mesto.'

'Natalia, if I can get you Kaplan's Lenin, can you get the head out and put the bust back together without anyone being the wiser?'

'It would take a few days.'

Burlane grinned. 'I'll work something out. Do not tell these people. Do not.' James Burlane was elated. 'Well! I think we should have a little celebration, don't you think? That's what defectors would do.' He stood in the aisle of the plane and said loudly, 'Okay, now, on your feet Isaak Avraamovich!' He took Ginsburg by the shoulder and gave him a tug.

Ginsburg, confused, rose uncertainly.

Burlane raised his arms high with his fingers spread wide. 'Okay, you Jewish dude. You slick mother. Give me ten. Let me have 'em. Don't be a stolid Russian now. Give 'em to me! That's it. Yes!'

Isaak Ginsburg let himself be shown how to give the Company's money man a magnificent, triumphant ten, in the manner of victorious athletes in the United States. Ginsburg didn't understand exactly what the giving of ten was all about, but he couldn't help but know it was a celebration.

James Burlane was unabashedly jubilant. He danced, grinning, laughing. 'End zone! End zone! Hot damn! Putting it to 'em, my man! Yes! Yes! Yes!' Burlane slammed the palms of his hands into Ginsburg's again and again, while Natalia Kropotkina, who had been weeping from joy, wept even louder. Burlane pulled Natalia to her feet and embraced her. 'Come on, you too! Give me ten, Russian lady; it's your moment. You made it work. Show 'em the joy! Show 'em! You too, Nina. On your feet.' Burlane embraced the joyous conductress.

Natalia Kropotkina, still crying, feeling grand, gave James Burlane ten.

Isaak Ginsburg glanced uncertainly at the American secretary of state. He turned and lifted a glass to James Burlane. 'Shall we drink, then? To Jaan Birk, a hero of the people!'

'A hero of the people!' Burlane drank, wondering who Birk was.

'To Comrade Jin! A worthy foe!' Ginsburg grinned.

'To Jin!' Burlane took a hard slug.

'To Mikheyev for his inspiration. I'll tell you the story one day, James Burlane.'

'Hell, yes, to Mikheyev!' Burlane said.

Natalia said, 'To Leonid for his inspiration and Ivan Dmitrov for his help.'

Ginsburg said, 'To the coughing *zek*, and Serafim Korenkho, and my old friend, Lado Kabakhidze.' He toasted and gave the weeping Nina a hug.

'To Comrade Lenin!' Burlane called up the aisle. 'Mr Secretary, we would like to drink a toast to your bust of Lenin. Will you join us?'

Stuart Kaplan grinned and held up the bust of Lenin. The cabin cheered. Kaplan stood up and took a stroll down the cabin, holding the bust of Lenin high for everybody to see.

James Burlane remembered the football spiraling his way in the darkness at Fossil . . .

Coming at him . . .

The world's greatest novelists now available in paperback from Grafton Books

Eric van Lustbader

Jian	£3.50 ☐
The Miko	£2.95 ☐
The Ninja	£3.50 ☐
Sirens	£3.50 ☐
Beneath An Opal Moon	£2.95 ☐
Black Heart	£3.50 ☐

Nelson de Mille

By the Rivers of Babylon	£2.50 ☐
Cathedral	£1.95 ☐
The Talbot Odyssey	£3.50 ☐

Justin Scott

The Shipkiller	£2.50 ☐
The Man Who Loved the Normandie	£2.50 ☐
A Pride of Kings	£2.95 ☐

Leslie Waller

Trocadero	£2.50 ☐
The Swiss Account	£2.50 ☐
The American	£2.50 ☐
The Family	£1.95 ☐
The Banker	£2.50 ☐
The Brave and the Free	£1.95 ☐
Gameplan	£1.95 ☐

David Charney

Sensei	£2.50 ☐
Sensei II: The Swordmaster	£2.50 ☐

Paul-Loup Sulitzer

The Green King	£2.95 ☐

To order direct from the publisher just tick the titles you want and fill in the order form.

GF781

The world's greatest thriller writers now available in paperback from Grafton Books

Anthony Price

Soldier No More	£2.50	☐
The Old Vengeful	£2.50	☐
Gunner Kelly	£1.95	☐
Sion Crossing	£2.50	☐
Here Be Monsters	£2.50	☐

Julian Rathbone

A Spy of the Old School	£1.95	☐
Nasty, Very	£2.50	☐

Matthew Heald Cooper

To Ride A Tiger	£2.50	☐
When Fish Begin to Smell	£1.95	☐

Donald Seaman

The Wilderness of Mirrors	£2.50	☐

Dan Sherman

The Prince of Berlin	£1.95	☐

To order direct from the publisher just tick the titles you want and fill in the order form.

GF1781

All these books are available at your local bookshop or newsagent, or can be ordered direct from the publisher.

To order direct from the publishers just tick the titles you want and fill in the form below.

Name _____

Address _____

_____

Send to:
Grafton Cash Sales
PO Box 11, Falmouth, Cornwall TR10 9EN.

Please enclose remittance to the value of the cover price plus:

UK 60p for the first book, 25p for the second book plus 15p per copy for each additional book ordered to a maximum charge of £1.90.

BFPO 60p for the first book, 25p for the second book plus 15p per copy for the next 7 books, thereafter 9p per book.

Overseas including Eire £1.25 for the first book, 75p for second book and 28p for each additional book.

Grafton Books reserve the right to show new retail prices on covers, which may differ from those previously advertised in the text or elsewhere.